The Mainstream of Civilization

Since 1500

Fourth Edition

Harcourt Brace Jovanovich, Publishers

San Diego / New York / Chicago / Washington, D.C. / Atlanta
London / Sydney / Toronto

JOSEPH R. STRAYER
Princeton University

HANS W. GATZKE
Yale University

The Mainstream of
Civilization

Since 1500
Fourth Edition

The Mainstream of Civilization *Since 1500*
Fourth Edition

Cover: Galleria Vittorio Emanuele II, Milan, Italy. Photo © Francisco Hidalgo/The Image Bank West.
Maps by Jean Paul Tremblay

ISBN: 0-15-551578-0

Library of Congress Catalog Card Number: 83-81467

Printed in the United States of America

Source of Illustrations on pages 849–53 constitutes a continuation of the copyright page.

Preface

It requires a certain amount of courage to attempt to write a history of civilization in one volume. Once the task has been accomplished, however, it is easier to do it a second, third, and even a fourth time. As before, we have deliberately omitted certain details so that we could discuss as fully as possible the basic characteristics of each civilization and of different periods in the history of each civilization. We have tried to emphasize connections and interrelations—the ways in which politics, economics, art, scholarship, and religion all influence one another. We have tried to capture the flavor of each age—the unique combination of beliefs, activities, and institutions that distinguishes one society from another. In choosing the illustrations and the inserts in the text we have tried to give some idea of the diverse and ever-changing ways in which people have looked at and lived in their world. Finally, we have tried to consider the most difficult of all historical questions—the nature of and the reasons for change in human communities. Why and how do new institutions, new activities, new ideas rise and flourish? Why do they fade away? There are no easy answers to these problems; all we can do is suggest lines of inquiry that the reader may wish to pursue.

Obviously, it is easier to assess the characteristics and achievements of earlier periods than those of the age in which we live. The English Revolution of the seventeenth century ended long ago; the communist revolutions of the twentieth century continue to develop in unpredictable ways. Obviously also, it is more important to know details about the nature and background of problems that are still with us than details about problems that have been solved (at least partially). For these reasons the book broadens as it reaches the nineteenth century. More information is provided and more events are described in the hope that the reader will better understand the present state of the world.

We trust that no one will passively accept our interpretations or believe that our book is an adequate summary of human history. Our work is only an introduction, an attempt to persuade the reader to think deeply about history and to study it in detail. We are convinced that historical-mindedness is a necessity of human life. Consciously or unconsciously, we all base our estimates of the future on our knowledge of the past. It is important, then, that our knowledge of the past be as accurate and as deep as possible.

We remember with gratitude the contribution of the late Professor E. Harris Harbison to the first edition. He left us a framework that has been useful in subsequent revisions. We have also found the contribution of our former collaborator, Professor Edwin L. Dunbaugh, to be helpful in our work.

We owe special thanks to Conrad Schirokauer, City College of the City University of New York, for his contribution of Chapters 6 and 15.

The authors are greatly indebted to the following historians, who critically read *The Mainstream of Civilization* and made many valuable comments and suggestions: Bernard Bacharch, University of Minnesota; Shiva Bajpai, California State University at Northridge; Stanley Chodorow, University of California at San Diego; Tony Grafton, Princeton University; Frank Kidner, San Francisco State University; Ronald P. Legon, University of Illinois; David Luft, University of California at San Diego; Edward Malefacis, Columbia University; Don McLarney, Highland Community College; M. Gwyn Morgan, University of Texas at Austin; Frederick Murphy, Western Kentucky University; Kenneth Pennington, Syracuse University; and William Sewell, Jr., University of Arizona.

J. R. S.
H. W. G.

Foreword *The Study of History*

Consciously or unconsciously, all of us are historians. We can plan for the future only because we remember the past. We can add to our knowledge only because we do not lose memory of former experiences. Everyone, from the peasant to the scholar, tries to meet new situations by discovering familiar elements that make it possible to evoke analogies with the past. An individual who has lost his memory, who has forgotten his own history, is helpless until he has recovered his past or has slowly built up a new past to which he can refer.

What is true of individuals is also true of societies. No community can survive and no institution can function without constant reference to past experience. We are ruled by precedents fully as much as by formal laws, which is to say that we are ruled by memories of the past. It is the memory of common experiences that unites individuals into communities, and it is the memory of his own experiences that makes a child into an adult. Some of the memories may not be happy ones, but in reacting against them we are still linked to the past that produced them.

If everyone is his own historian, if individuals and societies necessarily draw on their memories of the past in order to deal with the present, then what is the need for formal, scholarly history? Isn't it enough to remember only the history that serves our immediate needs?

It is not enough, for two reasons. Human memory is fallible; individuals and societies forget many things that might be useful in solving their problems. This is why we have written records (which are a kind of formal history); this is why illiterate peoples try to preserve their customs and traditions through repeated oral recitations by the elders of the tribe. Second, the more complicated a society becomes, the narrower the range of individual experience in proportion to the total of possible experiences. A peasant living in a medieval village shared most of the experiences of his neighbors, and village custom gave solutions of a sort even to rare and unusual problems. No one living in an urbanized society shares many of the experiences of his neighbors, let alone the experiences of the millions of people throughout the world with whom he is connected by political and economic ties. No one can sum up the past experiences of his society, and of the societies with which his own interacts, with a few customary formulas; and yet these past experiences place a heavy burden on the present. In facing any problem, we look for familiar elements; if these are lacking, we feel fearful and helpless. Knowledge of history increases the chance of finding something familiar in a new and difficult situation.

Certain card games show how this process works at an elementary level. There is almost no chance that one distribution of cards will be repeated in a subsequent deal in bridge. Yet a person who has played several thousand hands of bridge should be able to make intelligent decisions and predictions even though every deal presents a new situation. He should be able to use his high cards and long suits effectively; he should be able to make some shrewd guesses about the location of cards in other hands. Not every experienced player will develop these skills. Some people are unable to generalize from their past experiences, and others cannot see analogies between the present and the past. But, generally speaking, an experienced player will make better use of his cards than a person who has played only ten hands. There is such a thing as a sense of the realities and possibilities of social activity, which can be developed from a knowledge of history.

At the very least, the past has left us the problems that we are trying to solve and the patterns of living that we are seeking to modify. At the most, we may find in the past suggestions for understanding and coping with the present. It is the historian's task to study the behavior of man in the past, to uncover facts, sort them, mass and link them, and so provide connections between past and present.

At the same time the historian must avoid certain pitfalls along the way. Connections with the past cannot be broken, but they can be misrepresented or misunderstood. Primitive peoples have little sense of chronology; they are apt to stir all their memories into a timeless brew of legend. At a more sophisticated level, the past has been used as a means of justifying present values and power structures. Many writers, from ancient times down to the present, have found historical examples to prove that their people were specially favored by the gods, that their state was founded and strengthened by heroes of superhuman ability, that virtue and wisdom (as defined by the author) have always brought success, while folly and vice have led to disaster. "History is philosophy teaching by example," said an ancient Greek (Dionysius of Halicarnassus), and it was more important for the examples to be edifying than for them to be true.

But it is not difficult to avoid deliberate distortions of the past. What *is* difficult is to avoid distortions caused by the incompleteness of our knowledge of the past. Many human activities have left few traces, especially in written records. For example, for thousands of years agriculture has been the chief occupation of the human race, but there are still serious gaps in our knowledge of the history of agriculture. "The short and simple annals of the poor" are short because information is scanty. If we had better information we would probably find that the life of a poor man in any period was anything but simple; it must have been filled with an unending series of nagging problems. In general, we know more about political history than social history, more about the privileged few than the unprivileged masses, more about the history of art than the history of technology, more about the ideas of philosophers and religious leaders than the beliefs of the common people.

Historians have become more skillful in recent years in finding material that gives a better-balanced picture of the past. Archeology reveals not only the palaces of kings, but the homes of ordinary people with their tools, their toys, their cooking utensils, and even fragments of their food. Gods and heroes may dominate the great works of art, but the common folk going about their ordinary business are there too—on Greek vases, Roman tombs, and portals of Gothic cathedrals. Discoveries of hoards of coins reveal unexpected trade relations. Aerial photography can bring out traces of ancient methods of plowing land and dividing fields. Even the written records, which have been studied for centuries, contain hitherto unused facts about such things as family life, migrations, and changes in economic patterns. There are still many holes in the record, but there is no reason to complain about lack of material.

The historian's greatest difficulty is not in discovering facts, but in deciding what facts can be ignored, or merely sampled, or clumped together in a single generalization. No one could master all the facts in yesterday's issue of the *New York Times,* and there are files of newspapers that run back to the eighteenth century. No one could master all the facts brought out in a single session of the Supreme Court, and the records of American courts and of the English courts from which they were derived go back to the twelfth century. To deal with the overwhelming mass of facts, historians have to arrange them, link them together, establish meaningful sequences of causes and effects.

The massing and linking of facts is not only essential, if history is to rise above the level of a catalogue; it is also inevitable, since it is the way the human mind deals with past experience. We do not recall every word we have exchanged when we decide that a certain person is a good friend. We do not remember every paragraph we have read when we decide that we like a certain book. But, while the process of massing and linking is essential and inevitable, this operation is the point of greatest danger in any kind of historical thinking. Consciously or unconsciously, one can mass facts to produce a misleading impression, even though each individual fact is true. Any governmental system can be made to appear obnoxious by discussing only the cases in which there is clear evidence of corruption or oppresion. Any society can be wreathed in a golden haze by dwelling only on its accomplishments in art, literature, and scholarship. Individuals and communities can become convinced that the whole world is conspiring against them if they remember only the occasions when they were treated unjustly. The nature of the sources themselves may cause distortion. For example, it is very easy to find material on political life in the city of Rome during the first century of the Roman Empire. It is difficult to collect evidence on provincial government or on social and economic development. The natural tendency is to overemphasize court intrigues and to pay little attention to such topics as economic growth or the spread of Latin culture throughout the West.

There is no easy way to overcome these problems, but an understanding of the principle of interconnectedness will help. No one is a purely political or economic or ideological being, and societies are composed of such varied human beings. Historians must look for the ways in which these (and other) forces interact. For example, the kind of food men eat can affect their whole social structure: a society dependent on olive oil for its fats will differ in many ways from one that depends on animal products such as lard, butter, and cheese. Religion can have an influence on trade: medieval churchmen aided the growth of Mediterranean commerce by importing silk for their vestments, incense for their ceremonies, and precious stones for their altar vessels and relic boxes. Trade in turn can influence the development of a religion: often it has been the merchant who prepared the way for the missionary. Ideas, technologies, institutions, social patterns, shifts in consumer preferences interact in complicated and bewildering ways. For example, increased use of easily washable cotton clothing in modern Europe improved personal hygiene and thus may have reduced death rates and contributed to growth of population. At the same time, increased demand for cotton encouraged the extension of slavery in the United States and thus was one of the causes of the Civil War.

Full realization of the connections among all human activities should lead to three conclusions. First, there are multiple causes for every event; single explanations for change are almost always wrong. Second, change in any one part of the social pattern may affect any other part of the pattern. Finally, the connections lead back into the past, and therefore the past influences the present.

The relationship between continuity and change is an interaction that the historian must watch with special care. All societies change, and yet all societies retain some connection with the past. The most "traditional" society is less traditional than it realizes; the most "modern" society is more influenced by tradition than it would like to believe. The Anglo-Saxons, theoretically bound by immemorial custom, invented the office of sheriff about the year 1000 A.D. The Americans, theoretically free to create an entirely new political structure, have preserved the office of sheriff with many of its original powers. Conquests and revolutions do not break all the connections with the past. Even where there has apparently been a complete break, the roots of a society may again grow down into its past. Roman law practically vanished from the West after the fifth century A.D.; it reappeared as a powerful force in the thirteenth century.

If there were no continuity, there would be no use in studying history, since nothing in the past would have any bearing on what is done today. If there were no change, there would be no history; a few years of practical experience would teach anyone all he needed to know about human behavior in society at any time and in any place. But, in the world as it is, the forces that would make for change are modified and even distorted by habit and custom, the forces that make for continuity are weakened and limited by new desires and new ideas. It is of some importance to understand where, why, and to what degree the desire for change prevails.

It is easy to see multiple, interlocking activities and rapid rates of change in the modern world. It is less easy to get a sense of the complexity and capacity for change of premodern and non-European societies, which is why the history of such societies often seems flat and uninteresting. The European Middle Ages are summed up as an "Age of Faith"; the history of much of Asia is dismissed with talk of the "unchanging Orient." Yet the Middle Ages were also a period of state building, economic growth, and technological invention—activities that have influenced the modern world fully as much as the Christian Church. The "unchanging Orient" produced all the great world religions, and each of these religions was a powerful force for change. Moreover, there are advantages in studying societies that are less complex and in which rates of change are less rapid than in our own. It is easier to observe and to draw conclusions about human behavior when the number of variables is small and changes do not come so fast that their effects are blurred.

A good historian, then, will try to give adequate attention to a wide variety of human activities, to discuss the interactions among these activities, and to trace the connections between past and present. But these principles cannot be applied mechanically. A writer who is careful to give an exactly equal amount of space to politics, economics, religion, the arts, and scholarship will probably not produce an adequate description of a society. The importance and even the identity of each of these activities varies with time and place. Religion had more influence on Indian than on Chinese society. Economics and politics merge in primitive societies, such as that of the early Germans. It is probably true that the vast majority of the world's scientists were born in the twentieth century; this could not be said of theologians. Thus the impact of scholarship on early societies is different from its impact on modern societies. To understand such variations and transformations, the historian must be more than a meticulous scholar. He must develop a feel for the period he is writing about, a sense of how people lived and worked and thought. It takes time and experience to acquire this feeling for the past, but once it has been acquired historians can give reasonably accurate, and occasionally penetrating, descriptions of earlier societies.

It is this understanding of the development of human society that gives history its chief value. History, even at its worst, gives us the comforting and necessary feeling that there are some familiar elements in a changing world and that there is some hope of understanding the changes that do occur. History at its best gives us a chance of reacting sensibly to problems as they arise. It does not guarantee the correctness of our responses, but it should improve the quality of our judgment. Good judgment about human behavior in society is badly needed today.

A Note on the Paperbound Editions

This volume is one of a number of variant printings of the Fourth Edition of *The Mainstream of Civilization*. It is not a revised or condensed text. Many users of the Third Edition found the various paperbound versions of that edition useful because the variant printings made it possible for them to fit the text into their own patterns of teaching and scheduling. In the Fourth Edition, the publishers have continued the practice of preparing separate paperbound volumes. Users may choose the volume that best corresponds to the chronological period covered by their courses. The variants are:

1. A two-volume edition

   The first volume (Chapters 1 through 21) starts with the beginnings of western civilization in the ancient Middle East and continues to the eighteenth century. The second volume (Chapters 20 through 35) begins with the seventeenth century and carries the account forward to the present day.

2. A three-volume edition

   The first volume (Chapters 1 through 14) starts with the beginnings of western civilization in the ancient Middle East and continues to the end of the Middle Ages. The second volume (Chapters 13 through 23) begins with the late Middle Ages and ends with Napoleon. The third volume (Chapters 23 through 35) begins with the French Revolution and Napoleon and carries the account forward to the present day.

3. *Since 1500* (one volume)

   Since 1500 (Chapters 16 through 35), after a Prologue that summarizes events to the year 1500, begins with the Renaissance and carries the account forward to the present day.

In all the variant printings, the pagination, index, illustrations, maps (except for the color maps in the three-volume printing), and other related materials from the one-volume version are retained. The difference between the one-volume and the other versions of this book is a difference only in form.

Contents

23

24

32

746 The Rise of Totalitarianism

33

772 The Second World War and Its Aftermath, 1939–1950

List of Maps

Introduction

This is a history of civilization, with emphasis on the civilization developed by the peoples of Europe. Like all histories, it must be selective. Incomplete as our record of the past is, it is still too full to permit discussion in a single book of all civilizations or even of all events in the history of one civilization. The principles that have guided our selection of topics may be indicated by a definition of our subject. We must answer two questions: What is civilization, and what has been the role of western civilization in creating the conditions that we find in the world today?

Civilization is derived from the Latin word for city, *civitas*. There is reason to emphasize this derivation, for every great civilization has had great cities, and the basic characteristics of civilization are easiest to observe in cities. Civilization is first of all *cooperation*—men working together to satisfy their material and spiritual needs. It requires *organization*—as soon as several people start working together there must be some sort of social, political, or economic pattern to regulate their activity. It encourages *specialization*—as soon as several people begin to cooperate in an organized way there are obvious advantages in dividing the work so that no one man has to do everything for himself. The character of a particular civilization is determined by the type and degree of the organization and specialization of that civilization. Ten thousand Greeks living in a small city-state could accomplish much more than ten thousand Indians scattered through the forests of North America. A few hundred men specializing in science have done more to change our civilization in the last few centuries than millions of artisans working through past ages. Intensive organization and specialization can produce spectacular results, and they can also create spectacular problems.

Civilization requires faith in certain ideals and values as well as skill in organization and techniques. The immediate and direct advantages of organization and specialization are not very apparent to most people. Organization sets limits on personal freedom, and specialization makes a man dependent on other men who may not be wholly trustworthy.

In the long run the advantages are greater than the disadvantages, but farseeing, enlightened self-interest is a very rare human quality, probably rarer than altruism. And if men hesitate to give up present benefits for advantages in their own future, they will be even more hesitant if the advantages are to be gained only by their descendants. There is always resistance to increasing the scale and scope of organization; there is usually resistance to new types of specialization. This resistance can be overcome only by belief that there is something more important than the individual—a religion that emphasizes cooperation, a divinely appointed ruler or ruling class, a nation that has become almost a divinity, a theory of society that has taken on the aspects of a religion. There is a close connection between the dominant beliefs of a people and the kind of civilization it creates.

This history of civilization examines, more than anything else, how and why people have worked together. It is concerned with political history because the political record helps us to understand why people have been more successful at some times than at others in organizing on a large scale, and why some types of organization have proved more effective than others. It is concerned with economic and social history because economic and social organization has a direct effect on both political organization and the type and degree of specialization. It is concerned with the history of ideas and their manifestations in art and literature because organization and specialization are possible only within a framework of accepted beliefs. The interactions among political organizations, economic institutions, and dominant beliefs determine the character and development of a civilization.

Western civilization is only one, and by no means the oldest, of the civilizations that has left a historical record. The earliest civilizations touched Europe and the West only slightly; they centered in the river valleys of Egypt, the Near East, and China. Only with the appearance of the Greek city-states after 1000 B.C. can we see the beginnings of a civilization that belongs to the same family as our own. The Greeks drew heavily on the older civilizations of their neighbors, but they reorganized their borrowed materials and added significant elements to them. Ideas and forms of organization that have remained important in western civilization for over twenty-five hundred years first appear in ancient Greece. The Romans followed the Greeks as the dominant people in the Mediterranean basin. Like the Greeks, they borrowed from their predecessors, rearranged the old materials in new ways, and added ideas of their own, especially in government and law. Roman civilization is the direct ancestor of the civilization of modern European countries. There has never been a time, from the first conquests of the Roman Republic down to the present, when Roman law and Roman political ideas were not being discussed in some parts of the Continent.

Yet, while there is unbroken continuity between the civilization of the Greeks and the Romans and that of the modern West, it is well to remember that continuity is not identity. Much has been added—for example, the ideas brought in by Christianity—and much has been changed. Greco-Roman civilization was neither western nor European; it was Mediterranean. It was most highly developed on the eastern shores of the Mediterranean, and it was greatly influenced by the Orient. France and Spain were colonial outposts that contributed little to Greco-Roman civilization; Germany, Scandinavia, and the Slavic countries were outside the limits of the civilized Mediterranean world.

This Mediterranean civilization ran into trouble in the fourth and fifth centuries A.D. The economic organization proved unsatisfactory, and loyalty to the political organization weakened. As the Roman Empire slowly crumbled, the unity of the Mediterranean basin was destroyed, never to be restored. The southern and eastern shores became part of an Arab empire, part of the non-European Moslem civilization. A remnant of the old Roman Empire, centering around Constantinople, became the Byzantine Empire. This empire developed its own civilization—Christian in belief, Greek in language, but strongly influenced by the East in organization. Byzantine civilization made a great impression on the Slavic peoples of eastern Europe and had some influence on the Latin and Germanic peoples of the West. But it was never fully integrated with the civilization that grew up in western Europe. The western Europeans thought of the Byzantines as remote and somewhat untrustworthy relatives, who might hand out valuable gifts from time to time but who were too eccentric to live with. This attitude, in turn, has made it difficult to integrate eastern and western Europe, since the eastern countries borrowed much more from Byzantium than did those of the West.

With the Arab and Byzantine empires developing separate civilizations, the western European remnant of the old Mediterranean world was thrown back on its own resources. These were at first not very great. Western Europe saved only a fragment of its Roman inheritance, and this Roman inheritance was itself only a fragment of the old Mediterranean civilization. Moreover, the Germanic peoples of northern and central Europe, who had never been included in the Mediterranean world, were for a time dominant in western Europe. They brought in some new ideas and institutions, but they were backward in both political and economic organization. They were slow in assimilating the fragments of Roman civilization that remained, and even slower in developing effective types of organization. In the same way, the Christian religion, which eventually had great influence on European civilization, was only slowly absorbed by the half-barbarized Latins and the half-civilized Germans. For six centuries Europeans struggled with the problems of assimilating the Roman inheritance, integrating Latin and Germanic peoples, and implementing the basic ideas of Christianity. Only when this triple task was done did western Europe at last achieve an independent and consistent civilization. Only then could it profit from its contacts with the more highly developed civilizations of the Arab and Byzantine worlds.

Once it was established as a separate and viable entity, western Europe civilization developed rapidly. Many of our basic institutions and ideas, such as universities and representative assemblies, were worked out in the twelfth and thirteenth centuries. But this western European civilization was confined to a very small area. Its center was in the north, in a triangle bounded by Paris, Cologne, and London. The peripheral countries—Spain, Ireland, Norway, Sweden, Poland, Bohemia, and Italy—did not share in all the manifestations of this civilization, though they accepted its basic ideas. And beyond these countries the influence of western European civilization dropped off sharply. It had little effect on the Moslem world and none whatever on the peoples of Africa and Asia who lived beyond the limits of Moslem influence. It had some impact on Byzantium, but not enough to erase the differences that separated Byzantium from the West. There were some contacts with Russia, but the Russians were probably more influenced by the Byzantines. And the Mongol conquest of the thirteenth century weakened the ties that the Russians had with the West and forced them to face east for two centuries.

Meanwhile, another group of civilizations had developed in the Far East, in India, China, and Japan. Each had its own characteristic values—religious in India, secular and political in China, military in Japan. All three tended to become somewhat self-satisfied and isolated; neither India nor China, for example, was as interested in foreign voyages in the sixteenth century as it had been earlier. In all three the economic system was still based largely on village agriculture. Finally, in spite of promising beginnings, none of the Far Eastern civilizations had developed a strong scientific tradition. These characteristics put the Far Eastern countries at a disadvantage in dealing with Europeans, who were deeply interested in strange lands and peoples, were beginning to develop an economy based on machine production, and were just about to make their first important scientific discoveries.

The great voyages of exploration and the great mechanical inventions, both of which began in the fifteenth century, enabled western European civilization to emerge from its narrow corner and to spread throughout the world. Eastern Europe gradually accepted much of the civilization of the West, though the process was never complete. Three new continents—North America, South America, and Australia—were occupied by Europeans, and a fourth, Africa, was dominated by them. Asia, with its old civilizations and its dense population, was not so easily overrun, but even Asia was profoundly influenced by the European impact. Thus, for the first time, all the peoples of the world were brought into contact with a single civilization. The results of this great experiment are only beginning to be apparent.

There is some justification, then, for the conventional division of history into Ancient, Medieval, and Modern. Ancient history deals with the period in which some of the basic elements of western civilization were developed and passed on to later peoples. But ancient history must be focused on the Near East and the Mediterranean, not on Europe. It must give greater weight to Greece, Asia Minor, Syria, Mesopotamia, and Egypt than to Gaul, Britain, or Germany. Medieval history deals with the period in which a distinct western European civilization appeared. But this civilization was confined to a small part of the European peninsula, and it had little influence outside that area. During the Middle Ages each great region of the world had its own civilization, and no one civilization was able greatly to modify another. Modern history deals not only with the rapid development of western European civilization in its old homeland but also with relations between that civilization and the rest of the world.

This growth and diffusion of western civilization has gone so far that we have perhaps entered a fourth period in its history. This period is marked by the appearance of distinct types of western civilization in the different areas occupied by Europeans, and, even more, by the revitalization of other civilizations following their contact with the West. Both the appearance of different types of western civilization and the revival of old civilizations are stimulating factors; they should help to prevent ossification and decay. Unfortunately, a stimulus can also be an irritant, and the reactions among competing civilizations may lead to efforts for mutual destruction rather than for mutual instruction.

The history of civilization begins in obscurity and ends with a question mark. Yet past experience is our only guide in solving present and future problems, and knowledge of our history may help us answer the great question with which we are faced today, that of the survival of civilization in any form.

Color Maps

Since 1500

EXPLORATION IN SPACE

Mars
142,000,000
miles from
sun

Uranus
1,782,000,000
miles from sun

VOYAGER 1 & 2 (1977) USA
Launched to investigate outer
planets: Jupiter (1979),
Saturn (1981), Uranus (1986)

Pluto
3,664,000,000
miles from sun

VIKING 1 (1975) USA
First soft landing
on Mars (1976)

Neptune
2,792,000,000
miles from sun

Mercury
36,000,000
miles from
sun

MARINER 10 (1973) USA
Flew within 3300 miles
of Venus and 625 miles
of Mercury (1974)

SUN

Venus
67,000,000
miles from
sun

Saturn
886,000,000
miles from sun

PIONEER 5 (1960) USA
First solar orbit

Jupiter
483,000,000
miles from
sun

APOLLO 11 (1969) USA
First men on moon

VENERA 5 (1969) USSR
First probe to impact
on a planet

GALILEO (projected 1981) USA
First satellite to orbit
Jupiter

VENERA 9 (1975) USSR
First definite soft
landing on Venus (1976)

PIONEER 10 (1972-73) USA
Passed within 87,000 miles
of Jupiter. First object
to leave our solar system

Moon
238,900
miles from
Earth

SPUTNIK 1 (1957) USSR
First satellite to
orbit Earth

Earth
93,000,000
miles from
sun

PIONEER 11 (1973) USA
Flew within 25,000 miles
of Jupiter (1974) and is
scheduled to fly by
Saturn (1979)

LUNA 10 (1966) USSR
First lunar orbit

VOSTOK 1 (1961) USSR
First man in orbit

SALYUT (1971) USSR
First space station

ENTERPRISE (1979) USA
First reusable space
shuttle

APOLLO/SOYUZ (1975) USA/USSR
First international space
docking

GEMINI 7 & 6A (1965) USA
First successful space
rendezvous

VOSKHOD 2 (1965) USSR
First "space walk"

ge v. kelvin

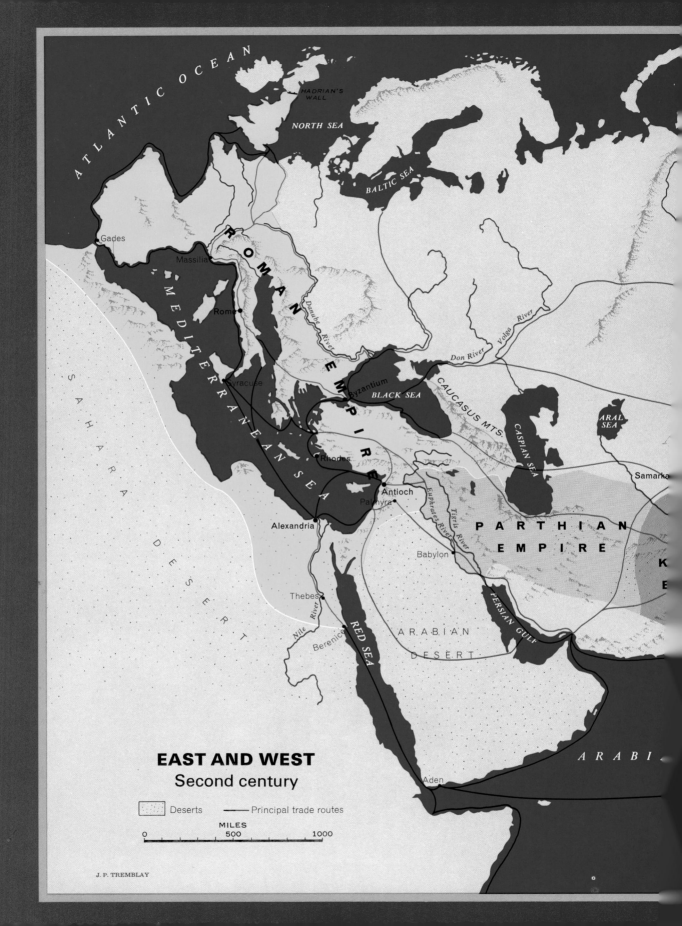

ATLANTIC OCEAN

HADRIAN'S WALL

NORTH SEA

BALTIC SEA

Gades

Massilia

ROMAN

MEDITERRANEAN SEA

Rome

Danube River

Syracuse

Byzantium

BLACK SEA

CAUCASUS MTS.

Don River

Volga River

CASPIAN SEA

ARAL SEA

Samarka

Rhodes

EMPIRE

Antioch

Palmyra

Euphrates River

Tigris River

PARTHIAN

EMPIRE

K

E

Alexandria

Babylon

SAHARA

DESERT

Nile River

Thebes

Berenice

RED SEA

PERSIAN GULF

ARABIAN

DESERT

Aden

ARABI

ARABIA

EAST AND WEST
Second century

Deserts   Principal trade routes

MILES

0   500   1000

J. P. TREMBLAY

PACIFIC OCEAN

SEA
OF
JAPAN

EAST
CHINA SEA

SOUTH
CHINA SEA

Amur River

HUNS

ALTAI MTS.

H U N S

GOBI DESERT

GREAT WALL

L A T E   H A N

E M P I R E

Yellow River

Loyang

Hankow

Yangtze River

EN SHAN MTS.

Kashgar

Yarkand

Khotan

A N

R E

Brahmaputra   River

HIMALAYA MTS.

Ganges River

Pataliputra

EMPIRE
OF THE
ANDHRAS

BAY
OF
BENGAL

Mangalore

DIAN OCEAN

ATLANTIC OCEAN

NORTH SEA

🛆 St. Andrews

York

BAY OF BISCAY

ENGLISH CHANNEL

Salisbury ✚
London 🛆
Winchester 🛆
Canterbury ✚

Bremen 🛆

Magdeburg 🛆

Elbe River

Amiens 🛆
Cologne 🛆
Aachen 🛆
Rhine R.
Fulda ✚

Rouen 🛆
Bec ✚
St. Denis ✚
Laon ✚
Reims ✚
Trier 🛆
Mainz 🛆
Worms 🛆

Paris 🛆
Chartres ✚
Seine River
Clairvaux ✚
Strasbourg 🛆

Loire River
Tours 🛆
Bourges 🛆
Cîteaux ✚
Cluny ✚
St. Gall 🛆

Bordeaux 🛆
Garonne River
Clermont 🛆
Lyons 🛆
Le Puy 🛆
Vienne 🛆
Milan 🛆
Aquileia 🛆
Po River

Santiago de Compostela 🛆
Toulouse 🛆
Albi 🛆
Avignon 🛆
Arles 🛆
Bobbio ✚
Ravenna 🛆

Duero River
Ebro R.
Narbonne
Rhône R.
Pisa 🛆
Siena 🛆
Florence 🛆

Lisbon 🛆
Tagus River
Toledo 🛆
CORSICA
Rome ✚

SARDINIA
Monte Cassino ✚

Seville 🛆
BALEARIC IS.
Naples 🛆

Monreale ✚
Palermo ✚
SICILY

MEDI

THE SPREAD OF CHRISTIANITY IN EUROPE To 1417

	Christianity to 600	🛆	Principal cathedral cities
	to 900	✚	Principal monasteries
	to 1200		
	to 1417		
	Temporarily lost to Islam		

MILES
0   100   200   300

BALTIC SEA

✚ Novgorod

✚ Moscow

Gnesen

Vistula River

ROMAN CHURCH
GREEK CHURCH

Kiev ✚

Dnieper River

Volga River

Don River

✚ Cracow

na

Gran

Danube River

B L A C K   S E A

Constantinople ✚

Thessalonica ✚

Tigris River

AEGEAN
SEA

Euphrates River

CYPRUS

CRETE

ANEAN   SEA

Nile R.

J. P. TREMBLAY

EUROPEAN CIVILIZATION Fifteenth century

AREAS OF WARFARE

▦ Fall of Granada, 1492

▨ Wars of the Roses, 1454-85

▤ Hussite Wars, 1420-36

▧ Hundred Years' War, 1338-1453

▲ Members of the Hanseatic League

══ Principal trade routes

MILES

0   100   200   300

Novgorod

Moscow

Volga River

BALTIC SEA

Königsberg

Danzig

Thorn

Vistula River

P O L A N D - L I T H U A N I A

Kiev

Crącow

Dnieper River

Don River

Buda

H U N G A R Y

Danube River

B L A C K   S E A

O T T O M A N

Salonika

Constantinople

Tigris River

E M P I R E

AEGEAN SEA

RHODES

CYPRUS

Euphrates River

CRETE

ANEAN SEA

Nile R.

J. P. TREMBLAY

COLONIZATION Seventeenth century

English   French   Dutch   Desert
Spanish   Russian   Portuguese

PACIFIC

OCEAN

JAPAN

Okhotsk,
1648

Amur River

Lake Baykal

Yeniseisk 1618

C H I N A

Yellow River

EAST
CHINA
SEA

Yangtze River

PHILIPPINE
IS.

SOUTH
CHINA
SEA

S P I C E I S.
(MOLUCCAS)

AMBOINA

EAST INDIES

*ARAL
SEA*

*CASPIAN
SEA*

HIMALAYA MTS.

Brahmaputra R.

Ganges R.

Indus River

Calcutta,
1690, 1756

JAVA

A U S T R A L I A

BAY OF
BENGAL

I N D I A

Madras, 1639
Pondicherry, 1674

Bombay,
1661, 1665

ARABIAN SEA

I N D I A N   O C E A N

J. P. TREMBLAY

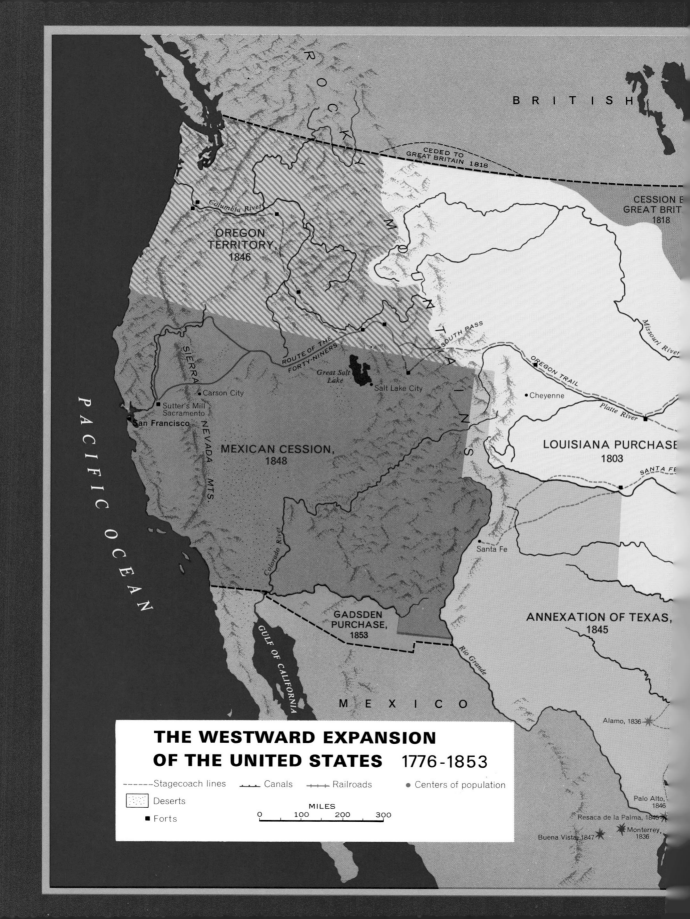

**THE WESTWARD EXPANSION
OF THE UNITED STATES** 1776-1853

‑‑‑‑‑Stagecoach lines ‑‑‑‑Canals ‑+‑+‑Railroads ● Centers of population

▨ Deserts

■ Forts

MILES

0   100   200   300

NORTH AMERICA

LAKE SUPERIOR

Northwest Territory

LAKE MICHIGAN

LAKE HURON

Battle of Lake Erie 1813

Detroit 1812

Chicago

Toledo

Cleveland

LAKE ERIE

L. ONTARIO

Lundy's Lane 1814

Chippewa, 1814

Buffalo

Plattsburg, 1814

VT. N.H.

MASSACHUSETTS

Boston

NEW YORK

Albany

CONN. RHODE ISLAND

New Haven

New York

Newark

PENNSYLVANIA

Harrisburg

Trenton

NEW JERSEY

Philadelphia

1800

1810

DEL.

Springfield

ROAD

Indianapolis

CUMBERLAND

Columbus 1840

1820

1830

Baltimore

Washington, 1814

MD.

Washington

1850

VIRGINIA

Richmond

St. Louis

Ohio River

WESTWARD
EXPANSION
TO 1783

APPALACHIAN

Kansas City

NORTH
CAROLINA

Mississippi River

Memphis

SOUTH
CAROLINA

Atlanta

Charleston

GEORGIA

Savannah

Mississippi Territory

New Orleans, 1815

New Orleans

Galveston

FLORIDA
PURCHASE,
1819

ATLANTIC OCEAN

GULF OF MEXICO

St. Lawrence River

J. P. TREMBLAY

ATLANTIC OCEAN

NORTH SEA

KINGDOM OF DENMARK AND NORWAY

KINGDO OF SWEDE

UNITED KINGDOM
OF
GREAT BRITAIN AND IRELAND

London

ENGLISH CHANNEL

Hanover   Berlin

WESTPHALIA

CONFEDERATION
OF THE
RHINE

Leipzig

SAXONY

Jena

Waterloo

Paris   Valmy

Seine River

Loire River

Rhine R.

1809

1805

NAPOLEONIC
EMPIRE

BAY OF
BISCAY

SWITZERLAND

KINGDOM
OF
ITALY

1797

Garonne River

Rhône R.

1814-15

Po River

Marengo
1800

1808

Duero River

Ebro

Salamanca

Madrid

Toulon

ELBA

CORSICA

Rome

KI

KINGDOM OF PORTUGAL

Lisbon

Tagus River

R.

KINGDOM OF SPAIN

KINGDOM
OF
SARDINIA

Trafalgar

KINGDOM
OF
SICILY

M E D.

NAPOLEONIC EUROPE   1812

Napoleonic Empire

States under French control

States allied to France

→ Routes of Napoleon

MILES

0   100   200   300

BALTIC SEA

Moscow

Borodino

1812

Tilsit

GDOM
PRUSSIA
Friedland

DUCHY
06 - 07
OF
WARSAW

Vistula River

R U S S I A N   E M P I R E

Volga River

Dnieper River

Don River

Austerlitz

Wagram

STRIAN EMPIRE

BESSARABIA

Danube River

BLACK SEA

OTTOMAN

AEGEAN
SEA

EMPIRE

Tigris River

Euphrates River

CES

1798

ANEAN SEA

1799

Abukir Bay

Nile R.

J. P. TREMBLAY

RUSSIAN EXPANSION   To 1914

Russia in 1533
Acquisitions to 1689
Acquisitions to 1801
Acquisitions to 1914

MILES
0   500

O C E A N

ALASKA
(Russian 1787?–1867)

BERING SEA

OKHOTSK SEA

P A C I F I C   O C E A N

E M P I R E

Lena River

Yenisei River

ALTAI MTS.

Lake Baykal

Amur River

MANCHURIA

SAKHALIN
Russian,
(1875–1905)

KURILE IS.
(Russian 1711–1875)

RUSSIAN SPHERE OF INFLUENCE

OUTER MONGOLIA

Vladivostok

SEA
OF
JAPAN

J A P A N

Tokyo

KOREA

Seoul

Peking

Port Arthur
(Russian 1898–1905)

Yellow River

C H I N A

Shanghai

EAST
CHINA SEA

Yangtze River

maputra   River

YA – MOUNTAINS

BHUTAN

River

Mekong River

Hong Kong

alcutta

BURMA

SIAM

FRENCH
INDO-CHINA

SOUTH
CHINA SEA

BAY OF
BENGAL

J. P. TREMBLAY

WORLD POPULATION

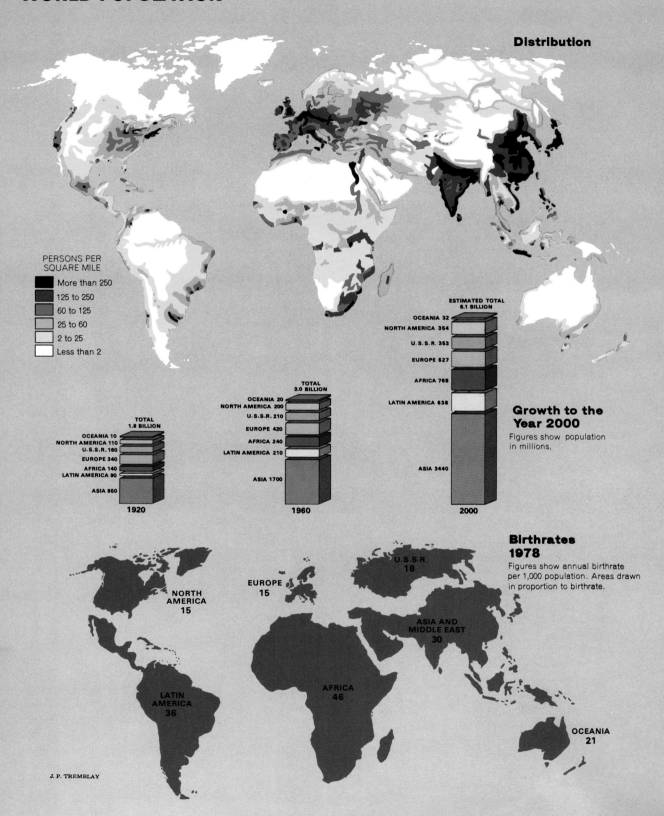

Distribution

PERSONS PER SQUARE MILE

- More than 250
- 125 to 250
- 60 to 125
- 25 to 60
- 2 to 25
- Less than 2

Growth to the Year 2000

Figures show population in millions.

ESTIMATED TOTAL 6.1 BILLION

- OCEANIA 32
- NORTH AMERICA 354
- U.S.S.R. 353
- EUROPE 527
- AFRICA 768
- LATIN AMERICA 638
- ASIA 3440

2000

TOTAL 3.0 BILLION

- OCEANIA 20
- NORTH AMERICA 200
- U.S.S.R. 210
- EUROPE 420
- AFRICA 240
- LATIN AMERICA 210
- ASIA 1700

1960

TOTAL 1.8 BILLION

- OCEANIA 10
- NORTH AMERICA 110
- U.S.S.R. 160
- EUROPE 340
- AFRICA 140
- LATIN AMERICA 90
- ASIA 950

1920

Birthrates 1978

Figures show annual birthrate per 1,000 population. Areas drawn in proportion to birthrate.

- NORTH AMERICA 15
- EUROPE 15
- U.S.S.R. 18
- ASIA AND MIDDLE EAST 30
- LATIN AMERICA 36
- AFRICA 46
- OCEANIA 21

J. P. TREMBLAY

The Mainstream of
Civilization

Since 1500
Fourth Edition

Prologue:
From the Beginnings to 1500

Three words appear repeatedly in this book that look simple and are actually very difficult to define. They are *civilization, western,* and *modern.* It is easy enough to use them; it is not so easy to say what they mean. What is civilization? When and how did a distinct type of civilization—western civilization—develop in Europe? And when did this western civilization begin to manifest traits that we call modern?

Every group of scholars that is interested in man and society gives a different meaning to the word *civilization.* Even historians are by no means in full agreement, though during the last century a good many of them have reached a consensus. When they speak of a civilization, they mean a society in which there is some degree of economic and political organization, some measure of occupational specialization, and a set of beliefs or values that is accepted by most members of the society. Organization, specialization, and common beliefs in turn combine to generate a distinct pattern of living that can be recognized, despite continuing change, over long periods of time.

Organization in its simplest form provides security against external and internal enemies, some control of the environment (for example, irrigation, community building, or collective agricultural operations), and some reasonably stable means of exchanging products. Without this minimum degree of organization each family or small group of families has to strive for self-sufficiency

and so is doomed to live at a bare subsistence level. No one will stop procuring his own food and spend his time making cloth unless he has some assurance that he can exchange that cloth—safely and regularly—for food. And if everyone has to give over his days to hunting animals or collecting grain, then no one is likely to become a very good clothmaker. Conversely, as soon as a group of people has attained an acceptable level of security and has set up regular procedures for exchanging goods, then individual members of the group can develop specialized skills. Effective organization, even in a small community, can stimulate a high degree of specialization. A few thousand Greeks working together in a city-state managed to produce or acquire almost every object they wanted in the entire Mediterranean world, in spite of the poverty of their soil and their lack of other natural resources. A few thousand North American Indians divided into small, wandering bands barely managed to survive, though they lived in a much richer country.

Organization requires a certain amount of cooperation from the people who make up the community. Cooperation is not achieved by coldly rational appeals to self-interest, nor can it be maintained simply through threats and punishments. If, however, men share common beliefs, they are likely to cooperate in carrying out the tasks of their society. So long as a group believes that it is working toward generally accepted goals through forms of organization that

The Parthenc
at Athens.

Old Stone Age | New Stone Age | Era of Civilization

B.C. | A.D.

Art of the Old Stone Age:

Harpoon

Dart thrower
of reindeer antler

Baton de commandement
of reindeer antler, showing
wild horses

seem right and proper, it will attain at least some of its objectives and it will survive as a group. Once a group, or some members of a group, loses this assurance, either an altered set of beliefs or a restructured society will emerge. One of the problems faced by every civilization is how to maintain common beliefs and common values in the face of technical, economic, and social change. Internal decay, resulting from a loss of common beliefs and values, is the real destroyer of civilizations; external attack usually knocks over empty shells.

THE ANCIENT MIDDLE EAST

The earliest examples of organization, specialization, and cooperation based on common beliefs are found in the city-states of the great river valleys of Eurasia—first in the Tigris-Euphrates Valley of Mesopotamia, next in the Nile Valley of Egypt and the Indus River Valley of India, and last in the Yellow River Valley of China. *City-state* is too grandiose a term for the earliest settlements; they were hardly more than big villages. But the emergence of the village itself marks an important stage in organization and specialization; it was the product of a social and economic revolution that took place at the end of the Old Stone Age, about 10,000 B.C.

When men began to grow their food in cleared fields instead of relying on hunting and food gathering, when they settled in one place rather than roaming over a wide area, when they built permanent homes instead of throwing up temporary shelters, they experienced a more pressing need for organization and richer opportunities for specialization. A sedentary population is more vulnerable to external attacks and suffers more from internal disputes than a migratory population. It cannot solve its problems simply by moving away from an exposed site or by splitting up into smaller groups. The members of a village using primitive agricultural techniques have to cooperate in clearing and planting fields, herding animals, and controlling the water supply. At the same time, the existence of a settled community means that there is a permanent market in which specialized craftsmen can produce and exchange goods. Even in the very earliest settlements there was a differentiation of social, economic, and political roles. There was a governing group, a priestly group, a merchant group, an artisan group, and an agricultural group. One person may have played several roles—ruler and priest, or priest and businessman—but the differentiation in roles was already well advanced.

The big villages grew into cities, and the cities into states. The influence of an urban center spread farther and farther into the countryside until it touched the area dominated by another urban center. The frictions that developed when two spheres of influence met often led to war, and a series of wars in turn sometimes resulted in the establishment of a fairly large kingdom. War itself was likely to strengthen the effectiveness of political institutions, and the creation of a kingdom required an elaboration of all forms of organization. The creation of a kingdom also required a conscious attempt to build up common beliefs and loyalties. The victors might, for example, substitute their gods for the gods of the defeated, or they might simply subordinate the gods of the defeated to the greater gods (who had proved their greatness by giving victory), or the victors and the vanquished might decide that they had been worshiping the same gods under different names. A good deal of local variation in worship was tolerated so long as special respect was paid to the ruler's god or to the ruler himself as an embodiment of that god.

This brief introduction cannot trace the long history of the kingdoms that grew up in India and in China. China, for some time, had few contacts with the rest of the world. India was in fairly close touch with Mesopotamia; but while Indian ideas reached the countries to the west, they were absorbed into existing patterns of thought and did not persist as a separate cultural tradition. On the other hand, the kingdom of Egypt and the various kingdoms and empires that succeeded one another in the Mesopotamian area laid the foundation for the ancient Mediterranean civilization out of which western civilization was to grow.

And just as important as Egypt and Mesopotamia were the border states that grew up in Asia Minor and Persia, and in the contested lands that lay between Egypt and the successive masters of the Tigris-Euphrates area. The Hebrews and the Phoenicians are the best known of these border peoples. When we remember that the Phoenicians invented (or at least perfected) the alphabet and that the Jewish tradition lies at the root of two great world religions, we see what significant contributions could be made by even the smaller communities of the Middle East.

There were some striking differences among the peoples of the ancient Middle East. The king of Egypt was a god, owner of the whole country, master of all its inhabitants. The Mesopotamian kings were only servants of the gods, and their subjects had full rights over their own property and considerable freedom of action. Egypt built in stone, Mesopotamia in brick. The chief agricultural problem in the Nile Valley was irrigation;

The gold-plated inner coffin of the pharaoh Tutankhamon (*ca.* 1340 B.C.).

THE ANCIENT MIDDLE EAST

the chief problem in Mesopotamia was drainage. There are dozens of other examples, but behind the diversity was a degree of uniformity. With very few exceptions, all the societies of the Middle East were agricultural societies. A vast number of agricultural workers supported a much smaller population of artisans and traders, and an even smaller elite of priests, bureaucrats, nobles, and members of the royal family. No one family of agricultural workers could produce much of a surplus, but the surplus from the labors of many thousands of workers could be funneled into very narrow channels and used to support artisans, bureaucrats, nobles, and kings.

The surplus could also be used to finance wars, and every kingdom—even the little kingdom of the Hebrews—went through a phase of empire building. Through war, through migration, and through trade there was a considerable amount of mixing of peoples and an extensive exchange of ideas and techniques. In fact, the real problem is not to explain similarities in social structures or the diffusion of ideas, but rather to explain why a few ideas did not spread very far. Every Middle Eastern society had invented or borrowed the technique of writing; yet only a small number of the border peoples accepted the immense improvement in writing made possible by the invention of the alphabet. Many peoples, notably the Egyptians, were intensely interested in religion, yet none of them adopted the rigid monotheism of the Jews. But such cases were rare, and their rarity simply demonstrates that there was a common fund of experience and knowledge in the ancient Middle East that could be drawn on by all the peoples of the area.

This fund of experience and knowledge was rich and varied. By the end of

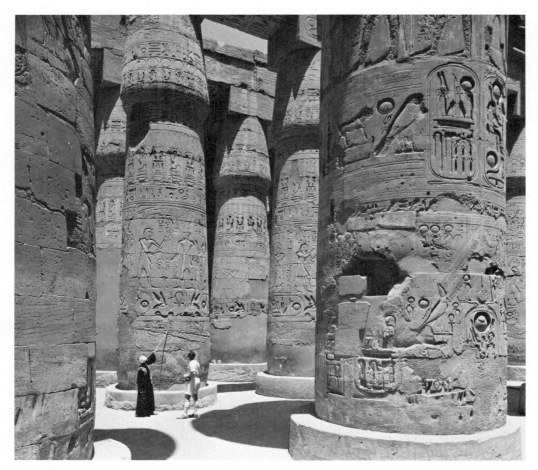

Ramses II, ruler of the Egyptian Empire at its height, built this temple to Amon at Karnak (*ca.* 1500 B.C.).

...mite prisoner inscribed
... a relief at the temple of
...xor (perhaps dating from
... period of Hebrew
...sidence in Egypt).

THE GREEKS

On the western edge of this Middle Eastern civilization lived the Greeks. They were almost certainly invaders from the north who had settled in the Greek peninsula, the Aegean Islands, and the coast of Asia Minor about 2000 B.C. The physical features of the area, in which small patches of fertile land are cut off from one another by rocky hills and barren mountains, encouraged the establishment of many small kingdoms. Each king had a fortified palace or town from which he could protect the farmers in his district. The invasions continued for many centuries, and the first settlers naturally viewed the successive newcomers with hostility. Persistent warfare strengthened the tendency toward political fragmentation. The Greeks were never able to unite; they clung to their separate states until in the fourth century B.C. Alexander the Great forced them to become part of a Mediterranean empire.

Geography had another effect on Greek life: it almost forced the Greeks to become a maritime people. Every path led toward the sea; almost every Greek grew up with the smell of salt water in his nostrils. Inland one could make only a bare living from the thin soil, but overseas were rich countries that could provide cheap food and attractive luxuries. Soon after the first invasions, certainly by 1700 B.C., there were Greek sailors in the Aegean seeking unoccupied land, trading with wealthy neighbors, sacking enemy towns. The early Greek traders had many competitors and few commodities to offer in foreign markets, but in the long run they managed to dominate the commerce of the eastern Mediterranean. Greek colonies along the coasts of Thrace, the Black Sea, and southern Italy supplied grain to the older settlements. As a result, the richer farmers of the homeland could concentrate on raising grapes and olive trees that flourished on the hillsides where grain would never grow. Exports of wine, olive oil, pottery, and metal work, together with shipping and middlemen's profits, produced a favorable balance of trade. It took a long while to work out this trading system, but even in the second millennium B.C.

the second millennium B.C., political organization had reached a stage where vast areas and hundreds of thousands of people could be governed from a single center, where power could be safely delegated to provincial administrators, where large armies could be raised and kept in the field year after year. Economic organization had produced not only a host of local traders and specialized artisans but a class of merchants who traveled thousands of miles every year. Masterpieces of architecture, sculpture, and painting had been produced, and religious writers had expressed ideas that are still significant. Some knowledge of astronomy, arithmetic, and geometry had been acquired. In short, by 1000 B.C. the ancient Middle East had achieved a level of civilization equalled only by China and India, and far beyond that of the rest of the inhabited world.

ca. 2000 B.C.		ca. 1700	ca. 1480		ca. 1100	ca. 800	ca. 600		404	323	

Minoan Civilization on Crete				"Dark Ages"	Dominance of City-states of Asia Minor	Dominance of Athens and Sparta	Hellenistic Era
Arrival of Greeks		Mycenaean Civilization in Aegean Area					

Decline of
City-state System and
Conquest by Macedon

the Greeks were clearly trying to build up their commerce, and by the seventh century B.C. they had become the most successful merchants of the Mediterranean.

Finally, geography put the Greeks into close contact with some of the most advanced peoples of the Middle East. At the time of the first Greek settlements, a remarkable civilization was flourishing on the island of Crete. This Minoan civilization, named after the legendary King Minos, had been influenced by all the peoples of the Middle East, and especially by Egypt. But the Minoans had added a quality of grace and elegance that was all their own. Instead of the

heavy, massive buildings and statues of Egypt that dwarfed the observer, the Minoan style was restrained, sensitive, proportioned to the human body. The Minoans may have passed these qualities on to the Greeks; certainly they influenced the Greeks in many ways. Even more than the Greeks, the Minoans had to be a maritime people. Their ships frequented the Aegean; they traded with the Greeks; they may even have established a sort of overlordship over some of the little Greek kingdoms. Later (about 1480 B.C.) a great disaster struck Crete, perhaps a terrific volcanic explosion. The people who rebuilt the ruined palaces and cities wrote a primitive form of

THE AEGEAN WORLD *ca.* 1500–146 B.C.

Greek, which would suggest that roles had been reversed and that the Greeks were now lords of Crete. In any case, the earliest form of Greek civilization—the Mycenaean—had many affinities with the Minoan civilization.

The Greeks who settled along the western coast of Asia Minor also learned from their immediate neighbors. Asia Minor was fully integrated into the ancient Middle Eastern civilization, and it was from this region that the Greeks acquired some of their earliest ideas about astronomy, mathematics, and philosophy. They also learned the use of coined money, a notable invention made about 700 B.C. in a kingdom of Asia Minor. Using coins instead of weighing out chunks of precious metals made trade easier, an advantage that the mercantile-minded Greeks greatly appreciated.

The peak of influence of Asia Minor on the Greeks came centuries after the peak of Minoan influence. In between lies a dark period during which the Greeks almost vanish from view, probably because new invasions from the north had shattered the old Mycenaean society. When the Greeks reappear, they are still divided into small kingdoms built around fortified towns; they are still bothered by their agricultural problems; and they are still trying to expand their overseas trade. Two new—or if not really new, greatly strengthened—traits appear: an insatiable curiosity about everything in the world and a willingness to try out new ideas and new forms of organization.

The Greeks seem to have realized that small states could survive in a world of large states only by making the fullest use of their human resources. Under monarchical or aristocratic government most citizens were barred from the political process and hence were unable to devote their full energies to the common welfare. So there was a trend toward democracy, a system in which more men could hold responsible positions in the army and in government. In Athens by the fifth century B.C. every citizen could vote and hold office. Slaves and natives of other cities (perhaps half the population) were still excluded, but Athens and

Cretan fresco of court ladies seated around a pillar shrine at a public festival, from the palace at Knossos (*ca.* 1500 B.C.).

Greek city-states like Athens provided more political freedom than any other contemporary government.

Curiosity, and the stimulation of individual talents through the responsibilities and opportunities offered to all free citizens, encouraged men to speculate about social and natural phenomena. The Greeks argued and wrote about politics and ethics, about philosophy and poetry, about mathematics and science. They tried to find out first principles and general laws that could be applied universally. They borrowed many of their facts from other peoples, but they had an ability to generalize that their predecessors had lacked. Their one weakness was to rely too much on logical reasoning—formal logic was a Greek invention—and to generalize too rapidly on the basis of incomplete evidence. A good example of the Greek mind at work is Euclid's geometry (*ca.* 300 B.C.). Many of his propositions had been known before (for example, the square of the hypotenuse) but had never been properly proved nor fitted into a coherent, consistent, logical system. Yet Euclid's whole system rests on axioms, truths that he thought were so self-evident that they needed no proof.

Pericles on Athens and Sparta

This oration, inserted by the Greek historian Thucydides in his *History of the Peloponnesian War,* does not give Pericles' exact words, but it does express admirably the pride of the Athenians in their city and its form of government.

We are called a democracy, for the administration is in the hands of the many and not of the few. But . . . the claim of excellence is also recognized, and when a citizen is in any way distinguished, he is preferred to the public service, not as a matter of privilege, but as the reward of merit. . . . Our city is thrown open to the world, and we never expel a foreigner or prevent him from seeing or learning anything of which the secret, if revealed to an enemy, might profit him. . . . In the matter of education, whereas the Spartans from early youth are always undergoing laborious exercises which are to make them brave, we live at ease, and yet are equally ready to face the perils which they face. . . . For we are lovers of the beautiful, yet simple in our tastes, and we cultivate the mind without loss of manliness. . . . Such is the city for whose sake these men fought and died; . . . and every one of us who survive should gladly toil on her behalf.

From Pericles' Funeral Oration, in Thucydides, *The History of the Peloponnesian War,* trans. by B. Jowett in Francis R. B. Godolphin, ed., *The Greek Historians* (New York: Random House, 1942), Vol. I, pp. 648–50.

Greek vase of the late sixth century B.C. depicting a foot race. The vase was awarded to the winner of the foot race contest at the Panathenaic festival in Athens.

In philosophy, Plato's emphasis on the importance of abstract ideas and Aristotle's theory of development through impressing form on matter were brilliant intuitions that were to lead to centuries of discussion, but they were based on logical argument rather than on observation.

The free Greek spirit also expressed itself in art and in literature. Man was always the measure, but man at the height of his powers. Temples were built to a human scale; the gods were glorified human beings just as heroic men were demigods. Drama dealt with the fate of man in an unfriendly world, and especially with the fate of men who lack moderation and a sense of the fitness of things. History—again an area in which the Greeks improved greatly on earlier work—dealt with the triumphs and failures of individuals.

There was a darker side to the Greek character, a side that expressed itself in the frenzies of secret religious rites and in the violence of Greek political life. One reason why the Greeks stressed rationality, moderation, and a sense of proportion was their painful awareness that they were often emotional, overly ambitious, and wildly partisan. The Greek city-states were never able to work together, even when their very existence was threatened. The Persian Empire, the last of the great Middle Eastern monarchies, nearly overran the Greek world in the fifth century B.C. because the Greek cities fought individually instead of under a common command. The elation that followed the defeat of Persia may have encouraged Greek artists and writers to produce their masterpieces; it certainly led politicians to incredible excesses. Athens and Sparta, the two states that had done most to defeat Persia, began playing crude power politics in an attempt to gain the leadership of Greece. Athens tried to build a maritime empire; Sparta countered by forming an alliance system on the mainland. The long and bitter Peloponnesian War that followed (431–404 B.C.) left the Greeks so exhausted that they could not resist the next threat to their independence.

That threat came from Macedon, a half-Greek kingdom that lay to the north

The Parthenon, built in the fifth century B.C., stands on the crest of the Acropolis, the hill that dominates Athens. Though the Parthenon is almost as large as a football field, its basic qualities are harmony and proportion; it is constructed on a scale that can be measured and understood by the human eye.

of the Aegean. Philip of Macedon defeated a badly organized Greek alliance in 338 B.C. Philip's son, Alexander the Great (356–323 B.C.), permitted the Greeks a large measure of local autonomy but made it clear that they were expected to cooperate in building up an eastern empire. Since he succeeded in conquering all the ancient Middle East (Asia Minor, Syria, Egypt, Mesopotamia, Persia) plus western India, the Greeks had plenty of chances to cooperate.

Alexander had no respect for Greek politicians, but he had great respect for Greek culture. All through his vast empire he built new cities on the Greek model (such as Alexandria in Egypt) or installed Greeks or Hellenized* natives as the rulers of old cities. Greek became the language of the upper classes; Greek art and literature furnished the models

*The Greeks called their country Hellas. People who accepted the Greek way of life were said to be Hellenized.

ALEXANDER'S EMPIRE 336–323 B.C.

Idealized statue of Alexander, probably the work of an artist of Pergamum in Asia Minor.

for artists and writers. True, Greek culture never spread beyond the large cities, and even there the Greek veneer was sometimes very thin. Yet the Greeks left an indelible mark on a large part of the ancient world. Alexander's early death made little difference; the generals who divided his empire continued his policy of Hellenization. For almost a thousand years the ruling group and the literate classes of the Middle East followed a tradition that was largely Greek. One example of this pervasive Greek influence will suffice: although Jesus almost surely spoke Aramaic and certainly did not speak Greek, the New Testament was written in Greek by his followers.

Actually, the political collapse of Greece during and after the war between Athens and Sparta was not quite so disastrous as it is sometimes said to have been. Plato wrote after the defeat of Athens; Aristotle was the tutor of Alexander. Euclid composed his geometry about 300 B.C. The greatest achievements of Greek science, such as the measurement of the circumference of the earth or the hypothesis that the earth moved around the sun, came in Alexandria during the Hellenistic period. The Greeks had lost none of their ingenuity, though they had lost the self-confidence that came from being free citizens of free cities. The philosophies that they developed during the Hellenistic period emphasized withdrawal from the world, the simple life, the search for internal harmony. The most successful of these philosophies—Stoicism—did teach that men should perform public functions when duty called them, but the Stoics also believed that no one should seek public office and that a private citizen could lead a better life than a statesman. On the other hand, a sense of the insignificance of the private citizen in a great empire made the Greeks less arrogant and more tolerant of other peoples than they had been. Hellenistic philosophy emphasized the brotherhood of all men and the existence of a universal law. All these ideas—withdrawal from the world, self-control, a sense of duty, the equality of all men under a single law—passed from the Hellenistic philosophers to the new lords of the Mediterranean world, the Romans.

THE ROMANS

The Romans were one of various Italic peoples, closely related to the Greeks, who had settled in the Italian peninsula during the second millennium B.C. They had more good land than the Greeks, fewer good harbors, and no chain of islands to lure them out to sea. Rome and its neighboring communities remained agricultural while the Greeks were building their commercial empire. But Rome was surrounded by enemies, and the Romans learned almost as early as the Greeks that a small community could survive in a hostile world only if it could get the wholehearted support of all its inhabitants. The Romans learned this lesson even better than the Greeks. Not only did they eventually give the right to vote and to hold office to all free Romans; they also extended Roman citizenship to residents of their military colonies and to some of their allies. Conquered cities were allowed to keep their own autonomous governments so long as they helped Rome in time of war. Thus Rome was able to extend its authority over the Italian peninsula and to draw a large, well-disciplined army from the growing population of free Roman citizens and citizens of allied cities.

The test of this system came when the expanding Roman state moved into the sphere of influence of an expanding North African state—Carthage. Carthage was a Phoenician settlement that had become far more powerful than the mother country itself; it controlled what is now Tunisia, much of Sicily, and the eastern part of Spain. Rome defeated Carthage in two long and perilous wars (264–241 and 218–202 B.C.), largely because Rome could always raise one more army, while Carthage, even though it won many victories, eventually exhausted its resources. With the collapse of Carthage, Rome became master of the western Mediterranean. But it was hard for the dominant power in the West to avoid friction with the states of the East. One by one, Rome defeated the kingdoms that had grown out of Alexander's empire. Macedon, Greece, Asia Minor, Syria, and, last of all, Egypt came under Roman rule. Meanwhile Julius Caesar completed the process of subduing all the countries bordering on the Mediterranean by conquering Gaul (France) in a series of campaigns that lasted from 59 to 52 B.C. Britain and a small part of western Germany were added later, but the basic work of building a Roman Mediterranean empire had all been accomplished before the birth of Christ.

The structure of the Roman state was severely strained by the annexations that followed the defeat of Carthage and the

EARLY ITALY ca. 275 B.C.

	Roman territory *ca.* 326 B.C.
	Rome and its allies at the start of the Second Punic War, 218 B.C.

eastern kingdoms. Rome continued to be generous with grants of Roman citizenship, but most citizens lived far from Rome. Since the Roman constitution was still that of a city-state, power theoretically lay in the hands of assemblies of all citizens. But since Rome never developed the idea of representation, power actually lay in the hands of the inhabitants of the city of Rome. A citizen who could not get to Rome could not vote. The populace of Rome was not well informed and was easily swayed by cheap oratory, bribes, and threats of force. For some generations it followed the lead of the Senate, an assembly of rich landholders, heads of patrician families, and exofficials. Most officeholders and generals were selected from senatorial families and took their seats in the Senate when their terms had expired. The leaders of the Senate were ruthless and selfish men who made fortunes out of provincial governorships and army commands. So long as the most prominent senators remained more or less united, they were able to preserve a fair degree of stability. After 100 B.C., however, they began to quarrel more and more openly over the spoils of office. Each faction sought the support of the Roman voters. Elections became so corrupt and tumultuous that eventually they could not be held at all. Riots in the city became civil wars that spread throughout the state. Just when Rome was completing the task of uniting the Mediterranean world, rival military commanders threatened to destroy that unity.

In the end, however, one general became supreme. The Gallic wars had given Julius Caesar great personal prestige and control over an army of veterans. He used these assets to eliminate his rivals and to begin the rebuilding of the Roman government. His assassination (44 B.C) put an end to those efforts and triggered a new round of civil wars. But Caesar's grandnephew and heir, Octavian, succeeded, after years of intrigue and battle, in destroying all his opponents. By 27 B.C. he was in full control of the Roman world. As the restorer of peace and prosperity, he was hailed by the Senate as Augustus (the revered, the majestic one). And as Augustus he became the first emperor of the Roman people.

Augustus' power rested on his command of the army (*emperor* is merely the English form of the Latin *imperator*, commander-in-chief) and on his position as First Citizen (less politely, boss) in the Roman political structure. But the early Empire was far from being a monolithic despotism. Although popular assemblies soon withered away, the Senate retained a good deal of its political influence and continued to administer some of the more peaceful provinces. Neither Augustus nor his immediate successors had a bureaucracy large enough to rule all parts of the Empire directly. The emperor was there to keep the peace and to intervene where trouble seemed to be looming, but not to take over local administration.

In the old Roman fashion, most of the work of government was done by allied or subject city-states, with only general supervision by imperial authorities. Where city-states did not exist, as in parts of Gaul and Spain, they were created by Roman governors. This division of the West into city-states was one of the most important results of Rome's conquest of the Mediterranean world. Through the city-state the culture of Rome and of Greece flowed into less developed areas. Because the business of a city-state had to be conducted in Latin and according to Roman forms, knowledge of Latin and of Roman laws and institutions began to spread throughout non-Roman populations. The lasting influence of Rome on western Europe was not due to authoritarian controls; it was due to the fact that it was to everyone's advantage to learn Roman ways.

The East was another matter. Here was an older civilization that felt culturally superior to Rome, however weak it might be militarily. There could be no Latinization of the East, but for several centuries there was a fruitful interchange of ideas between the Greek-speaking and Latin-speaking halves of the Empire. In the East as in the West, Roman law and administrative techniques made a strong impression. In return, the West took from the East literary and artistic standards and a wide assortment of philosophies and religions. There was one important omission in the exchange of

Bust of Julius Caesar early in his political career.

ideas: the Latin part of the Empire never showed much interest in Greek science. But on the whole, by the end of the first century A.D. the organization of society and the ways of living and thinking were much the same throughout the Mediterranean world. A Roman citizen was as much at home in Beirut or Alexandria as he was in Marseilles or Naples.

Religious writers have said for many centuries that Jesus chose to be born in the reign of Augustus because then, for the first time, the civilized world was at peace and was so well unified that it was ready to receive the new revelation. Certainly the Roman Empire had created a home for and a need for Christianity. Jesus lived and died among the Jews, but his message quickly reached the Greek-speaking peoples of the East and took only a little longer to become known in Italy and Gaul. Paul's letters take us right around the Mediterranean coast—Galatians, Ephesians (Asia Minor), Philippians, Thessalonians (Macedonia), Corinthians (Greece), and finally Romans. As for the need, both Greeks and Romans had long been dissatisfied with their old religions and had grown increasingly unhappy as the individual became lost in the vast multitudes of the Empire.

Philosophies such as Stoicism could help a few individuals—in fact, Stoicism became almost an official creed for the Roman governing class—but Stoicism was too cold and rational for most people. For those who wanted more assurance that the individual was significant and that the world was meaningful, there were the mystery religions, cults in which a god sacrificed himself for his people and through his own resurrection assured the salvation of his followers. While the mystery religions offered consolation to many, they offended thoughtful and fastidious men. They bore traces of dark origins—magical incantations and animal sacrifices—and they had polytheistic tendencies. A very fearful man might belong to two or three cults at the same time; he might worship Isis and Osiris in Egypt, and the Great Mother in Asia Minor.

Christianity grew out of the pure monotheism of the Jews; it rejected all other religions and showed its confidence in the truth of its message by its intolerance. For the poor and the humble, it was enough to know that God was a loving Father who had sent his only Son to redeem mankind through his death on the cross. For the educated classes, Christianity was free of the inconsistencies and crudities that marred other religions. One could talk about Christianity in the language of Greek philosophy or of Roman law—as Paul did, and as the author of the Fourth Gospel did. Christianity spread slowly through the Empire, but it spread steadily, and occasional persecutions did nothing to stop it.

The Roman Empire flourished in the first century, in spite of palace squabbles and some detestable emperors. It flour-

This fresco found in a villa on the outskirts of Pompeii depicts initiation rites of a Dionysian mystery cult, but they are rendered in such a way as to make precise interpretation difficult for the outsider.

ished even more in the second century, when the "five good emperors" ruled, and when the Roman administrative system was perfected. A decline began about 180 A.D. with the death of Marcus Aurelius, a Stoic and the last of the "good emperors." But for fifty years more the Empire suffered no disastrous setbacks, and it was in those years that Roman law saw its classical period.

The Romans had long realized that the early laws of their own city were archaic and could not be applied throughout a world empire. They were quite ready to allow subject peoples to use their own laws in their own communities. But what was to be done when citizens of different communities sued each other, or sued a Roman? Obviously some common rules must be found that would be acceptable to men of different origins and traditions. For generations

Roman lawyers tried to formulate these general rules, encouraged by the emperors and by the Stoic belief in universal law. They sought justice and equity, and they came as close to achieving these ends as any jurists have ever done. The "law of nations" that they worked out became the common law of the Empire; even the Romans of Rome found that this new jurisprudence was superior to their old customs. And as the whole Mediterranean world came under the same law, the old distinctions between Roman citizens, allies, and subjects became meaningless. Soon after 200 A.D. almost every inhabitant of the Empire was considered a Roman citizen.

Roman law was the most lasting achievement of the Empire. The basic principles had been worked out by 235 A.D., but the law continued to grow until it was summarized and codified in the

Scenes from everyday life in first-century Rome. Left: grain from African colonies is being unloaded. Right: a Greek slave appears to be tutoring his master and mistress.

sixth century by the emperor Justinian. Justinian's Code, in turn, became the basic text for medieval and early modern lawyers. The law of most European states has been strongly influenced by Roman law, and Europeans inherited the Roman fascination with legal problems. In no other civilization have those trained in the law exerted the influence that they did in Rome and still do in Europe and countries of European origin.

Just as the Empire was reaching a peak of administrative efficiency and legal learning, it was struck by a series of disasters from which it never recovered. Civil wars devastated many provinces and opened the way for invasions by barbarians pressing on the frontiers. Poverty and insecurity weakened the cities so that they could no longer perform their old functions in local government. For fifty years—235 to 285 A.D—the Empire was almost in a state of anarchy, and the partial recovery that came after 285 was achieved only by making the emperor a military dictator.

The most obvious reason for this collapse was political. Rome had never worked out a regular, generally accepted way of choosing a new emperor. A competent emperor could nominate his successor, but the choice of a weak emperor was ignored. In the latter case, senior generals fought for the throne, and the frontiers were neglected while the armies destroyed one another. In the third century the generals were particularly agressive; even the few able emperors who emerged could not survive long enough to restore order.

Lack of fixed rules of succession was a problem, but it had been a problem in the first century when the Empire was strong. Economic weakness probably

Cicero and Ulpian on Justice

Cicero was an able lawyer as well as one of the leading Roman politicians of the first century B.C.

Since reason is given to all men by nature, so right reason is given to them, therefore they are also given law, which is right reason in commanding and forbidding; if law, therefore justice . . . thus a sense of what is right is common to all men.

From Cicero, *De legibus,* I, 33.

Ulpian was one of the great Roman jurists of the early third century A.D. These passages from Ulpian were quoted by Justinian's lawyers at the beginning of the *Digest,* an authoritative treatise on Roman law.

Justice is a constant and perpetual will to give every man his due. The principles of law are these: to live virtuously, not to harm others, to give his due to everyone. Jurisprudence is the knowledge of divine and human things, the science of the just and the unjust.

Law is the art of goodness and justice. By virtue of this we [lawyers] may be called priests, for we cherish justice and we profess knowledge of goodness and equity, separating right from wrong and legal from the illegal. . . .

Roman soldier and barbarian warrior (detail from a third-century Roman sarcophagus).

created greater difficulties. During the centuries of expansion, Rome had lived off the plunder of conquered lands; a Rome with fixed boundaries had to live off its own resources. These resources were not great. The mines, the forests, and the soil around the rim of the Mediterranean were nearly exhausted, and the Romans had not settled in large numbers in the richer lands to the north. There was relatively little manufacturing for anything but local markets. Rome had an unfavorable balance of trade because of its desire for luxury goods from the Orient, and the resulting drain of money depressed prices in the Empire. Most citizens were very poor, so the cities had trouble collecting the taxes needed for local government. Most citizens produced goods only for a local market or for a great landlord in their district; the collapse of the Empire could not make their position worse and might make it better by removing imperial (as opposed to local) taxes. And for the soldiers (who were recruited from the poorest classes and were miserably underpaid), the one chance for wealth was to support a general who was claiming the throne. There would be loot during the campaign and gifts after the final victory. In fact, a good many generals had the imperial purple forced on them by soldiers who simply wanted a chance to raid the treasury.

Finally, there was a psychological problem that had begun long before and that grew worse with every century—the feeling that the individual did not count, that nothing mattered, that no change (or at least no change for the good) would ever happen, that there was no use trying to keep the machinery going. This feeling, as we have seen, stimulated interest in the mystery religions, but all the religions, even Christianity, counseled withdrawal from the world rather than participation in war and politics. Only a handful of soldiers, public officials, and

aristocrats imbued with the old Roman traditions really wanted to keep the Empire going. It is remarkable that they succeeded, though they did so only at a price. That price was the transformation of the Empire into an absolute monarchy. The cities lost their autonomy. Peasants, artisans, and even minor officials were bound to their jobs for life. The emperor became an Oriental despot whose will was law.

These measures, begun by Diocletian (284–305), preserved a united Empire for over a century. It was not a wasted century, in spite of the growing rigidity of the social and political structure. Diocletian's successor, Constantine (307–337), first tolerated and then actively encouraged the Christian Church. He certainly believed in the Christian God; he may also have realized that Christianity represented the most vital force in the Empire. The leading writers and thinkers were Christian, and Christian art was replacing the decaying classical style. Constantine also built a new capital, named for himself, at the strategic point where the Black Sea empties into the Aegean. Constantinople, with its almost impregnable fortifications, preserved the independence of the eastern part of the Empire for over a thousand years.

Constantine's heirs completed the process of making Christianity the official religion of the Empire. They also completed the process of barbarizing the army. For a long time the only Romans in the army had been peasants from the more backward provinces; now the peasants, bound to the soil, could no longer be used to fill the ranks. For a long time barbarians from across the frontiers had been enlisted as auxiliary troops; now they formed the bulk of the army. By 400 A.D. almost every "Roman" general and almost all the soldiers were Germans. These men were not disloyal, so long as they were paid, but they had no particular attachment to the Empire and no great understanding of Roman ways.

As a result, when the next crisis came, a large part of the Empire simply disintegrated. An invasion of central Europe by the Huns (an Asian people) set the Germanic tribes milling about and pushed some of them up against the Rhine-Danube frontier. There they met some resistance, but not enough to stop all of them all of the time. Most Romans had lost their old enthusiasm for the Empire, and their initiative and sense of responsibility had been stifled by generations of authoritarian rule. The Germanized Roman army was not always eager to fight other Germans, and in any case it was not large enough to defend the whole frontier. So the Germans moved in, usually without much fighting or looting, and occupied most of the West. The last emperor in the West was deposed in 476 A.D.; after that Spain, Gaul, Britain, and Italy came under the rule of Germanic kings.

The declining creativity and technical skill of the artists of the late Roman Empire can be seen in the Arch of Constantine in Rome (312–315).

THE LATE ROMAN EMPIRE *ca.* 395 A.D.

This fragment from the crown of the Lombard king Agilulf shows the king being greeted in the cities he conquered (early seventh century).

THE END OF MEDITERRANEAN UNITY

This collapse of the Empire in the West was, curiously enough, the first step in creating a distinctively western civilization. For the East did not fall to the Germans, partly because Constantinople formed a shield for the provinces of Asia Minor, Syria, and Egypt, partly because the economic situation was better in the East, partly because the government in the East had a little more political skill and a little more courage. An emperor continued to rule in Constantinople and for a time preserved the fiction that the western kings were his deputies. But the fiction had no substance and was soon forgotten, not because the Germanic kings were hostile to the emperor, but because they simply did not understand what the Empire was. The Roman machinery of government in the West ran down and stopped; the cities dwindled and died; the number of educated men decreased sharply; and commerce with the East declined. The West could no longer draw on the cultural or physical resources of the East. It remained to be seen what the West could do with its own resources.

Those resources were potentially quite valuable. They included the fertile northern plains that the Romans had neglected or had never occupied, a large and steady supply of water power (also neglected by the Romans), and large deposits of iron and other metals. They included the highly developed Latin language (far richer than the primitive Germanic dialects), Latin literature and philosophy, and Roman law (though the latter barely escaped with its life). Last, they included the Christian Church, which did its best to preserve Roman traditions of organization and learning. The only great loss to the West (and even this was repaired after some centuries) was the loss of Greek works in mathematics, logic, and science. Even before the collapse of the Empire in the West, fewer and fewer Romans had taken the trouble to learn Greek. After the collapse, the Greek texts practically disappeared.

The West had valuable resources, but it was a long time before they could be exploited. The Latin-speaking majority was apathetic; the ruling German minority was ignorant and inexperienced. Large-scale organization and widespread cooperation became almost impossible. Germanic kings, who had ruled only a few thousand warriors, did not know how to govern large kingdoms. They could not preserve the Roman bureaucracy or the Roman tax system; they simply delegated their authority in each county to counts who struggled vainly to keep the peace. The vast majority of the population made its living from agriculture, but agricultural techniques were primitive (especially in the north) and there was a chronic shortage of food. There was relatively little long-distance trade. The working political and economic unit was a small rural district in which no one lived more than a day's journey from the local market and the neighborhood court.

The one large-scale organization that did survive, the Catholic Church, had trouble preserving its unity and reaching the people. The Church had always been a city-centered institution. The bishops and most of the clergy lived in the cities; the faithful came to the cities to hear services and to receive the sacraments. There were few rural parishes, and almost none north of the Alps. Now the cities were dying, and the Church had to deal with a vast rural population—half-Christian, Latin-speaking peasants and heathen Germans. It took time to convert the Germans; it took about three centuries to establish rural parishes throughout the Germanic kingdoms. Until this was done, most people had little contact with Christianity, and Christianity had little influence on their behavior.

By the time of the Empire's collapse, it had been generally accepted that the pope, bishop of Rome and successor of St. Peter, was head of the Church, or at least head of the Latin-speaking part of the Church. This preeminence might be contested by the patriarch of Constantinople, but it was never challenged in the West. After the breakdown of the Empire, however, the pope had difficulty exercising any administrative authority. A bishopric was a profitable position, and barbarian kings named as bishops friends and relatives who were often ignorant and vicious men. Even when good bishops were appointed, the kings tried to dominate them. The kings continually ignored requests and pleas from the pope to respect the privileges and property of local churches.

The most helpful allies of the popes were the monks, men who had renounced the world and who lived in tightly organized religious communities under the rule of an abbot. They formed a disciplined force in an age when discipline was rare; they were more respected and less often harassed by secular rulers than the rest of the clergy; they were, on the whole, obedient to the pope. During the seventh and eighth centuries the popes began to use the monks to strengthen the Church. Monks were sent as missionaries to the heathen Anglo-Saxons in England, and the Anglo-Saxons, with the zeal of new converts, soon sent missionaries to the Low Countries and to Germany. The churches founded by missionary monks proved more obedient to the pope than churches in areas, such as Gaul, that had long been nominally Christian. Eventually a reform movement spread from the missionary areas into the rest of western Europe. The character and learning of the bishops improved, and the influence of the pope increased. But the reform succeeded only because it was supported by the kings, and the Church remained very loosely organized and subject to local pressures. It was only after the year 1000 that the pope began to gain administrative control over the Church.

Meanwhile the Mediterranean area, the center of the old classical civilization, suffered new blows after a temporary recovery under the emperor Justinian (527–565). Justinian resolved to restore the splendor and the unity of the Roman Empire. His building program (including Hagia Sophia in Constantinople) and his codification of Roman law left enduring monuments of his ability and his ambition. But his effort to reconquer the West was a complete disaster. He succeeded only in destroying the Gothic kingdom of Italy, the most advanced Germanic state, and in exhausting the resources of his eastern provinces. Italy soon fell into the hands of another Germanic people, the Lombards, who were far less capable rulers than the Goths had been. Syria, Egypt, and North Africa were oppressed by heavy taxation and were angered by Justinian's obvious willingness to sacrifice their interests in order to strengthen himself in the West. In theological disputes, Justinian steadily supported doctrines of the Latin Church and opposed those of Egyptian and Syrian theologians. Since religion was almost the equivalent of patriotism for the easterners, loyalty to

Mosaic portraits of Justinian and his wife, Theodora, San Vitale, Ravenna (*ca.* 547).

Islamic door with ivory panel (eighth century).

the emperor was shaken. Justinian forced his bishops, most of whom were Greeks, to follow his policy, but in doing so he simply released long-suppressed feelings of resentment on the part of native Egyptians and Syrians against domination by a Greek-speaking minority. During the crisis of the fifth century the East had held together. In the crisis that was soon to come, the Egyptians and Syrians made almost no effort to preserve their ties to the Empire.

The new crisis was caused by the rise of a new religion—Islam. The prophet Mohammed (*ca.* 570–632) had gradually convinced his fellow Arabs that he had received a revelation from God that superseded all earlier revelations. He accepted much of Jewish and Christian tradition, but he emphasized strict monotheism (in opposition to the Christian doctrine of the Trinity) and the joys of Paradise and the pains of hell (in opposition to Jewish uncertainties concerning the afterlife). His religion was simple and easily taught. No priest or theologian was necessary. To become a Moslem—that is, a convert to Islam—one had only to believe in Allah and in his prophet, Mohammed, to accept Mohammed's sayings (the Koran) as the word of God, and to

pray each day and fast for one month of the year.

Mohammed was not only a prophet; he was a political and military leader. Before his death he had united most of the scattered Arab tribes. His successors, the caliphs, used this united force to conquer the Middle East. Syria, Egypt, and North Africa fell after brief struggles. Persia, weakened by repeated wars with the Roman Empire, came under Moslem domination at the same time. Not all the conquered peoples became converted, but enough of them accepted Islam so that new armies could be raised for new wars. In the West the Moslem armies took Morocco, overran most of Spain, and raided Gaul. In the East they pushed as far as the Indus Valley. In just about a century the Moslems had created an empire larger than that of Rome at its greatest extent.

The Mediterranean world was now split into three unequal fragments. Largest and richest were the lands of the Moslem caliphate. The remnant of the Roman Empire now included only Greece, the Balkans, and Asia Minor, but it was a wealthy and well-organized state. Because it now was completely centered on Constantinople, whose old name was

THE GROWTH OF THE ISLAMIC CALIPHATE   632–750

Northumbrian cross (*ca.* 700).

Byzantium, this fragment of the old Roman state is usually called the Byzantine Empire. Finally, there was western Europe, poor, backward, and barbarous.

The shock of Justinian's wars and of the Moslem wars of conquest separated the West even more sharply from its old neighbors than had the earlier Germanic invasions. Not all contacts were broken, of course. Trade between East and West continued; the Byzantine Empire for a long time held enclaves in Italy and sent embassies to western courts; pope and patriarch remained in communion with each other until the eleventh century. But the West was profoundly suspicious of the Byzantines, who seemed arrogant, oversophisticated, and unreliable, and it was profoundly hostile to the Moslems, who were raiding Italy and southern Gaul. On the other hand, neither Byzantines nor Moslems saw much advantage in trying to expand relations with an undeveloped and poverty-stricken area. For several centuries western imports from the East, whether of goods or of ideas, remained at a low level.

Another result of Justinian's wars and the Moslem conquests was the destruction of the Germanic kingdoms that touched the Mediterranean. The Franks, whose strength lay on the lower Rhine and in northeastern Gaul, were far enough removed from the Mediterranean turmoil to escape damage, and they gradually picked up fragments of other kingdoms in southern France, northeastern Spain, and northern Italy. By the end of the eighth century the Franks were dominant in western Europe. The little Anglo-Saxon kingdoms in Britain had not yet united to form an English state; there was only a bare beginning of political organization in Scandinavia, and not even a beginning among the Slavs of central Europe. But the Frankish kings ruled lands that stretched from the Ebro to the Elbe and from the North Sea to Rome. Given the strength of local feeling and the weakness of Germanic administrative methods, this was far too large an area to remain long united. But for about a century the Frankish empire held together, and during that century some decisive steps were taken in founding a distinctively western civilization.

REVIVAL OF THE WEST

This fruitful period is usually called the Carolingian Age, after the most famous of Frankish kings, Charlemagne, or Charles the Great (768–814). Charlemagne, however, in many ways simply continued the work of his father and grandfather, and many of his own plans (especially in cultural matters) were fulfilled only in the reigns of his son and grandsons. The basic policy, from the beginning to the end of the Carolingian dynasty, was close cooperation between king and pope. The kings protected the pope from his enemies and supported missionary work in Germany. They encouraged reform in Gaul and closer connections between pope and bishops. They also encouraged a great increase in the number of rural parishes. As a result, the Church in the West improved the quality of its personnel, began to improve its administrative system, and had more frequent contact with the mass of the population. In fact, it was only with the Carolingian period that most men north of the Alps began to have a real chance to practice the Christian religion.

In return, the Church gave its spiritual support to the Carolingians and called on its prelates to take an active part in the administration of the kingdom. Since the clergy by this time were the only educated class, their assistance was absolutely necessary if the government was to operate. Moreover, the bishops and abbots were usually more loyal to the king than to the counts (the district governors), and they were often used by the Carolingians to balance the influence of local strong men. Finally, since the prelates were drawn from all parts of Europe, they helped to spread a common culture across the continent.

This common culture was the most lasting achievement of the Carolingian Age. Charles and his successors were eager to improve the education of the clergy, and with their encouragement a basic curriculum was established that was followed in all church schools. The Latin classics had to be studied to improve skill in the use of the language; as a result, books that were on the verge of disappearing were recopied and preserved. The Bible had to be explained in detail, so copies of the Bible were multiplied and errors in earlier texts were corrected. The Church Fathers furnished the authoritative explanations of the Scriptures, and again a vast effort of copying and emendation was needed. Added to this was a reform in handwriting that made reading much easier. It was only in the Carolingian Age that a large enough number of men in western Europe began to understand and to use their Latin and Christian intellectual heritage to help mold western society.

The culmination of the papal–Carolingian alliance came in 800, when the pope crowned Charles emperor in St. Peter's Church in Rome. This act symbolized Charles's supremacy in the West and his role as protector of the Church. It added somewhat to his moral authority over his subjects, though it did not increase his political power. On the other hand, it irritated the Byzantine emperor and thus helped to widen the rift between eastern and western Europe. The revival of a "Roman" Empire also created problems that were to plague the West for centuries. What authority did the emperor have over Italy, and especially Rome? If the pope could make an emperor, could he then depose him? And if a pope could depose an emperor, could he not also depose kings?

In the years that followed Charlemagne's death, however, the problems of the Empire became submerged in the greater problem of whether any political unit could survive. Internal strife among the Franks and a new wave of invasions from the north, east, and south threatened all forms of organization. Charlemagne's grandsons, after a bloody civil war, split the family lands into three shares. One grandson took France; another took the nucleus of what became Germany; the eldest received a middle kingdom, including the Netherlands, Belgium, Lorraine, part of Switzerland, Provence, and northern Italy. This long, narrow strip lacked cohesion, and soon the kings of France and Germany began to fight over fragments of the middle kingdom, a fight that has continued into our own century. Meanwhile the Scandinavian vikings began to raid and then conquer parts of Ireland, England, France, and Germany; the Magyars (a group of Asian nomads) occupied the Hungarian plain and plundered Germany and northern Italy; and the Moslems terrorized the coasts of Italy and southern France. Under the impact of war and invasion the Carolingian Empire dissolved. The empire split into kingdoms, the kingdoms into principalities, the principalities into counties, and the counties into castellanies (small areas ruled by the lord of a castle).

The fragmentation went farthest in France and in western Germany, and by 900 a new type of political organization was beginning to appear—a type that was later to be known as feudalism. In feudalism the actual work of government was done by a lord assisted by a band of armed retainers. Some lords ruled only the district around a castle; some were able to unite several castellanies; a very few lords (for example, the Duke of Normandy) had effective power over many counties. But large or small, the territory ruled by a lord was an autonomous political unit. There was a face-saving theory by which the lord owed allegiance and obedience to the king, or to some superior (a duke or a count) who stood be-

The Coronation of Charlemagne 800

Now when the king upon the most holy day of the Lord's birth was rising to the mass after praying before the tomb of the blessed Peter the Apostle, Leo the Pope, with the consent of all the bishops and priests and of the senate of the Franks and likewise of the Romans, set a golden crown upon his head, the Roman people also shouting aloud. And when the people had made an end of chanting praises, he was adored by the pope after the manner of the emperors of old. For this was also done by the will of God. For while the said Emperor abode at Rome certain men were brought to him who said that the name of Emperor had ceased among the Greeks, and that there the Empire was held by a woman called Irene, who had by guile laid hold on her son the Emperor and put out his eyes and taken the Empire to herself. . . . Which when Leo the Pope and all the assembly of the bishops and priests and abbots heard, and the senate of the Franks and all the elders of the Romans, they took counsel with the rest of the Christian people, that they should name Charles king of the Franks to be Emperor, seeing that he held Rome the mother of empire where the Caesars and Emperors always used to sit.

From *Chronicle of Moissac*, trans. by J. Bryce, *The Holy Roman Empire* (New York: Macmillan and St. Martin's Press, 1911), p. 54.

Ninth-century statue of Charlemagne on horseback. He wears a crown and carries an orb, symbol of royal power.

of government that met the needs of the time. The effective political unit—county or castellany—corresponded fairly closely with the working economic unit—a district centered around a few local markets. Local defense could be better secured by a local lord than by a distant king. Since the lord thought of his government as his private property, it was to his interest to improve that government, thereby making it more profitable. In time, feudal government became far more effective and far more popular than either the Germanic kingships or the late Carolingian monarchy had been. Most modern European states grew out of feudal states.

The immediate advantage of feudalism was that it gave increased security to many parts of the West. Inside the larger lordships relative peace prevailed; the frontier skirmishing and the quarrels of petty lords did far less damage than civil wars among Frankish kings had done. Feudal lords did their share in beating back the invasions of the Northmen and the Moslems, though kings and popes also won significant victories over these intruders. (The Magyar threat was blunted largely by the efforts of the king of Germany.) Altogether, in the century after the year 1000, there were very few major wars and almost no large-scale invasions of Europe.

Increased security, limited though it was, meant increased population. An increased population, in turn, required more food, and so stimulated improvements in agricultural techniques. These improvements produced enough food to support a rapid growth of the urban and professional classes. Industry and commerce expanded; for example, fine woolen cloth made in Flanders could be exchanged with Byzantines and Moslems for eastern luxuries. Political stability and economic expansion brought the West above the subsistence level for the first time in centuries.

Just as significant as increased production was the increased influence of the Church. It had taken a long time for Christianity to get under the skins of the people of the West. The slow extension of the parish system, the setbacks caused by repeated invasions by non-Christian

tween him and the king. This theory was to be helpful later in furnishing an excuse for reconstituting large political units, but in the tenth century it was meaningless. The chain of obedience was broken at many points, and each break marked the existence of an independent lordship.

The retainers of the lords were knights, men who never had independent political power but who gradually emerged as a landlord class. Most lords had a great deal of land, worked by free or unfree peasant farmers, while their castles were small and crowded. So it was easier to give a knight some land and the services of the peasants who worked the land than it was to support him in the lord's household. By 1100 most knights possessed estates, or even whole villages, and they gradually acquired a sort of police-court jurisdiction over their peasants. But the knights always remained politically dependent on greater men—barons, counts, or kings.

Feudalism was a rudimentary form of organization in which the ruler treated his rights of government as if they were private property. It was, however, a type peoples, the ignorance of many of the clergy, and the weak administrative system of the Church were all responsible for this lag. But during the eleventh century the Northmen and the Magyars were converted, and a new reform movement, much more widespread than that of the Carolingians, improved the quality of the clergy and increased the administrative authority of the pope. Laymen became more devout (if not more virtuous), more eager to demonstrate their attachment to the faith, and more willing to accept the leadership of the Church. For the first time in centuries the West had ideals and goals that commanded the ardent support of almost all members of society.

Some aspects of the life of a feudal knight—accompanying a traveling king and feasting (details from eleventh- and twelfth-century manuscripts).

THE CIVILIZATION OF WESTERN EUROPE IN THE MIDDLE AGES

These improvements in the condition of western Europe after the year 1000 created a burst of energy that lasted for more than two centuries. One of the first problems was to find land for the increasing population. Even though the towns were growing, they absorbed only about 10 percent of the population. Everyone else had to make a living by farming. All over Europe forests were cleared and swamps and marshes were drained. The Germans began to push into the half-empty Slavic lands that lay between the Elbe and Oder rivers. Some peasant families traveled hundreds of miles in order to obtain small farms on this eastern frontier. The Norman Conquest of England in 1066 was not just a military adventure: northern France was overpopulated; England was underpopulated; and most of William's army was composed of poor knights looking for land. The less well-known Norman conquest of southern Italy and Sicily was also accomplished by poor knights who could not make a living in their own country. And the long, slow reconquest of Spain from the Moslems was spurred on by the existence of empty land in the disputed area that lay between the little Christian kingdoms of the north and the Moorish states of the south.

Another problem was to make governments strong enough to put down internal disorder. In pursuit of this goal, however, rulers ran head-on into one of the strongest movements of the eleventh and twelfth centuries: the drive to reform the Church. No government could operate without the help of the clergy; members of the clergy were better educated, more competent as administrators, and usually more reliable than laymen. Kings and the greater feudal lords naturally wanted to control the appointment of bishops and abbots in order to create a corps of capable and loyal public servants. On the other hand, the reformers wanted a Church that was completely independent, a Church that would instruct and admonish lay rulers rather than serve them. The conflict between the two points of view led to a struggle that lasted for half a century, from the 1070s to the 1120s.

The leading figures in the struggle were the pope and the king of Germany. Germany had suffered less from civil war and invasion than had France and had consequently been less severely fragmented. The king had some power in most parts of the country, largely through the support given him by bishops and abbots whom he had appointed. In 962 a German king was strong enough to conquer northern Italy and to revive the title of emperor, which had lapsed after Charlemagne's empire had collapsed in the late ninth century. Almost all German kings after 962 were also emperors, titular rulers of northern Italy, and protectors of Rome and of the pope. In this last capacity they frequently installed men of their own choice in the papal office and on at least one occasion deposed a pope.

Such a situation was obviously intolerable to the reformers. Pope Gregory VII (1073–85) forbade the emperor to interfere in papal elections; henceforth the pope was to be chosen only by the cardinals. Gregory also tried to keep the emperor from naming bishops and abbots. The emperor Henry IV (1056–1106) in turn tried to depose the pope. Gregory then released Henry's subjects from allegiance to their ruler, and a rebellion broke out in Germany. Henry was so

weakened that he had to seek the pope's forgiveness at Canossa (1077). This was not a complete victory for Gregory (Henry later succeeded in driving him from Rome), but it did prove that some

Norman troops on horseback engaging Anglo-Saxon foot soldiers in battle (detail from the Bayeux tapestry, late eleventh century).

Principles of Gregory VII
ca. 1075

This document was certainly drawn up in Gregory's circle, and probably by the pope himself. It expresses the views of those who were trying to increase papal power in both Church and state.

1. That the Roman church was founded by the Lord alone.
2. That only the Roman pontiff is rightly called universal.
3. That he alone can depose or reestablish bishops.
4. That his legate, even if of inferior rank, is above all bishops in council; and he can give sentence of deposition against them. . . .
12. That it is permitted to him to depose emperors. . . .
18. That his decision ought to be reviewed by no one, and that he alone can review the decisions of everyone.
19. That he ought to be judged by no one.
20. That no one may dare condemn a man who is appealing to the apostolic see.
21. That the greater cases of every church ought to be referred to him.
22. That the Roman church has never erred nor will ever err, as the Scripture bears witness.
23. That the Roman pontiff, if he has been canonically ordained, is indubitably made holy by the merits of the blessed Peter. . . .
24. That by his precept and license subjects are permitted to accuse their lords. . . .
27. That he can absolve the subjects of the unjust from their fealty.

From *Dictatus Papae Gregorii VII*, trans. by E. Lewis, *Medieval Political Ideas* (New York: Knopf, 1954), Vol. II, pp. 380–81.

concessions would have to be made by lay rulers. Eventually a compromise was reached by the successors of Gregory and of Henry, a compromise that paralleled agreements reached between the pope and other rulers. Papal independence and papal administrative authority over the Church were clearly recognized. Royal influence over the appointment of bishops was admitted, and many bishops continued to act as advisers and officials of kings. The pope, however, could give orders to and discipline any bishop.

The net result of the struggle was to put the Church in a position rarely enjoyed by a religious organization. It was completely independent of the state. It had shown that it had enough support among men of all classes to shake the structure of any government that opposed it. The Church had taken over the leadership of western Europe.

An early demonstration of this leadership was the First Crusade (1096–99). Pope Urban II had many reasons for inaugurating the movement. Sending belligerent knights and nobles to fight the Moslems would distract them from their petty wars in Europe. If western warriors could help the Byzantines to regain some of their lost provinces, the quarrels between the Greek and the Roman Churches, which had culminated in the mutual excommunications of pope and patriarch in 1054, might be healed. Finally, Urban earnestly desired that the Holy Land be under Christian rule. His appeal for an expedition to the East had enormous and unexpected success. Men from all parts of the West responded to Urban's summons and under the leadership of a papal legate marched through Europe, Asia Minor, and Syria to capture the city of Jerusalem. No secular ruler could have raised such an army or persuaded men from so many different countries to cooperate. Only the pope could make full use of the religious fervor of the people. For two centuries the protection of the Holy Land through crusades was a primary goal of western Christians, and in the interests of the crusades the pope could intervene in every aspect of European life.

The new energy of the West, guided by the Church, also led to remarkable achievements in art and scholarship. A vast number of churches were built between 1000 and 1300, and a completely new architectural style emerged. The earlier Romanesque churches still had some affinities with buildings of the late Roman Empire, but about the middle of the twelfth century the first Gothic churches appeared in northern France. The new style was marked by height and light, with emphasis on vertical rather than horizontal lines and on enlarging window space as far as possible. To fill the windows, stained glass was needed; to adorn the exterior and especially the portals, large numbers of statues were required. All the arts worked together to make the Gothic style one of the most beautiful ever conceived.

In scholarship it was much the same story. By the twelfth century there was a sharp increase in the number of students and a desire to go beyond the work of the late Roman Empire. To teach large numbers of students, a new institution had to be invented—the university. To acquire new knowledge, texts that had been neglected or little used had to be studied. At Bologna the study of Roman law, as codified under Justinian, became the principal pursuit. Thousands of men from all parts of Europe studied at Bologna and carried home with them new ideas about the nature of the state and the meaning of justice. At Paris, the emphasis was on theology, and on logic as an indispensable tool in the understanding of theology. Since only a few basic texts on logic were known, a search was made for new material. This material could be found only in Greek, or in Arabic translations from the Greek. Several generations of devoted scholars spent their lives translating these books into Latin. In the process, all of Aristotle's works on logic were recovered, and much more besides. The Greek scientific and mathematical tradition, amplified by the Arabs, became, for the first time, part of the intellectual heritage of the West. The Romans had neglected science, but from the twelfth century on, western Europeans showed an increasing interest in scientific studies.

For the scholars at Paris, however, theology, not physics or mathematics,

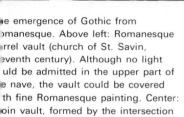

e emergence of Gothic from
omanesque. Above left: Romanesque
arrel vault (church of St. Savin,
eventh century). Although no light
uld be admitted in the upper part of
e nave, the vault could be covered
th fine Romanesque painting. Center:
oin vault, formed by the intersection

of two barrel vaults (Mont-Saint-Michel,
twelfth century). The walls could now
be pierced with windows. Above right:
late Romanesque rib vault (Mont-
Saint-Michel). Ribs reinforce the groin
vault, but the effect is still heavy. Below
left: early Gothic rib vault (Mont-Saint-
Michel). Greater height and light are

now being exploited. Below right:
Gothic rib vaulting on a grand scale
(the nave of Chartres Cathedral, 1194–
1220). Great height and light have
been achieved; the upper (clerestory)
windows are larger and more useful
than those at floor level.

A university lecture, as portrayed in a fourteenth-century Italian miniature. Attention to the lecturer is not undivided; several students are talking, and one is certainly asleep.

was the "queen of the sciences." With great effort they managed to weave all their knowledge into a pattern of Christian theology and philosophy. The final synthesis was achieved by St. Thomas Aquinas (1225–74). Thomas believed that all learning, even that of the pagans, was inspired by Divine Reason, and that it was impossible for a truth known by natural reason to contradict a truth known by revelation. Thus a great deal of Greek and Moslem scholarship could be absorbed into western thought.

The Church led Europe, but it could not do everything. It admitted that lay governments were necessary to keep the peace and to repress crime. It taught that the chief duty of a ruler was to do justice. This view was reinforced by the revival of legal studies and by the self-interest of kings and princes. In the twelfth and thirteenth centuries the best way to strengthen a state was to improve the administration of justice and to persuade or force subjects to come to the law courts. The European states that began to

emerge in the twelfth century were more firmly based on law than any other political units that had existed before.

The process of state-building went farthest and fastest in England and France. England had avoided fragmentation, partly because it was a small country, partly because the old Anglo-Saxon aristocracy that might have set up autonomous provincial governments was wiped out by the Norman Conquest. The new Norman aristocracy was created by the king, was dependent on him, and had very limited powers. The kings had land, officers, and courts in every part of England. So it was very easy for them to develop a reasonably efficient financial administration that centered royal revenues in one place. It was almost as easy to attract people to the royal courts. The kings sent their judges around on regular circuits; they protected the possessions of all free men; they used the jury to determine the facts in law suits instead of depending on such superstitious practices as trial by battle. By 1300 uniform taxes had been imposed, and all important cases were tried by royal courts.

The king of France had greater difficulties. At first he ruled directly only a small district running north and south of Paris. Even in this limited area there were unruly and disobedient lords; outside it were the feudal principalities (Normandy, Flanders, Burgundy, and others) where he had no power at all. His first job was to get full control of the Paris region; this was done early in the twelfth century. Next was the delicate task of finding ways of annexing the great lordships. Some came in by way of marriages between royal princes and heiresses; a few of the smaller ones came by purchase; but the most effective means was judgment by the king's court. Respect for the court grew during the twelfth century; by the thirteenth century a lord who defied its jurisdiction or disobeyed its orders could be punished by confiscation of his lands. King John of England lost the duchy of Normandy in this way—a lesson that made a deep impression on other lords. By 1285 the greater part of France was ruled directly by the king, and the part still held by feudal lords was reasonably obedient to him.

France, however, was less unified than England. In England there was one law and one system of courts. In France each province was allowed to keep its old laws and courts even after it was annexed to the crown. English royal courts dealt directly with the people. The French royal court at Paris dealt largely with appeals from provincial officials and feudal lords. Imperfect unity in turn reduced royal income. General taxes in France started a century later than in England, and even then strongly entrenched local privileges cut down the yield. France had four or five times the population of England, but the revenues of the two kings were often about the same.

Other countries were less advanced. The Spanish kingdoms were still occupied with their struggle against the Moors; the Scandinavian kingdoms were still unstable; the Slavic kingdoms were just beginning to get organized. Germany and Italy had been shattered by the struggle between pope and emperor. The typical political unit in Germany was to be the principality, and in Italy the city-state. But even in these areas there had been improvement since the period of invasion and civil war that followed the collapse of the Carolingian Empire. Almost everywhere secular rulers—kings, princes, city magistrates—were repressing internal violence and providing greater security for all classes.

The thirteenth century, which was on the whole a peaceful and prosperous period for the West, was a time of troubles for eastern Europe. Crusaders who had originally planned to attack the Moslems in the Holy Land were misled by Venetian politicians and Byzantine exiles and instead took the city of Constantinople (1204). The Greeks held on to fragments of their empire and eventually drove the westerners out of the capital city (1261), but the restored Byzantine Empire was never very strong. It could not resist the advance of the Turks, which began in the fourteenth century, and the Byzantines became even more suspicious of the West than they had been.

Russia was hit even harder. In the thirteenth century the Mongols started the greatest series of invasions in the history of the Asian nomads. They took China, Persia, and Mesopotamia and drove clear across Russia to the frontiers

EUDAL FRANCE   Late eleventh century

KINGDOM OF ENGLAND

ENGLISH CHANNEL

FLANDERS

LORRAINE

HOLY

Rhine R.

Rouen
Seine R.
Reims
NORMANDY
CHAMPAGNE
Paris
BRITTANY
B L O I S
ANJOU
Blois
Orléans
DUCHY OF BURGUNDY
Dijon
Loire R.
Tours
Cluny
POITOU
Lyons
ROMAN EMPIRE
KINGDOM OF BURGUNDY
BAY OF BISCAY
AQUITAINE
AUVERGNE
Rhône R.
Bordeaux
Garonne R.
GASCONY
TOULOUSE
Toulouse
Fraxinetum
NAVARRE
MEDITERRANEAN SEA
BARCELONA
EMIRATE OF SARAGOSSA

■ Royal Domain

0   MILES   100

of Hungary. Russia had been Christianized by the Greek Church and had drawn most of its intellectual and artistic tradition from the Byzantines. Now the Russian princes were forced into the northern forests, and even there they had to pay tribute to the Mongols. Contacts with Constantinople decreased; contacts with the West almost ended. Russia turned in on itself, proud of its orthodox faith and its old traditions, suspicious of all outsiders.

Thus the division between East and West that had begun centuries before was accentuated. The Byzantines could not forget the conquest of 1204, and the heirs of the Byzantine emperors were to be Turkish sultans, not Christian kings from the West. Russia had become isolated and for many generations was to look south and east to the camps of the Mongol khans, rather than west to Latin Christendom. The Moslems succeeded in converting the Mongols who had occupied their lands, but in the process they too became somewhat Orientalized and withdrawn. Moslem civilization of the twelfth century had been much more akin to western civilization than was the Moslem civilization of the fourteenth century.

THE CRISIS OF THE LATER MIDDLE AGES

The West once more stood alone. But it was in a far stronger position than it had been when the old Mediterranean world broke into fragments. By the thirteenth century the main outlines of what we call medieval civilization were well established. This medieval civilization was clearly a western civilization, unlike any that had existed before and unlike any of its contemporaries. Its ideals were largely Christian; its intellectual tradition was a unique combination of Greek, Roman, and Moslem thought, with some Jewish and even some Hindu influence. The West had an art that was entirely its own and habits of thinking that were becoming more and more original. It had built new institutions—the Church, the law-based monarchy, the university. It had improved its technology and had reached an economic level not inferior to that of earlier civilizations. In fact, per capita income in western Europe in the thirteenth century was probably higher than it had been in the same area in the best days of the Roman Empire. But this western civilization was no richer, no stronger, no more impressive in its intellectual and artistic production than contemporary civilizations in China, India, or the Moslem world. It was still based largely on peasant agriculture; industrial production was still low; even the rich lived under conditions that would appall a slum-dweller today. As for the poorest peasants and textile workers, their lives were short, miserable, and hopeless. By modern standards, western Europe in the

Turkish miniature depicting an Asiatic bowman. Unencumbered by armor, he could move swiftly on his small, strong horse.

thirteenth century was an underdeveloped society.

Moreover, western civilization was beginning to show signs of strain. The strain appeared first in the Church, which in exercising its leadership had found itself more and more involved in wordly affairs and less and less able to understand the affairs in which it was involved. For example, the Church drew most of its income from the land and did not fully understand the behavior and the problems of the urban classes. The Church had encouraged rulers to seek peace and justice but failed to see that their very success in this endeavor was strengthening men's loyalty to secular rulers. The Church still sought independence from lay authority, but thirteenth-century popes confused independence with their desire for a particular political configuration in Italy, one in which there was no strong state in the peninsula. In resisting the emergence of a strong Italian state they drifted into a long series of wars with German emperors, who by this time held Sicily and Naples and were trying to unite these southern territories with Lombardy and Tuscany. During the wars (1229–68) the popes taxed the clergy to support papal armies, gave indulgences to their supporters, and called on the kings of France and England for assistance. By playing politics, the papacy became politicized; by relying on secular rulers, the papacy lost much of the independence that it was trying to preserve; by preventing the creation of a strong Italian state, the papacy created such anarchy that the fourteenth-century popes had to abandon Rome and take refuge in France. By 1300 there was much less respect for the Church as an institution than there had been in 1200.

Western Europe remained more attached to the Christian faith than to the institution that embodied that faith. Two new religious orders, the Dominicans and the Franciscans, founded early in the thirteenth century, tried to reach the people who were alienated from or neglected by the rest of the clergy. These orders gained considerable support from townspeople, intellectuals, and secular administrators. But while they helped to preserve the faith, they had little influence on men's conduct. Western Europeans became more worldly, more selfish, more critical of the administration of the Church. The conflict between belief and behavior, the contrast between revivalistic piety and cynical resistance to papal orders, led to a dangerous instability in society.

Meanwhile, secular governments were growing in power and prestige. The thirteenth century was, on the whole, a peaceful age; even the papal–imperial wars were fought mostly on a local level and only occasionally led to large-scale battles. If men did not settle their quarrels by fighting, they had to settle them by law suits; and the more cases that came to the courts, the stronger the governments became. In these circumstances it was easy to transfer loyalty from a Church that did not seem to be doing its job very well to secular states that did seem to be. The showdown came at the

U el · iij · manieres de genſ que
L i philoſofe poſerent au mõd

leyue
regne
oz e a
paris
Enſi 9
ele fu
1a dis
a athe
nes q
ſiet en
grece

b ne ate de gũ nobleſe
a philoſofe q loez furent

Representatives of the three estates—a clergyman, a knight, and a laborer—from a late–thirteenth-century manuscript. The chapter heading over the picture says: "Of the three sorts of people whom the philosophers place in the world."

Medieval coins. Top to bottom: Florentine gold florin (thirteenth century); Venetian gold ducat (thirteenth century); obverse and reverse of a silver penny of Henry III of England (thirteenth century); gold agnel of Philip VI of France (fourteenth century). The gold coins were used for large-scale transactions; the silver, for wages and household purchases.

end of the century when major wars broke out again between France and Flanders, England and Scotland, and France and England. The kings of England and France ordered their clergy to pay taxes to support these wars, even though the clergy were supposed to be free from secular burdens. The pope at first forbade the clergy to pay, but this prohibition caused such a storm of protest that he had to admit that the clergy could be taxed for defense of the state. A few years later the king of France arrested a bishop on charges of treason. When the pope ordered the bishop's release and criticized the king's behavior, an agent of the king tried to arrest the pope on trumped-up charges of heresy. The attempt very nearly succeeded, and the ensuing propaganda attack against the pope became so nasty that in the end the papacy fully absolved the king and his ministers. In a head-on collision between Church and state, the Church had backed down. The people, including a large number of the clergy, had supported their king rather than the pope. The threat of a Church-inspired rebellion against a disobedient ruler was no longer credible.

These events put an end to the leadership that the Church had exerted in lay affairs for two centuries. Logically, the victorious states should have succeeded to that leadership. But the states were not quite ready to assume the responsibility. Their administrative structures were not yet complete; for example, no state had a foreign office or a war department. There was still a good deal of localism that limited the effectiveness of actions by the central governments. Worst of all, no state was able to solve a host of new problems that arose in the fourteenth century, and at times even strong states like England were almost as discredited as the Church. Therefore, the state did not emerge as the controlling force in western civilization until the end of the fifteenth century, and this emergence may be taken as one sign of the beginning of the modern period. Meanwhile, Europe floundered for a century and a half with no leadership of any kind.

The problems of the fourteenth century were grave enough to perplex the

ablest men. The economy had reached its limits; until new techniques, new industries, and new markets were discovered, Europe could neither produce more from its own resources nor acquire more from other areas. Population was pressing heavily on the land. Many peasants were barely at subsistence levels, but the labor market of the overcrowded cities offered them no relief. Landlords were finding it hard to live on their rents and had to borrow money at high rates of interest. So did most kings and princes. But the bankers from whom they borrowed were no better off; almost all of them went bankrupt during the century. In short, western Europe had entered a long and serious economic depression.

Population pressure was relieved by the Black Death, an outbreak of bubonic plague that entered Europe in 1347, swept through the West in a great arc— Italy, France, England, Germany—and returned several times during the century. In the areas that were hardest hit a third or more of the population died. The psychological shock of such a mortality rate and the economic shock of adjusting to a completely new population pattern were enormous. Peasants were better off, since they could now concentrate their work on the richest lands; artisans were worse off, since they had lost many customers and had to pay higher prices for food. It took a long time to strike a new balance between rural and urban producers. Meanwhile, society was dangerously unstable. There were frequent revolts by peasants eager to exploit their advantageous position, and by artisans trying to avoid loss of income and status.

With no economists and only a few badly trained doctors, governments could not have been expected to do much about the problems of depression and disease. They might, however, have avoided war. But in an age when many men were suffering from diminishing incomes, pressures for war were great. Nobles and landed gentry, who raised and commanded companies of soldiers, could make a good living out of army wages and could always hope for a windfall—the plundering of a town, for example, or the ransoming of a prominent prisoner. Merchants and mariners could try to eliminate their competitors. Kings could add new provinces to their domains and could forget their other problems in the excitement of conflict. Uncertain boundaries and attempts by feudal lords, such as the Count of Flanders, to assert their independence from higher authorities were also excuses for fighting. The thirteenth century had been relatively peaceful; the fourteenth and early fifteenth centuries were periods of almost constant warfare.

The longest and most costly war was the Hundred Years' War between England and France, which lasted officially from 1337 to 1453. Actually, neither country could afford continuous fighting, and the war was interrupted by long truces. Nevertheless, it used up most of the income of the two governments and devastated large areas of France. Other wars, in Scandinavia, Germany, Italy, and Spain, were less spectacular but caused a great deal of suffering.

The net result of all these conflicts was to confirm patterns that were already emerging in the thirteenth century. Germany remained a divided land ruled by many independent princes, of whom the Habsburg rulers of Austria were the strongest. Northern Italy remained a region of city-states, now wealthier than most of the other cities of Europe because the Italians had gained a virtual monopoly over the eastern trade. Wealth, however, led not to political stability but to factional quarrels, and by 1500 France and Spain were taking advantage of this weakness to intervene in Italy. The district around Rome claimed by the pope was almost in a state of anarchy, and southern Italy was occupied by a decaying monarchy. The three Spanish kingdoms of Portugal, Castile, and Aragon had driven the Moors to the southernmost tip of the peninsula, and marriages that would lead to the merger of Castile and Aragon into a kingdom of Spain were being prepared. Most important of all, the outcome of the Hundred Years' War confirmed the unity of France and forced the English to give up their hopes of holding territory on the Continent. When a peasant girl, Joan of Arc, became convinced that her religious duty and her loyalty to the French royal house re-

quired her to drive out the English and then secured enough support to persuade armies to follow her against the invaders, it became clear that the English were facing forces they could not defeat. It is too early to speak of nationalism, but

Scenes of everyday life in the fourteenth century—buying clothes and a smithy at work (detail from a contemporary manuscript illumination).

The Black Death in England

Then that most grievous pestilence penetrated the coastal regions by way of Southampton and came to Bristol, and people died as if the whole strength of the city were seized by sudden death. For there were few who lay in their beds more than three days or two and a half days; then that savage death snatched them about the second day. In Leicester, in the little parish of St. Leonard, more than three hundred and eighty died; in the parish of the Holy Cross, more than four hundred, and in the parish of St. Margaret, more than seven hundred. . . .

And the price of everything was cheap, because of the fear of death, there were very few who took any care for their wealth, or for anything else. For a man could buy a horse for half a mark [about 7 shillings] which before was worth forty shillings, a large fat ox for four shillings, a cow for twelve pence, a heifer for sixpence, a large fat sheep for four pence. . . . And the sheep and cattle wandered about through the fields and among the crops, and there was no one to go after them or collect them. They perished in countless numbers everywhere, for lack of watching . . . since there was such a lack of serfs and servants, that no one knew what he should do. For there is no memory of a mortality so severe and so savage. . . . In the following autumn, one could not hire a reaper for less than eight pence [per day] with food, or a mower at less than twelve pence with food.

From Henry Knighton, *Chronicle*, in *The Portable Medieval Reader*, ed. by J. B. Ross and M. M. McLaughlin (New York: Viking, 1949), pp. 218–19.

dislike of English rule had brought the French very close to nationalistic ideas. The English burned Joan as a heretic in 1431, but twenty years later they had lost all their French lands except Calais.

The wars also tended to sharpen an already existing difference between the institutions of England and those of other kingdoms. England was a unitary state, not an assemblage of provinces. Therefore England had a single representative assembly, the Parliament, instead of an assembly for each province or region. Representative assemblies had been introduced into most European states by thirteenth-century rulers who had found them useful instruments for influencing public opinion. Occasionally the assem-

blies were asked to give advice on policy or the making of statutes; more frequently, they were asked to consent to taxation. But where there were many provincial assemblies the opposition of one province made little difference; and where the pressure of war was greatest, as in France, there was a tendency to let the king collect taxes for defense without bothering about getting consent.

The English Parliament, on the other hand, spoke for the whole country, and England never had to face a dangerous invasion. The representatives of the propertied classes—the landowners and businessmen—who sat in Parliament agreed on basic issues, so class disputes did not weaken the assembly. Moreover,

The battle of Formigny, which was fought at the end of the Hundred Years' War. Notice that the Englis (right) are on foot and are flanked by bowmen, while the French are delivering a cavalry charge. Usually the English won in such circumstances, but this tim they were defeated.

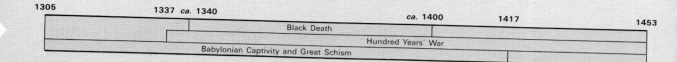
the members of Parliament were drawn from among the same men who collected local taxes and who, as Justices of the Peace, maintained order in the towns and counties. The government needed the support of these men, especially since it was weakened by factions among the nobility and by civil wars that resulted in the death of five of the nine kings who ruled between 1307 and 1485. All English governments in this period had to seek public support and the appearance of legitimacy. Parliament could give both. Therefore, Parliament became an essential part of the machinery of government; no statute could be enacted and no tax imposed without its consent. On the Continent, representative assemblies seldom played an important role in government, and what influence they did have dwindled in the fifteenth century. The English Parliament survived both the disorders of the fifteenth century and the strong monarchs of the sixteenth century and by the seventeenth century occupied a unique position in Europe.

Futile wars, heavy taxes, bad administrations, and factional quarrels had decreased respect for secular governments. But the Church was unable to profit from this decline because the Church suffered from similar troubles. Early in the fourteenth century, French influence, coupled with disorders in Italy, persuaded the popes to abandon Rome for Avignon, a city just across the Rhône from France. There they stayed for over seventy years (1305–78). This "Babylonian Captivity" hurt the prestige of the Church. The Avignon popes were good administrators but not good spiritual leaders; they were suspected (wrongly) of being puppets of the king of France; and a pope who was not at Rome hardly seemed a true pope. But worse was to follow. Pope Gregory XI moved back to Rome and died there in 1378. His successor, Urban VI, who was chosen under some pressure from

the Roman mob, soon succeeded in angering the cardinals. They fled back to Avignon, repudiated their choice of Urban, and elected a rival pope, Clement VII. All attempts to heal the dispute failed, and for forty years there were two lines of popes, one at Rome and one at Avignon. This Great Schism left Europe completely confused and divided. No one was entirely sure who the rightful pope was, and everyone was disgusted by the bickering between the two camps. Heresy, belief in witchcraft, and cynical immorality flourished. The Great Schism was one of the events that prepared the way for the Protestant Reformation.

In the darkest days of the fourteenth century it looked as if the western civilization that had so recently emerged was about to collapse. But there was a sur-

THE GREAT SCHISM   1378–1417

0 MILES 300

Land giving allegiance to Rome

Land giving allegiance to Avignon

Shifting and divided

prising toughness in European society. Almost everything seemed to be working badly, but almost nothing stopped working altogether. The Church continued to function, and the vast majority of the people remained fervently Christian. Kings and ministers might be overthrown, but monarchies endured. The nobility gained power because it commanded the armed forces, but it remained dependent on central governments because the governments paid the troops. There was no new fragmentation of the European political structure such as had occurred after the death of Charlemagne. War and plague did not stop the production of goods nor the exchange of commodities. In fact, in some areas per capita production actually increased as peasants concentrated on the best land and as artisans moved into country districts where they were less hampered by urban regulations on hours of labor and techniques of production. Pessimism about the state of the world did not kill the intellectual life of the universities. Some of the most subtle theological reasoning of all time appeared in the fourteenth century, as did the first really original European contri-

butions to scientific theory. For example, scholars at Oxford worked out a close approximation to the correct law of accelerated motion. This interest in science was important because other peoples, notably the Moslems, were losing interest in the subject. Between 1300 and 1500, western Europe gained a practical monopoly of the study of science.

During the same period some notable advances in technology were made. Ocean-going sailing ships were perfected, and voyages were made to distant Atlantic islands, such as the Azores. Blast furnaces were improved, so that the production of iron increased. The discovery of gunpowder did not immediately change the art of war, because early cannon were too clumsy for anything but siege operations, but it did put new demands on the art of metallurgy. In light industry, new types of textiles were developed and the first mechanical clocks appeared. Western technology was not yet superior to that of any other region, but the West was experimenting with a very broad range of technologies. There was growing interest in rather complicated machinery—for example, blast-furnace bellows driven by waterpower

Mechanical clock made in 1410. The first clocks had only one movable hand.

A fifteenth-century representation of Geoffrey Chaucer from the Ellesmere manuscript of the *Canterbury Tales.*

and multiple pumps to pull water out of deep mines. Both the wide range of skills and the fascination with machinery were to be important influences in the future.

There was a great potential for growth in western civilization in the fifteenth century. Many men were aware of this potential; they felt that if they could just get back on the right track all their troubles would vanish. They already had a good start on building a powerful political instrument (the sovereign state), on expanding manufactures and long-distance commerce, and on reaching a new level of competence in science and technology. The problem was to get rid of or minimize the disruptive forces that prevented western Europe from making the most of these assets. One of the most common words in the writings and speeches of the period was *reform*. And it was through the effort to reform its society that western Europe entered the modern age.

An early gun, lighter and more portable than the first cannon. The gun is placed on a forked stand and is braced against the ground by its long tail (illustration from a German manuscript, *ca.* 1405).

Suggestions for Further Reading

Note: Asterisk denotes a book available in paperback edition.

W. H. McNeill, *The Rise of the West** (1963), in spite of its title, deals largely with the ancient world and is an excellent book. V. G. Childe, *What Happened in History?** (1964), is a good summary of ancient history before the Greeks. M. I. Rostovtzeff, *A History of the Ancient World,* 2 vols. (1926), is a little out-of-date, but the superb illustrations and the emphasis on social and economic history make it worth consulting. The book covers Greece and Rome as well as the ancient Middle East.

M. I. Finley, *The Ancient Greeks** (1963), is a good introduction to Greek history. The standard textbook is G. W. Botsford and C. A. Robinson, *Hellenic History,* 5th ed., rev. by D. Kagan (1969). M. Grant, *The World of Rome** (1964); M. P. Charlesworth, *The Roman Empire** (1951); and H. Mattingly, *Roman Imperial Civilization** (1959), are all worth reading.

F. Lot, *The End of the Ancient World** (1931), is a classic study of the collapse of the Roman Empire. A recent and stimulating book is P. Brown, *The World of Late Antiquity** (1971). L. M. Duchesne, *Early History of the Christian Church,* 3 vols. (1912–24), is still one of the best surveys of the subject.

C. Dawson, *The Making of Europe** (1934), is an excellent account of the early Middle Ages. It should be supplemented by F. L. Ganshof, *Feudalism,** 3rd Eng. ed. (1964), and R. Latouche, *The Birth of the Western Economy** (1961). R. W. Southern, *The Making of the Middle Ages** (1953), is a first-rate account of the culture of the High Middle Ages. See also C. Brooke, *The Twelfth Century Renaissance** (1969). On institutions, see R. S. Lopez, *The Birth of Europe* (1967), and J. R. Strayer and D. C. Munro, *The Middle Ages,* 5th ed. (1970).

W. K. Ferguson, *Europe in Transition* (1962), and D. Hay, *Europe in the Fourteenth and Fifteenth Centuries* (1967), are good introductions to the problems of Europe in the later Middle Ages.

16 The Revival of Europe

During the course of the fourteenth century economic depression, plague, and war had weakened western Europe. Secular rulers, who in 1300 had seemed close to establishing absolute monarchies, had lost much of their power over the privileged classes and thus much of their ability to maintain law and order. The prestige of the Church had declined during the Babylonian Captivity and the Great Schism. Most men believed in monarchy as the best form of government; almost all believed in the Church as the only source of salvation. But with both these traditional authorities functioning badly, there seemed to be little hope for religious reform or a revival of security and prosperity. Everyone desired peace, a healing of the schism in the Church, better government, and increased production and trade. But there was little agreement on where to begin, and none of the many projects for reform was very successful.

By the end of the fifteenth century, a startling change had taken place. The economic depression had ended; new industries at home and new trade routes overseas had opened up new opportunities and created new wealth. Kings and princes had clearly gained the upper hand over the privileged classes, especially in France, Spain, and England. The papal schism was ended, and Rome was once more the capital of Western Christendom. New forms of learning based on an intensive study of the classics were competing with or modifying older stud-

ies. New forms of art were challenging the late Gothic style. Most important, there was a note of optimism and confidence, of excitement and enjoyment. There was talk of a "new age" dawning, a "dark age" past, a rebirth of the best qualities of classical civilization. By 1500 the basic characteristics of our "modern" world were becoming visible: its dynamic economy and fluid society, its sovereign nation-states and international anarchy, its secular ideals, and its intellectual and moral values.

We can now see that the political and economic revival of Europe was led by the north, while intellectual, literary, and artistic innovations were largely the work of Italy. But this sharing of responsibilities was less obvious in the fifteenth century than it was later, and in the transition from the medieval to the modern world the Italians had the great advantage of being the first to realize that a transition was taking place. They were the ones who talked of a new age, of a break with the barbarous past; they were the ones who believed that a new civilization could be created that would be a worthy heir of Greece and Rome. As a result, in the two centuries between the death of Dante (1321) and the sack of Rome by mutinous imperial troops (1527), Italy exerted increasing influence over the rest of Europe. Italians set the style in architecture, sculpture, and painting; they dictated the literary taste that Europe was to follow for generations. By combining the old ideal of the

Opposite: Donatello, equestrian statue of the Venetian *condottiere* Erasmo di Nardi, who was called Gattamelata (*ca.* 1445–50), in the Piazza del Santo, Padua.

chivalric, courtly knight with their own interest in learning, they developed a genuinely new social ideal, that of "the gentleman," and the educational ideal of a "liberal education." Italy was the school of Europe. Northerners flocked there by the thousands, and Italians, in turn, appeared in every northern court, even in remote Muscovy.

There were several reasons for Italy's leadership in the change from medieval to early modern ways of life. Italy had always been somewhat different from the rest of Europe during the Middle Ages. It was never completely feudalized, and it early rejected most feudal institutions. It rejected a unified monarchy under the German emperor even more decisively.

Scholasticism never dominated Italian thinking, nor did the Gothic style ever dominate Italian art. Since the medieval tradition in Italy was weak, it could easily be rejected. Moreover the Italian cities had great wealth, large populations, and complete independence. When they tried new experiments in art, literature, and politics, they became powerful instruments of social change.

THE CITY-STATES OF NORTHERN ITALY

The northern Italian cities were dominated by international trade. A third of the population of Florence lived by im-

A Renaissance prince and his wife: Giovanni Bentivoglio, lord of Bologna, and Ginevra Bentivoglio (details from paintings by Ercole Roberti, *ca.* 1480).

porting wool from agricultural countries and selling finished cloth all over Europe and the Levant. Almost all the population of Venice depended directly or indirectly on trade in Oriental goods such as silk and spices. In such communities, capitalists—the banker, the export merchant, the large-scale manufacturer—were the most important figures.

The Italian towns controlled the countryside around them as most northern European towns did not. They had broken the power of the landed nobility and had absorbed the defeated class into their own communities. Peasant villages and small market towns had been annexed by large urban centers. Thus city-states were created—that is, a strong city government controlled not only its own immediate area but hundreds of square miles of rural territory.

There were sharp differences among the people of these city-states. Obviously there were differences in wealth, from the international merchants and bankers—the *popolo grasso*, or "fat people"—through the craftsmen, shopkeepers, and all the lesser bourgeoisie—the *popolo minuto*, or "little people"—down to the growing proletariat of wage workers, and the peasants living outside the city walls. But Italian urban politics cannot be explained in terms of a class struggle. The wealthy men did not stick together. By and large the old rich disliked the new rich, but one old family might dislike another old family even more than it did an upstart neighbor. Men with common interests and ambitions formed political groups that cut across all class lines. The basic rules of the game were to build up the group through alliances among influential families, to gain support among middle and lower income groups through granting protection and political favors, to find a plausible slogan (usually no more complicated than "throw the rascals out!"), and then to stage a *coup d'état* or a revolution. Sometimes there was merely a change in the holders of the principal offices; sometimes there was a fairly drastic revision of the town constitution to ensure the perpetuation of the new dominant oligarchical group; very rarely, as in Florence in 1378, the lower classes demanded, and got, some social and economic reforms. Such reforms

were not only infrequent, they were also short lived.

During the fourteenth century few Italian towns went as long as thirty years without a *coup d'état*. This instability caused material damage and forced many useful citizens into exile (the most eminent example was Dante). Thus when an able man, backed by a strong coalition, gained power (often by perfectly constitutional means) and tried to put an end to political turbulence, his advent was usually accepted with some relief. Some of these leaders were at first not much more than military dictators (for example, the Sforza in Milan). Some of them were primarily very capable political bosses (for example, the Medici in Florence). They allowed no opposition; those who turned against them were eliminated by exile, imprisonment, or execution. On the other hand, these "despots," as they were eventually called, were usually careful to improve the city's public works, strengthen its defenses, devise efficient systems of taxation, and tighten internal security. By and large these programs were helpful to business, but one can hardly say that the despots were principally concerned with the welfare of the business community. They were wise enough to see that their power depended on attention to the common welfare. In return, they could spend much of the money derived from the fruits of restored political stability on "glory" (wars with their neighbors) and "splendor" (buildings and works of art). One should note, however, that Venice, the most prosperous Italian town, had no despot, and yet was just as warlike and just as lavish in expenditures on art as its neighbor, Milan, which is often taken as the typical example of despotism.

War and Diplomacy

Oligarchs and despots realized that the merchants and shopkeepers disliked military service and that armed subjects might easily turn against their rulers. Therefore they replaced citizen militias, which had never been very effective, with mercenary troops called *condottieri*. These soldiers were well trained and fairly reliable—as long as they were paid. In a pinch, however, their first loyalty was to their generals rather than to their employers. Moreover, as time went on, the generals sought to preserve their military assets by winning wars through clever maneuvers and negotiations rather than by pitched battles. But while they did not fight very much, they did have a monopoly of military power, and some generals displaced weak despots or divided city governments and became despots themselves.

What distinguished northern Italy most sharply from the rest of Europe was the total independence of its city-states from any central government. From Venice, oldest and proudest of the city-states, on down to towns of a few thousand inhabitants, city governments acted as if they were subject to no superior power. Motivated by economic and political self-interest, each city-state engaged in endless wars, making and breaking alliances, and jealously watching the most powerful state of the moment to make sure that it did not become strong enough to conquer the peninsula. Early in the fifteenth century the Italian city-states began to maintain resident ambassadors at the courts of foreign states to keep rulers in constant touch with governments that might one day become either useful allies or dangerous enemies.

In the second half of the century, a kind of "balance of power" began to operate among the five leading states in Italy—Venice, Milan, Florence, the Papal States, and the Kingdom of Naples—in response to an unwritten (and perhaps instinctive) understanding that no one of the five must be allowed to gain enough power to threaten the others. When France and Spain intervened in Italy at the close of the fifteenth century, both these practices—the basic machinery of modern diplomacy and the balancing of power among a group of sovereign states—spread to the larger stage of Europe. By the mid-sixteenth century, resident ambassadors were common throughout central and western Europe, and a rough balance of power had been established between the ruling dynasties of the two most powerful states, France and Spain.

Milan, Venice, and Florence

Behind these generalizations lie the striking variety and individuality of the Italian cities of this era. Milan, the largest city of the Po Valley, was perhaps the most typical. It submitted early to a despot, and about 1400 a Milanese ruler, Gian Galeazzo Visconti, came as close as any strong man of the time to eliminating

THE ITALIAN CITY-STATES   1454

his rivals and uniting northern Italy. He failed, but the fear he inspired persisted, and no other despot managed to come so close to dominating northern Italy. On the other hand, he did make Milan one of the leading manufacturing and trading towns of the peninsula, and he encouraged improvements in agriculture, which is more than some of his rivals did.

Venice, the greatest commercial power of the peninsula, was absorbed in its widespread Mediterranean interests and was relatively isolated from Italian politics until it began to acquire territory on the mainland in the fifteenth century. Its republican constitution was the oldest and its government the most stable in Italy. There was no despot in Venice—the doge, or duke, was a figurehead—but a tight-knit commercial aristocracy ran the city through a small and tough-minded executive committee, the Council of Ten. Perhaps because the energies of the whole population were so absorbed in commerce, there were no real revolutions and few conspiracies in Venetian history. The constitution of the "most serene republic" (the official title of Venice) stood as a model of republican stability to other Italians.

Florence, like Venice, was proud of being a republic among the welter of despotisms and was especially proud of having helped to frustrate Gian Galeazzo Visconti's attempt to snuff out republican liberties in Italy. But in every other respect Florence and Venice were unalike. Venice lived primarily by commerce; Florence primarily by banking and industry. The most astute bankers and the finest textiles in Europe were both to be found in Florence. The energies of Venetians were directed outward toward the sea; the energies of Florentines were focused on industry and politics within Tuscany. Venetian society and Venetian government exhibited a high degree of stability, whereas nothing seemed stable in Florence. Political intrigues were a constant problem, and changes in the constitution were frequent.

During the fourteenth and early fifteenth centuries the Florentines tried to solve their political problems by riots, by changes in electoral procedures and in governmental structure, and even by

The rise of the Medici: Cosimo de' Medici has the look of the wily businessman, while his grandson Lorenzo appears every inch the prince. Above: Cosimo, detail from a fresco by Gozzoli. Below: Lorenzo, by an unknown artist.

calling in outside mediators (who usually did more harm than good). In the end, the Florentines settled for boss rule. In 1434 a new-rich party within the oligarchy, led by one of the city's wealthiest and shrewdest bankers, Cosimo dé Medici, gained power. For almost sixty years Cosimo, his son Piero, and his grandson Lorenzo the Magnificent (d. 1492), ran the city by seeing that their candidates won elections, and by tinkering with the republican constitution. Cosimo was a banker who had been forced to play politics in order to save his financial interests. Lorenzo was more of a politician, little concerned with the family banking business. But each devoted his energy, his money, and his taste to the job of protecting, expanding, and beautifying the city. The most glittering example of Italy's golden age was Florence under the Medici.

ITALIAN URBAN CIVILIZATION

In these busy, crowded cities of northern Italy the structure of society and the ideals of the upper classes had to be modified. There had been a good deal of upward mobility during the fourteenth and early fifteenth centuries, and a new aristocracy was being formed—an aristocracy that included both descendants of old landed families who had prospered in the cities and wealthy merchants and bankers. The Medici, for example, had not been feudal lords, yet they eventually became dukes and married their daughters to kings of France. In the smaller towns, on the other hand, the despot was often a member of the old nobility who had learned how to deal successfully with urban problems. The situation was complicated by the growing prominence and wealth of writers, artists, and scholars. Most of these men did not, and never would, belong to the aristocracy, but their services and talents were necessary for the adornment of aristocratic life and their ideas of beauty, good taste, right behavior, and sound learning were accepted by the aristocracy. Finally, the aristocracy had to pay some attention to economic problems—problems far more complicated than those of managing landed estates. Communities dependent on continental markets and faced with sharp competition from their neighbors produced revenues that varied sharply from year to year. Frequent wars could bring even prosperous towns to the edge of bankruptucy. Loans had to be floated and new taxes devised. The oldest and most stable of the Italian aristocracies, that of Venice, was very skillful in managing its economic affairs; others were less successful.

The new ideal of the Italian aristocracies was a combination of old feudal-chivalric values and new urban-cultural values. It might be expressed as the ideal of the cultivated gentleman. A famous sixteenth-century book by Baldassare Castiglione, *The Courtier*, summed up this ideal. The courtier has all the chivalric virtures—physical dexterity, courage, skill in combat, courtesy—and all the new virtues—knowledge of the classics, appreciation of art and literature, eloquence, and good taste. Above all, he has grace; he excells in each activity without visible effort.

But besides the aristocrats there were the self-made men—not many, it is true, but just for that reason conspicuous. There was the *condottieri* general Sforza, who made himself ruler of Milan; the low-born artists, such as Leonardo da Vinci; the famous scholars, such as Lorenzo Valla; even a pope (Pius II) who may have had noble ancestors but who made his reputation as a scholar. How could these people be fitted into a common scheme? The answer was that they were men of *virtù*. This was the quality that made a man a free man (Latin, *vir*). It meant more than "virtue" in the modern sense; it also meant "virtuosity," that combination of genius and determination that made for greatness in statesmanship, artistic creation, or literature. In fact, by the time of Machiavelli, the word *virtù* was losing its moral connotation, and simply meant the qualities that led to success.

Individualism

At the upper levels of this society, there was growing individualism. Few of the old authorities carried the weight they had once carried for the aristocrat or highly talented city dweller. If his local government oppressed him, he could always move to another city. Many painters and sculptors were members of gilds, but gild regulations could not control their work. Scholars did not need university appointments in order to concentrate on their work, nor were they dependent on a single patron; a well-known writer could draw subsidies from many sources. And although the Italians considered themselves good Christians, they had little respect for the pronouncements of the clergy and accepted clerical rulings only when they were backed by strong ecclesiastical sanctions.

Thus for the upper classes and the cultural leaders there was a new emphasis on man as a private person, mainly concerned with himself, his own immediate family, his friends, and his own self-development. Such individualism sometimes went to extremes, as it did in the case of Benvenuto Cellini (1500–71), a sculptor and goldsmith who described his violent and colorful career in a famous *Autobiography*. Cellini assumed

A Man of Virtù

Benvenuto Cellini, a Florentine goldsmith and sculptor, had struck medals and coins for Pope Clement VII (1523–34). He claimed that he had been insulted by a jeweler named Pompeo (who also worked for the pope), and after several quarrels, Cellini stabbed Pompeo to death in a street brawl. Clement VII had just died; Cardinal Farnese was elected pope on October 13, 1534, and took the name of Paul III.

After he had put affairs of greater consequence in order, the new Pope sent for me, saying that he did not wish any one else to strike his coins. To these words of his Holiness one of his gentlemen named Latino Juvinale [a Humanist] answered that I [Cellini] was in hiding for the murder of Pompeo of Milan, and set forth what could be argued for my justification in the most favorable terms. The Pope replied: "I know nothing of Pompeo's death but plenty of Benvenuto's provocation, so let a safe-conduct be at once made out for him." A great friend of Pompeo's was there; he was a Milanese called Ambrogio [Ambrogio Recalcati, a papal secretary]. This man said: "In the first days of your papacy it is not well to grant pardons of this kind." The Pope answered: "You know less about such matters than I do. Know then that men like Benvenuto, unique in their profession, stand above the law."

From Benvenuto Cellini, *The Life of Benvenuto Cellini*, trans. by John Addington Symonds (New York: Scribner's, 1926), p. 144.

Minters making silver thalers (from which comes our word *dollar*). A heated metal disk has been placed on top of the die, another die has been placed on top of the disk, and the minter is striking the top die with an iron mallet (detail from the Miners' Altar by Hans Hesse, Church of St. Anne, Annaberg, Saxony).

houses and fine clothes, rich food and drink, and enjoyment of leisure—and that the ascetic and otherworldly ideals of the medieval Church seemed more and more remote to them. Their tastes and attitudes are already evident in the ribald stories of Boccaccio's popular *Decameron (ca.* 1350). The heroes and heroines are not exactly irreligious or critical of Christian ideals, but they despise the hypocrisy of priests and monks, and they rejoice in the triumph of clever people of the world over clerical busybodies.

The secularism of Italian society can thus be broken down into two components: preoccupation with worldly pursuits, and contempt for those who professed the ascetic ideal but did not live up to it. There were a few pagans or atheists. But most men simply thought more constantly of this world than of the next, without denying the ultimate importance of the next. There was a latent conflict between the older and the new ideals. This conflict troubled many writers and artists even in the most worldly cities, such as Florence. In fact, tension between worldly and otherworldly ideals was more typical of the period than was the frank and untroubled enjoyment of temporal pleasures.

Humanism

The third mark of Italian urban society was its enthusiasm for classical antiquity. The men most deeply concerned with the classics were called Humanists— from the Latin *humanitas,* as used by Cicero to describe the literary culture proper to a well-bred man. The Middle Ages had always lived in the shadow of Rome, and interest in classical literature was nothing new. John of Salisbury in the twelfth century had a first-rate knowledge of Latin literature, and the greatest medieval poet, Dante, made it his conscious concern to blend the best of both classical and Christian ideals throughout the *Divine Comedy.* However, Francesco Petrarca, or Petrarch (1304–74), is rightly called the father of a new Humanism. His enthusiasm for Cicero, his admiration for Rome (he said he wished he had been born in the ancient world instead of his own), and his feel for the style of classical Latin were con-

that the ordinary laws of morality were made for ordinary people and that they neither could nor should be enforced in the case of geniuses like himself. He also assumed that autobiography, a literary form that had been very rare in the Middle Ages, was a natural form of expression and one that would find eager readers. He begins his book: "All men of whatsoever quality they be, who have done anything of excellence, . . . ought to describe their life with their own hand." Later he remarks, "I make no profession of writing history. It is enough for me to occupy myself with my own affairs." Cellini was obviously interesting to himself, and he was sure he was interesting to others.

Secularism

The second mark of this new society was its predominantly secular tone. This does not mean that it was pagan or anti-Christian. It means that the things of this world increasingly occupied the time and attention of the Italian townspeople—the balance of profit and loss, well-built tagious. He loved the classics for their own sake, not only because they could be used to explain the language of the early Church Fathers but also because he believed that they taught the central ethical values later embodied in Christianity. Within a generation or two after his death Petrarch's followers were busily discovering classical manuscripts in monastic libraries, writing letters to one another in impeccable Ciceronian Latin, pouring contempt on the Latin style of medieval scholastic philosophers, and, most important, getting jobs as secretaries at the papal Curia and the courts of the despots, or as teachers of the children of the ruling classes in the cities.

These professional Humanists were something new in European society. Generally they were laymen who made a living by their learning, not clerics or monks devoting spare time to classical study. They were self-made men who were peddling a new type of scholarship to their contemporaries—and who found the market very good. Enthusiasm for the classics was heightened after 1395, when refugee scholars from the Byzantine Empire began to teach Greek to eager students in Florence and elsewhere. And by the end of the fifteenth century a few Italians were even beginning to learn Hebrew and Arabic. Humanism was both a scholarly movement and a social fad. The Humanists revived the study of classical Latin, Greek, and Hebrew, and they got the ruling classes of the Italian cities excited about what they were doing.

The Humanists initiated a revolution in educational theory and practice. Formal education in the Middle Ages had been dominated by the clergy and directed mainly to the production of clerics. Even the students of law were technically members of the clergy, and many of them ended their careers as cathedral canons, as bishops, or even as popes. The nobility had its own program of training knights to hunt and fight and behave properly at court. But neither of these systems of education offered much to the sons of business and professional town dwellers, and by the thirteenth century, if not earlier, there were town schools, primarily for laymen, that taught arithmetic and Latin grammar. The Human-ists of the fifteenth century rediscovered what Greco-Roman writers had meant by the "liberal arts": the liberating effect on mind and imagination of the study of great literature and philosophy. To this they added courteous behavior and athletic skill and so formed a new pattern of education. The result was a program designed to produce well-read laymen, able to write classical Latin and perhaps Greek, well mannered and at home in polite society, physically strong, and skillful in the art of war. "We call those studies liberal," wrote one Humanist educator, "which are worthy of a free man . . . that education which calls forth, trains, and develops those highest gifts of body and of mind which ennoble men." In practice this education too often degenerated into a narrowly literary training, floundering in the grammatical details of dead languages. It was available only to a few, and it was consciously aristocratic in its ideals. But at its best it passed on to later generations, including our own, the goal of turning out well-balanced human beings, devoted to both classical and Christian ideals, and able to become better businessmen or lawyers or statesmen because of their liberal education.

Young student reading Cicero (detail from a painting by Vincenzo Foppa).

Petrarch on the Classics and Christianity

You are well aware that from early boyhood of all the writers of all ages and races the one whom I most admire and love is Cicero. You agree with me in this respect as well as in so many others. I am not afraid of being considered a poor Christian by declaring myself so much a Ciceronian. [This is an allusion to a famous vision of St. Jerome in which God told him: "You are a Ciceronian and therefore not a Christian."] To my knowledge, Cicero never wrote one word that would conflict with the principles proclaimed by Christ. If, perchance, his works contained anything contrary to Christ's doctrine, that one fact would be sufficient to destroy my belief in Cicero and in Aristotle and in Plato. . . .

Christ is my God; Cicero is the prince of the language I use. I grant you that these ideas are widely separated, but I deny that they are in conflict with each other. Christ is the Word, and the Virtue and the Wisdom of God the Father. Cicero has written much on the speech of men, on the virtues of men, and on the wisdom of men—statements that are true and therefore surely acceptable to the God of Truth.

From a letter to Neri Morando, 1358, in *Petrarch's Letters to Classical Authors*, trans. by M. E. Cosenza (Chicago: University of Chicago Press, 1910), pp. 18–19.

Historical Self-Consciousness

The fourth and final mark of this urban society was its historical self-consciousness. The historical sense of the Middle Ages was not highly developed. The crucial events of the Christian drama had already happened, and time now had only to run on and out to its conclusion in the Last Judgment. Caesar and Charlemagne wore the same costume in medieval drawings. Frederick Barbarossa thought it perfectly reasonable to insert his own edicts in the *Corpus Juris* of Justinian. There had been no essential change since the triumph of Christianity. There was no significant difference between Constantine and Otto III, or between St. Peter and Innocent III. The passage of time brought only minor variations in a persisting pattern.

Petrarch and his Humanist successors in the fifteenth century revolutionized this conception of the past. They became more interested in this world and its history. Their enthusiasm for classical antiquity enabled them for the first time to see the ancient world as a civilization that had run its course. It had been born, it had flourished, and it had died. They talked of the "Fall of Rome" and of a "Dark Age" that had followed. Above all, they talked of a "rebirth," or "revival," that was beginning in their age. Rome had had its golden age and had fallen; darkness had succeeded, but now the light was beginning to dawn again. The Humanists and their followers were highly conscious of their position in history and of their historical mission.

THE "RENAISSANCE"

While the Italian Humanists were sure that they lived in an age of rebirth, they were not nearly so sure of the profound implications of their work as were later historians. Chief of these was the Swiss Jacob Burckhardt, who wrote a brilliant book called *The Civilization of the Renaissance in Italy* (1860). Thanks to Burckhardt, western historians accepted the idea that there was a "Renaissance," or rebirth, after the Middle Ages, that it marked a sharp break with medieval ideals and practices, and that it was centered in Italy. There was much truth in Burckhardt's thesis, but he exaggerated

both the sharpness of the breach with the medieval past and the uniqueness of Italy compared with the rest of Europe.

The term *Renaissance* is most useful when it is applied to the revolutionary change in the arts, in literature, and in the concept of man that took place in Italy in the fourteenth, fifteenth, and early sixteenth centuries. It is less useful when applied to political and ecclesiastical history because it is hard to say what "rebirth" means in these areas. And it is quite useless when applied to economic and social history, in which changes are always slow and in which the important developments began as far back as the eleventh century. Historians of art and literature are relatively sure of what *Renaissance* means; other historians are unsure in varying degrees to the point of total doubt. This does not mean that artistic and literary develpments had no connection with economic and social change. They created new opportunities for able young men and they modified the behavior of the upper classes. It means simply that the word *Renaissance* is best used to describe the changes in artistic and literary taste and skill that occurred at the close of the Middle Ages.

Literature, Philosophy, and Scholarship

Wherever there were classical models to fall back on, the tendency at first was for both writers and artists to lose themselves in simple imitation, in the first flush of excited rediscovery. It was easy, for instance, for Humanists to imitate the letter writing, the orations, the moral essays, and even the poetry of the Romans—and they did, relentlessly, in the early fifteenth century. When it became possible for educated Florentines to read Plato in the original Greek, the Medici fostered an informal group of scholars who became known as the Platonic Academy. Their leading members, Marsilio Ficino (1433–99) and Pico della Mirandola (1463–94), tried to reconcile Platonism and Christianity, as Thomas Aquinas had tried to reconcile Aristotelianism and Christianity. It was the one serious attempt at philosophical synthesis during the Renaissance, and it was a failure. But enthusiasm for Plato and Platonism was infectious and had widespread influence on poets and painters throughout Europe in the next century. In fact, Plato dominated the imagination of the Renaissance as Aristotle had earlier dominated the thought of medieval scholars.

All was not mere imitation in Italian thought and writing, however. Modern critical scholarship, in the sense of careful linguistic and historical analysis of the literary remains of the past, dates from the Renaissance, and particularly from one of the keenest minds of the age, Lorenzo Valla (ca. 1405–57). Valla analyzed the language and the historical background of the so-called Donation of Constantine, one of the main bulwarks of the popes' claims to temporal power, and proved beyond a shadow of a doubt that the document was a clumsy forgery of the early Middle Ages. He further compared several Greek manuscripts of the New Testament with the accepted Latin translation, the Vulgate, and showed that the translation was full of errors and distortions. The critical spirit and scholarly technique that he inaugurated influenced Erasmus, Pierre Bayle, and Voltaire and resulted in the "scientific" scholarship of the nineteenth century.

Social and Political Thought

Much of Renaissance thought about the relation of man to man simply paraphrased the ethics and political theories of the Greeks and Romans. But sometimes a man wrote freshly from his own experience and spoke directly to the members of his own society. For example, Leon Battista Alberti (1404–72) in his book *On the Family*, described the interests and ideals of the Florentine families he knew: prudence and thrift, strong family feeling and little concern for larger causes outside, appreciation of comfort, planning and foresight, and pride in owning a house in the city and an estate in the country to produce all the family's food. It is one of the earliest idealized portraits of what will later be called the bourgeois virtues.

A social stratum just above that described by Alberti is sketched in the earlier mentioned work of Baldassare Castiglione (1478–1529), *The Courtier*. This book, based on Castiglione's memories of the court of the Duke of Urbino, describes the gentleman—graceful, attractive, courteous, liberally educated, noble in spirit if not necessarily in birth, at home either on the field of battle or

The Adimari Wedding, by an anonymous painter (*ca.* 1450). The painting shows the parade of guests at the wedding reception, held under a canopy outside a church in Florence. Such paintings often adorned the bride's *cassone,* a wedding chest designed to hold her trousseau.

Machiavelli on Cruelty and Clemency

Is it better to be loved than feared or feared than loved? It may be answered that one should wish to be both, but it is much safer to be feared than loved when one of the two must be chosen. Men on the whole are ungrateful, fickle, false, cowards, covetous. As long as you succeed, they are yours entirely. They will offer you their blood, property, life, and children when the need is distant, but when it approaches they turn against you. And a prince who, relying entirely on their promises, has neglected other precautions, is ruined. . . . Men have fewer scruples in offending one who is beloved than one who is feared, for love is preserved by the link of obligation which, owing to the baseness of men, is broken at every opportunity for their advantage, but fear preserves you by a dread of punishment which never fails.

Nevertheless, a prince should inspire fear in such a way that if he does not win love, he avoids hatred; because he can endure very well being feared while he is not hated, and this will be true as long as he abstains from taking the property of his subjects or their women. But when it is necessary for him to take the life of someone, he must do it with proper justification and for manifest cause, and above everything he must keep his hands off the property of others, because men more quickly forget the death of their father than the loss of their heritage.

From Niccolò Machiavelli, *The Prince,* trans. by W. K. Marriott (London: Dent, n.d.), pp. 134–35.

Machiavelli on the Policy of Princes

You must know, then, that there are two methods of fighting, the one by law, the other by force: the first method is that of men, the second of beasts; but as the first method is often insufficient, one must have recourse to the second. It is therefore necessary for a prince to know well how to use both the beast and the man.

A prince being thus obliged to know well how to act as a beast must imitate the fox and the lion, for the lion cannot protect himself from traps, and the fox cannot defend himself from wolves. One must therefore be a fox to recognise traps, and a lion to frighten wolves. Those that wish to be only lions do not understand this. Therefore, a prudent ruler ought not to keep faith when by so doing it would be against his interest, and when the reasons which made him bind himself no longer exist. If men were all good, this precept would not be a good one; but as they are bad, and would not observe their faith with you, so you are not bound to keep faith with them.

From Niccolò Machiavelli, *The Prince,* in *The Prince and the Discourses,* ed. by Max Lerner (New York: Modern Library, 1940), Ch. 18, p. 64.

among cultivated ladies. The concept of "the gentleman" owed much to chivalry and other traditional sources, but Castiglione presented it as a genuinely fresh ideal in the history of European civilization.

In the case of Niccolò Machiavelli (1469–1527), wide reading in the classics illuminated years of practical political experience. Machiavelli's career as ambassador and secretary of the Florentine government during a period when the Medici were out of power helped him to understand the political history of Rome as described by Livy, and Livy helped him to understand the power politics of his own age. Exiled by the restored Medici to his country home in 1512, he began to read widely and to reflect on what makes states expand and grow, what are the causes of political breakdown, how political leaders get and hold power, what can be learned from the past.

Machiavelli set down his reflections in a long, rambling book, *Discourses on Livy,* and in a briefer and more famous essay, *The Prince.* He made it clear that he was describing things as they were, not as they ought to be. Ideal states he left to others; in the world as it is, power is what counts. The Roman Republic, he thought, was the best example in history of successful state building. Its constitution was a masterly blend of monarchy, aristocracy, and democracy; it had good laws and a good citizen army; its religion supported the civic virtues of justice, prudence, and courage, not those of patience and humility; its rulers knew that the good of the state came before the dictates of individual morality. And so Rome, unlike any Italian city-state of Machiavelli's day, had been able to unite the whole of Italy and to endure for centuries.

But Machiavelli realized that this ideal, real though it once had been, might be too difficult for a corrupt and divided group of Italian city-states to revive. Perhaps a prince of real *virtù,* with the courage of a lion and the cunning of a fox, might be able to learn the laws of politics from history and experience and use them to build a strong state in Italy. He would know that men in their collective relations with one another are bad, and therefore he would not be held back by any moral scruples. If others broke faith with him, as they certainly would, the prince must be prepared to break faith with them for the good of his state. Fortune might frustrate his work, but a man of *virtù* had at least an even chance of overcoming bad luck. If his generation had both the intelligence and the will, Machiavelli believed, something could be done about the helpless state of Italy, which was falling under the heels of France and Spain.

Machiavelli's *Prince* was to become a grammar of political and diplomatic practice to heads of state as remote as Mussolini and Hitler. In its origin it was a perfect example of the fruitful combination in Renaissance thought of classical "rebirth" and contemporary "new birth," of historical example and practical experience. Both Machiavelli's disillusioned analysis of things as they were and his passionate plea for reform were entirely characteristic of the age.

The Arts

The influence of classical examples was strong also in the visual arts, but here original elements were even more noticeable than in social and political thought. Roman buildings survived, of course, all over Italy. Brunelleschi (1377?–1446), the greatest architect of his generation, absorbed their spirit and designed new churches in semiclassical style after 1420, thus inaugurating a return to the classical from the Gothic style in architecture. The late Roman sculpture that was dug up (hardly any of the Greek works of the classical age were yet known) inspired sculptors to imitation. But there were no ancient paintings to look at (Pompeii was not unearthed until the eighteenth century), and so Italian painters had to depend on the inspiration of their medieval predecessors and their own genius in elaborating their art.

Italian Renaissance painting, like that of France and Flanders, tended more and more toward realism. Giotto (1266?–1337), the first Italian to develop the new style, was little influenced by northern art; later on some ideas were borrowed from the Low Countries (notably the use

A late–sixteenth-century portrait of Niccolò Machiavelli by Santi di Tito. The artist has tried to suggest both the intellectual brilliance and the shrewdness of the man.

of oil paint). But north or south, the dominant interest of fourteenth-century writers, artists, and philosophers was in the concrete, individual thing as it actually existed, not in the general idea or eternal truth behind and in all things, which had been the typical concern of earlier medieval thinkers. Late medieval artists and writers tried to represent nature and man more and more realistically—to model a leaf as it actually appeared in nature, to chisel the features of a real man or woman, to sketch the character of a person in concrete detail, as both Boccaccio and Chaucer did with such success in their collections of tales. In fifteenth-century painting, particularly in the Netherlands, this effort resulted in the most astonishing skill in representing the smallest details of visual reality.

It was an Italian painter, however, who first realized that surface realism is not enough, that the artist must conceive the human figure as a whole, place it in three-dimensional perspective, and arrive at a more sophisticated realism that sacrifices minute details to organic unity. This painter was Masaccio (1401–28?), the founder of Renaissance painting and

Donatello's *David* (*ca.* 1430–32). Compare this statue with the *David* by Michelangelo on the opposite page.

one of the great innovators in the history of the art.

Italian painting of the fifteenth and sixteenth centuries is far too rich in content and varied in technique for us to describe in detail. Some of its general characteristics may be suggested, however. The first thing that strikes the historical observer is the separation of painting and sculpture from architecture. It was as if the sculptured prophets and many-colored saints had stepped down from their niches and stained-glass windows in the great medieval cathedrals to be reincarnated in bronze statues in Italian public squares or painted portraits in Italian palaces. Painting and sculpture were no longer arts subordinate to architecture. Painters began to adorn the walls of monasteries and houses with frescoes. After they had learned from Flemish artists the technique of painting with oils, the Italians went on to develop the easel painting, meant to be hung in a palace or house and to be enjoyed for its own sake. Donatello (1368–1466), in his *David,* was the first sculptor since the ancients to model a free-standing nude figure, and from then on to the great works of Michelangelo (1475–1564) sculptors developed their art with no thought but of its own perfection.

The zest for solving fresh problems infected architects as well as painters and sculptors. Brunelleschi went far beyond classical or medieval models in designing and building his famous dome over the transept of the cathedral in Florence (1420–36). Architecture, sculpture, and painting each went its own way. An individual artist might turn his hand to all three, and a painter might borrow ideas from sculpture. But in each case the artist could create as he pleased without subjecting one art to another.

The second characteristic worth noting was the heightened individuality and social prestige of the artist. A famous passage in Cellini's *Autobiography* describes the unveiling of his bronze statue of Perseus in the central square of Florence in 1554. "Now it pleased God," he wrote, "that on the instant of its exposure to view, a shout of boundless enthusiasm went up in commendation of my work, which consoled me not a little." Such a shout might have greeted the proclamation of a crusade in the eleventh century or the triumphant conclusion of a world war in the twentieth. But the public appreciation of a work of art, the assumption that great art is the product of individual "genius," which is something to be nurtured—these were as characteristic of the Renaissance as they were atypical of ages before and after. Artists and writers felt that they should be to the age of the Renaissance what the saint had been to the Middle Ages. Reality did not always correspond to their expectations; some patrons treated their painters and architects like any other employees. On the other hand, some mediocre men received excessive adulation and high rewards. By and large, Italy's Golden Age was the golden age of the artist and the writer.

In seeking a higher realism, Italian painters studied the laws of spatial perspective about the same time that Humanists were restudying the temporal or historical perspective of their day. As a result, the artists pictured real persons whom they knew, in recognizable space. Some of them spent their lives probing the psychological depths of human beings and trying to put on canvas what they found. The chief of these was the lonely scientific and artistic genius Leonardo da Vinci (1452–1519), whose curiosity about the secrets of nature was as insatiable as his curiosity about the nature of man. In painting *The Last Supper,* he chose not the moment when Christ breaks the bread and remarks, "This is my body . . . ," as a medieval artist might have done, but the more humanly dramatic and startling moment when he announces, "One of you will betray me." The resulting psychological crisis experienced by each disciple is carefully portrayed. The climactic episode of the Creation, as Michelangelo painted it on the ceiling of the Sistine Chapel in St. Peter's, was the creation of Adam—an almost superhuman man at the threshold of self-consciousness, languid, wondering, awakening—almost as if he were a symbol of the man of the Renaissance. In one of his most famous sculptures, Michelangelo chose to portray Moses at the moment when he has caught sight of his people's idolatrous Golden Calf and is struggling to control himself.

These few examples typify the Renaissance point of view. The central concern is man here in this world, troubled, striving, with unknown possibilities. Thus Renaissance art is humanistic in the broader, more philosophical meaning of the word. Not that the artists rejected God or ignored nature. God is still there, and Renaissance landscapes are charming. But God is seen through man, through man's heroism and his tragedy; and generally nature is of interest only as background or setting to the human drama. The most important question is what is to become of man. Pico della Mirandola, in a famous *Oration* on man's dignity (1486), pictured God as giving man something he had given to no other creature, the unique gift of freedom:

> Thou, constrained by no limits, in accordance with thine own free will, in whose hands We have placed thee, shalt ordain for thyself the limits of thy nature. . . . We have made thee neither of heaven nor of earth, neither mortal nor immortal, so that with freedom of choice and with honor, as though the maker and molder of thyself, thou mayest fashion thyself in whatever shape thou shalt prefer.

Every other creature had its pattern and its limits, but to Pico man's nature and destiny were in his own hands. The men of the Renaissance had not lost belief in God, but they were convinced, in a way their medieval ancestors would not have understood, that man was on his own.

The greatness of Italian art lay in the fact that it reflected all the tensions and contradictions in the prevailing attitudes toward man. There was no party line in Renaissance art; there were no premature solutions of sharp differences, no accepted syntheses. Some artists were realists, others idealists. Donatello modeled despots as he saw them, with hard and observant realism, while Raphael (1483–1520) a generation later idealized the peasant girls he knew as calm and self-possessed Madonnas of ethereal beauty. Some artists were scientists and psychologists like Leonardo, who tried to peer into the souls of men and women, while others were like the Venetian Titian

(1477–1576), who was more interested in the external marks of character and the glorious play of color on the objects about him. Michelangelo, perhaps the most typical as well as the greatest artist of them all, gave his life to attempting the impossible: to reconciling the classical ideal of harmony, balance, and "nothing in excess," with the limitless goals and boundless love of Christian piety. This attempt to reconcile the Greco-Roman and Hebraic-Christian worlds was the central striving of the Renaissance. It failed, but the failure left an imperishable record in the arts.

Michelangelo's *David* (1501–04). Instead of representing David after his victory over Goliath, as Donatello had done, Michelangelo chose to represent him as watchful of the approaching foe, with muscles tensed in gathering strength.

Michelangelo, *Creation of Adam* (fresco from the ceiling of the Sistine Chapel of the Vatican, 1508–12).

Leonardo da Vinci, *Ginevra d' Benci* (*ca.* 1481).

Raphael, detail from *Madonna with the Goldfinch* (1505–06).

Natural Science

The Renaissance contributed relatively less to the progress of natural science than to the arts, but the contribution was still important. The Humanists in general were more interested in man than in nature and more absorbed in literature than in mathematics and physics. Nevertheless, even at the height of the Renaissance, the Humanists never had full control of higher education. The old medieval curriculum, which included mathematics and physics, drew as many students as the new curriculum based on the classics. And on the practical side, the desire of the upper classes for greater comfort, and the striving of artists for greater realism, led to significant advances.

Moreover, the interest in Greek meant that new Greek scientific texts became available, and the interest in Latin led to criticism of works such as Pliny's *Natural History.* Above all, the emphasis on man on this earth gave confidence that man could understand and shape his environment.

Some of this confidence was based on a mistaken reliance on ancient texts on magic, but some of it derived from actual experience. As craftsmen, mechanics, and engineers, the Italians were the best in Europe. In the science of perspective, their painters worked out the mathematical principles of representing figures in space. Their artists and doctors together advanced the knowledge of human anatomy beyond where it had been left by the Greeks. The *Notebooks* of Leonardo da Vinci, a landmark in the history of both art and science, show how closely the two interests were related in the fifteenth-century mind. His studies of anatomical detail, for instance, are of equal interest to painters and doctors. Furthermore, the medieval interest in science survived in the northern Italian universities, particularly Padua. There the study of mathematics flourished, and the arguments over Aristotelian laws of motion, which had been begun at Paris and Oxford, continued. Padua eventually passed on to Galileo a theory of scientific method in something like its modern form.

THE COUNCILS AND THE PAPACY

Italian energy and enthusiasm did something to dissipate the pessimism of the late fourteenth century. But Europe was still profoundly Christian and could not be entirely satisfied until its religious problems were solved. Of the three difficulties that faced the Church in 1400—the schism, heresy, and administrative reform—only one was completely overcome. By the mid-fifteenth century there was only one pope in Rome, even if the prestige of his office had not regained its thirteenth-century height. The most dangerous heresies had been walled off or driven underground, but the religious atmosphere was still heavy with discontent and revolt. And the more men talked of religious and administrative reforms in the Church, the more impossible it seemed to effect them.

The Great Schism had imposed an almost intolerable psychological burden on Europe. In theory there could not possibly be two true Vicars of Christ, yet there was no way of being sure which of the two claimants was the real successor. Men felt as if they were in a sinking ship: "If we remain in it," a contemporary wrote, "we must perish with it, and if we stray outside, salvation escapes us, since outside the ship there is no salvation." Many Lollards and other heretics had strayed outside. Those who remained on board tried desperately to find some solution.

The stubborn behavior of the two lines of popes at Rome and Avignon, in refusing to resign or to submit to arbitration, had increased antipapal feeling among both clergy and laity throughout Europe. In 1395 the French became so exasperated with their own pope that the French clergy, under pressure from the government, withdrew their obedience from him for five years. This was the first appearance of a policy that was to have an ominous future: secession from papal jurisdiction by the clergy of a large nation under the pressure of the secular government. Even in the fifteenth century there were signs that Christendom might dissolve into independent national churches.

Mobile bakers, one of the various groups who provided for the delegates to the Council of Constance (1414–18). Notice the "pretzels" in the upper right corner (detail from a manuscript version of Ulrich Richental's *Chronicle*, 1465).

The Conciliar Movement

As early as 1379, the year after the schism developed, scholars at the University of Paris had suggested a more conservative and practical scheme than the withdrawal of obedience. They urged that a general council of the Church be called. The leading advocates of the idea at the university picked up and amplified a concept of the Church that had been advanced in the thirteenth and fourteenth centuries to support their proposal. The Church, they argued, was not centered in the papacy but was made up of the whole body of believers. Thus the final authority in the Church was a council representing all the faithful, and the pope was only a limited monarch responsible to this representative assembly. The so-called fullness of power, which canon lawyers claimed for the pope, was a usurpation. Authority in the Church came from the bottom up, not from the top down. This conciliar theory of the constitution of the Church was to have strong appeal to secular rulers who were looking for a club to hold over the papacy. It was also to have a strong attraction for reformers during the next century.

In 1408 most of the cardinals of both sides deserted their popes and summoned a general council to meet at Pisa the next year. For a moment, a group of cardinals without a pope confronted two popes without any cardinals, but the result was simply the election of a third pope by the council. Unfortunately, neither the Roman nor the Avignonese pope resigned, as had been hoped. After five more years of confused negotiations, the German emperor Sigismund compelled the Pisan pope, John XXIII, to summon a genuinely representative assembly.

This great council, which met at Constance in Switzerland from 1414 to 1418, made a strong impression on the imagination of the age. It healed the schism by bullying John XXIII into resigning, persuading the Roman pope to resign after he had gone through the formality of resummoning and approving the council himself, and deposing the Avignonese pope, who by now had fled to Spain and was supported only by Aragon. In 1417 the council elected a new pope, Martin V, who soon commanded the allegiance of all western Christendom. The council was less successful in instituting reform. The English and German delegates worked in vain to have reform considered before the election of a new pope; the Latin nations were more anxious to heal the schism first and let reform come later. Once Martin V was elected, interest flagged in even the mild report of a committee to study abuses, and the council dispersed without ever really facing the complicated malpractices in the hierarchy. On the other hand, the council dealt energetically, though shortsightedly, with the problem of heresy.

John Hus

The danger spot in 1414 was Bohemia. Here during the preceding century the emperor Charles IV (who was also king of Bohemia) had helped to foster a national and cultural awakening among the Czechs. But Czech scholars ran into two obstacles: a corrupt and leaderless Church, and a steady influx of

Germans into the cities and into the newly founded University of Prague. Since the Czechs tended to be reformers, while the Germans generally supported the status quo, the gifted group of Czech preachers and teachers who attacked ecclesiastical abuses soon found themselves leading a movement that was as much patriotic as it was religious. In 1402 a brilliant young leader appeared in John Hus (ca. 1369–1415). The burden of his preaching was that faith must be based on the Bible as the only source of authority, that Christ, not the pope, was the true Head of the Church, and that a man is saved by God through Christ, not by trusting in ceremonies and in a mediating priesthood that was thoroughly corrupt. Hus knew and used the ideas of Wiclif, whose books had been brought to Bohemia by Czech students returning from England, but he had developed his basic theories independently. By 1414 Hus had been excommunicated by the Roman pope, but he was at liberty and his ideas were accepted by a majority of the Czech people.

Hus eagerly seized the opportunity to journey to Constance to present his case before the council. He was almost immediately imprisoned for heresy. The emperor, who had granted him a safe-conduct, withdrew his protection the moment the dreaded charge of heresy was made. The conciliar leaders would have preferred a public recantation that could have been publicized throughout Bohemia, but Hus stood firm. In the dramatic trial that followed, the essential issue was whether the Bible and a man's conscience are the ultimate religious authority, as Hus argued, or whether the Catholic Church represented by the clerical hierarchy is the sole authority, as the council declared. Hus was condemned and burned at the stake outside the walls of Constance in May 1415. His follower, Jerome of Prague, was burned on the same spot the following spring.

Before the council disbanded, civil and religious warfare had broken out in Bohemia. It lasted for almost twenty years. The upshot was an agreement in 1436 between the more conservative Hussites and the Church. This agreement recognized a national church in Bohemia with local control over ecclesiastical ap-

pointments and with its own liturgical practices, notably the right to offer the cup as well as the bread to the laity when giving communion. For the first time the Church had made an agreement on equal terms with condemned heretics after excommunicating them and solemnly preaching a crusade against them. Wiclif's Lollards had been driven underground in England, but the Hussite heresy had simply been walled off in Bohemia.

The Papacy's Triumph over the Conciliar Movement

The restored papacy, which owed its existence to the Council of Constance, was more successful in defeating the conciliar movement than it was in extirpating heresy. The fathers had decreed at Constance that general councils must be summoned every ten years. But the superior diplomacy and the more efficient administrative machinery of the Roman papacy soon made this provision a dead letter. The temper of the times was changing; the idea that a ruler should be controlled by an assembly now seemed to lead only to confusion. Just as most European kings weakened their parliaments and humbled their nobles, so the popes weakened the conciliar ideal, stopped holding councils at regular intervals, and humbled the princes of the Church, the cardinals. By the time Nicholas V became pope (1447–55) the threat

John Hus being burned at the stake in 1415. He wears a fool's cap with pictures of the Devil and the word *heresiarch* (leader of heretics).

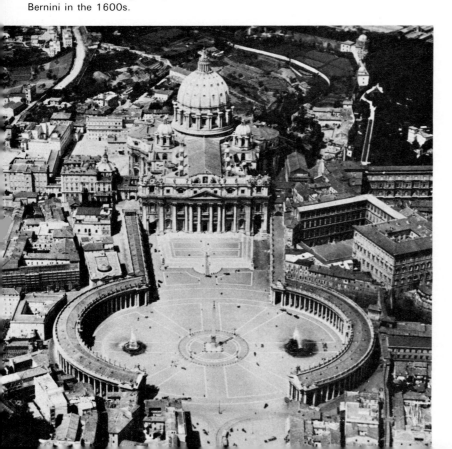

Aerial view of St. Peter's in Rome. In 1505 Pope Julius II commissioned Bramante to construct a church that would mirror the classical-Christian aspirations of the sixteenth century. The plans were changed several times, and the building was not completed until 1626. Michelangelo designed the dome; the colonnades were designed by Bernini in the 1600s.

that the Church might be transformed into a limited monarchy was over. Never again was there a general council of the Church that the pope could not control.

The popes' triumph over the councils left the papacy stronger in some respects but weaker in others. No one within the Church itself could challenge the papal "fullness of power," but the victory had been bought by making wide concessions to secular rulers. In opposing the reforming element in the councils, the popes had isolated themselves from clerical and lay leaders of opinion, particularly in the north of Europe. As a result, the popes depended on the support of lay rulers and could not resist their efforts to control the clergy within their own realms. In 1438 the king of France summoned an assembly of the French clergy and issued a solemn decree known

as the Pragmatic Sanction of Bourges. This decree strictly limited the pope's power of appointment and taxation in France and in effect set up a national, or "Gallican," Church, as it was called. In later years the popes were able to persuade the French monarchs to modify this one-sided action by "concordats," or agreements, between the papacy and the French crown. But in these agreements the monarchy always retained its control over appointments to the higher clergy. With some differences, the kings of England and Spain established similar limitations on papal power during the fourteenth and fifteenth centuries. In Germany, where there was no central government strong enough to stand up to the pope, papal rights of appointment, taxation, and jurisdiction were not limited as they were in the stronger monarchies. The popes had eliminated all their clerical rivals for power, only to be faced by much more greedy and formidable lay rivals—the monarchs.

The Renaissance Papacy

The eighty years between the accession of Nicholas V to the papacy (1447) and the sack of Rome (1527) are often called the period of the Renaissance papacy. It was a brilliant but tragic era in the history of the Church. Some of the popes of the period were patrons of Humanism and the arts, notably Nicholas V, founder of the Vatican Library, and Julius II (1503–13), builder of St. Peter's. Pius II (1458–64) had been Aeneas Sylvius, a celebrated Humanist, before his election. Two were particularly noted for their wars: Sixtus IV (1471–84), who was rumored to have died of rage at the conclusion of a peace settlement; and Julius II, who was known to his generation as "the Warrior Pope." More than one was notorious for his nepotism, as favoritism to relatives, including bastard children, was called. Roderigo Borgia, Alexander VI (1492–1503), was by far the worst of the lot. His mistresses lived openly with him; his voracious Spanish relatives got whatever they asked for; and his illegitimate son, Cesare Borgia, made a bloody attempt to become the ruler of all central Italy with his father's help.

All the accumulated evils of many years seemed to become intensified in the papal court: simony, nepotism, immorality, involvement in secular politics and warfare. Two centuries before, Innocent III had been immersed in secular diplomacy, but it had been on a Europe-wide scale, and the excuse had always been the advancement of the Church's cause. Now the scale of involvement was limited to the Italian peninsula, and the popes were generally motivated by selfish family interests. As time went on, the papacy became thoroughly Italianized, perhaps out of fear of another schism. (Since the end of the schism in 1417, only two non-Italian popes have been elected, in 1522 and 1979.) Most secular rulers came to assume that as ruler of the Papal States the pope would act like any Italian despot, at the dictates of his own personal and family interests—with the unfair competitive advantage, of course, that he was considered to be the Vicar of Christ. But even when the papacy seemed to be simply another Italian principality it was sustained by the basic belief that the office was greater than the man, that the moral character of the pope did not lessen his authority in spiritual matters.

The open corruption of the papal Curia during the fifteenth century had much to do with the Protestant revolt that began in 1517. As one historian has put it, the popes of the Renaissance tried to substitute splendor for reform. In the hands of an intelligent and devoted Humanist like Nicholas V this was not an unworthy idea. To him it meant reconciling Christianity with the best in ancient civilization and rebuilding Rome as the capital of a revived Christendom. But this ideal did not satisfy the mystical and moral strivings of thousands of the faithful, particularly those outside Italy. Significantly, it was under a cultivated son of Lorenzo de' Medici, Pope Leo X (1513–21), that much of Germany rebelled against the papacy, and under an illegitimate son of Lorenzo's brother, Pope Clement VII (1523–34), that England set up a national Church.

ECONOMIC GROWTH IN THE NORTH

While Italy was building city-states on the wealth derived from its monopoly of Mediterranean trade, northern and western Europe was building nation-states based on new industries and new trade routes. The cumulative effects of technological change began to stimulate the transalpine economy during the fifteenth century. Thus gradual improvements in building and rigging sailing ships made possible the great voyages of Vasco da Gama to India and of Columbus to America. Da Gama's voyages gave the Atlantic countries an increasing share of the lucrative trade in Oriental goods. Columbus gave the same countries a monopoly of the wealth of a New World. Even though Italian trade remained close to its old level, it was dwarfed by the much greater trade of Portugal and Spain, of France, England, and the Netherlands.

In Europe, new and profitable industries began to appear. For example, improved techniques in metallurgy made it possible to take full advantage of the discovery of gunpowder and to make cannon for sieges and naval warfare. Since more metal was needed, mining methods had to be improved and blast furnaces had to be enlarged to enable metal workers to acquire an increased supply of iron. The Atlantic states were able to gain control of world sea lanes not only because their ships were slightly better than those of their rivals but because they were more powerfully armed with naval cannon. On land the use of siege cannon weakened the noblemen and strengthened the monarchs, and so increased security. The noble's castle was no longer a secure retreat, and no ordinary noble could afford the vast cost of heavy guns. If they were to maintain their military tradition, the nobles had to become officers in the armies of kings

Cesare Borgia, anonymous copy of an authentic portrait.

and princes who could afford to buy the new weapons. They were not always well-disciplined officers, but they were no longer independent war-lords.

As we have seen, the invention of printing from movable type also depended on advances in metallurgy. And that invention, in the middle of the fifteenth century, had even more revolutionary effects than the invention of the cannon. So long as books had to be laboriously copied by hand, only a few men could aspire to higher learning. But as printing presses spread rapidly from the Rhine Valley to Italy, the Netherlands, France, Spain, and England, Europeans had a flood of books available at prices that would have been unbelievable a century earlier. There were "standard editions" of the Bible, the Church Fathers, and the classical writers in both Greek and Latin, scientific works, devotional treatises, and popular manuals in the vernacular languages. Like all mechanical inventions, printing brought

An early printing press, as shown in an early–sixteenth-century French print.

both good and evil in its train. The "standard editions" could multiply errors as well as corrections, and the pamphlets that were now so easy to print and circulate in large numbers could mislead as well as inform. But one thing was clear: learning would never again be the monopoly of a small upper class in European society. Anything human beings had written could now be multiplied and placed quickly and cheaply in the hands of anyone who could read.

Industry and Agriculture

New industries such as cannon founding and printing required large initial investments in plant and machinery. They were organized from the start as capitalistic enterprises—that is, enterprises in which accumulated wealth was deliberately used to produce more wealth. In addition to capital, these industries needed and attracted free laborers from town or country who could be employed for a wage and dismissed when business slacked off.

Even in rural areas capitalistic methods calculated to produce a profit were occasionally being applied to the land. Landlords had long realized that raising sheep for wool might be more profitable than accepting a customary rent. Legally or illegally, many of them, particularly in England, managed to fence off, or "enclose," lands formerly reserved for the common use of villagers, or to convert ploughed land to pasture. Since tending sheep required far fewer man-hours than raising food on the same amount of land, many families were displaced from the soil. Occasionally "improving landlords" turned to more intensive cultivation of the soil in order to produce a larger cash crop of food for the growing urban markets, often riding roughshod over the preference of villagers for timeworn methods.

In short, capitalism was being applied to industry and agriculture wherever individual entrepreneurs saw profit to be made in producing books, weapons, clothing, or food for sale in the open market. For some peasants and workers this meant new opportunity. Many an ambitious peasant was able to better his position, as Martin Luther's father did by becoming a miner. But a great deal of misery and unemployment also resulted from the breaking down of customary economic relationships, the eviction of peasants from their holdings, and the movement of population to the new industrial centers. "Sturdy beggars" and "vagabonds" were a constant problem for sixteen-century town governments; eventually prisons and workhouses had to be built to contain them.

Wealth derived from the new industries and commerce tended to concentrate in a few hands in a few places. For a brief period the most powerful banking house was that of the Fuggers of Augsburg in south Germany. Jakob Fugger (1459–1525), as banker for the Habsburgs and the pope, could invest in Austrian mines and Spanish colonies and carry on dealings with every part of the Continent. On the whole, however, from about 1476 to 1576 Antwerp was the Wall Street of northern Europe, with Lyons not far behind. Then, for a century after 1576, it was Amsterdam. The wealth that poured in from the Orient and the New World had a way of gravitating to the commercial centers of the Netherlands. Where the investment market was freest, where the largest and most aggressive firms transacted most of their business, here were the nerve centers of European finance. Italy was losing its old place as the banking center of Europe. Financial power was clearly shifting to the north.

POLITICAL CONSOLIDATION AND CENTRALIZATION

The most highly developed monarchies of western Europe—England and France—had undergone a severe crisis in the fourteenth century (see Chapter 13). The successors of Edward I and Philip the Fair allowed their political ambitions to outstrip their financial resources. The Hundred Years' War (1337–1453) exhausted both France and England, and plague and social revolt added their toll of misery to war. The monarchs were not equal to the strain. As the fifteenth century opened, France was ruled by a king who had periods of insanity (Charles VI), and England was ruled by a usurper who owed his throne to his fellow barons and

THE FINANCIAL EMPIRE OF JAKOB FUGGER
ca. 1485–1525

Jakob Fugger with his bookkeeper. The cabinet in the rear lists the names of cities where Fugger had branch offices—Innsbruck, Nuremberg, and Lisbon, among others (detail from a painting by Matthaus Schwartz, 1516).

to Parliament (Henry IV). The future did not seem very bright for the monarchies that had been so painfully built up in the twelfth and thirteenth centuries.

The later fifteenth century, however, saw a remarkable recovery of monarchical institutions in western Europe. As people grew more and more weary of war, violence, and anarchy, the forces striving to restore some semblance of law and order rallied to the support of the monarchs in France, the Spanish kingdoms, and England. Even weak rulers profited from the demand for peace and strong government. And economic growth made it easier to support stronger armies and more effective bureaucracies.

France

At times during the Hundred Years' War the authority of the French king had almost disappeared, but there had been considerable recovery before the war ended in 1453. Charles VII was not a great king, but he was clever enough to find able men to work for him (he was known in his time as Charles the Well-served). He began his reign by using the widespread enthusiasm aroused by Joan of Arc to expel the English and to restore law and order to the French countryside. In 1438, by the Pragmatic Sanction of Bourges, he asserted his authority over the French clergy at the expense of papal power. In the 1440s he solved the financial problem of the crown by obtaining consent from the Estates to a broad-based tax on land called the *taille;* he then continued to levy the tax on his own authority. He organized a small standing army (at most, 25,000 men) under direct royal control, gained the support of wealthy merchants who supplied him with a siege train of heavy artillery, and methodically ousted the English from all their strongholds on the Continent except Calais.

Louis XI (1461–83) carried on his father's work and left the monarchy stronger than it had been since Philip IV. Louis, a slovenly and superstitious man with a morbid fear of death, had none of the majesty of kingship. He was called "the Spider" because he preferred to trap his enemies in diplomatic webs than to fight them. Machiavelli admired him, with reason. The greatest threat to the French monarchy was the powerful state that the dukes of Burgundy had built up on France's eastern frontier, including the wealthy provinces of the Netherlands as well as Burgundy proper. Louis never actually defeated his rival, Charles the Bold, Duke of Burgundy (1467–77), but he shrewdly helped Charles defeat himself. Louis encouraged quarrels between Charles and his eastern neighbors, and in the end the duke was killed in battle against the Swiss. The richest portion of his inheritance, the Netherlands, fell to the Emperor Maximilian (1493–1519) through his marriage with Mary, daughter of Charles the Bold; but the strategically located Duchy of Burgundy went to the king of France. At home, Louis encouraged trade and kept a firm rein on the nobles and higher clergy. His successor Charles VIII (1483–98) married the heiress of Brittany and so brought the last remaining feudal duchy under direct royal control.

With France fully under control, Charles felt strong enough to invade Italy (1494) in order to assert his claims to Naples as the remote heir of Charles of Anjou (see Chapter 12). Spain, which also had claims in Italy, quickly reacted, and foreign armies fought over the peninsula for half a century. The Italian city-states were helpless; even if they had been united they probably could not have resisted such powers as France and Spain. As it was, Spain gradually gained a dominant position in Italy, and with the loss of independence Italian life lost much of its vigor and excitement. On the other hand, while France suffered financially because of its losses in the Italian wars, the position of the king was not weakened and France remained one of the most influential states in Europe.

Spain

As we have seen, the Iberian Peninsula had suffered almost as severely as France from war and anarchy in the fourteenth and early fifteenth centuries. In 1469, however, a momentous marriage took place between Ferdinand of Aragon (1479–1516) and Isabella of Castile

			Joint Reign of Ferdinand and Isabella
750	1085	1252	1479 1504

| Moslem Rule in Spain | | *Reconquista* in the North | Amalgamation of Kingdoms into Portugal, Aragon, and Castile |
| | | Moslem Rule in Granada | |

1481 1492

Reconquest of Granada

(1474–1504). The marriage brought no organic fusion of the political institutions of the two states, but husband and wife followed a common foreign policy and their heir could properly be called king of "Spain." A new national monarchy had been born from a dynastic union.

Isabella reestablished the authority of the crown in Castile and with her husband led a successful eleven-year "crusade" (1481–92) to expel the Moors (as the Moslems in Spain were called) from their last holding in Spain, the kingdom of Granada. The victory touched off a wave of national patriotism and religious intolerance, which had been slowly gathering force during the later fifteenth century. In 1492 all Jews in both kingdoms were ordered either to become Christians or leave the land, and ten years later, in spite of promises of toleration when Granada fell, all Moors in Castile were offered the same choice. In 1478 some Dominicans had persuaded the pope to authorize Ferdinand and Isabella to set up the Spanish Inquisition. This dreaded instrument became a powerful force toward royal absolutism when the monarchs directed it against "converted" Jews and Moors who were suspected of secretly adhering to their old beliefs. There was thus a note of religious fervor and racial hatred, which was lacking elsewhere, in the birth of Spain as a great power.

A second marriage was greatly to affect Spain's European destiny in the sixteenth century. The Emperor Maximilian and his wife, Mary of Burgundy, had a son, Philip, who was heir to Austria through his Habsburg father and to the Netherlands through his mother. Philip married Joanna, the daughter of Ferdinand and Isabella. Their son Charles, born in 1500, eventually became king of Spain (1516–56) and ruler of the Netherlands, Austria, Milan, Naples, and the Spanish possessions in America. In 1519 the German princes elected him

emperor as Charles V. Thus Spain was thrust out into the full stream of European politics and world empire by coming under the Habsburg dynasty in 1516.

Spain was not a wealthy country, nor were its two halves, Castile and Aragon, ever thoroughly amalgamated. Even today Catalonia is markedly different from Castile. But the Spanish armies soon proved themselves the best in Europe during campaigns in Italy and

Illumination of Ferdinand and Isabella of Spain— known as the "Catholic Kings"—with their daughter Joanna.

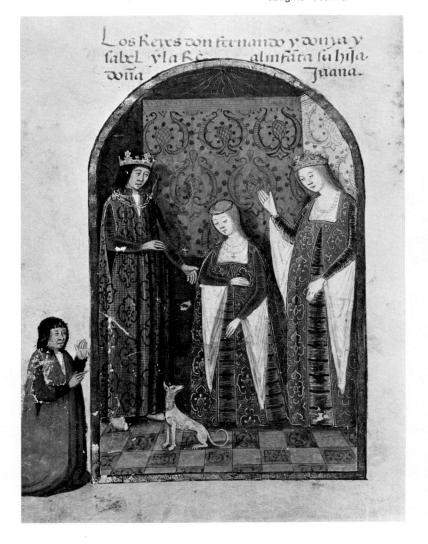

the Netherlands, and Columbus' discoveries brought in a stream of gold and silver from the New World that surpassed all European dreams of wealth. As a result, Spain was to become the leading power in Europe in the sixteenth century.

England

The Hundred Years' War had been a heavy burden on England. But the most severe trial followed the end of the war, when a restless nobility and professional soldiery returned from France to plunge into thirty more years of intermittent civil strife in the Wars of the Roses (1454–85). The excuse for the wars was the rivalry between the House of Lancaster and the House of York (both descended from Edward III) for the throne. Actually the

Effigies on the tombs of Ferdinand of Aragon and Isabella of Castile, who created a united Spain.

wars were contests between shifting factions of nobles for control of the government. When it was all over, the first of the Tudors was on the throne as Henry VII (1485–1509), by right of conquest and a dubious hereditary claim. The bloodshed and violence of the wars had sickened the people, and plots and counterplots had killed off most of the leaders of the nobility. Taking advantage of the opportunity to restore the monarchy, Henry proved himself one of the ablest rulers in English history. He kept England out of foreign wars, encouraged trade, restored the sources of royal revenue, and eliminated all pretenders to the throne. His son, Henry VIII (1509–47), inherited a full treasury, a united nation, and (for its day) an efficient administration. Henry VIII soon wasted the treasury surplus in war with France, but he and his overbearing minister, Cardinal Wolsey, did manage to concentrate power in their own hands. Henry VIII's England could compare well with either France or Spain in governmental efficiency and potential military strength, even though it had only about half Spain's population and a fourth that of France.

The Monarchs and the Nobility

Louis XI, Ferdinand and Isabella, and Henry VII all had common problems, which they met in strikingly similar ways. The chief obstacle in the path of rebuilding royal authority in the later fifteenth century was the military, political, and economic strength of the great nobles in each country (the kings were wise enough never to attack the social prestige of the nobility). The monarchs used various expedients in their cold war with overmighty subjects. The key to success was to make the royal Council an effective agency of central government. Councillors were selected from among nobles who were loyal to the king and from members of the upper middle class (especially lawyers) who sought power and promotion. Key councillors, often at their own expense, developed groups of agents who kept them informed about internal and external threats to the security of the state. At the same time the Council, or one of its committees, was given supreme judicial power so that it could act quickly in any emergency. Thus in England the Secretaries of State, who were the most influential members of the Council, were well aware of plots against the throne through their close contacts with local authorities, with English ambassadors abroad, and with a network of spies. The Star Chamber, the judicial arm of the Council, could be used to suppress any manifestations of aristocratic independence, and the ordinary courts almost never failed to convict men accused by the Council. In France and Spain the Council was equally well informed and had even greater judicial power.

The Monarchs and the Representative Assemblies

A second possible obstacle to royal absolutism was the representative assembly: the Estates General in France, the Cortes in the Spanish kingdoms, and Parliament in England. These assemblies had reached the peak of their influence in the fourteenth century. In the fifteenth century, they declined everywhere but in England. This was due more to the ineffectiveness of assemblies than to the hostility of monarchs. Except in England, provincial feeling was so strong that it was difficult to reach agreement on any issue. Assemblies were more ready to grumble than to act. In France, for example, the Estates General, in spite of repeated requests, neither supported, nor proposed clear-cut alternatives to, royal policies. It is also true that the kings had weakened the Estates by depriving them of their financial powers; old taxes were continued and new ones imposed by royal authority alone. Thus the Estates General of France were weak and useless and gradually ceased to meet. In Spain, the monarchs played off class against class by summoning only the represent-

atives of the cities when they needed money, thus depriving the townsmen of the possible aid of the great nobles. Anxious to support royal authority, the town representatives usually consented readily to whatever taxes the king demanded. Deprived of any real power, the Cortes of Castile, like the Estates General of France, met less and less frequently after the end of the fifteenth century.

In England Henry VII apparently had little respect for Parliament and, after the first years of his reign, seldom summoned it. But since the English Parliament could speak for all the privileged classes and all parts of the country, it was more difficult to ignore than the weak and divided assemblies of other countries. In England provincial rivalries scarcely existed; landowners and the bourgeoisie usually cooperated, and no general tax could be levied without Parliamentary consent. When Henry VIII got into trouble with the pope, he summoned Parliament to give him support. This use of Parliament as an accomplice had unanticipated results. By 1600, thanks to the frequent use Henry VIII and his successors made of it, Parliament had become a more powerful force in English government than ever before. By that time the representative assemblies on the Continent, in states governed by absolute monarchs, had become hollow forms.

The Monarchs and the Church

The final obstacle to the development of monarchical power was the Church. Against this obstacle the kings moved cautiously. Louis XI was proud to be called "Most Christian King" of France; Ferdinand and Isabella were proud to be known as the "Catholic Kings"; and Henry VIII was especially proud of his title "Defender of the Faith," which the pope granted him in 1521. But on the three crucial questions of appointment of the higher clergy, taxation of the clergy, and the appeal of ecclesiastical cases to Rome, not one of the monarchs admitted the full papal claims. The kings of England and France had established their right to tax their own clergy by 1300. The French kings had asserted their right to control clerical appointments in the Pragmatic Sanction of Bourges (1438), and the pope had granted Francis I the right to nominate the higher clergy and to settle the bulk of ecclesiastical disputes in France in the Concordat of Bologna in 1516. Even the "Catholic Kings" of Spain asserted and maintained their right to appoint, to tax, and to reform the clergy within their kingdoms, despite papal objections. Thus long before the Protestant Reformation, kings were trying to build "national churches"— churches that looked to the authority of the secular ruler in matters of appointment, taxation, and even jurisdiction, although not in doctrine.

Consolidation and Centralization Elsewhere in Europe

These tendencies in western Europe toward the consolidation of territory and the centralization of political power also appeared in the kingdoms of Norway and Sweden. They appeared too in Russia, where Ivan the Dread (1533–84) ruthlessly broke the power of the aristocracy. In Italy, however, there was no central government to be strengthened (much to the despair of observers like Machiavelli). In the German Empire the central government was a sham. There was no imperial army and no effective system of imperial taxation. There was an imperial supreme court, but it was so inefficient that it had little authority. An attempt at the close of the fifteenth century to strengthen the imperial government was almost a total failure. When Charles V became emperor in 1519, his real strength lay in the fact that he was duke of Austria, lord of the wealthy towns of the Netherlands, and king of Spain, with its well-equipped armies and overseas treasure. Becoming emperor added something to his prestige, much to his responsibilities, but little to his power. Many German princes expanded their territories at the expense of weaker neighbors and increased their authority within their principalities by methods very similar to those of the kings of western Europe. But in 1500 there was no central authority in Germany strong enough to resist papal exactions, foreign intervention, or the spread of heresy.

This lack of central authority was to be of crucial importance for the future. On the one hand, it meant that the Protestant Reformation, once it started, could not be brought under control. On the other, it meant that the emperor could rely only on his own hereditary domains in meeting a new threat that came from the East. The Turks had advanced steadily after the fall of Constantinople in 1453. The greatest of their sultans, Suleiman the Magnificent (1520–66), captured Belgrade, won most of Hungary in the battle of Mohacs (1526), and almost took Vienna in 1529. With a divided Germany behind him and a dangerous enemy facing him in the Danube Valley, the emperor could not play his old role of defender of Christendom until he had built a new state out of the old Habsburg territories.

Suggestions for Further Reading

Note: Asterisk denotes a book available in paperback edition.

General J. Burckhardt's great "essay," *The Civilization of the Renaissance in Italy* * (1860), is still the starting point for study. W. K. Ferguson, *The Renaissance in Historical Thought* (1948), traces the development of the idea of "rebirth" from the Humanists themselves through Burckhardt to the present. His *Europe in Transition: 1300–1520* (1963) is a good survey of the period. So is L. W. Spitz, *The Renaissance and Reformation Movements,* * 2 vols. (1971). M. P. Gilmore, *The World of Humanism: 1453–1517* * (1952), makes excellent use of recent monographic material and offers a critical bibliography. D. Hay, *The Italian Renaissance* * (1977), is a newer work of considerable value. See also his *Europe in the Fourteenth and Fifteenth Centuries* (1971).

Italian Society and Politics   There is interesting material on Renaissance businessmen and bankers in M. Beard, *A History of the Business Man* (1938), and R. de Roover, *The Rise and Decline of the Medici Bank* * (1963). I. Origo, *The Merchant of Prato* (1957), is an enjoyable study of a small-town businessman. G. Mattingly, *Renaissance Diplomacy* * (1955), traces the origins of modern diplomacy in Italy in a fascinating way. There are histories of all the major Italian states, but the most important for an understanding of the Renaissance are those on Florence. G. Brucker, *Renaissance Florence* (1969), is the best brief treatment in English. D. Herlihy, *Pisa in the Early Renaissance* (1958), and W. M. Bowsky, *The Finances of the Commune of Siena* (1970), provide the histories of two other leading cities. H. Baron, *The Crisis of the Early Italian Renaissance,* * 2 vols. (1966), is an important study of Florentine politics and culture in the early fifteenth century. Perhaps the best single volume on Machiavelli is F. Chabod, *Machiavelli and the Renaissance* * (1958). Felix Gilbert, *Machiavelli and Guiccardini* (1965) is also very good. D. Merejkowski's novel, *The Romance of Leonardo da Vinci* * (1902), gives a vivid and unforgettable picture of Italian society based on sound historical scholarship. D. S. Chambers, *The Imperial Age of Venice: 1380–1580* * (1970), examines Venice's power as a commercial enterprise. On another kind of enterprise, see M. Mallet, *Mercenaries and Their Masters* (1974), an excellent study of the *condottieri.*

Literature and Art   Most of the general works listed above contain discussions of the literary and artistic achievements of the age. The classic literary history, still well worth reading, is F. de Sanctis, *History of Italian Literature* (1870; trans. 1931), R. R. Bolgar, *The Classical Heritage* (1954), traces Greek and Roman influences on western literature. P. O. Kristeller, *Renaissance Thought,* * 2 vols. (1961, 1965), is a brief but penetrating analysis. The best introduction to the educational theories of the Humanists is W. H. Woodward, *Vittorino da Feltre and Other Humanist Educators* * (1905). Of the many works on Italian Renaissance art, three by masters of their subjects may be mentioned: B. Berenson, *The Italian Painters of the Renaissance,* * rev. ed. (1930), E. Panofsky, *Renaissance and Renascences in Western Art,* 2 vols. (1965) and M. Baxendall, *Painting and Experience in Fifteenth Century Italy* (1972). An older handbook, still useful, is H. Wölfflin, *The Art of the Italian Renaissance* * (1903; edited as *Classic Art,* 1952). A. C. Krey, *A City That Art Built* (1936), is an interesting brief attempt to relate cultural flowering to economic and political circumstances in Florence. See also A. Smart, *The Renaissance and Mannerism in Italy* (1971), and A. Blunt, *Artistic Theory in Italy, 1450–1600* * (1962).

Contemporary Writings   It is easy to become acquainted with the thought of Renaissance writers because of the number of readily available translations. Two source collections are particularly good: *The Renaissance Philosophy of Man,* * ed. by E. Cassirer (1948), which includes Pico's *Oration,* and *The Portable Renaissance Reader,* * ed. by J. B. Ross and M. M. McLaughlin (1953), which includes a selection from Alberti's *On the Family.* See also W. L. Gundersheimer, *The Italian Renaissance* * (1965). There are many editions of Boccaccio's *Decameron,* Cellini's *Autobiography,* and Castiglione's *The Courtier.* N. Machiavelli, *The Prince and the Discourses* * (trans. 1940; Modern Library), is the most convenient edition. C. B. Coleman has edited *The Treatise of Lorenzo Valla on the Donation of Constantine* (1922), and E. A. McCurdy has edited *The Notebooks of Leonardo da Vinci,* 2 vols. (1938). *The Vespasiano Memoirs* * (trans. 1926) offer contemporary thumbnail sketches of Humanists, artists, and princes. G. Bull has translated Vasari's *Lives of the Artists* * (1965).

The Church   There is a full account of the councils of Constance and Basel and of the Renaissance popes in the five-volume work by an Anglican bishop, M. Creighton, *A History of the Papacy from the Great Schism to the Sack of Rome* (1919). The best account, however, based on the Vatican archives, is the still larger work of the Swiss Catholic L. Pastor, *History of the Popes,* 40 vols. (trans. 1891–1953). On conciliar ideas, see B. Tierney, *Foundations of the Conciliar Theory* (1955), and E. F. Jacob, *Essays in the Conciliar Epoch* (1953). H. Jedin, *A History of the Council of Trent,* Vol. I (trans. 1957), gives a good account of the events leading up to the council.

Technological and Economic Growth in the North   On printing, see P. Butler, *The Origin of Printing in Europe* (1940); D. C. McMurtrie, *The Book: The Story of Printing and Bookmaking,* 3rd rev. ed. (1943); E. P. Goldschmidt, *The Printed Book of the Renaissance* (1950); and V. Scholderer, *Johann Gutenberg* (1963). R. Ehrenberg, *Capital and Finance in the Age of the Renaissance* (trans. 1928), is a study of the Fuggers. The Fugger Newsletters of the later sixteenth century are available in *News and Rumor in Renaissance Europe.* * E. Eisenstein, *The Printing Press as an Agent of Change* (1979) is a good account of this great innovation. On science, see M. Boas, *The Scientific Renaissance, 1450–1630* * (1962), W. Wightman, *Science and the Renaissance,* 2 vols. (1962), and F. A. Yates, *Giordano Bruno and the Hermetic Tradition* (1964).

17 Reform and Revolution in Western Christendom

At the opening of the sixteenth century, the Roman Church was in greater danger than it had been at any time since the Great Schism. Suspicion of Church policy and contempt for the leadership of the Church were widespread. Even the peasants were annoyed by the financial demands of the clergy and bored by routine services. Laymen would flock to their churches for the great feasts or to Rome for a papal jubilee, but many of them were also ready to respond to radical evangelical preachers. There had always been some tension between the Church and the bourgeoisie. The Church had never been able to incorporate business ethics into its system of values, and the bourgeoisie had never been happy about the Church's special financial privileges. The better educated the townsmen became, the more clearly they saw the weaknesses of the Church. The nobility either denounced the corruption of the Church or profited from it.

Most dangerous of all were the secular rulers who were limiting the papacy's powers of taxation, jurisdiction, and appointment. Caught in the maelstrom of Italian power politics, the popes of the fifteenth century found themselves threatened by leagues of Italian princes and thus forced to seek help from and make concessions to more distant and more powerful rulers. The popes had no military power of their own. Moreover, by 1500 they were regularly in debt, with little prospect of finding any easy way out of their financial straits.

THE NEED FOR REFORM IN THE WESTERN CHURCH

Even able and devoted Vicars of Christ might have had difficulty defending the independence of the papacy and raising its moral prestige. But this was the era of the Renaissance popes—at best, good administrators and patrons of artists and scholars; at worst, corrupt and immoral men with secular tastes and interests. Some, like Alexander VI, used the contributions of the faithful to carve out principalities for their illegitimate sons. Most of them, under financial pressure, sold justice in their courts and appointments to office in their councils.

Bishops and archbishops throughout Europe were generally of noble blood, and many of them had been nominated by monarchs or by the pope for loyal service rather than for their piety or administrative ability. Some held more than one bishopric, although this was contrary to canon law, and some rarely visited their sees (one bishop visited his only once, when he was buried there). Even conscientious bishops found that their power to appoint the clergy and to reform abuses within their dioceses had diminished. Many powers that properly belonged to the bishop had either fallen into the hands of local laymen or had been "reserved" by the pope. The ignorance and immorality of the parish clergy were bywords among contemporary writers. The parish priest in fact was no better or worse than he had been for centuries, but moral sensitivity to clerical misconduct had been rising. Furthermore, the tithes that the priest levied and the fees that he charged for baptisms, marriages, and burials were burdensome to peasants and small craftsmen. In earlier centuries monks and friars had made up for many of the deficiencies of the parish clergy, but by 1500 the religious orders had little influence on laymen. Monastic life no longer attracted the pious, as it had several centuries earlier, and monasteries now had to search out recruits to keep their numbers up.

The most widespread complaints were caused by practices that could be interpreted as the selling of spiritual benefits. The Church was rich in land but poor in the newer forms of wealth. It cost money to maintain such a large institution, and the clergy had a right to ask for a fair share of the growing wealth of Europe. But the methods used to raise money and the purposes for which the money was spent (such as waging war to regain territory claimed for the Papal States) outraged many believers. Papal demands for money were passed from the bishops to the parish clergy to the people. Thus some priests demanded the best garment of a deceased parishioner as a "mortuary fee" and had regular tables of charges for other religious rites. Even worse were the abuses that the pope allowed to creep into the sale of indulgences.

Indulgences

Indulgences, in fact, were the raw nerve of the Church's whole financial system. An indulgence was a remission of the temporal penalty for sin (penances in this life and the pains of Purgatory after death) imposed by a priest in the sacrament of penance. It was granted on condition of true contrition for the sin and in consideration of some pious deed performed, such as going on a crusade or

Lucas Cranach the Younger, *Martin Luther and the Wittenberg Reformers* (*ca.* 1543).

A pair of woodcuts by Lucas Cranach the Elder contrasting Jesus and the pope. On the left, Jesus is driving the moneychangers from the temple; on the right, the pope is taking money for indulgences.

a pilgrimage. During the Middle Ages a money "contribution" became the normal consideration, and the necessity for contrition was often forgotten by the believer. In the fourteenth century the popes developed the doctrine that Christ and the saints had accumulated a "treasury of merits" from which Christ's Vicars could dispense benefits to the faithful through indulgences. In the fifteenth century Sixtus IV, on the strength of this doctrine, claimed the power to release the souls of the dead from the penance they were undergoing in Purgatory as the temporal penalty for their sins. This claim helped make the indulgence trade even more lucrative. It was hard to withhold a contribution that would release the soul of a dead parent from years of suffering in the next world. In theory, the money was a "contribution" for pious purposes. But many laymen concluded that the Church was selling salvation at a price—and was then wasting the money on petty wars and luxurious living.

The Dangers of Criticism

Criticism of the Church was not new. Though the Church was divinely instituted, everyone knew that it was administered by fallible human beings—that is,

by sinners. The moral level of the clergy was probably better in 1500 than in the year 1000. But the world of 1500 was far different from that of 1000, and it is well to review some of the main differences in order to understand why criticism now constituted a real danger to the Church.

The European world of 1500 was more secular in its interests and ideals, as we have seen. The artist, the despot, the sea captain, and the businessman were pursuing careers that seemed more exciting than sainthood, and the medieval interpretation of life in this world as a pilgrimage to life after death seemed unsatisfying, even though it was not yet openly rejected. Granted that salvation was the goal of mankind, some men began to ask: Was renunciation of the world the only, or even the surest, way to gain that goal?

While the fifteenth century was an age of increasing secular interests for some, it was an age of heightened religious sensitivity and piety for others. Both the worldly minded and the devout were becoming critical of the growing complexity of the Church's sacraments and ceremonies. Popular piety of the late Middle Ages had nurtured a luxuriant growth of religious practices that seemed to verge on superstition and idolatry. The cult of the saints and the veneration of

In the first of this pair of woodcuts, Cranach shows Jesus kissing the feet of his disciples as he washes them. The other woodcut shows the pope offering his foot to be kissed by kings and nobles.

relics became a kind of obsession. For almost every human ill there was a saint, who, if properly approached, could prevent or heal the affliction. And as the number of sacred symbols and ceremonies multiplied, their religious significance almost disappeared. A fifteenth-century French artist painted a sensual, photographic portrait of the French king's mistress as the Virgin Mary, apparently without being conscious of any blasphemy. As a modern historian has put it, the religious atmosphere of the later Middle Ages was "supersaturated," and the most observant church leaders of the fifteenth century grew worried. They saw that the Church was becoming dangerously vulnerable to radicals who might ask: What is the core of Christianity? Is it to venerate an image of St. Anthony, to avoid meat on Fridays, and to go on a pilgrimage? Or, rather, is it to love one's neighbor and to live a Christlike life?

A final reason why ecclesiastical abuses were so dangerous to the Church in 1500 was that there were now secular rulers strong enough to use the cry for reform for their own purposes. The monarchs of western Europe were already appointing and taxing the clergy. The upper classes all over Europe coveted the wealth of the Church. Many secular rulers, should they so decide, now had the power to confiscate the Church's lands, buildings, and revenues in the name of reform. Reform by royal command sometimes had good results. In Spain, Cardinal Jiménez de Cisneros, strongly backed by Ferdinand and Isabella, instituted many reforms in the Spanish clergy at the opening of the sixteenth century. But there was always the danger that reform by a secular power might result in state control of the Church and confiscation of its property.

Failure of Fifteenth-Century Reform Movements

Various schemes for reform had been advanced in the fifteenth century. In the Rhineland, the Brethren of the Common Life, a group of laymen who devoted themselves to communal living and biblical piety, emphasized direct, intimate communion with God in their communities and schools. In Florence between 1494 and 1498 one of the most remarkable preachers of the age, the Dominican monk Girolamo Savonarola, moved multitudes to repentance and encouraged the crowds to follow an old custom of making bonfires of their wigs, makeup, and other "vanities" during Lent. These reformers still held to the medieval conception of reform. According to that conception, the Church itself was divinely constituted and so could not be "reformed," but the individuals who composed it could and should be regenerated. The leaders at the councils of Constance and Basel were reformers of a more modern sort. They meant to reform the institution itself by giving more power to representatives of the clergy, thus making the pope a limited monarch. Hus wanted to reform both the individual and the institution by returning to the Bible as the standard of Christian living and ecclesiastical practice.

Each of these differing conceptions of reform was to take root and bear seed in one way or another during the sixteenth century. But before 1500 the impetus of each movement was soon spent, and the institutional abuses remained untouched. The councils failed to make permanent changes in the constitution of the Church, and both Hus and Savonarola were burned as heretics. Whenever attempts at reform threatened to undermine the status of the clergy as mediators between God and man, or the power of the pope as the Vicar of Christ, they were declared heretical and stamped out. It seemed that the strength of vested interest and the dead weight of authority were so strong that the Church would never be roused from its complacency.

Christian Humanism

A new and hopeful type of reform movement emerged in the sixteenth century—Christian Humanism. Under the inspiration of the classical revival in Italy, a number of scholars in northern Europe began to recommend a return to the best of both the classical and the Christian traditions through a study of the classics and the Bible. They argued that if men could appreciate the ethical perfection of Socrates and Jesus, of Plato and Paul, then the absurdities of theological hair splitting and the irrelevance of many ecclesiastical practices would become evident. Reform would inevitably follow from a better understanding of the simplicity of primitive Christianity—and of the noble ideals of the Greeks and Romans, which they felt to be complementary rather than antagonistic to Christi-

anity. Let the Church take for its guides the Bible and the early Fathers rather than the scholastic theologians of the Middle Ages. Abuses would disappear if laymen and clerics alike would recognize that Christianity was an attitude of mind and a way of life, not a complex set of dogmas and ceremonies.

This program was fundamentally conservative, designed to save the Church from itself. It had a radical element in its demand for lay participation in reform and for vernacular translations of the Bible so that the laity would understand the need for reform. Nevertheless, its leaders were almost without exception loyal to Rome. They were obviously optimistic in their estimate of human nature. They rated the power of reason and education very high, and encouraged historical and literary studies in the hope that they would reveal earlier and purer practices. Cardinal Jiménez in Spain set scholars to producing a monumental edition of the Bible that presented the original Hebrew and Greek texts in parallel columns with the Latin. In Germany, Johann Reuchlin defended the study of Hebrew literature as a means of understanding the Old Testament, even though a group of Dominicans wished to destroy all Hebrew books. In France, Lefèvre d'Etaples studied the Epistles of Paul and translated the New Testament into French (1523) in an effort to enlighten his contemporaries and further the cause of reform. For Sir Thomas More in England, study and reform were also closely related. In his famous *Utopia*, More wrote a searching analysis of the most glaring social, political, and ecclesiastical evils of his day from the point of view of a scholar steeped in Humanism and the Gospels as well as in the monastic tradition of the Middle Ages.

Erasmus

The acknowledged leader of these Christian Humanists was Erasmus of Rotterdam (*ca.* 1469–1536). Erasmus' enthusiasm for the Greco-Roman classics matched his enthusiasm for the Bible and early Christian writings. He devoted his life to scholarship in the conviction that sound learning would help save the Church. He edited the New Testament in the original Greek (1516), with a preface urging that it be translated into all the vulgar tongues, and he published editions of the early Church Fathers. His hundreds of letters and his briefer books were even more influential. In them, with lively humor, underlying seriousness, and an unsurpassed command of the Latin language, he argued for what he called "the philosophy of Christ," the love of God and neighbor that he saw as the essence of Christianity. He insisted that this love be expressed through an active life. He feared that the Church of his day had obscured this essential truth with useless forms and ceremonies. In a typical passage he ridiculed monkish ideas of religion. When the final reckoning comes, one monk will point to his fastings and ceremonies for credit; "another will boast that for sixty years he never touched money, except when his fingers were protected by two pairs of gloves." Christ will interrupt their boasts and say, "Whence comes this new race of Jews [that is, Pharisees]? I promised the inheritance of my Father, not to cowls, prayers, or fasts, but to works of charity." This device of imagining how Christ himself would judge the world of the 1500s was characteristic of Christian Humanism.

Christian Humanism offered the last chance of peaceful reform. But it was a movement that needed time, patience, and understanding to have any impact on the upper classes, and it never had much appeal for the mass of the population. It influenced every effort, both Protestant and Catholic, to reform the Church, but as a practical program it was doomed to failure. It was too aristocratic and too intellectual. The times were revolutionary, and the remedies that Europe was to adopt were both sterner and simpler than Erasmus' "philosophy of Christ."

LUTHER'S REVOLT FROM ROME

On October 31, 1517, an Augustinian friar serving as Professor of Bible in the little University of Wittenberg in Saxony prepared ninety-five theses, or propositions, for academic debate on the subject of indulgences. The author, Martin

Luther (1483–1546), was outraged by the unscrupulous salesmanship of a Dominican friar named Tetzel who had been hawking indulgences in Magdeburg. "So soon as coin in coffer rings," Tetzel was reported as preaching, "the soul from Purgatory springs." The proceeds from this particular sale of indulgences were meant to go toward the building of St. Peter's church in Rome, though half

Portrait of Erasmus by Albrecht Dürer.

Erasmus' Preface to His Edition of the New Testament

I utterly dissent from those who are unwilling that the sacred Scriptures should be read by the unlearned translated into their vulgar tongue, as though Christ had taught such subtleties that they can scarcely be understood even by a few theologians, or, as though the strength of the Christian religion consisted in men's ignorance of it. The mysteries of kings it may be safer to conceal, but Christ wished his mysteries to be published as openly as possible. I wish that even the weakest woman should read the Gospel—should read the epistles of Paul. And I wish these were translated into all languages, so that they might be read and understood, not only by Scots and Irishmen, but also by Turks and Saracens. To make them understood is surely the first step. It may be that they might be ridiculed by many, but some would take them to heart. I long that the husbandman should sing portions of them to himself as he follows the plough, that the weaver should hum them to the tune of his shuttle, that the traveller should beguile with their stories the tedium of his journey.

From Erasmus, "Paraclesis," *Novum Instrumentum,* trans. by Frederic Seebohm, in *The Oxford Reformers* (New York: Dutton, 1914), p. 203.

Ihr deutschen merctet mich recht/
Des heiligen Vaters Papstes Knecht/
Bin ich/und br ing euch ist allein/
Zehen tausent und neun hundert carein/
Gnad und Ablaß von einer Sünd/
Vor euch/ewer Eltern/Weib und Kind/
Sol ein jeder gewehret sein
So viel ihrleg t ins Kästelein/
So bald der Gülden im Becken klingt/
Im hup die Seel im Himel springt/

Contemporary caricature of Johann Tetzel hawking indulgences. The last line of the jingle is: "So soon as coin in coffer rings, the soul from Purgatory springs."

of it actually ended up in the pockets of the Archbishop of Mainz and of the Fugger banking firm. Luther's theses were immediately printed and debated not only in Wittenberg but all over Germany. The sensation they caused marked the start of the Protestant Reformation. Luther's chief propositions were:

> There is no divine authority for preaching that the soul flies out of purgatory immediately the money clinks in the bottom of the chest. . . . It is certainly possible that when the money clinks in the bottom of the chest, avarice and greed increase. . . . All those who believe themselves certain of their own salvation by means of letters of indulgence will be eternally damned, together with their teachers. . . . Any Christian whatsoever, who is truly repentant, enjoys plenary remission from penalty and guilt, and this is given him without letters of indulgence.

At the time, Martin Luther was a strong-willed, keen-minded, high-strung man in his early thirties. He was the son of a prosperous peasant turned miner, who had been able to give his boy a university education. The young Luther had experienced several severe emotional crises; the most acute one led him to become a friar. But in his convent he had become increasingly dissatisfied with the

emphasis his teachers laid on good works. He had been a most conscientious friar; he had fasted and prayed and confessed without end. If good works could win a man salvation, surely they should win it for him, he thought. Yet performing the acts commanded by the Church gave him no inner certainty that he was forgiven, only a growing sense of guilt, despair, and deepening spiritual crisis. Peace came to him when he suddenly understood what St. Paul had meant when he said that a man is saved not by doing the works of the Jewish law but by his faith in Christ. The ceremonies and religious practices of the medieval Church seemed to Luther a new Jewish law. Man is too corrupted by sin to meet the demands of such a law by his own efforts, and so he must rely on his faith in God's mercy. It is unthinkable that a man can buy God's favor by doing a good deed or performing some sacramental act. In the matter of saving a man's soul, Luther concluded, God does everything, man can do nothing.

It took Luther some time to work out the revolutionary implications of this thought. If man is saved by faith alone, then ceremonies and sacraments, pilgrimages and indulgences, everything the medieval Church called "good works," are at best irrelevant and at worst dangerous. Indulgences were the first "good work" at which Luther struck. Within a short time after his attack their sales dropped off sharply in Germany. When the Dominicans, chief sellers of the indulgences, persuaded Pope Leo X to condemn his theses, Luther was gradually driven to deny the authority of the pope. Soon afterward, when he came to believe that John Hus had been right on certain matters in spite of his condemnation by the Council of Constance, he denied the authority of general councils as well. By April 1521 Luther was standing before the Emperor Charles V at an imperial diet at Worms and declaring that he was bound by the authority of the Scripture and his own conscience rather than by that of either pope or council. He could not recant any of his writings, he added, because his conscience was "captive to the Word of God" and because it was "neither safe nor right to go against conscience." The

Bible and conscience—these were to be the two chief pillars of Protestant Christianity.

Luther was not burned at Worms, as Hus had been at Constance. His safe-conduct was respected, and he was allowed to return to the protection of his ruler, Frederick, the Elector of Saxony. For twenty-five years, till his death in 1546, he taught, preached, and wrote at Wittenberg. Meanwhile the revolt against the papacy that he had started gathered momentum and spread over northern Europe. In the end, the unity of Western Christendom was permanently destroyed.

Lutheran Principles

In breaking with the papacy, Luther was guided by three main principles: salvation by faith, not by works; the ultimate authority of the Bible; and the priesthood of all believers. The three were closely related. It was through study of the Bible that Luther came to his belief in salvation by faith, and it was to the Bible that he always appealed against the authority of tradition or the papacy. His greatest literary work was a German translation of the Bible (completed in 1534), which he wrote in order that God's Word might be put into the hands of every devout person in Germany who could read. There was no essential difference between a priest and a layman, he insisted. A dedicated layman reverently reading the Scripture was closer to divine truth than a worldly pope proclaiming dogma for the Church. Christ had meant every believer to be a priest to his neighbor; He had not intended a special few to act as mediators between man and God. A Christian can serve God as well by being an honest merchant or a faithful housewife as by becoming a monk or a nun. Thus Luther encouraged the dissolution of the monastic orders, and in order to dramatize his convictions he married a nun and became the happy father of six children.

Luther's original protest had been a purely religious matter, rooted in his own spiritual experience. But to gain support he had to appeal to the nationalistic and financial grievances of his fellow Germans. "What has brought us Germans to such a pass that we have to suffer this robbery and this destruction of our property by the Pope?" he asked in 1520.

Portrait of Martin Luther by Lucas Cranach (1533).

Luther on Justification by Faith

For the word of God cannot be received and honored by any works, but by faith alone. Hence it is clear that, as the soul needs the word alone for life and justification, so it is justified by faith alone and not by any works. For if it could be justified by any other means, it would have no need of the word, nor consequently of faith. . . .

It is evident that by no outward work or labor can the inward man be at all justified, made free and saved, and that no works whatever have any relation to him. And so, on the other hand, it is solely by impiety and incredulity of heart that he becomes guilty and a slave of sin, deserving condemnation; not by any outward sin or work.

Therefore the first care of every Christian ought to be to lay aside all reliance on works, and strengthen his faith alone more and more, and by it grow in the knowledge, not of works, but of Christ Jesus, who has suffered and risen again for him.

From Martin Luther, *On Christian Liberty*, trans. by H. Wace and C. A. Buchheim, in *First Principles of the Reformation* (London: Murray, 1883), pp. 107–08.

"If the kingdom of France has resisted it, why do we Germans suffer ourselves to be fooled and deceived?" Luther appealed to princes eager to confiscate church property, to businessmen unhappy about papal finance, to German patriots resentful of the Italians who dominated the papacy and the College of Cardinals, and to devout laymen and conscientious priests who were shocked by the corruption in the Church. His principles of salvation by faith and of serving God in one's secular calling appealed especially to laymen, who found in them a way of reconciling Christian devotion with an active concern about worldly affairs. High-minded and low-minded motives were inextricably mixed in the minds of those who accepted Luther's arguments.

Luther had no intention of breaking away from the true Church of Christ or of setting up a rival organization. But after 1520 he was convinced that the Church founded by Christ and the Apostles had wandered from the true path somewhere in the Middle Ages, and that the bishop of Rome was not the Vicar of Christ, but rather the Anti-christ. Much of the dogma and ritual of the Church of his day, Luther believed, was the work of men, not of God. Such accretions must be swept away, leaving only the pure faith of the Apostles and the early Church Fathers. In the purified Church there would be only two sacraments (Baptism and Holy Communion) in place of seven, a simplified ritual in German rather than in Latin, and more emphasis on the congregation's participation in the service. But Luther did not want to set up a "new" church; he sought only to reform *the* Church. There could be only one true Church, into which all men were received in baptism. Either Luther was right in defying the pope, or the pope was right in excommunicating Luther. At first there were not two churches, one "Catholic" and one "Lutheran," but an irreconcilable argument over the nature of the one true Church.

The Spread of Lutheranism

Luther's ideas were spread by his students and by the books and pamphlets that poured from the new printing presses. During the early years of the movement, publishers overwhelmingly supported Luther. Leopold Ranke calculated that in 1523 there were almost four hundred books and pamphlets written by Luther and his supporters compared with only twenty or so pro-Catholic works. Many of the younger Humanists supported Luther's ideas and gave his movement intellectual respectability, and even the older Humanists greeted the attack on indulgences with joy. As Luther became more vehement in his criticism of the Church, the older Humanists retreated to the fold of the Catholic Church, but with some reluctance. Even Erasmus, who came to consider Luther a fanatic, broke with him only in 1524, after repeated pleas for moderation had failed.

Many priests and monks, on the other hand, were convinced by Luther's arguments and were among his first converts. These converts were especially numerous in the German cities, and the cities gave Luther his first solid basis of support. The town governments had their own grievances against the Church. The clergy could avoid most local taxes,

Luther on the Church

Thus it may come to pass that the Pope and his followers are wicked and not true Christians, and not being taught by God, have no true understanding, whereas a common man may have true understanding. Why should we then not follow him? Has not the Pope often erred? Who could help Christianity, in case the Pope errs, if we do not rather believe another who has the Scriptures for him? Therefore it is a wickedly devised fable—and they cannot quote a single letter to confirm it—that it is for the Pope alone to interpret the Scriptures or to confirm the interpretation of them. They have assumed the authority of their own selves. And though they say that this authority was given to St. Peter when the keys were given to him, it is plain enough that the keys were not given to St. Peter alone, but to the whole community. . . . Moreover, if the article of our faith is right, "I believe in the holy Christian Church," the Pope cannot alone be right; else we must say, "I believe in the Pope of Rome," and reduce the Christian Church to one man, which is a devilish and damnable heresy. Besides that, we are all priests, as I have said, and have all one faith, one Gospel, one Sacrament; how then should we not have the power of discerning and judging what is right or wrong in matters of faith?

From Martin Luther, "Address to the Christian Nobility of the German Nation," in *Luther's Primary Works,* ed. by H. Wace and C. A. Buchheim (London: Hodder and Stoughton, 1896), pp. 170–71.

and at the same time the financial demands of the Church bore especially heavily on the urban population. The worldly life of the higher clergy and the ignorance of many parish priests were offensive to pious laymen. The towns had already taken over responsibility for most social services (education and charity); why should they not assume responsibility for religion as well? Thus in town after town, with very little violence, the conservative clergy were replaced by followers of Luther. Considering that many towns were in fact independent political entities, they were establishing the first state churches. They did so a decade or more before some of the German princes made Lutheranism a state religion. Luther was not entirely happy about this development (he would have preferred no secular control), but he realized that if the truth, as he saw it, was to prevail, it must be protected by secular rulers.

The peasants were excited by Luther's message at first, but he lost most of them after the Peasants' Rebellion of 1524 to 1525. This was the largest and bloodiest of the many peasant uprisings that resulted from complex economic and social causes during the later Middle Ages. The rebels' chief aim was to abolish serfdom and the burdens of the manorial system. "Therefore do we find in the Scripture that we are free," they argued, "and we will be free." Luther was close enough to his peasant origins to sympathize with their demands, but the freedom he was interested in was an inner religious freedom, freedom from an ecclesiastical system, not from social or political bondage. He felt that the peasants were perverting his message, and their violence further turned him against them. Finally he wrote a bitter condemnation of the uprising. The rebellion was put down with atrocities that went beyond those of the rebels. The peasants felt that Luther had betrayed them, but the middle and ruling classes welcomed his social conservatism. After 1525 he and his followers fought as hard against radicals, who wanted to carry the religious revolt too far, as they did against the Roman Catholics, who wished to wipe out Lutheranism.

There was at first no effective resist-ance in Germany to the spread of Luther's ideas. The emperor Charles V never wavered in his orthodoxy, but the task of holding together his scattered dominions proved so difficult that he was unable to bring political or military pressure to bear on cities and states that had turned Lutheran. From 1522 to 1559 Charles and his son Philip were caught up in a series of conflicts with France that absorbed much of their energy and income. Meanwhile Charles and his brother Ferdinand were also trying to stem the tide of Turkish conquest in the Mediterranean and the Danube Valley. The French in the West and the Turks in the East, sometimes in alliance with each other, allowed the emperor only a few intervals of peace in which to turn his attention to the religious division of Germany.

By the time of Luther's death in 1546, the German principalities were about evenly divided between the two faiths, while the majority of the free cities supported the Lutheran movement. In 1547, during a peaceful interlude in his international struggles, Charles V finally found an opportunity to attack the Lutheran states. The confused war that followed proved that neither side could destroy the other, and in 1555 the emperor reluctantly allowed his brother Ferdinand, who was ruler of Austria and later emperor, to conclude the Religious Peace of Augsburg. This peace allowed the city-states and princes of the Empire to choose between Lutheranism and Catholicism and bound them to respect each other's rights. *Cuius regio, eius religio*, as someone later summed up the

Title page of the first German translation of the Bible, by Martin Luther, printed in 1534 with the approval of the Elector of Saxony.

Contemporary engraving depicting a noble lady and her son kneeling before peasant rebels to plead for their lives during the Peasants' Rebellion (1524–25).

THE SPREAD OF PROTESTANTISM — Sixteenth century

Map legend:
- Anglicans
- Lutherans
- Calvinists
- Anabaptists
- Roman Catholics

ATLANTIC OCEAN — NORTH SEA — BALTIC SEA — MEDITERRANEAN SEA

Cities shown: Leiden, Antwerp, Canterbury, Münster, Wittenberg, Worms, Strasbourg, Augsburg, Vienna, Bourges, Basel, CALVINISTS, Geneva, Lyons, Trent, Bordeaux, Manresa, Rome, Madrid

0   MILES   300

southern Germany remained mostly "Catholic." The division remains today about as it was in 1560. Outside Germany, Lutheran ideas spread widely but took root only in Scandinavia, where Denmark, Norway, and Sweden became Lutheran before mid-century. Perhaps because Luther spoke so forcefully in the German idiom to his follow Germans, his teaching was not so well adapted to export as was the teaching of John Calvin.

CALVINISM

Luther's University of Wittenberg was not the only center from which reform ideas radiated. Other important centers were Zurich, Basel, Strasbourg, and especially Geneva. In these southern German and Swiss cities there developed a type of Protestantism closely related to Lutheranism but different in emphasis. There was more reliance on a highly developed system of theology and church organization and more stress on moral conduct and political action. The members of this second family of Protestant churches are generally called "Reformed" churches, in contrast with the "Lutheran."

Among the early Swiss and south German reformers were the Humanists Ulrich Zwingli of Zurich (1484–1531) and Martin Bucer of Strasbourg (1491–1551). Neither man agreed entirely with Luther. Zwingli took a more radical position on the sacraments, arguing that Communion was essentially a memorial service commemorating the Last Supper. Bucer tried to reconcile various Protestant groups and was more tolerant than most of the other reformers.

More influential than either Zwingli or Bucer was John Calvin (1509–64). Calvin had been trained as a lawyer and a Humanist in his native France before he became converted to Protestantism and settled down as a pastor in Geneva. He learned much from Luther, as well as from Zwingli and Bucer. Through these influences and through his early training, he became the chief theologian and organizer of second-generation Protestantism. His *Institutes of the Christian Religion* served as the basic handbook of Protes-

Sketch of John Calvin drawn by a student, perhaps during a lecture.

principle: the ruler determines the religion for the region. People who disliked the ruler's choice might migrate to another state. Lutherans were allowed to keep any church lands they had seized before 1552, but it was agreed that every Catholic bishop or abbot who turned Protestant in the future would have to resign his title and leave his lands in Catholic hands. This last clause was difficult to interpret and caused trouble later. The chief flaw in the settlement, however, was the exclusion of Calvinists, whose numbers were growing rapidly, from the benefits of the peace.

The Peace of Augsburg was the first official recognition, however grudging, that Western Christendom had been rent asunder and would have to continue as a house divided. It was not religious toleration, but it was a step along the way. In the end, northern Germany became mostly "Protestant" (as Lutherans had been called since 1529, when they presented a "protest" at an imperial diet);

The more rigid Protestants objected to all religious paintings and sculpture as leading to idolatry. In this engraving of 1579, Calvinists are pulling down statues of saints and destroying stained-glass windows.

tant principles for two centuries. It was a clear, well-organized, well-written book in both its Latin and its French versions, and its argument had all the logic a trained lawyer could bring to it. Calvin's two polar principles were the absolute sovereignty of God and the radical depravity of man. No acts of sinful man can merit salvation; God, through his inscrutable will, has destined some to be saved and some to be damned. This doctrine of "predestination," of course, made "good works" in the Catholic sense useless. It did not, however, condone fatalism; men were always God's instruments to carry out His will. Good works might not save a Calvinist—but they might be evidence that God was working through him. Good works were a "sign" that a man was probably one of the Elect.

As time went on, Calvin's church in Geneva became the model for Presbyterian or Reformed churches in France, England, Scotland, the Netherlands, the Rhineland, Bohemia, and Hungary—later in North America and Dutch South Africa. Calvin advocated that each local congregation have a ruling body composed of both ministers and laymen (presbyters, or elders) who were to watch carefully over the moral conduct and beliefs of the faithful. These officials then met in synods that linked up the Reformed congregations of a whole district or nation. Thus in place of the Roman Catholic hierarchy of bishops and priests

under the pope, and in place of Luther's state churches, Calvin devised a peculiarly tough and flexible system of church government that resisted control by the state, maintained strict discipline, and, in the lay elders, included a potentially democratic element. Unlike Lutheranism, Calvinism met the two conditions for

Calvin on Predestination

Predestination we call the eternal decree of God, by which he has determined in himself, what he would have to become of every individual of mankind. For they are not all created with a similar destiny; but eternal life is foreordained for some, and eternal damnation for others. . . .

In conformity, therefore, to the clear doctrine of the Scripture, we assert, that by an eternal and immutable counsel, God has once for all determined, both whom he would admit to salvation, and whom he would condemn to destruction. We affirm that this counsel, as far as concerns the elect, is founded on his gratuitous mercy, totally irrespective of human merit; but that to those whom he devotes to condemnation, the gate of life is closed by a just and irreprehensible, but incomprehensible, judgment. . . .

How exceedingly presumptuous it is only to inquire into the causes of the Divine will; which is in fact, and is justly entitled to be, the cause of everything that exists. . . . For the will of God is the highest rule of justice; so that what he wills must be considered just, for this very reason, because he wills it.

From John Calvin, *Institutes of the Christian Religion*, trans. by John Allen (Philadelphia: Westminster Press, 1930), Book III, Ch. 21, pars. 5, 7; Ch. 23, par. 2.

Radical Protestantism: The Teaching of Menno Simons

Menno Simons (1496–1561) was one of the ablest leaders of the radical wing of the Reformation. Simons' followers formed the Mennonite Church, which still exists. His ideas also contributed to the development of the Baptist Church. He never summed up his doctrine in a single document; it has to be put together from scattered pamphlets.

We do not find in Scripture a single word by which Christ has ordained the baptism of infants, or that his apostles taught and practiced it. We say that infant baptism is but a human invention. . . . To baptize before that which is required for baptism, namely faith, is to place the cart before the horse.

Never should any commandment be observed which is not contained in God's holy Word, either in letter or in spirit.

The regenerated do not go to war nor fight. . . . How can a Christian, according to Scripture, consistently retaliate, rebel, make war, murder, slay, torture, steal, rob, and burn cities and conquer countries?

Where have you read in the Scriptures, that Christ or the Apostles called upon the power of the magistracy against those who would not hear their doctrine or obey their words? . . . Faith is a gift of God, therefore it cannot be forced on anyone by worldly authorities or by the sword.

We must be born from above, must be changed and renewed in our hearts and thus be transplanted from the unrighteous and evil nature of Adam into the righteous and good nature of Christ, or we cannot be helped in eternity by any means, divine or human.

From "Selections from the Writings of Menno Simons," in *The Medieval World and Its Transformations*, Vol. II, ed. by G. M. Straka (New York: McGraw-Hill, 1967), pp. 463, 466, 467, 468, 470.

on the Dutch Netherlands. Calvinist minorities formed a kind of revolutionary international society throughout Europe in the later sixteenth century. Like their chief rivals, the Jesuits, the Reformed ministers were often able to elicit a religious loyalty that transcended loyalty to secular rulers and nations. Calvinism was the militant, international form of Protestantism.

THE RADICALS

Some reformers wanted to move much further and faster along the road of religious revolution than Luther, Zwingli, or Calvin. Throughout Germany workers and peasants had been hard hit by the economic changes of the fourteenth and fifteenth centuries. Often their discontent took on a religious coloring, combining easily with what survived of earlier heresies—Waldensian, Lollard, and Hussite, for example. These uneducated men and women took most of Luther's ideas literally—the Bible as ultimate authority, the priesthood of all believers, the freedom of true Christians from man-made ecclesiastical laws and organizations. During the 1520s in Switzerland and in the upper Rhine Valley particularly, little groups of such people came together proclaiming that a true church of Christians was a voluntary association of converted believers, not an official or established institution like that of the Lutherans or Catholics. Most of them believed that until a man came of age and knew what he was doing, he should not be admitted to the church through baptism. Thus, since they had to rebaptize most of their converts, their enemies called them Anabaptists, or rebaptizers. Their ritual was simple, and generally they took the Bible literally. Most of them would not take an oath in a law court, accept public office, or serve as soldiers; some practiced communism of goods on the model described in the second chapter of Acts.

They were cruelly persecuted by Catholics and conservative Protestants alike as dangerous heretics and social radicals. A small but violent minority gave temporary excuse for such persecu-

successful export all over Europe: it possessed a systematic theology, and it offered a practical substitute for medieval church organization.

By the 1550s Calvinism was spreading rapidly. Except in a few cities like Geneva, the nerve center of the movement, and in Scotland, Calvinists never became a majority. But the Calvinist minorities were stubborn, well organized, and widely distributed over Europe. Calvinism left a deep imprint on English society in the form of Puritanism, on France through the Huguenots, on Hungary, and tion by capturing the city of Münster and conducting a reign of terror there for over a year (1534–35). But generally they were pacifists and eager to suffer as their models, the Apostles, had done. After the 1530s the Anabaptists were to be found mainly in the Netherlands, Bohemia, Poland, and England, having been stamped out in southern Germany, where they had originated.

In addition to such "evangelical" groups, which tried to return to the first-century Gospel even more literally than Luther, there were other religious radicals. Some, like the Quakers in the seventeenth century, continued the medieval mystical tradition by following an inner voice rather than the letter of the Scripture. Others were more rationalistic, anticipating the doctrine that the nineteenth century was to call Unitarianism, the belief that there is only one God, not a Holy Trinity, and that Jesus was not God but man at his best. No one in the sixteenth century went quite this far, but the Spanish physician Michael Servetus (1511–53) combined a rationalistic denial of the divinity of Jesus with a rationalistic ethical program. He was imprisoned by the Catholic Inquisition, escaped, and in 1553 was burned at the stake in Geneva as a result of Calvin's influence.

The ideas of these religious radicals, who went too far not only for Roman Catholics but also for Luther and Calvin, were of great importance in the religious history of the Anglo-Saxon peoples. It was in England during the seventeenth century and later in the English colonies in America that Anabaptist ideas were fully realized. There the doctrine that the church should be a voluntary association, "a free church in a free state," organizing itself and electing its pastor, was accepted without any restrictions. Modern Baptists (who believe in adult baptism only), Congregationalists (who emphasize the autonomy of local congregations of Christians), and Quakers (who rely on the "inner light" and tend toward pacifism) all look back to the religious radicals of the sixteenth century as their remote ancestors. American Protestant conceptions of the place of the church in society derive more from the Anabaptists than from either Luther or Calvin.

ANGLICANISM

The peculiarity of the English Reformation is that it was initiated by a king for reasons that had almost nothing to do with religion. Henry VIII cut England off from the papacy much as the king of France had cut his realm off from the papal obedience in 1395. But in England the jurisdictional breach with Rome was followed by a decisive religious change.

In 1527, ten years after Luther had written his ninety-five theses, both England and its king seemed entirely orthodox. Parliament had restricted papal rights of appointment and jurisdiction in England, but England had not gone so far toward developing a national, or "Anglican," Church as France had in "Gallicanism." Lutheran ideas, strongly opposed by the king, had taken only shallow root in England among a few merchants, monks, and university scholars. There was some anticlericalism and opposition to papal taxation among the people, and

Title page of Daniel Featley's *Description* of 1645, known also as "The Dippers Dipt," a satirical view of the Anabaptists.

some talk of reform among the intellectuals, but no organized movement of revolt. Henry, however, found himself in a personal quandary that was to lead him into direct conflict with the pope, Clement VII. After eighteen years of married life, Henry's wife, Catherine of Aragon, had given him only one living child, a daughter. He knew that the lack of a male heir might well throw England into a new War of the Roses, and he knew that Catherine could bear him no more children. Furthermore, he was infatuated with a lady of the court named Anne Boleyn. Henry therefore asked the pope to annul his marriage with Catherine so that he might marry Anne. It was not hard to find technical grounds for the annulment. Catherine had been married to Henry's short-lived elder brother, and it was against Church law to marry the widow of one's brother. But it was hard to persuade the pope to grant the annulment because he was in the power of the emperor Charles V, and Charles was the nephew of Catherine.

Henry, a strong-willed man convinced that he was right, was skillful in political manipulation. In 1529 he summoned Parliament, determined to make the nation his accomplice in whatever he might have to do. He and his chief minister, Thomas Cromwell, deftly built up anticlerical sentiment in Parliament and forced the English clergy to acknowledge that the king was "Supreme Head of the Church in England." Then Henry threatened to withdraw all revenue and obedience from the pope. When Clement still refused to grant the annulment, Henry carried out his threat. He had the marriage annulled in England by Thomas Cranmer, whom he had just persuaded the pope to name as Archbishop of Canterbury, married Anne, and then, in 1533 to 1534, had Parliament cut all ties between the Roman papacy and England by a series of statutes. Conscientious monks, priests, and laymen who resisted this separation were executed. The most prominent martyr was Sir Thomas More (1478–1535), author of *Utopia* and chancellor of England from 1529 to 1532, who was proclaimed a saint in the twentieth century. Henry was now a kind of pope of the Church of England, except that as a layman he never claimed the power to administer the sacraments. Between 1535 and 1539 he and his agents demonstrated the extent of his authority by dissolving all English monasteries, turning their inmates out into the world, and confiscating their lands. Because Henry needed ready money to carry on a war with France, most of these lands were eventually sold to nobles, gentry, and merchants. The result, probably unforeseen, was to bind a whole new class of landowners to the English crown and to the new religious settlement.

In breaking with the papacy, Henry had no intention of breaking with orthodox Catholic belief and practice. He made it clear to his people that the breach with Rome meant no letting down of the bars against heresy, whether Lollard, Lutheran, or Anabaptist. It was impossible, however, to seal England off from the influx of Protestant tracts and ideas, and Henry himself approved the

A Catholic, Sir Thomas More, on the Church

1557

The true Church of Christ is the common known church of all Christian people not gone out nor cast out. This whole body both of good and bad is the Catholic Church of Christ, which is in this world very sickly, and hath many sore members, as hath sometime the natural body of a man. . . . The Church was gathered, and the faith believed, before any part of the New Testament was put in writing. And which was or is the true scripture, neither Luther nor Tyndale [translator of the New Testament into English] knoweth but by the credence that they give to the Church. . . . The Church was before the gospel was written; and the faith was taught, and men were baptised and masses said, and the other sacraments ministered among Christian people, before any part of the New Testament was put in writing. . . . As the sea shall never surround and overwhelm the land, and yet it hath eaten many places in, and swallowed whole countries up, and made places now sea that sometime were well-inhabited lands, and hath lost part of his own possession in other parts again; so though the faith of Christ shall never be overflown with heresies, nor the gates of hell prevail against Christ's Church, yet in some places it winneth in a new people, so may there in some places by negligence be lost the old.

From *The Workes of Sir Thomas More*, pp. 527, 852, 853, 921.

distribution to churches of an English translation of the Bible. By the time of Henry's death in 1547, the Protestant wing of the English clergy led by Archbishop Cranmer was growing in power. During the brief reign of Henry's sickly son Edward VI (1547–53), the government moved rapidly toward building a church that was moderately Protestant in doctrine and ritual. Cranmer gathered together the most impressive parts of the ancient liturgies of the Catholic Church and translated them into majestic English in the Book of Common Prayer. This collection served as the rallying point of Anglicanism, as Luther's hymns did for Lutherans and Calvin's *Institutes* for Calvinists.

This new official Protestantism had no time to take root among the people. In 1553 Catherine of Aragon's daughter, Mary, the most honest and least politic of all the Tudors, came to the throne. She tried to vindicate her mother and atone for her father's sins by turning the clock back to 1529, abolishing all antipapal legislation, and restoring England to the papal obedience. But she outraged her people's patriotism by marrying a foreigner, Philip II of Spain, son and heir presumptive of Charles V, and she shocked their humanity by allowing three hundred Protestants to be burned for heresy in about three years. The courage with which Cranmer and more obscure victims went to their deaths, together with the arrogance of Philip's courtiers, left an indelible impression on the English people. Patriotism and Protestantism became identified in the public mind.

When Anne Boleyn's daughter, Elizabeth I (1558–1603), came to the throne, there was little possibility that she would keep England in the Catholic camp. Elizabeth cautiously guided her Parliaments and her bishops into a compromise religious settlement. She accepted the title of "Supreme Governor" of the Church in England, but she saw to it that revised articles of the faith and the Book of Common Prayer could be accepted by both moderate Catholics and Protestants. For the rest, she refused "to make windows into men's souls," as she put it; that is, she persecuted only open oppo-

Sir Thomas More, after Hans Holbein (1527).

nents of her policies but not those who quietly dissented from them. After the pope excommunicated her in 1570 she was forced to treat over-zealous Catholics who denied her right to rule as traitors, but unpolitical Catholics were tolerated. Elizabeth was rather more annoyed with the "Puritans," who wished to go much

Henry VIII, after Hans Holbein. (*ca.* 1540).

further than she in purifying the English Church of Catholic traditions. The Puritans were strong in Parliament, but when they became obstreperous, Elizabeth clapped some of them into jail. The idea that patriotism required independence from Rome became dominant during her reign, and in the end England was the largest single state to secede permanently from the Roman obedience. The secession cost less in bloodshed that it did elsewhere, largely because of the firm control that Henry VIII and Elizabeth exercised over the pace of religious change in England.

England under Elizabeth was clearly Protestant, but it accepted a conservative form of Protestantism, a form that looked on Presbyterians with suspicion and on Baptists with contempt. This conservatism grew during the religious disputes of the seventeenth century. Today many Anglicans would follow Henry VIII in insisting that their church is not "Protestant" at all. According to this theory, it was the Roman papacy that in effect had "seceded" from the Catholic tradition during the Middle Ages, and it was Henry VIII and Cranmer who restored the true continuity between the Church of the Fathers and the Church of the sixteenth century. Elizabeth always took the position that the Church of England occupied a middle ground between a Catholic minority that wished to bring England back to Rome and a Puritan minority that wished to build a more radically Protestant church in England.

THE CATHOLIC REFORMATION

Luther, Calvin, Cranmer, and the radical reformers thought of what they were doing as a "reformation" of the Church, and to this day the movement is generally called the Protestant Reformation. To Roman Catholics, however, the movement was a "revolt" against the divine authority of the Vicar of Christ, a religious revolution. From this point of view the only true "reformation" was the successful effort finally made by the Roman Church to reform itself, partly in response to the Protestant attack, partly as a result of internal pressures. Historians call this movement the Catholic Reformation, or the Counter Reformation.

This movement was both a religious revival and a counterattack on Protestantism. Before Luther appeared on the scene, some distinguished members of the clergy founded the Oratory of Divine Love at Rome in the hope of beginning a spiritual revival among the clergy. They directed their efforts toward the monastic orders and the papal court itself. In the course of the sixteenth century they succeeded in transforming the atmosphere at the Vatican. The bloody sack of Rome in 1527 by undisciplined imperial troops practically ended papal hopes of becoming powerful Italian princes. Italy was now effectively under Spanish control. As dreams of temporal power waned, better popes were chosen, who in turn appointed better cardinals. In the second half of the century, several of the popes were zealous, almost fanatical, men who would have seemed utterly out of place in the Renaissance papacy a century earlier. Politics still influenced religion and certain administrative abuses persisted, but the popes of the later sixteenth century were spiritual leaders, not Italian princes.

The driving forces behind the Catholic Reformation, especially the political forces, originated in Spain. Years of crusading against the Moors had given Spanish Catholicism a peculiarly intense quality lacking in the rest of Europe. King Philip II of Spain (1556–98), the son of Emperor Charles V, was a devoted Catholic who felt that it was Spain's destiny to stand as the bulwark of Roman Catholicism against the Protestants in Europe. He tended to give orders to the popes rather than to take orders from them, but during his reign Spanish armies and navies, Spanish diplomacy, and Spanish saints constituted the hard core of a revived and militant Catholicism all over Europe.

The most powerful single agency in restoring papal power, in rolling back the tide of Protestantism, and in carrying Catholic missions overseas was a new order founded by one of the most single-minded and influential saints in Christian history, a Spaniard of Basque descent named Ignatius of Loyola (1491–1556). While he was fighting the French in the service of his king, Ignatius' leg was fractured by a cannon ball. During a long and painful convalescence, he devoured the lives of the saints, which were the only reading matter at hand, and decided to enlist as a kind of Christian knight in the service of the Virgin Mary. During a lengthy period of trial and temptation he perfected the "spiritual exercises" that he later passed on to generations of followers. These exercises consisted in the believer's concentrating his imagination on the most vivid details of hell and of the life and death of Christ in order to strengthen his will and to direct it toward salvation. While Ignatius was a student at the University of Paris (about the same time as Calvin), he enlisted nine friends, who became the nucleus of a new order. This new order, which was approved by the pope in 1540, was the Society of Jesus. Its members became known as Jesuits.

The rules of the new order were designed to develop a flexible, disciplined, and efficient body of ecclesiastical shock troops for the papacy. The Jesuit wore no distinctive habit; he dressed as his job might require, as priest, teacher, missionary, or secret agent. He swore a special oath of obedience to the pope. He was carefully selected and trained for the most dangerous and difficult tasks the Church might require, from serving as confessor to a king, to venturing into Protestant countries where he might be executed as a traitor, to voyaging to foreign lands as remote as Brazil or India. The Jesuits were spectacularly successful. They strengthened the pope's control over the Church itself; they ran the best schools in Europe; and during the late sixteenth century they won back most of Bohemia, Poland, Hungary, and southern Germany from Protestantism.

The Roman Church strengthened itself against the Protestant attack in other ways as well. A general council was held at Trent in three sessions between 1545 and 1563 to define Catholic dogma and to reform abuses. Since the papal representatives and the Jesuits controlled the deliberations from the beginning, there was no danger of a revolt against the papacy as there had been in the councils of a century before. In reply to the central doctrines of Protestantism, the council declared that salvation is by both faith and works and that final religious authority is in the Bible and tradition as interpreted by the Roman Church. A beginning was made at reforming financial and administrative abuses in the ecclesiastical organization (the final and most drastic changes were made by the pope).

Seminaries were set up for the training of priests. The council defined the Church's teachings much more sharply than they had ever been defined before and recognized the absolute supremacy of the pope over the clerical hierarchy. Rome had lost much in the struggle with heresy, but the Catholic Church of 1563 was far better able to cope with future heresies than it had been in 1500. New forms of the Inquisition had been established in Spain (1480), the Netherlands (1523), and Italy (1542), and a system of censorship of printed books (the Index) was instituted by the pope in 1559 and approved, with some additions, by the Council of Trent in 1563. All the faithful were forbidden to read any book on the Index.

The Roman Church had found a new religious vitality and had closed its ranks against the Protestant threat. By the second half of the sixteenth century a relatively monolithic Catholic Church, reorganized from within and backed by Spain, the strongest military power in

Engraving showing the third session of the Council of Trent (1562–63). An amphitheater was set up in the church of St. Maria Maggio.

Europe, faced the divided Protestants on somewhat better than even terms.

SIGNIFICANCE OF THE REFORMATIONS

It is not easy to sum up the significance of the Protestant and Catholic Reformations. They were religious movements, phrased in theological terms, rooted deep in the religious experience of men like Luther and Loyola, and resulting in a religious fragmentation of western Christendom that has lasted to the present day. But Luther's angry protest against indulgences would not have had such far-reaching results had not the economic, social, and political conditions been just right. The religious upheaval was intermingled with the growth of capitalism, of secularism, of national sentiment, and of absolutism in government. It is difficult to say precisely what was cause and what was effect. While German princes, for example, took advantage of purely religious protests to confiscate church property for their own interests, religious reformers also utilized purely secular events, like Henry VIII's desire to get rid of his wife, to advance the Protestant cause.

One thing is clear. The era of reform and revolution in the Church temporarily arrested the trend toward the secularization of culture that had begun in the last centuries of the Middle Ages. The century that followed Luther's death was a religious age; its most serious arguments were religious arguments; its wars were intensified by religious fanaticism; and most of its leading figures were either men of religion or men considerably affected by religion. Intensified interest in religion introduced a new and intolerant "ideological" element into the economic and political causes of conflict in European society. The hatred among Catholic, Lutheran, Calvinist, and Anabaptist was as profound in the sixteenth century as the hatred among fascist, communist, and democrat in the twentieth, and for somewhat the same reasons. No man could believe that he or his family or his society was safe so long as opposing religious groups were allowed to exist. Only in time did it become evident that differing religious beliefs did not necessarily lead to civil war and the collapse of the state. Religious toleration was an eventual result of the Reformation but not of the efforts of the reformers.

For over a century the long-term effects of the Protestant Reformation on the economic, political, and cultural development of Europe have been vigorously debated by historians. It has been argued and denied that Protestantism, with its emphasis on serving God in one's secular calling and with its appreciation of the bourgeois virtues of honesty, thrift, and self-discipline, provided the necessary religious sanction for the development of capitalism. It has been argued and denied that Lutheranism aided the growth of divine-right monarchy, whereas Calvinism provided a spur toward the development of constitutionalism, and Anabaptism toward the development of modern socialism. It has been argued and denied that Protestantism wrecked the development of art by destroying religious sculpture and paintings and by rejecting most religious symbolism. And it has been argued and denied that by dissolving monasteries, the old centers of scholarship and philanthropic activity, Protestants deprived the poor of intellectual and physical support. Both the good and the bad in modern capitalism, modern nationalism, and modern secularism have been attributed to Protestantism by one historian or another.

The historical data are far too complex for dogmatic judgments in such matters. The permanent schism of western Christendom and the temporary intensification of religious motives in European politics can justly be attributed to the Protestant movement. Beyond this, all that can be said surely is that Protestantism allied itself with developments that had their origins far back, sometimes intensified them and accelerated their growth, occasionally blocked or countered their expansion. Capitalism, democracy, nationalism, and the secularization of culture appeared in Catholic as well as Protestant lands, and none of these phenomena can be explained by a simple chain of causes leading back to Luther and his revolt from Rome.

Luther tweaks the beard of Calvin as both of them pull the hair of the pope. This satirical engraving presents a Catholic view of the Reformation controversy.

Suggestions for Further Reading

Note: Asterisk denotes a book available in paperback edition.

Background of the Reformation

For the background of the Reformation, see S. Ozmont, *The Reformation in Medieval Perspective** (1971); G. Strauss, *Pre-Reformation Germany** (1972); and the famous "essay" by J. Huizinga, *The Waning of the Middle Ages** (1924). Huizinga's *Erasmus** (1952), and R. H. Bainton, *Erasmus of Christendom** (1969), are perceptive biographies. Erasmus' best-known writings are available in many modern editions, for example, J. P. Dolan, ed., *The Essential Erasmus* (1964).

The Religious Upheaval

An old, but still useful, work is P. Smith, *The Age of the Reformation** (1920), a lively and opinionated book. H. J. Grimm, *The Reformation Era* (1973), does religious developments fuller justice than Smith and is abreast of recent scholarship, particularly on Luther. H. Holborn, *A History of Modern Germany: The Reformation* (1959), is excellent on Germany. See also B. Moeller, *Imperial Cities and the Reformation* (1972) and Gerald Strauss, *Luther's House of Learning* (1978). There are briefer treatments of the period in general in R. H. Bainton, *The Reformation of the Sixteenth Century** (1952), and E. H. Harbison, *The Age of Reformation** (1955). The best recent work is L. W. Spitz, *The Renaissance and Reformation Movements*, Vol. II (1971). See also O. Chadwick, *The Reformation** (1964), and H. J. Hillerbrand, *The World of the Reformation** (1973). J. Lortz, *The Reformation in Germany*, 2 vols. (1969), is a fair statement of the Catholic position. A. G. Dickens, *The German Nation and Martin Luther* (1972), stresses the urban nature of the Reformation. F. Wendel, *Calvin, The Origin and Development of His Religious Thought* (1963), is excellent. See also G. Rupp, *Luther's Progress to the Diet of Worms** (1964), and R. H. Fife, *The Revolt of Martin Luther* (1957). There are many translations of the writings of Luther, Calvin, and other reformers, for example in the *Library of Christian Classics*. A good anthology of contemporary writings on the movement is H. J. Hillerbrand, *The Protestant Reformation: A Narrative History* (1964).

For the radicals, see G. H. Williams, *The Radical Reformer* (1962). Good introductions to different aspects of the "left wing" of the Reformation are offered in F. H. Littell, *The Free Church* (1958); R. H. Bainton, *The Travail of Religious Liberty** (1951); and C. L. Clausen, *Anabaptism: A Social History* (1972).

The best work on England is A. G. Dickens, *The English Reformation* (1964). See also the brief and authoritative accounts by F. M. Powicke, *The Reformation in England* (1941), and T. M. Parker, *The English Reformation to 1558** (1950). J. J. Scarisbrick, *Henry VIII** (1968), is a brilliant work. A good Catholic account is by P. Hughes, *The Reformation in England*, 3 vols. (1950–54). For the Puritans, see P. Collinson, *The Elizabethan Puritan Movement* (1967).

An excellent discussion of the Catholic Reformation is H. Daniel-Rops, *The Catholic Reformation,** 2 vols. (1961). The best biography of St. Ignatius is by the Jesuit P. Dudon (1949). For a less favorable treatment, see R. Fülöp-Miller, *The Power and Secret of the Jesuits* (1930). Jedin is engaged in writing a definitive *History of the Council of Trent*, the first two volumes of which have appeared in translation (1957). See also A. G. Dickens, *The Counter Reformation** (1969); M. R. O'Connell, *The Counter-Reformation, 1560–1610** (1974); and H. O. Evennett, *The Spirit of the Counter-Reformation** (1968). There is useful material in J. C. Olin, *The Catholic Reformation, Savanarola to Loyola* (1969).

Results of the Reformation

On the economic, political, and cultural consequences of the Reformation there are wide differences of opinion. A famous "essay" by M. Weber, *The Protestant Ethic and the Spirit of Capitalism** (1905), became the starting point of a long controversy about the economic significance of Protestantism, which still continues sporadically. *Protestantism and Capitalism: The Weber Thesis and Its Critics,** ed. by R. W. Green (1973), is a convenient collection of selections from the literature of this controversy. Other collections are L. W. Spitz, *The Reformation: Basic Interpretations** (1972), and R. Kingdom and R. Linder, *Calvin and Calvinism: Sources of Democracy** (1972). K. Holl, *The Cultural Significance of the Reformation** (1911), is inclined to view Luther as the prophet of modern Germany and of twentieth-century culture in general. For a readable and perceptive survey of the period, see A. G. Dickens, *Reformation and Society in Sixteenth-Century Europe** (1966).

and the Greatness of Spain

A sixteenth-century sailing ship, with its navigator (left center) sighting the sun to determine his latitude. The foremast (right) is square-rigged for running with the wind. The mainmast and the mizzenmast astern (left) are lateen-rigged for better tacking against the wind.

The Protestant Reformation struck a Europe that was already in the throes of a different sort of revolution. That revolution was launched by Portuguese voyages down the northwest coast of Africa; it quickened with the discovery of America and the sea route to India; and it continued unabated throughout the sixteenth century. For Europeans this was an age of discovery without parallel. For the first time they found themselves in direct contact with all the continents on the globe and with all the civilized peoples who inhabited them. That contact began to have a profoundly disturbing effect on the economy and the politics of Europe just as the Peace of Augsburg was bringing a respite from religious strife.

THE DEVELOPMENT OF OCEANIC COMMERCE

In 1400 Europeans knew scarcely more about the earth than the Romans had. The oceans around the Continent were still impenetrable barriers; the only long voyages ever taken by Europeans were the almost forgotten expeditions of the Northmen to Greenland and America. Franciscan friars and the Polos of Venice had shown that China could be reached by land and that the steppes linked Europe and Asia. But after the collapse of the Mongol Empire in the fourteenth

Top: Mediterranean war galley with lateen sail (ca. twelfth century); middle: lateen-rigged vessel, much like Columbus' *Niña* (early fifteenth century); bottom: Spanish galleon of sixteenth century, the typical long-distance ship for Spanish commerce.

of world-communication." Europeans had mastered both the technological and the psychological problems of making long voyages over the sea. Their ships had crossed and recrossed the Atlantic Ocean, rounded the southern tips of Africa and South America, pushed into the Indian Ocean, and crossed the Pacific. Before this time men had believed that there was far more land than water on the surface of the globe. Now explorers were discovering that there was far more water than land, and that the water could serve as a highway to any coast in the world for men who knew how to use its winds and ride its waves. The Mongol Empire had rested on mastery of the steppes. The empires of the future would rest on mastery of the oceans. When the first ship to circumnavigate the globe finished its voyage in 1522, Europe had begun to cast a web of communication and influence around the earth. During the next four centuries that web was to draw all the civilizations of the world under the influence of Europe.

Conditions for Maritime Discovery

By the year 1000, Norsemen from Iceland and Greenland had coasted North America in small, open boats. They were too few, however, to make any permanent settlement, and their discoveries were unknown to the rest of Europe. Before Europeans could make a sustained drive to push out across the Atlantic they needed better ships, more reliable aids to navigation, and stronger motivation.

Better ships were long in coming. Oar-propelled galleys had already mastered the Mediterranean, and by the thirteenth century Genoese and Venetian galleys were venturing out into the Atlantic to Morocco and Flanders. But on the open seas mariners needed sails rather than oars and broad, round hulls rather than long, narrow galleys. By the fifteenth century the Portuguese had devised a craft capable of long ocean voyages: the squat, three-masted caravel, with two masts generally square-rigged and one mast lateen-rigged (see the illustration at left). The caravel preserved the advantages of both the northern Eu-

century the routes across the steppes were no longer safe for missionaries or merchants. Arab sailors now became the middlemen between the Orient and Europe. They brought the spices and textiles of India and the East Indies to Alexandria and Beirut, whence the Venetians distributed them to the rest of Europe. The Europeans themselves had no direct contact with the East.

By the end of the sixteenth century an almost incredible geographical revolution had taken place. Arnold J. Toynbee defines it as "the substitution of the Ocean for the Steppe as the principal medium ropean square-rig, which was better for running before the wind, and the Arab lateen-rig, which was better for sailing close to the wind. It was slower than the galley, but it had more space for cargo and for supplies on long voyages.

Galleys had generally stayed close to land, hugging the shoreline. Before ships could venture straight out to sea, shipmasters needed some way of determining their direction and their whereabouts. The compass (used in Europe by the thirteenth century) gave them a sense of direction in dark weather; the astrolabe (known since the eleventh century) enabled them to determine their latitude with fair accuracy by measuring the elevation of the sun and stars; and the portulan charts (first developed for the Mediterranean) gave them confidence that they could recognize the approaches to most European ports. (No precise way of determining longitude was known until the eighteenth century.)

City-states were the original bases for long-range navigation. Venetian and Genoese merchants linked the Black Sea and Egypt with Italy and England, and the Germans of the Hanseatic League traded from Russian Novgorod to French Bordeaux. But transoceanic exploration, trade, and colonization required a broader base for support. The new monarchies of western Europe were better situated geographically than the Italian or German city-states to open up the Atlantic. They also had advantages in manpower, resources, and political centralization. After 1400 the western monarchies gradually replaced the cities as the major centers of commercial enterprise.

It is not easy to determine the motives that prompted Europeans—rather than Chinese or Moslems—to "discover" the rest of the world by taking to the sea. The Moslems had been crossing the Indian Ocean for centuries, and the Chinese regularly sailed up and down the East Asian coast and into the Indian Ocean; but neither people tried to go farther. Certainly the crusade ideal influenced Portuguese and Spanish rulers. To convert the heathen and to weaken Islam by placing Christian allies in the Moslem rear was the goal of many explorers. Crusading zeal was not the main impetus of the great discoveries, but it could be used to inspire enthusiasm for dangerous ventures and to sanctify more worldly motives.

Of those more worldly motives, the need to find precious metals was the most compelling. In an age without refrigeration, the spices that helped preserve meats and make them more palatable—pepper from India, cinnamon from Ceylon, ginger from China, nutmeg and cloves from the East Indies—were luxuries that were almost necessities. The

An illustration from a sailing book, *Art de Naviguer* (1583), demonstrating how to determine latitude by observing the sun's height.

long journey from India or the Moluccas and the Arab-Venetian trade monopoly made such spices expensive. But Europeans needed them (and other luxuries such as cotton and silk cloth) more keenly than Asians needed anything Europe had to offer except gold and silver; so there was a steady flow of precious metals from Europe eastward. This drain limited the supply of specie (hard coins) in Europe at a time when it was increasingly needed as currency. Before credit systems became widely used in the seventeenth and eighteenth centuries, the only practical way to provide the money needed by burgeoning commerce and industry was to increase the supply of bullion. European mines had never been very productive and were nearly exhausted by 1400. Fifteenth-century rulers were acutely aware of their need for gold. They knew that they had to have hard cash in their treasury to hire soldiers, equip navies, and maintain bureaucracies, and they knew that European supplies of precious metals were limited.

By the late fifteenth century a restless, energetic, and bold seafaring population was scattered along Europe's Atlantic coastline. Resourceful sailors, fishermen, and merchants had developed the techniques and the ships for making long voyages. They had religious and economic motives strong enough to overcome their superstitious fears of what lay beyond known waters, and their governments were often ready to back them. Europe needed direct contact with Asia, and some Europeans believed that it would not be too difficult to reach Asia by sea. Ptolemy in the second century had underestimated the size of the globe and had overestimated the span of Asia, and the geographers of the fifteenth century, accepting his miscalculations, were convinced that Japan and China lay only a few thousand miles west of Europe. The size of Africa was also underestimated, so that an eastern route did not seem to be too difficult. Either an eastern or a western voyage seemed possible, and the material and psychological environment was favorable for an age of discovery.

Portuguese Exploration

Perhaps the most interesting figure of the whole age stands at its very beginning: Prince Henry the Navigator (1394–1460), the younger son of King John I of Portugal. Prince Henry was obsessed with the desire to learn more about Africa; he devoted his life to organizing, equipping, and sending out fleets that pushed farther and farther down the African west coast. In a remarkable observatory at Sagres on Cape St. Vincent, the southwestern tip of Portugal, he brought together the scientific and the seafaring knowledge of his day. He had vague notions of outflanking Islam by reaching lands that the Moslems had never touched (such as the mythical kingdom of Prester John in East Africa), but his main objective was to find gold. When the Portuguese reached the Gold Coast of Africa in the 1450s this objective was achieved.

After Henry's death the impetus of exploration was lost for a time. Clusters of small islands (the Madeiras, the Azores) were found and settled, but they were not very profitable. (On the other hand, if there was land eight hundred

---

Toynbee on the Age of Discovery

Since A.D. 1500 the map of the civilized world has indeed been transformed out of all recognition. Down to that date it was composed of a belt of civilizations girdling the Old World from the Japanese Isles on the north-east to the British Isles on the north-west. . . . The main line of communication was provided by the chain of steppes and deserts that cut across the belt of civilizations from the Sahara to Mongolia. For human purposes, the Steppe was an inland sea. . . . This waterless sea had its dry-shod ships and its quayless ports. The steppe-galleons were camels, the steppe-galleys horses, and the steppe-ports "caravan cities." . . . The great revolution was a technological revolution by which the West made its fortune, got the better of all the other living civilizations, and forcibly united them into a single society of literally world-wide range. The revolutionary Western invention was the substitution of the Ocean for the Steppe as the principal medium of world-communication. This use of the Ocean, first by sailing ships and then by steamships, enabled the West to unify the whole inhabited and habitable world.

From Arnold J. Toynbee, *Civilization on Trial* (New York: Oxford University Press, 1948), pp. 67–70.

miles out in the Atlantic, there was reason to hope that larger islands existed farther west.) Henry's grandnephew, King John II (1481–95), however, was interested in voyages to the east and speeded up the effort to find an all-water route to India that would short-circuit the Venetian-Arab monopoly. By 1488 Bartholomew Dias had discovered the Cape of Good Hope, and in 1497 Vasco da Gama rounded the cape with four ships, reached Calicut on the Malabar Coast of India in 1498, and was back in Lisbon with two of his ships in 1499. In 1500 a larger fleet, commanded by Cabral, touched the coast of Brazil and then headed for India in Da Gama's wake.

This first contact by sea with India was to have momentous consequences, but neither side was particularly impressed by the other on first meeting. The Hindus had only contempt for the bedraggled sailors who had spent months aboard Da Gama's ships, and the Europeans soon made it clear that they found nothing to respect in the civilization of India. When the Hindus asked Da Gama what he sought in India, he is said to have replied laconically, "Christians and spices."

During the sixteenth century the Portuguese strove to build a commercial empire in the Indian Ocean. Affonso de Albuquerque, the brutal but able Portuguese governor from 1509 to 1515 and the real founder of that empire, understood the relationship between trade, sea power, and strategic bases. He seized Goa on the western coast of India to serve as his headquarters, Malacca on the Strait of Malacca to control the trade between the Spice Islands and the Indian Ocean, and Ormuz to dominate the Persian Gulf. He failed to capture Aden, a base from which he could have strangled the Arab-Venetian trade through the Red Sea. He was as ruthless in disciplining his own men as he was in terrorizing Hindu princes and fighting Arab seamen. At Albuquerque's death in 1515 the Portuguese had a large share of the spice trade (though not a monopoly) and controlled strategic bases all the way from Africa to the East Indies.

It was easy for the Portuguese and other Europeans to seize footholds in India because the Moslem and Hindu princes of the coastal districts were weak, and the Mughal Empire of the North had little power in the South. The Portu-

The Portuguese as others saw them. Above: African bronze sculpture of a Portuguese man. Left: detail from a seventeenth-century Japanese screen painting showing a Portuguese sailor playing a game of *go* with a Japanese friend in a native ship.

guese, however, established only trading posts, not colonies of settlement, in India, and even the trading posts soon ceased to be very profitable. The early voyages had made large profits for their backers. But the cost to the Portuguese government of equipping fleets and maintaining fighting forces soon ate up the profits. Portugal was a relatively small and poor country, with a small merchant class. Italian, German, and Flemish bankers soon dominated the Portuguese trade, and the spices that arrived at Lisbon were sent on directly to Antwerp, which proved to be a better point from which to distribute them to Europe. The burden of empire was already proving heavy when Portugal fell into the grip of Spain in 1580.

Columbus and Spanish Exploration

In 1484, before the Portuguese had reached the Cape of Good Hope, a Genoese sailor named Christopher Columbus had tried in vain to persuade King John II of Portugal to back him in a voyage of exploration to the west. Columbus was convinced by all the evidence at hand that it would be comparatively easy to reach Cipangu (Japan) by sailing due west. But for years he was unable to persuade any monarch to back him. At last the rulers of Spain, who had conquered the Moorish Kingdom of Granada in January 1492, were free to turn their attention elsewhere. And so it was under Castilian auspices that Columbus sailed on his famous voyage. It took the Portuguese almost a century of patiently organized effort to reach the Old World eastward, while the Spanish reached the New World westward in one brilliant voyage. There was a large element of luck in the founding of Spain's empire in the New World.

Columbus touched land in the Bahamas on October 12, 1492, thinking he had struck some small islands in the Japanese archipelago. Throughout four voyages and until his death in 1506, he remained convinced, even after touching the mainland, that it was the Old World

Christopher Columbus, the Genoese sailor who sailed west in search of Japan and found the New World. This portrait of Columbus is thought to be the closest existing likeness of him. It is a copy, made in about 1525, of an earlier painting that has been lost.

a hundred leagues west of the Cape Verde Islands was favorable to Spain, at least in the Western Hemisphere. The Portuguese were unhappy, perhaps because most of the unknown regions of the Atlantic were left to Spain, and in 1494 they persuaded the Spanish to sign the Treaty of Tordesillas. By this treaty a line was drawn from pole to pole 370 leagues west of the Cape Verde Islands, separating Portugal's claims to the east from Spain's to the west. The Portuguese assumed that the line applied only to the Atlantic (it gave them Brazil, though they did not know this in 1494). The Spanish preferred to believe that the line extended round the world, cutting it in half as a knife cuts an orange. They hoped that this interpretation might give them the Moluccas, the heart of the Spice Islands, and, in fact, it would have given them part of what is now Indonesia. But Spain was soon too busy in the Americas to concentrate on the East Indies, and in 1527 it sold all its claims to these islands to Portugal.

Vasco da Gama.

of Japan and China that he had discovered. And so, although it was Columbus who named the "Indians" he found on the shores of Haiti and Cuba, it was the Florentine Amerigo Vespucci who gave his name to the continents Columbus had discovered. Amerigo, director of the Medici branch bank in Seville, sailed on both Spanish and Portuguese voyages and described what he saw in letters that were widely read throughout Europe. In one he referred to the great southern continent in the west as *Mundus Novus*, a New World. Later map makers labeled the two new continents "America," after the man who first realized that it was a new, not an old, world that was opening up to view.

The Treaty of Tordesillas, 1494

Since both Spain and Portugal were seeking the same lands, they soon had to appeal to the pope for an adjudication of their rival claims to unoccupied and heathen lands around the globe. The pope, Alexander VI, was a Spaniard, and the line of demarcation that he drew in 1493

Magellan

By 1512 the Portuguese were in the Moluccas, and in 1513 the Spaniard Balboa sighted the Pacific from the Isthmus of Darien in Central America. In the years to come, the Spanish, the English, and others tried again and again to discover a strait through the New World by which they might sail westward into the Pacific and reach the Spice Islands. The Portuguese navigator Magellan was convinced that he could do just that by rounding the southern tip of South America. He knew that Portugal would never back him in such an expedition because it would create a Spanish-dominated route to the islands, so in 1519 he sailed with Spanish backing. It was the third of the truly great voyages—along with those of Columbus and Da Gama. Magellan negotiated the straits that are named for him and got across the Pacific after incredible hardships, only to be killed by natives in the Philippines. His navigator, Sebastian del Cano, brought one of the five original ships back to Lisbon by way of the Cape of Good Hope in 1522, the first ship to sail round the world.

Magellan plotting his position (detail from an allegorical portrait by De Bry).

THE SPANISH EMPIRE IN THE AMERICAS

From 1520 to 1550 the conquistadors of Spain carved out an empire in the Americas. As the Spaniards on the Caribbean islands began to hear exciting tales of wealthy, half-civilized empires, they turned from exploration to conquest. The most notable of the conquistadors were Hernando Cortes, who from 1519 to 1521 conquered the formidable Aztec Empire in Mexico with six hundred men, sixteen horses, and a few cannon, and Francisco Pizarro, who from 1533 to 1534 conquered the Inca Empire in Peru with even fewer followers. Their firearms, steel swords, and horses gave the Spaniards an advantage over the more primitively armed groups that faced them, but it was primarily their daring, their discipline, and their fanatical faith that accounted for their fantastic early successes. Later on, diseases imported from Europe (especially smallpox) reduced native populations to such an extent that revolt was impossible.

Las Casas on the American Indians in the Sixteenth Century

It has been written that these peoples of the Indies, lacking human governance and ordered nations, did not have the power of reason to govern themselves—which was inferred only from their having been found to be gentle, patient and humble. It has been implied that God became careless in creating so immense a number of rational souls and let human nature, which He so largely determined and provided for, go astray in the almost infinitesimal part of the human lineage which they comprise. From this it follows that they have all proven themselves unsocial and therefore monstrous, contrary to the natural bent of all peoples of the world.

. . . Not only have [the Indians] shown themselves to be very wise peoples and possessed of lively and marked understanding, prudently governing and providing for their nations (as much as they can be nations, without faith in or knowledge of the true God) and making them prosper in justice; but they have equalled many diverse nations of the world, past and present, that have been praised for their governance, politics and customs, and exceed by no small measure the wisest of all these, such as the Greeks and Romans, in adherence to the rules of natural reason.

From Bartolomé de las Casas, *Apologética historia de las Indias,* in *Introduction to Contemporary Civilization in the West,* 3rd ed. (New York: Columbia University Press, 1960), Vol. I, p. 539.

Within a generation Spanish soldiers, lawyers, and friars unexpectedly found themselves the undisputed rulers of vast stretches of territory and millions of human beings. Often the new ruling class simply stepped into the place of former conquerors like the Aztecs and Incas, living on the tribute from subject populations that had supported their predecessors. But the Spaniards needed labor to exploit the new lands fully, and the upland Indians already decimated by European diseases could not survive in the rich, but unhealthy, lowlands. Thus when sugar became an important crop, Negro slaves were imported from Africa to do the work. Until the seventeenth century, however, the industry most favored by the Spanish government was the mining of gold and silver. After the discovery of enormously rich silver mines in both Mexico and Peru in 1545, the extraction and shipment of silver became the main business of the Spanish Empire as a whole. Every spring after 1564 the plate fleet of twenty to sixty vessels gathered at Havana harbor to be convoyed by warships to Seville. And every year the Spanish government waited anxiously until the bullion, which everyone agreed was the key to national strength, was safely in harbor.

The empire that grew out of these exploits and these economic activities was a kind of compromise between what the Spanish settlers, the Christian friars, and the Spanish government at Madrid would each have liked to see develop in America. The settlers, many of them former conquistadors, would have liked to set themselves up as manorial lords living on the forced labor of the natives, unmolested by any political direction from Madrid. The Franciscans and other friars, particularly the great Dominican, Bartolomé de las Casas, would have liked to see the natives treated as fellow Christians and fellow subjects of the Spanish crown. Las Casas worked tirelessly to protect both the legal and the moral rights of the Indians in the face of relentless pressure from the settlers to exploit them. The government in Spain was determined to centralize all decision making in Seville or Madrid, and to protect the natives so far as possible, as the friars

ycpolínhq mexuca

Cortes accepting the surrender of Quauhtemoc, last king of the Aztecs. The artist was a Spanish-trained native from Tlaxcala, who chronicled Cortes' conquest of Mexico. Notice the mixture of European and Indian styles.

urged. However, it was difficult to enforce orders when they took weeks to be received and when provincial authorities never had enough manpower to police the vast areas for which they were responsible.

The policy of the Spanish Empire, as it had unfolded by the end of the sixteenth century, was remarkably sensible and humane by contemporary standards. The settlers were allowed to command the forced labor of the subject Indians, but this labor was regulated by public authority, not by private right. There were serious abuses, especially in Mexico, and the long arm of the home government was often exasperatingly slow in dealing with local problems. But as time went on the Spanish came close to ac-

complishing what the Portuguese failed to accomplish in the East and what the English never attempted in North America: the Christianization and Europeanization of a whole population. The Spaniards took seriously the papal bulls of 1493, which gave them the heathen peoples of the New World to convert and nurture in the Christian faith. In theory, the natives were considered Christians and subjects of the king (unlike the unfortunate Negroes, who had been enslaved by West African rulers and who gained no new rights when they were sold to Europeans). The gulf between Spaniard and native was never entirely closed, in either religion or culture. But Spanish and Portuguese in the end became the languages of all but the most isolated Indians, and Roman Catholicism the dominant religion. Intermarriage was so common that the mestizos, or descendants of mixed marriages, eventually became more numerous than the purebred of either race. The Spanish (and the Portuguese in Brazil) made a serious attempt to convert the New World to western civilization.

SPAIN UNDER PHILIP II

In the later sixteenth century Spain was the dominant power in Europe as well as in America. The accession of the Habsburg Charles to the throne of Spain in the early sixteenth century had thrust the Spanish into the full stream of European politics and diplomacy at a moment when the Protestant revolt was beginning to spread, the Turks were expanding up the Danube Valley, and the job of exploring and colonizing America was demanding a huge expenditure of energy. To roll back the threats of heretics and infidels while conquering a new world was a heavy task for a state so recently formed. But for a brief and brilliant time, the Spanish under the Emperor Charles V (1515–56) and his son, King Philip II (1556–98), were almost equal to the challenge. The sixteenth and early seventeenth centuries were the golden age of Spain.

In 1555–56 Charles V divided his family holdings between his brother Ferdinand and his son Philip. To Ferdinand went the Habsburg possessions in Austria, Bohemia and a slice of Hungary, and the imperial crown (still elective in theory, but by now always bestowed on a Habsburg). To Philip went the crowns of Castile and Aragon, with Castile's possessions in the New World, the Kingdom of Naples and the Duchy of Milan (which meant control of Italy), and the Netherlands. Thus for a century and a half after 1556 there were "Austrian Habsburgs" and "Spanish Habsburgs," separate ruling houses but houses that cooperated closely in matters of dynastic policy. Except for the Netherlands, which might well have gone to Ferdinand because of the Netherlands' close cultural and geographical ties with the Empire, the possessions of Philip II formed a more tight-knit and centralized state than his father's holdings.

Philip II was thoroughly Spanish in speech, thought, and character. After the conclusion of peace with France in 1559, he returned from the Netherlands to Spain to remain until his death almost forty years later. He caught the imagination of his people as few of their rulers had done. To the Spanish he is still "Philip the Prudent," one of their greatest kings. Distrustful of his advisers, unable to delegate authority even in minor matters, slow in coming to a decision, strongly Catholic in religion (his enemies would have said "bigoted"), convinced of his divine right to govern Spain as an absolute ruler strictly accountable to God but to no one else, Philip devoted his country to the ideal of a restored Catholic Christendom with the Spanish monarchy as its leading power and defender. For centuries the Spanish had fought the Moors. To Philip, the crusade would continue against half-converted Jews and Moors at home and against Turks and Protestants abroad until the Christian Commonwealth of the Middle Ages had been restored. Meanwhile the Catholic faith would be carried to the New World. Since Spain was the divinely chosen agent of this mission, what was in the interest of Spain was naturally in the

Philip II of Spain, by Titian.

On Philip II of Spain

The pallor of his complexion was remarked on by all observers, and most of them drew the proper conclusion, namely, that it indicated a weak stomach and lack of exercise. Reddened eyes were a penalty of his excessive devotion to the written word both day and night. . . . Reading and writing occupied the major portion of Philip's day. . . . He had taken deeply to heart his father's injunction to direct everything himself, and never to give his full confidence even to the most faithful of his ministers, and the natural result was that his time was completely occupied with receiving and answering reports and letters. . . . Reports, reports, and even more reports; Philip was literally submerged with them in his later years, and moreover he did not stop at reading them; he annotated them, as he went along, with comments on matters as absurdly trifling as the spelling and style of the men who had written them—all in that strange, sprawling hand of his, one of the most illegible hands of an age more than usually replete with chirographical difficulties.

From R. B. Merriman, *The Rise of the Spanish Empire in the Old World and in the New* (New York: Macmillan, 1934), Vol. IV, pp. 21–24.

interest of Christendom as a whole. Or so it appeared to Philip and to most of the Spanish nobility.

If ever there was a monarchy and a ruling class with a sense of destiny, it was the Spanish of the sixteenth century. This spirit was evident in the Spanish Jesuits who guided the Council of Trent and helped to reconvert much of central Europe to Catholicism, in the Spanish friars who labored to convert the American Indians, in the conquistadors who toppled native empires in the New World, and in the tough Spanish infantry who, for over a century, defeated every organized army they met in Europe, and gained at least a draw in their struggle with the Dutch guerillas. Philip II's Spain was the strongest military power on the Continent, the strongest naval power in the Atlantic (in spite of the defeat of the Armada in 1588), and the wealthiest state in Europe. Spain was the nerve center of the Catholic Reformation. No wonder the terror of the Spanish name lived on into

the seventeenth century long after Spanish strength had begun to waste away.

Economic Policy

The economic basis of Spain's predominance was the gold and silver that flowed to Seville in a swelling stream from the New World. Early in the sixteenth century the bullion imported was almost entirely gold. But after the discovery in 1545 of the rich mines in Peru and Mexico, it was mostly silver. The value of the treasure that reached Spain rose enormously between 1500 and 1600. In very round figures the average yearly value of bullion imports at the beginning of the century was something under $300,000; by about 1550 the value had increased fifteen times; and by 1600 over forty times, to about $12,000,000. Then a steady decline set in, until about 1660 the average was down to around $1,200,000. The Spanish crown received about a quarter of the total as its share.

Contemporary map showing Spain as the head and crown of sixteenth-century Europe.

This influx of precious metals, combined with internal financial problems, contributed to a steep rise in prices. At first the rise was slow and generally stimulating to Spanish industry and commerce. But it had become precipitous by the middle of the century, amounting to a severe inflation that struck first Spain and then the rest of western and central Europe as the metal flowed out of the Iberian peninsula (in spite of all government prohibitions). It has been estimated that prices quadrupled in Spain in the course of the century. Since prices rose faster than taxes could be increased, Philip II was forced to repudiate his government's debts three times, in 1557, 1575, and 1596. (His successors had to follow the same course in 1607, and 1627, and 1647.) The effect of inflation on Spanish industry was eventually disastrous. Since prices always rose faster in Spain than elsewhere, it was relatively more expensive to manufacture goods in Spain than in other countries. This meant that Spanish producers could not sell their goods abroad and that cheaper foreign products captured the Spanish market.

In the short run, Spain's silver enabled it to maintain supremacy in Europe by paying its armies in cash and buying what goods it needed abroad. In the long run, this policy helped to ruin Spain's industry and commerce, and even to undermine its agriculture. There were other reasons for Spain's economic troubles in the seventeenth century, such as the expulsion of its best farmers, the Moriscoes, as the converted Moors were called. But the influx of precious metals was probably the major reason for both the rapid rise and the equally rapid decline of Spain as the leading power in Europe. Spain lived for a century on the windfall of American treasure, but when the supply of bullion dwindled in the seventeenth century Spain found that the real sinews of its national strength—native industry and agriculture—were ruined.

Religious Policy

Philip II's religious policy was the most narrowly intolerant of his time. He abhorred heresy and unbelief with a holy hatred and said he would rather be king in a desert than in a land of heretics. He feared Islam as the ancient enemy both of Christendom and of his people. In his eyes and in those of most of his countrymen, the Moors who had been forcibly Christianized after the conquest of Granada in 1492 were still Moslems at heart. Furthermore, they were more prosperous than most Spanish farmers, and they were reputedly in league with the Moslems of North Africa. In 1566 Philip ordered them to stop using the Arabic language and learn Castilian, to give up their Moorish dress, and to stop taking hot baths, as was their custom. In 1569 the exasperated Moriscoes broke into a revolt, which was savagely suppressed. They were driven out of Andalusia and scattered over Spain. In the years after 1609 they were driven out of the country entirely. Their numbers and importance have sometimes been exaggerated, but there is no doubt that their loss helped to weaken the Spanish economy.

At the height of the revolt of the Moriscoes in 1570, the Turks captured Cyprus from the Venetians. Once again Europe trembled before the threat of Islamic expansion. Philip II immediately allied himself with the pope and the Venetians to counter the danger, and in October 1571 a Spanish and Venetian fleet won a famous victory over a large Turkish fleet at Lepanto in the Gulf of Corinth. Nothing decisive came of the battle because the Christian forces were unable to follow up their victory. But the event had considerable importance for European morale because it was the first time a Turkish fleet had been defeated.

The Apogee of Spanish Prestige

Philip's prestige probably never stood higher in Europe than in the years immediately following Lepanto. He was popular at home, and his defeat of the Turks gave him the undisputed political leadership of Catholic Europe. France, potentially the strongest monarchy in Europe, was torn by civil war during most of Philip's reign and so was unable to contest his leadership. England seemed weak and divided by religious controversies, and its queen had been excommunicated by the pope in 1570.

Meanwhile the Empire was safely in the hands of Philip's Habsburg cousins. It seemed as if his dream of a resurgent Catholic Christendom dominated by Spain was about to become a reality.

This dream was shattered during the last quarter of the sixteenth century by the revolt of the Netherlands, the rise of English sea power, and the accession of a former Protestant to the throne of France. In his struggle with the embattled forces of Protestantism in northern Europe, Philip overreached himself, exhausted his resources, and started his nation on its long decline.

THE REVOLT OF THE NETHERLANDS

The Netherlands were the wealthiest and most densely populated of Philip II's dominions. The 3 million people dwelling beside the mouths of the Rhine and the Meuse had lived by their industry and commerce since the early Middle Ages. The looms of the southern provinces turned out great quantities of linen and woolen cloth, while the fisheries and shipping of the northern provinces steadily increased in value. The comfortable houses of Bruges, Ghent, Antwerp, and Amsterdam were built with the profits of this flourishing industry and trade.

The seventeen provinces of the Netherlands had been united in a personal union by the dukes of Burgundy. But when Charles V inherited the territories in 1519 through his grandmother, Mary of Burgundy, there was little in the way of national feeling or common institutions to bind them together. Charles, who was brought up in Flanders and spoke Flemish as well as French, was the closest thing to a native ruler the united Netherlands had ever had, but he regularly sacrificed their interests to his broader imperial aims. During his reign the faint beginnings of a Netherlandish national consciousness appeared.

The provinces were a crossroads for ideas as well as for commerce. The Humanism of Erasmus as well as the teachings of Luther took early root in the Netherlands, to be followed by Anabaptist ideas. But in the 1550s a militant, disciplined Calvinism spread rapidly and soon became the dominant form of Protestantism. When Philip II took over the rule from his father in the fall of 1555, Calvinists constituted tight-knit minorities in most of the cities of the seventeen provinces.

Within ten years after his accession, Philip had alienated most of the nobility and bourgeoisie of the provinces. Legally he was not king of the Netherlands, but only duke or count of provinces that had their own individual liberties and customs. Philip paid no attention to these traditional restraints on his power. Native nobles were displaced in favor of Spaniards in the governing council, a policy that hurt the pride of the upper classes. A threat to enforce the laws against heresy with new efficiency and severity sent a chill of terror through the

The baptism of Moslem women, from a Spanish relief (1520).

Calvinist merchants and ministers. Madrid was almost a thousand miles away from Brussels, and Philip's Spanish-Catholic mind was even more remote from the interests and concerns of his busy, prosperous Dutch and Flemish subjects, whether they were Calvinist or Catholic. The revolt that ensued was partly a provincial reaction against centralization, partly a patriotic movement directed against foreign rule, and partly a religious protest against an inquisitorial Catholicism.

In 1566 Calvinist mobs began to break images of the saints and smash the stained-glass windows in Catholic churches throughout the Netherlands. Philip decided to make a frightful example of the iconoclasts. He sent the Duke of Alva and about ten thousand Spanish regulars to the Netherlands with orders to bring the troublemakers either to the block or to the stake. Alva set up what came to be called a "Council of Blood" and boasted (with some exaggeration) that within the six years of his residence in the Netherlands (1567–73) he had executed close to eighteen thousand people. In addition to spilling so much blood, Alva and his council confiscated large amounts of property and imposed a 10 percent sales tax that injured the trade of the country during the year or two it was in force. The Netherlanders never forgot these six years. Instead of crushing the opposition to Philip, Alva's policy solidified the resistance, at least for a time.

William the Silent and Dutch Independence

By 1572 the resistance movement had found a leader in William the Silent, Prince of Orange, the wealthiest landowner in the provinces. William was no military genius—he lost almost every battle he fought against the Spanish—but he had political wisdom, integrity, and patience, a rugged kind of patriotism, and a deep hatred of religious fanaticism, whether Calvinist or Catholic. He tried his best to hold the Calvinists in check, keep all seventeen provinces united against the Spanish, and still find a solution that would leave Philip as titular ruler. For a few years it looked as if he might succeed. In 1576 Calvinist excesses

provoked a frightful sack of Antwerp by Spanish troops known as the "Spanish Fury." This was enough to frighten all seventeen provinces into an agreement to stick together. The agreement was called the Pacification of Ghent.

Within three years, however, both Protestant and Catholic radicals had got out of hand, moderates had lost influence, and animosity between Catholics and Protestants had begun to undermine the universal hatred of Spain. The almost unanimous opposition to Alva and his successors gradually gave way to a savage civil war in which the Calvinists, the best-disciplined minority, took over leadership of the opposition to Philip. Most of the Catholics rushed back into the arms of Spain for protection. The seventeen provinces split in two as Calvinists fled to the Dutch provinces in the north beyond the great rivers, where they were better able to defend themselves, and Catholics fled to the Walloon provinces in the south, where Spanish troops could be maintained and supplied from the upper Rhine. In 1579 the Dutch provinces in the north formed the Union of Utrecht. This union ultimately became the foundation of the United Provinces, or Dutch Netherlands, which formally declared their independence of Philip II in 1581. And so the unanticipated result of the revolt of 1566 was that the seven northern provinces broke away from Spanish rule, while the ten southern provinces remained under Habsburg control and eventually (in 1830) became the kingdom of Belgium.

The Rise of the United Provinces

The Dutch Netherlands had to fight for their independence for two generations after 1581. They got some help from French and English troops at various times, but the price that the French Duke of Anjou and the English Queen Elizabeth asked for their help was often dangerously high. In the long run it was dogged determination, geography, and the rivalry of their enemies that won the Dutch their independence. William the Silent was assassinated in 1584, but his descendants carried on his tradition of able and disinterested leadership as

William the Silent, by Anthony Moro.

stadtholders (regents) of one or more of the seven provinces. The "United Provinces" never formed more than the loosest sort of political federation, but the Dutch fought with stubbornness when they had to. The Duke of Parma, who became Philip's representative in the Netherlands in 1578, was one of the best military commanders of his day, but he was unable to reconquer the provinces beyond the bend of the Rhine and the Meuse, especially since he lacked control of the sea. The Dutch "Sea Beggars," or privateers, won as many battles against the Spanish on the water as William's armies lost on the land. When Philip's "Invincible Armada" was broken up in 1588 by the English and the weather, reconquest of the northern provinces became impossible. Finally, in 1648, the king of Spain recognized the independence of his former Dutch subjects.

By this time the new Dutch state had become one of the great powers of Europe. Most long wars exhaust even the victors, but the Dutch came out of this war the most powerful commercial nation in Europe. By the early seventeenth century they were building more ships each year than all other nations combined (two thousand, it was said), and they were better ships than any others. During the first half of the seventeenth century the Dutch captured more and more of the carrying trade not only of Europe but of the world. Their rates were cheaper, their business methods more efficient, their handling of cargo more skillful. Antwerp (in the Spanish Netherlands) had been ruined by the Spanish soldiery and blocked off from the sea through the closing of the Scheldt River by the Dutch. Thus Amsterdam (in the United Provinces) took Antwerp's position as the commercial and financial center of Europe. Until their own vulnerability to attack by land became evident after 1660, the Dutch had no rivals who could contest their power.

The sheer geographical extent of Dutch commercial operations was remarkable. Dutch ships handled much of the grain trade of the Baltic and a large part of the carrying trade of England, France, Italy, and Portugal. When Philip II seized the crown of Portugal in 1580 and stopped the Dutch from visiting Lisbon (whence the Dutch were accustomed to distribute Portuguese spices to the rest of Europe), the Dutch with characteristic daring went out to the source of the spices themselves in the Moluccas. In 1602 the Dutch East India Company was formed and soon established its headquarters at Batavia on the island of Java. By the middle of the century the Dutch had seized the richest part of Portugal's eastern empire—the Moluccas, Malacca, and Ceylon. For over a century the company paid very large dividends, mainly by ruthlessly monopolizing the production of spices and limiting it to keep up

Example of a propaganda badge worn by Dutch "Sea Beggars." The insurgents' hatred of Catholicism is expressed in the inscription: "Better the Turks than the pope."

THE DIVISION OF THE NETHERLANDS 1581

Amsterdam harbor, center of a worldwide trade (detail from an engraving by Pieter Bast, 1597).

prices. In 1652 the Dutch founded a colony at the Cape of Good Hope as a way station to the East. A few decades earlier they had come close to ousting the Portuguese from Brazil. At about the same time (1624) they founded a settlement on Manhattan Island named New Amsterdam that became the center for a large Dutch carrying trade in the New World. When the French and British embarked on overseas trade and colonization, they found not only the Spanish and Portuguese but the Dutch ahead of them all over the world.

So it was an economic giant that Philip II conjured up when he set out to crush his rebellious subjects in the Netherlands. The revolt of the Netherlands may be considered as a kind of dress-rehearsal-in-miniature for those larger popular and patriotic revolts against absolute monarchy, beginning with the Puritan Revolution in England and continuing through the American and French revolutions, that marked the next two centuries. There are many differences among these movements, but there are many similarities in the mixture of economic, patriotic, and religious grievances, the blindness of the absolute monarchs, and the ultimate triumph of "middle-class" interests.

ELIZABETHAN ENGLAND

Philip of Spain was almost as unfortunate in his dealings with England under Queen Elizabeth I as he was in his dealings with the Netherlands. England was crucial to his plans. If he could have added control of England to his control of Spain, Milan, and the Netherlands, France would have been encircled and the vital sea routes between Spain and the Netherlands would have been safer. For a few years (1554–58), while Philip was married to Queen Mary of England, it seemed as if the emperor's dream would be realized: England had been brought within the Habsburg orbit and restored to Roman Catholicism. But Elizabeth's accession to the throne in 1558 changed everything.

Queen Elizabeth I (1558–1603) is generally accounted the greatest of the Tudors and one of England's ablest rulers, though to some critics she was simply a stingy and narrow-minded woman. Whatever the judgment, England was immeasurably stronger at her death than at her accession, and she died beloved by the great majority of her people. At twenty-five, when she came to the throne, she had already lived through disgrace, humiliation, and even danger of execution during her sister Mary's reign. She had seen how Mary had lost the love of her people by marrying a foreigner and by burning heretics. These early experiences left her a strong-willed and shrewd young woman, aware of how precarious both her own situation and that of her nation were, determined to put politics before religion and to follow a purely national policy.

Elizabeth's instinct was always to temporize and compromise. As the daughter of Henry VIII and Anne Boleyn, Elizabeth could never allow England to submit to papal authority. But she wanted a religious settlement that would not alienate patriotic Catholics, and she hoped she could deceive the Catholic powers of Europe for a time into thinking that she could be won back to Rome. On the other hand, she resented the attempt of the left-wing Protestant minority (a group that was gradually gaining the appellation of "Puritan") to dictate a radical religious settlement and a risky, pro-Protestant foreign policy. However, Elizabeth never completely broke with her patriotic Puritan subjects and never lost their loyalty, even when she punished them for advocating radical measures. Elizabeth's policy was nationalist first and Protestant second, but the long-term result was to encourage that fusion of patriotism and Protestantism that became a permanent characteristic of English public opinion.

She compromised and temporized in her foreign policy as well. Her instinct was to avoid clear-cut decisions, to keep a dozen intrigues afoot so that there were always avenues of escape from any policy, and to avoid war at almost any cost. The chief danger at her accession was from French influence in Scotland. The French had long been allies of the Scots, and Mary Stuart, Queen of Scots, was married in 1558 to the heir to the French crown. A year later John Knox, who had become a Calvinist, returned to his native Scotland from Geneva and began a religious revolution. Catholicism and French influence on the Scots were both undermined. Moreover, since Mary Stuart's husband was now king of France, it was clear that France would make every effort to defeat the Calvinists. For once Elizabeth made a rapid decision: to ally with the Calvinist party in Scotland and keep the French out. By 1560 Knox, the Kirk (Scottish Church), and the pro-English party were in control, and the French had lost all influence in Scotland. The way was paved for the union of the English and Scottish crowns in 1603.

Mary, Queen of Scots

Mary Stuart returned to Scotland in 1561 after her husband's death. She was a far more charming and romantic figure than her cousin Elizabeth, but she was no stateswoman. A convinced Catholic, she soon ran head-on into the granitelike opposition of Knox and the Kirk. Her second marriage, to her cousin Lord Darnley, turned out badly, and she became involved in a plot resulting in his murder. In 1567 she was forced to abdicate, and in the following year she fled from Scotland and sought protection in England from Elizabeth. No visitor could have been more unwelcome. Mary, as Henry VII's great-granddaughter, had the best hereditary claim to be Elizabeth's heir, but she was a Catholic and a foreigner. Elizabeth would never formally recognize her as her successor, nor would she marry in order to produce another heir, nor would she do anything to harm her fellow sovereign, except keep a close watch on her through her agents. This policy exasperated Elizabeth's Puritan advisers and left Mary free to become the center of almost every French or Spanish

plot against Elizabeth's life during the next twenty years.

The Anglo-Spanish Conflict

Though there were many sources of friction between them, Elizabeth and Philip of Spain remained on relatively good terms for over twenty years. As time went on, however, it became increasingly difficult to keep the peace. England was a small country with less than half the population of Spain, but during the quarter-century of peace that Elizabeth's cautious temporizing gave her people, English industry, commerce, and shipping expanded considerably. For reasons we have already suggested, the Spanish were unable to produce the goods needed by their colonies. And Spanish shipping was incapable of supplying the insatiable colonial demand for African slaves. An aggressive merchant named Sir John Hawkins was the first Englishman to carry both goods and slaves direct to the Spanish settlements in 1562. It was profitable but dangerous work. In 1569 he and his cousin, Sir Francis Drake, were almost wiped out by a Spanish fleet. In revenge, Drake seized the annual silver shipment from Peru on its way across the Isthmus of Panama. From 1577 to 1580 he followed Magellan's route around the world and demonstrated the vulnerability of the Spanish Empire. Meanwhile English sailors were boldly probing the coasts of North America in a vain search for a Northwest Passage that would short-circuit the Portuguese route to the Indies. Like their fellow Protestants, the Dutch, the English were contesting the Spanish-Portuguese monopoly of overseas trade.

It was the revolt of the Netherlands, however, that finally brought England and Spain to blows. For centuries the economic ties between England and the Low Countries had been close. The Eng-

Elizabeth I of England, and her signature. The silver medal commemorates the defeat of the Spanish Armada (1588).

Mary Stuart, Queen of Scots, and her signature. Lead medal by Jacopo Primavera (ca. 1572).

lish people sympathized with Alva's victims, and English Sea Dogs cooperated informally with Dutch Sea Beggars to prey on Spanish shipping and to cut Spanish communications by sea with the Netherlands. Philip's ambassadors in England became deeply involved in one plot after another against Elizabeth's life, usually with the object of setting Mary Stuart on the throne. In 1587 Elizabeth reluctantly consented to Mary's execution when confronted with unmistakable evidence of her complicity in these plots. Philip immediately planned an attack on England. In 1588 he sent his "Invincible Armada" north to hold the Channel while Parma ferried his Spanish veterans across to conquer England for Spain.

The story of the defeat of the Armada has become an allegory of the triumph of a young, vigorous nation over an old and senile nation. The Spanish ships were large and slow, equipped with inferior cannon, and commanded by a landlubber. The fleet was conceived as a means of transporting troops, not of fighting battles at sea. The English ships that put out from Plymouth to harry the Spanish up the Channel were smaller and more maneuverable, trained to fire their cannon at longer range. When the Spanish

reached Calais and anchored there, Parma had still not completed his plans. The English sent in fire ships among the Spanish ships as they lay at anchor, drove them northward in panic, and attacked them fiercely off Gravelines. Stormy weather completed what the English had begun. Hardly half the galleons that had left Spain made their way back northward and westward around Scotland and Ireland. The victory gave a lift to the morale of Englishmen and of Protestants everywhere. It ended all further thought of Spanish conquest of England—or reconquest of the Netherlands, for that matter. It did not mean the end of Spanish sea power, which was still greater than that of any other country. But when peace was finally signed in 1604, the English, with the Dutch, stood close to the Spaniards as powers on the sea.

THE FRENCH WARS OF RELIGION

One obvious reason for Spain's ascendancy in the later sixteenth century was the fact that France, traditionally the chief obstacle to Habsburg expansion, was torn by a series of civil and religious wars that prostrated the monarchy and devastated large areas of the country between 1562 and 1593. Almost overnight France was transformed from an aggressive national monarchy into a victim of intervention by neighboring states.

Background of the Civil Wars

France, with a population about double that of Spain, was the largest nation in Christian Europe under a single government. But, impressive as the French monarchy was, it was far from having absolute power. There was still a powerful and turbulent aristocracy in France, and French provinces clung jealously to local customs and privileges. The country was imperfectly unified; there was no body that could speak for the whole realm, as Parliament could for England. Class differences were sharp, and the bureaucracy was overworked, corrupt, and inefficient. Other countries had the same weaknesses; few other countries had to face the same internal and external threats.

The Armada

When the Spanish Armada challenged the ancient lords of the English on their own grounds, the impending conflict took on the aspect of a judicial duel in which as was expected in such duels, God would defend the right. . . . So when the two fleets approached their appointed battleground, all Europe watched. For the spectators of both parties, the outcome, reinforced, as everyone believed, by an extraordinary tempest, was indeed decisive. The Protestants of France and the Netherlands, Germany and Scandinavia saw with relief that God was, in truth, as they had always supposed, on their side. The Catholics of France and Italy and Germany saw with almost equal relief that Spain was not, after all, God's chosen champion. From that time forward, though Spain's preponderance was to last for more than another generation, the peak of her prestige had passed. . . . So, in spite of the long, indecisive war which followed, the defeat of the Spanish Armada really was decisive. It decided that religious unity was not to be reimposed by force on the heirs of medieval Christendom, and if, in doing so, it only validated what was already by far the most probable outcome, why, perhaps that is all that any of the battles we call decisive has ever done.

From Garrett Mattingly, *The Armada* (Boston: Houghton Mifflin, 1959), pp. 400–01.

1328

Civil
Wars

1562 ⌐ ¬ 1593

1793

House of Valois

House of Bourbon

1589

Moreover, during the sixteenth century church leaders and political theorists had worked out a formal justification of the right of subjects to resist their rulers when the rulers were doing wrong. Obviously the greatest wrong was to impose a false religion on the people. This doctrine was invoked in the Netherlands against Philip of Spain and in Scotland against Mary Stuart, but it had the most disastrous effects in France. For in a monarchy that was only halfway to absolutism, the strong irritant of religious conflict was injected about the middle of the century in the form of militant Calvinism. The rational theology and disciplined organization of Reformed Christianity—not to mention the superb French style of Calvin's writings—appealed widely to many nobles and bourgeois throughout France. The French Calvinists were nicknamed Huguenots. On the eve of the civil wars they boasted about 2500 churches. They probably never numbered more than a sixth of the population (some scholars say as low as a twelfth), but they were an aggressive and well-organized minority, sure of their faith, and confident of the support of a few men, such as Admiral Coligny, at the very top of the social hierarchy. Arrayed against them were strongly Catholic noble families, and, more important, the University of Paris and the Paris *parlement* (High Court). Most important of all was the fact that the Concordat of Bologna had given the kings of France full control over the appointment of the higher clergy as well as considerable indirect control of papal taxation and jurisdiction. In short, the king and his advisers could see no advantage in religious change, and consequently the Huguenots remained a permanent minority in France.

The Course of the Wars

The wars that broke out in France in 1562 were at once social, political, and religious. When Henry II died in 1559,

the royal authority fell into the hands of the Queen Mother, Catherine de' Medici, during the reigns of her three weakling sons, Francis II (1559–60), Charles IX (1560–74), and Henry III (1574–89). Catherine was an astute woman who put politics before religion and did her best to keep the feuding factions at court and the religious fanatics throughout the country from flying at one another's throats. But she lacked formal authority, and by now the animosities had become bitter. Calvinists allied themselves with discontented nobles and upholders of local autonomy. On the other side were Catholics, royal agents, and defenders of the status quo. Fanatics on both sides appealed for foreign aid, the Huguenots to the English, the Dutch, and the Germans, the Catholics to Spain. Both England and Spain sent troops, mostly at the beginning and again at the end of the wars.

Fighting was of the savage and bitter kind that characterizes civil wars. The Catholics won most of the pitched battles but were unable to wipe out the Hugue-

Massacre of St. Bartholomew's Day, 1572 (detail from a painting by an eyewitness, François Dubois).

nots. In 1572 Catherine was persuaded by the Catholic fanatics that one sharp blow might end all the trouble. At two o'clock on the morning of St. Bartholomew's Day, Catholic armed bands set upon the Huguenots in Paris, where many of their leaders were gathered for the wedding of the king's sister to the Protestant Henry of Navarre. Coligny and many others were killed. The slaughter spread quickly to other French cities, and before it was over probably ten thousand Protestants had been massacred. This was the most spectacular of innumerable atrocities on both sides. It horrified Protestants throughout Europe and, according to one story, made Philip II laugh aloud for the only time in his life. But it had little effect on the conflict in France.

Catherine de' Medici in 1561, by an unknown artist.

Henry of Navarre

The wars dragged on for twenty more years, becoming more and more confused and purposeless until the Huguenot Henry of Navarre came to the throne in 1589 as Henry IV (1589–1610). Though he was the nearest male heir, he was only remotely related to the previous king. He had a difficult time making good his claim to the crown against a Catholic League that held Paris and against troops of Philip II that intervened from the Spanish Netherlands under Parma. In the end he found that the only way he could capture Paris was to renounce his faith and become a Catholic, which he did in 1593. He did not forget his former fellow Protestants, however. By the Edict of Nantes in 1598 the Huguenots were granted freedom of conscience, freedom of worship in specified places, equal civil rights, and control of some two hundred fortified towns throughout France. In short, the edict simply recognized a religious stalemate, and zealots on both sides of the religious fence considered it only temporary. But it constituted the first formal recognition by a European national monarchy that two religions could be allowed to exist side by side without destroying the state, and growing numbers of Frenchmen who preferred civil peace at any price to the anarchy and fanaticism of the past forty

Henry of Navarre in court dress (seventeenth-century enamel).

years supported it. With the conclusion of peace with Spain and the publication of the Edict of Nantes in 1598, France was ready to resume building a strong monarchy.

THE GENERAL CHARACTER OF THE LATER SIXTEENTH CENTURY

The age of Philip II and of Elizabeth of England has been called the Age of Religious Warfare. It is true that religion was often the spark that set aflame the combustible materials of sixteenth-century society, but early nationalism, economic instability, and social unrest also played their part. A more precise description of the period might be the Age of Religious Politics. Until the Reformation, European politics and diplomacy had slowly grown less religious and more secular. Now for a century, thanks to the religious schism, politics and diplomacy became once more strongly motivated and embittered by religion. The monarchies were faced by religious ideologies that often commanded fiercer loyalties than could the dynasties themselves. A Jesuit might scheme and work and die for an ideal that obviously transcended all state boundaries. In the same way a Scottish Presbyterian, a Dutch Calvinist, and a French Huguenot might have more in common than subjects of the same king. Thus religious differences sometimes undermined the power of monarchs, as they did in France and the Netherlands. And sometimes religious zeal reinforced loyalty to the dynasty, as it did in Spain and among English Protestants. Perhaps the best symbol of this Age of Religious Politics was the Escorial, which Philip II built for his residence near Madrid. The building was half-palace, half-monastery; and the private chamber of the king was connected directly with the chapel of the monastery. A century later a palace would be built at Versailles that would express the spirit of a quite different age.

The European Witch-Craze

The Age of Religious Warfare coincided with a tragic episode of western civilization: the European witch-craze. The witch-craze began in the mid-sixteenth century and continued for over a hundred years; before it ended, thousands of persons had been hanged or burned at the stake as convicted witches. The exact number of victims may never be known, but it is certain that the overwhelming majority of them were completely innocent.

Superstitious beliefs and practices—often dating back to pre-Christian times—had always lurked beneath the surface of European life. It was widely believed that some people had occult powers that could be used to assist neighbors in distress—or to harm them. Almost every community had its wizard or cunning woman, someone who offered cures and consolations when the efforts of priest or doctor had proved to no avail. From time to time throughout the Middle Ages, people had also been convicted of malevolent witchcraft; that is, of attempting to use occult means to inflict death or disease on others.

During the sixteenth century, however, the number of people accused of witchcraft began to increase dramatically. In one community after another a single accusation, which formerly might have led to a single witch-trial, triggered a chain reaction of arrests. Most of the victims were females—since witches were popularly assumed to be reclusive old women who had relieved their loneliness by making a "compact" with the Devil—but some men and even children were also arrested. Under torture, the suspects were forced to confess participation in lurid "witches' sabbaths" and diabolical schemes to harm or kill their neighbors. Having confessed, the suspects were then forced to name "accomplices," who in turn would be arrested and convicted. Dozens, even hundreds, of victims were often led to the stake in a single community. (In England, more humanely, the suspects were spared torture, and executions were by hanging.)

Historians are still puzzled about why the witch-craze exploded in sixteenth-century Europe. Certainly its occurrence reflected a growing interest in the "science" of demonology, which had begun to flourish in the late Middle Ages. It is

The Escorial, Philip II's monastery-palace near Madrid.

no accident, however, that the actual increase in accusations and executions coincided with the Age of Religious Warfare. The religious passions unleashed by the Reformation had generated deep hostilities on a level unprecedented in European history. Protestants regarded the pope as Antichrist; Catholics believed that Luther had been spawned by the Devil. Prominent intellectuals, such as King James I of England, felt obliged to publish extensive treatises about the works of Satan and his minions. In such an atmosphere, people of every class could become suspicious of their friends and neighbors, while judges took even the most unlikely accusations seriously,

Religion and Patriotism

A Spanish ambassador reporting the words of a French Catholic in 1565:

Nowadays Catholic princes must not proceed as they once did. At one time friends and enemies were distinguished by the frontiers of provinces and kingdoms, and were called Italians, Germans, Frenchmen, Spaniards, Englishmen, and the like. Now we must say Catholics and heretics, and a Catholic prince must consider all Catholics of all countries as his friends, just as the heretics consider all heretics as friends and subjects whether they are their own vassals or not.

◇　◇　◇

An English Protestant writing in 1589:

All dutiful subjects in this land desire with all their hearts the continuance of God's religion; the preservation of Queen Elizabeth; and the good success of the English navy. These particulars, I grant, are not expressed in flat in the Lord's Prayer; but they are contained within the compass of, and may be deduced from the petitions of that excellent prayer. Whosoever doubteth of this is void of learning.

As quoted in Erich Marks, *Die Zusammenkunft von Bayonne* (Strasburg: K. J. Trübner, 1889), p. 14; as quoted in Benjamin Hanbury, *Historical Memorials Relating to the Independents* (London: Congregational Union of England and Wales, 1839–44), Vol. I, p. 71.

and interrogated suspects in the most ruthless possible fashion.

Why did the witch-craze end? In the first place, religious warfare died out in the mid-seventeenth century, and with its passing came a cooling of the religious passions that had inflamed post-Reformation Europe. Even more importantly, the emergence of a modern scientific outlook (see Chapter 21) made the belief in invisible spirits and occult forces increasingly untenable among serious intellectuals. By 1660 the witch-panics were on the wane; by 1700 they all but disappeared. But the witch-craze, like the religious wars themselves, showed the instability of sixteenth-century society.

"Golden Ages"

It is characteristic of the history of civilization that periods of intense political and social conflict sometimes coincide with great creative achievements. Thus the late sixteenth and early seventeenth centuries witnessed a "golden age" of literature and the arts in three of the nations under consideration. Shakespeare's plays and Spenser's poetry in Elizabethan England, Cervantes' *Don Quixote* and Velasquez' paintings in Spain of the early seventeenth century, and Vondel's poetry and Rembrandt's portraits in Holland of the mid-seventeenth century represent a kind of summit of achievement in the history of the arts in these three nations. Shakespeare (*ca.* 1564–1616), Cervantes (1547–1616), and Vondel (1587–1679) are still the greatest figures in the literary history of their native countries, and, though Eng-

land produced no great painter, Frans Hals (*ca.* 1580–1666) and Rembrandt van Rijn (1606–69) are the towering figures in Dutch painting, as El Greco (*ca.* 1548–1614) and Velasquez (1599–1660) are in Spanish.

In each case the artistic flowering accompanied or, as in Spain, immediately followed a period of heroic national struggle, effort, and achievement. It is tempting to say that ages of national expansion and excitement, times of heroism and "crusade," provide great artists with the stimulation and the receptive audiences they need. On a more mundane level, it is clear that "golden ages" depend on the existence of a class of people with enough education, wealth, and leisure to appreciate luxuries like books and paintings. The historian can record the existence of such classes and the occurrence of heroic national effort in England, Spain, and the Dutch Netherlands during these years. But he cannot account satisfactorily for Shakespeare's extraordinary appreciation of the complexities of human motivation, Cervantes' sympathy for all sorts and conditions of men, or Rembrandt's penetration of the depths of the religious soul. All these are manifestations of purely individual genius. Nor can he account for the appearance in France during a time of troubles of three writers who have profoundly influenced the French mind: Montaigne (1533–92), Descartes (1596–1650), and Pascal (1623–62). The historian can explain something about the conditions and characteristics of "golden ages." He cannot explain the appearance of genius.

Suggestions for Further Reading

Note: Asterisk denotes a book available in paperback edition.

Geographical Discovery

Two brief general studies provide a good introduction to the subject: J. H. Parry, *Europe and a Wider World, 1415–1715* (1949), and C. E. Nowell, *The Great Discoveries and the First Colonial Empires** (1954). J. H. Parry gives a more detailed account in *The Age of Reconnaisance* (1963). W. C. Abbott, *The Expansion of Europe*, 2 vols. (1918), is an older but still valuable general account, including consideration of the effect of the discoveries on Europe. John H. Elliott, *The Old World and the New* (1970), is excellent. P. Sykes, *A History of Exploration* (1934), surveys the whole subject from ancient times on; H. H. Hart, *Sea Road to the Indies* (1950), describes the Portuguese exploits; J. B. Brebner, *The Explorers of North America, 1492–1806** (1933), and A. P. Newton, *The European Nations in the West Indies, 1493–1688* (1933), treat exploration in particular areas. E. Sanceau has written a good modern biography of Henry the Navigator (1947). S. E. Morison, *Admiral of the Ocean Sea,** 2 vols. (1942), is the best account of Columbus. A shorter discussion by Morison is *Christopher Columbus, Mariner* (1955), and he gives an excellent overall view in *The European Discovery of America* (1971). C. M. Parr, *So Noble a Captain* (1953), is a reliable account of Magellan. E. Sanceau, *The Land of Prester John* (1944), traces Portuguese interest in Abyssinia. The best correctives for older Anglo-Saxon notions of Spanish colonizing are C. H. Haring, *The Spanish Empire in America* (1947), and L. Hanke, *The Spanish Struggle for Justice in the Conquest of America* (1949). R. L. Reynolds, *Europe Emerges** (1961), is a good analysis of European expansion in general.

The Late Sixteenth Century

J. H. Elliott, *Europe Divided, 1559–1598** (1968), synthesizes the political history of this era. Volume III of the *New Cambridge Modern History* (1968) is also useful. F. Braudel, *The Mediterranean and the Mediterranean World in the Age of Philip II,** 2 vols. (1972–73), is a magisterial survey. For an introduction to the witch-craze, see H. R. Trevor-Roper, *The European Witch-Craze of the Sixteenth and Seventeenth Centuries and Other Essays** (1969). Among the best treatments of the witch-craze in specific countries are K. Thomas, *Religion and the Decline of Magic** (1971), for England; J. Caro Baroja, *The World of the Witches** (1965), for Spain; and H. C. E. Midelfort, *Witch Hunting in Southwestern Germany, 1562–1684* (1972). For a general social history of the years 1550 to 1650, see H. Kamen, *The Iron Century* (1971).

Spain

R. B. Merriman, *The Rise of the Spanish Empire in the Old World and in the New,* 4 vols. (1918–34), is a superbly written and scholarly account of Spain in Europe and overseas to the death of Philip II. J. H. Elliott, *Imperial Spain, 1469–1716** (1964), is a remarkable book. R. Trevor Davies, *The Golden Century of Spain, 1501–1621** (1937) and *Spain in Decline, 1621–1700** (1956), are well-informed, interesting, sometimes controversial accounts. J. H. Parry, *The Spanish Theory of Empire in the Sixteenth Century* (1940), studies the effect of empire on the Spanish monarchy. E. J. Hamilton, *American Treasure and the Price Revolution in Spain, 1501–1650* (1934), is the starting point for study of sixteenth-century inflation. G. Parker, *The Army of Flanders and the Spanish Road** (1972), discusses Spain's military decline, with emphasis on the actual life and problems of Spanish soldiers.

The Netherlands

The most scholarly brief account of the Dutch rebellion and its consequences is in the two books by P. Geyl, *The Revolt of the Netherlands, 1555–1609** (1932) and *The Netherlands Divided, 1609–1648* (1936). There is a beautifully written popular biography of William the Silent by C. V. Wedgwood* (1944).

Elizabethan England

There is a wealth of well-written, scholarly books on the period. J. Neale, author of three brilliant volumes on the parliamentary history of the reign, has written the best biography of Elizabeth, *Queen Elizabeth I** (1952). E. Jenkins, *Elizabeth the Great** (1959), adds insight on the purely personal side. C. Read's thorough biographies, *Mr. Secretary Walsingham,* 3 vols. (1925) and *Mr. Secretary Cecil* (Lord Burghley), 2 vols. (1955, 1960), provide intimate knowledge of the politics of the period. A. L. Rowse has written with zest on Elizabethan society in *The England of Elizabeth** (1950) and *The Expansion of Elizabethan England** (1955). J. A. Williamson, *The Age of Drake,** 3rd ed. (1952), is by a master of naval history, and G. Mattingly, *The Armada** (1959), is one of those rare books, a definitive treatment of its subject that is at the same time magnificent reading. A good brief survey is S. I. Bindoff, *Tudor England** (1959).

France

It is more difficult to find good reading in English on France than on England in the sixteenth century. John W. Salmon, *Society in Crisis: France in the Sixteenth Century* (1975), is the best general treatment. L. Batiffol, *The Century of the Renaissance* (trans. 1916), is an older general account of France in the sixteenth century. J. E. Neale, *The Age of Catherine de' Medici** (1943), is very useful, as is H. Pearson, *Henry of Navarre* (1963). There is a brief modern account of the period in F. C. Palm, *Calvinism and the Religious Wars* (1932). J. W. Thompson, *The Wars of Religion in France, 1559–1576* (1909), is older but still useful. A. J. Grant, *The Huguenots* (1934), is both scholarly and brief. W. F. Church, *Constitutional Thought in Sixteenth Century France* (1941), discusses with discernment the conflict of medieval and modern ideas of government during the civil wars. Social aspects of the wars of religion are well portrayed in N. Z. Davis, *Society and Culture in Early Modern France* (1975).

19 Political and Economic Crises of the Seventeenth Century

The seventeenth century, much more than the fifteenth or sixteenth, is the century in which modern European civilization took on recognizable form. It was also a century that was afflicted by severe political, social, and economic crises, crises at least as dangerous as those that had shaken the medieval civilization of Europe in the fourteenth century. Everywhere the growing power of the state was challenged, and in the 1640s the three strongest European monarchies—Spain, France, and England—were weakened by outright rebellions. War was endemic—the last of the religious wars merged with wars to preserve the balance of power, and these in turn with the first commercial wars. The ravages of war were compounded by bad weather, famine, and plague. Population growth leveled off, and in some areas, notably Germany, population declined. There was also a prolonged economic depression, running through the middle decades of the century. The flow of silver from the New World, which had stimulated the economy, dropped off sharply, and industrial production in Europe increased only slightly, if at all. Only gradually, after 1670, did growth in commerce and industry start spiraling upward again. Meanwhile, poverty exacerbated social unrest, and inadequate revenues limited the capabilities of governments.

Yet out of this unpromising environment a new Europe emerged. Governments, businessmen, and intellectual leaders struggled to keep the gains they had made in the last two centuries. Every challenge was met, at different dates and by different means in different countries. But the net result was that Europe was richer, controlled more of the world's commerce, and had more effective governments in 1700 than in 1600. And, there was at the same time an intellectual revolution, a sharp change in ways of thinking about man and the universe, that did more to change the nature of human life than any of the new ideas that had emerged during the Italian Renaissance (see Chapter 21).

Although seventeenth-century statesmen and writers recognized the importance of economic problems more clearly than had their predecessors, they still felt that political problems deserved primary consideration. They wanted to complete the process that had begun in the thirteenth century, the building of a sovereign territorial state. This process had been interrupted by the troubles of the fourteenth century and the religious conflicts of the sixteenth century; now it was to be pushed to a conclusion. From a theoretical point of view, this meant defining the concept of sovereignty ever more clearly. From a practical point of view, it meant concentrating supreme power in some organ of the state, either in the monarchy (as in France and most other states) or in the representative assembly (as in England).

FRANCE: IN SEARCH OF ORDER AND AUTHORITY 1598–1661

Seventeenth-century France still felt the effects of the anarchy and violence that had prevailed for almost half a century before the Edict of Nantes in 1598. Three weakling kings had tarnished the prestige of the monarchy, and the great nobles had become powerful and unruly. Merchants and manufacturers had been hard hit by the wars, and the peasants had suffered heavily from the ravages of undisciplined soldiers. The mass of the people were eager for security, but still somewhat suspicious of any authority that might violate local privileges and increase the burden of taxation. They could still rebel when they felt that government was pursuing an undesirable course.

Jean Bodin, the most penetrating political thinker of the tragic years just past, had seen what was needed. In his book *The Republic*, which he published in 1576, Bodin argued that in any well-ordered state, supreme power or sovereignty must be clearly lodged somewhere in some organ of the state, preferably the monarchy. Sovereignty he defined as the power of "giving laws to the people as a whole without their consent." Bodin did not think of this power as arbitrary or capricious: the sovereign was still subject to the laws of God and of nature. But he insisted that sovereign power must not be limited by any human agency—that

Opposite: Rembrandt van Rijn, *Syndics of the Cloth Guild* (1662).

Triumphal Entry of Henry IV into Paris,
large sketch by Peter Paul Rubens (*ca.* 1630).

Jean Bodin on Sovereignty

Jean Bodin was a sixteenth-century French lawyer who was interested in political and economic problems. The *fact* of sovereignty had been recognized for some time, but Bodin was the first writer to express the *idea* in clear and uncompromising terms.

Sovereignty is supreme power over citizens and subjects unrestrained by laws. . . . A prince is bound by no law of his predecessor, and much less by his own laws. . . . He may repeal, modify, or replace a law made by himself and without the consent of his subjects. . . . The opinion of those who have written that the king is bound by the popular will must be disregarded; such doctrine furnishes seditious men with material for revolutionary plots. No reasonable ground can be found to claim that subjects should control princes or that power should be attributed to popular assemblies. . . . The highest privilege of sovereignty consists in giving laws to the people as a whole without their consent. . . . Under this supreme power of making and repealing laws it is clear that all other functions of sovereignty are included.

From Jean Bodin, *Six Books Concerning the Republic,* from the Latin version of 1586 [the French version of 1576 is less coherent], trans. by F. W. Coker, in *Readings in Political Philosophy* (New York: Macmillan, 1938), pp. 374, 375, 376, 377, 380.

is, it must be "absolute" to be effective. He insisted that it could not be divided. Neither the *Parlements* (the highest French courts) nor the Estates General could veto or modify the decisions of the sovereign. Sovereignty must be recognized as legitimately residing in one person or one political institution. No one had defined sovereignty so clearly before or argued so persuasively for it as the only remedy for insecurity and civil war. Bodin's prescription for France's ills was fulfilled in the French absolute monarchy that became the model and envy of most of Europe.

Henry IV and Sully

The first steps toward restoring the power of the monarchy and the prosperity of the land were taken by Henry IV and his minister, Sully. Henry, first of the Bourbon dynasty, was a popular king—courageous, vigorous, humorous, tolerant, and sound in his judgment of men. But he spent much of his time in hunting and lovemaking and left the routine business of government to Sully and others. Sully was a puritanical Huguenot with a keen sense of economy and a hatred of dishonesty. He improved the financial condition of the monarchy, partly by avoiding expensive wars and partly by patching up the tax-collecting system. The French taxation system was inefficient, corrupt, and inequitable. Many taxes were "farmed"—that is, the right to collect them was granted to private collectors who paid the government a fixed sum and then collected all they could. The burden fell most heavily on the peasants, since the nobles and the upper bourgeoisie were exempt from major taxes. Sully could do nothing to make the system more just (nor could any French minister down to the Revolution), but he could make it work better by discharging dishonest and inefficient tax farmers. (It has been estimated that as a rule hardly half the taxes collected in France at this time reached the treasury.) Moreover, the reestablishment of internal peace and order, which allowed agriculture and commerce to recover, helped to increase the government's revenues, especially from customs duties. When Henry IV was assassinated by a Catholic fanatic in 1610 there was a sizable surplus in the treasury.

The Estates General of 1614

Within a few years the work of Henry and Sully was in ruins. Under the regency of Henry's widow, Marie de' Medici, the treasury surplus was sopped up by rapacious courtiers, and Spain began once more to intervene in French affairs, sometimes in a strange alliance with the Huguenots. In 1614 the Estates General were summoned to one of their rare meetings, but the deliberations soon turned into a struggle between the First and Second Estates (the clergy and the nobility) and the Third Estate (the bourgeoisie, who were represented largely by provincial royal officers). No group was willing to take responsibility; and no group had the power to demand reform. The assembly dissolved with a strong declaration that "the king is sovereign in France, and holds his crown

from God only." It was not to meet again until 1789, on the eve of the Revolution.

Richelieu

In 1614 Henry IV's son, Louis XIII, was only fourteen years old. He was soon to be married to Anne of Austria, daughter of Philip III of Spain, as a symbol of Habsburg influence on France. There was not much to be hoped for from the monarch himself—except that he might choose and support some able first minister. The man was already in sight—a brilliant young bishop named Richelieu—but it took him several years to become a cardinal (in 1622) and head of the king's council (in 1624). From 1624 to his death in 1642 Richelieu was the real ruler of France. Richelieu, rather than any member of the Bourbon dynasty, founded absolute monarchy in France.

There is no mystery about Richelieu, as there is about many other great figures in history. He had the clearest and most penetrating mind of any statesman of his generation. And he made his purpose perfectly plain: to enhance the power and prestige of the French monarchy beyond any possibility of challenge. He came to his task with a marvelous grasp of political and diplomatic possibilities, an infal-

Three studies of Richelieu by Philippe de Champaigne.

lible memory, and an inflexible will un-hampered by moral scruples. Richelieu admired Machiavelli's writings, and the heart of his political creed was *raison d'état*—the doctrine that the good of the state is the supreme good, and that any means may be used to attain it. He would coolly send an innocent man to his death in order to frighten other troublemakers, enhance the authority of the monarchy, and so save bloodshed in the end. "In judging crimes against the state," he ar-gued, "it is essential to banish pity." He was not irreligious, but the workings of his mind were overwhelmingly this-worldly. "Man is immortal; his salvation is hereafter," he once argued against some conscientious scruples of the king, but "the state has no immortality, its salvation is now or never." While his cardinal's robes helped protect him against assassination, his policy was that of an astute secular statesman who put public order before religious zeal. His reputation for diabolical cleverness went even beyond the reality and helped him to bewilder his enemies and gain his ends.

Richelieu had three concrete objec-tives that had to be carried out more or less simultaneously. First, he meant to break the political and military power of the Huguenots. Second, he meant to crush the political influence of the great nobles. And finally, he meant to destroy the power of the Habsburgs to intervene in French internal affairs.

The Edict of Nantes had allowed the Huguenots to garrison about two hun-dred towns, the chief of which was La Rochelle on the west coast. Richelieu persuaded Louis XIII that he would never be master in his own house until he had wiped out this "empire within an em-pire." Rumors that the government had decided to attack provoked the Hugue-nots to rebel, and Richelieu proceeded to besiege and capture La Rochelle. At the Peace of Alais in 1629, which settled the dispute, Richelieu was unexpectedly generous in his terms. He had no respect whatever for what he contemptuously called "the allegedly Reformed religion," but he allowed the Huguenots the right to worship as they pleased once he had attained his primary objective of elimi-nating their political and military auton-omy. He did not wish to alienate Protes-tants abroad who could help him in a war with Spain and Austria, and he hoped he could make loyal and useful citizens out of the Huguenots. In this he was successful. The Huguenots served the crown in the war that followed against the Habsburgs and loyally sup-ported the monarchy in the crisis of the Fronde.

Richelieu's attack on the political power of the nobility was less successful than his attack on the Huguenots, but it was just as determined. Until the very end of his career, he was constantly threatened by aristocratic intrigues. In response to this threat, he developed a network of spies, set up a special tribunal to try noble lawbreakers, and sternly forbade dueling, a privilege that marked the freedom of the aristocracy from ordi-nary restraints. He gradually weakened the power of the great nobles who were provincial governors and gave more local administrative responsibilities to direct representatives of the crown. These rep-resentatives, called *intendants*, were usu-ally drawn from the *noblesse de la robe*, ennobled officeholders of middle-class ancestry. They were therefore more de-pendent on the monarchy than the older nobility. Richelieu did nothing to lessen the economic or social privileges of the French nobility, but he did curtail its political power.

Richelieu was no financier, nor did he have any interest in bettering the condi-tion of the common people. He spent large sums on rebuilding the armed forces and even more in actual warfare against Spain. He left the government's finances and the nation's peasants in worse condition than he had found them. But through his subtle diplomacy and his well-timed intervention in the Thirty Years' War (discussed below), he made France, instead of Spain, the leading European power.

Mazarin and the Fronde

Richelieu's death in 1642 (Louis XIII died a few months later, in 1643) put his work to a severe test. Louis XIV was a child of five when his father died, and so his mother, Anne of Austria, was appointed regent. However, she left the business of government to the man whom Richelieu had picked and trained to succeed himself, an Italian cardinal named Mazarin. Mazarin had the subtlety and political skill of his master but not his inflexible will; he was both more adaptable and, as a foreigner, less popular than Richelieu. His two main objec-tives were to continue the war against Spain until the Habsburgs were defeated and to maintain the prestige of the monarchy at the level to which Richelieu had raised it. The nobility hated him as a foreign upstart, however, and the bourgeoisie hated him for the high taxes he imposed to carry on the war. The result was the last serious rebellion to take place against the monarchy until the French Revolution—a complicated and uncoordinated movement of resistance known as the Fronde (1648–52).

The word *Fronde* referred to a game of slinging clods at passing coaches, which was played by the more unruly children of Paris. The rebellion was like the game; it was annoying, but in the end it did not keep the monarchy from driving along the road to absolutism. The leaders did not want to destroy the French monarchy nor did they wish to upset the established social order. They were composed of several groups—the judges of the *Parlements* (the High Courts) and the chief financial officers, who were practi-

Outbursts during the Fronde in Paris (1648).

cally hereditary bureaucrats, and the nobles led by princes of the blood. Each group wanted to modify the structure of government so that it could have more influence. But no group could agree with others on a joint program, with the exception of the purely negative policy of exiling Mazarin. Thus the *parlements*, which began the struggle, stood for the privileges of the corporations of bureaucrats who controlled the courts and the financial bureaus. They wanted the king to rule with their advice, rather than with that of councilors whom he could make or break as it pleased him. They insisted especially that no tax could be imposed without their consent. The nobles, who joined the rebellion later, had no intention of letting the *parlements* become dominant in government; they wanted to get rid of the *intendants* and regain their old powers as provincial governors. In the provinces, many men rebelled to protect or enlarge local privileges, but they often found it hard to decide whether they should support a *parlement* or a noble governor.

The result might have been different if anyone had dared draw on the deep-seated resentment of the lower classes—a resentment that had been expressed during the first half of the century in many local riots against taxation and misgovernment. But while a few theorists talked of liberty and democracy, no one was willing to take the chance of unleashing forces that might not be controllable. Unlike the contemporary English rebellion, in which the middle and lower classes accepted radical doctrines and defeated the king (see p. 426), the Fronde remained dominated by the nobility and the upper bourgeoisie. Each group approached the brink of making unlimited war on the king even at the risk of social revolution, and each drew back in horror. This innate conservatism, combined with lack of unity among the leaders, led to the disintegration of the rebellion. There was very little hard fighting; by the end of 1652, Mazarin, who had had to flee the country, was once more back in the saddle. Most Frenchmen concluded that a strong monarchy was preferable to futile civil war. The young king, Louis XIV, was to profit from this reaction when he came of age. Meanwhile, he remembered with

loathing the violence and instability of the Fronde. He came to hate Paris, from which he had had to flee in 1648, to despise the mob, and to fear the nobles unless they were restrained by a firm royal hand.

In spite of the Fronde and the tax burden that continued to oppress the common people, Mazarin carried on the war with Spain until the Spaniards were forced to ask for terms in 1659. France gained two Pyrenees counties, and Maria Theresa, daughter of Philip IV of Spain, was married to Louis XIV. Both the treaty and the marriage symbolized the humiliation of Spain and the triumph of France as the leading power in Europe. Mazarin died in 1661, and Louis XIV announced to his ministers that he would henceforth be his own prime minister. Now the work of Richelieu had come to full fruition. The French monarchy no longer had anything to fear from Huguenots and nobles at home or from Habsburgs abroad. It was an absolute monarchy, endowed with a fuller sovereignty than any other yet seen in European history.

ENGLAND: IN SEARCH OF CIVIL AND RELIGIOUS LIBERTY, 1603–60

While Richelieu and Mazarin were laying the foundations of absolute monarchy by divine right, leaders in England were slowly developing a constitutional, parliamentary monarchy. Richelieu could see clearly where he was going, but the goal was never clear to English leaders during their century of conflict with the crown. Englishmen groped their way toward a conception of sovereignty as something rooted in law rather than in personal authority, something to be lodged in the hands of an assembly that represented the community, or at least its more wealthy and influential members. England was not alone in its resistance to absolute monarchy, but the result in most other countries, such as Poland, was anarchy and confusion. Only in England was a representative assembly able to increase its power without wrecking or at least weakening the state. When Queen Anne came to the throne in 1702 the English government was both a stronger and a more popular government than it had been in 1603 when James I succeeded Elizabeth I. The example of England, particularly as reflected in the writings of John Locke, was to have an enormous influence on western history throughout the following two centuries.

England, on the periphery of European civilization, had always been peculiar in its political development. For instance, although the strong monarchy of the Tudors (1485–1603) was part of a general European trend, the survival and strengthening of Parliament under such a monarchy was without parallel elsewhere. The Tudors continued to use Parliament in legislation and taxation, whereas rulers on the Continent felt that representative assemblies were usually either useless or obstructive. Parliament, particularly the House of Commons, slowly acquired a corporate feeling and a sense of being an integral part of the national government. The House of Commons, it will be remembered, represented both the mercantile classes in the towns and the landed gentry (knights and squires) in the country. The gentry had been increasing in numbers, wealth, and political influence since the dissolution of the monasteries. They governed England at the local level as justices of the peace (the English monarchy had no paid bureaucrats like the French *intendants*), and they dominated the lower house of Parliament by sitting as representatives not only of the counties but of many boroughs as well. In any other country they would have been considered members of the lesser nobility; in England they sat in the House of Commons with merchants and lawyers. This House had grown steadily in wealth and influence, until one member could boast in 1628 that the lower house could afford to buy the House of Lords three times over.

Thus the English Parliament in the early seventeenth century represented all the politically active classes of the nation in a way no other representative assembly in Europe did. There were no provincial estates or privileges in England as there were in France, and the class lines among peers, gentry, and wealthy burgesses were not so sharply drawn. The

rigid English rule of primogeniture meant that younger sons of the nobility, who were commoners, often went into the professions. On the other hand, English merchants were continually buying land and becoming gentry. This meant that if the monarch should ever fall out with Parliament—and with the social groups it represented—he would not be able to play class against class or district against district.

The Tudors

Queen Elizabeth had had arguments with her Parliaments, but the threat from abroad and the political good sense of both the queen and the opposition kept these arguments from becoming dangerous. It was generally recognized that only Parliament could make a law or impose a tax. It was also recognized that making policy, especially foreign policy, lay outside the competence of Parliament and within the sphere of what was called the royal prerogative.

The Tudors felt, however, that it was sometimes wise to confirm royal policy

Formal meeting of Parliament in 1625. The Lords are seated; the Commons stand outside the bar.

by parliamentary statute, particularly in the delicate field of religion. Henry VIII used Parliament to break with Rome; Mary had asked Parliament to restore England to the Roman obedience by statute; and Elizabeth had broken with the pope once more by statute. Elizabeth's Parliaments tried more than once to reform the Anglican Church in a Puritan direction and to nudge the queen on foreign policy—presumptuous acts for which Elizabeth scolded them sharply. But she was too popular for Parliament ever to make a real issue of the conflict and too astute ever to demand a clear definition of her prerogative. Tudor "despotism" was a popular despotism, and Tudor rulers found that they could exercise their sovereign power most effectively by seeking the cooperation of Parliament.

James I and Parliament

The Stuarts, who ruled from 1603 to 1714, either could not or would not cooperate with Parliament. James I (king of Scotland and of England, 1603–25), the son of Mary Queen of Scots, was a well-meaning but pedantic intellectual who never understood the social structure or the political realities of the kingdom he inherited from Elizabeth. He had been raised as a Protestant by the regents who ran Scotland after his mother's exile, but he had not greatly enjoyed his Presbyterian upbringing. His aims were praiseworthy—peace with Spain, toleration of the Catholic minority in England, union of England and Scotland, and a strong but benevolent monarchy—but he did not inspire confidence as a political leader. Moreover, many of his ministers were incompetent. Unlike Elizabeth, who often concealed her imperial will in cloudy and ambiguous language, James liked to have things dangerously clear. He had written a book, *The True Law of*

James I, by D. Mytens (1621).

Free Monarchies, in which he insisted that kings owed their position to God alone, were responsible only to God, and in fact were themselves like gods on earth.

His belief in a monarchy "free" of restraints, free to do as it pleased for the common good, did not appeal to the classes represented in Parliament. Some of James's policies might have really helped the poor; others simply transferred wealth from one privileged group to another. In either case, opposition to the king could not endanger the country. The Tudors had long ago ended the threat of aristocratic violence, and peace with Spain in 1604 removed the danger of foreign conquest. Only their own king could now attack the beliefs or interfere with the property rights of the privileged classes. Parliament, fearing royal tyranny, began to criticize James's acts. James, fearing parliamentary intervention in policy matters, began to scold Parliament. The delicate Tudor balance was destroyed.

Friction rapidly developed over three related issues: religion, finance, and foreign policy. The Puritans and their sympathizers in the House of Commons wished to "purify" the Anglican Church of everything that savored of Catholic practice, from "popish" ritual to the authority of bishops. James was convinced that the Presbyterian system of church government, which he had known in his youth in Scotland, would not only destroy royal control of the church, but would threaten the monarchy itself. "No bishop, no king," he remarked within a year of his arrival in England. Parliament, annoyed by the extravagance of James's court and dubious about his policies, denied him enough money to meet the rising costs of government. James replied by raising money without parliamentary approval—for example, by increasing the customs duties on his own authority. When his right to take such actions was contested, the courts ruled in his favor—probably correctly, since the king controlled foreign trade as part of his control of foreign policy. But the seeming subservience of the courts to the royal will further disturbed Parliament.

Meanwhile James was following a foreign policy that exasperated the Puritan majority in Parliament. He was too friendly with Spain for the Puritan taste, he did little to defend Protestants abroad against the rising tide of Catholicism, and he tried in vain to marry his son Charles to the Spanish Infanta. When James chided the House of Commons in 1621 for even discussing his foreign policy, the House bristled and passed a unanimous Protestation defending its right to discuss "the arduous and urgent affairs concerning the King, State, and defence of the realm, and of the Church of England." This was revolutionary talk. James tore the resolution from the Commons' *Journal*, but he could not undo what had been done. The House of Commons, which Queen Elizabeth had kept under the control of her privy councilors, was now taking the initiative under leaders of its own. An aggressive and powerful element among James's subjects was demanding a voice in politics that he was utterly unwilling to grant.

Charles I
and the English Revolution

The situation rapidly worsened during the early years of the reign of Charles I, who came to the throne in 1625. Charles tried to please Parliament by attacking Catholic countries, but his incompetent favorite, the Duke of Buckingham, failed to capture Cadiz in Spain or to relieve the French Huguenots at La Rochelle. Parliament had urged war but had not granted adequate taxes, so the government tried to pay for the wars by levying a forced loan and by imprisoning those who objected to paying. Parliament in 1628 drew up a formal protest in the form of a Petition of Right, which they finally compelled Charles to approve. Its two main provisions were that no one should henceforth be compelled to pay any tax or loan "without common consent by Act of Parliament," and that

no one should be imprisoned without cause shown.

By the next year the House of Commons was roused to fury by Charles's assertions of his full control of Church and state. It declared that anyone who introduced anything savoring of Catholic practices in the Anglican Church was "a capital enemy to this kingdom and commonwealth," and that anyone who advised or submitted to the levying of taxes without parliamentary consent was "a betrayer of the liberties of England." The issue of "sovereignty" had finally been raised, and the word itself was being debated by lawyers and parliamentary orators. Where did the supreme power in England lie—in the king or in Parliament? The old answer, that it lay in the "king-in-Parliament," would no longer do. The royal prerogative and "the liberties of England" were not reconcilable any longer.

Charles I now took things into his own hands and ruled without Parliament for eleven years (1629–40). He was less intelligent and more stubborn than his father. James had always yielded before conflict became irreconcilable. Rather than yield, Charles was to resort to duplicity and falsehood in the crises ahead of him, and as a result he ended his life on the block, trusted by almost no one. Trying to duplicate Richelieu's brilliant work across the Channel, he chose tough-minded advisers: Thomas Wentworth, Earl of Strafford, in political affairs, and William Laud, Archbishop of Canterbury, in ecclesiastical affairs. With them and others, Charles devised new methods of nonparliamentary taxation that provided enough money to run the government so long as it stayed out of war. Laud began a movement toward more ritual and formality in the Anglican service, a movement the Puritans regarded as an attempt to restore Catholicism. All opposition, whether to arbitrary taxation or to innovations in worship, was sternly suppressed by the courts. Everything went well until Laud tried to force the Anglican Book of Common Prayer on stubbornly Presbyterian Scotland. Before long an angry and well-led Scottish army was encamped in northern England. Charles and Strafford,

Charles I, by D. Mytens (1631).

ENGLAND DURING THE ENGLISH REVOLUTION 1642–49

Districts controlled by Parliament at beginning of war

Districts controlled by Charles I

MILES 0 — 100

Edinburgh
DUNBAR, 1650
DROGHEDA, 1649
Dublin
MARSTON MOOR, 1644
NASEBY, 1645
EDGEHILL, 1642
Oxford
London

The Dutch view of Cromwell (detail from a print dated April 30, 1653).

finding themselves unable to raise an army to fight the Scots, had to summon Parliament to get the money to buy them off.

The Long Parliament, which met in November 1640 and was not dissolved until 1653, became a workshop of revolution. It sent Strafford and Laud to the block. It passed an act stating that a Parliament must be summoned at least every three years. It outlawed all non-parliamentary taxation and abolished the special royal courts (the Court of Star Chamber, which dealt with opposition to the government, and the Court of High Commission, for ecclesiastical affairs), which had been the chief instruments of the "Eleven Years' Tyranny." In other words, in less than a year (1640–41) Parliament had made absolute monarchy impossible in England. This much of its work won unwilling approval from Charles, since sentiment for it was virtu-

ally unanimous. But when the more radical Puritans in Parliament went on to abolish bishops in the Anglican Church and to seek control of the army, a party began to form around Charles in opposition to the parliamentary majority. And thus a civil war broke out in 1642 and lasted until 1649.

Enough has been said to suggest that the English Revolution was primarily a war of ideas, not of classes or of districts or even of interests, although the interests of merchants and gentry who were outraged by nonparliamentary taxation were certainly involved. Generally the towns, the middle class, and the economically advanced southeastern counties of England supported Parliament, while many rural areas, aristocrats, and the backward northwest supported Charles. But nobles, squires, and artisans from all parts of England were to be found on both sides. Unlike the Fronde, in which narrow interest groups failed to work out programs with broad appeal, the English Revolution offered a real alternative to the established order: parliamentary monarchy instead of benevolent absolutism, and a Presbyterian Church governed by elected "presbyters," or elders, instead of an Anglican Church governed by bishops appointed by the crown. Unlike the Fronde again, the English Revolution was able to attract and to accept men with really radical ideas—men who wanted neither a monarchy, nor an established church, nor power in the hands of landlords.

As the civil war intensified, Parliament proved to be more successful than the king in raising money and in building a strong army. A brilliant cavalry officer named Oliver Cromwell formed a "New Model Army" largely from among his fellow Independents, or Congregationalists. The Independents were Bible-reading Puritans of strict morals who believed in independent congregations democratically organized, with little or no national organization. Many of them were of lower economic status than either Anglicans or Presbyterians (though Cromwell and his chief aids would have ranked as gentry). Cromwell and his army finally defeated the king's forces in 1645, only to fall out with the Presbyterians, who had dominated Parliament since the Anglicans withdrew in 1642 to join Charles. With Parliament and the army at loggerheads about what to do with the king and about what sort of government to set up in England (many in the army wanted a truly democratic regime), the king was able to escape and make one last bid for victory before being finally defeated by Cromwell in 1648. Cromwell and the Independents in the army were determined now to get at what they considered the root of the trouble. They "purged" Parliament of its Presbyterian members, executed King Charles I in 1649, abolished monarchy and the House of Lords, and set up a republic, or "Commonwealth," with the "rump" of the Long Parliament as its government and Cromwell as its moving spirit.

Cromwell

Cromwell proved to be a revolutionary leader unlike almost any other in western history. He was a deeply religious man who tried in vain to avoid becoming a dictator. Yet he was ruthless and determined when he felt his policies were threatened. He massacred the Catholic Irish when they rebelled, defeated the Scots when they intervened in favor of the son of Charles I, fought a commercial war with the Dutch from 1652 to 1654, and boldly dissolved what was left of the Long Parliament in 1653. In a few short years he had decisively won a civil war, united the British Isles under one government for the first time, made England again the terror of the seas, and apparently wiped the slate clean for any political experiment he wished to try. The rest of his career until his death in 1658, however, was a tragic search for answers to insoluble problems: how to guarantee religious toleration to all kinds of Protestants except determined Anglicans, and at the same time how to develop some constitutional basis for his government. Cromwell tried to rule through a written constitution (the first in the history of any major state) and with the assent of a Parliament. He took the title of Lord Protector instead of king, but he quarreled with his Parliaments as bitterly as the Stuarts had quarreled with

theirs. At one point Cromwell had to set up an open military dictatorship to keep his Parliament from disbanding his army and persecuting his coreligionists. The plain fact was that most Englishmen were not ready for religious toleration, especially toleration of the radical religious minorities that made up a large part of Cromwell's army.

Furthermore, it became more and more evident that it was impossible in England to break utterly with history and to set up a new sort of government simply by writing a constitution. There was already a "constitution" deeply ingrained in the English political tradition, although it was nowhere written down. Soon after Cromwell's death even his own supporters saw that the only possible alternative to military dictatorship was Parliament, and that the only way to restore Parlia-

Oliver Cromwell, painting from the original panel by Samuel Cooper.

Democratic Ideas in the English Revolution

After it was sure of victory, the Parliamentary army began to worry about a proper government for England. A Council of the Army, including representatives of the ordinary soldiers, held a series of debates at Putney in 1647 on a constitution for the country. One of the basic issues was whether all men should be allowed to vote.

Major Rainborough: I think that the poorest he that is in England hath a life to live, as the greatest he, and therefore truly, sir, I think it's clear, that every man that is to live under a government ought first by his own consent to put himself under that government, and I do think that the poorest man in England is not at all bound in a strict sense to that government that he hath not had a voice to put himself under.

General Ireton [Cromwell's son-in-law]: Government is to preserve property. . . . The objection does not lie in the making of the representation more equal but in the introducing of men . . . in this government who have no property in this kingdom. . . .

Sexby [a representative of the soldiers]: I see that though liberty were our end, there is a degeneration from it. We have ventured our lives to recover our birthrights and privileges as Englishmen, and by the arguments urged there is none. There are many thousands of us soldiers that have ventured our lives; we have had little property . . . yet we have had a birthright. But it seems now, except a man hath a fixed estate in this kingdom, he hath no right in this kingdom. I wonder we were so much deceived.

From *Puritanism and Liberty*, ed. by A. S. P. Woodhouse (Chicago: University of Chicago Press, 1951), pp. 53, 62, 69.

The restoration of King Charles II: the crowning in Westminster Abbey (from a contemporary print).

ment was also to restore the monarchy. In 1660 the monarchy, Parliament, and the Anglican Church were all restored when a "Convention Parliament" invited Charles II to return from France and take up the crown.

The Restoration

At first glance nothing more remained in England after twenty years of civil war and revolutionary experiment than had remained in France after the defeat of the Fronde. To this day Englishmen refer to the events just described as the "Puritan Rebellion." They do not call it a revolution because it was succeeded by the "Restoration." But one thing at least had been decided: there was to be no absolute monarchy in England. All acts of the Long Parliament passed before the outbreak of civil war were still valid, and these acts put severe limitations on royal power, even if the balance of power between king and Parliament was still un-

certain. Strafford and Laud had tried to do for Charles I what Richelieu and Mazarin had done for Louis XIV, but all three Englishmen died on the block, while all three Frenchmen died in their beds. The turmoil of the first half of the seventeenth century left most Englishmen with certain half-expressed convictions whose effects can be traced in English history for generations. Among these convictions were a fear of allowing any one individual to acquire too much political power, a deepened respect for government by law rather than by personal command, a reverence for Parliament as the defender of individual rights against arbitrary despotism, and a distaste for standing armies.

The early seventeenth century was a brilliant age in the history of English literature, including Shakespeare's mature work, the Authorized, or King James, Version of the Bible (1611), and Milton's formative years. It was also a brilliant period in political thinking, as statesmen and pamphleteers argued for royalist, parliamentary, or radical principles of government.

Perhaps Thomas Hobbes's *Leviathan* (1651) best represented the political insights and fears, if not the greatest hopes, of these turbulent years. Writing in the midst of civil war and in exile, Hobbes pictured the life of man without government as "solitary, poor, nasty, brutish, and short." Without some authority to enforce law, there is no society, no order, only "a war of every man against every man." Men in general are inclined to "a perpetual and restless desire of power after power." So they set up a sovereign power by agreement or contract (it makes no difference whether the sovereign is a king or a Parliament), by which all men agree to obey the sovereign, but only so long as he is able to maintain order. The sovereign is not bound by anything in the contract. No clearer argument for might as the necessary basis of all right had ever been written. Hobbes took Bodin's argument for a legitimate sovereign authority and subtly transformed it into justification of sheer arbitrary power. His book could be used equally well to support Charles I or Cromwell. In a sense the main effort of Englishmen during the seventeenth century was to find some way to refute Hobbes—to subject political power to the restraint of law and to increase its responsibility to the governed. They finally succeeded in 1688.

GERMANY: DISINTEGRATION AND DISASTER, 1618–48

While France was building the strongest monarchy in Europe and England was undergoing a constitutional crisis from which it was to emerge with new strength, the German-speaking peoples were caught up in one of the most futile and destructive wars in the history of Europe. The Thirty Years' War (1618–48) was really four successive wars that began in Bohemia, spread to the rest of the Empire, and finally involved most of the major powers on the Continent. It was a savage and demoralizing conflict that left "Germany" poorer and weaker than the western European states.

The Causes of the Thirty Years' War

The war sprang out of a complicated mixture of religious and political grievances. Lutherans and Catholics had not fought each other since the Peace of Augsburg (1555), but the Catholics were disturbed by the fact that, in spite of the provisions of the peace, most of the Catholic bishoprics in northern Germany had fallen into Lutheran or secular hands. This gave some grounds for creating an ultra-Catholic movement headed by the Jesuits and the German Catholic princes, particularly Maximilian, Duke of Bavaria. The spread of Calvinism introduced a new source of friction because

Title page of Thomas Hobbes's *Leviathan,* a great landmark in the making of the modern state. Hobbes calls the sovereign power of the state, usually conferred on one man, "that great Leviathan, or rather (to speak more reverently) that mortal God, to which we owe under the Immortal God, our peace and defence."

Calvinists had been excluded from the Peace of Augsburg. When Maximilian roughly disciplined the Protestant town of Donauwörth, Frederick V, the Calvinist ruler of the Palatinate, a small state on the middle Rhine, took the lead in forming a Protestant Union among the German princes and cities in 1608. In reply, a Catholic League was organized the next year under the leadership of Maximilian. By 1609 two illegal military alliances faced each other within the Empire, each afraid of the other and each determined to keep the rival religion from making any further gains.

Revolt in Bohemia

As these examples show, each component of the Empire was a virtually independent state. The Habsburgs, who held the imperial title, realized that the only way to rebuild and expand imperial authority was to establish firmer control over what had been their old family domains—Austria, Bohemia, and Hungary. Thus the Austrian Habsburg, Ferdinand of Styria, got himself elected king of Bohemia in 1617.

Bohemia was a flourishing kingdom in which two nationalities (Germans and Czechs) and several religions (Catholicism, Lutheranism, Calvinism, and remnants of the Hussite movement of two centuries earlier) lived fairly peaceably together under earlier Habsburg promises of toleration. Ferdinand, a zealous Catholic, began systematically to undermine this toleration and to re-Catholicize the country. This action provoked rebellion by the Bohemian Estates, which were dominated by a strong Protestant majority. In May 1618 two of Ferdinand's councilors were tossed from a castle window in Prague, and civil war broke out between the Habsburg ruler and the Estates. The Estates raised an army, deposed Ferdinand, and offered the crown of Bohemia to Frederick V of the Palatinate. When Frederick unwisely accepted, the Protestant Union became involved in defending the Bohemian Estates, while Maximilian of Bavaria brought the Catholic League to the support of Ferdinand. In 1619 Ferdinand was elected emperor. Thus a war that might have remained a local affair soon spread throughout the Empire.

The Bohemian phase of the war was soon ended. The forces of the emperor and the League won an overwhelming victory in 1620. Frederick fled, and the emperor proceeded to work his will on the prostrate Bohemians. Half the property in the country changed hands through confiscation. The Jesuits, with strong secular backing, set out to reconvert the country to Catholicism, and within ten years they had succeeded. The prosperity of the country was ruined, Protestantism was stamped out or driven underground, and Czech nationalism was crushed for two centuries to come. The Habsburgs and their Catholic allies had won the first round decisively.

Danish Intervention

The fall of Bohemia terrified German Protestants and elated the Catholics. The Spanish Habsburgs came to the aid of their fellow Catholics, and the armies of the League were everywhere triumphant. In spite of the common danger, the Protestants could not unite. The Lutherans had been more afraid of a Calvinist victory in Bohemia than of an imperial triumph, and so Lutheran Saxony had ac-

Soldiers and siege artillery of the Thirty Years' War (copper engraving by Merian in "Theatrum Europeam").

tually helped Ferdinand put down the revolt. Although Frederick V was the son-in-law of James I, Protestant England gave no help because James and Charles were too involved in difficulties at home.

In 1625 the Protestant king of Denmark intervened, partly to save the cause of his coreligionists but primarily to pick up some territory in northern Germany. Within a year he was beaten in battle by a large army raised by the most inscrutable figure of the war, a wealthy war profiteer and professional soldier named Wallenstein, who had offered the emperor his services. Wallenstein had no serious religious convictions, and his political aims have puzzled generations of historians. His immediate aim seems to have been to build an imperial Habsburg military machine of such strength that it could not only eliminate all Protestant opposition but could operate independently of all other forces in the Empire, including the Catholic League. Before long Wallenstein and the League were as much at loggerheads on one side as Calvinists and Lutherans were on the other. Religion slowly receded in significance as the war became a struggle for the hegemony of Europe.

The high-water mark of Habsburg triumph and Catholic recovery was reached in 1629. Denmark withdrew from the war, leaving Wallenstein's army supreme. The Catholic League and Jesuit advisers persuaded Ferdinand to issue the Edict of Restitution, which restored to Catholic hands all ecclesiastical lands lost to Protestantism since 1552. It was evident that this edict could not be carried out without more bloodshed, because it meant that Catholic bishops were to be restored throughout northern Germany. Such an act would destroy the rough balance between Catholicism and Protestantism in Germany and weaken the northern states for the benefit of Austria and Bavaria. This threat finally roused the Lutherans inside and outside Germany to a sense of their peril.

Swedish Intervention: Gustavus Adolphus

In 1631 growing Habsburg power was blocked by the intervention of Sweden, a

The siege of Magdeburg in 1631 by Habsburg and Catholic forces. This siege resulted in one of the bloodiest massacres of the Thirty Years' War.

country that had not appeared before on the stage of international politics. Gustavus II (Gustavus Adolphus) was the ablest ruler of his generation. His country was sparse in population and resources, but he had cultivated its iron and timber industries, united the nation behind him, and built the best army of the day. It was not large, but it was well

The Sack of Magdeburg

1631

Then was there naught but beating and burning, plundering, torture, and murder. Most especially was every one of the enemy bent on securing much booty. When a marauding party entered a house, if its master had anything to give he might thereby purchase respite and protection for himself and his family till the next man, who also wanted something, should come along. It was only when everything had been brought forth and there was nothing left to give that the real trouble commenced. Then, what with blows and threats of shooting, stabbing, and hanging, the poor people were so terrified that if they had had anything left they would have brought it forth if it had been buried in the earth or hidden away in a thousand castles. In this frenzied rage, the great and splendid city that had stood like a fair princess in the land was now, in its hour of direst need and unutterable distress and woe, given over to the flames, and thousands of innocent men, women, and children, in the midst of a horrible din of heartrending shrieks and cries, were tortured and put to death in so cruel and shameful a manner that no words would suffice to describe, nor no tears to bewail it.

From Otto von Guericke, in *Readings in European History*, ed. by James Harvey Robinson (Boston: Ginn, 1906), Vol. II, pp. 211–12.

equipped (with the first uniforms and an improved musket), well disciplined, and inspired by high morale. Gustavus had already come close to making the Baltic a Swedish lake in wars with Denmark and Poland. He now stepped into the fray as the sincere champion of Lutheranism, hoping apparently to set up a federation of Protestant states in Germany under Swedish leadership.

Gustavus arrived too late to save Magdeburg from a terrible sack by the Habsburg Imperialists in May 1631, but in the fall of 1631 he overwhelmed the Imperialist armies at Breitenfeld in Saxony. He then marched triumphantly to the Rhine. Wallenstein, whom the emperor had dismissed under pressure from the Catholic League, was recalled, only to be beaten by Gustavus at Lützen in 1632. Gustavus himself was killed in the battle, however, and by 1634 his army had finally been outnumbered and beaten. Wallenstein had been murdered by one of his staff, and another phase of the war had come to an end. Swedish intervention had saved German Protestantism but had not gained a decision. The most powerful state of all had been watching the course of events closely and was now about to intervene with decisive results.

French Intervention: Richelieu

Since coming to power in 1624, Richelieu had kept in close touch with the progress of the war through his ambassadors and agents. But for ten years he did not feel that the French army was strong enough to intervene in Germany. His major purpose was to crush the Habsburgs, both Austrian and Spanish, and he was ready to ally with anyone, Protestant or Catholic, who was opposed to them. The Dutch, who went back to war with their old enemies the Spanish, were his first allies, and in 1631 he subsidized the invasion by Gustavus Adolphus. When the Swedes were finally defeated in 1634, Richelieu saw that he would have to intervene directly if he was to check Habsburg expansion in, and perhaps control of, Europe. And so in May 1635 he sent a French herald to Brussels to declare war on the king of Spain.

The Thirty Years' War had lasted for seventeen years with no decisive result, and it was to continue for thirteen more dreary years while French, Swedish, and Dutch armies fought against the Spanish and Austrian Habsburgs. Spain was weakened by the successful rebellion of Portugal and the almost successful rebellion of Catalonia (1640). In 1643 the French finally destroyed the legend of Spanish invincibility by crushing a Spanish army at Rocroi in the Netherlands. It was the first time in 150 years that a Spanish army had suffered a major defeat. The emperor's allies deserted him, and by 1648 the Swedes were threatening Vienna and storming Prague. The dream of Emperor Ferdinand II (who had died in 1637) of re-Catholicizing Germany and establishing Habsburg control over the Empire lay in ruins.

The Peace of Westphalia, 1648

A peace was finally worked out at the Congress of Westphalia (1643–48), Europe's first great peace conference and the first international gathering of importance since the Council of Constance (1414–18). But it was a far different gathering from that of two centuries earlier. The atmosphere and the business at hand were now entirely secular, and the communities represented were sovereign territorial states that recognized no earthly superior and only the most shadowy common interests. "Christendom" had dissolved, and the word *civilization* would not be generally used until the next century to express in secular terms what *Christendom* had once meant to Europeans in religious terms.

Almost every act of the Congress emphasized the importance of the sovereign state. For example, it recognized the right of each German principality to make alliances and to declare war on its own. This constituted practical recognition of the disintegration of the Empire into over three hundred separate sovereignties. Switzerland and the Dutch Netherlands were finally recognized as sovereign states, independent of all ties to the Empire. France acquired some very ambiguous rights to Alsace, Sweden acquired strips of German territory along the shores of the Baltic and the North Sea, and the two German states of Brandenburg and Bavaria ended up with increased territory and prestige. As for religion, the old principle of *cuius regio, eius religio* was reaffirmed. Calvinism was simply added to Catholicism and Lutheranism as one of the recognized faiths. The ownership of church lands was settled as of 1624, meaning in general that northern Germany remained Protestant and southern Germany, Catholic. France and Spain were unable to reach agreement, so their war continued until French victory was finally recognized in the Peace of the Pyrenees in 1659. France

received some territory along the Pyrenees and in Flanders, and the Spanish princess, Maria Theresa, married Louis XIV. In general, the peace settlements of the middle of the century left France the strongest power in Europe, Spain prostrate, the Empire shattered, and a kind of power vacuum in the center of Europe.

The Social Results of the War

The Thirty Year's War was one of the most brutal and destructive wars of which we have record until the twentieth century. Armies robbed, raped, and murdered their way back and forth across Germany. The lack of any modern supply system meant that they had to live off the land. There are gruesome records of towns totally wiped out, cities reduced to a small fraction of their original population, and cultivated land reverting to waste. Destruction of livestock was even more serious than the loss of crops. The fields could be resown when the armies had passed, but work animals took years to replace. Thus starvation and disease killed more than the sword. It is impossible to be sure of the total decline in population, but some historians believe that Germany lost almost a third of its inhabitants. Even if the destruction was not so great as contemporary sources would suggest, the social and psychological effects were certainly frightful. A whole generation grew up accepting violence and brutality as normal. The fragmentation of the Empire into practically independent states hampered economic recovery. Cultural and political provincialism were to go hand in hand for the next two centuries in German history. In fact, it is almost impossible to find any good result of the generation of aimless fighting in Germany known as the Thirty Years' War.

DUTCH UNREST AND SPANISH DECLINE

England, France, and Germany were not the only countries to experience political crises in the first half of the seventeenth century. Political upheavals in this era touched every part of Europe. Even faraway Russia underwent an anarchic "Time of Troubles" before settling down uneasily under the rule of the first Romanov tsar in 1613. In the West, there were violent upheavals in the Netherlands and in Spain.

The northern Netherlands had achieved effective independence from Spain by the beginning of the century and were enjoying enormous economic success. Yet the United Provinces were riven by political and religious conflicts. One party, supported by orthodox Calvinists and led by the House of Orange (William the Silent's family), pressed for an aggressive war against Spain in the southern Netherlands. A second party, supported by the religiously tolerant Arminians (who were unwilling to accept the doctrine of predestination) and led by the mercantile class, favored a policy that might open the way to peaceful trading with Spain. As the Thirty Years' War approached, this tolerant "peace party" was overthrown: war with Spain resumed in 1621 and continued until the Peace of Westphalia. Tensions between the House of Orange and a "regent class" of mercantile interests continued throughout the century. For two decades after 1650 the "regents" dominated Dutch affairs. But when invasion again loomed in 1672—this time France, not Spain, was the enemy—the old conflicts surfaced again. The leading regent, Jan de Witt, was torn to pieces by a mob in The Hague, and the head of the House of Orange—the young Prince William III— was summoned to lead the Dutch war effort.

In Spain, problems that had been building up for decades exploded all at once in 1640. The resumption of warfare in the Netherlands, in Germany, and, finally, with France, put intolerable financial burdens on the Spanish state. Efforts by the leading minister, the Count-Duke of Olivares, to impose a more efficient centralized government and a more effective system of tax collection on the different sections of the Spanish kingdom led to two bitter rebellions in 1640. Portugal (which had been united with Spain since 1580) successfully broke away and regained its independence. And in the same year a revolt broke out in the province of Catalonia. Aided by the French, the Catalans held out for over a decade. Meanwhile unrest also broke out in Spain's Italian provinces.

All of these problems contributed to the decline of Spain and made inevitable its surrender to France in 1659. Yet behind Spain's political troubles lay an even deeper source of trouble: the diminishing strength of Spain's overseas empire. For the decline of Spain was caused largely by changes in the European (and world) economy during the seventeenth century.

THE MERCANTILE ECONOMY OF EARLY MODERN EUROPE

Seventeenth-century kings and ministers were aware that political power depended on economic strength. They sought to increase the wealth of their own countries and to decrease the wealth of rival countries, or at least to prevent its growth. Agriculture, of course, was still the chief occupation in every part of Europe, but very little could be done either to increase home production or to decrease foreign production of food and fibers. Industry was more susceptible to state interference, but none of the major countries was very dependent on industry. On the other hand, the volume and value of European trade had increased enormously. Growth between 1500 and 1600 had been so spectacular that some historians have described it as a "Commercial Revolution." And the countries that were assuming political leadership in Europe were becoming the centers of trade. The main routes now led to Amsterdam, London, and Paris rather than to Venice, Lisbon, and Seville. In the Netherlands, England, and France, the merchant was far more important than the industrialist and far more influential than the farmer.

Therefore, a ruler who wanted to use economic controls as a political weapon thought primarily in terms of altering the patterns of international trade. This policy seemed so natural that no one bothered to give it a name. In 1776, however, Adam Smith, looking at the process with some disapproval, coined the phrase "the mercantile system." This phrase, or its equivalent "mercantilism," has been used ever since.

Problems of Economic Organization

By the end of the sixteenth century it was evident that old forms of economic organization were not able to deal with the vast increase in the volume of trade. The gilds, which controlled production in many towns, could not supply the growing demands of merchants and governments. Most gilds were geared only to local markets and insisted on following traditional, and often inefficient, methods of work. Many governments tried to regulate gilds in order to get uniform, nationwide standards of production, but except for a few luxury articles, this policy proved a failure. It was easier to let the merchants deal with the problem of industrial organization.

One method, already used by the end of the Middle Ages, was called the putting-out system. For example, in the textile industry an entrepreneur might buy wool, pass it out to peasants to be spun into thread, carry the thread to others to be woven into cloth, take the cloth to the dyers, and finally sell the finished product. This system had the double advantage of bypassing the gild restrictions in the towns and of tapping new sources of cheap labor in the countryside. Underemployed peasants with only a few acres were glad to have any extra income; in England they took almost all the work away from the old textile towns. In the same way, English merchants bought Swedish iron, gave it out to Sheffield toolmakers, and sold the product abroad. (The English were the best precision-toolmakers in Europe.) The putting-out system was hard on the laborers, but it increased production and lowered costs.

Another type of organization was the gathering-in system (the factory system). In industries like printing, cannon founding, mining, and shipbuilding, and even in some textile processes such as silk weaving and calico printing, it was more efficient to gather workers together at some central place where their work could be directly supervised and coordinated. There was not much division of labor; each man made a finished or semi-finished article. But transportation costs were cut, and quality could be controlled. In both the putting-out and the gathering-in systems, it was almost invariably a merchant, not the manufacturer or the technician, who did the organizing.

Joint Stock Companies

In commerce an important innovation was the joint stock company. The small partnerships of the Middle Ages (and even the Medici Bank was small by seventeenth-century standards) could not

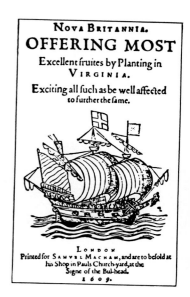

NOVA BRITANNIA.
OFFERING MOST
Excellent fruites by Planting in VIRGINIA.

Exciting all such as be well affected to further the same.

LONDON
Printed for SAMVEL MACHAM, and are to be fold at his Shop in Pauls Church-yard, at the Signe of the Bul-head.
1609.

Page from a pamphlet put out by the London Company in 1609 to persuade investors to support its enterprise in Virginia.

THE CENTER OF EUROPEAN ECONOMY   Early seventeenth century

raise the capital needed for large-scale, overseas voyages. So merchants formed associations called "regulated companies." Governments gave such groups a monopoly on trade to a given area, but each member of the group, while he helped meet common expenses, traded on his own account. They were associations of men, not of capital. What was needed, however, was a type of association that would attract the investments of men who had neither the desire nor the ability to qualify as active traders in a regulated company. The answer was the joint stock company, an amazingly flexible institution that was to be the parent of many other economic and political institutions on both sides of the Atlantic.

The joint stock company began as an association of investors, not of traders. Individuals bought shares in a venture, such as a trading voyage, and shared in the profits in proportion to their investment. When the association continued beyond a single venture, it became a joint stock company. This device had two advantages: it enabled anyone from a modestly wealthy man to Queen Elizabeth to invest in a business enterprise like Drake's voyages, and it associated businessmen with courtiers and statesmen at a time when both business sense and influence at court were necessary to the success of commercial ventures. The joint stock idea originated in southern Europe, but it was first applied to large-scale overseas enterprise in England in the Russia Company of 1553. The English East India Company, the companies that founded Virginia and Massachusetts, and the Bank of England were all joint stock companies. As these examples show, the first joint stock companies were dependent on government support (usually in the form of a trade monopoly) and were not concerned with industry. The joint stock company rapidly became the dominant form of commercial organization; it developed more slowly in industrial production.

The cumulative effect of these changes was to make the king, not the town, the chief regulator of economic activity. The unit of economic activity in the Middle Ages, apart from agriculture, had been the town or the city-state. As

stronger monarchs appeared at the end of the Middle Ages, urban economy was steadily absorbed into the national economy throughout much of Europe, except in Italy and Germany. The monarch stepped into the shoes of medieval town officials and regulated trade and production much as municipal governments had done, but on a larger scale.

Mercantilism

The original aim of economic regulation was to advance the common good, not to increase the wealth of individuals. But a king's definition of the common good was the strength and security of his realm, not a general rise in consumption or standards of living. During the seventeenth century monarchs began to believe that their goals could be attained by following the economic doctrine called mercantilism. This doctrine, as applied in the seventeenth century, assumed that there is only a certain stock of wealth in

An Englishman on the Importance of Trade
ca. 1630

Although a kingdom may be enriched by gifts received, or by purchase taken from some other nations, yet these are things uncertain and of small consideration when they happen. The ordinary means therefore to encrease our wealth and treasure is by foreign trade, wherein we must ever observe this rule; to sell more to strangers yearly than we consume of theirs in value. For suppose that when this kingdom is plentifully served with the cloth, lead, tin, iron, fish and other native commodities, we do yearly export the overplus to foreign countries to the value of twenty-two hundred thousand pounds; by which means we are enabled beyond the seas to buy and bring in foreign wares for our use and consumptions, to the value of twenty hundred thousand pounds; by this order duly kept in our trading, we may rest assured that the kingdom shall be enriched yearly two hundred thousand pounds, which must be brought to us in so much treasure; because that part of our stock which is not returned to us in wares must necesarily be brought home in treasure. . . .

Behold then the true form and worth of foreign trade, which is, the great revenue of the king, the honour of the kingdom, the noble profession of the merchant, the school of our arts, the supply of our wants, the employment of our poor, the improvements of our lands, the nursery of our mariners, the walls of the kingdoms, the means of our treasure, the sinews of our wars, the terror of our enemies.

From Thomas Mun, *England's Treasure by Foreign Trade* (New York: Oxford University Press, 1933), p. 5.

the world at any given time, and if one country gains wealth another loses it. (This is a fairly typical assumption in a period of depression; it had already emerged in the fourteenth century and is not unknown today.) To prevent loss, home industries and shipping should be encouraged and colonies founded to provide raw materials that would otherwise have to be bought from foreigners. By regulating trade in these ways a country's stock of precious metals might be increased and surely would not decrease. This was not an unreasonable precaution in an age when credit devices were in their infancy and when, in case of war, a country had to have a reserve of gold and silver to pay its suppliers and soldiers.

The obvious way to build such a reserve—short of discovering new mines or capturing a Spanish plate fleet—was for a nation to export more than it imported. Foreign buyers would have to settle their balances in precious metals. At the very least there should be a balance of trade, so that more money would not leave the country than stayed in it. And so mercantilism called for tariffs to discourage imports and various benefits to encourage export industries. But it was thought that some exports, such as gold and silver, scarce raw materials, and skilled workmen, would weaken a state and should therefore be forbidden. Logically, mercantilist theory called for the abolition of all internal tariffs and all internal barriers to trade in order to build up the home market, though it was impossible to accomplish this except in England. At the core of mercantilism was the conviction that trade is the most important of all economic activities, that the regulation of trade is the government's most important economic concern, and that regulation should result in self-sufficiency and readiness for war.

As we shall see (p. 440), when new colonial policies were developed during the seventeenth century, mercantilists favored tropical colonies that enhanced the strength of the mother country by furnishing products such as sugar and tea and by buying home manufactures. They had no use for colonies that raised crops or produced manufactured goods that competed with the home country's products, nor for colonies that traded directly with other nations. The integration of colonies into the home economy was a cardinal mercantilist principle.

Mercantilism has necessarily been made to seem more clear-cut and consistent than it actually was in practice. It differed from one country to another, in response to the interests of the ruling group. In France the system was often called Étatisme, or state-ism. The hand of the government was very heavy in France: government intervention in commercial enterprise was direct and positive; regulation was intense; and relatively little initiative was left to individual enterprise. In England mercantilism also meant regulation of the economy in the government's interest. But even before the Revolution of 1688, and especially afterward, the English government was more responsive to the pressures of businessmen than was the French. It is often very difficult to tell whether English economic policy represented the interest of the state as a whole or the interests of individual entrepreneurs. In the United Provinces, where the federal government was in effect a government of businessmen, the interest of the state and the interests of the business community practically coincided. Dutch mercantilism was not so much the regulation of trade by the state as it was the control of economic policy by organized business. In the rest of Europe, however—in Spain, Portugal, Austria, Prussia, and Sweden—mercantilism represented primarily the interest of the monarchy and so followed the French model more than the Dutch.

Financial Problems

The rise in prices that had marked the sixteenth century slowed down in the seventeenth, and may even have been reversed for a while. It has been estimated that while prices more than quadrupled between 1500 and 1600, they rose no more than 20 percent during the next hundred years, and most of that gain came during the first two or the last two decades of the century. The problems of inflation had been hard enough to handle. With prices rising faster than government income, bankruptcy was always just around the corner. In Spain, with its heavy military commitments, the government had had to repudiate its debts at frequent intervals (see p. 404). But the problems of deflation were even more serious. Taxes brought in less, while government expenditures (mostly for wars) continued to increase. The optimism that comes with inflation, at least to the classes able to profit from it, decreased. The classes that had profited from the inflation of the sixteenth century—merchants, bankers, men who invested in land (like the English gentry)—found the financial atmosphere of the seventeenth century rather chilling. This is one reason why taxation seemed so oppressive after 1600.

Spain never managed to solve its problems and continued to hang on the edge of bankruptcy until late in the century. France did better, partly because its taxes fell most heavily on the peasants, and agricultural prices remained at a higher level than prices of other commodities, thus giving the peasants enough of a surplus to pay for the extravagances of the court and the waste of war. But the French taxation system was antiquated, and trouble was simply postponed to the eighteenth century. In England the Stuarts were never able to build a sound system of government finance because they lost the confidence of Parliament, which controlled the major part of the royal revenue. But after 1688 a government that had gained the confidence of Parliament as well as the business community was able to construct an exceptionally strong system of public finance that included parliamentary taxation, a national bank, and a permanent public debt. In large measure this system was modeled on Dutch governmental finance, the most successful of the age. Since the rulers of the United Provinces were representatives of the business community, they had little difficulty, at least for a century, in raising the money and credit they needed for their overseas empire building and their wars. In an age dominated by trade, a state that had a flourishing commerce and could command the confidence of its merchants could weather any financial storm. A state that had little commerce, or in which commerce was growing slowly while merchants were discouraged, was likely to find itself in financial difficulties.

EUROPEAN COLONIES IN THE SEVENTEENTH CENTURY

European expansion overseas was checked briefly in the seventeenth century, and picked up again only after some fundamental changes were made in patterns of colonial settlement. The earliest and easiest type of colony to establish was a fortified trading post, to which the natives brought readily salable commodities, such as gold, spices, and slaves. This was the Portuguese pattern, and, as the Dutch gradually ousted the Portuguese from the East Indies, it was the pattern that the Dutch tried to follow. But even the Dutch eventually found that they had to go inland and take over responsibility for governing large numbers of people in order to maintain the flow of commodities, and no other colonizing power found it possible to avoid administrative responsibilities for more than a brief period. The Spaniards, for example, could not exploit the wealth of America without taking over the Aztec and the Inca Empires.

Moreover, it became harder and harder to get riches without effort. There was an apparently inexhaustible supply of slaves in Africa, which is why European colonies there could remain at the trading post level. But the market for spices was soon glutted, and, once the pillaging of the American Indians ended, gold and silver could be acquired only by laborious and expensive mining operations. A new type of colony was needed, a colony that produced goods desired by Europeans with its own labor. The first such colonies were the sugar islands of the Caribbean; later came the tobacco, tea, and coffee colonies.

The East

At first the Dutch, the English, and the French tried to cut in on the Portu-

Miniature by an Indian artist of a foreigner, possibly a merchant of the East India Company (*ca.* 1600).

guese trade in India, Ceylon, and the East Indies. The English East India Company was founded in 1600, the Dutch in 1602, the French in 1664. The Dutch discouraged English trade with the Spice Islands—they killed ten English merchants in 1623—so the English withdrew to India. There they set up "factories," or trading posts, on the Portuguese model. Until the breakup of the Mughal Empire in central India early in the eighteenth century, it was never possible for Europeans to penetrate very far into the subcontinent of India. Their footholds on the coast depended entirely on sea power for support; and as Portuguese sea power declined in the seventeenth century and as the Dutch busied themselves farther east, the English were able to establish themselves at Bombay, Madras, and Calcutta. Meanwhile, the French at Pondicherry had become their most important potential rivals. The stage was set for a struggle in the next century between the British and the French East India companies over India's commerce and riches.

The Caribbean

In the Caribbean the Dutch, the English, and the French were all searching for footholds around the periphery of the Spanish settlements. After an unsuccessful attempt to take Brazil from the Portuguese, the Dutch seized Curaçao as a base from which to raid Spanish commerce. The English settled Barbados in 1624 and acquired Jamaica in 1655. Meanwhile, the French settled Guadaloupe and Martinique. These acquisi-

tions were made just as the new colonial model—the colony as a producer of tropical goods—became popular. All the West Indian islands rapidly became rich sugar-producing areas, thanks to slave labor. So the English and the French, who came to the Caribbean to trade and buccaneer in the Dutch manner, stayed on to become plantation owners in the Spanish manner. The English and French sugar islands were the darlings of mercantilists at home. The planters cultivated a crop that could not be grown in Europe; they developed no industries to compete with home industries; and they were entirely dependent on their mother countries for shipping. Not surprisingly, the sugar islands were the center of attention among financiers and diplomats for over a century.

The chronic dearth of manufactured goods and slaves in the Spanish colonies meant that foreign smugglers who could slip by the Spanish navy were always welcome. As Portuguese control of the slaving stations on the western coast of Africa relaxed, the Dutch and English stepped in to supply the Spanish West Indies with the slaves needed on their sugar plantations. The brutality of this trade has become a byword, but it aroused no protest whatever in any European nation during the seventeenth and early eighteenth centuries.

North America

In North America a new wave of colonial expansion was beginning that was to have more far-reaching results than

The Javanese port of Batavia, from a Dutch engraving of 1682. Notice the Dutch architecture, entirely inappropriate for the climate.

West Indian sugar planting, though it was long overshadowed by the economic success of the tropical islands. There were many reasons why the Dutch, the English, and the French became interested in North America at the opening of the seventeenth century. For some time their sailors had been searching for a northwest passage to the Indies. Their ships were already engaged in cod fishing on the Newfoundland Banks. It was evident that North America could supply vast quantities of furs and timber. There might be precious metals, and it might turn out that sugar could be grown farther north than the Caribbean. Permanent settlements could support all these economic activities and at the same time help turn the flank of the Spanish in the New World.

Sir Walter Raleigh's unsuccessful attempt to found a colony in Virginia during the 1580s, however, had revealed some of the difficulties of settling the land the Spanish had left unoccupied. Colder climate, poorer soil, and hostile natives discouraged a plantation type of economy. To plant a permanent colony in North America a whole labor force would have to be transported and supported, perhaps for years, until the settlement became self-sufficient. This called for a large investment of capital and a large number of settlers. Furthermore, it called for strong belief and determination.

The Dutch, the French, and the English

It was the English and, to a lesser degree, the French, not the Dutch, whose determination proved strongest. The Dutch explored the Hudson in 1609 and settled New Amsterdam on Manhattan Island by 1624, but their colony of New Netherland never became more than a center for maritime trade and the export

The Indian village of Pomeiock in "Virginia" (actually North Carolina), watercolor by John White, an artist who took part in Raleigh's attempt to establish a colony at Roanoke in 1585. In his text White notes that mats and the bark of trees were used to cover the dwellings; the town was encompassed by poles instead of a wall.

of furs. Unsupported by the company that founded it, it fell to the English in 1664. The French were more successful. From Cartier, who discovered the St. Lawrence in 1535, to La Salle, who coursed the Mississippi in 1682, their explorers were more adventurous, their fur traders better able to adapt to the country, and their Jesuit missionaries more determined, than the representatives of any other European nation in the New World. In 1605 there were French settlers in Acadia, and in 1608 Champlain founded Quebec. By 1640 there were perhaps three thousand Frenchmen in Canada; by the end of the century about ten thousand.

The growth was slow for several reasons. The settlement of French Canada was marked by paternalism and relatively little individual initiative. Only when the French government actively encouraged Frenchmen to emigrate, as it did under Colbert in the 1660s and 1670s, did the colony grow appreciably. Since land was granted in large blocks, or *seigneuries*, to a few proprietors under semifeudal conditions, there was little inducement for peasants to emigrate. The government strictly prohibited the Huguenots, who wanted to emigrate, from going to Canada (they went to the English colonies instead). A fairly solid block of settlements grew up in the St. Lawrence Valley, but the slow-growing colony of *seigneurs* and *habitants* (as the peasants were called) was soon outdistanced by the English settlements to the south.

The founding of the English colonies in North America was the result of a peculiarly favorable set of historical circumstances in the mother country. The idea that colonization meant wealth had been skillfully sold to ordinary Englishmen by enthusiasts and businessmen before Queen Elizabeth's death. London and Bristol merchants were ready for colonizing ventures and able to organize such ventures by means of joint stock companies. The constitutional and religious conflicts that troubled England through most of the seventeenth century provided many people with both material and idealistic motives for wishing to emigrate. Finally the English government,

whether it was that of the Stuarts or of their revolutionary opponents, encouraged but did not interfere with colonizing projects. In particular, it put no bar in the way of religious minorities that wished to emigrate.

The first successful colony, planted at Jamestown by the Virginia Company in 1607, had a difficult time until the settlers discovered that by concentrating on a single crop, tobacco, they could buy the goods they needed from England. The little band of religious dissenters who landed at Plymouth in 1620 lost half their number during the first winter and survived only by sheer heroism. But the Massachusetts Bay Company, which founded Boston, was able to profit by the Pilgrims' experience. In 1630 it transported nine hundred settlers across the ocean in a large and well-planned operation. Within ten years the population had increased to about fourteen thousand in Massachusetts and within twenty years there were about twenty thousand in New England as a whole. This population had developed a surplus of food for export, and had plenty of fur, fish, and timber to ship back to the mother country. By the end of the century more colonies had been established, either as offshoots of the original settlements or by royal grants to "proprietors," until there were twelve in all (the thirteenth was added in 1732). It has been estimated that by 1700 there were almost two hundred thousand English settlers in North America, as compared with about ten thousand French. It was already clear that most North Americans would someday speak English.

English and French Colonies

The English colonies were more divided and less well controlled by the home government than were the French. New France was under one central administration at Quebec, whereas the English colonies were under twelve separate governments. Each of the twelve eventually elected representative assemblies that controlled local legislation and taxation. The royal governors were not responsible to these assemblies, but, since they were generally dependent on the assemblies for their salaries, their power was effectively limited. In the 1660s Parliament did its best to impose strict mercantilist theories on the colonies—for example, by ruling that certain exports must be sent directly to England in English or colonial ships. These measures caused complaints, and after the Revolution of 1688 the English government gradually became less insistent on asserting its authority. The colonists accepted parliamentary regulation of their trade so long as the regulations were not too strictly enforced, but they became more and more accustomed to running their own affairs to suit themselves.

Without conscious design, the English in the seventeenth century fashioned a new kind of colonial empire in North America, quite different from either the Portuguese or the Spanish. The Portuguese Empire (and, to a large degree, the Dutch) was based on armed trade. The Spanish Empire was based on the efforts of a ruling class of soldiers, planters, and missionaries to convert the natives and exploit their labor. But the Protestant English (and Protestant Dutch) were never particularly interested in converting the natives. They never felt responsible for the Indians as the Spanish did, partly because there was no possibility of exploiting their labor. So they simply displaced the natives from the land on which they settled. The English transferred a whole European population to a new environment and permitted it to blend the traditional institutions it brought from home with the innovations and improvisations evoked by the new surroundings. Not surprisingly, these innovations tended toward economic, political, and religious freedom. The breeze was blowing in this direction in England, and it was blowing even more strongly in the colonies.

The Russians in Siberia

While the French and the British in North America were pushing westward from the Atlantic seaboard toward the

Codfishing in the waters off Newfoundland (ca. 1720).

A Cossack warrior.

Pacific, the Russians were pushing eastward from the Ural Mountains across Siberia toward the Pacific. The two movements were strikingly similar in many respects, but the Russians had no ocean to cross at the start and they reached the Pacific first. In 1581, groups of Cossacks—"pioneers," or "frontiersmen," who had earlier pushed back the Tartars and Turks and had settled in the lower valleys of the Dnieper, the Don, and the Volga—began to move eastward from the Urals under a leader, Ermak, who became famed in song and story. Like the French in Canada, the Cossacks were mainly in search of furs, particularly sable, and so they followed the dark pine forest, not the steppe to the south. The great rivers of Siberia—the Obi, the Yenisei, and the Lena—flow north into the Arctic Ocean, but in their upper reaches they branch out so that they almost touch one another. Thus the Cossacks could move easily across the continent by water. The movement was not planned or organized. The settlers simply flowed eastward through the sparsely settled wastes of Siberia in search of furs, occasionally stopping to form widely separated settlements, and reached the Pacific in the early 1640s, barely two generations after the movement began. The distance covered was greater than that across North America, but there were no wide mountain barriers until near the end and no serious resistance from natives until the Cossacks met the Chinese in the Amur Valley. There the Russians were checked by a superior, civilized state, and in 1689, by the first treaty concluded between Russia and China, the Russians withdrew from the Amur basin. They remained behind the Stanovoi Mountains for the next 170 years.

Like the English, the Cossacks were in search of freedom as well as furs, and their early communities in Siberia were often wild and lawless, like the later towns of the American "Wild West." But the tsar's government soon reached out across the vast distances to establish its administration and to tax the lucrative fur trade—more like the French than the English government in North America. By 1700 there were perhaps half again as many Russian settlers in Siberia as there were French and British in North America. By the end of the century, Russian traders were venturing across the Bering Strait into Alaska and down the North American coastline in search of seals. Thus long before the English colonists in America had reached the Pacific, the Russians, by a combination of individual daring and government backing, had staked out a claim to the northern half of Asia and had even reached out far enough to touch the shores of the Western Hemisphere.

Suggestions for Further Reading

Note: Asterisk denotes a book available in paperback edition.

General Works on the Seventeenth Century

There are several successful attempts at a synthetic treatment of the period. D. Ogg, *Europe in the Seventeenth Century,** 8th ed. (1960), is a sound and interesting narrative of the major developments on the Continent, arranged by country. G. N. Clark, *The Seventeenth Century** (1931), is a more analytical discussion of different aspects of the period: for instance, population, industries, military organization, political thought, science, religion. C. J. Friedrich's volume in the *Rise of Modern Europe* series, *The Age of the Baroque, 1610–1660** (1952), combines narrative and analysis and makes use of recent interpretations of baroque style. C. J. Friedrich and C. Blitzer, *The Age of Power** (1957), is a brief and thoughtful survey of the century, based on Friedrich's larger work. The essays in T. Aston, ed., *Crisis in Europe, 1560–1660** (1965), are uneven, but the best ones are very good. Geofrey Parker, *Europe in Crisis* (1979) is a new and excellent work on the period.

Mercantilism and Economic Growth	L. B. Packard, *The Commercial Revolution, 1400–1700* (1927), is the briefest reliable treatment of mercantilism. J. W. Horrocks, *Short History of Mercantilism* (1925), and P. W. Buck, *The Politics of Mercantilism** (1964), are somewhat longer studies. The fullest and best treatment is E. F. Heckscher, *Mercantilism*, 2 vols. (1935). H. Sée, *Modern Capitalism* (trans. 1928), is the best extensive discussion of the subject. F. L. Nussbaum, *History of the Economic Institutions of Modern Europe* (1933), summarizes the work of the great German historian of capitalism, W. Sombart. D. Hannay, *The Great Chartered Companies* (1926), is a good introduction to its subject. J. U. Nef, *Wars and Human Progress* (1950), argues that war is a detriment, not a stimulant, to technological and economic progress, particularly in this period. Up-to-date surveys of economic topics are available in C. Cipolla, ed., *The Fontana Economic History of Europe,** Vol. II (1974) and in Cipolla's own book, *Before the Industrial Revolution* (1976).
Expansion Overseas	In addition to the works cited for Chapter 18 on geographical discovery, the following are useful on special topics: B. H. M. Vlekke, *The Story of the Dutch East Indies* (1945); C. R. Boxer, *The Dutch Seaborne Empire* (1965); C. Gibson, *Spain in America* (1966); and H. A. Wyndham, *The Atlantic and Slavery* (1935). On the rivalry of France and England in America, the many fascinating volumes of F. Parkman dating from the 1860s are still worth reading, especially the earlier ones. G. M. Wrong, *The Rise and Fall of New France*, 2 vols. (1928), is the standard modern account. The *Cambridge History of India*, 5 vols. (1922–37), is useful for reference. Vol. IV of the *Cambridge Economic History of Europe* (1967) emphasizes overseas expansion.
France	J. Boulenger, *The Seventeenth Century** (trans. 1920), is a standard one-volume account in English. G. Treasure, *Seventeenth Century France** (1966), is a recent survey. F. C. Palm, *The Establishment of French Absolutism, 1574–1610* (1928), and P. R. Doolin, *The Fronde* (1935), are good special studies. Of the many books on Richelieu, the most trustworthy short account is C. V. Wedgwood, *Richelieu and the French Monarchy** (1962). C. J. Burckhardt, *Richelieu: His Rise to Power** (1964), is a solid piece of work. The French social structure is described in P. Goubert, *The Ancien Régime: French Society, 1600–1750** (1973).
England	The classic one-volume account, Whiggish in sympathy and brilliantly written, is G. M. Trevelyan, *England Under the Stuarts* (1904, 1946). The standard modern account is G. Davies, *The Early Stuarts, 1603–1660*, 2nd ed. (1959), in the *Oxford History of England* series. The detailed narrative history of S. R. Gardiner, published in eighteen volumes (1863–1903) and covering the years 1603 to 1656, is a major achievement of English historical scholarship to which all later accounts are indebted. C. V. Wedgwood has published three volumes of a history of the Puritan rebellion: *The King's Peace* (1955), *The King's War* (1958), and *A Coffin for King Charles* (1964). D. L. Keir, *The Constitutional History of Modern Britain, 1485–1937,** 4th ed. (1950), and J. R. Tanner, *English Constitutional Conflicts of the Seventeenth Century** (1928), together constitute a good introduction to some of the more technical constitutional issues of the period. There are many biographies of Cromwell, but the best is still C. H. Firth, *Oliver Cromwell and the Rule of the Puritans in England* (1900, 1925). W. Notestein, *The English People on the Eve of Colonization, 1603–1630** (1954), is a good introduction to the social history of the period, and B. Willey, *The Seventeenth Century Background** (1934), a good introduction to its intellectual history. A. S. P. Woodhouse, ed., *Puritanism and Liberty* (1951), is a selection of sources illustrating the ferment of democratic ideas during the rebellion. See also W. Haller, *The Rise of Puritanism** (1938); M. Walzer, *The Revolution of the Saints** (1965); and L. Stone, *The Crisis of the Aristocracy, 1558–1642** (1967). For a vivid introduction to the social history of seventeenth-century England, see P. Laslett, *The World We Have Lost,** 2nd ed. (1971).
Germany	There are good chapters on the Thirty Years' War in Ogg and Friedrich (first section, above), and in H. J. Grimm, *The Reformation Era* (1973), and H. Holborn, *A History of Modern Germany: The Reformation* (1959). Far and away the best general account in English is C. V. Wedgwood, *The Thirty Years War** (1938). The scholars' argument over how destructive the war was may be followed in S. H. Steinberg's criticism of Wedgwood in *History*, Vol. XXXII (1947), pp. 89–102. T. K. Rabb, ed., *The Thirty Years' War** (1964), gives readings on the causes and effects of the war. The Swedish phase of the war is well described by M. Roberts, *Gustavus Adolphus* (1953–58). J. Polišenský, *The Thirty Years War* (1971), examines the social effects of the war, especially in Bohemia. For a wider treatment of the period see Robert W. J. Evans, *The Making of the Hapsburg Monarchy* (1979).

20 Absolutism and Constitutionalism 1660–1715

During the latter half of the seventeenth century France was the leading nation in Europe. Its population was twice that of Spain and over four times that of England. Its land was fertile and its commerce and industry were growing.

FRANCE UNDER LOUIS XIV

There were no disturbing arguments over forms of government; absolute monarchy was accepted by almost all Frenchmen as necessary, reasonable, and right. By the Peace of the Pyrenees (1659) the French army had displaced the Spanish as the strongest military machine on the Continent. As time went on, it seemed as if not only French generals, French military engineers, and French diplomatists but also French architects, painters, dramatists, and philosophers were the best in Europe. French fashions in dress dominated the Continent; the French language became the leading language of diplomacy and polite conversation, and the French court with its elaborate etiquette and ceremonial became the model for countless smaller courts throughout Europe.

As Florence had been the nerve center of the Italian Renaissance and Spain of the Catholic Reformation, so France was the nerve center of late–seventeenth-century politics, diplomacy, and culture.

How much of this predominance is to be attributed to the long reign of Louis XIV is one of those questions that historians can speculate about but never answer. No one doubts that French (and European) history would have run in different channels had Louis never lived—or had he not lived so long. He was born in 1638, became king in 1643, took the reins of power into his own hands in 1661 at twenty-three, and died in 1715 at the age of seventy-seven, leaving the throne to his great-grandson. By temperament and training Louis was the very incarnation of divine-right monarchy—the idea that hereditary monarchy is the only divinely approved form of government, that kings are responsible to God alone for their conduct, and that subjects should obey their kings as the direct representatives of God on earth. In an age that put its trust in absolute rulers, the achievements of the French people at the peak of their greatness cannot be separated from the personality of their ruler, even if it can be proved that many

447

The emblem of the Sun King.

of those achievements were unrelated to, or even accomplished in spite of, the ruler.

Louis is said to have remarked, "I am the state." Even if the remark is apocryphal, the words reveal more of the true importance of his reign than anything else he said or wrote. Louis XIV set out early in his reign to personify the concept of sovereignty. He dramatized this aim immediately after Mazarin's death by ordering his ministers thereafter to report to him in person, not to a "first minister."

To be the real head of a large and complicated government required long, hard work, and Louis paid the price. His education was poor, and he had little imagination, no sense of humor, and only a mediocre intelligence. But he had common sense, a knack of picking up information from others, and a willingness to work steadily at the business of governing. "If you let yourself be carried away by your passions," he once said, "don't do it in business hours." Painstakingly he caught up all the threads of power in his own hands. All major decisions were made in four great councils, which he attended regularly. These decisions were then carried out by professional "secretaries" at the head of organized bureaucracies. In the provinces, the *intendants* more and more represented the direct authority of the central government in justice, finance, and general administration. The old French monarchy imposed its authority through judicial decisions and had frequently consulted local and central assemblies. The new monarchy, begun by Richelieu and perfected by Louis XIV, imposed its authority through executive decisions. Louis reduced the importance of the *parlements*, never summoned the Estates General, and, so far as such a thing was humanly possible in his century, built a government that was himself.

Colbert and the Economy

Colbert, Louis XIV's Controller General of Finance, systematically ordered the economic life of the country under royal direction. He was an extreme mercantilist; everything he did was consciously or unconsciously meant to strengthen the country for war. He set up high protective tariffs to help home industry, fostered new export industries, encouraged the French colonies in Canada and the West Indies, and did everything he could to develop a powerful navy and a strong merchant marine. Some historians suspect that his minute regulation of industry and commerce did more to hinder than to help the French economy. But until the burden of foreign wars became heavy in the 1680s, national production and wealth were increasing. Colbert also cut down waste and corruption in the collection of taxes, as Sully had once done, but he was unable to make the burden of taxation much more equitable because of the exemptions held or purchased by members of the nobility and the bourgeoisie, the classes best able

Louis XIV on the Duties of a King   1661

During the early period of his direct rule, Louis XIV prepared notes for the instruction of his son in the art of ruling. He had assistance in this task, and the texts do not necessarily give his exact words. They do express his ideas.

I have often wondered how it could be that love for work being a quality so necessary to sovereigns should yet be one that is so rarely found in them. Most princes, because they have a great many servants and subjects, do not feel obliged to go to any trouble and do not consider that if they have an infinite number of people working under their orders, there are infinitely more who rely on their conduct and that it takes a great deal of watching and a great deal of work merely to insure that those who act do only what they should and that those who rely tolerate only what they must. The deference and the respect that we receive from our subjects are not a free gift from them but payment for the justice and the protection that they expect to receive from us. Just as they must honor us, we must protect and defend them, and our debts toward them are even more binding than theirs to us, for indeed, if one of them lacks the skill or the willingness to execute our orders, a thousand others come in a crowd to fill his post, whereas the position of a sovereign can be properly filled only by the sovereign himself.

. . . of all the functions of sovereignty, the one that a prince must guard most jealously is the handling of the finances. It is the most delicate of all because it is the one that is most capable of seducing the one who performs it, and which makes it easiest for him to spread corruption. The prince alone should have sovereign direction over it because he alone has no fortune to establish but that of the state.

From Louis XIV, *Memoires for the Instruction of the Dauphin*, ed. by Paul Sonnino (New York: Free Press, 1970), pp. 63–64.

to pay. During the crisis of Louis' last war an attempt was made to tax these upper classes in order to stave off bankruptcy, but the attempt set no precedent.

The Nobility

The most dangerous potential opponents of royal absolutism, as Louis XIV knew from his own experience during the Fronde, were the members of the nobility. Louis completed Richelieu's work of destroying the political power of the French nobility. He excluded the nobles completely from all responsible positions in government and cheapened their status by increasing their numbers. An army commission came to be almost the only major outlet for a noble's ambition, which meant that the nobles as a class generally constituted a war party at court. All important positions in Louis XIV's government, such as the secretaryships and intendancies, were filled by men of bourgeois or recently ennobled families. At the same time, he followed earlier precedents in enhancing the splendor of his court and the participation of the nobility in his splendor.

Louis did not attack the social privileges of the nobility; he used them to make the nobles utterly dependent on him. In 1683 he moved the court and government from the Louvre in Paris to Versailles, fifteen miles away. He had hated Paris since the riots of the Fronde, and now in the formal gardens and ornate chateaux of Versailles, which he had built on waste marsh at considerable cost of human lives and treasure, he felt at home. He also felt safe; Versailles was the first royal residence that was completely unfortified. At Versailles, the king lived in an utterly artificial atmosphere, as far removed from reality as Versailles was physically removed from the bustle of Paris. Here the great nobles were compelled to live. Here a ball seemed as important as a battle, and holding the

basin for the king's morning ablutions was a job as much to be coveted as commanding the king's armies. Instead of competing for political power, nobles squandered their fortunes and exhausted their energies in jockeying for social prestige.

The regular rectangular shapes of the gardens, the balanced classical lines of the baroque architecture, the bright glint of mirrors and chandeliers, all these seemed to symbolize and emphasize the isolation of Versailles from nature, from the French nation, from the real world. Through all this Louis moved with impassive dignity. Years of self-conscious practice in kingship had given him a kind of public personality—cool, courteous, impersonal, imperturbable—which carried out perfectly the artificiality of the little world at Versailles. At his death he left to his successors a privileged nobility shorn of all political power and responsibility, demoralized by the empty pleasures and petty intrigues of court life and uneasily aware of its uselessness. It was a dangerous legacy.

Religious Policy

The only other potential opponents of Louis' absolutism were religious groups. The king had his differences with several popes who disliked his Gallican principles, which stressed royal control over the Church in France. These quarrels, however, never led to a real breach. Louis was always a good Catholic in a formal sense. He disliked and persecuted the Jansenists, an austere group of Catholic "puritans" who emphasized the teachings of St. Augustine on original sin, the depravity of man, and the need for divine grace. They felt that the Jesuits were far too optimistic about man's ability to work out his own salvation, and far too ready to compromise with the world. Louis, whose confessors were Jesuits, thought the Jansenists subversive (they

The medal above, issued in 1661, celebrates Louis' accessibility to his subjects. The medal below was struck in 1685 to commemorate the restoration of military discipline in Louis' reign.

Cartoon of 1686 showing a "missionary" of the king (an armed dragoon) "converting" a Huguenot to Catholicism.

had been condemned by the pope) and impertinent (they disapproved of his numerous mistresses). After 1680, though never a particularly religious man, he seems to have become increasingly concerned about the fate of his own soul. When his queen, Maria Theresa, died in 1683, he gave up his mistresses and secretly married Madame de Maintenon, a

pious Catholic whose parents were Huguenots. In 1685 he shocked Protestant Europe by revoking the Edict of Nantes, by which Henry IV had granted religious toleration to the Huguenots.

There were about a million Huguenots out of a total population of perhaps 18 million in France at the opening of Louis XIV's reign. After Richelieu deprived them of their military and political privileges, they had become good citizens and had remained loyal to the crown during the Fronde. Many were successful in industry and the professions, though few had attained the civil and military positions that were theoretically open to them. The French Catholic clergy had long tried to persuade Louis XIV that the continued exercise of the Protestant religion in France was an insult to his dignity and authority, and as the king became more concerned about his salvation the idea of atoning for his sins of the flesh by crushing heresy became more attractive to him. The Edict was "interpreted" more and more strictly. Protestant children were declared of age at seven and converted to Catholicism, and any attempt by their parents to win them back was punished by imprisonment. Money was offered to converts, Protestant chapels were destroyed, and troops were quartered on prominent Huguenots to make life miserable for them. Finally Louis, aided and abetted by his Jesuit advisers, announced that since all the heretics had finally been reconverted to Catholicism there was no further need for the Edict of Nantes, and it was therefore revoked. Protestant churches and schools were closed, and all Protestant children were baptized as Catholics. The Revocation was enforced by imprisonment, torture, and condemnation to the galleys, but many Huguenots continued to practice their faith in secret. Others fled to England, the Dutch Netherlands, Brandenburg, and the New World. The industry and skill of the 200,000 or so Huguenots who escaped contributed appreciably to the economic life of their new homes. To France the Revocation brought both economic and moral loss.

There were only two other examples of such brutal treatment of religious minorities in the seventeenth century: the

Bishop Bossuet on Absolutism

Jacques Bénigne Bossuet was tutor to Louis XIV's son in the 1670s.

The royal power is absolute. With the aim of making this truth hateful and insufferable, many writers have tried to confound absolute government with arbitrary government. But no two things could be more unlike. . . . The prince need render an account of his acts to no one. . . . Without this absolute authority the king could neither do good nor repress evil. . . . God is infinite, God is all. The prince, as prince, is not regarded as a private person: he is a public personage, all the state is in him; the will of all the people is included in his. As all perfection and all strength are united in God, so all the power of individuals is united in the person of the prince. What grandeur that a single man should embody so much! . . . Behold this holy power, paternal and absolute; behold the secret cause which governs the whole body of the state, contained in a single head: you see the image of God in the king, and you have the idea of royal majesty. God is holiness itself, goodness itself, and power itself. In these things lies the majesty of God. In the image of these things lies the majesty of the prince.

From Jacques Bénigne Bossuet, "Politics Drawn from the Very Words of Scripture," in *Readings in European History*, ed. by James Harvey Robinson (Boston: Ginn, 1906), Vol. II, pp. 275–76.

systematic impoverishment and degradation of the Irish Catholics by their English conquerors, and the ruthless suppression of Bohemian Protestantism by the Habsburgs. But in both these cases, unlike that of France, national hatred complicated religious differences. The Revocation of the Edict of Nantes was an anachronistic act of religious intolerance that gained Louis XIV little and lost him much.

Arts and Literature

To dramatize his conception of kingship and to underscore the dependence on the monarch of all other persons and institutions in the state, Louis chose as his emblem Apollo, the sun god. The symbol of the sun, on whose rays all earthly life is dependent, was worked into the architecture and sculpture of the palace of Versailles. The Sun King patronized the arts and gave historians some reason to call his reign the "Augustan Age" of French culture. As befitted such a patron, the prevailing taste was classical, insisting on form, order, balance, and proportion. The ideals of literature and art were "order, neatness, precision, exactitude"—and these were presumed to be the ideals of all reasonable men of all ages.

Pierre Corneille (1606–84) was the father of French classical tragedy. In 1636 he had written *Le Cid*, the first of his powerful dramas that glorified will power and the striving for perfection. Corneille was still writing when Louis XIV began his personal reign, but he was soon eclipsed by his brilliant younger contemporary, Jean Racine (1639–99). Racine wrote more realistically about human beings in the grip of violent and sometimes coarse passions, bringing French tragedy to its highest point of perfection in the years between 1667 and 1677. Then he underwent a religious conversion and renounced playwrighting as an immoral occupation. Some who thrilled to his and Corneille's tragedies had little respect for the comedian Molière (1622–73), but Molière's wit and satire became the unsurpassable model for future French dramatists. From 1659 to his death in 1673 he was the idol of audiences at Versailles. All three playwrights concentrated on portraying types, not individuals—the hero, the man of honor violently in love, the miser, the hypocrite—embodiments of human passions and foibles who belonged to no particular time or place. As a result, French classical drama of the age of Louis XIV could be understood and appreciated by people everywhere, and French taste in writing came to be the dominant taste of other countries as well. So it was with architecture and the other arts. The baroque style, which ruled the design and decoration of the palace of Versailles, was intelligible and exportable. French artistic and literary standards became the standards of cultivated Europeans everywhere.

Caricature of Molière as an actor.

Engraving of a performance of *Le Malade imaginaire*, Molière's last play (1673). Molière died on stage on the fourth night of the performance.

The Wars of Louis XIV

Richelieu and Mazarin had begun the process of strengthening the French army, but French military power reached its peak under Louis XIV. Le Tellier and his son Louvois were the ministers of war for almost fifty years. They subordinated the aristocratic officer class to the royal authority, developed a supply system, coordinated infantry and artillery, and, like Gustavus Adolphus, supplied the soldiers with uniforms. Vauban, one of the great military engineers of history, invented the fixed bayonet and perfected the art of building—and of destroying—fortifications. All in all, Louvois provided his master with the largest and best-equipped army in Europe: one hundred thousand men in peace and up to four hundred thousand in war.

Strengthening the army provided the king with great temptations to use his power in foreign wars. War would please the nobles, who profited by it and who had little outlet for their ambitions at home. War would exercise and justify the enormous standing army. Above all, successful war would enhance the glory of the monarch, raise him still further above his subjects, and perhaps make him the arbiter not only of France but of Europe as well. No one better than Louis XIV exemplified a nineteenth-century historian's dictum, "All power tends to corrupt, and absolute power corrupts absolutely." For half a century Europe was ravaged by wars that were caused by Louis' desire to maintain French prestige and increase French territory. As Louis' thirst for power grew, so did his enemies' fear of him.

The aims of Louis' earlier wars were relatively limited and understandable. With Spain's power broken and the Empire in a state of collapse, he wanted to annex the Spanish Netherlands (later Belgium), Franche-Comté, and bits of western German territories. He fought two wars for these objectives, but each time, after early victories, he found himself thwarted by an alliance of other powers. By 1678 he had gained only Franche-Comté and a few border towns in Flanders.

For a time Louis tried legal chicanery in place of bullets to gain more territory. French courts called Chambers of Reunion were set up to "reunite" to France any land that at any time had been a dependency of a French territory. This process gave Louis control of the independent Protestant republic of Strasbourg in 1681, and it was long before European indignation subsided or Strasbourg became a contented part of France. The Revocation of the Edict of Nantes in 1685 was further evidence to European

The palace at Versailles (1668). Louis XIV is shown arriving in a carriage.

statesmen of Louis' intemperance, and in 1686 the defensive League of Augsburg was formed by the emperor, Spain, Sweden, and several German states. Europe was already at war when William of Orange, ruler of the Dutch Netherlands and Louis' most implacable enemy, became King William III of England in 1689. The circle was closed around France when the English and the Dutch joined the League.

This time France was on the defensive. At the very outset, in 1688, the French united their enemies by perpetrating one of the most senseless atrocities of the century, the systematic devastation of the Palatinate for no good political or military reason just before the occupying French troops withdrew. The War of the League of Augsburg was waged in India and America as well as in Europe, so it may be called the first of the modern world wars. After ten years of fighting, France agreed to the Peace of Ryswick (1697), by which France managed to retain its gains up to 1678 but was forced to renounce nearly all accessions after that date except Strasbourg. England came out of the war considerably stronger as a naval and military power; France came out of it a weaker power than it had been a decade earlier.

The War of the Spanish Succession, 1701–14

At the turn of the century all the fears and hatreds that had been built up during a generation of fighting were concentrated in a fourth struggle, the War of the Spanish Succession (1701–14). This war, like that of 1688 to 1697, was fought in America and India as well as in Europe. In its origins and its course, the older motives of dynastic ambition and preservation of the balance of power were mixed with the newer motives of commercial advantage and national sentiment. Religion now played no important part whatever.

In 1698 Charles II of Spain, who had for thirty years been a kind of walking medical exhibit of half a dozen fatal diseases, was finally dying. He was the last of the Habsburgs who had ruled Spain since 1516, and he had no direct heirs. The question was whether the Spanish

THE CONQUESTS OF LOUIS XIV 1661–1715

ENGLISH CHANNEL

ARTOIS
PICARDY
NORMANDY
ILE DE FRANCE
CHAMPAGNE
ALSACE
BRITTANY
MAINE
ORLÉANAIS
NIVERNAIS
BURGUNDY
FRANCHE-COMTÉ
ANJOU
TOURAINE
BERRY
POITOU
BOURBON-NAIS
AUNIS
MARCHE
LYONNAIS
SAINT-ONGE
ANGOUMOIS
LIMOUSIN
AUVERGNE
DAUPHINY
GUYENNE AND GASCONY
LANGUEDOC
ORANGE
C. OF VENAISSIN
PROVENCE
NAVARRE
BÉARN
FOIX
ROUSSILLON
MEDITERRANEAN SEA

France before 1668
Acquisitions by the Treaty of Aix-la-Chapelle, 1668
Acquisitions by the Treaty of Nimwegen, 1678
Acquisitions by the Treaty of Utrecht, 1713

0   MILES   100

Empire would fall to some member of the Austrian Habsburg family or to some member of the French Bourbon dynasty (both Louis XIV's mother and first wife had been Spanish Habsburg princesses) or would be partitioned or dismembered in some way. The English and the Dutch had obvious reasons for keeping France from gaining control of the Spanish colonial trade or of the Spanish Netherlands. Louis seemed willing to compromise and twice concluded secret treaties with the English and the Dutch to partition the Spanish dominions, but when news of the second treaty reached Madrid the dying king lost his temper. In order to preserve the Spanish Empire intact as a bulwark of Catholicism, he made a will leaving all his dominions to a grandson of Louis XIV. This grandson was proclaimed King Philip V of Spain shortly after the death of Charles II in November 1700.

Louis XIV soon decided to tear up the treaties by which he had accepted a more modest share of the Spanish Empire. He recognized the will of Charles II and sent French troops into the Spanish Nether-

Officer and musketeer of the French Guard (late seventeenth century).

lands. In 1701 William III of England concluded the Grand Alliance of the Hague by which the English, the Dutch, and the Austrian Habsburg emperor bound themselves to fight until they had ended the threat of Bourbon control of Spain and of the Spanish colonies. Louis XIV had made his last and most arrogant bid for the dominance of Europe, but this time he was forced to fight for France's life against enemies who proved as arrogant and unyielding as he. War was now a much more organized and professional use of force. Soldiers were rigidly disciplined, regimental offiers were experienced commanders and not heroic but untrained nobles, and coordination of infantry, cavalry, and artillery had greatly improved the allied forces. Under the brilliant command of Prince Eugene of Savoy and the English Duke of Marlborough, within a few years the allied armies had beaten the French in four bloody battles (Blenheim, 1704; Ramillies, 1706; Oudenarde, 1708; Malplaquet, 1709). The English navy had trounced the French at sea, and the English had seized Gibraltar. An allied army had even dethroned Philip V in Spain for a time.

Louis XIV, his country exhausted, sued for peace on almost any terms, only to be met by an allied demand that he contribute French troops to expel his own grandson from Madrid. This was too much for even a badly beaten monarch, and he refused, backed by a rising tide of national feeling in France. A similar national reaction in Spain in favor of their new Bourbon monarch, Philip V, resulted in the defeat of English and Austrian troops there. In 1710 a victory of the Tories over the Whigs, who had been the war party in England, brought in a government in London favorable to peace. And finally in 1712 the French won their only important victory of the war. In the end the allies paid the price for asking too much from Louis at the moment when he was almost helpless. The Peace of Utrecht (1713–14), which settled the war, was somewhat more favorable to France than it might have been if it had been signed four years earlier. Here at the very end of his career, the balance of power seemed to work in Louis XIV's favor by preventing the elimination of France from the ranks of the great powers.

The Peace of Utrecht, 1713–14

In theory, the Peace of Utrecht gave the French the prize that they had sought at the beginning of the war. Philip V remained on the throne of Spain, but only on condition that the crowns of Spain and France should never be worn by the same monarch. In every other aim, however, the French were thwarted. They gave up all conquests east of the Rhine, failed to win the Spanish Netherlands, and lost their bid for control of the Spanish colonial trade. England was the chief winner. England took Newfoundland, Acadia (modern New Brunswick and Nova Scotia), and Hudson's Bay Territory from France, and Gibraltar and Minorca from Spain. In addition, the English received the *Asiento*—the right to supply black slaves to the Spanish colonies, a privilege that proved very lucrative and provided an excuse for a large-scale smuggling trade with the Spanish Empire.

England came out of the war rich and powerful, in a position to dominate international commerce and with the strongest navy in Europe. France came out of it still a great nation, but with its people badly exhausted by high taxation and its government bankrupt and unpopular. The Austrian Habsburgs gained by being given the Spanish Netherlands (which now became the Austrian Netherlands), as well as Milan, Naples, and Sicily. Austria thus replaced Spain as the dominant power in Italy. Two new smaller powers, Brandenburg-Prussia and the Duchy of Savoy, came out of the war with increased territories and heightened prestige as a reward for having been on the winning side. A century and a half later Prussia was to unify Germany, and Savoy, as the Kingdom of Sardinia, was to take the lead in the unification of Italy. The Dutch kept the Scheldt River closed, thus blocking the trade of Antwerp, the chief port of the Austrian Netherlands. But they had suffered from the long strain of fighting against the French for half a century and were soon to disappear from the ranks of the great powers.

The Peace of Utrecht ended the first attempt by a European state to establish an overwhelming predominance of power since the days of Philip II of Spain. When Louis XIV died in 1715, rulers outside France breathed a sigh of relief; it was even said that the common people of his own land "openly returned thanks to God." His bid for European hegemony had been defeated by the workings of the balance-of-power principle, but the seeds of future war were unfortunately still deep in the European soil.

ENGLAND: THE EMERGENCE OF A PARLIAMENTARY MONARCHY

While Louis XIV was putting the finishing touches on the institution of absolute monarchy in France, the English, without any very clear idea of where they were headed, were completing the foundation of a constitutional monarchy controlled by Parliament.

The restoration of the king, Parliament, and the Anglican Church in 1660 had established a kind of equilibrium between the crown and Parliament, but it was soon evident that it was a very unstable balance. Who was really to control the government—the king or the wealthy landowners and merchants who dominated Parliament? What was the religious settlement to be, and who was to have the last word in making it? Who was to control foreign policy? These three main questions of the past two generations— the questions of politics, religion, and foreign policy—still awaited final answers. It took almost two more generations of domestic intrigue and foreign war for the answers to be found.

Charles II, 1660–85

Charles II was quite unlike his father—witty, worldly-wise, attractive, a man of easy morals and shrewd political sense. He had lived long in exile in France, and his cousin Louis XIV was his model. He would have liked to restore England to Catholicism and to set up an absolute monarchy on the French model, but he was too intelligent to ignore the difficulties in his way and too cautious to persist in the face of determined opposition. He was resolved not to risk exile or execution. He knew that if his goal was to be reached, it would be by intrigue, manipulation, and compromise, not by force or by open proclamation of his aims. The result was twenty-five years of infinitely complex party politics and secret diplomacy in which the issues were never very clear to the people or to the members of Parliament, or even to the king's ministers.

Cavalier Parliament, 1661–79

Parliament held a commanding position at the beginning of the reign. The "Cavalier Parliament," which met in 1661 and was not dissolved until 1679, was dominated by the landed nobility and gentry, who were now restored to their ancient influence in both local and national government. Both groups were strongly royalist for the moment, both determined to stamp out all remnants of religious and political radicalism. But at the same time they were not willing to see the crown recover any real financial independence of Parliament. In place of the old idea that "the king should live of his own," Parliament now granted Charles a regular income from customs and excise duties, but it was not enough. Charles found that he could not meet even the ordinary expenses of government, let alone the expenses of his extravagant mistresses, from his regular revenue. And there was certainly no money for foreign war unless Parliament approved the objectives. So for a time at least, Charles had to let Parliament have its way under the leadership of his father's adviser, Edward Hyde, Earl of Clarendon.

Parliament also had the last word in the religious settlement. The Cavalier Parliament was as strongly pro-Anglican as it was pro-royalist. In a series of statutes passed between 1661 and 1665 and known as the "Clarendon Code," Puritans who dissented from the established church were excluded from local government and Puritan ministers were rooted out of the Anglican clergy. Later legisla-

The House of Commons, on the Great Seal of England (1651).

tion made it illegal for a dissenter to sit in Parliament, to serve in the army or navy, or to attend the universities at Oxford or Cambridge. Behind this attempt to discourage dissent was the fear that Puritans were inevitably political radicals. But while the Clarendon Code lowered the social position and narrowed opportunities for dissenters, it did not greatly decrease their numbers. Presbyterians, Congregationalists, Baptists, and Quakers (also Methodists a century later) formed permanent but peaceful minority groups. The dissenters remained antagonistic to the ruling Anglican majority, but they were even more bitterly opposed to Catholicism.

Charles did not like the Clarendon Code. He would have preferred a policy that tolerated both Puritans and Catholics, but Parliament would not stand for this. In 1672 Charles issued a "Declaration of Indulgence," which suspended the operation of the laws against both groups. But the next year Parliament forced him to withdraw the declaration and accept a severe Test Act excluding all but Anglicans from civil and military office. To the Anglican gentry in Parliament, Puritans were still radicals and Catholics still traitors.

Foreign Policy

Two natural calamities, an outbreak of plague in 1665 and a fire that destroyed much of London in 1666, contributed to general unrest. Uneasiness increased as king and Parliament drifted apart over foreign policy. In 1665 Parliament forced Charles into a commercial war with the Dutch but did not give him enough money to win it. When victories failed to develop, Clarendon was unfairly held responsible and was exiled. After Louis XIV began his attacks on the Spanish Netherlands in 1667, the ordinary Englishman began to see the military power of Catholic France as more of a threat than the commercial rivalry of the Protestant Dutch. But to Charles II, Louis was still the ideal ally—powerful, wealthy, and an old personal friend.

In 1670 England once more allied itself with France against the Dutch, and Charles negotiated with Louis one of the most notorious deals in the history of English foreign policy, the secret Treaty of Dover. By this agreement Charles promised to declare himself a Catholic and to reconvert England to Catholicism in return for French money and, if necessary, French troops. Probably Charles himself was not sure how far he meant to go, but at the least he was ready to adopt a pro-French foreign policy. Between 1675 and 1681 four more secret agreements were concluded between Charles and Louis in which Charles promised he would thwart Parliament's anti-French moves in return for subsidies from France. The close understanding between Charles and Louis leaked out and gradually built up English fears of Catholicism and French dominance. The landed classes represented in Parliament were

Pepys's Account of the Great Fire of London
September 2–6, 1666

The fire started near the river, spread to warehouses full of combustible materials, and destroyed most of the old city of London, including St. Paul's Cathedral. This gave Christopher Wren the opportunity to build his famous churches. Samuel Pepys was an eyewitness to the fire and recorded its events in his diary.

[Pepys heard of the fire and took a boat down the Thames.] Everybody was endeavoring to remove their goods, and flinging them into the river or bringing them into lighters; poor people staying in their houses till the fire touched them, and then running into boats. And the poor pigeons, I perceived, were loth to leave their houses, but hovered about the windows and balconys till they burned their wings and fell down. Nobody, to my sight, endeavoring to quench it, but only to remove their goods and leave all to the fire—the wind mighty high and driving it into the city and everything, after so long a drought, proving combustible, even the very stones of the churches.

[That evening Pepys and his wife went out on the river.] We went as near the fire as we could for smoke and all over the Thames; with one's face in the wind, you were almost burned with a shower of fire-drops. This is very true; so that houses were burned by these drops and flakes of fire [even when] three or four—nay five or six—houses from another. When we could endure no more at the water, we went to a little ale-house on the Bankside and there saw the fire grow . . . as far as we could see up the hill of the city, in a most horrible malicious bloody flame, not like the fine flame of an ordinary fire. We stayed till we saw the fire as only an entire arch of fire from this to the other side of [London] bridge and in a bow up the hill for an arch of above a mile long. It made me weep to see it—the churches, houses and all on fire and flaming at once, and a horrid noise the flames made, and the cracking of houses at their ruin.

From *The Diary of Samuel Pepys* (many editions), entry for September 2, 1666.

suspicious of Charles, increasingly less royalist in sentiment than they had been in 1661, and ready to give way to panic if any incident should excite their fear of France and popery.

Whigs and Tories

In 1678 these accumulated fears were fanned into flame by a lurid incident known to history as the Popish Plot. A thoroughly disreputable character named Titus Oates concocted a story, accepted by almost the whole country, that there was a Jesuit plot afoot to murder the king and put his Catholic brother James, the Duke of York, on the throne with French help—"a damnable and hellish plot," Parliament called it, "for assassinating and murdering the king and rooting out and destroying the Protestant religion." Civil war seemed about to break out again.

A "Country Party" led by the Earl of Shaftesbury campaigned at the polls and supported a bill to exclude the Duke of York from the succession to the throne. An Anglican and royalist "Court Party" rallied to the support of Charles II and his brother, though at first without very much enthusiasm. Members of the first group were called Whigs (a name hitherto applied to fanatical Scottish Presbyterians); members of the second group were called Tories (a name for Catholic outlaws in Ireland). The Whigs controlled the three brief Parliaments that followed the dissolution of the Cavalier Parliament in 1679, and innocent men went to their deaths for complicity in the Popish Plot. But the Whig leaders soon overplayed their hand; public opinion swung back in favor of the king, and it was now the turn of innocent Whigs to suffer. By 1681 Shaftesbury had fled abroad, the inventors of the Popish Plot were disgraced or executed, and Charles was stronger than ever before. Until his death four years later he ruled without Parliament, thanks to Louis' subsidies, with his brother James by his side.

The origin of political parties in the modern sense—groups organized for the purpose of electioneering and controlling government through a representative assembly—lies in these chaotic years of English history. Instead of civil war, the eventual outcome was the "two-party system," which came to be characteristic of English and American politics. Whigs and Tories were the remote political heirs of the Parliamentarians and royalists of the 1640s. In turn they became the ancestors of the Liberals and Conservatives, the Democrats and Republicans, of two centuries later.

James II, 1685–88

The Duke of York, who succeeded Charles II as James II in 1685, was a very different sort of person from his brother—a bigoted convert to Catholicism without any of Charles's political shrewdness or tendency to compromise. Within three short years (1685–88) he managed to infuriate almost every group of any importance in English political and religious life, and in the end he provoked the revolution that Charles had succeeded in avoiding. Made overconfident by early successes, he introduced Catholics into the high command of both army and navy and camped a standing army a few miles from London. He surrounded himself with Catholic advisers and attacked Anglican control of the universities. He claimed the power to suspend or dispense with acts of Parliament. In a vain attempt to win the support of Puritans as well as Catholics, he issued a Declaration of Indulgence along the lines of his brother's. By revoking borough charters and browbeating sheriffs he tried to ensure the election of a Parliament favorable to his policies. Louis XIV's Revocation of the Edict of Nantes in 1685 had already terrified Protestants in England. They held back as long as James's immediate heir (his older daughter) was a Protestant, but their fears became unbearable when the hope of a Protestant succession was suddenly destroyed by the unexpected birth of a son to James's Catholic queen.

The "Glorious Revolution" of 1688

In spite of the intense political tension, civil war did not break out in 1688 as it had in 1642. Englishmen still remembered the horrors of civil war, and this time there was only one side. James had literally no support of any signifi-

Engraving of James II, after a painting by Kneller (1688).

Contemporary engraving showing the speaker of the House of Lords offering William and Mary the English crown.

cance, except for a handful of personal friends. He had alienated both Anglicans and nonconformists, Tories and Whigs, nobles and common people. The result, therefore, was a bloodless "revolution," a thoroughgoing political overturn that, as historians look back on it, answered all the main questions of the century in favor of a limited, or parliamentary, monarchy and established the constitutional pattern of English public life that has persisted to the present time.

James II had two daughters by his first wife (Clarendon's daughter), both of whom remained Protestants. The elder, Mary, was married in 1677 to the *stadtholder* of the Dutch Republic, William of Orange, who was Louis XIV's outstanding Protestant opponent on the Continent. In June 1688 a group of prominent and representative Englishmen, both Whigs and Tories, invited William to cross the Channel and save the Protestant cause in England. In the following November William landed on the southern coast of England with a Dutch army and marched slowly on London. There was almost no resistance. James II fled to France, and a Convention Parliament (an irregular assembly of men who had had parliamentary seats) declared that James had "abdicated" the throne by his flight. It then invited William and Mary to become joint sovereigns. A "Bill of Rights" was passed and the "Glorious Revolution" was accomplished.

The chief result of the Revolution was the establishment of parliamentary sovereignty over the crown. Parliament had made a king and could regulate the right of succession to the throne. Though William was a strong-willed man, especially in matters of foreign policy, he realized, though reluctantly, that Parliament had the final say. And though the supporters of James II and his son intrigued and even staged two abortive rebellions in the eighteenth century, there was no second Restoration. Parliament could criticize, influence, and eventually make the government's policy.

The Bill of Rights emphatically denied the king's right to suspend acts of Parliament or to interfere with the ordinary course of justice. It furnished a base for the steady expansion of civil liberties in the generation after 1688. Religious toleration and freedom from arbitrary arrest were established by law; censorship of the press was quietly dropped. The king had to summon Parliament every year because he could not pay or control his armed forces without parliamentary consent. These regular meetings strengthened the parties and made the king dependent on their support. In 1707 the monarch vetoed a parliamentary bill for the last time.

Struggles for control of policy were now no longer between king and Parliament, but between factions in Parliament. The Revolution did not establish democracy, but it did establish control by the wealthy landed proprietors and merchants over both the central and local organs of English government. Generally speaking, the greater noble landowners, the bankers and the merchants, and most dissenters were Whigs, while the smaller gentry, the Anglican parish clergy, and some great lords were Tories. But parties were still loosely organized, and small factions with selfish interests often held the balance of power. England was governed by shifting alliances among leaders of the propertied classes.

The Cabinet System

It took over a century for parliamentary leaders to work out a smooth and efficient way to run the government. The ultimate answer was to be the "cabinet system"—that is, government by a committee of leaders of the majority party in Parliament, holding the chief executive offices in the government, acting under the leadership of a "prime minister," and acknowledging primary responsibility to Parliament rather than to the crown for their actions. During the reigns of William and Mary (1689–1702) and of Mary's sister, Queen Anne (1702–14), the first fumbling moves were made that led to such a system, though parliamentary leaders had as yet no sense of their goal, and monarchs still considered ministers to be responsible to them rather than to Parliament. The privy council had long been too large and unwieldy for effective action, so that a "cabinet council," or inner circle of important ministers, had developed under Charles II. The members of this "cabinet" slowly found that it was better to discuss major questions among themselves and to present a united front to the monarch on matters of policy. Sometimes a leading member of the "cabinet" was referred to as "prime minister." In order to gain Parliament's indispensable support in war or peace, both William and Anne occasionally found that it was better to choose their ministers not from both parties but from the majority party. By the time Queen Anne died in 1714 it had become evident that the real government of England was slowly falling into the hands of

a cabinet of ministers who controlled a parliamentary majority, often by bribery, and felt themselves ultimately responsible to the political interests of this majority.

Religious Toleration

The Revolution also produced a certain measure of religious toleration. Broad-mindedness was becoming fashionable in educated circles, and both Anglicans and Puritans were now more afraid of Catholic France than they were of each other. Puritans had supported Anglicans against James II, and King William, who came from the most tolerant country in Europe, insisted on a religious truce. The result was the "Toleration Act" of 1689, which allowed dissenters to worship as they pleased and to educate their clergy and laity in schools of their own. Dissenters were still legally excluded from all civil and military offices, however, and there was no repeal of the long series of anti-Catholic statutes, although they were not enforced with any great rigor after 1689. Protestant fear that a Catholic might succeed to the throne was finally quieted by the Act of Settlement of 1701, which provided that the sovereign should always be an Anglican. The act also settled the succession, in case James II's two daughters should die without children, on the descendants of that daughter of James I who had married the ill-fated Elector of the Palatinate before the Thirty Years' War. In this way the elector of Hanover came to the throne in 1714, when Queen Anne died without issue, thus bringing the Stuart dynasty to a close.

Growth of English Power

A third result of the Revolution was to unite crown and Parliament on foreign policy as they had never been united under the first four Stuarts, and thus to turn the energies of a generation of Englishmen from domestic conflict to foreign war. Given English fear of Catholicism, King William had no difficulty bringing England into the Grand Alliance against Louis XIV, who was sheltering James II in exile. Parliamentary monarchy soon demonstrated that it was a more formi-

Medal of Queen Anne (1702–14), and her signature.

One hundred drown'd in a River.

Boys forced to kill the Proteſtants.

Anti-Catholic woodcuts showing "horrors" of the rebellion by Irish Catholics (1689).

dable foe than the absolute monarchy of the Stuarts had been. The English government was able to raise money to fight its wars in a way that was barred to all other European governments except the Dutch. The founding of the Bank of England in 1694 was an important event in the history of English public finance. Within a few days of its founding, it had raised over a million pounds of investors' money that it promptly lent to the government at 8 percent interest. So long as the government continued to pay the interest, the bank made no demand for repayment of this loan. Thus the present permanent, or "funded," national debt began. The merchants and tradesmen, large and small, who invested their money in the bank obviously had confidence in the government, and their investment bound them still more firmly to support the revolutionary settlement.

Throughout the next century English wealth combined with English sea power was to give the island kingdom a striking power out of all proportion to its area and population. During the reigns of William and Mary and of Anne, trade, which was more and more the foundation of English wealth, increased considerably. The Peace of Utrecht (1713) gave English sea power, the guarantor of English trade, an almost unrivaled position. The solution in 1689 of the chief political

and religious differences between crown and Parliament touched off an almost explosive release of English energies that by 1763 had rocketed England to the hegemony of Europe.

Ireland and Scotland

The Revolution also did something to further the unification of the British Isles, though indirectly. England, Ireland, and Scotland all had the same king from 1603 on, but union went no further than the common crown. The two smaller kingdoms, especially Ireland, suffered greatly during the seventeenth century through involvement in England's religious and political divisions. The native Irish were Catholic to a man, and the Protestant English both despised them and feared them as potential allies of the Catholic Spanish and French. By settling Protestant colonists in Ulster, James I began the policy of creating a Protestant majority in the northeastern region of Ireland. But the Ulster Protestants were Presbyterians and soon became anti-Stuart, while the rest of the Irish were generally loyal to the Stuart dynasty, and for that reason suffered cruelly under Cromwell. After the Revolution, James II tried to fight his way back to his throne by way of Ireland. He was defeated at the Battle of the Boyne (1689), an event whose memory still stirs up bitter feelings between Catholics and Protestants in Ulster. James's defeat led to a savage and systematic persecution of the Catholic Irish by English (and Irish) Protestant landlords, comparable only to Louis XIV's brutal treatment of the Huguenots. The Irish were exploited and bled white economically, their priests were persecuted, and their Parliament was reserved for Protestants only.

The Scots had somewhat better fortune in the end, although they too suffered by being involved in England's troubles through the century. Scotland had gained little by giving a king to England in 1603. It remained a poor but proud neighbor of a larger kingdom, excluded from the benefits of English trade, jealously guarding its own law and its own Parliament, and firmly defending its Presbyterian Church against Anglican attacks. Although it had been the Scots who touched off the revolution against Charles I, there was strong attachment to the native Stuart dynasty in Scotland, especially among Catholic clansmen of the Highlands. After 1649 and again after 1689 Scotland became a base for risings in support of the Stuarts. The Scots accepted the Revolution of 1688, but they did not accept the Act of Settlement of 1701. They threatened to choose a separate king of their own—possibly the exiled pretender James II—in case James's last daughter, Anne, died without issue. This frightened the English into serious negotiations. In 1707 an organic union between the two kingdoms was finally agreed on and was confirmed by an Act of Union. Scotland retained its own law and its established Presbyterian religion, but it surrendered its separate Parliament in return for representation in the English Parliament. Scottish nationalists were (and still are) angry over their loss of independence, but Scotland gained much in the next century by becoming an integral part of the Kingdom of Great Britain. Scottish merchants, administrators, and philosophers were to play a prominent part during the eighteenth century in building the British Empire and in furthering the Enlightenment.

John Locke

The Revolution of 1640 and the Glorious Revolution of 1688 together constituted the first of those revolutions in modern western states that ended absolute divine-right monarchy and eventually put the middle classes in control of government. English leaders did their best to insist to the outside world in 1688 and 1689 that they were doing nothing new or revolutionary at all, but they never succeeded in persuading foreigners that they were merely conservative supporters of ancient English liberties. Europe was more interested in the interpretation of the Revolution by John Locke (1632–1704), a friend of the Earl of Shaftesbury, the founder of the Whig Party. In *Of Civil Government: Two Treatises* (1690), Locke set down in plain, common-sense fashion the general principles underlying the long English strug-

gle for limited monarchy that culminated in the Revolution of 1688. Even if the logic was not always clear, the reasonableness of the discussion had great influence throughout the eighteenth century.

Locke directed his attack explicitly against the divine-right theory of monarchy, and implicitly against the more pragmatic absolute theory of Thomas Hobbes. He began with the rights to "life, liberty, and property," which he said all men possess naturally, and went on to insist that the sole reason for establishing any government is to preserve these rights. Legislative and executive powers are to be strictly separated; if the executive becomes tyrannical and invades the rights of individuals, the people must curb it through their representative assembly—or if all else fails, they may revolt and set up a new government. In other words, an ultimate right of revolution always resides in the people, and the dissolution of government does not necessarily mean the dissolution of society. Locke's book was probably written before 1688 as a sort of program for revolution, but it was not published until after the Revolution and so naturally became a kind of apology for what had been done. Inalienable rights, government by consent, separation of powers,

John Locke (1632–1704), champion of the "natural" rights of man.

Locke on Government by Consent   1690

Compare "Bishop Bossuet on Absolutism," p. 450.

Men being, as has been said, by nature all free, equal, and independent, no one can be put out of this estate and subjected to the political power of another without his own consent, which is done by agreeing with other men, to join and unite into a community for their comfortable, safe, and peaceful living, one amongst another, in a secure enjoyment of their properties, and a greater security against any that are not of it. . . . When any number of men have so consented to make one community or government, they are thereby presently incorporated, and make one body politic, wherein the majority have the right to act and conclude the rest. . . . Absolute, arbitrary power, or governing without settled standing laws, can neither of them consist with the ends of society and government, which men would not quit the freedom of the state of Nature for, and tie themselves up under, were it not to preserve their lives, liberties, and fortunes, and by stated rules of right and property to secure their peace and quiet.

From John Locke, *Of Civil Government: Two Treatises* (New York: Everyman's Library, 1924), pp. 164–65, 186.

NORTH SEA
Copenhagen
Hamburg
London
Amsterdam
Berlin
Warsaw
Cologne
Elbe
Paris
Prague
Vienna
Geneva
Buda
Venice
ADRIATIC SEA
Belgrade
MEDITERRANEAN SEA
Rome

The crown of the Holy
Roman Empire of the
German Nation, used from
961 to 1792.

the right of revolution—these were the ideas that Locke implied were at the heart of the Glorious Revolution. These were the ideas that seemed self-evident truths to Americans in 1776 and to Frenchmen in 1789 and that formed a link between the English, the American, and the French revolutions.

CENTRAL AND
EASTERN EUROPE
1648–1721

The economy of early modern Europe was divided into two sharply defined halves by an imaginary line running north from the head of the Adriatic Sea, around the Bohemian mountains, and down the Elbe River to the North Sea. West of this line was an area that was increasingly affected by the growth of towns and trade. The majority of the population still lived on the land, but most peasants were free workers and many of them small landowners. Most serfs in the West had become agricultural laborers for pay, and most feudal nobles had become landlords who hired labor for wages (particularly in England) or simply lived on rents. Though still a minority, the bourgeoisie were increasingly influential in society and politics.

East of the line was a society still largely agrarian and feudal, an area of few large towns and an insignificant bourgeoisie. Here in Hungary, Bohemia, Poland, Prussia, and Russia, the landed estates were larger and the landed nobility more powerful politically than in the West. During the sixteenth and seventeenth centuries the nobles of eastern Europe managed to reduce the great majority of the peasants to a state of serfdom in which the peasant was bound to the land and forced to work from two to five days a week for his lord. One reason for this drive to enslave the peasant was that grain prices were rising in western markets, and eastern landlords had every inducement to increase the production of their estates. Another reason was that the governments of eastern Europe were either dominated by nobles, as in Hungary and Poland, or favorable to the growth of serfdom because it supported the nobles

who served the state, as in Prussia and Russia. In western Europe, command of money was increasingly the key to power and influence; in the East, ownership of land and command of compulsory services were still the secrets of power.

Warfare was as common as in the West, and much more dangerous. States with no natural frontiers on the flat plains of central and eastern Europe could easily be wiped out. Modernized armies were needed, but such armies could be created only by strong, centralized administrations and supported only by effective tax systems. Neither centralization nor taxation was easy. Eastern rulers were facing roughly the same obstacles to the growth of centralized government that western rulers had faced two centuries and more earlier: a powerful landed nobility, a church that held itself above dynastic interests and owned a large portion of the wealth of the land, an agrarian economy with limited commerce and infant industries, a bourgeoisie still too small to bear the weight of heavy taxation, and an ignorant and exploited peasantry tied to the land and thus incapable of meeting the need of new industries for labor. To build a "modern" state in the face of these difficulties was beyond the capacities of all but the ablest rulers.

The Holy Roman Empire

The one large political organization bridging eastern and western Europe was the Holy Roman Empire. But although there was still an emperor, and a Diet, which met "perpetually" at Regensburg after 1663, the Empire was a political fiction. It had no central administration, no system of imperial taxation, no standing army, no common law, no tariff union, not even a common calendar. The Peace of Westphalia had recognized the sovereignty of the individual states, as well as the right of France and Sweden to take part in the deliberations of the Diet. In the welter of political units—free cities, ecclesiastical principalities, counties, margravates, and duchies, together with one kingdom (Bohemia)—that made up the Empire, almost every petty princeling fancied himself a Louis XIV and fashioned a court modeled as closely as possible on Versailles. Already the Empire fitted Voltaire's description a century later as "neither Holy, nor Roman, nor an Empire."

The ruling families of a few of the larger states—Bavaria, Saxony, Hanover, Brandenburg, and Austria—were trying hard to expand their territories by war or marriage and to gain royal titles. Augustus the Strong of Saxony, in addition to fathering (according to legend) more than three hundred children, managed to get himself elected king of Poland in 1696. In 1701 the Elector of Brandenburg obtained the emperor's consent to style himself king in Prussia. And in 1714 the Elector of Hanover became king of England. But only two great powers eventually grew out of the wreck of the Empire. These were Austria and Brandenburg-Prussia.

The Habsburgs and Austria

The attempt of Emperor Ferdinand II (1619–37) to revive and strengthen the Empire under Habsburg control was defeated in the Thirty Years' War. The Habsburgs thereafter turned to a policy that Ferdinand had also furthered: consolidating and expanding the hereditary lands of the family in Austria and the Danube Valley. Thus a centralized Habsburg monarchy might be developed that could hold its own with the states of the West. The Emperor Leopold I (1658–1705) was the chief architect of this policy, aided, and at times prodded, by some capable civil servants and one remarkable general, Prince Eugene of Savoy.

To weld a centralized monarchy together, Leopold had to reduce three separate areas—Austria, Bohemia, and Hungary—to some semblance of unity and obedience. In the Duchy of Austria and neighboring Tyrol, his lawyers were able to establish his ascendancy over a feudal nobility whose economic position was still strong. Bohemia, it will be remembered, had been reduced to obedience to Vienna early in the Thirty Years' War. A new nobility owing its titles to the Habsburg ruler replaced the old, and the crown of Bohemia, previously elec-

tive, was made hereditary in the Habsburg family in 1627.

The real problem was Hungary. Although the Habsburgs had usually been the elected monarchs of the kingdom since early in the sixteenth century, hardly a third of Hungary was actually in Habsburg hands. The rest was either directly or indirectly ruled by the Ottoman Turks. To establish their authority in Hungary, the Habsburg monarchs in Vienna had to deal not only with the powerful Hungarian nobility and the Hungarian Protestants but with the Turks and the French as well. The nobles were wealthy and unruly; the Protestants were numerous and inclined to side with the Turks against the Catholic Habsburgs. The Ottoman Empire was not the power it had been in the sixteenth century, but since 1656 it had been undergoing a revival under a vigorous line of grand viziers of the Kiuprili family, who in the 1660s began a new thrust up the Danube Valley directed at their old enemies, the Habsburgs. Louis XIV, also an inveterate enemy of the Habsburgs, allied himself with the Turks and Hungarian rebels against his Austrian foes. Thus building a monarchy in the Danube Valley was as much a foreign as a domestic problem.

The Siege of Vienna, 1683

The crisis came in 1683. In July of that year a Turkish army of more than one hundred thousand laid siege to Vienna. For two months the fate of Austria seemed to hang in the balance. Then volunteers began to flow in from all over the Continent to help the emperor in his extremity. The greatest pope of the century, Innocent XI, contributed moral and material aid, and King John Sobieski of Poland arrived with an army that helped rout the Turks by September. The retreat continued year after year as the impetus of Europe's last crusade carried on down the Danube Valley, until Eugene of Savoy broke Turkish military power at the battle of Zenta (1697).

The Peace of Carlowitz in 1699 gave the Habsburgs full control of Hungary. The Hungarian Protestants were crushed; many of them were executed for treason.

Emperor Leopold I (above) and Prince Eugene of Savoy, Habsburg commander, detail from a painting by Kupezky.

The castle of the Hohenzollerns (detail from a seventeenth-century engraving).

The landowning nobility was left in full control of its serfs and in possession of many of its old privileges, in return for recognizing the ultimate sovereignty of the chancellery at Vienna. The Habsburgs were thus content with what one historian calls "a loose framework of centralized administration." They left local administration much as they found it, but they had established a strong monarchy in the Danube Valley where none had existed before.

The Treaties of Ryswick (1697) and Carlowitz (1699) marked the appearance on the European stage of two new great powers: England and Austria. Each had risen in response to Louis XIV's bid to make himself the heir of Habsburg power in Spain and Germany. The two illustrated how diverse great powers could be in the seventeenth century: England, a parliamentary monarchy controlled by a commercial and landed aristocracy, its strength based on commerce and sea power; Austria, a bureaucratic monarchy with agriculture and a standing army its most conspicuous sources of strength. At about the same time two more powers were just beginning to appear, each as distinct and different as England and Austria. These were Brandenburg-Prussia and Russia.

The Rise of Brandenburg-Prussia

The story of the rise of the Hohenzollerns in northern Germany is somewhat parallel to that of the Habsburgs in the south, except that the Hohenzollerns started with less and had farther to go. Their achievements owed proportionately more to the genius and patience of one man, Frederick William (1640–88), called the Great Elector.

The Hohenzollerns had been margraves of Brandenburg since 1417 (a margrave was count of a "mark," or frontier province). To this small territory around Berlin they had added by inheritance two other areas: Cleves and some neighboring lands on the Rhine (1614), and the Duchy of Prussia on the Baltic coast to the northeast (1618). When the Thirty Years' War broke out there was nothing to suggest that the ruler of these three scattered territories had any

brighter future than a dozen other German princes. He was an Elector—that is, one of the seven princes who (theoretically) chose the emperor—and thus a member of the highest echelon of German princes. But his lands had no natural boundaries, no traditional ties with one another, poor soil, few resources, and sparse population, about a million and a half in all. Furthermore, they were especially hard hit by the Thirty Years' War. Swedish and Imperialist armies tramped back and forth across Brandenburg without hindrance. Berlin lost over half its population. And the Great Elector's dominions as a whole probably lost almost one-third of their people—a loss that took forty years to make up.

The Great Elector, 1640–88

Frederick William was twenty years old when he became Elector in 1640 during the later years of the Thirty Years' War. Though he was a devoted Calvinist, he nevertheless respected the Lutheranism of his subjects and was genuinely tolerant in an age of intolerance and fanaticism. The helplessness of Brandenburg during the war taught him that his first and foremost task must be the development of an army, and to this end he set himself with unrelenting effort.

"A ruler is treated with no consideration if he does not have troops and means of his own," he advised his son in 1667. "It is these, Thank God! which have made me considerable since the time that I began to have them."

In 1640 he had a poorly equipped and ineffective army of twenty-five hundred men. Before the end of the war in 1648 he had increased it to eight thousand and by his death in 1688 he had a peacetime force of thirty thousand which was once expanded in wartime to forty thousand. It was something of a miracle for a state with the meager population and resources of Brandenburg-Prussia to produce such a large, well-equipped, and well-trained standing army in so short a time. In forty years (1648–88) Brandenburg had become the strongest military power in Germany except for Austria. If there was any explanation, it was the single-minded devotion of the Great Elector to this goal and to any political, social, or economic policy that would help him reach it.

The first thing he had to do was to establish his authority over the Estates of Brandenburg and Prussia, which had almost complete control of taxation. In Brandenburg the Great Elector was strong enough to imitate the practice of the king of France by simply continuing to raise taxes that had once been granted by the Estates, which were never summoned again after 1653. In Prussia the townsmen were more stubborn and the Junkers (or nobles) more unruly. Their leaders turned to Poland for support, and Frederick soon had a fight on his hands. The fight ended only after he had executed the ringleaders of the resistance. In the end Frederick set up a taxation system for the support of his army that was common to all his territories, administered by civil servants of his own choosing, and independent of local control. The nobility were shorn of their power in the Estates and pressed into service to the Hohenzollern state as officers in the army. In return, the power of the Junkers over their serfs on their own estates was left untouched. Military strength, not social betterment, was the Great Elector's objective.

It could be argued, however, that much social betterment came indirectly from his building of a strong army, even if the Prussian peasants were sinking deeper into serfdom. The devastation of war was even worse than aristocratic oppression, and Frederick William protected a whole generation from invasion. He used his army as a weapon in diplomacy rather than in war by selling his support to one side or another in return for subsidies. The subsidies helped pay for the army, and the alliances seldom required much fighting. By pursuing this policy, the Great Elector and his immediate successors made substantial territorial gains. For example, by playing off Sweden against Russia, the Hohenzollerns gained Stettin and Pomerania in 1720. There was little sentiment and much shrewdness in this foreign policy, which showed its results in the steady growth of the army and the territorial expansion of the state.

Frederick William's economic policy was designed to develop his lands to the point where they could support his army without the need for foreign subsidies. He did much to revive and improve agriculture after 1648, and much to encourage industry and commerce. His tolerant policies made Brandenburg a haven for religious refugees—persecuted Lutherans, German Calvinists, and, above all, French Huguenots after the Revocation of the Edict of Nantes in 1685. These immigrants, together with Dutch, Swiss, and other newcomers, brought new skills in agriculture and industry, helped increase the population, and added considerably to the strength of the state. He welcomed even the more radical Protestant sects and the Jews, drawing the line only at admitting the Jesuits, whom he considered too intolerant.

The recognition of the Great Elector's son as King Frederick I in 1701 symbolized the appearance of a new power in Europe. Prussia (as the Hohenzollern lands came to be known) had devoted relatively more of its population, its resources, and its energies to military purposes than had any other German state during the later seventeenth century. It has been said that in Prussia the army created the state. The army was, in fact, the first institution common to all the Elector's lands, and its bureaus were the

Frederick William, the Great Elector, as a young man; painting by his contemporary Mathias Czwiczeic.

models for many organs of the later civil government. But while the needs of the army were especially important in Prussia, they played a significant role in the development of every great power in Europe except England.

Sweden

While Prussia was growing in strength, its neighbors, Sweden and Poland, were declining, for different reasons. Sweden had burst on the European horizon as a military power of first rank during Gustavus Adolphus' invasion of Germany (1631–32). During the latter part of the century the Baltic became a Swedish lake, and a Swedish empire grew up on both sides of the inland sea all the way from the Gulf of Finland to the North Sea. Copper, iron ore, and agriculture were the Swedes' chief resources, a technically superior musket their chief military advantage.

Swedish power, however, rested on shaky foundations. The country had a population of less than 2 million—not much larger than Prussia or the Dutch Republic. Its lines of empire were over-extended, and its enemies—from Russia and Poland to Prussia and Denmark—were hungry for revenge.

When young Charles XII (1697–1718) came to the throne, a coalition of Russia, Poland, and Denmark pounced on his Baltic territories. Charles XII proved to be a military genius and crushed his enemies in a series of lightning campaigns. But he became intoxicated by success and engaged in political adventures that far exceeded his country's resources. He marched deep into Russian territory and was totally defeated at Poltava in 1709. He failed to gain Turkish support, though he spent some years at the Ottoman court seeking an alliance. Finally, he lost his life in a raid on Norway in 1718. In the peace settlements of 1719 to 1721, the Swedish empire outside Sweden was divided among Hanover, Denmark, Prussia, and Russia. Sweden settled down gracefully enough in the eighteenth century to its earlier role of second-class power.

Poland

The case of Poland was quite different, though the results were somewhat similar. Poland, formed in 1386 by the union of the crowns of Poland and Lithuania, was, after Russia, the largest state in Europe. Polish prosperity and culture had reached their peak in the sixteenth century, when the Polish people, linked by their Roman Catholic religion to western Europe, had felt some of the effects of the Renaissance, the Protestant revolt, and the Catholic Reformation. By the beginning of the seventeenth century, however, economic and political decline had set in. The Polish monarchy had always been elective. Until about 1572 the nobles had usually elected the legal heirs of their monarchs, but after this they began to choose anyone whom they believed they could control. By 1700 the real power in Poland lay in the hands of the nobility. The monarchy was almost powerless, although petty German princes still sought election to gain the prestige of a royal title. The peasants were the most depressed in Europe, sunk deep in serfdom. There was almost no bourgeoisie, since the towns had not

THE BALTIC: A SWEDISH LAKE   1621–1721

Swedish territory, 1621-1721

Swedish gains and losses 1621-1721

MILES 0 — 300

ARCTIC OCEAN

TRONDHJEM, 1658-60

1645

KARELIA, 1617-1721

FINLAND

Bergen

Christiania

Viborg, 1721

BOHUS, 1658

ÖSEL, 1645

Stockholm

INGRIA, Narva 1617-1721

Novgorod

HALLAND, 1658

GOTHLAND, 1645

ESTONIA, 1561-1721

LIVONIA, 1629-1721

SCANIA, 1658

Riga

NORTH SEA

Moscow

Copenhagen

DENMARK

BALTIC SEA

Memel

Smolensk

Lübeck

Pillau, 1629-35

Königsberg

Vilna

Bremen

Hamburg

Danzig

Stettin

Elbing, 1629-35

Route of Charles XII

BREMEN-VERDEN, 1648-1719

Berlin

HITHER POMERANIA, 1648-1720

Dresden

Warsaw

POLAND

flourished. Political power was concentrated in the diet, which by now represented only the nobility, since representatives of the towns no longer dared to attend.

The diet was notorious for its futility; one negative vote (the *liberum veto*) could block any action. Moreover, by using the *liberum veto* any member might "explode" the diet—that is, dissolve the diet and wipe out everything it had done up to that moment. Of fifty-seven diets held in the century after 1652, all but nine were so "exploded"—one by a member who simply wanted to see what would happen. If legislation did succeed in running the gauntlet of this national assembly, there was still no way of getting it enforced in the provincial assemblies of lesser nobles or on the private estates of the landed barons. John Sobieski (1674–96), a native Pole of high integrity who made a serious effort to lead the country out of its weakness, was the last great king of Poland. After him the Polish crown became simply the prize of foreign intrigue, and Poland started down the path that led to extinction at the hands of more powerful neighbors at the end of the eighteenth century.

Russia

Throughout the seventeenth century there was no great power east of Sweden, Poland, and the Ottoman Empire. The Grand Duchy of Moscow had fallen on evil days after the death of Ivan the Dread in 1584. Disputes about the succession to the tsar's crown led to a "Time of Troubles," and the accession of the Romanovs, who were to rule Russia from 1613 to 1917, at first did little to strengthen the state. In the 1650s a near revolution was provoked by a reforming patriarch of the Orthodox Church, who ordered that the ritual and liturgy be revised in order to bring them closer to

the original Greek text of the Bible. This order exasperated vast numbers of the uneducated masses to whom the Slavonic texts were sacrosanct. For many years after, "Old Believers" resisted the official religious policy of the government in spite of executions and exile.

Russia was a victim state through most of the century, often unable to defend its frontiers against invading Swedes, Poles, and Turks, and still cut off from access to either the Baltic or the Black Sea. English merchants had made contact with Moscow in the 1550s through the White Sea, and German merchants were even more active in the capital. But while Russia absorbed some of the technology (especially the military technology) of the West, it remained relatively untouched by cultural changes in the rest of Europe. The Renaissance, the Reformation, and the scientific revolution, with all the ferment they brought to the West, remained almost unknown to the peoples living east of Catholic Poland.

Peter the Great, 1689–1725

In 1689 one of the most remarkable rulers in all European history came to power in Russia at the age of seventeen. He was a giant of a man, nearly seven feet tall (his enormous boots are still proudly preserved in the Kremlin), with large, skillful hands, inexhaustible energy, insatiable curiosity, and a hot temper. As a boy he had loved to play at war. He had also spent much of his time with the Dutch and Germans who lived in the "German Quarter" of Moscow, listening and learning. In these early years the great passion of his later life seems to have been born: to make Russia a great power by rapidly westernizing its technology, its civil and military institutions, and its popular customs. At his death in 1725 he had aggrandized, upturned, and

Medals celebrating the Treaty of Eternal Peace between Russia and Poland (1686). Above: King John Sobieski; below: personifications of Poland and Russia.

Peter the Great,
by Aert de Gelder.

exhausted his country and had earned the name by which he was to be known to later history: Peter the Great.

Peter's plans at first developed slowly. Using his old-fashioned army, he failed to capture Azov at the mouth of the Don from the Turks in 1695. Next year, after he had built a fleet on the river with Dutch help, Azov fell. Peter had learned a lesson: in order to build a navy and to modernize an archaic army, he would first have to learn a great deal from the West. From 1696 to 1698, thinly disguised as a private citizen, Peter visited Holland, England, and Germany. Here he learned how an utterly different society built its ships, made its munitions, ran its government, and conducted its diplomacy. He alternately shocked and amazed the Dutch and English who came to know him. Direct, spontaneous, and naive in temperament, he always had to try to do things for himself. He

worked in the shipyards, eagerly questioned everyone he met on western technology, and caroused through the night in drunken orgies with his Russian companions. He hired over seven hundred technicians of various sorts to return with him to Russia.

In Vienna word reached him of a revolt of the *streltsi*, the barbarous and undisciplined palace guard, which to Peter represented everything backward and reactionary about Russia. (The *streltsi* were in league with the "Old Believers" and were better at staging palace revolutions than at fighting an enemy.) Peter hastened back to Moscow and made a fearful example of the rebels, executing over a thousand of them and using torture on a scale that shocked even his countrymen, who were used to brutality. At the same time he forbade the wearing of beards and long robes by any Russian, as a sign of his determination to westernize even the personal habits and costumes of his subjects. His subjects wore beards because God was presumed to wear a beard and man was made in His image. But to Peter, beards symbolized the old Russia of reaction, rebellion, and religious fanaticism. The clean-shaven look was western. Typically, the tsar himself took a hand in shaving some of his courtiers.

There was nothing particularly original about what Peter did to reform the military, political, and social institutions of his country. He borrowed his ideas and techniques from what other statesmen were doing at the time in France, England, the Dutch Republic, Brandenburg, and Sweden. But his methods were more casual and informal, more brutal and ruthless, than were those of western countries.

An overwhelming defeat by the Swedes at Narva in 1700 spurred on Peter's efforts to improve his army. With the help of foreign officers and advisers he had trained a formidable force of over one hundred thousand by 1709, the year he annihilated Charles XII's forces at Poltava. At the time of his death the army numbered over two hundred thousand in a population of about 8 million. Years of warfare against the Turks were unsuccessful, and even Azov was lost

Peter the Great Tries to Westernize Russia

The Czar tried to reform fashions, or, to be more exact, dress. Until his time Russians had always worn long beards, which they cherished and preserved with great care. . . . The Czar, to reform that custom, ordered that gentlemen, merchants and all other subjects must each pay a tax of one hundred rubles a year if they wished to keep their beards. . . . Officials were stationed at the gates of the towns to collect that tax, which the Russians considered an enormous sin on the part of the Czar. . . . Many old Russians, after having their beards cut off, saved them to be placed in their coffins, fearing that they would not be allowed to enter heaven without their beards. . . . From the reform in beards, let us pass to that of clothes. Russian garments, like those of [other] Orientals were very long, reaching to the heel. The Czar issued an order abolishing that costume and commanding all the nobles and those who had positions at the court to dress in the French fashion. . . .

As for the rest of the people . . . a suit of clothes cut in the new fashion was hung at the city gates, with an order that everyone except peasants was to have their clothes made on this model. Those who entered the town with clothes in the old style were forced to kneel and have all the part of their garments that fell below the knee cut off. . . . Since the guards at the gates had a good deal of fun in cutting off long garments, the people were amused and readily abandoned their old dress, especially in Moscow. . . .

From Ivan Nestesuranoi, *Memoirs,* 1703, as translated in *Readings in Western Civilization,* ed. by Paul L. Hughes and Robert F. Fries (Paterson, N.J.: Littlefield, Adams, 1960), pp. 130–31.

once again. But decisive victories came in the north. In the Great Northern War Peter gained territory on the Gulf of Finland that had once belonged to Sweden. This gave him the "window on the sea," the direct contact with western Europe through the Baltic, that was his primary aim.

To man his army, Peter developed a conscription system. To pay for it was harder, since he could not borrow money. As expenses increased, he and his advisers taxed anything and everything they could think of: births, marriages, caskets, graves, and beards, among other things. By the end of his reign the combined burdens of heavy taxation, conscription for the army, and forced labor for industry and for building had resulted in a measurable decline in the population.

Political reforms followed military reforms, though more slowly. Peter's method of governing was informal and haphazard. To get something done, he would dash off a hastily written order and set up a commission to carry it out. Slowly, toward the end of his reign, some order was brought out of the resulting chaos. The first provincial governments were set up; the numerous commissions were brought under supervisory "colleges"; and a "senate," or central administrative body, was instituted to interpret the tsar's orders (which were sometimes confusing) and to carry out his will. A secret police also appeared to provide a check on all officials.

In Russia the imperial government did more and individuals or nonofficial groups did less than in any other European country. After 1700 no new patriarch was appointed, and the Orthodox Church was strictly subordinated to the state under a civilian official. When new industries were needed to support the army, government contractors founded them, using forced labor (serfs and criminals) granted by the tsar. One of Peter's most herculean achievements was to compel the ancient hereditary nobility to serve the state. He ordered many of the sons of the nobility to study abroad, then compelled them as well as their parents to serve for life in the army, in the government, or in industry. At the same time

he enlisted commoners for the service of the state, giving them land and titles of nobility. He thus created a "service nobility" out of older and newer classes. To support this service nobility, he allowed them a free hand in dealing with the serfs on their lands. A census for tax purposes resulted in greatly increasing the number of serfs in Russia by classifying doubtful cases as servile. Under Catherine the Great, who came to power a generation after Peter's death, the nobles were freed from the obligation of service to the state, but it took another century for the peasants to become free from the galling form of serfdom prevailing in Russia. In central Europe a serf was usually bound to the land, but in Russia he could be sold apart from the land like a slave and was generally at the mercy of his master—a fact that made it easier for new industries to acquire forced labor but degraded the Russian serf to a level even below that of his counterpart in eastern Germany and Austria.

In 1707 Peter moved the seat of his government to a new city that he had built on conquered territory at the eastern end of the Gulf of Finland and had named in honor of his patron saint. St. Petersburg was a perfect symbol of his work as a whole. It was a city unlike Moscow, without roots in the country's past, built new on a marsh by forced labor. The nobles were ordered to build houses in it, and merchants were ordered to settle in it. This seaport city looked westward to Germany, Holland, and western Europe, not to the interior, as landlocked Moscow had for centuries. The nobility and civil servants hated it at first, but in the end it became their capital—the political center of what has been called "a government without a people," and the social center of a westernized aristocracy out of touch with the Russian peasant. As Versailles came to stand for the France of Louis XIV, so St. Petersburg (later called Petrograd and then Leningrad) came to stand for the Russia of Peter the Great—a powerful autocracy with few vital connections with the people.

Historians still differ sharply in estimating the value of Peter's work, but on some things they are fairly well agreed. The older Russian institutions were

Contemporary cartoon of Peter cutting off the beard of a Russian noble. Those who wanted to keep their beards had to pay a tax and carry a license (below).

bankrupt, and western influences were beginning to have their effect even before Peter appeared on the scene. Peter hastened processes of change that were almost certain to have come in any case. He cannot be blamed for all the evil results that followed, since many of them (such as the intensification of serfdom) had their roots deep in the past and owed much of their growth to Peter's successors. Two things he did accomplish: he transformed Russia from a victim state into a great power, and he involved it irrevocably with the future development of Europe. Since his time, Russia has always been a factor in the European balance of power. Peter's westernizing policy ultimately provoked a strong nationalistic and orthodox reaction, leaving Russia divided to the present day between deep suspicion of everything foreign and eager admiration of western technology and culture. But never again was Russia able to turn its back on Europe.

Even more important than Peter's accomplishments were Peter's methods. His example created a tradition of dynamic autocracy. To future tsars and future dictators his reign was to be the classic example of what might be accomplished by a ruthless and demonic will.

CONCLUSION

The half-century between 1660 and 1715 thus saw significant changes in the political and social structure of Europe. Absolute divine-right monarchy reached the apogee of its development in the France of Louis XIV and was imitated from Madrid to St. Petersburg. It is difficult to imagine two more different personalities than Louis XIV of France and Peter of Russia, but their aims were essentially similar. A few smaller peoples like the Swiss had quietly rejected monarchy in favor of republican government, and the Dutch had become wealthy and powerful as a republic. But it took the English Revolution to demonstrate to Europe that there was a practical alternative to absolute monarchy that could serve great powers as well as small. So by 1715 the political alternatives of absolutism and constitutionalism were each embodied in a great power. At the same time there were important shifts of power within the European state system. The French bid for predominance failed, provoking the rise of England and Austria as great powers. Two great empires of the sixteenth century, the Spanish and the Ottoman, were in decline. Two peoples of limited resources and numbers, the Dutch and the Swedes, had bid strongly for great-power status in the mid-seventeenth century, but by 1715 their strength was spent. Two new powers had appeared in the East to join the balance, the small military Kingdom of Prussia and the vast semibarbarous Tsardom of Russia. The rivalries of these states— England versus France, France versus Austria, Austria versus Prussia, Austria and Russia versus the Ottoman Empire— were to become the dynamic elements in eighteenth-century war and diplomacy.

Suggestions for Further Reading

Note: Asterisk denotes a book available in paperback edition.

General   The best general accounts of the period are F. L. Nussbaum, *The Triumph of Science and Reason, 1660–1685** (1953); J. B. Wolf, *The Emergence of the Great Powers, 1685–1715** (1951); and J. Stoye, *Europe Unfolding, 1648–1688** (1969). All three of these books are particularly helpful as introductions to the history of eastern Europe, about which it is hard to find good reading in English. R. Hatton, *Europe in the Age of Louis XIV** (1969), is excellent on the social history of the period. A general study of an important subject begins with this period: E. Barker, *The Development of Public Services in Western Europe, 1660–1930* (1944). On the general theme of this chapter, see J. N. Figgis, *The Divine Right of Kings** (1896, 1922); C. J. Friedrich and C. Blitzer, *The Age of Power** (1957); and F. D. Wormuth, *The Origins of Modern Constitutionalism* (1949).

France Under Louis XIV

There are good chapters on Louis' reign in Ogg and Boulenger, mentioned at the end of Chapter 19. Two excellent short surveys are L. B. Packard, *The Age of Louis XIV** (1914), and M. P. Ashley, *Louis XIV and the Greatness of France** (1946). J. B. Wolf, *Louis XIV** (1968), is a good biography. A. Guérard, *The Life and Death of an Ideal: France in the Classical Age** (1928), is a more thought-provoking and comprehensive discussion, including both politics and culture within its scope. P. Goubert, *Louis XIV and Twenty Million Frenchmen** (1970), relates the career of the king to the social history of France during his reign. N. O. Keohane, *Philosophy and the State in France* (1980), is also useful. J. E. King, *Science and Rationalism in the Government of Louis XIV, 1661–1683* (1949), is an important study. On economic history, the three books of C. W. Cole are the best introduction: *French Mercantilist Doctrines Before Colbert* (1913), *Colbert and a Century of French Mercantilism*, 2 vols. (1939), and *French Mercantilism, 1683–1700* (1943). C. Hill, *Versailles* (1925), is one of many books on the life of the court. W. H. Lewis, *The Splendid Century** (1954), is a popular account of all aspects of the reign, full of fascinating material. The best guides to the literary history of the period are the various works of A. A. Tilley.

England

G. N. Clark, *The Later Stuarts, 1660–1714* (1934), in the *Oxford History of England* series, is a particularly fine synthesis. A more detailed narrative history of the period may be found in three books, all more or less Whiggish in sympathy: D. Ogg, *England in the Reign of Charles II,** 2 vols. (1934); the same author's *England in the Reign of James II and William III* (1955); and G. M. Trevelyan, *England under Queen Anne*, 3 vols. (1930–34). A. Bryant, *Charles II* (1931), is more pro-Stuart. The most recent interpretation of the whole period of revolution in England is C. Hill, *The Century of Revolution, 1603–1714** (1961). There is a good modern biography of James II by F. C. Turner (1948), and of William III by S. Baxter (1966). J. Pollock, *The Popish Plot* (1903, 1945), is the standard investigation of a tangled historical problem. On the economic history of the period, there is a good special study, *The Bank of England*, by J. Clapham, 2 vols. (1944), and a masterly brief sketch by G. Clark, *The Wealth of England, 1496–1760* (1947). C. H. Wilson, *England's Apprenticeship, 1603–1763* (1965), is a remarkable study of England's emergence as a great power. Pepys's *Diary* is the most deservedly famous contemporary account of the Restoration period. It is perhaps read best in the abridgment of O. F. Morshead, *Everybody's Pepys* (1926).

Eastern Europe

In addition to the general accounts in Nussbaum and Wolf (first section, above), two books are very helpful as an introduction to the problems of eastern Europe: S. H. Cross, *Slavic Civilization Through the Ages* (1948), and O. Halecki, *Borderlands of Western Civilization* (1952). For Germany as a whole, see H. Holborn, *A History of Modern Germany, 1648–1840* (1964). On Habsburg history, P. Frischauer, *The Imperial Crown* (1939), follows the history of the house to 1792 and is mostly concerned with personalities. R. W. J. Evans, *The Making of the Habsburg Monarchy* (1979), is even more useful. See also H. G. Hoenigsberger, *The Habsburgs and Europe* (1971). H. F. Schwarz, *The Imperial Privy Council in the Seventeenth Century* (1943), is concerned with constitutional matters. For the events of 1683, see J. Stoye, *The Siege of Vienna* (1964). On Prussia, S. B. Fay, *The Rise of Brandenburg-Prussia to 1786** (1937), is very brief but also very good. J. A. R. Marriott and C. G. Robertson, *The Evolution of Prussia* (1915), and F. L. Carsten, *The Origins of Prussia* (1954), are more detailed. Also, G. A. Craig, *The Politics of the Prussian Army* (1964) is excellent. F. Schevill has written an admiring biography of Frederick William, *The Great Elector* (1947). R. N. Bain, *Scandinavia: A Political History* (1905), and O. Halecki, *History of Poland** (1943), are useful national histories. J. A. R. Marriott, *The Eastern Question* (1917, 1940), is a reliable survey of the slow disintegration of the Ottoman Empire and of the resulting repercussions in Europe. The classic larger history of Russia is by V. O. Kliuchevsky; the standard Marxist account is by M. N. Pokrovsky. There are good one-volume histories by G. Vernadsky, rev. ed. (1944); B. Pares, new ed. (1953); and B. H. Sumner, rev. ed. (1947). B. H. Sumner, *Peter the Great and the Emergence of Russia** (1950), is a well-informed and judicious short account. Kliuchevsky's *Peter the Great* (1958) is an English version of an older but still useful book. R. J. Kerner, *The Urge to the Sea: The Course of Russian History* (1942), contains a valuable account of Russian expansion eastward to the Pacific. J. Blum, "The Rise of Serfdom in Eastern Europe," *American Historical Review*, Vol. LXII (July 1957), is a masterly examination of the differences in the economic development of eastern and western Europe. See also his *Lord and Peasant in Russia from the Ninth to the Nineteenth Century** (1961).

21 The Scientific Revolution and the Enlightenment

Until the seventeenth century the growth of civilized man's knowledge about the natural world around him had been slow, fumbling, and discontinuous. He had made many individual observations of natural phenomena and had derived some useful generalizations from these observations. But many generalizations were poorly stated, and others were entirely erroneous. "Experiments" in the modern sense were all but unheard of, and most people felt that scientific speculation was both unsure and impractical.

THE SCIENTIFIC REVOLUTION

By the eighteenth century a startling change had occurred. A large body of verifiable knowledge about nature had accumulated and has continued to accumulate at an increasing rate down to our own day. This knowledge has had revolutionary effects. Human society today has at its disposal more food, clothing, and shelter, faster ways of moving about the globe, quicker means of communicating across great distances, and more power than anyone could have dreamed of before about 1600. The characteristic mark of our civilization is that it is a "scientific civilization," and this quality began to be noticeable in the seventeenth century.

Discussion of a new method of inquiry—which we call the scientific method—began in the universities in the late thirteenth and fourteenth centuries and came to fruition in western Europe after 1600. The new method was essentially a combination of two elements: careful observation and controlled experimentation, and rational interpretation of the results of this observation and experimentation, preferably by use of mathematics. In A. N. Whitehead's words, science is "a vehement and passionate interest in the relation of general principles to irreducible and stubborn facts."

When Galileo and others began to apply this method in physics and astronomy, other brilliant "discoveries" followed. These discoveries fired the imagination and enthusiasm of European thinkers. Scientific societies were organ-ized, scientific journals began to appear, and "chain discoveries," each one resting on the results of the one preceding it, made their appearance. Science, hitherto the pursuit of occasional lonely individuals, became a social enterprise and has continued so to the present. Furthermore, it became fashionable. The Humanists had been little interested in science, but Newton's work made a profound impression on every writer in Europe. Finally, the gap between the theories of the scholar and the practical knowledge of the technician began to close.

The Medieval Universe

Precisely *why* all this took place when and where it did is still a puzzle. The one thing that can be said is that ever since the twelfth century the people of western Europe had been interested in scientific problems. But the medieval answers to these problems were based on deep-rooted, traditional assumptions about the nature of the universe. For example, it was generally believed that the universe was a finite sphere with the earth at the center. Between the center and the outermost limits were nine transparent spheres that carried the stars, the planets, the sun, and the moon in their daily revolutions around the earth, which remained motionless. On earth all was change, corruptibility, and decay. In the heavens all was perfection and incorruptibility—the perfect sphericity of sun and moon, the unvarying circular motion of the heavenly bodies, and the music of the spheres produced by their motion. And so what was the rule on earth was not the rule in the heavens. There was an earthly physics and a heavenly physics, and the laws of the one were not those of the other.

Even in the Middle Ages, however, not all men were satisfied with this relatively simple picture of the universe. In the thirteenth and fourteenth centuries a small but increasing number of scholars began to question existing explanations. Many of them were Franciscans, inspired perhaps by their founder's sensitive feeling for nature. Stimulated by the current study of Greco-Arabic science, a group of teachers at Oxford and Paris began to apply mathematical reasoning to prob-

Opposite: The Danish astronomer Tycho Brahe's underground observatory was the finest of the sixteenth century. Most of his instruments were under the protective domes.

lems of physics and astronomy, such as accelerated motion. Their speculations were continued by professors at the University of Padua in the fifteenth and sixteenth centuries. At Padua, a center of medical training for three centuries, the proper method of studying nature was vigorously debated in the course of arguments about Aristotle. Medieval universities kept interest in science alive, and the first faint beginnings of the scientific revolution were seen in Oxford, Paris, and Padua.

Most Europeans of 1500, however, did not question the standard Greek authorities. The normal state of everything in the universe was a state of rest: things moved only if they were pushed or pulled by a mover—so said Aristotle. Galen, in the second century A.D. had described the anatomy of the human body so convincingly that doctors still saw the human organs through his eyes. Ptolemy in the same century had worked out such an ingenious mathematical explanation of the observed irregularities in

the movements of the planets that no one in 1500 thought it could be improved on. All motion in the heavens was circular, Ptolemy assumed, but there were smaller circles, or "epicycles," whose centers moved around the circumference of larger circles, and on the circumferences of these smaller circles the planets moved. It took about eighty epicycles to do the job, but the system worked quite well in explaining the observed phenomena and predicting their reoccurence with mathematical precision. There seemed to be very little reason at the close of the Middle Ages to try to improve on either the observations or the theories of these ancient writers.

The Background of Change

In the fourteenth, fifteenth, and sixteenth centuries, however, certain forces in European society were preparing the way for a change in the general view of nature. Artisans and craftsmen were becoming more skilled in their techniques. The invention of the lens and the development of the glass industry, to take but one example, gave the promise of vastly extending man's powers of observing natural processes. New techniques in shipbuilding led to voyages of discovery, which in turn stimulated interest in nature and turned men's attention to problems of navigation.

The Renaissance, with its emphasis on literature and art and its veneration for the wisdom of the ancients, was in some of its aspects antiscientific. But the Humanists were interested in Greek scientific texts as well as in Greek literature, and patrons of the arts were also patrons of inventors and technicians. Humanistic study revealed conflicting opinions among the ancients on matters of science, just at the moment when the authority of Galen and Ptolemy was becoming shaky for other reasons. Anatomical studies by artists and the increasing practice of dissection suggested that Galen had made mistakes in observation. Growing skill in mathematics exposed the clumsiness of Ptolemy's explanations. In the opening years of the sixteenth century, conditions were ripe for change.

The Scientific Revolution

ALFRED NORTH WHITEHEAD

A brief and sufficiently accurate description of the intellectual life of the European races during the succeeding two centuries and a quarter up to our own times is that they have been living upon the accumulated capital of ideas provided for them by the genius of the seventeenth century. . . . It is the one century which consistently, and throughout the whole range of human activities, provided intellectual genius adequate for the greatness of its occasions. . . . The issue of the combined labors of four men [Descartes, Galileo, Huyghens, and Newton] has some right to be considered as the greatest single intellectual success which mankind has achieved.

HERBERT BUTTERFIELD

The so-called "scientific revolution," popularly associated with the sixteenth and seventeenth centuries, but reaching back in an unmistakably continuous line to a period much earlier still . . . outshines everything since the rise of Christianity and reduces the Renaissance and Reformation to the rank of mere episodes, mere internal displacements, within the system of medieval Christendom.

From Alfred North Whitehead, *Science and the Modern World* (New York: Macmillan, 1925), pp. 57–58, 67; from Herbert Butterfield, *The Origins of Modern Science* (London: Bell, 1949), p. vii.

1543: Vesalius and Copernicus

In 1543 two notable scientific works heralded the end of medieval science and the beginnings of a revolution in western man's conception of nature. Vesalius' *On the Structure of the Human Body* was for its day a marvelously careful description of human anatomy based on direct observation in dissection and illustrated by graphic and accurate plates. Vesalius did not free himself completely from the authority of Galen, nor was there much theory in his book. But it was an influential example of the power of observation. Copernicus' *On the Revolutions of the Heavenly Bodies* was a brilliant mathematical treatise that showed that the number of Ptolemy's epicycles could be reduced to thirty-four if one assumed that the earth turned on its axis once a day and moved around the sun once a year. Unlike Vesalius, Copernicus was not primarily an observer. He learned during his study at Padua in the early years of the century that there was an ancient opinion that the earth moved, and he found that this assumption made everything simpler to explain mathematically. Since medieval theory decreed that "nature always acts in the simplest ways," the simpler explanation must be the truer. And so with little experimental or observational proof, Copernicus presented his readers with a theory of a universe in which the earth was no longer the center. The experimental and the theoretical sides of the modern scientific method were perfectly exemplified in Vesalius' and Copernicus' books, but they were not yet conjoined in one man or one work.

In 1600 a monk named Giordano Bruno was tried as a heretic, condemned, and burned at the stake for preaching that the universe was not finite but infinite in extent, that it was filled with numberless suns and planets like our own, and that God was equally in every planet or atom in the cosmos. Bruno had been inspired by Copernicus, although Copernicus himself believed in the finite sphere of the fixed stars and the uniqueness of the earth. Nevertheless, this intuition of the infinity of the universe spread gradually among scientists.

The medieval cosmos based on the earth-centered Ptolemaic conception. Ptolemy's explanation of the universe as a closed and defined system seemed so perfectly put together that it was not criticized for fourteen centuries—until the discoveries of Copernicus and Galileo.

Bacon and Descartes

Two major prophets of the Scientific Revolution were Francis Bacon (1561–1626) and René Descartes (1596–1650). Bacon, an English lawyer, statesman, and essayist, waged a vigorous battle in his books against the deductive method of Scholasticism, which started from premises usually taken on authority and then deduced all the logical consequences. This method might help men to organize truths already known, he said, but it could never help them to discover new truths. Only inductive reasoning, which starts from direct observations of phenomena and goes on to develop the principles that explain these observations, can produce new truth. Bacon was as interested in controlling nature as in knowing its processes. He pictured an imaginary society of scientists whose end was to benefit mankind by conducting hundreds of experiments and discovering useful facts. Bacon failed to appreciate the importance of mathematical models

Scientific revolutionaries of the seventeenth century: Francis Bacon (above) and René Descartes.

in theoretical analysis (he was unconvinced by Copernicus), and although he praised experimentation, he performed almost no experiments but collected his data, in the traditional way—from books. Nevertheless, his writings did dramatize the importance of empirical research. The founding in 1662 of the Royal Society of London, the first scientific society in England, owed much to Bacon's inspiration, and in a sense he was the remote ancestor of the great research laboratories and research teams of today.

Descartes, a French mathematician and philosopher, was a more important figure than Bacon, but he lacked Bacon's intuitive understanding of the need for careful observations. To Descartes, the excitement of science lay in mathematical analysis and theory. In a famous autobiographical account, he told how the literature and philosophy he studied as a youth left him unsatisfied because they reached no certain conclusions, how mathematics charmed him by its precision and certainty, and how he set out to discover a "method of rightly conducting the reason and discovering truth in the sciences." In November 1619, in a moment of intuition, he saw the exact correspondence between geometry and algebra: the truth that any equation can be translated into a curve on a graph, and that any regular curve can be translated into an equation. This intoxicating vision suggested to him a new way of grasping ultimate truth. If only men would systematically doubt all notions based on authority or custom and start with clear and precise ideas they know to be true, the whole universe might be deduced from a few simple principles and thus comprehended as clearly as the coordinate geometry he had discovered.

Descartes was one of the first to believe that science could save humanity. His enthusiasm was infectious, but he moved too fast. He reduced the universe, including the body of man, to a mathematically intelligible machine. To do this he had to take mind out of the world of matter entirely and define it as a separate substance that comprehended the world of matter but did not exist in it. His generalizations in astronomy, physics, and anatomy were often premature, and his passion for system building went beyond his capacity to check by experiment. (He did do important work in optics, but this was hardly enough to justify his basic theories.) But his enthusiasm for scientific "method," his belief that everything could be reduced to mathematical terms, and his insistence on systematic doubt of all earlier theories left a profound mark on the thinking of scientists in the next two centuries. Descartes made it easier for his successors to reject old ideas, and they gradually came to accept his belief that the language of science must be mathematics.

Experiment and Mathematics

Both Bacon and Descartes were overoptimistic. Bacon thought that a generation of determined experimentation would establish a solid structure of knowledge about the universe. Descartes thought that a universal science could be deduced fairly soon from a few basic mathematical axioms. He also believed that the universe was much less complicated than it is; it was one of Descartes' pupils who described the world as a gigantic piece of clockwork.

Meanwhile, experimentation and mathematics were developing slowly and steadily in the hands of a growing host of scientists. William Gilbert used what little was known of the mysterious force of electricity to deduce that the earth itself was a great magnet (1600). William Harvey, who had studied at Padua, proved that the blood must circulate from arteries to veins to heart to lungs and back to heart and then arteries again. He did this by estimating the amount of blood pumped out by the heart in a minute and arguing that it must go somewhere (1628). Later in the century the new microscope revealed the tiny capillaries that actually connect arteries to veins. Torricelli, Pascal, and others investigated the ancient proposition that "nature abhors a vacuum," a proposition that had long been believed by most scholars. In order to prove the falseness of the proposition, the new investigators created vacuums in test tubes, invented the barometer, and discovered the pressure of the atmosphere. All these advances evidenced a growing precision in observation and an increasing sophistication both in controlling experiments and in quantifying their results.

At the same time, mathematics was making rapid strides. The invention of decimals and of logarithms early in the century facilitated calculation; Pascal inaugurated the study of probability; and at the end of the century Newton and Leibniz crowned the work of many others by simultaneously inventing the calculus, which provided the first method of analyzing regularly accelerating or decelerating motion.

Kepler

It was in astronomy and physics that observational techniques and mathematical methods found their most fruitful union. The German astronomer Johannes Kepler (1571–1630) was troubled by discrepancies in Copernicus' theory, which he nevertheless believed to be true. He worked from the observations of his master Tycho Brahe, which were far more accurate than those available to Copernicus. Copernicus had clung to the old belief that all heavenly bodies moved in circles. But to Kepler it was obvious that the planets' orbits were not circles. For years he worried about the geometry of these orbits and finally decided that the ellipse might be a good model. The properties of the ellipse had been studied since the time of the Greeks, and Kepler quickly saw that this solution fitted the observations. The planets' orbits, he announced, are elliptical, with the sun in one of the two foci of the ellipse. Further, a line from the sun to a planet sweeps out equal areas of the ellipse in equal times, and the cube of the distance of each planet from the sun is proportional to the square of the time of its revolution. Here was astounding proof of the intuition of Descartes and others that nature in some mysterious sense was mathematical. A geometrical figure, studied for centuries as an abstract form, was found to "fit" the facts of nature. The implication was that nature was perhaps really a machine, intelligible to careful observers equipped with the tools of mathematics.

Galileo

The first fruits of Kepler's work appeared in 1609. During the same year an Italian, Galileo Galilei (1564–1642), professor at Padua and Pisa, turned a newly invented instrument, the telescope, on the heavens and soon afterward published an account of what he saw. The changeless perfection and perfect sphericity of the heavenly bodies had dissolved before his gaze. The moon had craters and mountains; there were moving spots on the sun; there were rings around Saturn; and Jupiter proved to have four moons of its own. A bright new star had already appeared and been noted in 1572, and in 1577 a new comet had cut a path through what should have been crystalline spheres. The finite, spherical universe of the Middle Ages was shattered, and thoughtful men suspected strongly that they were looking out into boundless space, sparsely populated by stars like the sun and possibly by other solar systems as well. The old distinction between terrestrial and celestial physics was apparently dissolving. The moon and sun were not perfect globes, and the stars were not changeless. Perhaps the same forces and laws operated both on earth and in the heavens. Nor was the earth any longer the motionless center of the universe. The earth was a planet circling the sun like Jupiter or any other, and round about the solar system were infinite, silent spaces.

This was too much for obscurantists in the Church. The Copernican theory had been denounced in 1616, and in 1632 Galileo himself was condemned by the Roman Inquisition, threatened with torture, and forced to recant. Nevertheless, his brilliantly written dialogues contributed mightily to the overthrow not only of Ptolemy in favor of Copernicus, but also of Aristotle in favor of a new physics.

Galileo's physics was inspired by the speculations of the fourteenth-century Franciscans, but he went much further and was much more accurate in developing mathematical formulas to describe the laws of motion. He worked out the law of falling bodies. The result was a simple mathematical formula again: the distance covered increases as the square of the time. He saw that the path followed by a projectile is a regular curve, a parabola, produced by the operation of two forces on the projectile—the initial

Two of Galileo's telescopes.

Harvey Discovers the Circulation of the Blood
1628

Since calculations and visual demonstrations have confirmed all my suppositions, to wit, that the blood is passed through the lungs and the heart by the pulsation of the ventricles, is forcibly ejected to all parts of the body, therein steals into the veins . . . flows back everywhere . . . from small veins into larger ones, and thence comes at last into the vena cava and to the auricle of the heart; all this too in such amounts that it cannot be supplied from the ingesta [food] and is also in greater bulk than would suffice for nutrition.

I am obliged to conclude that in all animals the blood is driven around a circuit with an unceasing, circular sort of motion, that this is an activity of the heart which it carries out by virtue of its pulsation, and that in sum it constitutes the sole cause for the heart's pulsatile movement.

From C. C. Gillispie, *The Edge of Objectivity* (Princeton, N.J.: Princeton University Press, 1960), p. 71.

impetus and the pull of the earth. He came close to formulating the key concept of modern mechanics, the law of inertia: that all bodies tend to remain at rest or to continue in motion in straight lines unless acted on by outside forces. From this deceptively simple proposition—so fundamentally different from Aristotle's conception of motion as the result of some mover's action—was to spring the law of gravitation. Galileo prepared the way, but the actual formulation of the law was to be reserved for one who was born in the year Galileo died, 1642.

Newton

It was the genius of an Englishman, Sir Isaac Newton (1642–1727), that related Kepler's astronomy to Galileo's physics, destroyed all distinction between celestial and terrestrial physics, and accomplished at least part of Descartes' dream of establishing a "universal science." The basic intuition came to Newton while he was still a student in his twenties at Cambridge University. The thought occurred to him that the force that keeps the moon from flying off

at a tangent and bends it into an orbit about the earth must be exactly the same force that pulls an apple from its branch to the ground. There must be a reciprocal force of attraction between every body in the universe, and this force must be calculable—even if we do not know exactly what it is in itself. Newton's earliest calculations came close enough to mathematical proof to persuade him that it was in truth the same force that operated on the moon and the apple, and that this force varied "directly as the product of the masses" involved and "inversely as the square of the distance" separating the bodies. For some time he seems to have lost interest in his "law," but twenty years later a friend, the astronomer Edmund Halley, urged him to work out and publish his theory. Newton developed the necessary mathematics (the calculus) to prove his theory to his own satisfaction and published his conclusions, in Latin, in *The Mathematical Principles of Natural Philosophy* (1687). This proved to be one of the most influential books ever written in the history of science as well as in the history of human thought.

To scientists Newton's law of gravitation provided a single, simple explanation of a growing mass of data in astronomy and physics and laid the foundations of future research in both these sciences. Further, Newton gave scientific method its classic formulation in his "Rules of Reasoning":

> In experimental philosophy (i.e., science) we are to look upon propositions collected by general induction from phenomena as accurately or very nearly true, notwithstanding any contrary hypotheses (theories) that may be imagined, till such time as other phenomena occur, by which they may either be made more accurate or liable to exceptions.

Newton's support of the experimental, or inductive, approach was aimed at the premature generalizing of Descartes and his followers. But obviously he did not underestimate the value of mathematical theory, as Bacon had. In Newton the slow growing together of empirical observation and rational interpretation reached full maturity.

The Newtonian Universe

To the layman, who learned about Newton's work through popularizers, a new universe began to open up. It was a far cry from the small and finite medieval universe. It was a universe in which the significant objects were bodies or masses moving about in infinite space in response to regularly operating forces. Mass, force, and motion were the key concepts, and mathematics was the means of understanding them. Medieval man had been obsessed by the question "Why?" and had felt he understood whatever he encountered in nature once he had discovered its end or purpose. Seventeenth-century scientists limited themselves to asking "How?" and were satisfied when they found what appeared to be the regular patterns in natural processes. The world of Kepler, Galileo, and Newton was a vast machine, working according to laws that could be mathematically expressed, laws that were intelligible to anyone who followed the proper experimental and mathematical methods.

What was the place of God and of man in this universe? We shall see what the answers to this question were in the next century. But here it must be observed that no seventeenth-century scientist of prominence thought that he was reading God or man out of the universe. Descartes considered himself a good Catholic and was apparently not troubled by the dangers inherent in his sharp separation of the world of matter from the world of mind. Newton spent most of his energy in his later years in religious speculation. Contradictions between faith and science were not necessarily evident to the first modern scientists and their readers.

Still, the religious view of life was weakening in the later seventeenth century, and the development of science was in part the result of this decline. The charters of the scientific societies and academies that sprang up throughout Europe during the century usually contained clauses stating that purely theological or political discussion would not be tolerated and that "ultimate" or "final" causes were no part of the group's concern. In the earliest history of the Royal Society of London, published in 1667, it is clear that scientific discussions had offered a peculiar attraction to thoughtful men during a fanatical and bitter civil war like the Puritan Revolution. Science was impartial politically and theologically; it did not stir men's tempers; it would not start religious wars; and above all, it was useful—it could benefit mankind. Scientific truth was an alternative to theological truth that was more verifiable, more practical, more peaceful—or so at least some men argued. It was more than coincidence that modern science arose in a century that saw Europe's last violent struggles over religion.

One supremely sensitive philosopher felt the religious awe implicit in the new mechanistic picture of the universe. This was an obscure Dutch lens grinder, Baruch Spinoza (1632–77). To Spinoza the new universe of mass, force, and motion, operating in strict obedience to inexorable laws, was God. There was no need, he thought, to consider God as above, behind, or beyond nature. God is not a "free cause" apart from natural law. He is not "Creator" or "Redeemer." He is natural law. "God never can decree, nor ever would have decreed, anything but what is; God did not exist before his decrees, and would not exist without them." Nature is "a fixed and immutable order," with "no particular goal in view." Man, like everything else, is part of this order. So Spinoza could write a book called *Ethics Demonstrated in the Geometrical Manner* and say, "I shall consider human activities and desires in exactly the same manner as though I were concerned with lines, planes, and solids." The wise man contemplates this natural order with serenity and delight. This was Spinoza's religion. Naturally such arguments were called atheistical, and Spinoza was considered a dangerous radical by his contemporaries.

For most men, however, the new science did not destroy the traditional religion. Rather it compelled them to consider the religious significance of a greatly expanded and complicated universe. The telescope was revealing the immense size of the cosmos, displacing the earth and even the sun from the

Newton's design for a reflecting telescope.

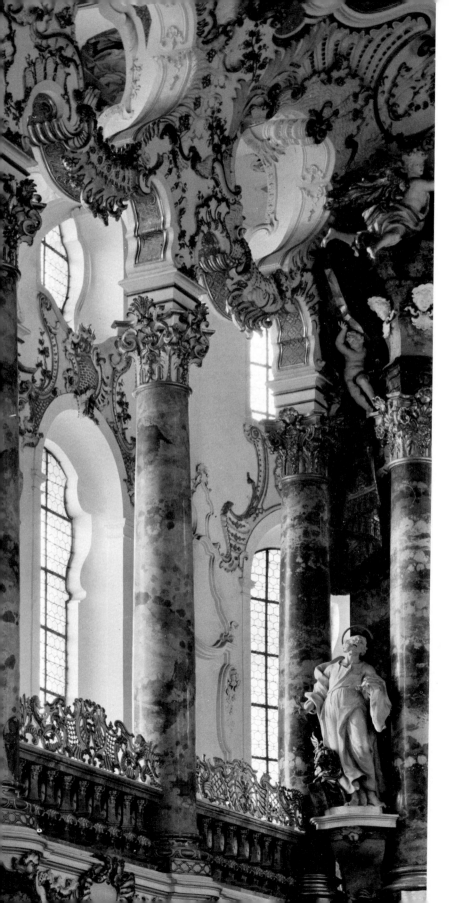

center of the universe. The microscope was beginning to reveal the wonders of the world's minutiae—the capillaries, the bacteria, the cells, the foundations of life. No one felt the two infinites—the infinitely great and the infinitesimally small—so keenly or speculated so profoundly about their religious significance as Blaise Pascal (1623–62). "The whole visible world is only an imperceptible atom in the ample bosom of nature," he wrote. The universe, he said, is "an infinite sphere, the center of which is everywhere, the circumference nowhere." "The eternal silence of these infinite spaces frightens me." Yet to examine a mite—"with its minute body and parts incomparably more minute, limbs with their joints, veins in the limbs, blood in the veins, humors in the blood, drops in the humors, vapors in the drops"—is equally astonishing. "What is man in nature? A Nothing in comparison with the Infinite, an All in comparison with the Nothing, a mean between nothing and everything." And yet man is greater than anything in the universe because he comprehends all this, and because Christ died on the cross for him. In this way, Pascal related the new universe to Christianity. Other Christians were not so concerned about the new science, and other scientists were not so concerned to articulate a Christian interpretation.

THE CULTURE OF THE SEVENTEENTH CENTURY

The Baroque Style in Art

The age of the scientific revolution was also the age of the "baroque" style in art—a style that sprang up in the later sixteenth century, reached its climax about the middle of the seventeenth, and came to its end around the middle of the eighteenth. The term *baroque* (French for "odd" or "irregular") was invented by eighteenth-century critics who regarded seventeenth-century art as a grotesque corruption of Renaissance art. But modern critics consider the baroque a great achievement; one of them has called it "the high-water mark of European crea-

View of the baroque interior of the church at Weiss in Germany.

tive effort." As a style it is difficult to define because it reflected all the contrasts and contradictions of seventeenth-century culture in general: its religious ecstasy and its sensual worldliness, its credulity and its rationalism, its violence and its respect for order. Baroque painters and sculptors were influenced by all these contradictions. They portrayed voluptuous women in repose, military heroes in battle, and saints in ecstasy with equal skill and zest.

In general, the dominant notes of the baroque were a sense of tension and conflict and a liking for the grandiose and dramatic. The conflicts of man and the universe, of man and man, and of man within himself were conceived on a more heroic, and often a more tragic, scale than they had been in the Renaissance. Renaissance painters and writers had been interested in man himself. Baroque painters and writers were fascinated by man in his environment—typical men torn by conflicting passions, confronted by human and supernatural enemies, buffeted by elemental forces beyond their control.

There were instructive parallels between the thought-worlds of the artists and the thought-worlds of the scientists of the period. To Galileo and Newton, bodies or masses moving through space in response to conflicting forces such as gravitation and centrifugal force were the objects of study. To the great French dramatists of the age—Corneille, Racine, and Molière—the objects of study were typical human beings acting and reacting in response to conflicting passions such as love and duty. Baroque painters were intrigued by space. Vermeer portrayed figures in a space that was bathed and suffused with light; Rembrandt spotlighted them in the midst of darkened space; and others pictured them floating through apparently infinite space (to baroque artists the supernatural was natural). The scientists' concern with "mass, force, and motion" seems closely related to the painters' and poets' concern with men caught in the tension between elemental forces in their whole natural or supernatural environment. The typical hero of baroque literature, it has been said, is Satan in Milton's *Paradise Lost.*

"To reign is worth ambition though in hell:/Better to reign in hell than serve in heav'n." So speaks Satan after the Fall, swayed by colossal passions, moving through vast three-dimensional spaces, commanding many of the natural forces in the universe, but ultimately checked and frustrated by God.

The most typical product of baroque architecture was the royal palace: Versailles in France, Schönbrunn in Austria, or Blenheim, Marlborough's regal residence in England. The style was fundamentally Renaissance classical, but grander, more ornate, and more complicated. These palaces were designed to be the stage settings of worldly greatness. The vast reception rooms, the halls of mirrors, the great sweeping staircases, and the long vistas of the formal gardens were designed to enhance the drama of royalty and aristocracy. Even the churches of the period—such as Bernini's colonnades framing St. Peter's in Rome—suggested the majesty of God rather than his mercy.

But it was the operas that originated in Italy early in the seventeenth century that were the most original creation of the baroque. The union of dramatic action and a less polyphonic, more direct musical style was a great popular success, and opera continued to grow as a distinct form of art down to the twentieth century. The grandiose and palatial stage settings (sometimes outdoors), the dramatic conflicts of the action, and the emotive power of the music exactly suited the taste of the period. Italian composers led the way until the end of the seventeenth century: Monteverdi, the father of the opera, Frescobaldi, Scarlatti, and Vivaldi. But an Englishman, Henry Purcell, wrote the most moving opera of the century, *Dido and Aeneas* (1687).

Opera singers of the baroque period. Detail from a drawing for an opera setting by Ludovico Burnacinia, Vienna (1674).

SEVENTEENTH-CENTURY THOUGHT ABOUT MAN

The seventeenth century developed conceptions about man that were based on Renaissance views but went beyond them. These conceptions may be conveniently summed up under three heads:

individualism, relativism, and rationalism tempered by empiricism. We are speaking here of the thought of the most adventurous and best-educated minds, not of the many, whose thought-world was still conventional and in many ways "medieval."

Individualism

Radical thinkers of the seventeenth century took an increasingly individualistic view of man in society. The most intense Christian piety of the period—whether it was the Catholic devotion preached by St. François de Sales, the stern conscience of Puritans and Jansenists, or the warm inner conviction of German Pietists—was highly individualistic. The trend was equally evident in political theory. The fashion was to start with the individual and then to ask how society and the state could have originated and how they could be justified. Supporters of the divine right of kings were still numerous, but advanced thinkers were arguing that the state was based on a contract, either explicit or implicit, between the people and the ruler. Some, like Hobbes, argued that this contract, once made, was irrevocable. Others, like Locke, insisted that if the ruler broke the terms of the contract, which were usually thought to provide for good government, the people might depose him and set up a new ruler in his place. This idea of a "political contract" between ruler and people had some basis in the Old Testament and had been reinforced by feudal "contracts" between lords and vassals. It had been revived as a fighting idea by religious minorities when they were resisting the tyranny of rulers.

As time went on, the idea of a "social contract" took its place by the side of the "political contract." This was the idea that society itself was the result of a voluntary agreement among individuals who had been absolutely independent in their original "state of nature." The two ideas were mixed, somewhat confusedly, in Locke and later theorists. In both contracts, the individual with his rights and his natural independence logically came first; then came society or the state. In contrast, the Middle Ages had thought of society as an organism or a "body" in which individuals were mere "members." The more radical thinkers of the seventeenth century were coming to think of society as an artificial organization of independent individuals based on voluntary agreement or consent.

Relativism

The greatest thinkers of the Middle Ages were sure that the people of Christendom were God's chosen people and that the truth had been revealed once and for all to Christians. During the sixteenth and seventeenth centuries, Humanism, the voyages of discovery, and the development of science greatly weakened this assurance.

Humanism had shaken this assurance by revealing Greco-Roman civilization in clearer historical perspective. Here—in a society long since dead, but still alive in its literature, its art, and its historical records—was an alternative to the medieval Christian view of life. Modern historical studies—history, archeology, philology—were born during the Renaissance and were carried on with even greater skill during the seventeenth century. This steady development of the "historical sciences," as they would be called today, slowly impressed on thoughtful Europeans that there had been other societies in other times with values, beliefs, and institutions quite different from those of the present. Thus the idea of relativism in time was born and grew. What had been right behavior for a Roman was perhaps not right behavior in other times.

The idea of relativism in space resulted from the geographical discoveries, as we have seen. The discovery in America of societies far less civilized than Europe and of societies in Asia more civilized in many respects than Europe had the effect of shaking European provincialism. Perhaps the "noble savages" of the New World were happier than the more cultured but more corrupt Christians of Europe. Perhaps Christians had something to learn from Persian sages and Chinese philosophers. Each society had different standards; was any set of standards absolutely right? So at least increasing numbers of Europeans began to think in the seventeenth and eighteenth centuries.

As the temporal and geographical horizons of the European imagination widened, the vision of man's place in nature was complicated by scientific discovery, as we have seen in considering Bruno and Pascal. European Christians were not unique in time and space, as they had once thought; nor, perhaps, was man himself unique.

The intellectual results of historical study, geographical exploration, and scientific discovery are best seen in the work of Pierre Bayle (1647–1706), the great scholarly skeptic of the later seventeenth century. Bayle, originally a Huguenot, was briefly converted to Catholicism, but he renounced all orthodox belief when his brother died in a dungeon during an attempted forced conversion. He took up residence in the relatively tolerant Dutch Netherlands and devoted the latter part of his life to a crusade against superstition, religious intolerance, and dogmatism in general. In 1697 Bayle published a huge rambling book, a *Historical and Critical Dictionary*, which had enormous influence on eighteenth-century thinkers. Into this book he poured all the relativism and skepticism that he had acquired through his extensive historical study, his amateur knowledge of science (he was an admirer of Descartes), and his personal experience. He argued that atheists might be good citizens and that there was no necessary connection between a man's religious beliefs and the way he behaved. Bayle insisted that there is nothing more abominable than to make religious conversions by force. He ridiculed the idea that stars and planets could influence human life and mercilessly attacked superstition on every front. He distrusted all historical authorities, including the writers of the Old Testament, unless he was sure that their account of events was inherently credible. His test of truth was reason—and few if any accounts of miracles met this rigorous test. All in all, Bayle was the most thoroughgoing skeptic and the most destructive critic of his generation.

Rationalism and Empiricism

The leading thinkers of the seventeenth century were predominantly rationalistic. Reason was the faculty that distinguished man from the beast, and the triumphs of seventeenth-century science proved that reason could be trusted. And so the conclusion was drawn that the man of reason could know and understand the world into which he was born if he made the right use of his mind.

This optimistic attitude was reflected in the growing belief in "natural law." The idea of a law of nature that served as a standard of moral behavior for all men at all times in all places originated with the Stoics and was developed by medieval scholars. During the Renaissance and the Reformation this idea went into eclipse, but the discovery of scientific "laws of nature" (like Kepler's laws of planetary motion) helped to revive the belief that natural laws of human behavior also existed. Cicero had given the idea classic formulation: "There is in fact a true law—namely, right reason—which is in accordance with nature, applies to all men, and is unchangeable and eternal. By its commands this law summons men to the performance of their duties; by its prohibitions it restrains them from doing wrong." This law was implanted in the minds of men by God himself. Its content was hazy, but it was understood to include respect for life and property, good faith and fair dealing, giving each man his due. These principles could always be discovered by reason, just as reason could discover the proof of a geometrical proposition. Hugo Grotius, a Dutch jurist and statesman, in his book *On the Law of War and Peace* (1625), turned to the law of nature in an attempt to find some basis for a "law of nations" that would transcend the religious fanaticisms of the Thirty Years' War. And in more general terms, if natural law is the same for all men, then it lessens the contradictions caused by the relativism in time and space that was perplexing seventeenth-century men.

The most influential example of this kind of thinking was John Locke's faith

Title page of John Locke's *Essay Concerning Human Understanding* (1690).

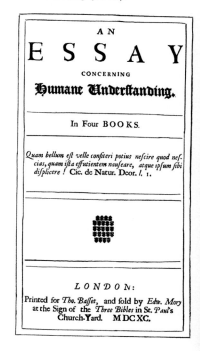

that there are certain "natural rights" vested in every individual in the "state of nature," notably life, liberty, and property. From this it follows logically, as conclusion from axiom, that men form societies and set up governments mainly to preserve these rights. Descartes had hoped to be able to deduce the universe from a few central mathematical principles; Locke in his *Second Treatise of Government* (1690) assumed that he could deduce society and government from a few simple axioms about man and natural law.

This enthusiastic rationalism in the study of man and society was qualified by an undercurrent of empiricism, of respect for sense-experience. Here again Locke led the way in his *Essay Concerning Human Understanding*. Many of its readers thought that it did for the study of man what Newton had done for the study of nature. Locke argued that all our ideas come from experience. The mind at birth is a *tabula rasa*, a clean slate, on which our sense-experiences gradually imprint conceptions. There are no "innate ideas," and no self-evident axioms (as Descartes had assumed). The mind and its ideas can be explained only by the outside forces that act on it.

This was the purest empiricism. Locke hoped that it would provide a weapon for getting rid of all the superstitions and prejudices that cluttered men's minds, but it could destroy many things besides superstitions, including some of Locke's own doctrines. Logically, Locke's theory of the mind did away with original sin (which was held to be born into all men), with revelation (which did not come through the senses), with mathematical axioms, and with all "natural rights" (which were considered innate and not based on experience). And so the rationalism of Locke's theory of society clashed with the empiricism of his theory of the mind—as the mathematical tendency clashed with the fact-finding tendency in seventeenth-century study of man in general. The eighteenth century was to inherit both: a strong faith in reason and natural law, together with a firm confidence in the value of sense-experience. Out of these two a new blend was to come in the "Enlightenment."

THE ENLIGHTENMENT

The task that the leading thinkers of the eighteenth century set themselves was to popularize the methods and principles of seventeenth-century natural science and to apply these methods and principles to God, man, and society. Scientific discovery continued, but the work that attracted the most brilliant writers of the age was that of applying the new scientific methods to long-festering human ills—economic, social, political, and ecclesiastical. Their concern was not so much to discover new truth about nature as to use the methods of natural science to reform society.

The eighteenth century's own name for this movement was the "Enlightenment." This term suggested the dawn of an age of light after a long night of darkness—the darkness of ignorance, superstition, intolerance, and slavery to the past. This new light was the light of science, as the poet Alexander Pope suggested:

> Nature and nature's laws lay hid in night;
> God said, "Let Newton be," and all was light.

There were "enlightened" writers and readers in every country of Europe from Russia to Spain and from England to Italy. Correspondence, exchange of publications, and travel linked these men together. Even in far-off America, Franklin and Jefferson were in close touch with and accepted by leaders of the Enlightenment. Nevertheless, this international movement was centered in France, and more particularly in Paris. There were good reasons for this. After the death of Louis XIV (1715) the French government became steadily more inept and ineffective, while the social tension between the privileged aristocracy and the less privileged, but powerful, wealthy bourgeoisie became more acute. Many leaders of the Enlightenment were bourgeois, and their writings often reflected bourgeois interests. These men of letters were angered by bureaucratic stupidity and aristocratic arrogance; they wanted to get rid of privilege and obscurantism. They learned to write with clarity and wit so that they influenced not only their fellow bourgeois but many members of the nobility as well. Government censors were either stupid or secretly in accord with critics of society. They could stop only the most blatant attacks; they were quite incapable of checking the criticism and satire that poured from the presses, particularly in the second half of the century.

For someone interested in ideas, Paris was the most exciting place in Europe during the eighteenth century. Here the intellectuals were in close touch with one another, excited by the feeling that they were helping to guide a revolution of ideas without precedent in European history, and bound together in a crusade to put an end to all the barbarities and absurdities of the old order. Such an intellectual conspiracy could develop only in Paris, capital of the largest and most civilized state in Europe. Other countries were too small or too backward to become major centers of "enlightened" thought and agitation. England, which had had its own Enlightenment or pre-Enlightenment with Hobbes and Locke, was a little too complacent to be-

come a center of the Enlightenment. But the Scots delighted in stirring up their duller neighbors to the south; David Hume and Adam Smith were major Enlightenment figures, and Edinburgh in the eighteenth century was one of the great European intellectual centers.

Voltaire

As a movement the Enlightenment is often dated from Voltaire's visit to England (1726–29). Voltaire (1694–1778)—his real name was François Marie Arouet—became the central figure and moving spirit of the Enlightenment, in part at least as a result of this trip. He already had reason to dislike the old regime in France, having been imprisoned for a short time in the Bastille. In England he read Newton and Locke, and he sensed the relative freedom of English society compared with his own. After his return to France he published his *Philosophical Letters on the English* (1733), in which he passed on to his readers Newton's main principles in watered-down form, as well as Locke's theories of human nature and

An assembly of *philosophes*: Voltaire (1), Adam (2), Abbé Maure (3), d´Alembert (4), Condorcet (5), Diderot (6), and Laharpe (7). Contemporary engraving by Jean Huber.

political freedom. He skillfully contrasted the rationality of Newton's method and the reasonableness of the English way of life with the more unreasonable aspects of church, state, and society in France.

These letters set the tone of "enlightened" propaganda in France for the next half-century or so. They were "philosophical"—that is to say, they reflected on the facts of life to discover their meaning, and they searched constantly for general principles that might be useful to mankind as a whole. And so the men of the Enlightenment called themselves *philosophes,* observers of the human scene with breadth of view and a sense of the practical. They were popularizers in the best sense of the word, crusaders for the application of the best intellectual tools of the century to the most vexatious social problems of their own day. Voltaire was the greatest of them—the most prolific, the wittiest, the most readable, and perhaps the angriest. His prime targets were religious intolerance, religious bigotry, and superstition. The close union in France of religious persecution and theological obscurantism with a capricious monarchical despotism exasperated him.

"*Ecrasez l'infâme*" (crush the infamous thing), he cried, in letters, pamphlets, stories, and satires. In an essay on "religion" he described a vision he had had of a desert covered with piles of bones, the bones of "Christians slaughtered by each other in metaphysical quarrels." He went on to report a "philosophical" conversation with the shades of Socrates and Jesus, who both deplored the spectacle he had just seen. And he attacked intolerance in his own day as vigorously as the barbarism of the past.

When Voltaire died in 1778, he was the most widely read author in Europe, the first writer to have made a fortune from the sale of his own writings. He was buried in Paris in a ceremony worthy of a king.

Montesquieu

Another leading figure of the Enlightenment, Montesquieu (1689–1755), tried to institute a "social science" by applying the methods of the natural sciences to the study of society. In *The Spirit of the Laws* (1748) he suggested that forms of government were related to climate and other environmental factors, and he tried to discover what form of government best fitted a given set of environmental conditions. The book was not "scientific" by later standards, but it was the first serious attempt since the Greeks to try to show the relationship of a system of government to its environment. (Voltaire later elaborated the concept in his *History of Civilization,* 1754). Montesquieu, like Voltaire, was impressed by Locke's theories about the English constitution. As a French nobleman he wished to limit the excesses of royal absolutism. He concluded that the ideal political form was a separation and balance of powers within government. This conclusion was to have great influence on the authors of the American Constitution.

Diderot
and the Encyclopaedia

A third major figure of the Enlightenment was Denis Diderot (1713–84), co-editor of a huge *Encyclopaedia* designed to sum up human knowledge and provide a kind of handbook of enlightened philosophy for the educated world. Diderot was an enthusiast for science, and he saw the relationship between science and technology more clearly than most of the *philosophes*. The plates showing machinery and industrial processes are one of the most remarkable features of the *Encyclopaedia*. Diderot was also full of confidence in man and his abilities, a kind of prophet of a this-worldly religion of man. His interests were reflected in the titles and content of the *Encyclopaedia*, which appeared in thirty-five volumes over the course of thirty years (1751–80). Much of the most trenchant writing of Diderot, Voltaire, and other *philosophes* (or Encyclopedists) was done in articles for the *Encyclopaedia*. The book succeeded in becoming a bible of the "enlightened" everywhere. Through it ran faith in man's reason, pride in his accomplishments, contempt for his follies, and confidence in his future.

Leading Ideas of the Enlightenment

No intellectual movement is successful unless it has followers as well as leaders, and the Enlightenment, like the Renaissance, produced its full quota of earnest, but dull, disciples and literary hacks who used Enlightenment language to create sensations or to attack their enemies. But the silent supporters of the Enlightenment were even more numer-ous than the writers who jumped aboard the bandwagon. As Robert Darnton has shown, the sales of the *Encyclopaedia* in tiny, provincial towns were astonishing. The main ideas of the Enlightenment struck root all over Europe and produced

A plate from Diderot's pictorial *Encyclopaedia* illustrating different kinds of domestic spinning devices, from the clumsy spindle and distaff (at left) to the more productive treadle-operated spinning wheel (fig. 2).

Key Words in History

If we could discover the little backstairs door that for any age serves as the secret entranceway to knowledge, we will do well to look for certain unobtrusive words with uncertain meanings that are permitted to slip off the tongue or the pen without fear and without research; words which, having from constant repetition lost their metaphorical significance, are unconsciously mistaken for objective realities. In the thirteenth century the key words would no doubt be *God, sin, grace, salvation, heaven,* and the like; in the nineteenth century, *matter, fact, matter-of-fact, evolution, progress;* in the twentieth century, *relativity, process, adjustment, function, complex.* In the eighteenth century the words without which no enlightened person could reach a restful conclusion were *nature, natural law, first cause, reason, sentiment, humanity, perfectibility.* In each age these magic words have their entrances and their exits. And how unobtrusively they come in and go out! We should scarcely be aware either of their approach or their departure, except for a slight feeling of discomfort, a shy self-consciousness in the use of them.

From Carl L. Becker, *The Heavenly City of the Eighteenth-Century Philosophers* (New Haven, Conn.: Yale University Press, 1932), p. 47.

a generation that had new ideas about religion and social organization. These ruling ideas may be summed up in five words, each of which bore a heavy freight of meaning in the eighteenth century: reason, nature, happiness, progress, and liberty.

The eighteenth century believed as passionately in reason as the seventeenth, but with a difference. Voltaire's "reason" relied more on experience and less on mathematics than Descartes'. It was a weapon of skeptical inquiry based on observed facts (or what he thought were facts) rather than an instrument of deduction from axioms. To the men of the Enlightenment, reason was the alternative to superstition and prejudice; it was the only sure guide to the principles that governed man and nature. Man's reason could discover the fundamental rationality of the universe, and it could also make human society more sensible. The *philosophes*, as shown by their writing for the *Encyclopaedia*, were less interested in "pure science" than in its applications, less concerned with system building than with specific reforms. Reason was now a pragmatic instrument, applicable not only to astronomy and physics but to agriculture, government, and social relations as well.

Nature was one of the favorite words of the Enlightenment. It was not always clear just what the *philosophes* meant by it, but it was clear enough that to nearly all of them "nature" or "the natural" were the proper standards for measuring God and man. If a thing was according to "nature," it was reasonable and therefore good. Voltaire and his contemporaries brought the idea of natural law to the peak of its prestige and the beginning of its decline. One of them devised this definition of natural law:

> The regular and constant order of facts by which God rules the universe; the order which his wisdom presents to the sense and reason of men, to serve them as an equal and common rule of conduct, and to guide them, without distinction of race or sect, towards perfection and happiness.

There is order and law, then, throughout the universe—laws of economics, of politics, of morality, as well as of physics and astronomy. These laws can be discovered by reason. Men may ignore or defy them, but they do so at their peril. To the enlightened, the way to happiness lay in conformity to nature and nature's laws. The man who broke nature's laws was looked on by the enlightened of the eighteenth century somewhat as the heretic who broke God's laws was looked on by the clergy in the Middle Ages: as a rebel against the order of the universe.

The end in view now was happiness, not salvation—happiness here in this world, not joy in the next. The Enlightenment was thoroughly secular in its thinking. When Jefferson included "the pursuit of happiness" along with life and liberty as an inalienable human right, he

Historical Relativism in Montesquieu: The Effects of Climate and Geography

In Asia they have always had great empires; in Europe these could never exist. Asia has larger plains; it is cut out into much larger divisions by mountains and seas . . . and the rivers being not so large form more contrasted boundaries. Power in Asia, then, should be always despotic; for if their subjugation be not severe they would soon make a division inconsistent with the nature of the country.

In Europe natural divisions form many nations of moderate extent, in which ruling by laws is not incompatible with the maintenance of the state: on the contrary, it is so favorable to it that without this the state would fall into decay. It is this that has formed a genius for liberty that renders each part extremely difficult to be subdued and subjected to a foreign power. . . .

Africa is in a climate like that of the south of Asia and is in the same servitude. America, being lately destroyed and repeopled by the nations of Europe and Africa, can scarcely display its genuine spirit, but what we know of its history is very conformable to our principles. . . .

Monarchy is more frequently found in fertile countries and a republican government in those which are not so, and this is sometimes a sufficient compensation for the inconveniences they suffer by the sterility of the land. Thus the barrenness of the soil of Attica established a democracy there.

From Charles de Secondat de Montesquieu, *The Spirit of the Laws*, Book XVII, Chs. 6, 7; Book XVIII, Ch. 1 (in the Bohn Standard Library edition), Vol. I, pp. 289–91.

was expressing the general agreement of the enlightened. The tendency of medieval Christianity to ignore misery in this life because it would be compensated for in the next angered the *philosophes*, who insisted that Christian ideals, if they were worth anything at all, must be realized here and now. Voltaire and his fellows were humanitarians. They abominated torture and cruelty, slavery and the callous treatment of the insane. An Italian, Beccaria, was the first to point out that savage penalties do not stop crime and to demand more rational treatment of criminals. The *philosophes* were also cosmopolitan and even pacifist in temper. Some of the bitterest passages ever written about the insanity of war and the absurdity of blind patriotism were penned by Voltaire. The "happiness" that he and others talked about was often materialistic. But it corresponded closely with Christ's injunction to feed the hungry, clothe the naked, and visit the sick and imprisoned. To the enlightened this was far more important than saving anything so vague as one's own soul.

The *philosophes* were the first sizable group of educated Europeans to believe in progress. They took the older Christian idea of the spiritual progression of mankind from the Creation through the Incarnation to the Last Judgment and secularized it. The progress of civilization, they believed, was now out of God's hands and in man's own. Once man had found the clue to discovering and using nature's laws in government, economics, and technology, progress was sure, if only research could prevail. There was some pessimism about this, but certainly both man and society were perfectible. On the whole, they thought that time was on man's side, not against him.

This was a major revolution in western thought. The Middle Ages could not have conceived of purely secular progress unrelated to God. Men of the Renaissance still felt themselves inferior to the heroic Greeks and Romans. But in a literary battle between "ancients" and "moderns" that began in 1687 the idea appeared that the "moderns" were as good as, and probably better than, the "ancients." By 1750 a French *philosophe* and economist, Turgot, suggested that

the essential element in history was man's slow struggle upward to his crucial discovery of the scientific method. In 1794 Condorcet, a mathematician under sentence of death during the French Revolution, wrote a *Sketch for a Historical Picture of the Progress of the Human Mind*, which summed up all the optimism of his century. He saw "the strongest reasons for believing that nature has set no limit to the realization of our hopes" and foresaw "the abolition of inequality between nations, the progress of equality within nations, and the true perfection of mankind." Progress, he concluded, was now "independent of any power that might wish to halt it" and "will never be reversed." The scientific method cannot be lost, scientific knowledge of natural law will accumulate, and so progress can never cease. It was an intoxicating vision, a vision shared by the majority of the enlightened.

All the French *philosophes* were concerned about liberty. They were acutely aware of the limitations on liberty that prevailed inside France: restrictions on freedom of speech, freedom of religion, freedom of trade, freedom to choose a job, and freedom from arbitrary arrest. Looking at England through slightly rose-colored glasses, they envied Englishmen their economic, political, and religious liberty. Their concern about liberty was potentially the most explosive part of their thinking, but almost none of them felt that violence was necessary. Their belief in liberty was tied to their belief in reason. Reason would soon reveal the true natural laws governing everything from trade and government to religion. The artificiality of French society, French government, and French religious practices would become evident, and a benevolent despotism, enlightened by this knowledge, would set things right. Or so at least Voltaire and the majority of the Encyclopedists believed.

The Enlightenment and Religion

These ideas inevitably affected the religious thought of Europe. The fashionable belief among educated persons in the eighteenth century came to be

Deism, the belief in a God who is Creator but not Redeemer. Like a watchmaker who designs and constructs a complicated piece of machinery to keep perfect time, so God created the universe and started it going and then stepped aside to let it run according to its natural laws. God does not concern himself with redeeming men or society. The essence of religion is awe and reverence before the rationality and perfection of the universe—a feeling reflected in the hymns of Isaac Watts, which are still sung in many Protestant churches. To a Deist (Voltaire was a good example) all talk of revelation or miracle, all belief in the special intervention of God in the natural order, was false. All dogma and ritual were superstition, since man needed only his reason to understand God. The heart of natural religion was the morality common to all mankind. "Light is uniform for the star Sirius," Voltaire wrote, "and for us moral philosophy must be uniform." Obviously, Deism tended to undermine orthodox Christianity and to substitute for it a rational belief in God as First Cause and natural law as man's moral guide. A few of the French *philosophes* went further and pushed beyond Deism to atheism. Baron d'Holbach, for example, argued that there is nothing but matter in the universe, that man himself is a conglomeration of atoms, and that everything that happens is determined by natural law. But in the end many Protestants were able to find a compromise between Christian beliefs and the Enlightenment's rationalism, humanitarianism, and tolerance. The result in the nineteenth century was Protestant Liberalism.

Others reacted against Deism in the direction of more intense piety. To the enlightened, religious fervor of any sort savored of the fanaticism that had caused the wars of religion, and so all enthusiasm was frowned on. But Deism could be understood only by the educated, and its cold rationality had no appeal to emotional natures. Hence the wide popularity of two warmly emotional Protestant movements, Pietism in Germany and Methodism in England and America. Both emphasized the importance of inner religious experience, of individual "conversion." Pietism was a second and

milder Protestant Reformation, directed this time not against the pope but against both the dogmatically orthodox and those who were inclined to Deism in Germany. Individualistic, tolerant, and unconcerned about creeds or ceremonies, the Pietists attracted followers among both Catholics and Protestants.

John Wesley (1703–91) was the leader of a somewhat parallel revival of a warm, personal Christian piety in England in the years following his conversion in 1738. Finding his efforts resisted by the respectable Anglican clergy, he took his message directly to the people, addressing huge congregations outdoors or in remote chapels, teaching them to sing their way to heaven with the hymns of his brother Charles, and sending out streams of pamphlets from his printing presses to the congregations he had established. In the end Wesley was forced to establish a new denomination outside the Anglican Church—the Methodist (originally a term of derision directed at the "methodical" piety of Wesley's followers). Methodism touched thousands upon thousands of Englishmen at home and in the colonies who cared nothing for the arid intellectualism of many of the Anglican clergy in the eighteenth century. More than one historian has suggested that it was Methodism that kept the English lower classes from turning to revolutionary violence during the first impact of the Industrial Revolution.

Social and Political Thought

The *philosophes* were interested in social and political problems, but they were reformers, not revolutionists. Their formula for reform was simple: discover by reason and experience the natural laws that should operate in any given situation, clear away all artificial obstacles to their operation, and the result will be progress toward happiness and freedom. The first "economists" in the modern sense used this formula to launch an attack on mercantilism. In 1758 François Quesnay published his *Economic Survey*, which argued for the existence of natural economic laws that must be allowed to operate freely. In 1776 the Scot Adam Smith published his *Wealth of Nations*,

John Wesley preaching in a private house.

which argued in parallel fashion that all nations would be wealthier if they removed restrictions on trade and let the natural law of supply and demand govern the exchange of commodities. Quesnay was primarily interested in agriculture and Smith in commerce, but both came to the same conclusion: that economic laws, like other natural laws, should be respected, that interference with these laws is dangerous, and that the greatest happiness and freedom come from allowing these laws to operate freely.

The same line of reasoning in political theory led to the theory of enlightened despotism. The *philosophes* hoped that divine-right monarchy would become benevolent monarchy, that monarchs would gradually become "enlightened" (or perhaps engage enlightened *philosophes* as advisers) and so govern their people according to natural law rather than according to their own caprice. To Voltaire and most of his fellows, government should be for the people but not necessarily by the people. A smaller group believed that reason pointed in the direction of a constitutional monarchy like the English, a government based on natural rights and contract, with a separation of powers as a further guarantee of political liberty. Finally, to enlightened despotism and constitutional government there was added a third theory, the theory of democracy, still too radical to be of much immediate influence but of enormous importance for the future. This was the theory obscurely but excitingly preached in *The Social Contract* (1762) by Jean Jacques Rousseau (1712–78).

Rousseau

Rousseau, a native of Geneva, turned up in Paris after a troubled and wandering youth, came to know Diderot and others of the *philosophes,* and for a time tried to become one of them. He was never easy in their company, however. He trusted reason, but he relied even more on emotion. He trusted nature, but to him nature was the unspoiled simplicity of precivilized man, "the noble savage." In a kind of conversion that he experienced in 1749, he became con-

vinced that mankind had lost more than it had gained by cultivating the arts and sciences, and so he surrendered his faith in progress. He grew more and more irritated by the artificiality of Paris society and finally broke with his former friends. Voltaire thought him mad, and Rousseau was haunted in his miserable later years by the illusion that he was being persecuted by everyone.

Rousseau was the great critic of the Enlightenment. By temperament he was a shy and sensitive misfit who vainly wanted to "belong." Deep down he knew himself to be good, but he felt that he had been corrupted and humiliated by an artificial society to which he did not and could not belong. To what kind of society or state could he give himself, then? Only to a society in which there were no hereditary rulers, no privileged aristocracy, no one with any right to lord it over others, none but those who had freely consented to become members of the society and had given up to the group all their individual rights. Perhaps Rousseau had an idealized Geneva in mind as he wrote *The Social Contract*—a community in which all the citizens knew and trusted one another—in which the minority accepted the majority's view with good grace because both felt themselves part of the same community. At any rate, he developed a theory of liberty as willing obedience to laws that the individual himself had helped to make as an active and loyal citizen, even though he might have been in the minority on any given issue. Locke and Montesquieu had thought that the way to obtain political liberty was to guarantee individual rights and to separate the organs of government so that no one of them could gain unrestricted control. Rousseau thought he would never feel free until he could find a community to which he could give up everything, on condition that all others did the same. In such a community there would be no division between rulers and ruled; the people would rule themselves. What magistrates there were would be mere servants of the community who could be instantly removed if they failed to carry out the people's will. If the people really governed themselves, there should be no checks and balances, no

Jean Jacques Rousseau.

Rousseau on the Social Contract

The problem is to find a form of association . . . in which each, while uniting himself with all, may still obey himself alone, and remain as free as before. This is the fundamental problem of which the Social Contract provides the solution: . . . the total alienation of each associate, together with all his rights, to the whole community. . . . Each man, in giving himself to all, gives himself to nobody. . . . Each of us puts his person and all his power in common under the supreme direction of the general will, and, in our corporate capacity, we receive each member as an indivisible part of the whole. . . . In order that the social compact may not be an empty formula, it tacitly includes the undertaking, which alone can give force to the rest, that whoever refuses to obey the general will shall be compelled to do so by the whole body. This means nothing less than that he will be forced to be free.

From Jean Jacques Rousseau, *The Social Contract* (New York and London: Everyman's Library, 1913), Book I, Chs. 6, 7, pp. 14–18.

separation of powers, no protection of rights.

Rousseau was picturing democracy in its purest and simplest form: a tight-knit community of loyal and active citizens, unhampered by any checks on their collective will because they unreservedly accepted this general will as their own. His book was highly abstract and difficult to understand. But when revolution actually flared up in France after his death, *The Social Contract* came into its own. It was not a work of the Enlightenment; its full force could be felt only in the new age of democratic revolution, nationalism, and Romanticism. And when romantic nationalism reached its peak, Rousseau could be used to justify dictatorship (which after all is supposed to embody the common will) as well as democracy.

So the two centuries that saw the Scientific Revolution and the Enlightenment might well be called the most revolutionary centuries in western intellectual history. The true watershed between what we call "medieval" and "modern" thought about God, man, and nature runs somewhere through these two centuries. The world of Luther and Loyola, of Charles V and Philip II, was still or-

ganically related to the Middle Ages. The world of Newton and Locke, of Voltaire and Rousseau, was unmistakably the father of our own.

ARTS AND LETTERS IN THE EIGHTEENTH CENTURY

The pervasive faith in the rationality, intelligibility, and order of the universe displayed by the scientists and philosophers of the age was reflected in the art and literature of the later seventeenth and early eighteenth centuries. Rationalism blended easily with classicism. The regularity and harmony of Newton's universe seemed to accord with the balance and proportion that Greek architects had admired as artistic ideals and with the rationality and restraint that the leading Greek and Roman writers had held up as literary ideals. The dictators of literary and artistic taste at the close of the seventeenth century were classicists, and when *philosophes* like Voltaire wrote dramas they accepted classical standards as unquestioningly as Corneille and Racine. Architects accepted classical rules of balance and unity with equal zeal in the "Georgian" buildings of England and the beautifully proportioned Place de la Concorde in Paris. Enthusiasm for classical antiquity reached its post-Renaissance climax in 1748, when the remains of the Roman city of Pompeii were discovered in startlingly well-preserved condition under the lava of Mt. Vesuvius.

An Age of Prose

The age of reason was an age of prose. Essays, satirical tales, novels, letters, and histories were the characteristic literary forms of the eighteenth century. Authors bent their energies to description and narrative rather than to suggestion and imagination. The essays of Addison and Steele, which began to appear in 1709, sketched a delightful picture of English rural society, while Jonathan Swift's *Gulliver's Travels* (1726) and Voltaire's *Candide* (1759) were more biting and satirical commentaries on human society. As the century progressed, the novel emerged as the favorite form of literary expression; the most mature example was Henry Fielding's *Tom Jones* (1749). Besides fiction, men read philosophy, economics, and history—of which Edward Gibbon's majestic *History of the Decline and Fall of the Roman Empire* (1776–88) was the most enduring example. Everything that could be done in prose—argument, satire, realistic description, historical narrative—was tried and done well by some French or British writer.

The elegance and aristocratic flavor of eighteenth-century society can be seen in its painting, and especially in the portraits, which were the most characteristic form of the art. The delicate-featured and exquisitely groomed women who look coolly down on the observer, and the worldly, sometimes arrogant, faces of their husbands under their powdered wigs suggest the artificiality of their society and sometimes the hardness of their characters. Furniture, tableware, and the great town and country houses of wealthy merchants and nobles reflect the same elegance and aristocratic spirit.

Not all the books, the arts, and the crafts were meant for the enjoyment of the aristocracy, however. The eighteenth century saw the appearance of the first newspapers, written for a wide audience of educated readers. William Hogarth (1697–1764) made engravings of his realistic satirical sketches of English society and sold them by the thousands. Above all, the novelists, the dramatists, and the musicians began to appeal to a middle-class audience that went far beyond the limits of the aristocracy. After the 1770s the plays and operas in Paris were apt to have a keen, satirical edge and to be directed at bourgeois listeners. The heroes and heroines of the novels were more often of middle-class origins than either upper- or lower-class. Music began to move from the aristocratic salon into the public auditorium.

Music

The greatest cultural achievement of the eighteenth century was its music. The musical world of the early eighteenth century was dominated by two great Germans: Johann Sebastian Bach (1685–1750) and George Frederick Handel (1685–1759) (who spent most of his life in England). Together they realized all the dramatic and emotive possibilities of the baroque style: Handel in his oratorios for chorus and instruments, Bach in his richly varied works for keyboard instruments, chamber groups, orchestras, and choruses. In the latter part of the century the orchestra, which had originated in the seventeenth century, was expanded and strengthened, the pianoforte invented, and music brought more and more into touch with a wider public. Franz Joseph Haydn (1732–1809), who wrote for both chamber groups and orchestras, developed the musical forms known as sonatas and symphonies. The other outstanding musical personality of the latter half of the century, Wolfgang Amadeus Mozart (1756–91), was possibly the most gifted musician who ever lived. A child prodigy, he lived only thirty-five years and died in poverty, but within this short span of time he produced string quartets, concertos, symphonies, and operas that were masterpieces of invention and form.

Wolfgang Amadeus Mozart, unfinished painting by Joseph Lange.

The Beginnings of Romanticism

Beneath the dominant tendency to respect rational structure and classical balance, however, there were countercurrents of revolt. Some evidence of these currents was seen in Pietism and Methodism, and in Rousseau's distrust of an exclusive reliance on reason. More clearly than Rousseau, the Scottish philosopher David Hume (1711–76) criticized reason as a method of knowing truth and defended the validity in human experience of feeling, conscience, and habit. French and English novelists developed sentimentalism to a fine art, putting their heroines through heartrending misfortune and mistreatment and trying at every turn to arouse the reader's anger, pity, love, or terror. The most influential example was Samuel Richardson's two thousand-page tearjerker, *Clarissa* (1748), which influenced Rousseau in writing his *Nouvelle Héloïse* (1761). The strange, the unusual, the offbeat, and the fantastic began to come into fashion. Gothic architecture and literature began to be appreciated once more, and a collection of poems (1762) ostensibly by a medieval poet named Ossian was very popular, though it turned out to be a forgery.

In Germany, which never came totally under the sway of the French Enlightenment, a "Storm and Stress" (*Sturm und Drang*) movement in literature emphasized the great elemental emotions and denied the supremacy of reason. Johann Gottfried von Herder (1744–1803) worked out a philosophy of history that emphasized the uniqueness and peculiarity of each nation or race, the individuality of its genius, and the falsity of any view that denied this uniqueness in the name of universal reason. Johann Wolfgang von Goethe (1749–1832) at the start of his long literary career published *The Sorrows of Young Werther* (1774), a morbid tale ending in a suicide, which appealed to lovers of sentiment and sensibility.

The greatest philosopher of the age, Immanuel Kant (1724–1804), a man who never traveled more than a few miles from Königsberg, his native city in East Prussia, launched a powerful attack on the rationalism of his age as too narrow and too dogmatic. Starting from David Hume's criticism of reason, Kant distinguished carefully between speculative (or scientific) reason and practical (or moral) reason in his very difficult book, *Critique of Pure Reason* (1781). The effect of his work was to enable Christians and idealists to make a new case for religion and morality based on the fact of man's conscience.

Taken together, these various tendencies heralded the beginnings of what was to be called Romanticism. The "Age of Reason" thus contained within itself the seeds of an age that would rely for its artistic, philosophical, and even social insight on emotion and conscience rather than on reason.

Suggestions for Further Reading

Note: Asterisk denotes a book available in paperback edition.

General J. H. Randall, *The Making of the Modern Mind* (1926, 1940), is the most successful one-volume survey of the course of western thought, by a philosopher with a sense for historical context. To Randall, "the modern mind" is essentially the scientific mind. C. Brinton, *Ideas and Men** (1950)—the material since the Renaissance has been published as *The Shaping of the Modern Mind** (1953)—is a more informally written and engaging narrative by a historian. Both books are particularly good on the seventeenth and eighteenth centuries. G. R. Sabine, *A History of Political Theory* (1938), is the most penetrating one-volume survey, particularly full on English political thought in the seventeenth century and French in the eighteenth. A. O. Lovejoy, *The Great Chain of Being** (1936), is a classic account of the underlying western conception of the universe as a hierarchical structure of being, from the Greeks to the nineteenth century. M. Ashley, *The Golden Century* (1968), is a well-written survey of seventeenth-century social and cultural history. J. Bronowski and Bruce Mazlish, *The Western Intellectual Tradition* (1974) puts the period in a general perspective.

The Scientific Revolution E. A. Burtt, *The Metaphysical Foundations of Modern Physical Science** (1924, 1955), and A. N. Whitehead, *Science and the Modern World** (1925, 1948), are famous philosophical inquiries into the origins of modern science, not easy reading, but rewarding to the serious student. A. R. Hall, *The Scientific Revolution** (1954), is the best modern account, well informed and critical. H. Butterfield, *Origins of Modern Science, 1300–1800** (1949), is a more readable discussion of the subject for the lay reader written by a general historian. A. Koyré writes absorbingly about the cosmological implications of the "revolution" in *From the Closed World to the Infinite Universe** (1957). C. C. Gillispie, *The Edge of Objectivity** (1960), is a brilliantly written essay on the growth of objectivity in the study of nature from Galileo to Einstein. T. S. Kuhn, *The Copernican Revolution** (1957), describes the transformation of astronomical thought. *The Structure of Scientific Revolutions** (1962), by the same author, is a controversial but brilliant discussion of scientific change in general. R. G. Collingwood traces the chief western conceptions of the natural order from the Greeks to the present in *The Idea of Nature** (1945). C. J. Singer, *From Magic to Science** (1928), is still valuable for its interpretation of the origins of modern science. On the social background of scientific development, three books are particularly valuable: M. Ornstein, *The Role of Scientific Societies in the Seventeenth Century* (1928); D. Stimson, *Scientists and Amateurs: A History of the Royal Society* (1948); and G. N. Clark, *Science and Social Welfare in the Age of Newton* (1937). See also R. K. Merton, *Science, Technology and Society in Seventeenth Century England* (1970). There are biographies and special studies, too numerous to list here. of every scientist mentioned in the text. But two studies of a famous case are worth noting: G. de Santillana, *The Crime of Galileo** (1955), and F. S. Taylor, *Galileo and the Freedom of Thought* (1938). The effect of scientific discovery on literature is the theme of M. Nicolson, *Science and Imagination** (1956). R. Hooykass, *Religion and the Rise of Science* (1972) is a good study of this topic.

Culture of the Seventeenth and Eighteenth Centuries	There is no full and reliable discussion in English on the baroque style in art, the basic studies being in German. The best introductions are in C. J. Friedrich, *The Age of the Baroque, 1610–1660** (1952) in the *Rise of Modern Europe* series, and Chapter 6 of H. Leichtentritt, *Music, History, and Ideas* (1938). The Pelican *History of Art** has good studies of individual countries for the period from 1600 to 1880. The latter third of G. N. Clark, *The Seventeenth Century* (1931), is devoted to art, literature, and philosophy. B. Willey's two volumes, *The Seventeenth Century Background** (1934) and *The Eighteenth Century Background** (1940), sketch a broad background for the study of English literature in the period. F. Fosca, *The Eighteenth Century* (1953), is probably the best introduction to the painting of the age. In addition to Leichtentritt, M. F. Bukofzer, *Music in the Baroque Era* (1947), is particularly interesting. There is no satisfactory general account of religious developments, but A. C. McGiffert, *Protestant Thought Before Kant* (1911), is a brief reliable account. M. J. Bradshaw, *The Philosophical Foundations of Faith* (1941), is illuminating on the religious attitudes of prominent seventeenth-century figures like Descartes. M. L. Edwards, *John Wesley and the Eighteenth Century* (1933), is one of many books on Methodism. See also G. R. Craig, *The Church in the Age of Reason* (1961).

Contemporary Literature	The best way, as always, to gain a firsthand knowledge of the thought and feeling of the period is through a study of some of the paintings, the buildings, the literary and philosophical writings, and the musical works of the age. This becomes increasingly easy to do after the sixteenth century because of the availability of reproductions, records, and inexpensive reprints. The student will have to make his own selection, but some of the following should be on any reading list (there are many editions of each except where specified): Descartes, *Discourse on Method;** Bacon, *New Atlantis;* Pascal, *Pensées;** Galileo, *Dialogue on the Great World Systems,* ed. by G. de Santillana (1953); John Bunyan, *The Pilgrim's Progress;** John Locke, *Second Treatise of Government** and *Essay Concerning Human Understanding;**Selections from Bayle's Dictionary,* ed. by E. A. Beller and M. D. Lee (1952); Beccaria, *Essay on Crimes and Punishments** (trans. 1953); *The Portable Voltaire,** ed. by B. R. Redman (1949); Rousseau, *Social Contract;** Henry Fielding, *Tom Jones;** Samuel Richardson, *Clarissa* (abridgment, Modern Library, 1950). *The Portable Age of Reason Reader,** ed. by C. Brinton (1956), is an excellent selection of readings from the *philosophes.*

The Enlightenment	The most significant study of the transition from the seventeenth century to the eighteenth, from the Scientific Revolution to the Enlightenment, is P. Hazard, *The European Mind: The Critical Years, 1680–1715** (trans. 1952). There are excellent chapters on the Enlightenment in W. L. Dorn, *Competition for Empire, 1740–1763** (1940), and in the *New Cambridge Modern History,* Vol. VII: A. Cobban, *The Old Régime, 1713–1763* (1957). The most searching interpretation of the movement as a whole is E. Cassirer, *The Philosophy of the Enlightenment** (1932, trans. 1951), which emphasizes the break with older ways of thinking accomplished by the eighteenth century. C. L. Becker's charming lectures, *The Heavenly City of the Eighteenth-Century Philosophers** (1932), emphasize the continuity with the past. G. R. Havens, *The Age of Ideas: From Reaction to Revolution in Eighteenth-Century France** (1955), is a sound study. On the idea of progress, besides Becker, see J. B. Bury, *The Idea of Progress** (1920, 1932); R. F. Jones, *Ancients and Moderns** (1936); and C. Frankel, *The Faith of Reason: The Idea of Progress in the French Enlightenment* (1948). C. R. Cragg, *Reason and Authority in the Eighteenth Century* (1964), is an excellent account of the Enlightenment on the English side of the Channel, and D. Mornet, *French Thought in the Eighteenth Century* (1929), of Enlightenment on the other. P. Gay, *The Enlightenment: An Interpretation** (1966–69), is an attempt to pull all aspects of the movement together. For the political thought of the *philosophes,* see K. Martin, *French Liberal Thought in the Eighteenth Century** (1929); and for the historical thought of Voltaire, Robertson, Hume, and Gibbon, see J. B. Black, *The Art of History* (1926). Two unfamiliar aspects of the Enlightenment are brought to light in R. Darnton, "The High Enlightenment and the Low-Life of Literature in Pre-Revolutionary France," *Past and Present,* no. 51 (1971), and *Mesmerism and the End of the Enlightenment* (1968).

22 Aristocracy and Empire, 1715–1789

The seventy-five years between the death of Louis XIV (1715) and the outbreak of the French Revolution (1789) have a character of their own. This was a period of stability and equilibrium. There were no religious wars and no social upheavals (except for an uprising of serfs in far-off Russia), and there appears to have been somewhat less social mobility than in the seventeenth century. Monarchy was the most prevalent form of government, with divine-right monarchy evolving into "enlightened despotism."

Closely examined, however, the governments of the European states in the eighteenth century, both monarchies and republics, are better described as "aristocracies." Everywhere landed or moneyed minorities controlled or strongly influenced the governments of Europe. The Whig nobles and merchants who dominated the English Parliament, the French nobles and lawyers who dominated the royal councils and the law courts of France after the death of Louis XIV, the Junkers who commanded the Prussian armies, the landed nobles who made a farce of the Polish Diet, the "service nobility" that ceased to serve any but its own interests after the reign of Peter the Great in Russia, the wealthy bourgeois who directly controlled the governments of the Dutch Republic and the German free cities—all were rich, well-born, and privileged, and thus fitted the eighteenth-century definition of aristocrats. Everywhere "aristocracy" was resurgent against absolute monarchy, and many of the gains of seventeenth-century monarchies were lost or compromised. Only where the monarch or the chief minister was a man of unusual ability was this revival of aristocratic influence turned to the benefit of the central government.

In this undeclared war between monarch and aristocrat a kind of compromise was generally reached. Eighteenth-century governments maintained an uneasy balance between centralization and decentralization, between absolute monarchy and aristocratic privilege. This might have been illogical, but strict adherence to basic principles had caused the bloody religious and civil wars of the last two centuries. Most men were glad to accept the structure of society and government as they found it after 1715. It was a glorious age to be alive in—if you were an "aristocrat." There was much abject poverty, injustice, and brutality in European society, but these could be forgotten if one centered one's attention on the brilliant "civilization" (the word first appeared in the 1770s) of the Paris salons or the London coffeehouses. To men who remembered the devastation of the Thirty Years' War or the fanaticism of Cromwell's "saints," social stability and political equilibrium were worth a fairly high price in injustice.

INTERNATIONAL RELATIONS

Equilibrium was also the rule in international relations. The defeat of Louis XIV's bid for a preponderance of power in Europe had been bloody and costly, and European statesmen were tacitly agreed that all such attempts to become "top dog" should be stopped at the outset. The balancing of power among the "great powers" of Europe—France, Britain, Austria, Prussia, and Russia (Spain, Holland, Sweden, Poland, and the Ottoman Empire could no longer qualify)—became the chief concern of diplomats.

The balance, of course, seldom remained steady for very long. Every country was constantly on the lookout for additional territory or for new colonies and trading opportunities abroad. In order to avoid large-scale wars like those needed to curb Louis XIV's ambitions, it became the custom for all the great powers to expect "compensation" whenever one of them was fortunate or daring enough to acquire new territory. This was hard on the weaker states, which were carved up to provide the "compensation," but it admittedly preserved the balance and often maintained the peace.

There were wars, and they were fairly frequent. But they were not so bloody or so exhausting as those of the seventeenth century. Generally they were "limited wars"—in two senses. First, they were limited in the numbers of persons who took part in them or were affected by them. Eighteenth-century armies were

Opposite: Frederick II of Prussia in 1778.

professional armies, often recruited or kidnaped from the dregs of society or composed of foreign mercenaries. Except in Russia, where serfs made up most of the army, there was no general conscription, and the civilian was usually little affected by wars. Warfare consisted of elaborate maneuvering by highly disciplined professional units rather than bloody mass combat. There was little pillaging, even in enemy territory, because it was bad business to devastate a territory that might be annexed.

Wars were limited also in their objectives. There were no wars of annihilation. The enemy of today might be the ally of tomorrow, and it was thought well not to defeat any power too thoroughly because that would disturb the balance. The religious hatreds of the seventeenth century had cooled, and the passions of revolutionary liberalism and nationalism had not yet sprung into flame. The statesmen and generals fought for comparatively definite and concrete political and economic objectives, not for ideologies. When the objectives were attained—or when it became clear that they could not be attained immediately—the statesmen made peace or arranged a truce. There was no need to fight through to unconditional surrender. In spite of cutthroat competition for "empire"—in the form of land, population, colonies, or trade— the monarchs, bureaucrats, and aristocrats of the eighteenth century felt themselves part of a common civilization. The competition was a jockeying for power

EUROPE IN 1715

among cousins rather than a fight for survival against deadly enemies.

The picture of a stable, well-balanced eighteenth-century society sketched here could of course be compared to Newton's picture of the universe—a beautifully stable order of perfectly balanced gravitational pushes and pulls in which every mass moved along discoverable lines of force. But this picture must not be exaggerated. The eighteenth century was also a dynamic age. Its precarious equilibrium was an equilibrium among rapidly expanding forces. Wealth and trade were increasing; something like a revolution in agriculture was in the making, and a revolution in industry had begun. European economy and diplomacy were rapidly becoming global rather than continental, and the struggle for empire was reaching the farthest corners of the earth. For the first time, battles fought in America, Africa, and Asia began to tip the balance of power in Europe. And in trying to keep the balance, each country accentuated its own particular sources of strength. England relied more and more on naval power and commerce, Prussia on its army and bureaucracy. Russia intensified its reliance on serfdom, while Austria made up for weakness in Germany by increasing its power in southeastern Europe. France, the one country that did not want to specialize, found itself coming out second-best in most fields—naval power, military power, and industrial growth. Its intellectual and cultural leadership masked, but did not remedy, these weaknesses. In short, differences in the bases of power among European nations increased rather than decreased during the period and made it harder to keep the balance. With growing political rivalry added to rapid social change, it can be seen that the eighteenth century was not all order and stability. It was pregnant with revolution as well.

The years from 1715 to 1789 may conveniently be divided into three periods of about twenty-five years each: (1) a generation of peace and prosperity, 1715–40; (2) a period of worldwide warfare, 1740–63; and (3) an interval of enlightened despotism, aristocratic resurgence, and revolutionary stirrings, 1763–89.

Aristocracy

[By the 1760s] the world had become more aristocratic. Aristocracy in the eighteenth century may even be thought of as a new and recent development, if it be distinguished from the older institution of nobility. In one way it was more exclusive than mere nobility. A king could create nobles, but, as the saying went, it took four generations to make a gentleman. In another way aristocracy was broader than nobility. Countries that had no nobles, like Switzerland or British America, or countries that had few nobles of importance, like the Dutch provinces, might have aristocracies that even nobles recognized as such. . . . Aristocracy was nobility civilized, polished by that "refinement of manners" of which people talked, enjoying not only superiority of birth but a superior mode of life. It was a way of life as pleasing as any that mankind has ever developed, and which the middle classes were to imitate as much and as long as they could, a way of life characterized by dignified homes and by gardens and well-kept lawns, by private tutors and grand tours and sojourns at watering places, by annual migration between town and country and an abundance of respectful and unobtrusive servants.

From R. R. Palmer, *The Age of the Democratic Revolution* (Princeton, N.J.: Princeton University Press, 1959), pp. 29–30.

PEACE AND PROSPERITY 1715–40

After the peace settlements of 1713 in western Europe and of 1719 to 1721 in eastern Europe, both governments and peoples were weary of war. The age that followed was unheroic, unexciting, and corrupt, like many other postwar periods. But peace restored law and order, and order stimulated an enormous expansion of trade, particularly in western Europe.

Increase of Trade and Wealth

Seaborne commerce was the key to wealth in the eighteenth century. Thanks to the enterprise of their merchants and the technical skill of their mariners, the foreign trade of Britain and France increased about five times during the eighteenth century. In the case of Britain the sharpest increase was in colonial trade. This meant that Britain needed a

The Baron, caricature of a member of the French nobility (1785).

Engraving from a seventeenth-century history of the West Indies showing the workings of a sugar plantation.

larger merchant marine than its rivals and forced the British to build the strongest navy in the world to protect its overseas trade. In the case of France the greatest increase was in trade with other European nations. In both cases the accumulation of wealth in the hands of the upper classes was spectacular. For the first time the wealth of Europe began to eclipse the wealth of Asia. The two preceding centuries of exploration and establishment of overseas trading connections had begun to pay off handsomely in material benefits. The dinner table of a merchant of Liverpool, for instance, was graced by sugar from the West Indies, wine from Portugal, and tobacco from Virginia. His wife might wear calico from India in summer and furs from Canada in winter. Their daughter might be married to the heir of a nobleman whose capacious Georgian house had been built on the combined profits from his land and his mercantile investments.

But many of the commodities on which this thriving trade was based were derived from the labor of slaves or serfs. Only African slaves could be forced to do the kind of work required on the sugar plantations of the West Indies, and even they survived only about seven years, on the average. There was an almost insatiable demand for black slaves in the sugar islands, a demand that was met largely by English slave traders, who procured their victims from the petty kings of the west coast of Africa, exchanged them for sugar in the West Indies, had the sugar converted into rum, then used the rum to debauch native rulers and village leaders and thus to secure more slaves in Africa. The serfs who toiled without recompense for their noble landlords in the grain-producing regions of eastern Europe were in much the same position in the economic order as the slaves of the West Indies. In short, a large part of the European economy was still based, as the economy of Greece and Rome had been, on servile labor.

There were signs in England, however, of the beginnings of revolutionary changes in both farming and industry. Eventually these changes were to result in an unprecedented expansion in the amount and variety of food, clothing, shelter, and luxuries that Europeans could produce. Historians speak of these changes as the "Agricultural Revolution" and the "Industrial Revolution," but these two revolutions picked up speed very slowly. For example, the first workable, though inefficient, steam engine was in use by 1700; the greatly improved Watts engine appeared three-quarters of a century later but was not widely used until after 1800. Since the results of the Agricultural and Industrial Revolutions were seen most clearly in the nineteenth century, they will be discussed in later chapters.

Mississippi and South Sea Bubbles

European commercial capitalism was still expanding its field of operations in the early eighteenth century. The period of peace after 1713 encouraged both private financial speculation and wildcat commercial ventures. The years 1719 and 1720 saw the first large-scale example of a typically modern phenomenon, a cycle of boom-and-bust, or, as contemporaries called it, a "bubble."

The wars of Louis XIV had burdened both the French and the English governments with large debts. When a Scottish promoter named John Law showed up at the court of France after the death of Louis XIV and offered to solve the government's financial troubles, he was given *carte blanche* to manage the French economy as he saw fit. He set up a bank to issue paper currency and organized a Mississippi Company to trade with France's colony in Louisiana. The company boldly took over the government's debt, accepting government bonds in payment for shares of its own stock. Then it promoted a boom in the price of its stock by spreading tall tales of its commercial prospects. When the price finally reached forty times its original

value, investors began to sell in order to cash in on their profits. Before long the price had plummeted, the bubble had burst, and Law had fled the country.

A similar episode occurred across the Channel in London. A South Sea Company had been organized to exploit the trade with the Spanish colonies provided for by the Peace of Utrecht. It too took over much of the government's debt, and it too deliberately promoted a boom in its own stock. In 1720, a few months after Law's failure, the South Sea bubble burst.

The collapse of the Mississippi and South Sea bubbles in 1719 and 1720 hampered the development of joint stock companies and ruined a good many individual investors. But the two companies had shown how to mobilize vast amounts of capital and how to find new sources of support for the public debt. Deliberate encouragement of speculation had tarnished both objectives, but the underlying commercial purposes of the two companies were essentially sound. When they were reorganized, both continued to make money for their investors for many years. French trade, particularly, was stimulated, although investors lost confidence in the French government. In contrast, the English government came to acknowledge the national debt as a public obligation and never again permitted private interests to assume responsibility for it, thus gaining the confidence of investors.

England Under Walpole

During the generation of peace that followed the death of Louis XIV, the English worked out some of their internal political problems. As had been determined by the Act of Settlement, the Elector of Hanover succeeded Anne as ruler of England in 1714. Compared with the Stuarts, the first two Hanoverian monarchs, George I (1714–27) and George II (1727–60), were colorless figures. Both were stupid men who spoke little or no English. They interfered constantly in minor details of government, but neither was capable of grasping the larger issues. As a result, the "inner cabinet" of ministers became more and more

George I of England (1714–27), and his signature. Medal by John Croker.

Caricature of George II drawn by a British officer about 1760.

responsible for policy decisions. Legally, the king was still free to choose his own ministers. Actually, he had to select men who could influence elections and control a majority in Parliament. These leading ministers had to meet frequently in order to concert policy. They began to force out of office colleagues who disagreed with the group's majority, and they usually accepted the leadership of the ablest or most powerful among them in presenting their policy to the king. These informal practices vaguely foreshadowed the "cabinet system" and "prime minister" of the nineteenth century.

Sir Robert Walpole (left), leader of the Whig government from 1721 to 1742, talking to the speaker of the House of Commons. Engraving after a painting by Hogarth.

Robert Walpole, a country squire who had family connections with both the landed and the commercial aristocracies, is generally considered the first prime minister in English history, though he would not have acknowledged the title. For some twenty years, from 1721 to 1742, he was the manager of the Whig party in Parliament and the leading minister in the government. The first two Hanoverians by necessity chose their ministers from Whigs, since the Tories were tainted by affection for the Stuarts and had little strength in Parliament.

Walpole was a good-natured, hard-headed politician who understood the landed and financial "interests" represented in Parliament and knew how to hold a parliamentary majority together by tact, persuasion, and, if necessary, bribery and corruption. The fact that he was addicted to hard drinking and off-color stories helped rather than hurt him in managing the Whig merchants and landed gentry who controlled Parliament and ran local government as justices of the peace. Walpole's motto was, "Let sleeping dogs lie." He took care never to stir up any issue, at home or abroad, that might arouse passion and conflict. In 1733, for instance, he proposed a sensible scheme for raising more revenue from excise taxes and less from customs duties in order to discourage smuggling and encourage legitimate trade. But when his scheme was met by a storm of irrational abuse ("No excise, no popery, no wooden shoes" was one slogan), he dropped it. So far as the colonies were concerned, he followed a policy of "salutary neglect," leaving them to grow in population and wealth by their own efforts. In foreign affairs he preserved the peace until 1739, when the London merchants and their spokesmen in Parliament forced him into a commercial war with Spain. Even then he tried to keep the war as limited as possible.

1589	1610	1616		1643			1715				1774	1793

Henry IV · Regency · Louis XIII · Richelieu · Mazarin · Louis XIV · Regency · Louis XV · Fleury · Louis XVI

1624 1642 1661   1723 1726 1743

On the whole, Walpole's ministry was a fruitful one for England. Both England and its colonies prospered; the credit of the government was never better; and the ruling aristocracy of landed and commercial wealth governed with a loose rein. When Voltaire visited England from 1726 to 1729 he may have idealized English society and government somewhat. But there was without question more equality before the law in England, more personal freedom, more sense of public obligation in the ruling class, more security of property, and more widespread prosperity than anywhere else in Europe.

Louis XV and Cardinal Fleury

The generation of peace that brought strength to Britain brought weakness to France. Louis XIV's great-grandson Louis XV (1715–74) was a child of five when he came to the throne. The Regency that governed in his name for eight years had to make concessions to all the powerful elements in French society that had been kept in leash by the Sun King. The result was an aristocratic reaction in French government. Nobles began to reappear as policymakers on the royal councils, and the *Parlement* of Paris boldly reasserted its ancient claim to register and enforce royal legislation or not, as it saw fit. The French monarchy remained as absolute as ever in theory, but after Louis XIV there was no strong hand to make the theory work. French government became inefficient and inconstant. Aristocratic privilege exasperated the middle classes and in the long run made it impossible for the government to avoid financial insolvency.

For a time the decline was arrested by Cardinal Fleury, the leading minister from 1726 to 1743. Fleury had ability, but he was no Richelieu. He was past seventy when he came to power, and his policy,

much like Walpole's, was to preserve the peace, make cautious compromises, and avoid direct confrontation with the holders of power—in this case the nobility. He dissociated himself from the statesmanlike attempt of another minister to tax the nobility like everyone else, but he stabilized the currency, encouraged trade, and did all he could to make the old system of tax-farming work. His monarch was too debauched and incapable to set a more constructive course.

Fleury lost power in his last years, and when he died at the age of ninety, Louis XV decided that he would govern for himself without a prime minister. This simply meant that France now had a king who could neither govern himself nor let anyone else govern for him. Louis XV's best-known remark, "After me, the deluge," perfectly expressed his attitude. The aristocracy naturally took full advantage of this situation and greatly increased its influence. France remained the largest and potentially the most powerful nation in Europe. French trade and industry were growing at a rapid rate, but the government was run by royal mistresses and favorites (Mme. de Pompadour was the most prominent), and the French state could not make full use of its resources.

Declining Monarchies and Empires

Elsewhere in Europe, with few exceptions, monarchical institutions were in decline as they were in France during the generation after the Peace of Utrecht.

In Spain the Bourbon whom Louis XIV established on the throne, Philip V (1700–46), managed to curb the nobility somewhat and to encourage trade and industry. But the dry rot had eaten too deep into Spanish society and government to allow a real revival of the nation's greatness. Neither the Spanish

Arms of Louis XV, from Diderot's *Encyclopaedia*.

Maria Theresa of Austria with her husband, Emperor Francis I, and eleven of their children. The future Emperor Joseph II stands in the right center. Painting by Meytens.

economy, nor the army and navy, nor the colonies made any significant gains.

Austria was an imperfectly united empire composed of three separate kingdoms (Austria, Bohemia, and Hungary) and two dependencies of quite different cultures and traditions (northern Italy and the southern Netherlands). The Habsburg Emperor Charles VI (1711–40) had to spend years in persuading his own subjects and foreign governments to accept a "Pragmatic Sanction" that provided that his daughter Maria Theresa (Charles had no sons) should succeed him as ruler of all his various lands. By the time of his death he had the agreement on paper of everyone concerned, but no one was sure just how long the agreement would be respected by greedy neighboring monarchs or restless Hungarian nobles.

Farther to the east, the Polish and Ottoman empires continued to decline. A desultory and trivial war over the succession to the Polish crown was fought between 1733 and 1738 by France and Spain against Austria and Russia. The Russian candidate for the throne won out, and all the losers were "compensated" by being given scraps of territory elsewhere—Spain in Naples and Sicily, for instance. At the same time Austria and Russia were once more at war with the Ottoman Turks. The Turks were never completely dominated by their neighbors, as were the Poles, but it was evident that neither state counted for much in the European power structure.

In the generation after Peter the Great's death in 1725 a series of palace revolutions placed the Russian crown successively on the heads of half a dozen children or incompetent women. German, particularly Prussian, influence was very strong at the court. As in France, the nobles managed to free themselves from many of the restrictions placed on them by earlier and stronger monarchs. The Russian nobles extended the power that Peter had given them over their own serfs but tried to renounce the obligation to serve the state that he had imposed on them in return. In Russia, as in Hungary and Prussia, the peasant sank deeper and deeper into serfdom during the eighteenth century, while the governments made one concession after another to the hereditary nobles in order to gain their favor. Until the accession of Catherine the Great in 1762 there was no strong hand at the helm of the Russian state, but Peter's work in raising his country to the position of a great power in European war and diplomacy proved to be permanent.

Frederick William I of Prussia

Probably the most successful ruler of his generation apart from Walpole—and for quite different reasons—was King Frederick William I of Brandenburg-Prussia (1713–40). While absolute monarchy seemed to be in decline elsewhere, this strange, uncouth, and furious man, who smoked tobacco and drank beer in Gargantuan quantities, continued the work of transforming one of the smallest and poorest states of Europe into a great military power. Following in the footsteps of the Great Elector, he centralized the administration in a so-called General Directory, pared civil expenditures to the bone, and worked his subordinates remorselessly, all with the object of building the best-disciplined and most formidable army in Europe. "Salvation is from the Lord," he remarked, "but everything else is my affair." When he was through he had increased the size of his army to over eighty thousand men, twice what it

Frederick William I, by Antoine Pesne.

505

had been under his father. But while Frederick William built the fourth largest and the most efficient army on the Continent, he drew back whenever he might have used it. He left his son a full treasury, an efficient civil bureaucracy, and a highly trained army—one that had not fought a battle in over a generation.

He despised his son, Frederick, for his unmilitary habits and his taste for reading Voltaire and playing the flute. On occasion he would break the flute, burn the books, and even have the young man publicly beaten. When Frederick finally tried to flee the country with a friend, his father had the friend beheaded before his son's eyes and put the young man to work in the bureaucracy. Strange to say, the treatment worked. Without losing his taste for literature and music, Frederick grew interested in administration and the army. He succeeded his father in 1740 as Frederick II (1740–86), better known to history as Frederick the Great.

WORLDWIDE WARFARE 1740–63

The peaceful generation just described was followed by a generation dominated by two wars, the War of the Austrian Succession (1740–48) and the Seven Years' War (1756–63), separated by a few years of intensive diplomacy. These wars grew out of two irreconcilable rivalries for power. One was the rivalry between the rising Hohenzollerns of Prussia and the more established Habsburgs of Austria for territory in central Europe. The other was the rivalry between Great Britain and France for trade and colonial empire in North America, the West Indies, Africa, and India. Twice these two rivalries became entangled with each other, although the partnerships changed between the wars. And in the final peace of 1763 England and Prussia gained at the expense of France and Austria.

The British Navy and the Prussian Army

These wars were to demonstrate that the most efficient fighting units in eighteenth-century Europe were the British navy and the Prussian army. The most obvious explanation of superiority in each case was the unrivaled excellence of the officers. But behind the two military arms were two sharply different societies and political systems, each well adapted to the particular sort of competition in which the nation found itself.

Great Britain had many advantages in the race for sea power. It was an island, safe from invasion by land, and therefore able to pour into ships the men and money that continental states had to pour into armies. Maritime enterprise was both profitable and patriotic; a seafaring career attracted enterprising younger sons of the nobility and gentry as well as yeomen and artisans. The reservoir of experienced sailors was larger in England than in France, its nearest rival, because the British had the largest merchant marine in the world. Finally, the government and the ruling classes recognized the importance of trade and sea power, and in spite of periods of neglect they supported naval construction and encouraged British shipping.

Britain's rival, France, had almost all the advantages England had—experienced sailors, a large merchant marine, warships superior in design even to the

Figures from recruiting signs for the Prussian army (1740).

Ships of the Line: the British Channel Fleet (1790).

British, and colonial bases overseas. But France had long land frontiers and a tradition of pushing those frontiers to the east and of intervening in the affairs of central Europe. This situation created an impossible dilemma. France could not be both the greatest land power and the greatest sea power, and if the army was favored, as it usually was, then the navy suffered.

The Prussian army was the creation of the Hohenzollerns, who had shaped a society and designed a state to support it. The Prussian bureaucracy and fiscal system had grown out of institutions devised to provide direct support to the army. The Junkers had been taught that their calling was to serve the king, in the army by preference, in the civil service if necessary. In return for their service they were given wide powers over the serfs who supported them. Enterprising members of the small middle class were also enlisted into the civil service, and serfs were conscripted when needed into the army. The proverbial discipline of the Prussian army pervaded to some degree both the society and the government. In England, central government by Parliament, local government by amateurs, and a considerable amount of freedom proved to be a good formula for produc-

ing sea power. In Prussia, centralized professional administration with an absolute monarch leading a disciplined aristocracy proved to be a successful formula for producing land power.

The War of the Austrian Succession, 1740–48

In 1740 Maria Theresa, a beautiful but inexperienced young woman, succeeded her father in the Habsburg dominions, to which her right of succession had been guaranteed by the Pragmatic Sanction. Frederick II of Prussia almost immediately threw his army into Silesia, one of her richest provinces, on the northeastern frontier of Bohemia. Frederick had published an anonymous little book against the immorality of Machiavelli, but he had learned some of the Florentine's precepts well. Silesia, with its million inhabitants, its linen industry, and its iron ore, would finally make Brandenburg-Prussia a great power. Both Maria Theresa and the European powers were caught off guard. Frederick seized what he needed and spent the next twenty years defending his gain.

For a time it was not too difficult. Frederick's boldfaced aggression encouraged every enemy of the Habsburgs to

22 / Aristocracy and Empire, 1715–1789   **507**

join in the attack: Bavaria, Spain, and finally France. Strangely enough, Hungary, which resented Habsburg rule, proved to be Maria Theresa's salvation. When she went to Budapest with her infant son and made an emotional appeal to the Hungarian Parliament, the chivalrous nobility rose tumultuously to her support. During the wars that followed, an able minister, Count Haugwitz, centralized the Habsburg administration and reorganized the army. Austria, a helpless victim state in 1740, was able to revive and become a formidable antagonist to the king of Prussia. Frederick's armies fought brilliantly, however, and the combined pressure of France, Bavaria, and Prussia—shaky though the alliance was—proved to be too much for Maria Theresa to overcome. In 1748, at Aix-la-Chapelle, she agreed to a peace treaty that left Silesia in Frederick's hands.

Meanwhile the Anglo-French rivalry had also broken out into war. When war began between England and Spain in 1739, it was only a question of time before France would be drawn in. France and Spain cooperated closely in the eighteenth century. Both had Bourbon rulers, and France had a large economic stake in the Spanish Empire since France supplied the Spanish colonies with most of their manufactured goods. English and French interests clashed in America and in India. In North America the English felt threatened by the French military hold on Canada and Louisiana, while the French felt threatened by the pressure of the English colonies expanding northward and westward. In the West Indies there was rivalry over the sugar islands. In India the death of the last strong Mughal emperor in 1707 had led to the collapse of all central administration. Both the French and the British East India companies were trying to influence native principalities, particularly around Madras and Pondicherry. From Canada

to the Carnatic Coast of India uneasy Frenchmen and Englishmen were ready to fly to arms.

In 1744 France declared war on Great Britain, and immediately the war in Europe and the war overseas merged into one. In 1745 the American colonists captured Louisbourg in Canada, and in 1746 the French seized Madras. Nothing decisive came of the conflict, however, because the English could not yet make up their minds whether to concentrate their efforts on a land war on the Continent against France or on the war overseas. The former policy was denounced by the "Patriots" in Parliament as "Hanoverianism"—that is, a pandering to the interests of the monarch, George II, who was Elector of Hanover in Germany. The English navy defeated the French; the French army defeated the English on the Continent; but neither side pressed its successes very far, either on sea or on land. A typical "limited" war, the War of the Austrian Succession ended in a stalemate so far as Britain and France were concerned. The French gave up their conquest of Madras, and the English government, much to the disgust of the American colonists, gave back Louisbourg. The French came out of the war with no gains over either Austria or England. The English came out of it with a clearer sense of how they should fight their next war with France.

The Diplomatic Revolution

England had fought in the War of the Austrian Succession in loose agreement with its old ally, Austria. France had fought in a still looser alliance with Prussia (Frederick deserted his ally twice to make truces with Austria). During the years between 1748 and 1756, a "diplomatic revolution" took place in which the chief antagonists in the first general war of mid-century changed partners in preparation for the second. This "revolution" illustrates nicely the main characteristics of eighteenth-century diplomacy.

The chief instigator of the "revolution" was Count Kaunitz, the Austrian chancellor. Burning with desire to crush Frederick and recover Silesia, he decided that the only practical way was to heal the ancient antagonism between Bourbons and Habsburgs and to gain the support of France—and if possible of Russia as well—in a new war against Prussia. Prussia, he was sure, could not last long against the three strongest powers on the Continent. Kaunitz worked carefully to bring the mistress of Louis XV, Mme. de Pompadour, around to his side, but it was a chain of calculations and miscalculations by other statesmen that finally persuaded France to agree to the alliance. The English ministry became worried about whether Austria had the will and ability to help England defend Hanover against France. Prussia was obviously better placed to defend Hanover, but when Frederick agreed to do so in return for British subsidies, the French were irritated. Since Frederick had made an agreement with France's ancient enemy, England, the French were now ready to reach an understanding with Frederick's enemy, Austria. Soon a coalition of France, Austria, and Russia was arranged, and it looked as if Prussia's situation was hopeless. Frederick saw that his only chance was to catch his enemies off guard, and, characteristically, he started the war with an offensive in 1756, almost a year earlier than his opponents had planned.

Conflict Overseas

War had already broken out between the British and the French overseas. In India, Joseph Dupleix had been trying since 1749 to make the French East India Company a political as well as a commercial power. By dominating native states, he hoped to increase the company's revenue and hamper British trade. The English East India Company soon became alarmed, and there were some armed clashes in which Dupleix's forces were defeated. In 1754 the company directors, afraid that Dupleix was leading them into serious conflict with the British, recalled him to France. Ironically, his idea of increasing the company's revenue through domination of native states was adopted by the British East India Company under its brilliant local leader, Robert Clive, and became the foundation of British territorial rule in India.

The situation in America was even more tense than in India. The French in Canada had used the interval of peace to build a chain of forts from the St. Lawrence down the Ohio to the Mississippi, and the British government had countered by sending ships and troops to the American colonies. The time was approaching when the two expanding empires of the North American continent were going to clash, and there were now perhaps a million and a half British subjects (including slaves) in North America and only about sixty thousand French—the ratio had grown to 25 to 1. British troops and colonists began to strike at the French forts. An attempt to capture Fort Duquesne, the most important link in the chain (on the site of modern Pittsburgh), was disastrously defeated in

Bengal miniature of about 1760 showing a British East India Company employee adapting to his Indian environment.

1755, and England and France were at war.

So in 1756 Europe was once more deep in conflict—this time France, Austria, and Russia against England and Prussia. The largest navy in the world had little to fear, but the odds were very great against the best army in Europe. If Prussia were defeated and partitioned, as seemed likely, any British gains overseas might well be wiped out at the peace conference. The Anglo-French and the Austro-Prussian rivalries had become inextricably mingled.

The Seven Years' War*
1756–63

England made no headway in the war until the summer of 1757, when William Pitt became virtual prime minister. Pitt, one of Britain's greatest war ministers, shrewdly focused the nation's war efforts on conquests overseas. His policy repre-

*This war, in its American phase, is known as the French and Indian War.

sented the commercial aims of the London business community, but it also appealed to the pride of the ordinary Englishman in the navy and the growing colonial empire. Pitt concentrated power in his own hands, and his energy and his enthusiasm stimulated his subordinates to unheard-of efforts. The "year of miracles" (1759) demonstrated Pitt's remarkable ability to direct a complex series of operations and to choose first-rate commanders. In this one year Quebec fell, Guadaloupe was taken, French military power in India was broken, and the French fleet was crushed off Quiberon Bay. England's control of the seas enabled it to hold both Canada and India, a classic example of the strategic importance of sea power.

While Britain was destroying the French Empire abroad, Prussia was fighting for its life on the Continent. England's "year of miracles" was a year of near disaster for Prussia. Its army was badly defeated by the Russians at Kunersdorf in 1759; the Prussians now needed a miracle just to survive. Only

View of the taking of Quebec by British forces in 1759. This eighteenth-century engraving is quite accurate in its depiction of military positions.

the divisions among his enemies allowed Frederick to prolong the war. Kaunitz had not promised enough of the spoils to France and Russia to stimulate an all-out effort from either country. Pitt's subsidies to German forces were just enough to pin the French down in bloody fighting in Westphalia. The war was unpopular in France and was putting a heavy strain on the already shaky French financial system. Austrian armies were poorly led, and the Austrian government was almost as afraid of the Russian army in the Oder Valley as it was of the Prussian. So Frederick held on, though his resources were almost exhausted, until the "Hohenzollern miracle" occurred. Empress Elizabeth of Russia died in 1762 and was succeeded by her nephew, Peter III, a warm admirer of the king of Prussia. Peter promptly withdrew from the war, and Austria now had only a crippled and sulky France as a major ally. With no hope of winning a decisive victory, Maria Theresa decided to end the war. Peace was made in 1763, leaving Prussia in permanent possession of Silesia. To have preserved the status quo was a moral victory for Frederick. Prussia had clearly established itself as one of the great powers.

The death of an empress saved Frederick the Great from possible defeat. The death of a king indirectly robbed Britain of some of the fruits of victory. When George III succeeded his grandfather in 1760 he wished to prove himself thoroughly English, unlike the first two Georges. This meant withdrawing from all involvement in German affairs, contrary to Pitt's advice. By October 1761, Pitt had been forced out of office. Lord Bute, George's Scottish favorite, deserted Frederick II and set himself to get peace with France at almost any price.

The Peace of Paris, 1763

The peace finally signed at Paris in January 1763 was overwhelmingly favorable to Great Britain, but it was not so severe on the French as Pitt would have wished. France received back from its conqueror most of its purely economic stakes around the world: trading posts in India, slave stations in West Africa, the rich sugar islands in the West Indies, and fishing rights off Canada, together with two tiny islands off Newfoundland, St. Pierre and Miquelon. But in India and in North America the new colonial system required control of large territories to supply the trading posts. Sugar islands could produce great wealth in a few square miles, and the French were happy to retain their possessions in the Caribbean. But in the long run it was the continents that counted. With the collapse of its political and military power in India and on the North American continent, the first French colonial empire was permanently broken. France agreed to maintain no more troops in India and to recognize the native rulers whom the British had set up. France ceded the whole of Canada and everything east of the Mississippi to Britain and handed over Louisiana west of the Mississippi to Spain. Henceforth the British had no serious competitors in North America.

"ENLIGHTENED" DESPOTISM 1763–89

During the twenty-five years that followed the Peace of Paris, the "enlightened" ideas and practices of a number of European monarchs fired the imagination of educated men. The ancient institution of monarchy seemed to take a new lease on life. It looked as if the major ideas of the Enlightenment—reason, natural law, happiness, progress, liberty—were filtering through to the rulers. The later *philosophes* had questioned aristocratic and ecclesiastical privilege, unequal taxation, and the unfair treatment of certain social classes. Was it reasonable? Was it natural? These were the fashionable questions in "enlightened" quarters, and some of the crowned heads of Europe became troubled by them. Further, the mid-century wars had left almost every European state in need of reform and reconstruction. Law and order had to be restored, trade revived, and government treasuries refilled. So the practical needs of a postwar era, added to the ferment of new ideas, produced what was known as "enlightened despotism."

This apparently new kind of monarchy was in many ways a revival of older monarchical ideas, and a reaction against the power that the aristocracy had gained in the eighteenth century. In rooting out irrational customs and vested interests, enlightened despots could curb the power of the nobility and the clergy and attack local and provincial privileges just as monarchs before them had been doing for several centuries. The difference was in the way the enlightened despots justified what they did. They talked little about divine right or hereditary title and a great deal about following reason and serving the public. Frederick the Great called himself "merely the first servant of the state," liable at any moment to render an account of his service to his subjects. But this did not mean that he or any other monarch felt he was really responsible to his people. Monarchs might be "enlightened," but they were still "despots." As one contemporary economist observed, "Whenever old disorders have been eradicated speedily and with success, it will be seen that it was the work of a single enlightened person against many private interests." *

* Quoted in R. R. Palmer, *The Age of the Democratic Revolution* (Princeton, N. J.: Princeton University Press, 1959–64), p. 105.

Few of the rulers who dominated the political horizon in the later eighteenth century measured up to the ideal of an enlightened despot. George III of England (1760–1820) did not even pretend to be "enlightened," and the English would not have been pleased if he had; they were satisfied with the status quo. Louis XV of France (1715–74) was hardly enlightened in any sense of the word, although some of his policies were. Among the minor monarchs, Gustavus III of Sweden (1771–92) and Charles III of Spain (1759–88) had good claims to the title, but the three rulers whom the *philosophes* cited most often as enlightened despots were Catherine the Great of Russia, Frederick the Great of Prussia, and Joseph II of Austria.

Catherine the Great of Russia

Catherine II (1762–96) was a German princess who became empress of Russia through a conspiracy of her friends that led to the assassination of her husband, Tsar Peter III (1762). Uneasily conscious of being a usurper, she tried to make Russia great in an effort to endear herself to her people. She had to make concessions to preserve the support of the nobility, including lavish gifts to a long succession of lovers whom she used as her chief officers of state. She read the books of the French *philosophes*, corresponded with Voltaire, persuaded Diderot to visit her court, and made much of her "enlightenment" for publicity purposes. In 1767 she excited her admirers by summoning a legislative commission to codify the laws of Russia and to give the nation a sort of constitution. The representatives were elected by every class in the land except serfs, and they came armed with statements of grievances. Very little came out of their deliberations, however: some slight religious toleration and some limitation of torture in legal proceedings. The members went home in 1768, and the Russian government was to make no further attempt to summon a representative assembly until the twentieth century.

The net result, in fact, of Catherine's reign was not enlightened government but the strengthening of the nobility and the extension of serfdom. From 1773 to

Catherine the Great, on a gold medal struck to celebrate her accession as empress of Russia.

1775 a vast and dangerous uprising of serfs broke out in the valley of the Volga, led by a Cossack named Pugachev. The revolt was directed at the local landlords and officials; and after it was broken and Pugachev had been brought to Moscow in an iron cage to be drawn and quartered, it was these landlords and officials who profited by the reaction. Peter the Great's idea of a service nobility had long been weakening. In 1785 Catherine freed the nobles from both military service and taxation and gave them absolute control over the serfs on their estates. Further, she gave away large tracts of crown land to noble favorites, thus subjecting hordes of relatively free peasants on these estates to serfdom. At the end of her reign it has been estimated that 34 million out of a population of 36 million Russians were in a state of serfdom—a state that was not very different from that of slaves in the American colonies. The net result of Catherine's reign was to encourage the forces that were making Russia a state built on slavery.

Catherine was called "the Great" not because of her enlightenment—if she had any—but because of her conquests. Peter the Great had pushed his possessions out to the Baltic Sea in the northwest at the expense of Sweden. Catherine expanded the frontiers of her state many hundreds of miles to the west and south at the expense of Poland and the Ottoman Empire. Russians were concerned about the large Orthodox minority in Catholic Poland. Furthermore, during a large part of the seventeenth century, the Poles had threatened Moscow, and the Polish frontier was still only about two hundred miles from the old Russian capital when Catherine came to the throne. The ancient Russian thirst for vengeance on the Poles was to be richly satisfied after 1763 when Catherine put one of her favorites, Stanislaus Poniatowski, on the Polish throne. From that time on, Russia and Prussia made it their business to see that the anarchy and confusion of Polish politics continued and that any suggestion of constitutional reform or revival of the national spirit was snuffed out.

The Partitions of Poland

In 1772 Catherine and Frederick the Great arranged the first partition of Po-

land. Frederick took West Prussia and so joined Prussia to Brandenburg territorially for the first time. Catherine took a generous slice of northeastern Poland. To preserve the balance of power they thought it wise to give Maria Theresa a share of the loot (Galicia). The pious empress hung back at first, but Frederick remarked that the more she wept for Poland, the more she took. This first partition shocked the Poles into a nationalistic revival. King Stanislaus himself was swept along by the patriotic fervor and forgot that he owed his throne to Catherine. In 1791 after the outbreak of the French Revolution, a remarkable reform constitution was instituted setting up a strong monarchy and abolishing the *liberum veto.* Catherine's answer was swift and ruthless. Early in 1792 she called off the war she was fighting against the Turks, rushed an army into Poland, abolished the new constitution, restored the old anarchy, and arranged a second partition of Polish territory in 1793, this time with Prussia alone.

These events were followed by a

THE PARTITIONS OF POLAND

genuinely popular uprising in what was left of Poland, led by a Pole who had fought for the Americans in their revolution, Thaddeus Kosciuszko. The end was inevitable. Kosciuszko was captured by the Russians, the revolt collapsed, and Stanislaus was forced to abdicate. The Kingdom of Poland was wiped off the map in a third partition in 1795 among

Russia, Prussia, and Austria. In the three partitions, Russia took almost two-thirds of the original Polish territory, and Prussia and Austria divided the remainder.

Catherine's successes against the crumbling Ottoman Empire were almost as decisive. In a series of wars running from 1768 to 1792 Catherine gained the Crimea and most of the northern shore of the Black Sea. The Treaty of Kuchuk Kainarji (1774) also gave Russia vague rights to protect Orthodox Christians in the Ottoman Empire—rights that were to be used later as excuses for Russian intervention in Turkish affairs. The Ottoman Empire escaped the fate of Poland because it was stronger internally and because its two chief enemies, Austria and Russia, were jealous of each other. But when Catherine died in 1796 there seemed to be little obstacle to a Russian advance to Constantinople and the Mediterranean.

Frederick the Great of Prussia

Frederick II of Prussia (1740–86) had a somewhat better claim than Catherine to be considered "enlightened." He had a first-rate mind and a real grasp of what the *philosophes* were talking about. He invited Voltaire to Potsdam, and although they soon fell to quarreling over the merits of Frederick's poetry, they both agreed that it was the job of a king to combat ignorance and superstition among his people, to enhance their wel-

Maria Theresa on the First Partition of Poland

This letter to a diplomat is doubtless sincere, but as Frederick the Great said, "Maria Theresa wept, but she kept on taking."

This unfortunate partition of Poland is costing me ten years of my life. . . . How many times have I refused to agree to it! But disaster after disaster heaped upon us by the Turks, misery, famine and pestilence at home, no hope of assistance from either France or England, and the prospect of being left isolated and threatened with war both by Prussia and Russia—it was all these considerations that finally forced me to accept that unhappy proposal which will remain a blot on my reign. God grant that I be not held responsible for it in the other world! I confess that I cannot keep from talking about this affair. I have taken it so to heart that it poisons and embitters all my days.

This abbreviated version of the letter is from *Readings in Western Civilization,* ed. by Paul L. Hughes and Robert F. Fries (Paterson, N.J.: Littlefield, Adams, 1960), p. 134.

fare, and to promote religious toleration. Frederick welcomed religious exiles of all sorts—even Jesuits expelled from France and Spain. He treated the Jews badly, but his general tolerance in religion was the best evidence of his enlightenment. He was a mercantilist in his economic policies; he sought national self-sufficiency and used protective tariffs to foster infant industries. Interested in the new scientific agriculture, he tried to encourage new methods by bringing foreign farmers to his kingdom. Some three hundred thousand immigrants entered Prussia during his reign. Finally, he rationalized and simplified the Prussian laws and court procedures—another typical objective of enlightened despotism.

In some respects, however, Frederick was not at all enlightened, though he was always a despot. He believed firmly in social rank and privilege. The Junkers served him well as officers in his army, and the army was the most important organ of the state. In return for their services, he allowed the nobles to keep full control over the peasants on their estates. He strictly defined the ranks of noble, bourgeois, and peasant and made it difficult if not impossible for a man to move from one class to another. Prussian

serfs were not so badly off as Russian and Polish serfs, but those who lived on private estates were almost as much at their lord's mercy. Frederick did something to improve the lot of serfs on his own estates, but otherwise he showed no taste for social reform.

In some respects the discipline, the machinelike efficiency, and the strict centralization of power in the Prussian monarchy were the results of a long Hohenzollern tradition, quite unrelated to the influence of the Enlightenment. The powerful state that Frederick II erected in twenty-three years of war (1740–63) and consolidated in twenty-three years of peace (1763–86) was the most striking political achievement of his time. But twenty years after the strong hand of the despot was removed, Prussia proved to be an easy victim for Napoleon. The weakness of enlightened despotism, as well as its strength, lay in the fact that everything depended on the monarch.

Joseph II of Austria

The monarch with the best claim to be called an enlightened despot was Joseph II of Austria. Although he professed contempt for the *philosophes*, he

THE GROWTH OF BRANDENBURG-PRUSSIA 1640–1795

Brandenburg-Prussia at the beginning of the reign of Frederick William, 1640

Acquisitions to the beginning of the reign of Frederick II, 1740

Acquisitions through the partitions of Poland, 1795

was more thoroughly converted to the main tenets of the Enlightenment than any of his fellow monarchs. And he was probably more sincerely devoted to his people's welfare than any of the others.

Frederick II's seizure of Silesia in 1740 was the signal for a reorganization of the Habsburg Empire. During Maria Theresa's long reign (1740–80) an imperial bureaucracy was developed that was able to centralize in Vienna the administration of all the divisions of the empire except Hungary. All parts of the empire but Hungary were brought into a tariff union in 1775. The nobles were compelled to assume at least some of the burden of taxation. Maria Theresa did more for the serfs in her kingdom than any other ruler

of her time by limiting the amount of labor they owed their lords and by curbing the lords' power to abuse them. In much of this she was aided and abetted by her son, Joseph, who became emperor and coregent after the death of her husband in 1765. But Joseph wished to move much further and faster than his mother. Until her death in 1780 he chafed under the compromises and conservatism that characterized Maria Theresa's policies, particularly in religion.

In the ten years of Joseph II's own rule (1780–90), literally thousands of decrees poured out from the imperial chancellery in Vienna. He proclaimed religious toleration for all Christians and Jews. He dissolved monasteries devoted solely to contemplation and turned their revenues over to the hospitals that were to make Vienna the medical center of Europe in the next century. He applied a system of equal taxation in proportion to income to everyone in the Habsburg dominions, regardless of rank or nationality. He imposed one language for official business, German, on all parts of the empire, including Belgium, Italy, and Hungary. Most significant of all, Joseph abolished serfdom. Early in his reign he issued a number of decrees that gave all serfs in the Habsburg dominions personal freedom—freedom to leave the land, to marry whom they pleased, to choose any job they liked. This much of Joseph's work was permanent. In later decrees he tried to relieve peasants who stayed on the land of all forced labor and to turn them into property-owners, but these decrees were repealed by his successors.

Joseph II made more and more enemies by his policy of centralization and reform: the clergy, the landed nobility, non-German parts of his empire like Hungary, even peasants who failed to understand his intentions. In 1789, when revolution broke out in France, peasants in the Austrian Empire began to plunder and to murder landlords to gain the rights Joseph had held out to them. In 1790 both Belgium and Hungary were in revolt against his rule. The Church was bitterly hostile to him. Joseph felt lonely and deserted. "I am the only one holding to the true course," he wrote his brother

Joseph II, an Enlightened Despot

The following two extracts show both sides of enlightened despotism. Joseph wanted to reform the state, but he could do so only by autocratic methods.

I have not confined myself simply to issuing orders; I have expounded and explained them. With enlightenment I have sought to weaken and with arguments I have sought to overcome the abuses which had arisen out of prejudice and deeply rooted customs. I have sought to imbue every official of the state with the love I myself feel for the wellbeing of the whole. . . .

The good of the state can be understood only in general terms, only in terms of the greatest number. Similarly, all the provinces of the monarchy constitute one whole and therefore can have only one aim. It is necessary therefore that there should be an end to all the prejudices and all the jealousies between provinces [and] all races which have caused so much fruitless bickering. [Circular letter of Joseph II, 1783.]

◆ ◆ ◆

Unity and the end of prejudices, however, were to be achieved by dictates of the monarch. A common language was needed; Joseph II determined what it should be.

The German language is the universal tongue of my empire. I am the emperor of Germany. The states which I possess are provinces that form only one body—the state of which I am the head. If the kingdom of Hungary were the most important of my possessions, I would not hesitate to impose its language on the other countries. [Letter to a Hungarian noble, 1783.]

From T. C. W. Blanning, *Joseph II and Enlightened Despotism* (London: Longman Group, 1970), pp. 131–32; from Louis Léger, *Histoire de l'Autriche Hongrie* (Paris, 1879), p. 373.

Leopold, "and I am left to labor alone. . . . I am without any assistance whatsoever." Worn out, he died in 1790, choosing as his own epitaph: "Here lies Joseph II, who was unfortunate in everything that he undertook."

It is clear why Joseph II has been called "the revolutionary Emperor." Like Peter the Great he had shown what a single determined will could accomplish in the face of stubborn private interests. Unlike Peter, he had been guided by the principles of reason, tolerance, and humanitarianism. But Joseph was a revolutionist without a party. He had to depend on an unimaginative bureaucracy and on the secret police that he found it necessary to set up. Enlightened despotism in his hands might have formed a bridge between divine-right monarchy and democratic revolution. But it also suggested that permanent revolution demanded a broader base of popular understanding and support than he had been able to command.

FRANCE, ENGLAND, AND THE AMERICAN REVOLUTION 1763–89

France and Great Britain were the centers of the Enlightenment, but neither had an enlightened despot as monarch. Perhaps as a result (such large generalizations are very difficult to prove), each suffered a revolution from below. The American colonists won their independence from England in the name of reason and natural rights, and the French bourgeoisie, fired by the same ideals, destroyed aristocratic privilege in France.

Abortive Revolution from Above in France

When the Seven Years' War ended in 1763, both the French and the British governments needed more revenue to carry the burden of their war debts and to meet the rising costs of administration. Louis XV proposed to continue a war tax that fell on nobles and commoners alike and to institute a new tax on officeholders. It was a statesmanlike proposal, but Louis' program was greeted by a storm of

opposition from nobles and wealthy bourgeois alike. The *parlements* resisted the new taxes on the ground that they went against the "fundamental laws" of the kingdom and the "natural rights" of Frenchmen. Louis answered by abolishing the *parlements* and instituting a new system of law courts. It looked like a minor "enlightened" revolution, but it did not last. Louis XV died in 1774, and his son, Louis XVI, was neither strong enough nor determined enough to continue the fight against privilege. The old *parlements* were restored, the new taxes were dropped, and the financial problem was passed on to more cautious ministers. In the end, Louis XV's abortive reforms resulted in a further aristocratic reaction. After 1774 the nobility and the *parlements* came back so strongly from their temporary defeat that the Bourbon monarchy became in effect their prisoner.

The Revolt of the British American Colonies

The political and social situation was different in England, but the course of events was somewhat similar. A reasonable attempt by the government to raise new revenue was met by a storm of opposition in the American colonies. As a result, the attitude of the English governing classes stiffened. Concessions either to the colonists abroad or to reformers at home became impossible, and an irreconcilable conflict broke out that ultimately split the British Empire.

For nearly half a century before the Seven Years' War the policy of the British government toward its American colonies, as we have seen, had been one of "salutary neglect." For all practical purposes, the thirteen colonies governed themselves. Governors were appointed by the ministry in London, but their salaries were paid by colonial legislatures that were in fact quite independent of the British Parliament. These legislatures were also elected more democratically than Parliament or than almost any other representative body in Europe. Before 1763 Parliament never tried to tax the colonies. It did impose customs duties on colonial trade, but the intent of these levies was not to raise revenue but to force trade to flow toward the mother country.

The Seven Years' War, by eliminating French military power from North America, made the colonists feel more confident and less dependent on Great Britain for protection. At the same time it induced Parliament to tax the colonies in order that they might carry a fair share of the financial burden of imperial defense. The colonists had not done much of the actual fighting against the French. English troops had carried the brunt of the war, and after its close it was English troops that had to put down an Indian uprising under the Ottowa chief Pontiac across the Alleghenies. The taxes paid by the average American colonist were less than one-twenty-fifth of those paid by an Englishman. It seemed only fair to ask British Americans to carry some of the cost of maintaining English troops in North America.

In March 1765 Parliament imposed a stamp tax on paper of all sorts, including legal documents, commercial agreements, and newspapers. Familiar to Europeans as such a tax was, it aroused furious opposition in America among lawyers, merchants, and editors—the most articulate groups. A congress of delegates from nine of the colonies urged "that no taxes be imposed on them but with their own consent," and went on to argue that there was no practical way for the British Parliament to get American "consent" to any taxation. A year after its passage, Parliament repealed the Stamp Act but at the same time declared that crown and Parliament had the right to tax the colonies if they wished to. In 1767 Parliament returned to the attack with an act imposing duties on imports into the colonies of tea, paper, paint, lead, and glass. This was met by a determined colonial boycott, and in 1770 all the duties but those on tea were withdrawn.

Up to this point the colonists had shown little appreciation of the financial and military problems of the Empire, and Parliament had shown little appreciation of the factors that made the colonists doubt or fear its authority. But so far there had been no irrevocable break. Beginning in 1773, however, matters came to a head. In that year Parliament took over political responsibility in India from the East India Company and set up a Governor General, thus founding British rule in India. In order to compensate the company for its loss of political power, it was allowed to sell its surplus tea directly to American retailers. This move would presumably lower prices, increase sales, and thus increase in turn the revenue from the tea duty. The idea that the British government might get more in taxes from the colonies so infuriated a radical minority in Massachusetts that a party of Bostonians disguised as native Indians boarded three East Indiamen in Boston harbor in December 1773 and dumped thousands of pounds' worth of tea into the water. Parliament reacted with a violence out of all proportion to the incident. The port of Boston was closed, and

George Washington at Princeton. Portrait by Charles Willson Peale.

the Massachusetts legislature was deprived of much of its power (1774). This reaction drove the twelve other colonies to rally behind Massachusetts out of fear for their own charters.

To make matters worse, an otherwise statesmanlike measure, the Quebec Act of 1774, was passed at a moment when it appeared to be a further attack on the English-speaking colonies by Parliament. The act guaranteed the preservation of the French language and the Catholic religion in Canada and defined Canada as including all territory north of the Ohio River and west of the Allegheny Mountains. Settlement beyond the mountains was forbidden, an act that annoyed both rich speculators and poor pioneers. By now the breach was irreparable. To George III, to a large majority in Parliament, and probably to a majority of Englishmen, the American colonists had proved to be thoroughly irresponsible rebels who must be taught a lesson. To a majority of the colonists, the policy of Parliament was leading directly to unbearable tyranny—the kind of tyranny that they now felt it had been their main purpose to escape when they had originally emigrated to America. Fighting broke out at Lexington and Concord in 1775. A Continental Congress was summoned to meet in Philadelphia, and on July 4, 1776, the colonies formally declared their independence of king and Parliament in a declaration whose words rang like a tocsin summoning the people to rebellion throughout the Old World.

The American War of Independence

The American War of Independence was in a certain sense a civil war within the British dominions on both sides of the Atlantic. The colonists had friends in England, and the Irish sympathized with American grievances. The Whig faction to which Edmund Burke belonged tried in vain to induce George III and his prime minister, Lord North (1770–82), to follow a more moderate policy. A group of true "radicals," inspired by a rather unlovable champion of freedom of speech and parliamentary reform named John Wilkes, attacked the king's influ-

ence in Parliament, urged the publication of Parliamentary debates, and agitated for more democracy in the election of members. These radicals were too small a minority to carry any weight, but their political faith was that of the Declaration of Independence: that government must be by consent of the governed. Conversely, there were "Tories" in the colonies who agreed with Parliament and deplored the breach with England. In all, sixty thousand of them were to emigrate to Canada, never to return.

The War of Independence (1775–83) was won by the American colonists with French help. Following the principles of balance of power, France wanted compensation for the loss of Canada by depriving Britain of its American colonies. French supplies before the battle of Sar-

George III of England.

atoga (1777) and French troops and ships after the battle were of inestimable help to General Washington in his struggle to wear down the British forces in the colonies. In the peace treaty of 1783 the thirteen colonies gained their independence and won title to all the land east of the Mississippi, north of Florida, and south of the Great Lakes.

During the war most of the colonies had summoned conventions and drafted written constitutions with bills of rights to form the basis of their new governments. In 1787 a constitutional convention of delegates from all the colonies met in Philadelphia and drafted a constitution that bound the colonies in a federal union. This union was so successful that in mid-twentieth century the government founded on it could boast the longest continuous political tradition of any in the world except the British. In the same year, in the Northwest Ordinance, the colonists decided momentously to extend the principles for which they had fought to their still unsettled western territories. When these territories became populated, they would become not colonies or dependencies but "states," equal in status to the thirteen original members of the union.

The Significance
of the American Revolution

The success of the American Revolution had profound effects on Europe and eventually on other parts of the world.

As the liberals in Europe saw it, a people had taken its destiny into its own hands, had revolted against its established rulers, and had set up a government and governors of its own choosing. It had gained its liberty without falling into license. John Locke's ideas—natural equality, unalienable rights, government by consent of the governed, and the ultimate right of revolution—had been vindicated. Montesquieu's theory of a separation of powers had been written into both state and federal constitutions across the Atlantic. The constitutional conventions of the former British colonies appeared to demonstrate that a people could create a society and a government by formal contract. Furthermore, events in America seemed to demonstrate that smaller political units could be federated into a larger union without recourse to despotism. In sum, the American Revolution dramatized and passed on to the western world two political ideas of great importance for the future: the idea of limited, or constitutional, government (which had a long history reaching far back into the ancient and medieval worlds), and the idea of popular sovereignty, or democracy (which was relatively new in an age still strongly aristocratic in its thinking).

The quarter-century between the Peace of Paris and the outbreak of revolution in France apparently opened to the western world three possible roads for future development: enlightened despotism, aristocratic domination, and democratic revolution.

Suggestions for Further Reading

Note: Asterisk denotes a book available in paperback edition.

General The best general account of the century in English will be found in the three relevant volumes of the *Rise of Modern Europe* series, each with excellent critical bibliographies: P. Roberts, *The Quest for Security, 1715–1740** (1947); W. L. Dorn, *Competition for Empire, 1740–1763** (1940); and L. Gershoy, *From Despotism to Revolution, 1763–1789** (1944). M. S. Anderson, *Europe in the Eighteenth Century* (1961), is a good recent survey. Volume VII of the *New Cambridge Modern History*, A. Cobban, *The Old Régime, 1713–1763* (1957), has good articles on every major aspect of the period but is not for continuous reading. A. Sorel, *Europe under the Old Régime** (1947), is a translation of the introduction to a famous larger work of 1895 to 1904. R. R. Palmer, *The Age of the Democratic Revolution* (1959–64), is a major work of interpretation that sees the American and French Revolutions, together with the smaller disturbances of the period, as manifestations of a single great "democratic revolution." Other useful studies are C. B. A. Behrens, *The Ancien Régime** (1967), and Leonard Krieger, *Kings and Philosophers* (1970).

Economic and Social

See the works on mercantilism and economic history noted for Chapters 18 and 19; E. Williams, *Capitalism and Slavery* (1944), argues that mercantilism was compatible with slavery, but that the new industrial capitalism undermined it. On the aristocracy, see *The European Nobility in the Eighteenth Century,** ed. by A. Goodwin (1953), a collection of essays by various authors, and F. Ford, *Robe and Sword: The Regrouping of the French Aristocracy after Louis XIV** (1953), a study of the French aristocracy. For the other end of the social spectrum, see O. Hufton, *The Poor of Eighteenth-Century France* (1974). A. Young, *Tours in England and Wales* (1932), is a selection from the journals of a very keen observer of the eighteenth-century countryside. As brief introductions to the Agricultural and Industrial Revolutions, the general economic histories of Europe by H. Heaton, rev. ed. (1948), and by S. B. Clough and R. T. Rapp (1975) are useful.

Expansion Overseas

W. B. Willcox, *Star of Empire: A Study of Britain as a World Power, 1485–1945* (1950), and H. I. Priestley, *France Overseas Through the Old Régime: A Study of European Expansion* (1939), are good general works. J. R. Seeley, *The Expansion of England* (1883), is a very influential older account. C. G. Robertson, *Chatham and the British Empire** (1948), is a brief modern discussion. On India, see H. Dodwell, *Dupleix and Clive* (1920); E. Thompson and G. T. Garratt, *The Rise and Fulfillment of British Rule in India* (1934); and H. Furber, *John Company at Work: A Study of European Expansion in India in the Late Eighteenth Century* (1948). On America, in addition to the books cited for Chapters 19 and 20, see L. B. Wright, *The Atlantic Frontier: Colonial American Civilization, 1607–1763* (1947), and M. Kraus, *The Atlantic Civilization: Eighteenth-Century Origins* (1949). On the economic history of the British colonies, see C. P. Nettels, *The Roots of American Civilization* (1938). On social history, see J. Henretta, *The Evolution of American Society, 1700–1815** (1973).

Political and Diplomatic

J. Lough, *Introduction to Eighteenth-Century France* (1960), is a very good starting point for study. The best brief introduction to England is J. H. Plumb, *England in the Eighteenth Century** (1951). B. Williams, *The Whig Supremacy, 1714–1760* (1939), in the *Oxford History of England*, is a more extended topical treatment. Two other books by J. H. Plumb offer interesting reading: *Sir Robert Walpole* (1956) and *The First Four Georges** (1957). The serious student of the English political system and how it operated should examine the various studies of L. B. Namier. On Prussia, there is excellent material in Dorn (first section, above); a first-rate biography of Frederick William I, *The Potsdam Fuehrer*, by R. Ergang (1941); biographies of Frederick the Great by P. Gaxotte (1941) and G. P. Gooch (1947); and an expert general account by W. H. Bruford, *Germany in the Eighteenth Century** (1952). See also H. Rosenberg, *Bureaucracy and Autocracy, the Prussian Experience* (1958). C. L. Morris, *Maria Theresa: The Last Conservative* (1937), is probably the best of several biographies, S. K. Padover, *The Revolutionary Emperor* (1934), and T. C. W. Blanning, *Joseph II and Enlightened Despotism* (1970), are both good on Joseph II. On Joseph's most important reform, see E. M. Link, *The Emancipation of the Austrian Peasant, 1740–1798* (1949). There are many biographies of Catherine the Great, but G. S. Thomson, *Catherine the Great and the Expansion of Russia** (1950), is the most informative from the historian's point of view. On the enlightened despots as a group, G. Bruun, *The Enlightened Despots** (1929), is brief but extremely good. The best accounts of the war and diplomacy of the age will be found in the *Rise of Modern Europe* series, but there is a very brief account in A. H. Buffinton, *The Second Hundred Years' War, 1689–1815* (1929); C. Petrie, *Diplomatic History, 1713–1933* (1946), helps provide the continuity lacking in separate volumes.

The American Revolution

Two volumes in the *New American Nation* series provide the best up-to-date introduction: L. H. Gibson, *The Coming of the Revolution, 1763–1775** (1954), and J. R. Alden, *The American Revolution, 1775–1783* (1954). L. Gottschalk, *The Place of the American Revolution in the Causal Pattern of the French Revolution* (1948), and E. S. Morgan, *The Birth of the Republic, 1763–1789** (1956), offer a somewhat broader perspective. On the origins of the Revolution, see C. Andrews, *The Colonial Background of the American Revolution* (1924); B. Bailyn, *Ideological Origins of the American Revolution** (1967); and E. S. Morgan and H. Morgan, *The Stamp Act Crisis* (1953). M. Beloff has selected an interesting set of contemporary sources in *The Debate on the American Revolution, 1761–1783** (1949). On the side of ideas, C. L. Becker's study of the text of *The Declaration of Independence** (1922, 1942) is consistently illuminating. The best recent studies include P. Maier, *From Resistance to Revolution** (1972), and R. M. Calhoon, *Revolutionary America: An Interpretive Overview** (1976).

23 The French Revolution and Napoleon

The French Revolution marked a turning point in European history. The events that began in 1787 and ended with the fall of Napoleon Bonaparte in 1815 unleashed forces that altered not only the political and social structure of states but the map of Europe. Many attempts were made, in France and elsewhere, to undo the work of the Revolution and to repress the ideas of liberty, equality, and nationalism that the Revolution had inspired. But the Old Regime was dead, in France at least, and a Europe dominated by monarchy and aristocracy and by a hierarchical social order could never be fully restored. With the coming of the French Revolution, then, we enter into a more modern world—a world of class conflict, middle-class ascendancy, acute national consciousness, and popular democracy. Together with industrialization, the Revolution reshaped the institutions, the societies, and even the mentalities of Europeans.

THE ORIGINS OF THE FRENCH REVOLUTION

By the last half of the eighteenth century, France appeared to have overcome the dismal cycle of famine, plague, and high mortality that, in the preceding century, had inhibited both demographic and economic growth. The majority of Frenchmen who lived in the villages and tilled the fields were better off than their counterparts in most of Europe. French peasants, for example, owned some 40 percent of the country's farmlands. The mild inflationary trend that characterized much of the eighteenth century increased the wealth of large landowners and surplus wealth in agriculture served to stimulate the expansion of the French economy as a whole. Modest advances in the textile and metallurgical industries, the construction of new roads and canals, and urban growth were other indications of economic development.

Yet, despite evident signs of prosperity, there was great discontent and restlessness in France in the 1780s. French institutions were obsolete, inefficient, and uncoordinated. They were controlled by the nobility and by self-perpetuating corporations of hereditary officeholders. To anyone touched by the ideas of the Enlightenment they seemed irrational and unjust. The middle classes, especially, were offended by the legal and social distinctions that kept them from attaining high office or exerting political influence. Every bishop in France was of noble birth; only nobles could receive commissions in the army; bourgeois

The French peasant supports the clergy and the nobility in this eighteenth-century cartoon. The rabbits and doves eating the peasant's grain were protected by law for the sport of the upper classes.

plans for economic reform were constantly thwarted by the privileged classes. The economy, particularly in agriculture, remained unstable and subject to fluctuations that could drive the peasants and urban poor to starvation. An inefficient and inequitable tax system yielded too small an income to support the state, discouraged economic growth, and fell most heavily on the poor. On the eve of the Revolution, France faced a conjuncture of crises. Three of these crises—agrarian distress, financial chaos, and aristocratic reaction—were particularly acute.

Agrarian Distress

Wretched weather and poor harvests in 1787 and 1788 weakened the agricultural economy. The poorer peasants lived at a subsistence level at best; with poor crops they starved. The purchasing power of well-to-do peasants declined. Grain shortages led to sharp increases in the cost of bread. Moreover, from the late 1770s the long-term growth of the French economy had been interrupted in several important areas, such as the wine trade, and between 1776 and 1787, agricultural profits generally declined, though not to the low levels of the first part of the century. Nevertheless, noblemen and other large landowners, who had become accustomed to high profits, sought to save their declining fortunes by demanding from their tenant farmers dues and obligations that had long been neglected. The countryside was ripe for revolution.

Financial Chaos

The finances of Louis XVI's government were a shambles. By 1787 one-half of the nation's tax revenues went to service the massive public debt that Louis XIV had left to his successors. France's involvement in the Seven Years' War and in the American War for Independence had driven the government further along the road to bankruptcy. Without a reform of the tax system the king could not meet his obligations. But such a reform would mean an attack on the privileges of the upper classes, and this Louis could never quite summon the courage to do.

Three ministers in succession struggled with the problem. The first, the Swiss banker Necker, was dismissed by the king in 1781 after he had proposed some modest reforms. Necker's successor, Calonne, thought he could carry on without much change. But as the deficit mounted he grew alarmed, and in 1786 he proposed a much more radical reform program than Necker's. The most striking provision of Calonne's program was a direct tax on all landowners—noble and commoner, lay and clerical. To oversee the assessment of the new tax, Calonne suggested that the king create local and provincial assemblies in which all men of property would be represented regardless of social status. In addition, older taxes, such as the *taille*, which weighed on the lower orders, were to be reduced. Calonne's reforms struck at the very heart of the system of privilege and the social hierarchy of the Old Regime.

Calonne, aware that there would be bitter opposition to his plans, persuaded Louis XVI to call a conference of notables in the hope that they could be induced to back his program. But the members of this assembly, which met in February 1787, were drawn largely from the privileged orders and refused to support Calonne.

The king now dismissed Calonne and put in his place one of Calonne's chief opponents, Lomenie de Brienne, Archbishop of Toulouse. This prelate, though a member of both the higher nobility and the higher clergy, soon came to the same conclusions as Calonne. He tried to enact a similar reform program, but the *Parlement* of Paris, the most privileged of all the corporations of officeholders, refused to register the royal edicts. It declared that only the Estates General could approve such measures. When Brienne tried to break the opposition by exiling the magistrates of the *Parlement* and by abolishing the high courts, he touched off furious protests by many members of the upper bourgeoisie and the nobility. In the face of these attacks, the government backed away from its reform program. In July 1788, the king yielded to the opposition and ordered a meeting of the Estates General for May 1789.

Aristocratic Reaction

During the 1780s, then, aristocratic demands on the peasantry were aggravating the distress of the countryside, and aristocratic resistance to tax reform was hampering the government in its attempts to revamp the nation's financial structure. These were two facets of the aristocratic reaction that was directly responsible for the coming of the French Revolution.

The tremendous strength of the French privileged classes had been built up steadily during the reigns of Louis XV and Louis XVI. At every turn the poor, the aspiring middle class, and enlightened reformers in government confronted the fact of privilege. Some men of the Enlightenment, in particular Voltaire, and such royal ministers as Turgot and Calonne encouraged the king to rationalize state finance and to bring a measure of justice to French society at the expense of the privileged groups. Louis XVI supported several of these plans for reform, but he always backed down when the privileged classes protested. By the 1780s it appeared that the French king was the prisoner of the nobility and that he would do nothing to displease them.

Moreover, the nobles were particularly skillful in confusing the issue. Certain privileges, such as those that protected the laws, institutions, and customs of the provinces from encroachments by the central government, limited the arbitrary power of the king. These privileges, or liberties, were compared with the restrictions on royal power in England, and the English were regarded as the freest people in Europe. Thus the nobles could resist royal attacks on privilege by asserting that the king was simply trying to get rid of all restrictions on his power. Through this argument, the nobility and the *parlements* were able to gain wide support and considerable sympathy when they resisted the arbitrary orders of the king, even when those orders were directed toward desirable ends.

There were those, however, who were not deceived by the rhetoric of the privileged orders. The hesitations of the king and the intransigence of the aristocracy

increased the bitterness of large sections of the population. They wanted to put an end to privilege, and they felt that the unreformed monarchy would not help them in this struggle. The attack on privilege and the demand for equality before the law were the driving forces in the Revolution from beginning to end. Privilege, it seemed, could be destroyed only by attacking aristocracy and monarchy.

THE FRENCH REVOLUTION AND THE KING

The Estates General, which had not met since 1614, was convened by the king at Versailles on May 5, 1789. The electoral process by which deputies were selected was a relatively generous one: all adult French males had the right to vote, indirectly, for representatives to the Third Estate, which served the interests of the commoners. Moreover, following some recent examples in provincial assemblies, the Third Estate was given twice as many representatives as the other two Estates. The First and Second Estates (the clergy and the nobility, respectively) represented the privileged orders. The king had asked that all local electoral assemblies draw up *cahiers de doléances*—lists of grievances—to submit to the Estates General when it met. Thus in the months preceding the convening of the Estates General, a great political debate occurred. Almost all politically minded men agreed that the monarchy should yield some of its powers to an assembly and seek consent to taxation and legislation. By 1788 some noblemen were willing to go part way in abolishing privileges and in equalizing taxation. But the early debates in the Estates General revealed that the lawyers and bourgeois who represented the Third Estate were bent on a much more drastic reform.

The Estates General and the National Assembly

The mood of the Third Estate was best expressed by one of its deputies, the Abbé Sieyès. In a famous pamphlet, *What Is the Third Estate?*, Sieyès argued that the real French nation was made up of people who were neither clergymen

Caricature of the Abbé Sieyès.

nor noblemen, and that this majority should have the decisive voice in all political matters. This idea was translated into action during the opening debate on voting procedures in the Estates General. Since the Third Estate had as many representatives as the other two combined, it wanted the three Estates to meet and vote together. A few liberal nobles and a number of the lower clergy were sure to support the Third Estate. The king and the privileged orders, on the other hand, demanded that the Estates vote separately. This was traditional procedure, and it assured that the first two Estates would retain control.

The Third Estate not only rejected the king's plan for separate meetings: on June 17 it declared itself the National Assembly of France and invited the other Estates to sit with it. The National Assembly then assumed the right to approve all taxation and to withhold all taxation if its political demands were not met. In the face of this bold initiative, the king hesitated but finally resorted to a show of force. On June 20 Louis XVI had the Third Estate barred from its usual meeting place. The deputies then convened in a nearby indoor tennis court and took an oath not to disband until they had drafted a constitution. This Tennis Court Oath was the first great act of the bourgeois revolution in France.

In a dreary repetition of the political ineptitude he had shown in previous crises, Louis missed his chance to act as impartial mediator between the hostile Estates. On June 23 he went before the Estates General and offered a program of reform that only partly satisfied the demands of the Third Estate for tax reform and did nothing to abolish the privileges of the nobility. At about the same time, the king began to concentrate troops around Versailles and Paris. By now, however, neither partial reform nor brute force was a sufficient answer to the political crisis. The revolution had become a battle between those who desired a more equal and open society and those who wanted to preserve the privileges of the aristocracy.

The Popular Revolt

Most of the deputies in the Third Estate were lawyers, professional men, and lesser officeholders. Their aspirations were those of the French bourgeoisie. In the urban centers and the countryside resided yet another element of the Third Estate—the mass of artisans, shopkeepers, and peasants who lived in poverty or on the edge of it. Their aspirations and needs were not identical with those of the deputies at Versailles. But in the summer of 1789 a series of spontaneous popular disturbances and revolts broke out that linked, for the moment at least, the bourgeoisie and the common people in an uneasy alliance against the aristocracy.

Notable among these uprisings was an attack on July 14 (still France's national holiday) on the Bastille, a royal fortress and prison in Paris. By the end of June the city of Paris had grown tense. The economic depression of the 1780s and the poor harvests of 1788 and 1789 had reduced the urban poor to misery, and to misery was now added the fear that the king and the aristocrats were conspiring to dissolve the Estates General. When the king's troops appeared on the outskirts of the city, the immediate reaction of the citizens was to arm themselves. It was their search for arms that brought the leaders of the Parisian electoral assembly and a crowd of journey-

---

The Tennis Court Oath   June 20, 1789

The National Assembly, considering that it has been summoned to establish the constitution of the kingdom, to effect the regeneration of public order, and to maintain the true principles of monarchy; that nothing can prevent it from continuing its deliberations in whatever place it may be forced to establish itself; and finally, that wheresoever its members are assembled, *there* is the National Assembly:

Decrees that all members of this Assembly shall immediately take a solemn oath not to separate, and to reassemble wherever circumstances require, until the constitution of the kingdom is established and consolidated upon firm foundations. . . .

From *A Documentary Survey of the French Revolution*, ed. by John Hall Stewart (New York: Macmillan, 1951), p. 88.

men and workers to the Bastille. The commandant at first barred the gates and fired on the crowd. He then lost his nerve, opened the gates, and the crowd stormed in and slaughtered the garrison.

The fall of the Bastille was an event of small consequence in itself, but its implications were immense. The attack was regarded as a blow against royal depotism. It demonstrated that the Revolution was not simply a debate over a constitution. Of greatest importance, it brought the city of Paris and the political leaders of Paris to the forefront. A new, revolutionary municipal government was formed; henceforth Paris would shape the direction of the Revolution. Finally, the events in Paris set off revolts in the provinces.

The French peasants, also disappointed with the slow pace of reform, now began to take action of their own. Like the poor of the cities, the peasants had been heartened by the political promise of the winter of 1788/89. They had patiently drawn up their *cahiers* and they had chosen their electoral committees; then they had waited confidently for relief to follow. The Estates General met in May. Spring passed and summer came, but the peasants were still poor; they were still not allowed to till the unused land of the nobles; and they still had to pay their customary dues.

Then, during July 1789, the month of the storming of the Bastille, rumors spread through rural France that there would be no reforms and that the aristocrats were coming with troops to impose reaction on the countryside. The result was panic and rioting throughout the country. During the "Great Fear," as it is called, frightened peasants gathered to defend themselves against the unnamed and unseen enemy. Once assembled and armed, however, they turned against the enemy they knew—the local lord. Though the lords themselves were rarely in residence, peasants burned their châteaux, often tossing the first brand into the countinghouse, where the hated records of their payments and seigneurial obligations were kept.

The Destruction of Privilege

The popular revolts and riots had a profound impact on the king, the aristocracy, and the deputies of the Third Estate alike. Already in June, before the storming of the Bastille, Louis XVI had recognized the National Assembly and

The Oath at the Jeu de Paume, by Jacques Louis David. The deputies of the Third Estate, joined by some of the clergy and nobility, swear not to disband until they have drafted a constitution.

Storming the Bastille (July 14, 1789). The revolutionary leader is accepting the surrender of the prison.

French Women Become Free. Print from the General Collection of Caricatures about the Revolution (1789).

ordered the clergy and the nobles to sit with the Third Estate. He also recognized the revolutionary government of Paris and authorized the formation of a national guard composed largely of members of the bourgeoisie. But the king received no credit for his concessions from the revolutionary leaders, who felt, quite rightly, that his sympathies were still with the nobles. At the same time, Louis' indecision had discouraged many of the strongest supporters of the Old Regime. The most reactionary noblemen, headed by the king's brother, the Count of Artois, began to leave the country. Other members of the aristocracy sought to preserve their property by making dramatic concessions to the call for reform.

On the night of August 4, one nobleman, the Viscount de Noailles, stood before the Assembly and proposed that all feudal levies and obligations be abolished. In a performance at once impressive and bizarre, nobles, clerics, and provincial representatives arose to renounce noble privileges, clerical tithes, and provincial liberties. In effect, the Old Regime was dismantled in one night, and the way seemed clear for the Assembly's main business—to draft a constitution. The implementation of the concessions of August 4, however, was half-hearted. The structure of aristocratic privilege was indeed abolished along with tax exemptions and hereditary officeholding, but peasants were to continue paying customary dues to their lords until they had redeemed them. Only when the Revolution reached a more radical stage was this obligation abolished.

The Declaration of the Rights of Man

On the whole, the National Assembly had succeeded in wiping out the privileges of the upper classes, the corporations of officeholders, and the provinces. Now it faced the task of creating new political, legal, and administrative structures for the country. The ideological framework for this task was set forth by the constitution-makers in the Declaration of the Rights of Man, which they adopted on August 27, 1789.

In this preamble to a constitution, the members of the National Constituent Assembly (that is, the National Assembly acting in its constitution-making role) established a set of principles idealistic enough to sustain the enthusiasm of the mass of Frenchmen for the Revolution and sweeping enough to include all humanity. The basic ideas of this document were personal freedom, equality under the law, the sanctity of property rights, and national sovereignty. The first article declared that "men are born and remain free and equal in rights." There were to be no class privileges and no interference with freedom of thought and religion. Liberty, property, and resistance to oppression were declared inalienable and natural rights. Laws could be made and taxes levied only by the citizens or their representatives. The nation, not the king, was sovereign. Thus was established the framework for a system of liberty under law. The Declaration was a landmark in the fight against privilege and despotism, and it had a great appeal to revolutionary and democratic factions throughout Europe.

The Declaration of the Rights of Man
August 27, 1789

1. Men are born and remain free and equal in rights; social distinctions may be based only upon general usefulness.
2. The aim of every political association is the preservation of the natural and inalienable rights of man; these rights are liberty, property, security, and resistance to oppression.
3. The source of all sovereignty resides essentially in the nation; no group, no individual may exercise authority not emanating expressly therefrom.
6. Law is the expression of the general will; all citizens have the right to concur personally or through their representatives in its formation; it must be the same for all, whether it protects or punishes. All citizens, being equal before it, are equally admissible to all public offices, positions, and employments, according to their capacity, and without other distinction than that of virtues and talents.
10. No one is to be disquieted because of his opinions; even religious, provided their manifestation does not disturb the public order established by law.
11. Free communication of ideas and opinions is one of the most precious of the rights of man. Consequently every citizen may speak, write, and print freely, subject to responsibility for the abuse of such liberty in the cases determined by law. . . .

From *A Documentary Survey of the French Revolution,* ed. by John Hall Stewart (New York: Macmillan, 1951), p. 114.

The October Days

The Declaration of the Rights of Man was not simply a page lifted from John Locke, the *philosophes,* and the Americans. It was a highly political document hammered out in an Assembly that was showing itself to be increasingly divided. There were those among the moderate leaders of the Assembly who found the Declaration too radical and sweeping. These men desired to reconcile Louis XVI with the Revolution and to construct a constitutional system on the English model with a monarch guided by an assembly controlled by the rich and the well-born. The issues that divided the crown and the country could not, however, be compromised. Louis simply refused to give formal approval to the decrees and the Declaration that followed the night of August 4.

The king's recalcitrance, the divisions in the Assembly, and the food shortages combined to produce yet another popular explosion. On October 5, 1789, a crowd of some twenty thousand armed Parisians, including a large number of women, marched on Versailles, demanding bread and insisting that the royal family return to Paris. The king considered flight, but he was persuaded by Necker, who had been recalled to the government, and by Lafayette, leader of the National Guard, to appease the crowd and leave Versailles. On October 6 the royal family drove into Paris surrounded by shouting crowds, and established themselves at the Tuilleries palace. A few days later, the National Constituent Assembly followed.

The Parisians seemed satisfied with the king's capitulation, and the Assembly, together with the king and his ministers, turned to the question of the constitution. Henceforth, however, the deliberations of the Assembly were to take place in the heated atmosphere of Paris. Here in the capital many political clubs were formed to debate the issues and settle on policy. Here too were political agitators, journalists of all opinions, and, above all, crowds that could be mobilized to bring pressure on the Assembly. From the autumn of 1789 on, the Revolution became more and more a Parisian affair.

The Achievements of the National Constituent Assembly, 1789-91

It took two years to make the constitution. By the end of that time the government had been reorganized, the Church had been dispossessed of its lands, and the rights of Frenchmen had been more clearly defined. These are the main results of the Assembly's complex and lengthy deliberations:

The Monarchy. By acts passed in September 1789, Louis XVI was reduced from his position as a king by divine right to the role of a constitutional monarch. He was given the right of suspensive veto over legislation that allowed him to delay the passage of laws for two years. The monarchy remained hereditary, and the king retained control of military and foreign affairs.

The Legislature. The Constitution of 1791 provided for a unicameral Legislative Assembly, elected for two years. The Assembly had the power to initiate and enact legislation and to control the budget. It also had the exclusive right to declare war. Members of the Constituent Assembly were forbidden to serve in the new legislature, an unfortunate decision that barred experienced men from a body that had few precedents to guide it.

The Electorate. The Constitution did not provide for universal manhood suffrage. It divided Frenchmen into active

The three Estates "hammer out" a new constitution in this contemporary engraving.

LIBERTÉ DES CULTES

Playing cards of the French Revolution. Personifications of Liberty and Equality have taken the place of kings and queens.

and passive citizens. Only the former, who met a property qualification, had the right to vote. The active category comprised some two-thirds of the adult male population. Active citizens voted for electors, who in turn elected the Legislative Assembly. These electors, as well as officeholders in the Assembly, were drawn from some fifty thousand of the country's wealthiest men. Even with these restrictions, a far larger percentage of the population could vote and hold office than in England.

The Administration. The elimination of aristocratic privilege invalidated most of France's local administration, which had been controlled by the nobility or small oligarchies of officeholders and rich bourgeois. The Assembly completed the process of dismantling the administrative apparatus of the Old Regime by abolishing all former provinces, intendancies, and tax farms. On a clean administrative map they drew eighty-three departments, roughly equal in size, with uniform administrative and judicial systems. Administration was decentralized and put in the hands of some forty thousand local and departmental councils, elected by their constituents.

The Church. The reorganization of the French Church was decreed by the Civil Constitution of the Clergy, promulgated in August 1790. It was one of the most important and fateful acts of the Revolution. The Assembly confiscated the lands of the Church and, to relieve the financial distress of the country, issued notes on the security of the confiscated lands. These notes, or *assignats*, circulated as money and temporarily relieved the financial crisis. Clergymen henceforth became paid officials of the state, and priests and bishops were to be elected by property-owning citizens.

The Constitution of 1791, together with the Declaration of the Rights of Man, summed up the principles and politics of the men of 1789. In its emphasis on property rights, its restrictive franchise, and its fiscal policy, the Constitution had a distinctly bourgeois bias. To look upon the document simply as a product of selfish interest, however, would be to underestimate its achievements. A new class of peasant proprietors had been created. The framework

for a society open to talent had been established. Administrative decentralization, it was thought, would overcome the prevailing fear of despotism. Equality before the law, if not political equality, had been made a fact. These were impressive and revolutionary changes. But to succeed and mature, the new order needed peace, social stability, and the cooperation of the king. None of these was forthcoming. Within a year the Constitution of 1791 had become a dead letter, and the Revolution had entered a new phase.

The Failure of Constitutional Monarchy

The Constitution of 1791 was most certainly an imperfect instrument. The Civil Constitution of the Clergy, for example, offended the pope. Many bishops and priests refused to accept it, and they found broad support in the country. Schism in the Church became a major factor in the eventual failure of the Assembly to create a stable government. Moreover, the restrictive franchise opened the constitution-makers to the charge that they wanted to substitute a wealthy oligarchy for an aristocracy. Such obvious defects, however, were not alone responsible for the failure of constitutional monarchy. The principal culprit was the monarch himself.

At the head of the government stood a king who was thoroughly discredited. In June 1791, Louis XVI tried to escape from France in order to join the forces of counterrevolution abroad. He very nearly succeeded but was caught at Varennes, near the eastern frontier, and was brought back to Paris. This humiliating episode destroyed what little authority Louis still possessed. He now swore to obey the new constitution; but he was only a figurehead.

At this point the situation was complicated by outside pressures. Louis' fellow monarchs were unhappy over the way in which their royal colleague was being treated. The privileged orders in other countries feared that the leveling principles of the Revolution would spread. The English, many of whom had sympathized with the Revolution so long as it seemed to be following an English model, began to denounce the radicalism and violence of the French. Edmund Burke, in particular, saw clearly the radical nature of the Revolution. In his *Reflections on the Revolution in France* (1790) he insisted on the importance of tradition in preserving an orderly society and declared that it was folly to abandon time-tested institutions in favor of new ones based on abstract ideas. He did not convince radical writers or some of the articulate craftsmen, but he convinced almost everyone in power in England. Hostility to France was an old tradition; Burke gave new reasons for continuing it. And everywhere French refugees spread counterrevolutionary propaganda urging Europe's monarchs to intervene.

The Legislative Assembly
September 1791–September 1792

The Legislative Assembly met in an atmosphere of intrigue, fear, and factional strife. There were two issues on which it was almost impossible to find a solid majority. The first was the position of the king. He could not be trusted, and he would not commit himself to the principle of equality, on which everyone did agree. Was it worth compromising with the king in order to preserve the constitution and the unity of the country? If not, how far should the Assembly go in restraining or in punishing the king?

The second problem, which caused even sharper divisions, was that of defining "equality." Was the emphasis to be on equality before the law, or on equality of opportunity, or on political equality, or on economic equality, or on a mixture of two or more of these ideals? Here there was not only no clear majority, but no consistency within groups and even within individuals.

There were no parties in the Assembly, but there were the "clubs," loosely organized associations with affiliates in the provinces. One of the largest and best-organized groups was the Jacobin Club, with 136 members out of the 745 representatives. The Jacobins were republicans and wanted to get rid of the king. But they were also well-to-do bourgeois. They were far from agreement on political and economic equality, or on the pace at which change should take place. They were divided into at least two

factions. One faction was led by Brissot de Warville, the ablest politician in the Assembly. The other, composed mainly of Parisians, eventually found a leader in Maximilien Robespierre.

As it turned out, the issue that temporarily united the Assembly was that of declaring war on Austria. Inept diplomacy by European monarchs, even more inept politics in the French royal court, and a very real threat of counterrevolution convinced millions of patriotic Frenchmen that the forces of reaction were about to destroy all that had been gained since 1789 and that war was the only way to save their country and their freedom. The emperor of Austria and the king of Prussia in the Declaration of Pillnitz (August 1791) proclaimed that European monarchs must unite to restore order and monarchy in France. This was largely bluff, but it sounded ominous. Some conservative ministers thought that a victorious war against Austria would strengthen the king and allow him to end the Revolution. However, Louis XVI and his Austrian queen, Marie Antoinette, apparently hoped for a French defeat that would lead to the restoration of royal authority.

External threats and court plots played into the hands of Brissot's republican faction. Brissot believed that a crusade to unseat the monarchs of Europe would rekindle the revolutionary fervor of the French people and rally them around his plan to establish a republic in France. He was opposed in the Jacobin Club by Robespierre, who feared that a war would strengthen the conservatives and lead to dictatorship. But Brissot proved the stronger, and the powerful Jacobin Club passed a resolution advocating a declaration of war. Brissot took the issue before the Assembly, and in April 1792 all but seven deputies voted for war with Austria.

The First War
of the Revolution

The declaration of war transformed the Revolution. With war came the end of the monarchy and the constitution. With it also came terror and dictatorship. France became not simply the home of the Revolution but the exporter of revolutionary ideals. Finally, under the stress

Anonymous contemporary portrait of Robespierre.

and emotions of war, France became a modern, unified nation-state.

The war began badly. The French army lacked leadership and discipline. The government was short of money and hampered by factional disputes. The royal family and their supporters encouraged the enemy. It is not surprising that the Austrians and their allies, the Prussians, were soon able to advance along the road to Paris.

Two things saved the Revolution. The Austrian and Prussian generals, who were at least as incompetent as the French, delayed and divided their forces. And there was a genuine outburst of patriotic and revolutionary enthusiasm in France. It was during this crisis that the *Marseillaise* was composed, a stirring appeal to save the country from tyranny. The French kept on fighting, despite their failures. As a result, when the Austro-Prussian army was checked at Valmy, one hundred miles from Paris, in September 1792, its cautious commander decided to call off the invasion. The allies had lost their best chance to crush the Revolution before it gathered strength.

THE FRENCH REPUBLIC

During these gloomy months, when everything seemed to be going wrong, the radical politicians of Paris gained a commanding position in the government. These Jacobins—Robespierre and Georges-Jacques Danton were the most important—based their power on national guards summoned to protect the capital, on the Parisian crowds, and, from August 10, 1792, on an insurrectionary Paris Commune that replaced the legal municipal government. The poorer classes were suffering from economic depression and political uncertainty, and they were afraid that the Old Regime might be revived. The bourgeois radicals in the Assembly never fully sympathized with the desire of Paris artisans and workers for economic equality, but they could agree with them on the need for drastic political changes. In August the Jacobins touched off an uprising in Paris that forced the Legislative Assembly to suspend the king from office and to issue a call for a revision of the constitution. A

National Convention, elected by universal manhood suffrage, was to determine the new form of the French government. The events of August triggered what is often called the Second French Revolution. This revolution began with the deposition of Louis XVI; it ended in a bloody terror that consumed its own leaders. In many ways it confirmed Edmund Burke's most dire prophecies. And yet the Second French Revolution did not follow inexorably upon the first. War created its own necessities, survival being the most pressing.

The Convention and the Jacobins

The National Convention met in Paris on September 21, 1792, in the wake of a fierce bloodletting earlier in the month—the so-called September massacres. These massacres, which took the lives of some thirteen hundred prisoners in Paris, were part of a pattern of fear, terror, and revolutionary justice that persisted throughout much of the Convention's three-year rule.

The delegates to the Convention were elected by a minority of Frenchmen, despite universal manhood suffrage. Many citizens were repelled by the deposition of the king and the violence of the summer of 1792. Others were intimidated. Some were excluded from the electorate by governmental decree. Thus the most radical elements of the French population had disproportionate strength in the elections. Not surprisingly, many of the delegates were Jacobins.

The Jacobins, however, were divided. The followers of Brissot, now called the Girondists, made up one faction. They dominated the Convention in its early months. In general, the Girondists represented the interests of provincial republicans, and they were bitterly opposed to the Paris Commune. Their foreign policy was aggressive and expansionistic. It was they, for example, who issued a manifesto in November 1792 offering France's aid to all revolutionaries throughout Europe. In domestic affairs, the Girondists were relatively moderate—at least when compared with their Parisian enemies. On the prime issue of 1792, the fate of the king, the Girondists urged that Louis

XVI be imprisoned for the duration of the war. There was little doubt then—and less now—that Louis was guilty of treason. But the resolution condemning him to death passed by only one vote. He was guillotined on January 21, 1793. This victory for the so-called Mountain—Robespierre and Danton's faction—was followed by a purge of the Girondists in June 1793. The architects of France's war policy were among the first victims of that policy.

The Jacobins and the War

The Girondists fell before their Jacobin opponents in the wake of crushing French defeats by an overwhelming new coalition of European powers. The execution of Louis XVI, France's designs on Holland, and its annexation of Savoy and Nice prompted England, Spain, Portugal, and several lesser states to join Austria and Prussia in the war against France. In the face of such a formidable combination, the French armies suffered a series of reversals. The victor of Valmy, General Dumouriez, was badly defeated in Belgium, and, in the spring of 1793, he defected to the enemy.

Now the government, under the direction of a Committee of General Defense (later the Committee of Public Safety), undertook to organize the entire nation for war. It applied conscription on a nationwide scale for the first time in modern European history. It raised huge armies, far larger than those that could be called up by the old-fashioned monarchies against which France was fighting. And it supported those armies by means of confiscation and heavy taxes. The armies were organized by a military genius, Lazare Carnot, an engineer who made a science out of the service of supply.

The monarchies of Europe, which were used to fighting limited wars with limited resources for limited gains, were overcome by a French nation organized for war. They could not afford to arm all their people; they still depended on the old officer corps for their leaders. And, much as they despised the Revolution, they were still not prepared to sacrifice all their resources to put it down. Other problems distracted the crowned heads

Portrait of Louis XVI during his imprisonment at the time of the Revolution, by Joseph Ducreux.

The Execution of Louis XVI

The carriage proceeded thus in silence to the Place de Louis XV,* and stopped in the middle of a large space that had been left round the scaffold: this space was surrounded with cannon, and beyond, an armed multitude extended as far as the eye could reach. . . . As soon as the King had left the carriage, three guards surrounded him, and would have taken off his clothes, but he repulsed them with haughtiness: he undressed himself, untied his neckcloth, opened his shirt, and arranged it himself. The guards, whom the determined countenance of the King had for a moment disconcerted, seemed to recover their audacity. They surrounded him again, and would have seized his hands. "What are you attempting?" said the King, drawing back his hands. "To bind you," answered the wretches. "To bind *me*," said the King with an indignant air. "No! I shall never consent to that: do what you have been ordered, but you shall never bind me. . . ."

Many voices were at the same time heard encouraging the executioners. They seemed reanimated themselves, in seizing with violence the most virtuous of Kings, they dragged him under the axe of the guillotine, which with one stroke severed his head from his body. All this passed in a moment. The youngest of the guards, who seemed about eighteen, immediately seized the head, and shewed it to the people as he walked round the scaffold; he accompanied this monstrous ceremony with the most atrocious and indecent gestures. At first an awful silence prevailed; at length some cries of "Vive la République!" were heard. By degrees the voices multiplied, and in less than ten minutes this cry, a thousand times repeated, became the universal shout of the multitude, and every hat was in the air. . . .

*Now the Place de la Concorde.

From *English Witnesses of the French Revolution*, ed. by J. M. Thompson (Oxford: Basil Blackwell, 1938), pp. 230–31.

of Europe: England was seeking colonial conquests, and the eastern powers were still concerned with the Polish problem. So the French recovered from the blows of 1793 and by the late spring of 1794 had broken through into the Low Countries. When the Convention ended its work in 1795, France was stronger and held more territory than it had under Louis XIV at the height of his power.

The Instruments of Jacobin Rule

Military success was achieved only through the intensive and often brutal organization of the French people. The Constituent Assembly's program of administrative decentralization had left France without any effective chain of command linking the National Convention in Paris to the provinces. Moreover, the Convention was an ungainly body, incapable of swift action. Into this void moved the radical Jacobins. In the provinces, Jacobin clubs virtually replaced local governing bodies and through their committees of surveillance controlled public life. At the center, executive power was entrusted to two committees—the Committee of Public Safety and the Committee for General Security. The former wielded almost dictatorial power over France from July 1793 until July 1794. It had twelve members, of whom Robespierre was the most prominent.

The genuine achievement of the twelve capable men who composed the Committee of Public Safety, in coping with internal unrest and external war, is often overlooked because of the "Reign of Terror" they imposed on France. The Terror must be put into the context of the problems that confronted Robespierre, Carnot, and their colleagues. From early 1793 there had been a series of internal rebellions against the government. Conservative peasants of the Vendée, a region in the west of France, had revolted against the national conscription and in favor of their priests who opposed the Civil Constitution. Later in the year, the Girondists, who opposed what they thought was excessive centralization, stimulated local uprisings in some large provincial towns. In the heat of war, such rebellions appeared treasonable, and the Terror was used as a political weapon to impose order. Also, during much of the Committee's tenure, Parisian politicians, both to the left and to the right of Robespierre, maneuvered to secure power. Terror, against Danton among others, was a weapon in these internecine conflicts. There was an economic terror directed against war profiteers and hoarders. Finally, there were local terrors, uncontrolled from the center, in which Jacobins and undisciplined representatives of the government took revenge on their enemies. In the end, the Terror gained a certain momentum of its own, and the list of suspects grew. Among the factors in Robespierre's fall was the fear of the Convention that its remaining members would soon become victims of revolutionary justice.

In all, some forty thousand people were killed by the government and its agents. The largest number of victims were peasants; next came rebellious citizens of provincial towns, and politicians. Some hundreds of thousands of suspects were imprisoned. Even the Committee of Public Safety finally divided over the excesses of the Terror. When military successes restored a measure of stability to France, the National Convention reasserted its authority. Among its first acts was the arrest and execution of Robespierre in July 1794.

Jacobinism and French Society

The militant phase of Jacobinism was relatively short. The Committee of Public Safety ruled for a year, and Robespierre had complete authority for only four

Here Lies All of France. An engraving of Robespierre guillotining the executioner after having guillotined everyone else in France.

months. Thus, beyond the brilliant organization of the national defense, the Jacobins made few permanent contributions to French institutions and society. Certain of their acts, however, have remained of symbolic significance to the French Left. Among these were the guarantees of the right to a public education for all and the right of public welfare for the poor; these guarantees were set forth in an abortive constitution drawn up in 1793. In addition, the Jacobins were responsible for price controls and for the division of confiscated property among the poor. These decrees, however, were not the product of a conscious social philosophy; they were opportunistic acts designed to win over the disaffected crowds in the cities and the landless peasants in the countryside. The Jacobins were radical democrats who believed deeply in political equality; they were not socialists. With their fall in the summer of 1794, the Revolution fell back into the hands of the propertied bourgeoisie. It was this class that in the end gained most from the Revolution.

The Thermidorian Reaction and the Directory, 1795–99

The demise of Robespierre and the Jacobins touched off a wave of reaction against the excesses of the Terror. This "Thermidorian reaction," named after the month in the revolutionary calendar when Robespierre was executed (Thermidor/July), turned against the austerity of Jacobin rule and at times took the form of a "white terror" against the radicals in Paris and the provinces.

In 1795 the Convention finally presented France with a constitution, the third since 1789. It provided for a five-man executive board, called the Directory, and a two-house legislature. Even the republican-oriented Convention had been sufficiently sobered by the Terror to abandon its promise of universal suffrage, and the franchise was weighted in favor of the propertied classes. Once in office, the Directory proved both corrupt and incompetent. It maintained a militantly aggressive foreign policy and allowed the French economy to deteriorate disastrously. A more or less communistic

movement led by "Gracchus" Babeuf received some support from the poor, but was easily suppressed. The French poor were still largely artisans and peasants—property owners and not wage-earners. More dangerous was a royalist revival. Elections in 1797 demonstrated such an upsurge in royalist sentiment that the results had to be cancelled. The Directory's single source of strength was the army. With the economy foundering and popular unrest increasing, the Directory was ripe for the *coup d'état* that in 1799 brought one of its most successful generals, Napoleon Bonaparte, to power.

NAPOLEON'S RISE TO POWER

Napoleon Bonaparte was born on the island of Corsica in 1769, shortly after the

The Thermidorian Reaction

In two days after the execution of Robespierre, the whole Commune of Paris, consisting of about sixty persons, were guillotined in less than one hour and a half, in the Place de la Révolution; and though I was standing above a hundred paces from the place of execution, the blood of the victims streamed under my feet. What surprised me was, as each head fell into the basket, the cry of the people was no other than a repetition of "*A bas le Maximum!*"* which was caused by the privations imposed on the populace by the vigorous exaction of that law which set certain prices upon all sorts of provisions, and which was attributed to Robespierre. The persons who now suffered were all of different trades; and many of them, indeed, had taken advantage of that law, and had abused it, by forcing the farmers and others who supplied the Paris market, to sell at the maximum price, and they retailed at an enormous advance to those who could afford to pay. I did not see Robespierre going to the guillotine; but have been informed that the crowd which attended the wagon in which he passed on that occasion, went so far as to thrust their umbrellas into the wagon against his body. . . . It now became a measure of personal safety, to be able to declare that one had been imprisoned during Robespierre's tyranny. It was dangerous even to appear like a Jacobin, as several persons were murdered in the streets, by *La Jeunesse Parisienne*,† merely because they wore long coats and short hair.

*"Down with price controls!"
†"The (gilded, aristocratic) Paris youth."

From *English Witnesses of the French Revolution*, ed. by J. M. Thompson (Oxford: Basil Blackwell, 1938), pp. 248–49.

The interior of the Great Pyramid, as depicted in the *Description of Egypt* (1809–26), published by the scholars who accompanied Napoleon on his campaign in Egypt. They explored ancient monuments and provided the first modern survey of Egypt.

island had been annexed by France. The Bonapartes were members of the minor nobility, and at the age of nine Napoleon was admitted to a military school in France. From that time on, he knew no other life than the army. When most of the aristocratic officer corps left France after the fall of the monarchy, Napoleon stayed on to serve the Republic. He rose to become a brigadier general in 1793 at the age of twenty-four. He helped to reconquer Toulon—one of the towns that rebelled against the Convention in 1793—and he suppressed a royalist riot in 1795. By 1797, when the Directory felt its power slipping, Barras, one of the Directors, realized that Napoleon's support could be valuable. He sought Napoleon's friendship first by introducing the young general to one of his cast-off mistresses, Josephine Beauharnais (whom Napoleon married), and then by giving him command of an army that was preparing for an invasion of Lombardy, a province in northern Italy under the control of Austria.

The Italian campaign of 1797 removed Austria from the war, gave France control of northern Italy, and established Napoleon's reputation as an outstanding general. After the defeat of the Austrians only England was still at war with France. In 1798 Bonaparte took an army by sea to Egypt, where he hoped to sever England's lifeline to India. He easily defeated the Egyptians, but the English admiral Horatio Nelson sank the French fleet near the mouth of the Nile. Napoleon's army, trapped in Egypt, was soon decimated by disease. In the midst of this crisis, Napoleon heard that the Directory was in danger of falling and that some of the Directors wanted to create a military dictatorship. Leaving his army in Egypt, he made his way secretly back to France to offer his services to the conspirators.

The most important Director was the Abbé Sieyès, and it was with this former leader of the First French Revolution that Napoleon conspired. On November 9, 1799, he used military force to compel the legislators to abolish the Directory and substitute a new government in which a board of three consuls would have almost absolute power. The conspirators asked Napoleon to serve as one of the consuls. They hoped he would provide the personal popularity and military power needed to support a regime that would be dominated by the other two consuls. But when the new constitution was written—at Napoleon's orders—the general emerged as First Consul and virtual dictator. When the French people were invited to endorse the constitution in a plebiscite, they voted overwhelmingly to accept it. To Frenchmen exhausted by years of revolution, terror, and economic instability, Napoleon seemed to be the guarantor both of the gains of the Revolution and of order.

NAPOLEON AND DOMESTIC REFORM

Bonaparte was, above all, a soldier, and his fortunes always hinged on military success or failure. Yet his domestic reforms were profound and enduring. If the French Revolution gave the country an ideology that, henceforth, would both inspire and divide Frenchmen, Napoleon gave France many of its characteristic institutions. Better than any eighteenth-century monarch, Bonaparte fulfilled the *philosophes'* dream of an enlightened despot.

Between 1799 and 1801 Napoleon led a series of successful campaigns against the coalition that England, Austria, and Russia had formed to defeat him. He wanted to win a favorable peace so that he could devote himself to consolidating his position in France. Hostilities ended in 1801 and did not break out again on any major scale until 1805. Napoleon used those four years to restore domestic concord and economic stability and to establish a network of administrative institutions that gave coherence and uniformity to his government.

Perhaps Napoleon's most characteristic contribution was the *Code Napoléon.* From the laws left by the several legal systems of the Old Regime and the succession of revolutionary governments, Napoleon's advisers compiled a uniform legal code that is still the basis of French law. The *Code* maintained in theory the revolutionary concept of equality before the law, but it was in fact far less egalitarian than the laws of the revolutionary era. It emphasized, for instance, the authority of the government over its citizens, of employers over their employees, and of male heads of families over their wives and children. Property rights received particularly strong protection under the *Code*.

Other Napoleonic reforms followed a similar pattern. They often upheld in principle the ideals of the Enlightenment and the Revolution but served in practice to strengthen France's new authoritarian state. Napoleon retained, for instance, the division of France into eighty-three uniformly administered departments. He used the departmental system, however, not to foster local responsibility, as had been intended, but to create a highly centralized administration controlled directly by the First Consul through field administrators called prefects. He also instituted a nationwide system of public schools that not only educated the young—an ideal of the *philosophes*—but imbued them with an exaggerated patriotism and devotion to their ruler.

In reforming France's finances Napoleon followed the British and American examples by chartering a privately owned national bank as a depository for government funds and a source of credit for French businessmen. With government deposits as security, the bank issued paper money as legal tender. Increased currency, a stable franc, and improved credit helped to strengthen France's shaky economy. Napoleon also resolved that perennial problem of the Old Regime—taxation—by developing uniform taxes collected directly from each individual by paid officials.

Although Napoleon was far from devout, he understood better than his republican predecessors that domestic peace could not be achieved until the religious question had been settled. Accordingly, he signed with Pope Pius VII the Concordat of 1801, which regularized the situation created by the Revolution. Although the document recognized that the majority of Frenchmen were Roman Catholics, the Catholic Church was not to be the established church in France. Church properties confiscated during the

Revolution were not restored. Moreover, the First Consul retained the right to appoint bishops. Through the Concordat of 1801, Napoleon regained the loyalty of French Catholics and at the same time won the gratitude of owners of former church properties.

Although Napoleon brought a form of enlightened despotism to France, he did so at the expense of much of the individual liberty that had been a basic principle of the Enlightenment. The legislative institutions created by the Constitution of 1799 were a sham. Political opposition was punished and the press was strictly censored. Napoleon's training was military, and too often his solution to political and social problems was force. Nevertheless, his government in its early years was popular. He preserved the property of those who had gained from the Revolution. He satisfied the

Unfinished portrait of Napoleon by Jacques Louis David, the imperial court painter.

Political Maxims of Napoleon

These extracts from communications to the Council of State (1801–04) come from the period when Napoleon was First Consul and was trying to construct a civilian government.

We have finished the romantic period of the Revolution; we must now start to make it into history, to see only what is real and possible in applying its principles and not what was speculative and hypothetical. To follow any other policy today would be to philosophize and not to govern.

I shall respect public opinion when its judgments are legitimate, but it has whims that must be scorned. It is the duty of the government to enlighten public opinion, not to follow it in its errors.

One can lead a people only by promising it a future; a chief of state is a seller of hopes.

Constitutions should be short and obscure. . . . A constitution should be drafted in such a way that it will not hinder the actions of a government and not force the government to violate it. . . . If there are problems with a government that is too strong, there are many more with a government that is too weak. Things won't work unless you break the law every day.

My system is very simple. I believe that in the circumstances, it is necessary to centralize power and increase the authority of the government in order to build a nation. I am the constitution-making power.

Translated from Edouard Driault, *Napoléon: Pensées pour l'Action* (Paris: Presses Universitaires de France, 1943), pp. 30–34.

A cast of the imperial seal of Napoleon, ''Emperor of the French, King of Italy, Protector of the Confederation of the Rhine.''

social ideal of the Revolution by maintaining legal equality, equality in taxation, and careers open to talent. In his administration, he incorporated royalists, constitutionalists, and Jacobins. With such accomplishments, he easily won popular approval when he declared himself First Consul for life in 1802. And two years later, on December 2, 1804, the nation rejoiced when, in the presence of the pope, he crowned himself Emperor of the French.

THE NAPOLEONIC EMPIRE

Napoleon did not create French imperialism; he inherited and had been an agent of the aggressive expansion undertaken by the Convention and the Directory. A satellite republic had already been established in Holland in 1795, and during the victorious campaigns against Austria toward the end of the decade, French armies had extended French power to Switzerland and parts of Italy. This burst of French expansion had come to an end when Napoleon signed peace treaties with Austria in 1801 and England in 1802. Large-scale hostilities were resumed in 1805, and from that time until Napoleon's ultimate defeat ten years later, France was almost constantly at war.

If Napoleon could have avoided war he might have consolidated his European empire. But his own ambition and the continuing enmity of England made war almost inevitable. England was determined to keep France from becoming the dominant political and economic power in Europe. French control of the Low Countries had already violated a basic rule of English foreign policy—namely, to keep these invasion bases and commercial centers out of the hands of a strong power. The British and their ablest statesman of the period, William Pitt the Younger, furthermore, were convinced that Napoleon was using the peace to ready France for yet another war. Pitt soon was able to persuade other continental states that they must join England to restore the balance of power and resist the spread of French influence in central Europe.

Napoleon was just as ready for war as was England. He felt that his empire could never be secure and that his plans for Europe could never be achieved until England had been thoroughly defeated. The two states drifted into war in 1803, and other continental powers—Austria, Russia, and finally Prussia—joined England.

It was a difficult war for the two major contestants. Napoleon could not gain control of the sea, and without this control he could not subdue England. He made his greatest effort in 1805 when he concentrated his army at Boulogne and tried to entice the British fleet out of the Channel by an elaborate set of naval feints in the Atlantic. But the English were not deceived. While one fleet guarded England against invasion, another, under Nelson, caught the French off Cape Trafalgar and annihilated them (October 21, 1805). Napoleon was never again able to threaten England with invasion.

The English, on the other hand, could not defeat the French on the Continent and were dependent on the armies of their allies. By the fall of 1805 the armies of the Russian and Austrian emperors assembled in central Europe for a combined assault. Instead of waiting for the attack, Napoleon marched an army deep into central Europe and took the Austrian and Russian generals by surprise. He defeated the Austrian and Russian forces first at Ulm, and then again in the most spectacular of all his victories, at Austerlitz, on December 2, 1805.

With Austria defeated and Russia in retreat, Napoleon followed up his victory

1789		1795		1799			Napoleon	1814
Revolutionary Governments			Directory		Consulate		First Empire	

1804

with a complete reorganization of the German states. He helped end the Holy Roman Empire and eliminated most of the small German principalities. Out of these petty states he created a satellite system composed of fourteen larger states that were united in a Confederation of the Rhine, with Napoleon as protector.

Prussia, which had not at first joined the coalition against Napoleon, entered the fray in 1806 and was soundly defeated at Jena in October of that year. King Frederick William III was forced to accept a humiliating peace and to become an ally of France. The following spring, Tsar Alexander I of Russia again sent an army against Napoleon, only to have it defeated at Friedland in June 1807. In three campaigns in three successive years, Napoleon had defeated the three strongest powers on the Continent and established his position as master of Europe. Russia was too large to occupy, but Napoleon had taught Tsar Alexander the futility of opposition. A few weeks after Friedland, Napoleon and Alexander held a dramatic meeting near Tilsit in eastern Prussia. Alexander recognized Napoleon's supremacy in the West, and Napoleon agreed not to intervene in Russia's internal affairs or to prevent Alexander from extending Russian influence into the Ottoman-controlled Balkans.

Napoleonic Europe and the Continental System

Napoleon had reached the summit of his power. All Europe, save England, was under his control (see color map "Napoleonic Europe"). France, Belgium, Germany west of the Rhine, and parts of Italy and Illyria constituted a French Empire ruled directly by Napoleon. Holland, Westphalia (a Napoleonic creation in Germany), and southern Italy were theoretically independent kingdoms, over which Napoleon placed three of his brothers as kings. Northern Italy was also a kingdom, with Napoleon himself as king. The Grand Duchy of Warsaw was carved out of Prussia's Polish territories and given to France's ally, the king of Saxony. In 1808, the Bourbon monarch of Spain was overthrown and replaced by Napoleon's brother Joseph.

England alone resisted the tide of French expansion. From 1806 on, Napoleon tried to weaken England by wrecking British trade with the Continent. This so-called Continental System imposed heavy penalties on anyone trading with England and put a heavy strain on the economies of the continental countries. England made the strain worse by blockading all countries that subscribed to the French system. The English blockade drove Denmark into a close alliance with France and helped cause the War of 1812 with the United States. But the blockade caused less ill will than Napoleon's decrees. It was impossible for the European economy to function properly without English trade. Smuggling became a highly organized and profitable business, and attempts to enforce French regulations strengthened the opposition to Napoleon everywhere. Most important of all, the blockade led to a quarrel between Napoleon and Alexander of Russia.

Tsar Alexander had not been happy with the results of his alliance with Napoleon. France had gained vast territories; Russia had acquired only Finland and Bessarabia. Napoleon's creation of the Grand Duchy of Warsaw menaced Russia's control of the Polish lands it had seized in the 1790s. But the greatest grievance of the Russians was the Continental System. Russia needed English markets for its grain, and Alexander would not and could not enforce the rules against trade with England. Napoleon, bent on the destruction of England,

Contemporary engravings of French soldiers of Napoleon's era. Left: a sharpshooter of the Imperial Guard; right: a cannoneer.

could not tolerate this breach in his system. He requested Alexander to stop the trade; when Alexander refused, Napoleon prepared to invade Russia.

The Weaknesses of the Napoleonic Empire

When Napoleon undertook his Russian campaign in June 1812, his hold on Europe and even on the French had begun to weaken. French expansion had at first been greeted with enthusiasm by many of the inhabitants of the Low Countries, Germany, and Italy. Enlightenment ideas were strong in these regions, and their governments were unpopular. In the northern Netherlands there was opposition to the domination of the House of Orange and the urban oligarchy. In the Austrian Netherlands (Belgium), nationalist feelings had led to a revolt against Austrian rule as early as 1789. Italy was dominated by Spain and Austria, and growing nationalism and spread of the Enlightenment made the ideas of the French Revolution attractive to many Italians. In Germany the writings of the *philosophes* had been eagerly read, and there was general disgust with the archaic structure of the Holy Roman Empire and the stodgy governments of the petty principalities. In short, there had been serious political unrest in much of Europe in the 1780s and 1790s, and the invading French armies had often been

hailed as liberators. Napoleon took full advantage of this feeling. He was able to break the archaic political and social structures of many states. Within the Empire, the *Code Napoléon* was established, the privileges of the Church and aristocracies were abolished, and fetters on local industry and commerce were removed. Napoleon saw himself as the "revolution on horseback" and sought to impose a new order on Europe—a new order that was enlightened, rational, and French.

This vision of Napoleon's was, at best, only partially achieved, and even those who had most enthusiastically received the invading French armies soon perceived that imperialism was a more important component of the Napoleonic system than was liberation. The Continental System contributed to a general economic crisis in Europe that alienated the commercial and industrial interests. High taxes and conscription were imposed on the tributary states. And the French system was enforced by tight police surveillance. Napoleonic tutelage, even at its most benevolent, appeared incompatible with the libertarian and nationalistic ideals of the French Revolution.

Increasingly, Napoleon was beset by the growth of nationalistic feelings and national resistance to his rule. In Germany, Italy, and Spain, national awakening was intimately linked to opposition to French hegemony. This opposition took many forms. In Italy and Germany cultural movements gained momentum that emphasized the common history, language, and literature shared by these fragmented countries. In Spain resistance was expressed more violently when rebellions broke out in 1808 against the regime of Joseph Bonaparte. In was here that Napoleon first confronted guerrilla warfare and encountered serious failure. A Spanish victory at Baylen in 1808 was the initial break in the emperor's record of invincibility. By 1813, the Spanish rebels, with the help of an English army under Wellington, had driven the French from Madrid and had organized a constitutional government that controlled more than half the country.

The appearance of a well-organized

English army on the Continent was one indication that the balance of power in Europe was shifting against Napoleon. There were other signs, the most important of which was the recovery of France's nominal ally and potential enemy, Prussia. After the humiliating defeat at Jena, the process of reconstructing the kingdom was begun. Under Generals Gneisenau and Scharnhorst, the Prussian army was modernized and universal military training was introduced. To revitalize the country, another reformer, Baron vom Stein, persuaded the king to abolish serfdom and to grant a large measure of liberty to Prussian municipalities. Stein's social reforms were limited in their effects, but the military reforms allowed Prussia to play a significant role in the final defeat of Napoleon.

As his enemies were strengthening themselves and challenging the French monopoly of force, Napoleon began to lose his grip at home. Economic domination of Europe, which had been the goal of the Continental System, failed to materialize, and France, like the rest of the Continent, suffered from the economic crisis that marked the last years of Napoleon's rule. Internally, the regime grew more repressive, and Napoleon became increasingly intolerant of criticism. After his divorce from Josephine and his marriage to Marie Louise of Austria, Napoleon more and more took on the airs of an Old Regime monarch. Those Frenchmen who had provided him with his magnificent and spirited army were now exhausted by the burdens of empire.

The Invasion of Russia and the Fall of Napoleon

In June 1812 Napoleon marched into Russia with six hundred thousand men, the largest army ever assembled up to then. Most had been recruited in the German states or in other dependencies. Napoleon expected to deliver a fast and decisive blow, but the Russians, greatly outnumbered, did not give battle. Instead they retreated, drawing Napoleon behind them. After one costly but inconclusive engagement at Borodino, Napoleon occupied Moscow in September and waited

for Alexander to offer peace terms. But no message came.

After five weeks Napoleon realized that he could not keep so large a force in Russia through the winter, and in October he began the long march westward. Since the land through which he passed had already been devastated, he lost thousands of men to disease and starvation. When the cold weather came, the weakened soldiers were no match for the elements. As the remnants of Napoleon's army stumbled closer to the frontier, Polish and German soldiers deserted and headed homeward. When Napoleon reached the German border in December, he could not muster one hundred thousand men. If Austria or Prussia had chosen to launch an attack at this time, the war could have been ended. But the allies did not know the extent of the disaster.

Once in German territory, Napoleon hurried to Paris and organized a new army that he marched eastward in the spring of 1813. But defeat had ended Napoleon's glory, and he was badly beaten by the combined armies of Austria, Prussia, and Russia at Leipzig in October. Napoleon lost about two-fifths of his men and retreated back across the

Napoleon I: A Self-Assessment 1817

In spite of all the libels, I have no fear whatever about my fame. Posterity will do me justice. The truth will be known; and the good I have done will be compared with the faults I have committed. I am not uneasy as to the result. Had I succeeded, I would have died with the reputation of the greatest man that ever existed. As it is, although I have failed, I shall be considered as an extraordinary man: my elevation was unparalleled, because unaccompanied by crime. I have fought fifty pitched battles, almost all of which I have won. I have framed and carried into effect a code of laws that will bear my name to the most distant posterity. I raised myself from nothing to be the most powerful monarch in the world. Europe was at my feet. I have always been of opinion that the sovereignty lay in the people. In fact, the imperial government was a kind of republic. Called to the head of it by the voice of the nation, my maxim was, *la carrière est ouverte aux talents* without distinction of birth or fortune. . . .

From *The Corsican,* ed. by R. M. Johnston (Boston: Houghton Mifflin, 1910), p. 492.

Retreat of Napoleon's army across the Beresina River (1812), by an anonymous painter.

cated for the second time. The allies now exiled him to St. Helena, a small and remote island off the Atlantic coast of Africa. The era of the Revolution and Napoleon had ended.

The era had ended, but it could not be effaced. The allies could restore a Bourbon to the throne of France, but the new king, Louis XVIII, could not restore the Old Regime. He had to keep many of Napoleon's officials. He had to preserve the Napoleonic administrative system and the Concordat with the Church. He had to accept both the revolutionary principle of equality under the law and the revolutionary land settlement. He had to grant a constitution to his people. It was a conservative constitution with a very limited electorate, but it meant that the king's rule was not absolute. And throughout Europe the great ideas of the Revolution—liberty, equality, and nationalism—lived on, and with them the new and dangerous concept of revolution as a means of attaining social and political goals. These ideas were only partially recognized in some countries and totally suppressed in others, but they persisted everywhere—smoldering coals that were to burst into flame again and again during the nineteenth century.

The political balance of power in Europe had been permanently altered. No one could restore the petty states of Germany or the feeble republics of Italy. No one could ignore the claims of Russia to have, for the first time, a voice in the affairs of western Europe. No one could fail to recognize the tremendous strides that England had made in industry and commerce during the wars. Conversely, for the first time in two centuries, France was no longer the richest and strongest European state. These were some of the new political facts with which the diplomats at Vienna had to deal.

Rhine. Meanwhile, Britain's general Wellington defeated another French army in Spain and crossed the border into southern France. On March 31, 1814, the allied armies entered Paris, and one week later Napoleon abdicated. After some debate, the allies restored the Bourbons to the throne of France and then called a conference in Vienna to settle the fate of the rest of Europe.

Napoleon was exiled to the island of Elba, off the Italian coast. But he still had one battle to fight. In March 1815 he escaped and landed in the south of France. The army proved loyal to the deposed leader, and Napoleon was soon in control of France once again.* But the allies were prepared. Napoleon was conclusively defeated at Waterloo on June 18, 1815, and three days later he abdi-

*The three months spanning Napoleon's escape from Elba, resumption of power, and second abdication following his defeat at the battle of Waterloo are known as the Hundred Days.

Suggestions for Further Reading

Note: Asterisk denotes a book available in paperback edition.

General   The best general work on the French Revolution is the authoritative study by G. Lefebvre, *The French Revolution* (1962–64). A somewhat different interpretation may be found in F. Furet and D. Richet, *The French Revolution* (1970). C. Brinton, *A Decade of Revolution, 1789–1799** (1934), in the *Rise of Modern Europe* series, is still a fine introductory summary. See also A. Soboul, *The French*

Revolution: 1787–1799* (1975), and M. J. Sydenham, *The French Revolution* (1966). Valuable source material may be found in J. H. Stewart, ed., *A Documentary Survey of the French Revolution* (1951), and P. Dawson, *The French Revolution* (1967). J. M. Thompson, *The French Revolution* (1943), is a solid standard work. R. R. Palmer, *The Age of the Democratic Revolutions*, 2 vols. (1959–64), places the French Revolution in its broad European perspective. He published a revised and shortened version as *The World of the French Revolution* (1971). The same is done in N. Hampson, *The First European Revolution: 1776–1815* (1969), and, with a neo-Marxian approach, in E. J. Hobsbawm, *The Age of Revolution: 1789–1848* (1962). W. Doyle, *Origins of the French Revolution* (1980), assesses the literature since 1939.

The Social History of the Revolution

An excellent brief introduction to the social history of the Revolution is N. Hampson, *Social History of the French Revolution* (1962). The essays in J. Kaplow, ed., *New Perspectives on the French Revolution* (1965), are indispensable for an understanding of the social movement. A. Cobban, *The Social Interpretation of the French Revolution* (1964), is an important revisionary statement. On the role of the masses, see G. F. E. Rudé, *The Crowd in the French Revolution* (1959). E. Barber, *The Bourgeoisie in XVIIth Century France* (1955), discusses the background of bourgeois discontent.

Major French Interpretations of the Revolution

Alexis de Tocqueville's *The Old Regime and the French Revolution* (1956) presents the classic view of the Revolution as the continuation of the centralizing tendencies of the Old Regime. G. Lefebvre, *The Coming of the French Revolution* (1947), gives an excellent picture of France in the first year of the Revolution and states precisely and clearly the nature and problem of the French Revolution as a whole. For a treatment from the republican side, see F. V. A. Aulard, *The French Revolution*, 4 vols. (1901, 1910). A. Mathiez, *The French Revolution* (1928), is a sympathetic leftist interpretation of the Revolution.

Special Topics

B. Stone, *The Parlement of Paris, 1774–1789* (1981), deals with this important institution. Perhaps the best introduction to the Convention and the Reign of Terror is the brief study by J. M. Thompson, *Robespierre and the French Revolution* (1953). R. R. Palmer, *Twelve Who Ruled* (1941), is a fascinating account of the Reign of Terror written from a biographical approach. D. M. Greer, *The Incidence of Terror During the French Revolution* (1935), is a statistical account of who was actually executed and how. The role of Paris in the Revolution is the subject of A. Soboul, *The Parisian Sans-Culottes and the French Revolution* (1964). C. Tilly, *The Vendee* (1964), is a sociological analysis of the counterrevolution. On party politics during the Legislative Assembly and the Convention, see M. J. Sydenham, *The Girondins* (1961) and *The First French Republic, 1792–1804* (1973). The fall of the Jacobins and the period of the Directory are dealt with authoritatively in G. Lefebvre's *The Thermidorians* (1937) and *The Directory* (1946). For a more recent treatment, see M. Lyons, *France under the Directory* (1975). A. Forrest, *The French Revolution and the Poor* (1981), is an important contribution.

Napoleon and the Napoleonic Empire

G. Bruun, *Europe and the French Imperium* (1938), in the *Rise of Modern Europe* series, is a good general introduction. Among the many biographies of Napoleon are those of J. M. Thompson, *Napoleon Bonaparte* (1952), and F. Markham, *Napoleon* (1966). The best guide to interpretations of the period and perhaps the best book on Napoleon in English is P. Geyl, *Napoleon: For and Against* (1949). The best treatment in any language are the two volumes by G. Lefebvre, *Napoléon* (trans. 1969). On Napoleon's domestic policy, see R. Holtman, *The Napoleonic Revolution* (1967). See also, I. Collins, *Napoleon and his Parliaments, 1800–1815* (1979). Both R. B. Mowat, *The Diplomacy of Napoleon* (1924), and H. C. Deutsch, *The Genesis of Napoleonic Imperialism, 1801–1805* (1938), remain standard works on foreign policy. See also S. T. Ross, *European Diplomatic History 1789–1815: France Against Europe* (1969). The best recent treatment of Napoleon's military career is D. Chandler, *The Campaigns of Napoleon* (1966). O. Connelly, *Napoleon's Satellite Kingdoms* (1965), deals with the rule of Napoleon and his relatives over most of Europe. G. H. Lovett, *Napoleon and the Birth of Modern Spain*, 2 vols. (1965), tells a dramatic story. Napoleon's relations with the two peripheral powers of Europe are treated in C. Oman, *Britain Against Napoleon* (1944), and in A. Palmer, *Napoleon in Russia* (1967). On the end of Napoleon's career, see C. Hibbert, *Waterloo: Napoleon's Last Campaign* (1969).

24 The Search for Stability, 1815–1850

The unrest that had prevailed in Europe since the French Revolution did not end with the defeat of Napoleon. Many of Europe's troubles stemmed from the long and costly series of recent wars. But there were other causes of unrest. Politically, Europe continued to feel the effects of the issues first raised by the French Revolution—notably liberalism and nationalism. Intellectually, the years after Napoleon saw the flowering of the Age of Romanticism, with its protest against the rationalism of the Enlightenment. Economically and socially, the Continent in the first half of the nineteenth century began to feel in earnest the effects of the "Industrial Revolution," which had already begun in England in the eighteenth century (see Chapter 25). This chapter concentrates on political and intellectual developments. But we must keep in mind that political tension was often the manifestation of underlying economic and social unrest. The rapid increase of Europe's population alone—from 192 million in 1800 to 274 million in 1850—could not help but have unsettling economic and political effects. And the fact that more and more people now lived in cities did much to change the everyday lives of many Europeans.

Europe's search for stability after 1815 was marked by a contest between the forces of stagnation and the forces of change. For a while it seemed as though the traditional agencies of power—the monarchs, the aristocracy, and the Church—might once again resume full control. But potent new forces were ready to oppose this relapse into the past. With the quickening of industrialization, there was now not only a growing middle class but a wholly new class, the urban workers. Each class came to have its own political and economic philosophy—liberalism and socialism, respectively—which stood opposed to each other as well as to the traditional conservatism of the old order. It was inevitable that these rival classes and ideologies should clash. The resulting revolutions did not end until 1850. By that time the forces of the past were still not defeated, and in some places were definitely on the offensive.

Economic growth and ideological unrest were not the only causes of revolution in the early nineteenth century. There was also the force of nationalism, which made itself increasingly felt among Europeans everywhere. Nationalism as an awareness of belonging to a particular nationality was nothing new. What was new was the intensity that this awareness now assumed. There were still some signs of eighteenth-century cosmopolitanism, especially among the aristocracy. But for the middle class, and later for the mass of the people, nationalism became their most ardent political emotion, and national unification or independence their most cherished aim.

Generally speaking, the early nineteenth century was a major phase in the slow change from an essentially hierarchical and agrarian order into an increasingly democratic and industrial society. The problem faced by leaders everywhere was to give political expression to the economic and social changes resulting from the industrial transformation of Europe. In trying to do this, they hoped to bring stability to their deeply unsettled world.

THE RESTORATION OF THE OLD ORDER

The first task facing the allies after defeating Napoleon was to bring order to a continent that had been disturbed by two decades of war. Europe's statesmen in the main tried to restore conditions as they had been before the French Revolution. In domestic affairs they adopted the principle of "legitimacy"—that is, they brought back the dynasties that had been ousted by revolution or war. In international affairs they tried to reconstruct the balance of power that had been upset by France. In retrospect this preoccupation with the past may seem shortsighted. But history shows that most peace settlements are made with a view to the past rather than a vision of the future.

The Congress of Vienna

Peace conferences are usually dominated by a few leading statesmen. In 1814 and 1815 the decisive figures were Austria's chancellor, Prince Metternich;

Opposite: the July Revolution of 1830 at Pont Neuf.

Prince Metternich (1773–1859),
by Sir Thomas Lawrence.

Britain's foreign secretary, Lord Castlereagh; Tsar Alexander I of Russia; the Prussian King Frederick William III; and France's foreign minister, Prince Talleyrand. The fact that the vanquished French were thus able to make their voice heard shows the moderation and common sense of the victors.

The final peace with France was concluded at Paris in November 1815. France was the first to experience the principle of legitimacy. The new French king, Louis XVIII, was the brother of Louis XVI and the uncle of the deceased dauphin, Louis XVII. Considering the many hardships the French had inflicted on Europe, the peace settlement was remarkably lenient. France lost none of its pre-1790 territories; it had to pay only a small

indemnity; and it had to endure a brief period of allied occupation.

The settlement with France, however, was only part of the work of restoration. A far more difficult task was to reorder the affairs of the rest of Europe. This was done at a separate conference in Vienna. The Congress of Vienna aroused high hopes among those Europeans who desired a stronger voice in government or who, like the Germans and the Italians, longed for national unification. Their hopes were disappointed. The statesmen at Vienna, notably Metternich, had been deeply disturbed by the excesses of revolution and war and thus were firmly opposed to the forces of liberalism and nationalism in whose name these excesses had been committed.

EUROPE IN 1815

Considering the conflicting aims of the powers, it is surprising how much was actually achieved at Vienna. Following the principle of legitimacy, the Bourbons were restored in Spain and Naples, and other legitimate rulers were put back on their thrones in the smaller Italian states. Yet the idea of legitimacy was frequently ignored, especially in the case of republics like Genoa and Venice, neither of which regained its independence. To maintain the balance of power and to keep France from avenging its defeat, the countries along its eastern frontier were either enlarged or otherwise strengthened. In the north, the Republic of Holland was given a king and was joined with the former Austrian Netherlands (Belgium). In place of the defunct Holy Roman Empire, a loosely joined confederation of thirty-nine states was set up in Germany. To provide an effective barrier to French expansion in the southeast, Switzerland was reestablished as an independent confederation and was declared perpetually neutral. The containment of France was completed by strengthening the Kingdom of Piedmont in northern Italy. In compensation for relinquishing Belgium, Austria received the Italian provinces of Lombardy and Venetia as well as the Illyrian provinces and the Tyrol (some of which Austria had ruled before 1789). This made Austria the dominant power in Italy and the leading opponent of Italian unification.

Most of these changes caused no major difficulties, chiefly because the great powers saw eye-to-eye on them. One issue, however, caused much disagreement and at one point threatened to plunge the powers into war. That issue was Poland. A favorite scheme of Tsar Alexander I at Vienna was to pose as the "liberator" of Poland by setting up a Polish kingdom under Russian tutelage. The other powers objected to this: Prussia and Austria because they expected the return of those parts of Poland they had held before Napoleon, and England because it had no desire to see Russia grow too powerful. To gain his end, Alexander promised the Prussians compensations elsewhere if they would support his Polish scheme. The result was a deadlock at Vienna, with England and

Austria facing Russia and Prussia. An armed conflict was narrowly avoided when Talleyrand threw the weight of France behind England and Austria. The compromise that was reached was more advantageous to Prussia than to Russia. Russia received part of Poland, though less than hoped for, while Prussia got compensations in northern and western Germany that made it a powerful contender for leadership within the newly formed German Confederation and the guardian of Germany's interests along the Rhine.

While most of the decisions reached at Vienna were on specific territorial issues, the Congress also addressed itself

Two contemporary views of the Congress of Vienna. The caricature portrays Talleyrand and Castlereagh (left) deliberating whether to join the merry dance of England's allies, Frederick William III, Metternich, and Alexander I. The king of Saxony fears the loss of his crown, while the Republic of Genoa (right) plays up to the powers in the hope of keeping its independence. The other view, a group portrait of the peacemakers by Isabey, dignifies the occasion.

to some general questions. Among them was the slave trade. There had been agitation against this scandalous practice since the late eighteenth century, and it had been outlawed in Britain in 1808. At Vienna, Lord Castlereagh succeeded in having the traffic in slaves condemned, but France, Spain, and Portugal did not comply until 1820. Even then it was only the trade, not slavery itself, that was outlawed. The British Empire abolished slavery in 1833, the United States not until a generation later.

Metternich

PRO

He was a statesman of unusual proportions: the greatest foreign minister that Austria ever had, and one of the greatest masters of international politics in the history of the modern European states. . . . He lifted Austria from its deepest downfall to a proud height. . . . He had the greatest part in bringing it about that for thirty years Europe enjoyed comparative international peace, and that during this time, in the center of the continent, learning and art could have a period of the most salutary, quiet cultivation, capital and the spirit of enterprise could undergo a strong increase, and religion and religious communities could experience intensification and consolidation.

CON

The question has often been raised whether he was not rather a good diplomat than a statesman. The question appears to be thoroughly justified: he lacked virtually all the characteristics necessary to a real and great statesman—courage, resolution, strength, seriousness, the gift of breadth of vision, the correct evaluation of the fruitful forces of the future, in brief, everything creative. . . . All revolutions, he held, came not from economic misery or dissatisfaction with bad political conditions, but arose from the secret societies, visionaries and doctrinaires. The new, world-moving force, the idea of national self-determination, counted for nothing with him. Peoples, in his eyes, were "children or nervous women," "simpletons." Liberalism to him was a "spectre" which must be banished by forceful action, a mere fog, which would disappear of its own accord.

From Heinrich von Srbik, *Metternich, der Staatsmann und der Mensch* (Munich, 1925); from Viktor Bibl, *Metternich, der Dämon Oesterreichs* (Vienna, 1936), as quoted in Henry F. Schwarz, ed., *Metternich, the "Coachman of Europe"* (Boston: Heath, 1962), pp. 15–16, 22–23.

The Congress of Vienna had accomplished a great deal, even though it had not lived up to everyone's hopes. In particular, the Vienna settlement ignored the stirrings of nationalism and the hopes for more popular government that the French Revolution had awakened. But more widespread than the middle-class dreams of nationalism and liberalism in 1815 was the hope for peace and order. It was in fulfilling this hope that the statesmen of Vienna scored their major success. There was no war among the great powers for forty years, and no war of worldwide dimensions for a whole century.

The "Holy Alliance" and the "Concert of Europe"

An indication of how sincerely the framers of the Vienna settlement sought peace may be seen in the arrangements they made to maintain it. The most famous of these, though the least important, was the "Holy Alliance" of Alexander I. The tsar had long thought of himself as a world savior. In this role he proposed to his fellow monarchs that they should conduct their relations with one another and with their subjects in a spirit of Christian love. To humor the tsar, most European rulers signed his "Holy Alliance"; but it never achieved any practical significance.

Of far greater importance than this "piece of sublime mysticism and nonsense" (as Castlereagh called it) was the Quadruple Alliance signed by England, Austria, Russia, and Prussia at the time of the final peace treaty with France in 1815. Its primary purpose was to prevent any further French violation of the peace settlement. But the powers also agreed to hold periodic conferences (ultimately to include France as well) to discuss matters of general European concern. This was an important innovation. For the first time statesmen seemed to realize that peace might be preserved by dealing with crises before they led to general war. The "Concert of Europe" was thus born.

As it turned out, however, this congress system was not a great success. At the very first meeting, at Aix-la-Chapelle in 1818, it became clear that the powers did not really see eye-to-eye on the fundamental purpose of their system of international government. To Castlereagh, the Quadruple Alliance was mainly an instrument for keeping France in its place and for maintaining international peace. To Alexander I, on the other hand, the Alliance seemed a convenient means of maintaining domestic peace as well. This difference was clearly revealed when Alexander proposed a new alliance that would guarantee not only the territorial status quo in Europe but also the existing form of government in every European country. This latter proposal met with determined opposition from Castlereagh, who did not want to extend the alliance "to include all objects, present and future."

The problem of whether to aid legitimate governments against revolution became acute shortly after Aix-la-Chapelle when a whole series of revolutions suddenly broke out over most of southern Europe. Here was a welcome opportunity for Alexander to repeat his plea for joint intervention. But Britain again voiced its opposition. And to underline his determination not to meddle in the affairs of other nations, Castlereagh refused to attend the Congress of Troppau (1820), at which such intervention was to be discussed.

With England absent, the other powers were able to adopt the "Troppau Protocol," which promised military aid to any government threatened by revolution. The effects of the Protocol became clear in 1821. In that year a third congress, at Laibach, commissioned Austria to send its forces into the Italian peninsula to put down the liberal* insurrections there. Britain protested, but in vain. Similar action was taken at the next and last congress, which met at Verona in 1822. Again the continental powers, against England's objections, sanctioned the dispatch of a French force to put down a Spanish revolution in 1823. Diplomacy by congress, so promising

*The term "liberal," as shown in the next chapter, has a variety of meanings. It is used here in the general sense of advocating political and economic reforms, primarily benefitting the middle class.

Detail from a print showing British troops charging protesters at the Peterloo Massacre.

at first, had thus failed. It had failed because of a fundamental divergence among the victors over the issue of political change, with Britain opposing and the rest of the powers supporting intervention in the domestic affairs of other states to prevent liberal or national uprisings. There were other efforts to hold congresses, but England refused to attend.

A Wave of Reaction

The revolutions of the early 1820s, which are discussed below, were caused by the wave of reaction that followed the peace settlements of 1815. Wherever a legitimate monarch returned, he attempted to restore conditions exactly as they had been before he was ousted. In Spain and Naples the returning Bourbons abolished the liberal reforms that had been granted in 1812. In the Papal States, Pope Pius VII abolished French legal reforms, reestablished the Jesuits, revived the Inquisition, and put the Jews back into ghettos. In Piedmont, Victor Emmanuel I had the French botanical gardens torn up by the roots and the French furniture thrown out of the windows of his palace.

Elsewhere in Italy and over much of Europe the picture was the same. Both Frederick William III of Prussia and Francis I of Austria favored rigorous measures of repression in their respective countries. By tradition as well as actual power, Austria dominated the Diet of the

Johann Wolfgang von Goethe (1749–1832), from a medal stamped by the French sculptor David d'Angers in 1829.

new German Confederation at Frankfurt. Here it was Metternich who used his influence to suppress liberal or national stirrings wherever they appeared in Germany. As protests against this repressive "Metternich System" grew more vociferous, Austria and Prussia in 1819 pressured the Frankfurt Diet into adopting the so-called Carlsbad Decrees, which strictly limited intellectual freedom, especially at the universities.

There were very few exceptions to this general rule of reaction. It was felt even in England, whose foreign policy at least was more enlightened than that of the continental powers. There was much unrest in postwar Britain, chiefly due to economic causes. Overproduction during the war caused prices to fall, which in turn led to lower wages and growing unemployment. To remedy Britain's ills, a number of middle-class radicals advocated that the government be liberalized through parliamentary reform. But any agitation for reform was met by stern repression. In 1819, after the so-called Peterloo Massacre—when the constabulary of Manchester charged into a peaceful public meeting on parliamentary reform, causing many casualties—Parliament passed the repressive "Six Acts," which was England's version of the Carlsbad Decrees.

THE AGE OF ROMANTICISM

Before considering the several waves of revolution that swept over Europe between 1820 and 1850, we must examine the intellectual climate in which these events took place. Much of the political turmoil of the generation after Napoleon had its counterpart and its cause in the spiritual ferment associated with the Age of Romanticism.

The Main Characteristics of Romanticism

The term *Romanticism* defies clear definition. It differed not only from country to country but from Romanticist to Romanticist. It inspired reactionaries as well as revolutionaries. It made conservatives look longingly to the past and liberals look hopefully to the future. It

meant escapism for some and a call to action for others. But with all these contradictions, there were certain characteristics that most Romantics shared. Most prominent among these was their protest against the rationalism of the eighteenth century. The Enlightenment, with its emphasis on the rational nature of man and the rational order of the universe, had ignored irrational forces. We have already seen some earlier reactions to this narrow rationalism. The French Revolution and the age of Napoleon had given further impetus to this protest. Reason, it seemed, was not the solution to man's problems that the *philosophes* had promised it to be. If reason had failed, what was there left to turn to but its opposite—faith? The typical Romantic followed his heart rather than his head. He was an individualist. The Enlightenment had spoken of Man, as though he were the same everywhere. The Romanticist stressed differences among men and felt that each should be a law unto himself. Much of Romantic writing was devoted to the strong personality, the hero, both in history and in fiction. One manifestation of Romanticism's interest in the individual was the growing vogue of autobiographies. One of the most revealing of these was Rousseau's famous *Confessions*. It was Rousseau also who regarded education as a means of realizing a person's individuality. The Enlightenment, with its belief in the essential sameness of human minds, had been interested in formal rather than individualized education. Rousseau held that children should be left to develop their own abilities and potentialities.

While many Romanticists took a lively interest in the world about them, others used their imagination as a means of escape. To the eighteenth-century *philosophe* the world had appeared as a well-ordered mechanism; to the Romanticist, on the other hand, nature was a mysterious organism whose moods expressed his innermost feelings. The Enlightenment had liked landscapes that showed the civilizing influence of man; Romanticism, by contrast, preferred its nature wild or dreamlike, as in the paintings of Constable and Turner in England or Caspar David Friedrich in Germany.

This Romantic love of the unusual or the unreal in nature was frankly escapist. As factories began to disfigure the landscape and cities began to encroach on their surrounding countryside, the Romanticists longed to return to an unspoiled and simple life. They abhorred the ugliness and artificiality of city life and extolled the virtues of country folk, whose customs, tales, and songs they hoped to preserve. The escapism of the Romanticists took other forms as well. Some Romantic writers let their imagination roam in faraway, exotic places; others preferred to dwell in the realm of the supernatural. Still others escaped into the realm of religious emotion.

Romanticism and Religion

The close relationship between Romanticism and religion, especially Catholicism, is obvious, since both stressed the emotional, irrational side of man. Catholicism in particular answered the Romanticist's need to "believe in something." The mystery of Catholic theology and the splendor of its ritual provided just the kind of emotional experience the Romanticist craved. As a result, many Romanticists turned to Catholicism, and the Catholic Church, which had been on the defensive since the French Revolution, was able to reassert itself. In 1814, the Jesuit Order was officially restored. In 1816, divorce, which had been permitted in France since the Revolution, was once again abolished. In Spain and parts of Italy, the Inquisition returned. And almost everywhere on the Continent, education once again became a monopoly of the clergy.

Veneration of the Past

The revival of religious interest was closely allied to the general Romantic veneration for the past. The Enlightenment had derived much of its inspiration from the ancient Greeks and Romans, whose civilizations had appeared both reasonable and attractive. The intervening period, from about 400 to 1300 A.D., had been merely "Dark Ages" of ignorance and superstition. It was to these hitherto neglected centuries that the Romanticists now turned, attracted by the mystery and the grandeur that had survived in medieval castles and Gothic cathedrals.

Cloister Graveyard in the Snow, Romantic painting by Caspar David Friedrich (1810).

The Romantic interest in the Middle Ages, by arousing an interest in the past, also awakened a general interest in the study of history. To the Romantic mind, the world was an organism that had grown slowly, changed constantly, and was still growing and changing. In an effort to retrace this gradual change, historians in the early nineteenth century developed a careful method of inquiry, using historical sources—documents and other remains—to gain a truer understanding of the past. Modern historical scholarship, as we know it today, originated in the Age of Romanticism.

Nationalism and Conservatism

One of the things a study of the past teaches us is that mankind has gradually come to be divided into separate groups defined by geographic area, language, and historic experiences. In time, all these elements together create a common feeling of "national consciousness." Some such feeling had existed in England, France, and even Germany since medieval or early modern times. To transform this national consciousness into nationalism, however, something more was needed—a sense not only of being different from, but superior to, other national groups. The first modern manifestations of nationalism may be seen in the French Revolution and the Napoleonic wars. With its appeal to the emotions, this new nationalism fitted quite naturally into the climate of Romanticism. To the Romantic, nationalism, like religion, provided something in which he could believe and for which he could sacrifice himself.

Nationalism in the early nineteenth century was a revolutionary creed. Since it aimed at the liberation of peoples from foreign domination or their unification into a common state, it posed a threat to the established order. In defense of that order, a new political philosophy had already appeared during the French Revolution, the philosophy of conservatism. Its leading proponent was the Englishman Edmund Burke. We have seen how Burke, in his *Reflections on the Revolution in France*, had warned against the ultimate consequences of that upheaval. He

had in particular attacked the revolutionaries for their eighteenth-century belief that man was innately good and endowed with certain natural rights. Far from having any natural rights, man, according to Burke, merely inherited the rights and duties that existed within his society. Since these rights and duties had developed through the ages, they constituted an inheritance that no single generation had the right to destroy. Burke also rebuked the eighteenth-century idea that government was the result of a contract among its citizens. Instead, he held that the state was an organism, a mystic community, to which the individual must submit.

Burke's conservatism, with its veneration for the past, its organic view of society, and its prediction of many of the dire consequences of the French Revolution, had great appeal to the generation after 1815. Like nationalism, conservatism greatly attracted the Romanticists, and Burke found ardent adherents and imitators on the Continent. Initially, conservatism and nationalism often conflicted. Nationalism, to achieve its ends, advocated revolution, which conservatives abhorred. Conservatism, on the other hand, often became indistinguishable from reaction, which opposed change of any kind. In the course of time, nationalism, once it had reached its goals, tended to become conservative in order to defend its gains.

There was one point, however, on which conservatives and nationalists agreed from the beginning, and that was their admiration of the state as the highest social organism. The leading advocate of the supreme importance of the state was the German philosopher Georg Wilhelm Friedrich Hegel. Like the conservatives, Hegel viewed the state as an organism that had evolved historically. Only in submission to a powerful state, Hegel held, could the individual achieve his true freedom. To be strong, a state must be unified, preferably under the authority of a monarch. Each state, according to Hegel, had its own particular spirit, and by developing that spirit it contributed to the World-Spirit. "The State," Hegel wrote, "is the Divine Idea as it exists on earth." As such it is not bound by the

A German peasant girl in her native costume; painting by Ludwig Emil Grimm (1828).

usual laws of morality; its only judge is history. The course of history had evolved in three stages: the Oriental, in which only a despot was free; the Greek and the Roman, in which a few were free; and finally the Germanic, in which all would be free. It was his stress on the unique position of Germany and of Prussia that endeared Hegel to German nationalists.

The Impact of Romanticism

Romanticism, as this brief synopsis shows, was a bundle of contradictions. It helps us understand the conservatives who made the Vienna settlement, as well as the liberals who tried to overthrow it. It was a movement affecting all aspects of human life and thought. It was particularly strong in the arts, not only in literature but also in painting and music. The influence of Romanticism was deep and widespread. All the nations of Europe contributed to it, and it also was a vital force in the United States. The Romantic protest, furthermore, or at least the Romantic attitude, did not end with the Romantic era. Its influence is felt to the present day.

Romanticism has been criticized as a rebellion against reason, and as a surrender to the murky passions and emotions of the human heart. The German poet Goethe, himself a Romantic in his youth, looked back with nostalgia to the reasonableness and clarity of eighteenth-century classicism. "Classic," he said, "is healthy; Romantic is sick." Romanticism, it is true, did destroy the clear simplicity and unity of thought that had prevailed during the Enlightenment. There was no longer one dominant philosophy that expressed the aims and ideals of western civilization as rationalism had done during the eighteenth century. But rationalism had provided a one-sided view of the world, ignoring whole provinces of human experience. Romanticism did much to correct that unbalance. By insisting that the world was not the simple machine it had seemed since Newton and that man was not a mere cog in that machine, Romanticism provided a more complex but also a truer view of the world. With its emphasis on evolution throughout the universe, and its stress on the creativity and uniqueness of the individual, Romanticism came as a breath of fresh air after the formalism of the Enlightenment. This was its major and lasting contribution.

THE FIRST WAVE OF REVOLUTIONS, 1820–29

The restoration of the old order saved Europe from major international wars, but it was also responsible for the almost

The Ingredients of Nationalism

1. A certain defined (often vaguely) unit of territory (whether possessed or coveted).
2. Some common cultural characteristics such as language (or widely understood languages), customs, manners, and literature (folk tales and lore are a beginning). If an individual believes he shares these, and wishes to continue sharing them, he is usually said to be a member of the nationality.
3. Some common dominant social (as Christian) and economic (as capitalistic or, recently, communistic) institutions.
4. A common independent or sovereign government (type does not matter) or the desire for one. The "principle" that each nationality should be separate and independent is involved here.
5. A belief in a common history (it can be invented) and in a common origin (often mistakenly conceived to be racial in nature).
6. A love or esteem for fellow nationals (not necessarily as individuals).
7. A devotion to the entity (however little comprehended) called the nation, which embodies the common territory, culture, social and economic institutions, government, and the fellow nationals, and which is at the same time (whether organism or not) more than their sum.
8. A common pride in the achievements (often the military more than the cultural) of this nation and a common sorrow in its tragedies (particularly its defeats).
9. A disregard for or hostility to other (not necessarily all) like groups, especially if these prevent or seem to threaten the separate national existence.
10. A hope that the nation will have a great and glorious future (usually in territorial expansion) and become supreme in some way (in world power if the nation is already large).

From Boyd C. Shafer, *Nationalism: Myth and Reality* (New York: Harcourt Brace Jovanovich, 1955), pp. 7–8.

unbroken series of domestic wars and revolutions that lasted for more than a generation. We have already noted the unrest in Germany and England shortly after 1815. In France, the assassination in 1820 of the Duke of Berri, who was in line to be Louis XVIII's successor, was the signal for abandoning the moderate course Louis had tried to steer. More serious, however, than these sporadic acts of violence was the whole wave of revolutions that swept through southern Europe in the 1820s.

Revolt in Southern Europe

The first of these revolutions broke out in 1820 in Spain, where the army rebelled against being sent to South America to put down the revolutions in the Spanish colonies. From Spain revolution spread to Portugal and somewhat later to Italy. In every case it was the army that took the initiative, forcing reactionary monarchs to grant liberal constitutions. The situation in Italy was particularly complicated. The Italian peninsula was still divided into a number of states of varying size, the most important being the Kingdom of the Two Sicilies in the south, the Papal States in the center, and the Kingdom of Piedmont in the north. In addition, Austria ruled directly over the northern provinces of Lombardy and Venetia and exerted influence over the rest of Italy through Austrian or pro-Austrian rulers in many of the smaller states. The revolutions in Italy, therefore, were directed not merely against the reactionary policy of the various local rulers but against the alien influence of Austria.

As a result of these upheavals, the old order in much of southern Europe seemed to be crumbling. But the initial success of the revolutions did not last. The revolutionaries everywhere constituted only a small minority, finding little support among the apathetic mass of illiterate peasants. In addition, there was much disagreement among the leaders when it came to establishing more liberal regimes. More harmful than lack of popular following and differences among the revolutionaries was the intervention of outside forces. Austria, with the blessing of Prussia and Russia, intervened in Italy in 1821, and France intervened in Spain in 1823. Only in Portugal was a semblance of parliamentary government maintained, thanks to the support of Great Britain.

The Monroe Doctrine

With reaction triumphant, there was now a possibility that the powers might try to help Spain recover its colonies in Latin America. Largely under the impact of the French Revolution and the Napoleonic conquest of their mother country, the Spanish colonies, beginning in 1810, had followed the example of the United States and declared their independence. In this they had the sympathy of both the United States and Great Britain, whose commercial interests were eager to gain access to the South American market. In 1822, Britain's new foreign secretary, George Canning, proposed a joint declaration by England and the United States to oppose any European intervention against the Spanish colonies.

Simón Bolívar (1783–1830), outstanding leader of the South American revolution against Spain and the greatest of Latin American heroes.

But the United States was concerned not only about South America but also about the possible extension of Russian influence southward from Alaska and about England's designs on Cuba. President Monroe, therefore, decided to act on his own. In a message to Congress in December 1823, he warned that any attempt by the powers of Europe to extend their influence over the Western Hemisphere would be considered a "manifestation of an unfriendly disposition toward the United States." The immediate effectiveness of the Monroe Doctrine, of course, depended on the backing of the British navy rather than on the insignificant power of the United States. For that reason, Canning was justified in his famous boast that he "called the New World into existence to redress the balance of the Old."

The Greek War of Independence

The revolutions in the Iberian and Italian peninsulas, in their aims as well as their failures, had been quite similar. But the most important revolution of the 1820s, the Greek War of Independence, was a different matter. That war was almost entirely motivated by nationalism. And while the other revolutions failed largely because of outside intervention, the Greek revolt succeeded because the powers helped rather than hindered it. The Greek revolt against the Ottoman Empire was merely the latest chapter in the slow disintegration of that sprawling state. The Serbs had already staged a successful revolt by 1815. Greek nationalism had been gathering force for some time, especially among the "Island" Greeks, whose far-flung commercial contacts had put them in touch with western ideas. The Island Greeks had founded a secret society, the *Philikē Hetàiria*, and it was this society that inspired the uprising in early 1821 that started the war against Turkey.

The Greeks, however, were no match for the Turks, especially after the sultan called in his Egyptian vassal, Mehemet Ali, to help him. The great powers watched events in Greece closely, but were kept from intervention through

James Monroe (1758–1831), by Gilbert Stuart.

The Monroe Doctrine

In the wars of the European powers in matters relating to themselves we have never taken any part, nor does it comport with our policy so to do. It is only when our rights are invaded or seriously menaced that we resent injuries or make preparation for our defense. With the movements in this hemisphere we are of necessity more immediately connected, and by causes which must be obvious to all enlightened and impartial observers. The political system of the allied powers is essentially different in this respect from that of America. . . . We owe it, therefore, to candor and to the amicable relations existing between the United States and those powers to declare that we should consider any attempt on their part to extend their system to any portion of this hemisphere as dangerous to our peace and safety. With the existing colonies or dependencies of any European power we have not interfered and shall not interfere. But with the governments who have declared their independence and maintained it, and whose independence we have, on great consideration and on just principles, acknowledged, we could not view any interposition for the purpose of oppressing them, or controlling in any other manner their destiny, by any European power in any other light than as the manifestation of an unfriendly disposition toward the United States.

From President James Monroe, message to Congress, December 2, 1823.

Mahmoud II (1784–1839), sultan of Turkey at the time of the Greek revolts.

Nicholas I, tsar of Russia, (1825–55); sketch by Sir Edwin Henry Landseer (1802–73).

mutual jealousies. Only when the very existence of the Greeks seemed at stake did they realize that something had to be done.

Public opinion in the West had favored the Greek cause all along, and the pressure of this "Philhellenism" was partly responsible for the intervention of the powers. In 1827, British, French, and Russian squadrons destroyed the combined Turkish and Egyptian navies in the battle of Navarino. The following year, Russia declared war on Turkey. After brief fighting, the Turks had to submit to the Treaty of Adrianople (1829). Its terms were moderate, except that Russia was given a protectorate over the Danubian principalities of Moldavia and Wallachia, which later became Rumania. After some further negotiations, Greece was set up as an independent kingdom.

The Decembrist Revolt in Russia

While the Greek uprising was still going on, there had been one other attempt at revolution, this time against the most powerful stronghold of reaction, the tsarist regime in Russia. Like the Spanish and Italian revolts, it failed. The enigmatic Alexander I, who liked to pose as a liberal while actually becoming more and more reactionary, left the direction of Russian affairs largely in the hands of his efficient but equally reactionary adviser, Alexis Arakcheiev, who used Alexander's fear of revolution to build a regime of ruthless political oppression.

This policy of oppression naturally aroused the opposition of the few liberal elements in Russia. Many members of the upper class had come in contact with western liberal ideas during the wars against Napoleon and the subsequent allied occupation of France. These officers founded several secret societies. An opportunity for the conspirators to act came in December 1825, when Alexander suddenly died and there was some doubt about which of his brothers would succeed him. The revolt failed, however, because it was mostly confined to the army, and its leaders were disunited and lacked popular following. Even so, this so-called Decembrist Revolt was signifi-

cant. Earlier uprisings in Russia had been entirely spontaneous. Here, for the first time, was a revolt that had been planned by a small minority with a definite program. The Decembrist uprising served as an inspiration to all later revolutionary movements in Russia. Meanwhile, the December events inspired in Alexander's successor, Nicholas I, an almost pathological fear of revolution. For thirty years he remained the leading proponent of reaction abroad and repression at home.

THE SECOND WAVE OF REVOLUTIONS, 1830–33

The first wave of revolutions after 1815, far from upsetting the old order, merely seemed to have strengthened its hold. The uprisings had been too sporadic, the work of small army cliques with no following among the mass of the people. The second wave of revolutions was different. It started among the people of Paris, and from there it spread over most of Europe, leaving behind some important political changes.

The French Revolution of 1830

The first years of the restored Bourbon monarchy in France had been peaceful ones. Louis XVIII had tried sincerely to rally his deeply divided country. But he found it increasingly difficult to do so. To the liberals, led by Lafayette, the new constitution, the Charter, with its limited franchise did not go far enough. To the royalists, or "Ultras," led by the king's brother, the Count of Artois, the Charter was the source of all France's ills. Up to 1820, Louis had been able to maintain a moderate, middle-of-the-road course. But after the assassination of the Duke of Berri, the royalist faction gained the upper hand and moderation came to an end.

Louis XVIII died in 1824 and was succeeded by the Count of Artois, as Charles X. Reaction now went into full force. While liberal opposition became more outspoken, the government's policy became more repressive. In 1829 Charles appointed as his first minister one of the most notorious reactionaries, the Prince de Polignac. In the past the king had always been careful to enlist parliamentary backing, but this situation now changed. In the spring of 1830, when the Chamber turned against the government, Charles simply dismissed it. And when new elections brought in another liberal majority, Polignac had the king promulgate the July Ordinances, which dissolved the Chamber, imposed strict censorship, and changed the electoral law to give the government a favorable majority.

Discontent with this arbitrary policy came to a head in the July revolution of 1830. The hope of the men who fought on the barricades—workers, students, some members of the middle class—was for a republic. But this was not what the more moderate liberals wanted. Much as they hated the high-handed government of Charles X, they were equally opposed to a republic, which recalled the violent phase of the earlier French Revolution. It was due to the careful machinations of these moderates that France emerged from its July revolution as a constitutional monarchy rather than a republic.

The new king was Louis Philippe, Duke of Orléans. Though a relative of the Bourbons, he had stayed clear of the royalists and had affected a thoroughly bourgeois mode of life. Events in France, of course, violated the status quo established in 1814 and 1815. But the other powers had been taken too much by surprise and were too little united to take any action. Their attention, furthermore, was soon caught by events elsewhere, as the French example set off a whole series of revolutions in other countries.

Revolution in Belgium

The first to follow the lead of France was Belgium. Its union with Holland at Vienna had not proved very successful. The only area in which the two countries got along was in economic matters, and even there the Belgians in time developed grievances. The main differences were political and religious. In August 1830, in part inspired by events in Paris, rioting broke out in Brussels. King William I tried to save the situation by granting a separate administration for

Louis XVIII, by F. Gerard (1823).

Belgium, but he was too late. The Dutch troops sent to quell the uprising were quickly defeated; but the ultimate fate of Belgium depended on the attitude of the great powers. France and England looked favorably upon the new state, but the three eastern powers were hostile. Since Austria and Russia were preoccupied with disturbances in Italy and Poland, however, any aid to Holland was out of the question. In December 1830 the five powers agreed to recognize the independence of Belgium. The new state was to remain perpetually neutral.

France and Belgium were the only nations in which the revolutions of 1830 achieved any lasting success. Yet there was hardly a country that did not feel the tremors of revolution. Across the Rhine the events in Paris caused wild excitement among German intellectuals, though there was little echo among the

Charles X of France portrayed as a reactionary lobster moving backward; anonymous caricature (1830).

people. Some of the smaller states rid themselves of rulers who were particularly corrupt and vicious, and others won moderately liberal constitutions.

The Polish Insurrection of 1830

The bloodiest struggle of all in 1830 took place in Poland. The Kingdom of Poland already had been a source of trouble to Alexander I. Under Nicholas I tension mounted further. Like revolutionaries elsewhere, the Polish insurgents had founded a number of secret societies to propagate nationalism and to prepare for revolution. When rumors reached Poland in 1830 that Nicholas was planning to use Polish forces to help put down the revolutions in France and Belgium, the conspirators decided to act. Had the Polish people stood united, the revolt might have succeeded. But the revolutionaries were split into moderates and radicals, with neither faction having much following among the mass of the peasants. The hope, furthermore, that England and France would come to their aid proved vain. Even so, it took almost a year before Russia was able to subdue the rebellious Poles and impose a regime

of severe repression. For the next generation Russian Poland remained a sad and silent land.

Revolt in Southern Europe

Southern Europe, the scene of revolutions a decade earlier, was also aroused by the news from Paris. In Italy, where secret societies such as the *Carbonari*, or "charcoal burners," were flourishing, revolutions broke out in several states. The revolutionaries hoped to receive aid from France, and had they done so they might have won. But Louis Philippe could not afford to antagonize Austria, and Metternich had a free hand. A few years later, struggles among rival claimants to the thrones in Spain and Portugal, together with disturbances fostered by liberals, created widespread confusion in those countries. Both nations finally emerged, at least nominally, as constitutional monarchies.

Reform in Great Britain

There was one other country besides France and Belgium where unrest in 1830 and after led to major political changes. More than any other nation, Great Britain had been feeling the effects of rapid industrialization. The change from an agrarian to an industrial society could not help but have political repercussions. That England was able to make this adjustment without a revolution was due to its long parliamentary tradition and able political leadership. Britain did share in the initial wave of reaction after 1815. With the incapable George IV succeeding George III in 1820, and with the Tories in control of Parliament, little relief was in sight.

Beginning in 1822, however, a new and more enlightened element within the Tory Party became aware of the political implications of economic change. The first sign that some relief from repression was imminent came with the reform of Britain's criminal code after 1822, which drastically reduced the number of capital crimes. In 1824 the Combination Acts, forbidding workers to organize, were repealed. In 1828 a new Corn Law modified the duties on foreign grain, thus lowering

The Great Reform Bill of 1832 is the subject of this contemporary cartoon. Political corruption is put through the "reform mill" to emerge as a triumphant Britannia.

THE REFORM BILL.

the price of bread. The most important reform of the 1820s, however, was the establishment of religious equality. In 1828 the Test and Corporations Acts, which barred Protestant dissenters from holding state offices, were repealed; and in 1829 the Emancipation Bill permitted Catholics to sit in Parliament.

In most of these reforms the moderate element among the Tories had the support of the Whigs. The leaders of the Whig Party differed little from their Tory rivals in social background and outlook. But while the main backing of the Tory Party continued to come from the landed gentry and the established church, the Whigs were supported by the rising merchant and manufacturing class. For that reason they became the main advocates of parliamentary reform. To the Whigs, parliamentary reform meant giving a fairer share of representation in Parliament to the well-to-do middle class. This they were finally able to achieve in 1832.

The Great Reform Bill of 1832 was passed only after domestic unrest had at times brought England to the verge of revolution. Under the new bill, the franchise was extended to about half again as many voters, and proper representation was given to the new industrial towns. As a result, one in five adult males was now able to vote. The workers, the poor, and all women were still left without a vote, but this was no different from the situation elsewhere in Europe. Even though there was no change in Britain's form of government, the Reform Bill was every bit as much a revolution as the overthrow of Charles X had been in France. Both were significant stages in the rise to power of the middle, or upper middle, class.

East and West

Because the revolutions in the early 1830s were successful only in western Europe, they helped widen the already existing gap between the powers of the East and the West. France and England, constitutional monarchies both, had seen to it that the revolution in Belgium succeeded. Austria, Russia, and Prussia, still essentially autocratic, had suppressed the

uprisings in Germany, Italy, and Poland. The main reason for the success of revolutions in the West had been their popular support. The middle class had taken the lead, but it had been aided by the urban lower class. East of the Rhine, revolutions had found little popular backing and had failed. Industrialization, which had bolstered the ranks of the middle and lower classes in the West, had as yet made little headway in the East. But while the revolutions in western Europe had been successful, they had chiefly benefited the middle class. The workers, who had done much of the rioting and fighting, were left with empty hands. In the West as in the East, therefore, the revolutions of 1830 left much unfinished. Here is the main cause for the third and largest wave of revolutions, which swept across Europe in 1848 and 1849.

THE THIRD WAVE OF REVOLUTIONS, 1848–49

The third wave of revolutions lasted for over a year and affected most of Europe. Among the major powers, only England and Russia were spared, though England came close to revolt. There were countless differences among the various upheavals, but there were also some notable similarities. Generally speaking, the revolutions of 1848 were a further attempt to undo the settlement of 1815. In Italy, Germany, Austria, and Hungary the fundamental grievance was still the lack of national freedom and unity. There was also the desire for more representative governments and for the abolition of the remaining vestiges of feudalism. But these were secondary aims. Nationalism was the dominant concern of the revolutionaries in central Europe. In western Europe, neither nationalism nor feudalism was any longer an issue. There the chief aim of revolution was the extension of political power beyond the upper middle class. The revolutionaries did not always agree on how far this liberalization should go. The middle class wanted merely to widen the franchise to include the more substantial citizens, whereas the working class wanted political democracy for everyone

Above: a French cartoon showing Louis Philippe courting the public; it was captioned, "Well, good people, do you want some? Here it is."
Right: a British cartoon, from *Punch* in 1848, shows Liberty extinguishing Louis Philippe's candle.

and some measure of social and economic democracy as well. With the revolutions of 1848, socialism for the first time became an issue in European politics (see p. 585).

Aside from these political causes, there were also economic reasons for the outbreak of revolutions. Despite, or because of, the unprecedented economic growth of Europe since 1815, there had

been several severe economic crises, the latest in 1846 and 1847. These upsets particularly affected the lower classes. The small artisan was fighting against the competition of large-scale industry. At the same time, the still fewer industrial workers in the new factories were eking out a marginal existence on a minimum wage. Most important, there were periodic crises in agriculture, primarily as a result of crop failures. Economic hardship in many cases preceded and helped precipitate political action.

There were other common features among the revolutions of 1848. They were all essentially urban. The leaders came from the middle class, with lawyers, journalists, and professors especially prominent. Much of the actual fighting was done by the urban lower classes, by artisans and workers. Students also played an important part. None of the revolutions had any agrarian program beyond the abolition of feudal dues and services. Once these had been abolished, the conservative peasants withdrew what little initial support they had provided the revolutions.

Europe, in the spring of 1848, was discontented and restless. The causes of discontent differed from middle class to workers to peasants. But so long as these three groups stood united, it was easy for them to overthrow the old order. When it came to building something new, however, all the differences among the revolutionaries asserted themselves. The history of revolution in 1848 is a frustrating tale of missed opportunities.

The "July Monarchy" in France

The key nation in the events of 1848 was again France. The reasons for the failure of Louis Philippe's government are not too obvious. France under the "July Monarchy" (so-called after the month of its birth in 1830) was prosperous and progressive, with a liberal constitution, a free press, and a competent king. Louis Philippe had all the bourgeois virtues—he was thrifty, kindly, and industrious. He was served by capable ministers, and until about 1846 trade and industry flourished. France, which had fallen behind England economically as a result of the French Revolution, had regained some lost ground. Yet with all these advantages, the July Monarchy was far from popular. Most Frenchmen still smarted from the defeat of Napoleon. Only a glorious foreign policy could wipe out that humiliation. But no sooner was there an opportunity for such a policy than the genuine pacifism of Louis Philippe spoiled it.

In time the opposition against Louis Philippe became crystallized in three groups: the Liberals, the Bonapartists, and the Republicans. The Liberals wanted a further extension of the franchise. The Bonapartists hoped to overthrow Louis Philippe in favor of Prince Louis Napoleon, the emperor's nephew, who promised to restore to France some of the glories associated with his uncle's name. As for Republicanism, it had its roots in the failure of the radicals to assert themselves in 1830. As the number of workers increased, Republican feeling became more widespread. And since the workers also began to make economic demands, Republicanism gradually became tinged with socialism.

Discontent in France mounted after 1846, primarily for economic reasons. In the fall of that year, Europe was hit by a severe depression. In France, as elsewhere, rising prices and growing unemployment particularly affected the workers. Yet the government made no effort to help them, and the lower classes became more and more restive. To ease the situation, Liberals and Republicans joined forces in the summer of 1847 to hold a series of political meetings to discuss parliamentary reform. In February 1848 the government's ban against such meetings brought on a peaceful popular demonstration. As a precaution, the king called out the army, and in the ensuing confrontation several of the demonstrators were killed. Blood had been spilled, and the revolution was on. Major casualties were avoided by Louis Philippe's decision to abdicate and go to England. On February 25 a republic was proclaimed.

The Second French Republic

In a very short time and with little loss of life, a tremendous change had been brought about. The people who had been cheated out of the fruits of revolution in 1830 now had reached their goal; the days of upper-middle-class predominance seemed to be over. But this radical phase of the revolution did not last. The new provisional government was faced with tremendous difficulties. Paris was in a constant state of turmoil, with several political factions jockeying for position. Some wanted to concentrate on domestic reforms; others were more concerned with carrying the revolution abroad. The socialists in the government proclaimed the right to work and introduced a system of "national workshops," advocated by the socialist Louis Blanc (see p. 586).

In this period of confusion, the elections to the new National Assembly came as a severe shock to the radicals. Of some nine hundred delegates elected, fewer than one hundred supported the radical Republicans. The main reason for this

The February Days in Paris

I spent the whole afternoon in walking about Paris. Two things in particular struck me: the first was, I will not say the mainly, but the uniquely and exclusively popular character of the revolution that had just taken place; the omnipotence it had given to the people properly so-called—that is to say, the classes who work with their hands—over all others. . . . Although the working classes had often played the leading part in the events of the First Revolution, they had never been the sole leaders and masters of the State. . . . The Revolution of July [1830] was effected by the people, but the middle class had stirred it up and led it, and secured the principal fruits of it. The Revolution of February, on the contrary, seemed to be made entirely outside the bourgeoisie and against it. . . .

Throughout this day, I did not see in Paris a single one of the former agents of the public authority; not a soldier, not a gendarme, not a policeman; the National Guard itself had disappeared. The people alone bore arms, guarded the public buildings, watched, gave orders, punished; it was an extraordinary and terrible thing to see in the sole hands of those who possessed nothing, all this immense town, so full of riches, or rather this great nation: for, thanks to centralization, he who reigns in Paris governs France. Hence the terror of all the other classes was extreme; I doubt whether at any period of the revolution it had been so great, and I should say that it was only to be compared to that which the civilized cities of the Roman Empire must have experienced when they suddenly found themselves in the power of the Goths and Vandals.

From *The Recollections of Alexis de Tocqueville*, trans. by Alexander Teixeira de Mattos, ed. by J. P. Mayer (New York: Columbia University Press, 1949), pp. 72–75.

Giuseppe Mazzini (1805–72), Italian nationalist.

Detail of a Dutch caricature of 1852 showing Pope Pius IX removing his "savior's" mask and revealing his true face when he resumed power in 1849.

sudden shift lay with the French peasantry, whose aims had been largely met by the first French Revolution and who had subsequently become staunchly conservative.

But the radical element did not give up without a fight. There now followed a series of clashes between the radicals in the provisional government and the moderate National Assembly. Tension came to a head in the bloody "June Days," when the Assembly dissolved the workshops, considered breeding-grounds of discontent. The workers again took to the barricades, and the resulting street fighting caused thousands of deaths. By the end of June 1848 the back of lower-class resistance had been broken, and the middle class once again prevailed. The Constitution of the Second French Republic set up a single Chamber of Representatives, to be elected by universal male suffrage. Executive power was vested in a powerful president, to be elected by the people.

The first presidential election took place in December 1848. The French middle class and the French peasants wanted a strong man as president who would banish the "red peril" of socialism. Such a man, they felt, was Louis Napoleon. The first Napoleon had taken over the reins of government after an earlier revolution fifty years ago, and he had brought order at home and glory abroad. Why should history not repeat itself? The victory of Louis Napoleon by an overwhelming majority was thus due chiefly to the glamor of his name. A sign that he was ready to live up to that name came four years later, in 1852, when he proclaimed himself Emperor Napoleon III.*

The Italian Revolution of 1848

In Italy revolution had broken out in Sicily as early as January 1848. From there it had spread north. By the middle of March, most of the Italian states except Lombardy and Venetia had won liberal constitutions.

*Napoleon I's son, known as Napoleon II, had never assumed the throne and had died in 1832. Louis Napoleon was Napoleon I's nephew.

The origins of the Italian *Risorgimento* (meaning "resurgence") go back to the eighteenth century. The agitation for national liberation and unification had gained momentum during the Napoleonic period. But the hopes of Italian patriots and reformers had been dashed repeatedly since 1815. Despite the failure of the uprisings of 1830, however, Italian intellectuals had continued making plans for the future. Out of the maze of their projects, three main schemes had emerged: Giuseppe Mazzini, a noted Liberal and an ardent Italian nationalist, advocated the formation of a free, united, and republican Italy. Vincenzo Gioberti, a liberal priest, objected to the republican and centralizing tendencies of Mazzini and instead proposed a federated monarchy with a liberal constitution, headed by the pope. The election of the reputedly liberal Pius IX, in 1846 gave special emphasis to Gioberti's proposals. A third scheme for the future of Italy looked to Italian unification under the leadership of the house of Piedmont-Sardinia. Here, then, were three different schemes for the liberation and unification of Italy. Each was tried, and each failed.

With Austria the main obstacle to Italian unification, the outbreak of revolution in Vienna (see following) naturally aided the Italian cause. As insurrections broke out in the Austrian provinces of Lombardy and Venetia, Charles Albert of Piedmont, in March 1848, gave way to popular pressure and declared war on Austria. Contingents from other Italian states joined the Piedmontese. Pius IX, however, could ill afford to support a war against the leading Catholic power of Europe. His neutrality and subsequent flight from Rome dashed the hopes of those who had looked to the pope as the leader of Italian liberation.

The war of Piedmont against Austria, after initial successes, likewise ended in failure. The forces of Charles Albert were no match for the seasoned troops of the Austrian general Radetzky, especially after the Austrian government had succeeded in putting down its revolution at home. The final defeat of Charles Albert at Novara in March 1849 ended, for the time being, the chance of uniting Italy under the leadership of Piedmont-Sardinia.

Mazzini's alternative for the unification of Italy, the creation of a republic, also was given a brief chance. With Pius IX away from Rome, radicalism had a free hand. In February 1849 a constituent assembly proclaimed the Roman Republic, under the leadership of Mazzini, and with an army led by another hero of Italian unification, Giuseppe Garibaldi. But as Austria regained its position in northern Italy and as the troops of the ousted King Ferdinand II regained control of the Kingdom of the Two Sicilies, the Roman Republic became a liberal island in a sea of reaction. To make matters worse, Louis Napoleon, newly elected president of France, tried to ingratiate himself with his Catholic subjects by sending an expeditionary force against Rome. It defeated the forces of Garibaldi and thus ended the dream of a republican Italy.

The revolution in Italy had failed. It had done so chiefly because the Austrians had once again proved too strong and because the Italians had proved too little united. Piedmont, having been the only state to put up any fight, earned the leadership in Italian affairs. To rally the rest of Italy behind the national cause, the people had to be promised not only unification but political liberty as well. This the government of Piedmont, now under Victor Emmanuel II, realized. Alone among Italian states, Piedmont kept the liberal constitution that had been adopted during the revolution. It thus became the hope of Italian nationalists and liberals alike.

Revolutions in the Habsburg Empire

In Italy, revolution had erupted before it did in France. But the outbreaks in Austria were directly touched off by the events in Paris. The Habsburg Empire had long been ripe for revolution. Its government was cumbersome and corrupt, and Metternich's efforts at reform had been of no avail. The main problem facing the Austrian Empire was its conglomeration of nationalities. Besides the Germans in Austria proper, there were the Magyars in Hungary, the Czechs and Slovaks in Bohemia and Moravia, the Poles in Galicia, and the Italians in Lombardy and Venetia. None of these regions, moreover, was entirely inhabited by one nationality; almost everywhere the peoples just mentioned, together with Slovenes, Croats, Serbs, Ruthenians, and Rumanians, created a situation of utmost ethnic confusion. With the advent of nationalism, this situation endangered the very existence of the Habsburg Empire.

In addition to the demands of these subject peoples for some measure of autonomy, there was also a growing demand for governmental reforms in Austria proper. Industrial progress had swelled the ranks of the middle class and had created an urban proletariat, both of which now added their voices to the liberal protests of university professors and other intellectuals.

The news of the revolution in Paris caused more excitement among the subject nationalities than it did in Austria. There were some student demonstrations and some violence in Vienna, and a deputation of citizens asked for the resignation of Metternich. But he resigned under pressure from the imperial family rather than from the populace. With Metternich gone, events moved swiftly and smoothly. The emperor removed himself to Innsbruck, and the citizens of Vienna elected a National Assembly to draft a constitution. One of its first acts was to lift the last feudal burdens from Austria's peasants, completing a process begun by Joseph II two generations earlier.

From Vienna, revolution spread to other parts of the Empire. The uprisings in Lombardy and Venetia have already been discussed. Bohemia, except for some local unrest, remained quiet until early in June of 1848. At that time, disturbances broke out in connection with the first Pan-Slav Congress in Prague, which proclaimed the solidarity of the Slavic peoples against the Germans. Popular demonstrations were quelled when Austria's military governor ordered the bombardment of Prague. This was a significant event, for it was the first major setback of revolution anywhere in Europe. In Hungary, meanwhile, the Austrian government had agreed to the March Laws, which guaranteed a large measure of self-government. Hungary also followed the Austrian example in abolishing the remains of feudalism. But

Prince Metternich (ca. 1858). This photograph of the Austrian statesman was taken shortly before his death.

while the Hungarians thus secured freedom for themselves, they refused to grant the same freedom to the Croats within their own borders. Austria could thus play one nationality against the other. In September 1848, Croatian forces with Austrian backing invaded Hungary.

With imperial armies scoring successes against the revolutionaries in Bohemia, Hungary, and Lombardy, the tide of revolution in the Austrian Empire was definitely turning. A second, more radical outbreak in Vienna in October 1848 was soon put down. The Austrian government was now entrusted to Prince Felix Schwarzenberg, a strong-willed reactionary who urged the emperor, Ferdinand I, to resign in favor of his nephew, Francis Joseph. In March 1849

Schwarzenberg dissolved the National Assembly and imposed his own centralized constitution on the whole Empire.

By early spring of 1849 the Austrian government was again in control everywhere except in Hungary. At this point Francis Joseph accepted the offer of Nicholas I of Russia to help put down the Hungarians. The tsar was motivated by feelings of monarchical solidarity and by the fear that revolution might spread to the Danubian principalities and Poland. Hungarian resistance was finally crushed by the joint invasion of Russian and Austrian forces and by simultaneous uprisings among the Slavic peoples of southern Hungary. By mid-August of 1849 Austria was once again in control of its own house.

The victory of reaction in Austria, as we have seen, affected the fate of revolution in Italy. It had a similar effect in Germany. There the chances for the success of revolution actually seemed most favorable. Unlike Austria, Germany did not suffer from ethnic disunity, nor was there any need to expel a foreign power, as there was in Italy. The failure of the revolution was due to many causes, most important among them the division of the country into many separate states and the general apathy of the population. The majority of Germans seemed content to lead a life of modest comfort and to pursue cultural rather than political interests.

Still, there was enough ferment among German intellectuals to keep alive the agitation for a united and liberal Germany. These aims also found support among the growing industrial middle class. The formation of a German customs union, or *Zollverein*, had eased the movement of goods throughout Germany and thus aided both commerce and industry. But industrialization had also brought many hardships, especially to the artisans. Another discontented group were the peasants in eastern Germany. Since their liberation from serfdom, they were often unable to make a living on their small holdings and instead had to become agricultural or industrial laborers. This economic discontent, which became especially strong during the 1840s, added a new dimension to the liberal and national aims of the German intellectuals. Had the revolutionary leaders understood and utilized this discontent, the results of the revolutions might have been different.

The first German uprising occurred in Bavaria before the events in France. With the news from Paris the revolutions became general. Because Prussia, next to Austria, played the leading role in the German Confederation, events in Berlin were watched with particular interest. Prussia, since 1840, had been ruled by the brilliant but unstable Frederick William IV. The new king started out with a series of liberal reforms, but his liberalism was largely a pose. When the

revolution came to Berlin in March 1848, Frederick William was easily frightened into appointing a liberal ministry and agreeing to a constituent assembly. But the old regime in Prussia was not really beaten, especially since the Prussian army had remained intact. While middle-class delegates were drawing up a constitution, the lower classes were agitating for more drastic changes—including universal manhood suffrage, socialism, and even a republic. These radical demands drove the middle class, including the well-to-do peasants, back into the arms of reaction. When news reached Berlin in the fall of 1848 that the

Carl Schurz's Recollections of 1848

One morning toward the end of February, 1848, I sat quietly in my attic chamber, working hard at the tragedy of "Ulrich von Hutten," when suddenly a friend rushed breathlessly into the room, exclaiming: "What, you sitting here! Do you not know what has happened?"

"No; what?"

"The French have driven away Louis Philippe and proclaimed the Republic."

I threw down my pen—and that was the end of "Ulrich von Hutten." I never touched the manuscript again. We tore down the stairs, into the street, to the market-square, the accustomed meeting-place for all the student societies after their midday dinner. Although it was still forenoon, the market was already crowded with young men talking excitedly. . . . In these conversations . . . certain ideas and catchwords worked themselves to the surface, which expressed more or less the feelings of the people. Now had arrived in Germany the day for the establishment of "German Unity" and the founding of a great, powerful national German Empire. First in line the convocation of a national parliament; then the demands for civil rights and liberties, free speech, free press, the right of free assembly, equality before the law, a freely elected representation of the people with legislative power, responsibility of ministers, self-government of the communes, the right of the people to carry arms, the formation of a civic guard with elective officers, and so on—in short, that which was called a "constitutional form of government on a broad democratic basis." Republican ideas were at first only sparingly expressed. But the word "democracy" was soon on all tongues, and many, too, thought it a matter of course that if the princes should try to withhold from the people the rights and liberties demanded, force would take the place of mere petition. . . . We were profoundly, solemnly in earnest.

From *The Reminiscences of Carl Schurz,* 3 vols. (New York: McClure, 1907–08), Vol. I, pp. 111–13, as quoted in Geoffrey Bruun, *Revolution and Reaction, 1848–1852* (New York: Van Nostrand, 1958), pp. 125–27.

The English Working Classes

If the English working classes were not as revolutionary in the late 1830s and 1840s as many frightened contemporaries thought or as many militant Chartists hoped, this does not mean to say that they were not often hungry. The debate on the effect of the industrial revolution on living standards goes on, and there is plenty of evidence, some of it conflicting, to suggest that some workers were 'better off' economically in the 1840s than they had been twenty years before. The consumption per head of some commodities was increasing, the real wages of particular groups of workers had increased, and some of the expressions of grievance were the result of better opportunities for self-expression and organization in the concentrated centres of population than had hitherto been the case. But there is general evidence too on the other side. The Leeds labour economist John Francis Bray wrote in 1839 that 'the millions are a doomed class . . . their constitution is unimprovable and their wrongs irremediable,' while the classical economist John Stuart Mill argued as late as 1848 that it was doubtful whether any of the inventions yet produced had 'lightened the day's toil of any human being.' 'They have increased the comforts of the middle classes,' he went on, 'but they have not yet begun to effect those great changes in human destiny, which it is in their nature and in their futurity to accomplish.'

From Asa Briggs, *The Age of Improvement 1783–1867* (London: Longmans, 1959), pp. 302–303.

Austrian government was successfully moving against the revolution in Vienna, Frederick William dissolved the Constituent Assembly and later imposed his own constitution. By the end of 1848, the revolution in Prussia had been defeated.

But German liberals did not give up hope. Since spring, another assembly had been in session in Frankfurt to draft a constitution for all of Germany, including Austria, rather than for Prussia alone. Its delegates had been elected by the people. The majority were professional people, including many professors. Deliberations dragged on for almost a year. The main argument developed over the question of whether or not the new German state should be under the leadership of and include Austria. The *grossdeutsch* (greater-German) faction, which favored this solution, was opposed by the *kleindeutsch* (small-German) group, which advocated the exclusion of Austria and the leadership of Prussia. The issue resolved itself when the victory of reaction in Vienna disqualified Austria in the eyes of German liberals.

The Frankfurt Constitution, which was finally adopted in March 1849, called for a constitutional monarchy with a parliament elected by universal male suffrage. The Frankfurt Parliament elected Frederick William IV as "Emperor of the Germans." But the king of Prussia refused a crown that was offered him by the people. He would accept it only from his fellow princes. With reaction everywhere triumphant, Frederick William's refusal all but finished the revolution in Germany. There were some last flashes of violence in the smaller states, but Prussian troops soon restored order. The attempt of the German people to build a unified nation under a government of their own choosing had failed.

England in the Age of Reform

The one country in western Europe where one might have expected revolution to strike first was Great Britain. And yet, except for a brief flare-up in Ireland, the British Isles proved the major exception to the rule of revolution in western Europe. The Reform Bill of 1832 had been merely the most prominent of a large series of reforms. Most important among these was the establishment of free trade. Britain's merchants and industrialists had long agitated against import duties, but tariffs had been defended on the grounds that the government needed the income. With the reintroduction of the income tax in 1842, however, that argument lost ground, and protective tariffs were gradually abolished. Only in agriculture did they survive. To fight for the abolition of agricultural tariffs, the Anti-Corn Law League had been formed in 1839. In 1846 its relentless pressure succeeded, and the Corn Laws were repealed.

Along with this agitation for economic freedom, there also arose during the 1830s a movement for greater political freedom. The Reform Bill of 1832 had been a disappointment to the lower classes, among whom the so-called Chartist Movement gained its major support. The movement took its name from the "People's Charter" of 1838, drawn up by a group of radical reformers and calling for a further democratization of Parliament. But Parliament repeatedly turned down petitions based on the Charter. By 1848 discontent had mounted to such a pitch that there seemed to be a real threat of revolution. The Chartists prepared a "monster petition" demanding universal manhood suffrage and other political reforms, and started a demonstration to present it to Parliament. Wanting to avoid bloodshed, however, the demonstrators let themselves be dispersed peacefully. The truth of the matter was that a good deal of the discontent in the Chartist Movement was economic, and had disappeared with the repeal of the Corn Laws and a general increase in prosperity. Henceforth workers were turning more and more to trade unionism as a means of improving their status. England thus remained a quiet haven of refuge in the upheavals of 1848, giving asylum to refugees from revolution and reaction alike, including Metternich as well as Marx. Many of the revolutionaries, however, preferred to leave Europe altogether; the United States received them with open arms.

Why Did the Revolutions of 1848 Fail?

The revolutions of 1848 thus had failed everywhere. They had done so because of weaknesses in the revolutionary camp, because of the continued strength of the forces of reaction, and because the economic conditions that helped bring on the revolutions did not last. The economic picture in many countries improved, despite the unsettling effect of revolution.

The weakness of the revolutionaries was due partly to the lack of well-defined programs or the existence of too many different programs and to the indecision of their leaders. This indecision lost valuable time, which the reactionaries used to prepare for counterrevolution. But the primary weakness of the revolutionaries was lack of widespread popular support outside the cities. The middle class, in most countries, did not really want a

revolution. It preferred to achieve its aims through reform, as had been done in England. But once revolution came the middle class tried to reap its benefits. Much of the actual fighting in the revolutions was done by the workers, and the workers wanted more than limited democracy for the well-to-do. They wanted complete democracy, political and, in some cases, economic as well. To the middle class, these demands, especially the socialist ones, not only threatened its political predominance but its very existence. This bourgeois fear of a "red peril" was exaggerated. Despite the incendiary language of *The Communist Manifesto* (which appeared in 1848; see p. 587), the majority of the lower class were perfectly ready to follow the leadership of the middle class if that would improve their condition. But the middle class did not live up to these lower-class expectations; as a result the lower class more and more came to distrust the men it had helped gain power.

Not only was there disunity among the revolutionary forces within each

Barricade in Milan, from the *Leipziger Illustrierte Zeitung* (1848).

country, there was no attempt to coordinate the revolutions in different countries. While the forces of reaction often worked together, there was little collaboration among the revolutionaries. On the contrary, almost everywhere their programs showed traces of a selfish nationalism. There was nationalism behind France's talk of spreading the blessings of revolution. The Germans wanted to unite all German-speaking peoples, but they also wanted to lord it over the Poles, and they actually carried on a brief war against the Danes. The Poles wanted to be liberated and united, but they did not want to see the Ukrainians win the same benefits. And the Hungarians behaved every bit as selfishly toward the Croats as the Austrians did toward the Hungarians.

Yet, though reaction won a full victory in 1849, the revolutions of 1848 had not been entirely in vain. Some changes for the better were preserved. In France political power had been somewhat broadened. In Italy some leaders had learned useful lessons of how to go about

achieving unification. In Austria the abolition of serfdom during the revolution could not be undone, and Metternich did not return to power. Even in Germany, where the failure of revolution probably had more tragic long-range consequences than anywhere else, a few lasting gains were made.

The mid-century revolutions came at a crucial time in European history. Up to this time, the economy of the Continent had still been largely agrarian. From now on, industrialization really took hold. Metternich, the dominant figure after 1815, had in many ways been a relic of the eighteenth century. The future was to belong to a more modern kind of politician. Two forces were henceforth to dominate the history of Europe—nationalism and socialism. Neither was new, but both had lost much of their earlier idealism and utopianism. Henceforth, nationalism and socialism respectively became the main issues in the struggle of nation against nation and class against class.

Suggestions for Further Reading

Note: Asterisk denotes a book available in paperback edition.

General The best general introduction to the period following the French Revolution is E. J. Hobsbawm, *The Age of Revolution, 1789–1848** (1962). G. F. E. Rudé, *Debate on Europe, 1815–1850** (1972), deals with recent historiography. Detailed histories are F. A. Artz, *Reaction and Revolution, 1814–1832** (1934), and W. L. Langer, *Political and Social Upheaval, 1832–1852* (1969). J. Droz, *Europe between Revolutions, 1815–1848* (1968), is an appraisal by a noted French social historian. Among national histories, the following are recommended: A. Briggs, *The Making of Modern England* (1959); T. S. Hamerow, *Restoration, Revolution, Reaction: Economics and Politics in Germany, 1815–1871** (1958); A. J. P. Taylor, *The Hapsburg Monarchy, 1809–1918** (1948); A. Cobban, *A History of Modern France,** Vol. II (1957); A. J. Whyte, *The Evolution of Modern Italy, 1715–1920** (1944); and R. Pipes, *Russia under the Old Regime** (1975). The emergence of liberalism is treated in G. Ruggiero, *History of European Liberalism** (1927), and H. J. Laski, *The Rise of European Liberalism* (1936). Standard works on nationalism are C. J. H. Hayes, *The Historical Evolution of Modern Nationalism* (1931); H. Kohn, *The Idea of Nationalism** (1944); B. C. Shafer, *Nationalism: Myth and Reality** (1955); and L. L. Snyder, *Varieties of Nationalism: A Comparative Study* (1976).

The Restoration of the Old Order The leading works on the diplomatic settlements after Napoleon are C. K. Webster, *The Foreign Policy of Castlereagh, 1812–1822*, 2 vols. (1931), and *The Congress of Vienna, 1814–1815** (1934). H. Nicolson, *The Congress of Vienna: A Study in Allied Unity, 1812–1822** (1946) makes charming reading. Good biographies of the leading figures at Vienna are: G. de Bertier de Sauvigny, *Metternich and His Times* (1962); C. Brinton, *The Lives of Talleyrand** (1936); A. Palmer, *Alexander I, Tsar of War and Peace* (1974); and J. C. Bartlett, *Castlereagh* (1967). See also P. K. Grimsted, *The Foreign Ministers of Alexander I* (1969). On Alexander's successor, see W. B. Lincoln, *Nicholas I: Emperor and*

Autocrat of All the Russias (1978). On Castlereagh's successors, see H. W. V. Temperley, *The Foreign Policy of Canning, 1822–1827* (1925), and C. K. Webster, *The Foreign Policy of Palmerston, 1830–1841*, 2 vols. (1951). The diplomatic aftermath of the Congress of Vienna is treated in H. G. Schenk, *The Aftermath of the Napoleonic Wars: The Concert of Europe* (1947); P. W. Schroeder, *Metternich's Diplomacy at Its Zenith, 1820–1823* (1962); and H. A. Kissinger, *A World Restored** (1957). The impact of the revolutions in Latin America is summed up in D. Perkins, *Hands Off! A History of the Monroe Doctrine** (1941). See also B. Perkins, *Castlereagh and Adams: England and the United States, 1812–1823* (1964).

Romanticism

A good introduction to the complexities of Romanticism is J. B. Halsted, ed., *Romanticism** (1965). I. Babbitt, *Rousseau and Romanticism** (1919), is a classic indictment. See also J. Barzun, *Classic, Romantic and Modern** (1961). More recent works are J. Clay, *Romanticism* (1980), and M. Le Bris, *Romantics and Romanticism* (1980). The impact of Romanticism on political thought is treated in the works on nationalism cited above, as well as in H. S. Reiss, *The Political Thought of the German Romantics* (1955); C. Brinton, *The Political Ideas of the English Romanticists** (1926); and R. H. Soltau, *French Political Thought of the Nineteenth Century* (1931). See also G. D. O'Brien, *Hegel on Reason and History* (1975). On conservatism, see R. J. S. Hoffman and P. Levack, eds., *Burke's Politics* (1949); E. L. Woodward, *Three Studies in European Conservatism* (1929); and K. Epstein, *The Genesis of German Conservatism** (1966).

Revolutions Before 1848

Accounts of the numerous upheavals in the 1820s and 1830s may be found in the general histories cited above. For developments in France, see J. Plamenatz, *The Revolutionary Movement in France, 1815–1871* (1952); R. J. Bezucha, *The Lyon Uprising of 1834* (1974); W. H. Sewell, Jr., *Work and Revolution in France: The Language of Labor from the Old Regime to 1848* (1980); and G. de Bertier de Sauvigny's proroyalist *The Bourbon Restoration* (1966). Biographies of leading figures include D. W. Johnson's *Guizot* (1963), and T. E. B. Howarth's *Citizen King* (1961), on Louis Philippe. For the Greek Revolution, see D. Dakin, *The Struggle for Greek Independence* (1973). Russia's Decembrist Revolt is the subject of M. Raeff, *The Decembrist Movement* (1966). On events in Belgium and Poland, see J. A. Betley, *Belgium and Poland in International Relations, 1830–1831.* (1960). The disintegration of the Ottoman Empire is admirably summarized in M. S. Anderson, *The Eastern Question, 1774–1923** (1966). Much has been written on parliamentary and social reforms in Great Britain. Especially recommended are N. Gash, *Aristocracy and People: Britain, 1815–1865* (1979); M. Brock, *The Great Reform Act** (1974); A. Briggs, ed., *Chartist Studies* (1960); J. T. Ward, *Chartism* (1973); and W. Thomas, *The Philosophic Radicals* (1979). On social unrest, see R. J. White, *Waterloo to Peterloo* (1957), and G. F. E. Rudé, *The Crowd in History 1730–1848** (1964), which deals with both England and France.

The Revolutions of 1848

The most successful attempts to present an overview of these confusing events are P. Robertson, *Revolutions of 1848: A Social History** (1952), and P. Stearns, *1848: The Revolutionary Tide in Europe** (1974). R. Postgate, *Story of a Year: 1848** (1955), describes vividly the revolutions as seen from England. A. Whitridge, *Men in Crisis: The Revolutions of 1848* (1949), concentrates on a few leading figures. R. Stadelmann, *The Social and Political History of the German 1848 Revolution* (1975), is admirable. On France, see R. Price, ed., *Revolution and Reaction: 1848 and the Second French Republic* (1976); and on Hungary, see I. Deak, *The Lawful Revolution: Louis Kossuth and the Hungarians, 1848–1849* (1979). Among specialized works on various aspects of the revolutions, the following stand out: D. C. McKay, *The National Workshops: A Study in the French Revolution of 1848* (1933); J. Blum, *Noble Landowners and Agriculture in Austria, 1814–1848** (1948); A. J. P. Taylor, *The Italian Problem in European Diplomacy, 1847–1849* (1939); L. B. Namier, *1848: The Revolution of the Intellectuals** (1947); and L. C. Jennings, *France and Europe in 1848: A Study of French Foreign Affairs in Time of Crisis* (1973).

25 The Coming of the Industrial Age

Much of the political tension in Europe during the first half of the nineteenth century was due to underlying economic unrest caused by the gradual transformation of Europe's economy from agriculture to industry. This change began around the middle of the eighteenth century, but it did not become pronounced until after 1815. From then on it gathered momentum, first in England and later on the Continent, until by the end of the nineteenth century most of western Europe had become industrialized.

The term *Industrial Revolution*, often used to describe this industrialization, has come in for some criticism. The change from agriculture to industry was a very gradual process. Moreover, it is only when one considers the total effect of this change that the term *revolution* seems justified. By vastly improving communication, industrialization made the world seem much smaller; by enabling more people to make a living, it made the world much more crowded; and by raising the standard of living, it made life more agreeable. Industrialization has elevated nations which heretofore tended to be weak and has demoted others that do not have the manpower or the raw materials that industry requires. Industrialization has dissolved a rigid and hierarchical social order and has substituted a fluid and egalitarian mass society.

Not all these changes have necessarily been for the better. While industry created wealth for some, it emphasized the poverty of others. While it made nations and individuals more dependent on one another, it also increased their rivalry for a share of the world's riches. The preoccupation of modern industrial society with material well-being has diverted mankind from more elevated concerns. But while one may wonder how beneficial the change from agriculture to industry has been, about the magnitude of that change there can be no doubt.

THE ROOTS OF MODERN INDUSTRIALISM

Modern industrialism we define as the mass production of goods by machines driven by generated power and set up in factories. There had been few machines before the eighteenth century. During the Middle Ages, goods had been produced by hand for local consumption. With the Age of Discovery and the "Commercial Revolution" in the sixteenth century, the demand for goods and their production had increased. Since the small artisan did not have the capital to buy large quantities of raw materials, to produce a large stock, and to sell it in a distant market, a class of wealthy capitalists and merchants began to join in the production process. They supplied the artisan with raw materials and sometimes with tools, and they took over the finished product to sell at a profit. This "domestic," or "putting-out," system had become quite common, especially in the textile industry, by the seventeenth century. There were even a few simple machines, but they still had to be operated by humans or animals, or by the natural power of wind or water. During the eighteenth century the trend toward larger-scale production was accelerated by numerous new machines. The most important step came with the application of steam power to these inventions. From here on the domestic system gradually declined as production shifted from home and workshop to factory.

It was no accident that modern industrialism should have had its start in the eighteenth century. The intellectual climate of the Enlightenment, its interest in science, and its emphasis on progress were favorable to such a development. The beginnings of modern industrialism fall into the period after 1760, and the growth of industrialism was most pronounced in England. England was a wealthy country with large overseas holdings; its parliamentary system gave some influence to the rising commercial and industrial middle class; it had sufficient surplus capital; and it had an ample supply of basic raw materials and manpower. Early industrialization in England was also aided by drastic changes in British agriculture—an "Agricultural Revolution"—which increased Britain's food supply and provided some additional manpower for industry.

Opposite: Coke smelting on the coal fields of Upper Sîlesia in Germany, lithograph made in 1841.

THE AGRICULTURAL REVOLUTION

Before the eighteenth century, most of Britain's land was still worked under the open-field system. The holdings of individual owners were scattered about in strips, separated from those of other landholders by a double furrow. Each landholder also shared in the common pastures and woodlands of his community. This arrangement was of particular advantage to the small farmers and cottagers, who shared in the grazing and fueling rights of the "commons." But the open-field system was inefficient and wasteful. The prevailing method of cultivation was still by the medieval system of three-field rotation, under which one-third of the land remained fallow each year. Any attempt to change this routine by experimenting with new crops was impossible, since all strips in a given field had to be cultivated at the same time and planted with the same crop.

The Age of Revolution, 1789–1848

Words are witnesses which often speak louder than documents. Let us consider a few English words which were invented, or gained their modern meanings, substantially in the period of sixty years with which this volume deals. They are such words as "industry," "industrialist," "factory," "middle class," "working class," "capitalism," and "socialism." They include "aristocracy" as well as "railway," "liberal" and "conservative" as political terms, "nationality," "scientist," and "engineer," "proletariat" and (economic) "crisis." "Utilitarian" and "statistics," "sociology," and several other names of modern sciences, "journalism" and "ideology," are all coinages or adaptations of this period. So are "strike" and "pauperism."

To imagine the modern world without these words (i.e., without the things and concepts for which they provide names) is to measure the profundity of the revolution which broke out between 1789 and 1848 and forms the greatest transformation in human history since the remote times when men invented agriculture and metallurgy, writing, the city and the state. This revolution has transformed, and continues to transform, the entire world.

From E. J. Hobsbawm, *The Age of Revolution, 1789–1848,* Mentor edition (New York: World, 1962), pp. 17–18.

The "Enclosure Movement"

Beginning at the time of the Tudors in the sixteenth century, an "enclosure movement" had started in England, under which the scattered strips of individual owners were consolidated into compact holdings surrounded by fences or hedges. Enclosure meant a gain of usable land because it did away with the double furrows, and it made cultivation much easier. But since enclosure also entailed a division of the commons, it worked to the detriment of the small farmer, who thereby lost part of his livelihood. As the population of England increased, agricultural production for the general market rather than for local consumption became more profitable. The trend toward more efficient large-scale farming, and especially sheep raising, through enclosures therefore gained momentum. Between 1702 and 1797, Parliament passed some 1,776 enclosure acts affecting 3 million acres. In each case the larger landowner profited at the expense of the smaller farmer. Left with too little land of his own and deprived of his share in the commons, the small farmer had no choice but to become an agricultural laborer or a tenant farmer or move to the cities. Many took the latter course, providing some of the manpower without which the rapid growth of Britain's industry could not have taken place.

The enclosure movement brought hardships to many, but it also brought a dramatic improvement in agriculture and animal husbandry. Freed from the restrictions of collective cultivation, landowners now could try new methods and new crops. The result was growing more food on the same amount of land. The improvement was such as to justify the term "Agricultural Revolution." Like its industrial counterpart, the Agricultural Revolution at first was almost entirely restricted to Britain. Only with the advent of industrialization did larger landholders on the Continent begin to experiment with British methods, new crops and crop rotation. The small peasants, on the other hand, continued in their backward ways. As new industrial centers developed, new markets for agricultural produce opened up. Improvements in transportation facilitated marketing, and the use of fertilizers brought larger crop yields. These and other developments brought renewed hope for western Europe's farmers, who, after first profiting from industrialization, were gradually beginning to feel the competition of the fertile agrarian lands of eastern Europe and America.

THE BEGINNINGS OF INDUSTRIALIZATION

Inventions and the Rise of the Factory System

The early history of industrialization is related to the rise of mechanical inventions. Their numbers increased rapidly as one discovery created the need for another. When John Kay invented the flying shuttle in 1733, enabling one weaver to do the work of two, the need arose for some new device to speed up spinning. This demand was met in 1764 by James Hargreaves and his spinning jenny, which permitted the simultaneous spinning of sixteen or more threads. Some years later, Richard Arkwright devised the water frame, and in 1779 Samuel Crompton perfected the "mule," a hybrid that combined features of both Hargreaves' and Arkwright's inventions. These improvements in spinning in turn called for further improvements in weaving. In 1787 Edmund Cartwright patented a new power loom. Once it was perfected, the demand for cotton further increased. Cotton production received a boost when an American, Eli Whitney, in 1793 developed the cotton "gin," which speeded up the removal of cotton seeds from the fiber. Most early inventions were made in the cotton industry: it was new, it had a large overseas market, and cotton lent itself particularly well to mechanical treatment.

Since most of the earlier devices were small, relatively inexpensive, and hand-operated, they could be used as part of the domestic system in the workers' cottages. Arkwright's water frame, however, was large and expensive, and it needed water power to operate. Arkwright, therefore, moved into the heart of the English textile region of Nottingham, where he opened the first spinning mill

A result of the Agricultural Revolution: a German threshing machine of the 1850s.

in 1771. By 1779 he was employing some three hundred workers operating several thousand spindles. Arkwright's example was soon followed by other manufacturers and ultimately led to the factory system.

The Steam Engine

Of all the inventions in the early years of industrialism, the steam engine was the most important. Until the advent of electricity it remained the chief source of artificial power. The development of the steam engine is closely related to the two industries that ultimately proved basic to all modern economic progress—coal and iron. In the early eighteenth century the smelting of iron was still done by charcoal. The depletion of Britain's wood supply, however, and the discovery of a process for smelting iron with coke, shifted the emphasis to coal. The mining of coal was made easier by a simple steam engine, developed by Thomas Newcomen, that was used to pump water from the coal mines. This early eighteenth-century engine was a long way from the steam engine that could be used to run other machines. The credit for developing such an engine belongs to the Scotsman James Watt, who patented his first steam engine in 1769. By 1800 some three hundred steam

Arkwright's water frame, patented in 1769. It was the first self-acting machine to spin threads fine and hard enough for a weaver to use as the cloth warp.

engines were at work in England, mostly in the cotton industry. The use of steam engines further increased the need for coal and iron. Improvements in iron production, on the other hand, in turn led to improvements in the making of steam engines. The interaction of one discovery with another thus continued to be a major feature of industrial development.

Early Industry on the Continent

Prior to 1815 the "Industrial Revolution" was chiefly a British phenomenon. An economic revival in France after 1763, helping to make up for the loss of the French colonies to Britain, had been interrupted by the French Revolution. But the Continental System of Napoleon, on the other hand, which excluded British goods from the Continent, had proved quite beneficial to French industry.

Elsewhere in Europe there were few signs of industrialization. Economic development in Germany was retarded by political disunity. The rich coal fields of the Ruhr, Saar, and Silesia were hardly worked before 1815, and what little industry there was, especially in textiles, still operated under the "putting-out" system. Russia, Italy, and Austria were almost wholly agrarian. After 1815, continental industries were slow to assert themselves against British competition. It was only after the advent of the railroad in the 1830s that the situation began to improve.

The Railway King, a Victorian caricature.

THE RAILWAY AGE

Transportation in the Eighteenth Century

Industrial development was closely related to the improvement of transportation. England again had a special advantage in being able to use coastal shipping for the movement of bulky goods. But like any other country it depended on roads and canals for inland transportation. As industrialization increased the need for transport and travel, the construction of toll roads and canals became a profitable business. England added thousands of miles to its system of roads and canals during the eighteenth century, and France before the Revolution had the finest highway system in Europe. Napoleon improved the situation further by pushing highways far into Germany and the Netherlands. In eastern Europe, however, paved roads were rare. Prussia's kings constructed canals and improved riverways, but the movement of goods was hampered by innumerable tolls and tariffs. Farther east, dirt roads that regularly turned to mud and rivers that ran shallow during the summer and froze during the winter were the only arteries of communication.

The Advent of the Railroad

The railroad, which was to change all this, again had its start in England. Well before 1800, horse-drawn carts, moving first on wooden and later on iron rails, had been used to haul coal and iron. During the 1820s there were several hundred miles of such "rail ways." The problem of providing a faster means of locomotion was solved by putting the steam engine on wheels. The first commercial steam railroad was opened between Stockton and Darlington in 1825. By 1840 Britain had some eight hundred miles of track, and by 1850 it had more than six thousand. On the Continent, the railroad was slower in taking hold. The first railroad in France was opened in 1837, and by the middle of the century there were two thousand miles of track. Germany then had three thousand miles, Austria one thousand miles, and Italy and Russia had merely a few fragmentary lines.

The opening of the Stockton–Darlington Railway on September 27, 1825; drawing by J. R. Brown.

The economic impact of the railroad was overwhelming. Here was an entirely new industry, answering a universal need, employing thousands of people, offering unprecedented opportunities for investment, and introducing greater speed into all commercial transactions. England, already far ahead of the Continent in economic development, took the Railway Age pretty much in stride. Britain had been the workshop of the world for some time, and there was no indication that it would cease to be. Railroad construction vastly increased the demand for coal and iron, and England continued to lead the world in the production of both.

England also maintained its lead in shipping. The shipping industry was slow to feel the impact of steam. Even though Robert Fulton's steamboat had made its first successful trip on the Hudson River in 1807, it was not until 1840 that Samuel Cunard established the first transatlantic steamer line. Even then the inefficiency of marine engines and the large amounts of coal needed for long voyages retarded the development of steamship service. Well into the second half of the nineteenth century the fast clipper ship remained the chief means of ocean transport.

There were other important innovations and inventions in the early nineteenth century, with England again leading the way. The introduction of the penny post in 1840 helped business and private correspondence alike. The telegraph, invented by the American Samuel Morse, was first used extensively by Julius Reuter's news agency, which was established in 1851, the same year in which the first submarine cable was laid under the English Channel. A reduction in the stamp tax in 1836 substantially lowered the price of newspapers, and by the middle of the century the circulation of the British press had risen more than threefold. The communication of news and ideas kept pace with the faster movements of goods and persons.

The Railway Age on the Continent

In May 1851 the "Great Exhibition of the Works of Industry of All Nations"

The "Crystal Palace" in London, which housed the Great Exhibition of 1851.

opened in London's "Crystal Palace." This first "world's fair" was dramatic proof of Britain's industrial world leadership, but it also showed that other nations were beginning to profit from its example. The country in which industrialization made the most rapid progress was little Belgium. An ample supply of coal and a skilled labor force were the chief reasons, but technical aid by British engineers and investment of British capital also helped.

In France, economic development was much slower. The French had lost some of their best coal mines to Belgium in 1815; and while European populations were increasing, the French birth rate, by the middle of the century, had actually begun to decline. Still, with the encouragement given to commerce and industry by the July Monarchy, the middle class could not help but prosper. Pig iron production, generally considered an index of industrial development, increased fourfold in France during the thirty years after 1825; but it was still only one-quarter that of Great Britain. While England's population by the middle of the century was more than half urban, France remained predominantly rural. Imports of food became unnecessary and accounted for a self-contained domestic market.

In both Italy and Germany political disunity slowed down economic growth.

Industry in northern Italy remained insignificant until later in the century. In Germany, the *Zollverein* (see p. 565) did much to aid industrial development. Machines, imported from England, were used more and more. With the sinking of the first deep pit in the Ruhr in 1841, coal production began in earnest. But France, despite much slimmer resources, still produced more coal than Germany. As for pig iron, the total German output in 1855 was only half that of France. However, railroad construction in Germany made rapid progress during the 1840s. Low wages and the absence of natural obstacles kept construction costs down. It was the progress in railroad building that gave some inkling of the tremendous economic vitality of the German people, which was merely awaiting political unification to assert itself.

Beyond western and central Europe, industrialization had made hardly any headway by 1850. Austria and Russia were still predominantly agrarian. Industrial development depended first and foremost on an abundant supply of free labor. This supply did not exist in Austria until after the last feudal restrictions were abolished in 1849, and in Russia it had to wait until the abolition of serfdom in 1861. Outside Europe only the United States was showing signs of industrialization. By 1850 New England had become largely industrialized, but the total output of American industry was still behind that of France and far behind that of Britain. Like Germany, America was to become a leading industrial power only toward the end of the century.

THE SOCIAL EFFECTS OF INDUSTRIALIZATION

The beginnings of modern industrialization in the eighteenth century appeared to bear out the belief of the Enlightenment that human reason and ingenuity had the power to perfect the world. The invention of labor-saving machines promised to transform man from a beast of burden into a creature of leisure. But that promise soon began to fade. The "Industrial Revolution," in the beginning at least, benefited only a minority, the middle class, while it brought utmost misery and destitution to the growing urban working class. Only after industrialization had outgrown its infancy did its blessings come to be shared by more and more people.

Population Growth

Many of the early hardships of industrialization were due to an unprecedented population growth. Between 1815 and 1914, the population of Europe increased from 200 million to 460 million. Another 40 million Europeans migrated to other parts of the world, especially to the United States. The rate of growth differed from country to country. It was largest in Russia, less in England and Germany, and least in France. Population growth was due both to an increase in the birth rate and to a decrease in the death rate. This decrease had many causes: improvements in medicine and public sanitation, absence of major wars, greater efficiency in government and administration, changes in agriculture leading to better diets and more ample food supplies, and, most important, the acceleration of industrial development. Industry provided the means whereby more people could live, and the increase of population, in turn, supplied the necessary industrial labor force and swelled the ranks of consumers. The growth of population and industry thus interacted upon each other.

Urbanization and Working-Class Misery

With the increase in population and the growth of industry there came a further important change in European society—the movement of people from the country to the city. Large-scale urbanization had been virtually unknown before the early nineteenth century. But as workers began to flock to the mills, small villages grew into crowded towns and quiet towns into noisy cities. This sudden influx of people brought on wretched housing conditions. Teeming slums lacking in sanitation facilities turned into breeding places of disease, vice, and crime. There was as yet no effective municipal administration to cope with these novel problems, and the

Close,
No. 118
High Street,
Glasgow
(1868–77).

Life in the Slums

It is impossible to give a proper representation of the wretched state of many of the inhabitants of the indigent class, situated in the confined streets . . . where each small, ill ventilated apartment of the house contained a family with lodgers in number from seven to nine, and seldom more than two beds for the whole. The want of convenient offices in the neighborhood is attended with many very unpleasant circumstances, as it induces the lazy inmates to make use of chamber utensils, which are suffered to remain in the most offensive state for several days, and are then emptied out of the windows. The writer had occasion a short time ago to visit a person ill of the cholera; his lodgings were in a room of a miserable house situated in the very filthiest part of Pipewellgate, divided into six apartments, and occupied by different families to the number of 26 persons in all. The room contained three wretched beds with two persons sleeping in each; it measured about 12 feet in length and 7 in breadth, and its greatest height would not admit of a person's standing erect; it received light from a small window, the sash of which was fixed. Two of the number lay ill of the cholera, and the rest appeared afraid of the admission of pure air, having carefully closed up the broken panes with plugs of old linen.

From "Report . . . from the Poor Law Commissioners on . . . the Sanitary Conditions of the Labouring Population of Great Britain," 1842, pp. 21–22.

Children working in a coal mine, illustration from the Shaftesbury Report (1842). The evidence presented in this report brought about the Coal Mines Act of 1842 and subsequent measures to alleviate industrial abuse.

Child Labor

PRO

I have visited many factories, both in Manchester and in the surrounding districts, during a period of several months, entering the spinning rooms unexpectedly, and often alone, at different times of the day, and I never saw a single instance of corporal chastisement inflicted on a child, nor indeed did I ever see children in ill-humor. They seemed to be always cheerful and alert, taking pleasure in the light play of their muscles—enjoying the mobility natural to their age. The scene of industry, so far from exciting sad emotions in my mind, was always exhilarating. . . . The work of these lively elves seemed to resemble a sport, in which habit gave them a pleasing dexterity. . . . As to exhaustion by the day's work, they evinced no trace of it on emerging from the mill in the evening; for they immediately began to skip about any neighboring playground, and to commence their little amusements with the same alacrity as boys issuing from a school.

CON

The report of the Central Commission relates that the manufacturers began to employ children rarely of five years, often of six, very often of seven, usually of eight to nine years; that the working-day often lasted fourteen to sixteen hours, exclusive of meals and intervals; that the manufacturers permitted overlookers to flog and maltreat children, and often took an active part in so doing themselves. One case is related of a Scotch manufacturer who rode after a sixteen years old runaway, forced him to return running before the employer as fast as the master's horse trotted, and beat him the whole way with a long whip.

From Andrew Ure, *The Philosophy of Manufactures,* 3rd ed. (London: Bohn, 1961), p. 301; from Friedrich Engels, *The Condition of the Working Class in England in 1844* (New York: Lovell, 1887), p. 101.

workers themselves were too poor to improve their condition.

Poor housing was not the only hardship afflicting the early workers. Since mechanized industry required little skill, there was always an abundance of manpower, and wages remained at a minimum. The average working day was between twelve and sixteen hours. Because even this rarely yielded sufficient pay to support a worker's family, women and children had to work as well. Since they were more docile and received less pay, they were much in demand. But women and children also suffered more than men did from the harsh conditions in factories and mines. No provisions were made for the workers' safety, and accidents resulting from strange machines were frequent. There was no insurance against mishaps, sickness, or old age. Furthermore, as more efficient machines were invented, unemployment added to the workers' hardships. As industrialization spread to the Continent, so did the abuses that accompanied it. Conditions in Belgium and France were almost as bad as those in England.

Middle-Class Indifference

The attitude of much of the middle class toward the misery of the working class was one of indifference. The new "captains of industry," had to be tough and ruthless men if they wanted to survive. Competition was keen and risks were great. The path of early industrialism was lined with bankruptcies. Economic booms burst; wars closed markets; machinery broke down or became obsolete; and the agrarian supporters of the old order fought stubbornly against middle-class efforts to gain economic and political influence.

In order to understand the seemingly callous attitude of the middle class toward the hardships of the workers, we must consider briefly the middle-class philosophy of liberalism, which helped justify such selfish behavior. It was the belief in economic liberalism that prevented any drastic measures of social reform in the early part of the nineteenth century. The absence of such reform, in turn, led to various protests on behalf of the workers, of which Marxian socialism became the most effective.

MIDDLE-CLASS LIBERALISM

The term *liberalism* has assumed so many different meanings that it defies clear definition. In the early nineteenth century, however, liberalism had definite meaning and aims. A liberal was a person who believed in freedom—freedom of thought, freedom of religion, freedom from economic restrictions, freedom of trade, and freedom from the political injustices of the old regime. Most of these freedoms had already been demanded by the Enlightenment. The *philosophes* held that every man had certain natural rights—life, liberty, and property. These rights the middle class had demanded before and during the French Revolution, and it continued to demand them. But as time went on, its claims were based not on natural law, as they had been during the eighteenth century, but on the grounds of utility, as the most useful way of bringing about the "greatest happiness of the greatest number." This attitude of applying utility to political and social institutions is called "utilitarianism."

"Utilitarianism"

The key figure in the transformation of liberal thought from the Enlightenment to the nineteenth century was the English philosopher and reformer Jeremy Bentham (1748–1832). To Bentham, the reasonableness of an institution depended on its utility. How was this utility to be determined? Bentham wrote: "For everyone, his own pleasure and his own freedom from pain is the sole good, his own pain and his own unfreedom the sole evil. Man's happiness and welfare consist exclusively of pleasurable feelings and of freedom from pain." Translated into politics, this meant that the best government was the one that ensured the most pleasure and gave the least pain to the largest number of people. The type of government most likely to produce that effect, said Bentham, was a democracy.

Bentham's philosophy found many disciples, especially in England. Many of the British reforms in the 1820s and 1830s were due to the agitation of the "Utilitarians," or "Philosophical Radicals." The most influential follower of Bentham was John Stuart Mill (1806–73). Mill was an active public servant, a leading reformer, and a prolific writer on a wide range of subjects. Among his most famous writings was the essay *On Liberty* (1859). Its purpose, according to Mill, was to set forth the basic principle according to which relations between the individual and society, between the citizen and his government, should be regulated. That principle, Mill said, is "that the sole end for which mankind may interfere with the liberty of action of the individual is self-protection. The only purpose for which power can be rightfully exercised over any member of a civilized community, against his will, is to prevent harm to others." Mill based his plea not on natural law, as earlier advocates of individual freedom had done, but on utility. "I regard utility," he said, "as the ultimate appeal on all ethical questions."

Mill's emphasis on the right of everyone to do as he saw fit as long as his actions did not conflict with society, had tremendous appeal to the middle-class industrialist and businessman of the nineteenth century. Here was a philosophy that frowned on any but the most necessary interference by the government in the affairs of the individual. "That government is best that governs least." In another essay, *Considerations on Representative Government* (1861), Mill discussed the purpose of government in terms that appealed to businessmen. "Government," he said, "is a problem to be worked like any other question of business. The first step is to define the purpose which governments are required to promote. The next is to inquire what form of government is best fitted to fulfill these purposes." In answer to the first question, what is the purpose of good government, Mill held that it was "to promote the virtue and intelligence of its people"; and in answer to the second question, what form of government is best, Mill, like Bentham, decided in favor of democracy.

Jeremy Bentham (1748–1832), detail from a painting by J. Watts.

John Stuart Mill (1806–73).

Portrait medal of Adam Smith (1797). The reverse side shows symbols of Smith's *Wealth of Nations*.

Mill's belief in democracy was not shared by most members of the middle class. Nor were his proposals that the government should intervene to protect working children and improve housing and working conditions. Mill was highly critical of the economic injustices and inequities he found in his own society. He was especially concerned about the inequality that women still suffered in Victorian England. His essay *The Subjection of Women* (1869) was a ringing indictment of male chauvinism, and it became the bible of the women's suffrage movement. It remains as meaningful today as it was more than a century ago. There were already in Mill signs of a new type of liberalism that was ultimately to replace the dogmatic liberalism of the early nineteenth century (see p. 652). But even though Mill showed compassion for the fate of the underprivileged, his demand that the government leave the individual alone as much as possible clearly expressed the sentiments held by the majority of the bourgeoisie throughout the nineteenth century.

Liberalism in Politics

The middle class was primarily concerned with economic matters and liberalism developed its own economic doctrine (see following). But the industrialists, merchants, and bankers also realized that economic freedom was of no value unless it was supplemented by political rights. The main guarantee of such rights was seen in a written constitution, like that of the United States or the French Constitution of 1791. There were many others between 1812 and 1849. Most of these constitutions favored limited constitutional monarchy rather than true democracy. To ensure the predominance of the middle class, property qualifications for voting and for holding government office were part of all liberal constitutions. Anyone who found this restriction unjust needed only to work hard and improve his economic status in order to gain a share in the government. Only in their guarantee of individual liberty did these constitutions advocate equality for everyone. Freedom of the press, freedom of conscience, freedom of association, and freedom from arbitrary arrest—these were shared by rich and poor alike, at least theoretically. Workers who organized in order to improve their condition through collective bargaining, however, or socialists who used the press to call attention to existing injustices, would soon find out that the individual liberties guaranteed in the constitutions of the early nineteenth century did not apply to them.

The political ideal of early nineteenth-century liberalism was limited democracy. It has been aptly characterized as government of the wealthy, for the wealthy, by the wealthy. It was this ideal that motivated the middle class in the various revolutions discussed previously and that accounted for the widening rift between the middle and lower classes in these revolutions.

The "Classical Economists"

As for the economic philosophy of liberalism, its roots, too, went back to the eighteenth century. Its basic elements were already contained in the writings of Adam Smith (1723–90). This Glasgow professor, in his *Wealth of Nations* (1776), had argued for a policy of individual self-interest, free from any government interference, as the surest road to economic prosperity for society as a whole. Smith had proposed this policy of laissez faire, of leaving things alone, in order to liberate the individual from the many governmental restrictions that had hampered economic progress under mercantilism. He was the first of several writers who are usually called the classical economists. These men, for the first time, formulated certain general economic laws that seemed to apply at all times and in all societies. The most prominent members of the group were Smith, Thomas Robert Malthus (1766–1834), and David Ricardo (1772–1823).

Malthus wrote his famous *Essay on the Principle of Population* in 1798. It grew out of an argument he had with his father. The elder Malthus, a typical product of the eighteenth century, believed that if the world were reformed along rational lines there would be no end to human progress. Young Malthus did not agree.

He pointed to the rapidly increasing population of western Europe as an insurmountable obstacle to progress. "The power of population," he wrote, "is indefinitely greater than the power in earth to produce subsistence for man. Population, when unchecked, increases in a geometrical ratio. Subsistence only increases in an arithmetical ratio." Here was the basic hypothesis of Malthusianism: people multiplied much more rapidly than the supply of food that was needed to keep them alive. Human misery, it seemed, was unavoidable. Poverty rather than progress was the normal state of human society.

Many objections can be raised to the dire prophecies of Malthus. Even in his own day, improvements in agriculture and the opening to cultivation of vast new regions in America and elsewhere were increasing the world's food supply. Since then there have been further changes, especially with scientific farming and the development of birth control, to help maintain the balance between population growth and food supply. In our own day, however, the threat of overpopulation has once again taken on a fearful reality.

To the majority of people in the early nineteenth century, the warnings of Malthus came as a shock. The future, which only recently had held such promise, now suddenly looked bleak; no wonder the new science of political economy was soon called the "dismal science." Yet it was not dismal to everyone. As industrialists were growing rich while workers were sinking into misery, some voices now favored a more equitable distribution of profits. Such proposals, however, could not stand up against Malthus' assertion that poverty was inevitable. The poor were already increasing much faster than the rich. Giving them more wages or charity, the middle class could argue, would only result in their having more children. The best solution was to keep the poor as poor as possible. Adam Smith had asked government to keep its hands off business; Malthus advocated a similar attitude of laissez faire in regard to social reform.

The pessimistic note that characterizes the teachings of Malthus is also

Thomas Robert Malthus (1766–1834).

found in the writings of David Ricardo. His basic work, *On the Principles of Political Economy and Taxation* (1817), was the first real textbook on economics. One of Ricardo's major contributions to the economic theory of early nineteenth-century liberalism was what his disciples called the "iron law of wages." Labor, to Ricardo, was very much like any other commodity. When it was plentiful, it was cheap; when it was scarce, it was expensive. As long as there is an ample supply of workers, wages will inevitably sink to the lowest possible level of subsistence, just above starvation. To try to remedy

Adam Smith on the Limitations of Government
1776

According to the system of natural liberty, the sovereign has only three duties to attend to; three duties of great importance, indeed, but plain and intelligible to common understandings: first, the duty of protecting the society from the violence and invasion of other independent societies; secondly, the duty of protecting, as far as possible, every member of the society from the injustice or oppression of every other member of it, or the duty of establishing an exact administration of justice; and, thirdly, the duty of erecting and maintaining certain public works and certain public institutions, which it can never be for the interest of the individual, or small number of individuals, to erect and maintain; because the profit could never repay the expense to any individual or small number of individuals, though it may frequently do much than repay it to a great society.

From Adam Smith, *An Inquiry into the Nature and Causes of the Wealth of Nations,* ed. by Edwin Cannan (New York: Random House, 1937), p. 651.

H. W. Egley, *In the Omnibus* (1859), captures the tone of the British nineteenth-century middle class.

were British. Since England had a larger and more influential middle class than most continental countries, this is not surprising. But the writings of these men had a deep effect on continental liberalism as well. Adam Smith's *Wealth of Nations*, in particular, supplied most of the ammunition for the attacks of continental liberals on the economic restrictions and regulations of their governments. There were some differences in the direction or emphasis of these attacks. French liberalism, for instance, was more concerned with economic matters than was liberalism in Germany, where the problems of political reform and national unification overshadowed all other issues. Outside England, France, and Germany, the philosophy of liberalism had few contributors. Liberalism, after all, was the credo of a class that had as yet made little headway outside western Europe.

SOCIAL REFORM

Given the laissez-faire attitude of liberalism, it is not surprising that efforts to solve social problems through government action found little support among the middle class. What social reforms were introduced owed much to the agitation of a few individuals, who were motivated either by humanitarianism or, as in the case of Britain's "Philosophical Radicals," by a desire to be utilitarian and efficient.

Factory Acts

Some of the most effective opposition to early nineteenth-century liberalism came from among the representatives of the old order. For political and economic but also humanitarian reasons, some Tories attacked the new industrial system in its most vulnerable spot, the terrible conditions in the mines and factories. As far back as 1802, Parliament had passed an act that cut down the working hours of apprentices. The first real factory act, passed in 1819, forbade the employment in cotton mills of children under nine years of age and limited the daily labor of children over nine to twelve hours. In 1831 night work was abolished for per-

this situation by lowering profits and raising wages would be futile, since it would merely increase the number of workers' children and, by limiting the supply of capital, cut down production. "Like all other contracts," Ricardo said, "wages should be left to the fair and free competition of the market, and should never be controlled by the interference of the legislature."

Here was another economic law as dismal in its prospects for the lower classes as Malthus' predictions on the increase of population. If there were people living on the verge of starvation, if wages were low and children had to work sixteen hours a day, that was unfortunate; but it was also, as Malthus and Ricardo had shown, inevitable. Attempts to change the situation through charity or legislation designed to improve wages and hours were opposed by middle-class liberals as interference with the beneficent principle of laissez faire.

Liberalism on the Continent

All the intellectual figures mentioned so far in this discussion of liberalism sons under twenty-one. In 1847 the maximum working day for women and children was set at ten hours. Two acts in 1842 and 1855 made it illegal to employ women and children in the mining industry.

Despite the best intentions on the part of their sponsors, however, these early factory acts were not very effective. They were not strictly enforced, and they applied chiefly to the cotton industry. Not until 1833 was their scope extended to include other industries, and only then was some system of inspection set up to enforce the new provisions.

Social Legislation

There were other reforms in England besides factory acts. The Municipal Corporations Act of 1835 enabled municipalities to cope more effectively with problems arising from rapid urbanization. To ensure some degree of uniformity in matters of public health, Parliament in 1848 set up a system of local boards of health. One of the most pressing social problems was the care of the poor. The New Poor Law of 1834 for the first time brought some order into the complicated system of poor relief. It was, however, a mixed blessing to the poor. The law abolished the traditional practice of "outdoor relief," under which the wages of the poorest workers had been supplemented from public funds. Henceforth, to be eligible for relief, the poor had to report to workhouses; and by making conditions in these establishments as unpleasant as possible, all but those who could not possibly make a living otherwise were discouraged from going on relief. Here was a measure, clearly utilitarian, that delighted the middle class. It discouraged idleness and cut the expense of poor relief.

On the Continent, little was done to reform the abuses of early industrialism. A French law in 1803 prohibited work in factories before 3:00 A.M. Under the reign of Louis Philippe, the employment of children under eight was prohibited, and the work of children under twelve was limited to eight hours a day. But enforcement of these laws, in France as in England, was very lax. In Belgium, nothing at all was being done to improve the lot of the workers. The only state with any industry in Germany was Prussia, and the Prussian government, in 1839, introduced a factory law that forbade the employment of children under nine and limited the working hours of older children to ten hours.

Liberalism and Education

The only field of social reform in which the Continent was ahead of Great Britain was education. Here, for once, liberalism was a great help. Like the *philosophe* of the eighteenth century, the nineteenth-century liberal was a firm believer in education as a means of improving the world and of helping children get ahead. Any governmental measure in favor of education, therefore, had liberal support. Both France and Prussia had a long tradition of public education, which they maintained during the nineteenth century. There was a brief reaction in favor of religious education under the Bourbons, but the Education Act passed under Louis Philippe again asserted the state's role in education. Britain's first provision of public funds for education was not until 1833. It was

An early photograph of a classroom in an English school (1856).

increased in subsequent years, but even so the amount set aside for education in 1839 was still only half of what it cost to maintain Queen Victoria's horses. Not until 1870 was the first general education act adopted in England. In the meantime, education depended on private initiative, in which the middle class played a leading and beneficial role.

As this discussion has shown, some genuine attempts were made in the first half of the nineteenth century to cope with the ills of early industrialism through social reform. But such attempts ran counter to the laissez-faire philosophy of liberalism. Economic liberalism was, to some extent, a mere rationalization of selfish interests by the middle class. But there was also in it much of the eighteenth-century belief that the world operated according to certain basic laws that could not be altered and that ultimately made for the greater happiness of the greatest number.

This passive acquiescence in things as they were, however, could not possibly satisfy the workers. They refused to believe that the only solution to their troubles was to do nothing, to let matters take their course. They demanded that remedial action be taken on their behalf, else they were prepared to act for themselves.

WORKING-CLASS PROTEST

The protest of the working class took various forms. Some of the discontent expressed itself in political action, as in the revolutions of 1830 and 1848. In another form of protest, workers vented their anger and frustration on the very instruments that to them seemed primarily responsible for their plight—the machines. There were sporadic instances of such "machine-breaking" during the early phase of industrialization, both in England and on the Continent. But these acts of despair could not halt the advance of the machine age. Instead of waging war against mechanization, workers increasingly tried to escape industrialization altogether by emigrating to the United States, where virgin lands offered them the opportunity of making a better living.

Early Labor Unions

There was another, more effective way in which the working class tried to fight the injustices of industrialism. As the workers grew in number, they became aware that they constituted a new and separate class whose interests conflicted with those of their employers. This growing class consciousness among the workers led them to organize their forces in an effort to gain better treatment for themselves.

The first country in which labor unions made any headway was again Great Britain. The British government, impressed by the radicalism of the French Revolution, had watched with apprehension labor's early efforts to organize. In 1799 and 1800 Parliament passed the Combination Acts, which prohibited workers from organizing to improve their condition. Labor's continued activities, however, together with the agitation of some middle-class reformers, finally made the government relent. In 1824 and 1825, as we have seen, the Combination Acts were repealed. Henceforth, trade unions in England were no longer illegal, though it was still prohibited to engage in strikes and other forms of protest. Even so, under the new dispensation local unions arose throughout Britain. The next logical step was the formation of a large labor organization. This step was taken first in 1834, and more successfully in 1845, with the organization of the "National Association for the Protection of Labour." In 1859 the Association pressured Parliament to allow peaceful picketing. In 1868 a Trades Union Congress representing more than one hundred thousand members met in Manchester. By 1875, trade unions in Britain had won full legal status, including the right to strike and to picket peacefully. The British labor movement had at last come into its own.

On the Continent, labor's efforts at self-help were less successful. Labor unions were forbidden in Belgium until 1866, and there was no labor movement in Germany to speak of until after 1870. In France, the right of workers to organize had been forbidden even during the Revolution. This ban was reiterated in the *Code Napoléon* of 1803. Some French workers organized secret societies that fomented strikes and local uprisings; but these only made the government more repressive. Still, there were some people in France, the early socialists, who took a more sympathetic view of the workers' fate. If England was prominent in defining the middle-class philosophy of liberalism, France was equally prominent in launching its counterpart, the working-class philosophy of socialism.

THE BEGINNINGS OF MODERN SOCIALISM

Socialism as a mode of life is nothing new. It always existed, and still does, in primitive communities where people work together and share the proceeds of their common labor. Socialism as an economic and social philosophy, on the other hand, is a relatively recent development, closely connected with the rise of modern industrialism. The term *socialism* did not come into common use until the 1830s. Like liberalism, it has assumed a wide variety of meanings. Today almost any kind of government interference with the free play of economic forces is called socialism, whether it be the communist system of Russia or the "welfare state" of the United States.

While there are many varieties of socialism, all share certain fundamental principles. All socialists think that the existing distribution of wealth is unjust, because it gives a few people far more than they need and leaves large numbers of people with barely enough to exist. To close the gap between the haves and the have-nots, socialists advocate common ownership of the resources and means of production that constitute and create society's wealth. The fruits of production—that is, the profits of human labor—socialists propose to distribute in such a way that every member of society receives an equal or at least an equitable share. All schools of socialism agree that there should be far-reaching changes in society in the direction of economic and social as well as political equality.

The Utopian Socialists

Historically, modern socialism is divided into pre-Marxian and post-Marx-

Slitting room of a pen factory in Birmingham (1851).

ian socialism or, in Marxist terms, into "Utopian" and "scientific" socialism. The Utopian socialists earned their epithet because of the unrealistic nature of their schemes. Most of the Utopians were French, and they all came from the middle or upper classes. Given the workers' poverty and lack of education, this is hardly surprising.

The first Utopian socialist to achieve any prominence was a French nobleman, Count Henri de Saint-Simon (1760–1825). Concerned by the social and economic injustices of a laissez-faire economy, Saint-Simon suggested that the state take a hand in organizing society in such a way that people, instead of exploiting one another, join forces to exploit nature. "The whole society," he held, "ought to strive toward the amelioration of the moral and physical existence of the most numerous and poorest class." Saint-Simon defined the principle according to which this amelioration should operate as: "From each according to his capacity, to each according to his work." In time this became one of the basic slogans of socialism.

Another prominent Utopian was Charles Fourier (1772–1837). Most of the ills of society, Fourier held, were due to the improper social and physical environment in which most people lived. To provide a more favorable environment, Fourier proposed the creation of so-called *phalanges*, or phalanxes. These were to be pleasant communities of some sixteen hundred to eighteen hundred people, living on five thousand acres of

Contemporary drawing of Robert Owen.

land, and forming a self-sufficient economic unit. Fourier's plans never materialized in Europe; but in the United States, where land was cheap and pioneering more common, a number of cooperative establishments were tried. None of them, however, became a lasting success.

The only one among the French Utopians to play an active role in politics was Louis Blanc (1811–82). Blanc realized that economic reform, to be effective, must be preceded by political reform. Once true democracy had been achieved, the state could initiate the new type of industrial organizations that Blanc proposed. These consisted of social or national workshops—that is, self-supporting units of production, owned and operated by the workers. Some kind of workshops were given a brief try by the revolutionary government of 1848, of which Louis Blanc was a member. The experiment failed, however, largely because the original purpose of the workshops was subordinated to the needs of the moment, the temporary relief of unemployment.

The most prominent Utopian socialist outside France was the British industrialist Robert Owen (1771–1858). Appalled by conditions he found when he took over the cotton mills at New Lanark in Scotland, Owen gave his workers decent housing, increased their pay, and shortened their working hours. In the model community he created, both productivity and profits increased, thus bearing out Owen's contention that satisfied workers were also better workers. Owen was less

fortunate with a project he attempted on this side of the Atlantic. The community of New Harmony in Indiana, conceived along the lines of Fourier's phalanxes, turned out to be a fiasco.

Utopian socialism, in fact, had little to show for its manifold efforts. Like the *philosophes*, the Utopians believed in the natural goodness of man and the perfectibility of the world. They soon discovered that most men were not naturally good and reasonable. But even the failure of the Utopians contained a useful lesson. It showed that idealism and the best intentions are not sufficient to reform society. A more realistic and more militant type of socialism was needed that would use the workers' potential economic and political power to wrest concessions from the middle class. This new kind of socialism was first presented in the writings of Karl Marx (1818–83) and Friedrich Engels (1820–95).

MARXIAN SOCIALISM

One of the reasons for the failure of the Utopian socialists was that they never sparked any substantial movement among the workers. There were some political working-class organizations during the 1830s and 1840s, but they had to operate as secret conspiracies rather than as open political parties. In France, Auguste Blanqui founded the "Society of Families" and the "Society of Seasons," both of them socialistic or communistic. Another such society, founded by German exiles, was the "League of the Just." Its program was originally supplied by Wilhelm Weitling, a German tailor who in 1842 published his *Guarantee of Harmony and Freedom*. These various underground organizations were all influenced by the writings of the Utopian socialists, but in their demands for complete economic equality, or communism, they went considerably beyond the demands of the middle-class Utopians.

Communism—that is, the abolition of all private property—ultimately became the basis of most socialist programs. A century ago, the term *communism* did not have the connotations it assumed after the Bolshevik Revolution. The number of communist socialists in the first half of the nineteenth century was very small, and few people realized the ultimate implications of their aims. In 1844 two young Germans, Karl Marx and Friedrich Engels, made contact with the "League of the Just." Soon thereafter its name was changed to the "Communist League," and from secret revolutionary conspiracy it now shifted to open propaganda. In 1847 Marx and Engels supplied the League with its new program, *The Communist Manifesto*.

Karl Marx and Friedrich Engels

Both Marx and Engels came from the middle class that they spent most of their lives attacking. As a university student in Germany, Marx had shown a lively interest in social issues. His early writings got him into trouble and in 1843 led to his first exile in Paris. There he met Engels, the son of a wealthy German industrialist with industrial holdings in England. Engels was already a communist, and there developed between the two men a close intellectual partnership. Engels is usually overshadowed by Marx, but his contributions to Marxian doctrine were considerable; besides, Engels through most of his life supported Marx financially.

The first result of their collaboration was *The Communist Manifesto*, which appeared during the revolutions of 1848. Marx welcomed the revolutions, and he was present during the upheavals in Paris. When the revolutions failed, he went to England, where he remained until his death in 1883. It was while in England that Marx wrote most of his basic works, notably *Das Kapital*, the first volume of which appeared in 1867.

The Communist Manifesto

The basic elements of Marx's social philosophy were contained in the brief and persuasive *Communist Manifesto*. Its fundamental proposition, as restated by Engels in his introduction to a later edition of the *Manifesto*, was

that in every historical epoch the prevailing mode of economic production

and exchange, and the social organization necessarily following from it, form the basis upon which is built up, and from which alone can be explained, the political and intellectual history of that epoch; that consequently the whole history of mankind (since the dissolution of primitive tribal society, holding land in common ownership) has been a history of class struggles, contests between exploiting and exploited, ruling and oppressed classes; that the history of these struggles forms a series of evolutions in which, nowadays, a stage has been reached where the exploited and oppressed class—the proletariat—cannot attain its emancipation from the sway of the exploiting and ruling class—the bourgeoisie—without, at the same time and once and for all, emancipating society at large from all exploitation, oppression, class distinctions, and class struggles.

Here are the two basic tenets for which Marx is most famous: his eco-

Family photograph of Karl Marx (right), his wife, and two daughters in the 1860s. Friedrich Engels is at left.

nomic, or materialistic, interpretation of history, and his theory of the class struggle. Other thinkers before Marx had recognized the influence of external circumstances and of the environment upon history. But Marx focused his attention on one particular aspect of environment that he considered fundamental: the means of production, the way in which people make a living. It is the economic structure of society, according to Marx, that determines its social, political, legal, and even cultural aspects. Historians before Marx, especially since the eighteenth century, had viewed history as an intellectually determined process. Marx took a diametrically opposite view, recognizing material, nonintellectual forces as the sole determining factors.

To illustrate his economic interpretation of history as well as his theory of the class struggle, in *The Communist Manifesto* Marx gave a brief survey of the history of western civilization as he saw it:

> The history of all hitherto existing society is the history of class struggles. Freeman and slave, patrician and plebeian, lord and serf, guildmaster and journeyman, in a word, oppressor and oppressed, stood in constant opposition to one another, carried on an uninterrupted, now hidden, now open fight, a fight that each time ended either in a revolutionary reconstitution of society at large, or in the common ruin of the contending classes.

Marx then examined the history of western society more closely, beginning with the Middle Ages. At that time, the economy of Europe was predominantly agrarian, with a large class of serfs supporting a small class of feudal nobles. Upon this society, material changes began to work: money, trade, the beginnings of a commercial, capitalist economy. As these changes took hold, a new class, a trading or bourgeois class, was formed. And between the old feudal nobility and the new middle class a struggle arose, which led to some preliminary victories of the bourgeoisie in England and Holland and culminated in the American War of Independence and the French Revolution.

The final victory of the middle class came in the nineteenth century. But this did not end the struggle. Because now a new struggle began, this time between the bourgeoisie and the proletariat. It was brought about by another change in the mode of production, the introduction of the factory system and the rise of industrial capitalism. The workers in this new struggle, which Marx saw going on around him, were now herded together in large factories, under the eyes of their "oppressors." They were held down by the iron laws of capitalist economics to a bare subsistence level. But there was one thing these workers could do, according to Marx: they could organize, they could become class conscious.

Marx felt certain that the bourgeoisie and the workers were already locked in their death struggle. And the victory of the proletariat in this struggle, Marx

---

Engels' Funeral Oration for Marx (1883)

Karl Marx was one of those outstanding men few of whom are produced in any century. Charles Darwin discovered the laws of evolution of organic nature on our planet. Marx is the discoverer of the fundamental law that determines the course and development of human history. . . .

Above all, he saw in science a great lever of history, a revolutionary force in the best sense of the term. And in this sense, he applied his immense knowledge, especially of history, to all the fields he mastered.

For he was truly a revolutionary, as he called himself. The struggle for the emancipation of the wage-earning class from the fetters of the modern capitalist system of exploitation was his true mission. . . .

Nobody can fight for a cause without making enemies. And he had many of them. Throughout the greatest part of his political life he was the most hated and most calumniated man in Europe. But he hardly paid attention to the calumnies. . . . At the end of his life, he could proudly glimpse millions of followers in the mines of Siberia as well as in the workshops of Europe and America. He saw his economic theories becoming the indisputable basis of socialism throughout the whole world.

From Saul K. Padover, *Karl Marx: An Intimate Biography* (New York: McGraw-Hill, 1978), p. 591.

held, could be predicted with the certainty of a scientific experiment—hence the term *scientific socialism.* By the laws of capitalist competition there were bound to be periodic crises, caused by "epidemics of overproduction." As a result of these crises, the poor would get poorer and the rich would get richer. And there would finally come a time when "it becomes evident, that the bourgeoisie is unfit any longer to be the ruling class in society . . . because it is incompetent to assure an existence to its slave within his slavery. . . . Society can no longer live under this bourgeoisie. . . . Its fall and the victory of the proletariat are equally inevitable."

So much for the collapse of capitalism. What then? What will the world be like after the proletariat has won? On that subject Marx was not too clear. At one point he envisaged a transition period—the "dictatorship of the proletariat," as he calls it—in which the proletariat by revolution will destroy the existing political machinery of the state, will convert the means of production into public property, and will gradually bring about a classless society. The state, as Engels put it, will gradually "wither away." Then what? "In place of the old bourgeois society, with its classes and class antagonisms," Marx concludes, "we shall have an association in which the free development of each is the condition for the free development of all." This is an idyllic picture, but also rather vague, and not very different from the kind of society certain eighteenth-century writers had envisaged. There was, in fact, a good deal of the eighteenth century in Marxism. It shared the *philosophes'* belief in progress, in the good life on earth, and in the natural goodness of man.

The Errors and Contributions of Marx

What about Marx's concept of classes, and of history as a series of class struggles? The concept of class certainly was a useful contribution; and if Marx did not make us class conscious, he helped our understanding of past and present society by making us aware of classes. But his definition of classes en-

tirely in economic terms is much too narrow; and by denying the role of the individual, it runs counter to the liberal belief in individualism. As for Marx's

What If Marx Had Never Lived?

No one can read the story of Karl Marx or ponder the somber prognostications of Marx the historian or the economist without asking, "Would history have been significantly different if Marx had not lived?"

It is a surprisingly difficult question to answer. To be sure, the trend of world capitalism would not have been deflected by so much as an inch if it had been deprived of the insights of Marx's masterwork, *Das Kapital.* Marxism as a system of thought has exerted virtually no direct influence on the internal economic evolution of American or European capitalism as such. But the influence of Marxism is not so easily summed up when we look at the revolutionary countries: at Russia or China or Cuba or at the bubbling cauldron of the underdeveloped world. And its effects on these countries has, in turn, affected the West.

A first glance would tell us that in these lands Marx was of the greatest importance. Whole political catechisms and, more than that, crucial political guidance have been wrested from the writings of Marx and his collaborator Friedrich Engels, writings which have on many occasions assumed the role of Biblical literature in a fundamentalist community. Even so relatively liberated a Marxist as the Yugoslav spokesman Edvard Kardelj wrote a polemic against the Chinese position on the question of coexistence in 1960 by leaning not so much on facts and empirical evidence as on what Marx or Engels said. If Marx said (or if one can "interpret" Marx to have said) that coexistence was possible, then it is possible; if he said not, it is not.

Thus Marx and Marxism have indubitably left their imprint on the vocabulary, the thought pattern and the discourse of the revolutionary nations. Yet it is difficult to believe that the revolutions themselves would not have occurred or that Communism (by whatever name) would not be a great world presence today had Marx not lived. The forces which finally burst through the crusts of tired and corrupt societies in Russia, China and Cuba—and which treaten to do so again in Latin America and Asia and Africa—may have been guided by Marxism, but they were not generated by Marxism alone. Had Marx never lived or written, old and incapable regimes would have given way to new and vigorous ones, no doubt with all the agonies by which such changes in history are usually accompanied. The world would have been different surely, but not perhaps all that different.

From Robert L. Heilbroner, in Isaiah Berlin, *Karl Marx: His Life and Environment* (New York: Time-Life, 1963), pp. xviii–xix.

view of the past as a series of class struggles, it does not really fit the facts of history, nor does his emphasis on merely two opposing classes. Marx recognized the existence of other classes, but he believed that they would ultimately be absorbed by one or the other of the two contending groups—the bourgeoisie and the proletariat. This prediction, like so many others Marx made, thus far has failed to materialize.

There were, then, a good many blind spots in Marx's socialist theories. While the rich were getting richer, the poor did not necessarily get poorer. The general standard of living in the world's industrial nations was to reach heights undreamed of by Marx. Man, furthermore, does not seem to be motivated exclusively, or even primarily, by economic concerns. Despite Marx's attacks on religion, the established churches continued to play an important part even in the lives of the lower classes. Another force that increasingly came to command the allegiance of rich and poor alike was nationalism. The great wars of the last century were fought not between workers and capitalists, but between the citizens of different nations, including the workers, for the defense or the greater glory of their own country.

Despite errors and shortcomings in his teachings, however, Marx's contributions to modern thought have been considerable. By bridging the gap between politics and economics, he enriched our understanding of the past. We may not accept the dominant role he assigned to economic factors, but we have come to realize the importance of these factors. Prior to Marx, the division of society into rich and poor, haves and have-nots, was accepted as a natural, unchangeable fact. It was chiefly due to Marx that society was jolted out of such complacent acceptance of the status quo. By predicting far-reaching changes, he made people aware that changes were possible. The threat of revolutionary change conjured up in Marx's writings did much to hasten the peaceful evolution that has so markedly improved the condition of the lower classes in industrial societies. Marxian socialism offered its followers a seemingly logical, scientifically certain answer to the many perplexities of modern society. This explains its appeal to workers and intellectuals alike. The ultimate success of Marxism lay in the almost religious fervor it inspired among its disciples.

OTHER FORMS OF SOCIAL CRITICISM

Marxian socialism, in its ultimate effects on society, turned out to be the most important attack on the capitalist philosophy of laissez faire. Other critics of this philosophy, however, tried in various ways to awaken their contemporaries to the social problems created by the industrialization of society.

Humanitarianism

Writers like Victor Hugo and Honoré de Balzac in France and Charles Dickens in England, by dwelling in their novels on the more sordid aspects of the new industrialism, played on human sympathy in the hope of creating a climate favorable to reform. The historian Thomas Carlyle, in his *Past and Present* (1843), showed deep concern over the growing division between the working classes on the one hand and the wealthy classes on the other. He turned against the "mammonism" and the "mechanism" of his age and admonished the new captains of industry to be aware of their responsibilities as successors to the old aristocracy. Benjamin Disraeli, one of the rising young Tories, in his social novel *Sybil* (1845), deplored the wide gap that industrialization had opened between the rich and the poor. It was, he said, as though England had split into two nations "between whom there was no intercourse and no sympathy."

Christian Socialism

Another body of social criticism arose within the Christian churches, first in England and later on the Continent. For centuries past, organized Christianity had been the chief dispenser of charity to the poor and the aged. The beginnings of modern Christian Socialism go back to a small group of English clergymen who

Charles Dickens (1812–70), at age forty-seven.

felt that the best way to attack the evils of industrialism was to reaffirm the gospel of charity and brotherly love. The leader of the Christian Socialist movement was the Anglican theologian Frederick Denison Maurice. Its best-known propagandist was the clergyman and novelist Charles Kingsley. In his famous tract, *Cheap Clothes and Nasty* (1850), written under the pseudonym of "Parson Lot," Kingsley attacked the condition of "ever-increasing darkness and despair" in the British clothing industry, whose sweatshops were "rank with human blood." To remedy a situation in which men were like "beasts of prey, eating one another up by competition, as in some confined pike-pond, where the great pike, having dispatched the little ones, begin to devour each other," Kingsley proposed the formation of cooperative enterprises in which everyone would be "working together for common profit in the spirit of mutual self-sacrifice." Christian Socialism, in appealing to the social consciousness of "every gentleman and every Christian," helped to modify the belief in laissez faire and to prepare the soil for the movement of social reform that gained momentum in the second half of the nineteenth century.

Anarchism

One other form of social protest of quite a different nature deserves mention here, even though its effects were not felt until later in the century. Anarchism, like socialism, was intended to overthrow capitalism. But while the socialists were ready to use the state as a steppingstone for the realization of their aims, the anarchists were deeply opposed to any kind of governmental authority and organization. One of the earliest theorists of anarchism was the French publicist Pierre-Joseph Proudhon (1809–65). In his pamphlet *First Memoir on Property* (1840) he asked the question, "What is property?" and replied with the well-known slogan, "Property is theft!" This seeming opposition to private property appeared to align Proudhon with communism and endeared him to Marx. The latter's admiration cooled, however, when he discovered that Proudhon was less inter-

ested in overthrowing the middle class than in raising the worker to the level of that class. Proudhon was against any kind of government, be it by one man, a party, or a democratic majority. "Society," he wrote, "finds its highest perfection in the union of order with anarchy."

The most famous proponent of anarchism was a Russian nobleman, Mikhail Bakunin (1814–76). A theorist of anarchism, he also practiced what he preached. Bakunin was involved in several revolutions, was three times condemned to death, and spent long years in prison and Siberian exile. Bakunin attributed most of the evils of his day to two agencies—the state and the Church—both enemies of human freedom. His ideal society was a loose federation of local communities, each with maximum autonomy. In each of these communities the means of production were to be held in common. The way to achieve this governmentless condition, Bakunin held, was not by waiting patiently for the state to wither away, as Marx held, but by helping matters along, if necessary by means of terrorism, assassination, and insurrection. The last decade of the nineteenth century, as we shall see, witnessed a whole series of assassinations attributed to anarchists. But anarchism never developed into a well-defined movement, partly because of Bakunin's death in 1876, partly because of the impracticable nature of its doctrine. Traces of it, however, survived into the twentieth century and contributed to another type of social protest, syndicalism (see p. 663).

By the middle of the nineteenth century, the coming of the Industrial Age, with its revolutionary political, social, and economic effects, had made itself felt over most of Europe. For the next two decades, people's attention became absorbed by momentous political developments. A series of wars radically changed the existing international order and overshadowed economic developments. Once the political situation had become stabilized, however, in the 1870s and 1880s, a second wave of economic change swept over Europe and the world, a wave of such magnitude that it has often been called a "Second Industrial Revolution."

The Reverend Charles Kingsley (1819–75), English author and noted Christian Socialist.

Mikhail Bakunin (1814–76).

Suggestions for Further Reading

Note: Asterisk denotes a book available in paperback edition.

General Historians' views of the Industrial Revolution have changed over the years, as is shown in E. E. Lampard's perceptive essay, *Industrial Revolution: Interpretations and Perspectives* (1957), and in D. Landes, *The Unbound Prometheus: Technological Change and Industrial Development in Western Europe from 1750 to the Present* (1969). A good account of early industrialization is P. Deane, *The First Industrial Revolution** (1965). H. J. Habbakuk and M. M. Postan, eds., *The Industrial Revolutions and After* (1965) (Vol. VI of the *Cambridge Economic History of Europe*), contains essays by noted specialists. W. W. Rostow's influential book, *The Stages of Economic Growth** (1960), introduced novel concepts like "take-off" into the debate on industrialization. The widening scope of industrialization is stressed in W. O. Henderson, *The Industrial Revolution on the Continent* (1961). A. P. Usher, *A History of Mechanical Inventions* (1929), and G. Fussell, *The Farmer's Tools, 1500–1900* (1952), discuss the importance of technological change; and T. McKeown, *The Modern Rise of Population* (1972), and W. D. Borrie, *The Growth and Control of World Population* (1970), deal with the beginnings of the current "population explosion." On urbanization, see L. Mumford, *The City in History* (1961). The same author's *Technics and Civilization* (1934), and S. Chase, *Men and Machines* (1929), view with some alarm the impact of technology on man.

Economic Changes in Britain Because England was the first country to undergo the transition to modern industrialism, its Agricultural and Industrial revolutions have been studied most intensively. Both P. Mantoux, *The Industrial Revolution in the Eighteenth Century* (1929), and T. S. Ashton, *An Economic History of England: The Eighteenth Century* (1955), deal with the roots of these developments, although with different emphases. A small volume by T. S. Ashton, *The Industrial Revolution 1760–1830** (1948), corrects many misconceptions about early industrialism. J. H. Clapham, *An Economic History of Modern Britain*, Vol. I (1926), covers the period between 1820 and 1850. Briefer treatments are W. H. B. Court, *A Concise Economic History of Britain from 1750 to Recent Times* (1954), and A. Redford, *An Economic History of England, 1760–1860* (1947). The changes in British agriculture are the subject of E. L. Jones, *Agriculture and Economic Growth in England 1650–1815* (1968); Lord Ernle, *English Farming, Past and Present* (1936); J. L. Hammond and B. Hammond, *The Village Labourer, 1760–1832* (1918); and J. P. D. Dunbabin, *Rural Discontent in Nineteenth-Century Britain* (1975). The following are detailed studies on special aspects of the Industrial Revolution in England: T. S. Ashton, *Iron and Steel in the Industrial Revolution* (1951); W. H. B. Court, *The Rise of the Midland Industries, 1600–1838* (1938); and A. Redford, *Manchester Merchants and Foreign Trade, 1794–1858* (1934). The most important single invention of early industrialism is the subject of H. W. Dickinson, *A Short History of the Steam Engine* (1939), and of G. N. Von Tunzelmann, *Steam Power and British Industrialization to 1860* (1978).

The Spread of Industrialism Besides England, only France experienced any noticeable industrial development during the eighteenth century. These beginnings are discussed in H. E. Sée, *Economic and Social Conditions in France During the Eighteenth Century* (1927), and S. T. McCloy, *French Inventions of the Eighteenth Century* (1954). Later developments in France are treated in A. L. Dunham, *The Industrial Revolution in France, 1815–1848* (1955), and R. E. Cameron, *France and the Economic Development of Europe, 1800–1914** (1961). British influence on economic developments abroad is traced by W. O. Henderson, *Britain and Industrial Europe, 1750–1870* (1954); E. J. Hobsbawm, *Industry and Empire* (1970); and L. C. A. Knowles, *Economic Development in the Nineteenth Century: France, Germany, Russia, and the United States* (1932). Other useful economic histories are: J. H. Clapham, *Economic Development of France and Germany, 1815–1914** (1936); S. B. Clough, *France: A History of Natural Economics* (1939); W. O. Henderson, *The Zollverein* (1939) and *The Rise of German Industrial Power, 1834–1914** (1976); P. I. Lyashchenko, *History of the National Economy of Russia to 1917* (1949); and J. Blum, *Lord and Peasant in Russia from the Ninth to the Nineteenth Century** (1961). See also the same author's admirably broad *The End of the Old Order in Rural Europe** (1978).

The Social Effects of Industrialization The traditional emphasis on the negative effects of early industrialism is evident in J. L. Hammond and B. Hammond, *The Town Labourer, 1760–1832* (1917), *The Skilled Labourer, 1760–1832* (1919), and *The Bleak Age** (1947). That emphasis has found confirmation in E. P. Thompson, *The Making of the English Working Class** (1963). A more neutral picture is drawn in A. Briggs, *The Age of Improvement*,

1783–1867 (1959); S. G. Checkland, *The Rise of Industrial Society in England, 1815–1885* (1964); and G. Kitson-Clark, *The Making of Victorian England* (1962). See also M. I. Thomis, *The Town Labourer and the Industrial Revolution* (1975). On urban growth, see A. S. Wohl, *The Eternal Slum: Housing and Social Policy in Victorian London* (1977), and E. Gauldie, *Cruel Habitation: A History of Working-Class Housing, 1780–1918* (1974); and on landed interests, see F. M. Thompson, *English Landed Society in the Nineteenth Century* (1963). The situation in France is dealt with in L. Chevalier, *Working Classes and Dangerous Classes in Paris During the First Part of the Nineteenth Century* (1971); V. R. Lorwin, *The French Labor Movement* (1954); and B. Moss, *The Origins of the French Labor Movement* (1976).

Economic Liberalism

The best way to study the utilitarians and classical economists is through their writings. The most important of these—J. S. Mill, *Autobiography** and *On Liberty;** T, R. Malthus, *An Essay on Population;** and D. Ricardo, *Principles of Political Economy and Taxation**—are available in several editions. The general development of modern economic thought is presented in C. Gide and C. Rist, *History of Economic Doctrines from the Physiocrats to the Present Day* (1913, 1948), and E. Roll, *A History of Economic Thought* (1942). The standard work on Bentham and the utilitarians is É. Halévy, *The Growth of Philosophic Radicalism** (1955). More recent treatments are J. Hamburger, *Intellectuals in Politics: John Stuart Mill and the Philosophic Radicals* (1965), S. H. Letwin, *The Pursuit of Certainty: David Hume; Jeremy Bentham; John Stuart Mill; Beatrice Webb* (1965), and W. Thomas, *The Philosophic Radicals* (1979). Among the latest works on Mill are the psychohistorical B. Mazlish, *James and John Stuart Mill* (1975), and the more traditional A. Ryan, *J. S. Mill** (1975). P. James, *Population Malthus: His Life and Times* (1979), is the first full biography of the classical economist.

Social Reform

Social reform in the first half of the nineteenth century was almost entirely restricted to Great Britain. W. M. Thomas, *The Early Factory Legislation* (1948), deals with the period between 1802 and 1853. Other notable reform efforts are dealt with in E. L. Woodward, *The Age of Reform, 1815–1870* (1938); L. Radzinowitz, *A History of English Criminal Law: The Movement for Reform, 1750–1833* (1948); and S. Webb and B. Webb, *English Local Government: English Poor Law History*, 3 vols. (1927–29). For accounts of early attempts by the working class to organize itself politically and economically, see G. D. H. Cole, *British Working Class Politics, 1832–1914* (1941); S. Webb and B. Webb, *History of Trade Unionism* (1920); and H. M. Pelling, *History of Trade Unionism* (1963). A good introduction to social reform is through the biographies of some of the leading reformers: G. D. H. Cole, *The Life of William Cobbett* (1942); G. Wallas, *Life of Francis Place* (1925); G. F. A. Best, *Shaftesbury* (1964); and G. M. Trevelyan, *Lord Grey and the Reform Bill* (1929).

Socialism

Good surveys of the subject are G. D. H. Cole, *Socialist Thought: The Forerunners, 1789–1850* (1962), and H. W. Laidler, *Social-Economic Movements* (1949). Less systematic but more readable is E. Wilson, *To The Finland Station** (1953). G. Lichtheim, *The Origins of Socialism* (1969), is brilliant. R. Owen, *The Life of Robert Owen, by Himself* (1920), gives insights into the thought of this leading Utopian reformer. Among several books on Owen, J. F. C. Harrison *Quest for the New Moral World: Robert Owen and the Owenites in Britain and America* (1969), is one of the best. F. Manuel, *The Prophets of Paris** (1962), deals with the French Utopian socialists. The literature on Marxian socialism is vast. A convenient collection of basic sources is available in *Karl Marx and Frederick Engels; Selected Works*, 2 vols. (1951). The easiest way for the layman to become acquainted with Marx's basic concepts is still K. Marx and F. Engels, *The Communist Manifesto** (1848), available in countless editions. G. D. H. Cole, *The Meaning of Marxism** (1948), offers one of many keys to an understanding of Marxist theory. G. Lichtheim, *Marxism** (1961), is an important contribution. See also B. D. Wolfe, *Marxism: One Hundred Years in the Life of a Doctrine* (1965), and S. Avineri, *The Social and Political Thought of Karl Marx* (1969). There are numerous biographies of Marx, some favorable, like F. Mehring, *Karl Marx: The Story of His Life* (1936), and others hostile, like L. Schwarzschild, *The Red Prussian: The Life and Legend of Karl Marx** (1947). A balanced treatment is I. Berlin, *Karl Marx: His Life and Environment** (1963). J. Seigel, *Marx's Fate: The Shape of a Life* (1978) is excellent. The role of Engels in the genesis of Marxian socialism is emphasized by G. Mayer, *Friedrich Engels* (1935). For a discussion of anarchism, see two excellent biographies of its founders: D. W. Brogan, *Proudhon* (1934), and E. H. Carr, *Michael Bakunin** (1937). J. Joll, *The Anarchists** (1965), deals mainly with the later activities of the anarchists.

26 A New Balance of Power, 1850–1871

The main concern of European statesmen in the first half of the nineteenth century had been to reconcile the traditional claims of the old monarchical and aristocratic order with the democratic demands of the rising middle and lower classes. By 1850 the middle class had won some notable victories in western Europe, but east of the Rhine, the Old Regime had stood its ground. In the past, the defenders of the old order and the advocates of the new had been divided along ideological lines, as conservatives tried to maintain the status quo and liberals hoped to change it. The men who rose to leadership after 1850 were more flexible. They were realists, ready to forgo some of their principles to achieve some of their aims. Demands for political reform continued; however the unprecedented economic growth of Europe helped divert the attention of the middle class from politics to economics.

Besides economics there was nationalism to absorb people's attention. Before 1850, domestic upheavals and international peace had been the order of the day; after 1850, the reverse was true. Five wars involving great powers were fought between 1854 and 1871, all of them prompted by nationalism. In the past, whenever the status quo reached at Vienna had been threatened or actually changed, the "Concert of Europe" had collaborated to see that peace was restored and the balance of power maintained. With the rise of nationalism, however, the European concert became more tenuous. Even before 1850 the powers had failed to agree on certain international issues. But it was not until after 1850 that the first major showdown occurred. The Crimean War (1854–55) was the first in a whole series of conflicts that put at least a temporary end to the Concert of Europe. By 1871, a new balance of power had emerged on the Continent, significantly different from the balance that had existed twenty years earlier.

THE EASTERN QUESTION

The Crimean War was the culmination of the latent crisis caused by the slow disintegration of Turkish rule in the Balkans.

The "Eastern Question" had already caused one brief war between Russia and Turkey in 1828–29. To ensure year-round navigation, Russia depended on free access to the Black Sea through the Turkish Straits. This it had gained for its merchant ships in 1774, and again in the Treaty of Adrianople (1829). Attempts to gain exclusive passage for Russian warships, however, had run into opposition from the rest of the powers, since such an arrangement would have guaranteed Russian predominance in the Black Sea and the passage of Russian warships into the Mediterranean. Instead the Straits Convention of 1841 affirmed the closure of the Straits to *all* foreign warships.

The Straits were not the only issue involved in the Eastern Question. Both France and Great Britain had considerable commercial interests in the Near East, and the British regarded the eastern Mediterranean as the chief approach to India. These interests, the western powers felt, were threatened by Russia's gradual encroachment on Turkey, as evidenced in its occupation of the Danubian principalities of Moldavia and Wallachia after 1829. While Russia was thus threatening to change the status quo in the Ottoman Empire, France and England hoped to maintain it.

Another source of friction, which was the immediate cause for the Crimean War, concerned the so-called Holy Places in Jerusalem and Palestine that were closely associated with the life of Christ. Christians within the Ottoman Empire had long been guaranteed certain rights by their Turkish masters, and foreign pilgrims had been granted access to the Holy Land. The interests of the western Christians were traditionally championed by France, while Russia considered itself the guardian of eastern, Greek Orthodox rights. Shortly after 1850, when conflicts between the two religious groups led to a number of incidents, the tsar tried to pressure Turkey into officially recognizing Russia's role as protector of Greek Orthodox rights in Turkey. In order to emphasize their own interests, Britain and France sent naval contingents to the entrance of the Straits in 1853. Russia replied by reoccupying the Danubian principalities that it had evacuated two years earlier. The Concert of Europe,

Opposite: *Napoleon III and Bismarck on the Morning after the Surrender of the French Army at Sedan,* by W. Camphausen.

595

A Consultation About the State of Turkey, a mid–nineteenth-century cartoon. The "Sick Man of Europe" (Turkey) is threatened by Death (Russia), while the physicians (France and England) hold their consultation.

later brought the western powers into the war on Turkey's side. For the first time in forty years, the great powers had become involved in war with each other.

The Crimean War and the Peace of Paris

The major action of the Crimean War was a year-long siege against the Russian stronghold of Sebastopol on the Crimean Peninsula. It was one of history's costliest operations, with most of the casualties caused by disease. One of its few positive effects was the creation of the first modern nursing and medical services under the direction of Florence Nightingale, from which ultimately arose the International Red Cross.

The Crimean War lined up most of the European powers against the Russians. As the war progressed, Austria drew closer to the western powers and finally concluded an alliance with them. Austria never did any actual fighting, but even so the Russians resented its "ingratitude" for the aid Nicholas I had given the Austrians during the Hungarian uprising in 1849. Prussia outwardly followed Austria's lead but actually maintained a friendly neutrality and secretly aided the Russian cause. The small kingdom of Piedmont-Sardinia also entered the war on the side of the western powers, hoping to gain as a reward their support of Italian unification.

After eleven months of siege, the fortress of Sebastopol fell in September 1855. Nicholas I had died in March, and his successor, Alexander II, was now ready to talk peace. The Paris Peace Conference met in the spring of 1856. To curtail Russian influence over the area adjacent to the Ottoman Empire, the Black Sea was neutralized, which meant that Russia could not have any warships or fortifications there. In addition, navigation on the Danube River was declared free and open to all powers, and Russia had to surrender part of Bessarabia at the mouth of the Danube to the Turkish principality of Moldavia.

The Paris Conference also discussed the future of the Danubian principalities. Moldavia and Wallachia, it was decided, were to be under the temporary supervi-

acting on Austrian initiative, vainly tried to keep tension from mounting. In October 1853 Turkey, trusting in British and French support, declared war on Russia. Pressure of public opinion and concern over the expansion of Russian influence

Florence Nightingale (1820–1910).

sion of the great powers. Each principality was given a separate government. This, however, failed to satisfy the national aspirations of the Rumanians, who made up most of the population of the two regions. In 1858, therefore, both principalities elected the same man, Prince Alexander Cuza, as their ruler. After further consolidation of their common institutions, the principalities were finally recognized by the great powers in 1862 as the single and autonomous state of Rumania. The principle of nationality had triumphed once again.

Among the other decisions of the Paris Conference was the formal admission of Turkey to the family of powers, upon promise that it would introduce much-needed reforms. The Conference also issued a declaration against privateering and specified that a blockade, to be effective, had to be backed by force. This principle of the "freedom of the seas" was intended to safeguard the rights of neutral countries in time of war. Finally, the Conference took notice, at least, of the "Italian Question" by permitting Cavour, the prime minister of Piedmont, to plead the cause of Italian unification before the assembled dignitaries.

The Peace of Paris, like the Vienna settlement forty years earlier, was an effort by the great powers to remove the sources of tension that had led to war and to restore the balance of power that had been threatened by one of them. But while the Vienna settlement had succeeded in restoring international stability, the Paris settlement left a legacy of unresolved tensions. The Russians, in particular, felt humiliated, and henceforth would try to recoup the losses they had suffered in the Crimean War. The French, having won an important victory, took pride in the fact that their emperor had emerged as the leading figure at the Paris Peace Conference. But Napoleon III's role as arbiter of Europe merely whetted his appetite for further foreign ventures, and he was soon to come up with new plans for revising the map of Europe. Furthermore, the fact that Cavour had been permitted to raise the question of Italy's future at the conference gave fresh hope to Italian national-

Participants in the Paris Peace Conference (1856). Seated: Baron Hübner (Austria), Ali Pasha (Turkey), Lord Clarendon (Britain), Count Walewski (France), Count Orlov (Russia), Baron de Bourqueney (France), and Lord Cowley (Britain). Standing: Count Cavour (Sardinia), De Villamarina (Sardinia), Count Hatzfeldt (Prussia), Count Vincent Benedetti (France), Mohammed Jemil Bey (Turkey), Baron Brunnov (Russia), Baron Manteuffel (Prussia), and Count Buol (Austria).

ists, whose aspirations could be fulfilled only by war against Austria.

Other than Russia, the country most seriously affected by the Crimean War was Austria. Austria had been seriously weakened not only by its estrangement from Russia but from Prussia as well. The latter, already restive under the domination that Austria had resumed in German affairs after 1850, was further alienated by Austria's attempts to involve the two leading German powers in the Crimean War. This isolation of Austria from its two traditional friends, Russia and Prussia, was perhaps the most significant result of the war. It was the more ominous because England, having learned a bitter lesson at Sebastopol, once more withdrew from continental affairs. Austria was thus left alone at the mercy of Italian and German national-

ism. The stage had been set for one of the most dramatic periods in European history. The tragic hero of this drama was the French Emperor, Napoleon III.

THE SECOND FRENCH EMPIRE

Napoleon III remains very much an enigma. After his fall from power in 1870, there was little doubt in anyone's mind that he was a fraud and a failure. More recently, however, historians have become somewhat more charitable in their judgment. In his domestic policy, Napoleon III gave France some of the best years in its history. And if in his foreign policy he showed an unerring instinct for doing the wrong thing, his motives were idealistic, and many of his reverses were due to forces over which he had no control.

Louis Napoleon became emperor by a cleverly managed *coup d'état*. Like most countries after 1848, the Second French Republic experienced a wave of reaction. Socialists were ejected from the legislature, the right to vote was curtailed, public meetings were restricted, and the freedom of the press was curbed. At the same time, however, France's new president, Louis Napoleon, was eager to gain the support of the French masses. In pursuit of this aim, he dissolved the Assembly in December 1851 and called for new presidential elections. There was some street fighting, but his *coup* succeeded. The French people once again endorsed the name Napoleon by a vast majority. A year later, the president finished his overthrow of the Republic by proclaiming himself Emperor of the French, thus pursuing further the historical parallel between himself and his uncle.

The analogy was carried still further in the Empire's political institutions, which closely followed those of the first Napoleon. There were two parliamentary bodies—an appointive senate and a legislature elected by universal male suffrage—both of which could merely discuss what the emperor saw fit to put before them. By carefully managing elections, furthermore, Napoleon was always

| 1804 | 1814 | 1830 | 1848 | 1852 | 1860 | 1870 |

| First Empire | Bourbon Restoration | "July Monarchy" | Second Republic | Second Empire (Authoritarian) | Second Empire (Liberal) |

in a position to command a parliamentary majority. Most major decisions were reached by the emperor himself in consultation with a Council of State made up of experts with purely advisory functions. The Second Empire, at least during its first ten years, was little more than a thinly disguised dictatorship.

The "Authoritarian Empire"

The authoritarian phase of Napoleon's rule was a period of relative content. The emperor gave his countrymen what they wanted most—prosperity at home and glory abroad. Like most dictators, Napoleon III tried to do something for everyone. The peasants, who had voted him into office and who continued to endorse his policy in numerous plebiscites, were helped by large-scale public works and improved credit facilities. The workers, who continued to remain cool to the new regime, were aided by social legislation and public housing. But the class with which Napoleon's relations were most harmonious, at least in times of prosperity, was the industrial and commercial middle class.

More than any other statesman of his time, the Emperor of the French realized the importance and implications of modern industrialization, and he did his best to create conditions favorable to industrial growth. French railway mileage during the 1850s alone increased more than fivefold. A French law of 1863 permitted the formation of "limited liability" companies which made investment less risky and thus attracted the savings of the proverbially thrifty Frenchman. In a series of commercial agreements, notably the Cobden-Chevalier treaty (1860) with England, Napoleon abandoned the traditional protectionism of France in favor of moderate free trade. As a result, French exports soon exceeded imports. France in 1870 was still the chief industrial com-

Napoleon III, in the uniform of a major general (*ca.* 1860).

petitor of Great Britain. French industrial expansion had some negative aspects as well. There was an air of gaudiness and vulgarity about the newly enriched middle class. Speculation and overexpansion led to periodic economic crises. But on the whole the new prosperity was sound and was shared by all classes.

As a symbol of the Empire's prosperity and splendor, Napoleon was instrumental in having the city of Paris transformed into the beautiful work of art it remains to the present day. The center of the city was completely rebuilt, with wide boulevards, stately squares, and lovely parks. Like so many of Napoleon's projects, this "urban renewal program" served a dual purpose. By providing employment and eradicating ugly slums, it aided the workers; but at the same time it did away with the breeding-grounds of radicalism and revolution. The wide avenues of the new city were unsuitable for erecting barricades, and they permitted the use of cavalry and artillery in case there should ever be another popular uprising.

The Second Empire came to an end on the battlefield in 1870. Before that time, however, domestic discontent had already forced Napoleon to abandon many of the authoritarian practices of his earlier years. Most of this discontent was provoked by his blundering foreign policy. The French people were not opposed to war, so long as they won. France's involvement in the Crimean War had been popular, and the same was true of a number of small colonial ventures. The occupation of Algeria was completed; new French settlements were established in West Africa; New Caledonia was occupied in 1853; and during the 1860s protectorates were secured over Cambodia and the region later called French Indochina. The French participation in the wars of Italian unification, on the other hand, while it brought some mili-

tary glory and new territory, was deeply resented by French Catholics, since it deprived the papacy of its territorial holdings. Still more disastrous in French eyes were Napoleon's futile efforts, between 1862 and 1867, to establish a French protectorate over Mexico (see p. 628). The crowning blow to Napoleon's prestige, however, came when he failed to secure territorial compensations for France during Prussia's unification of Germany (see p. 609).

The "Liberal Empire"

To pacify the growing domestic opposition, Napoleon, during the 1860s, attempted a gradual liberalization of French political life. The "Liberal Empire" was initiated in 1860, when restrictions on debate in the legislative body were lifted and parliamentary proceedings were made public. Subsequent decrees extended the powers of the legislature and relaxed the restrictions on public meetings and the press that had existed since 1852. But these concessions only helped to swell the ranks of the opposition. By 1869 the government had so lost its grip that the parliamentary elections of that year returned ninety-three opposition candidates, thirty of whom were republicans. With labor unrest prompting a growing epidemic of strikes, and with the republican program of Léon Gambetta gaining more and more adherents, the government made some sweeping last-minute efforts to save its life. In their totality, these reforms amounted to the establishment of a parliamentary regime. In May 1870 the French electorate endorsed these constitutional changes with a rousing majority. But it was too late. Two months later the war with Prussia broke out, sweeping away the Empire and bringing in the Third Republic.

THE UNIFICATION OF ITALY

The domestic events in France must be viewed against the background of Napoleon's foreign policy. He had two main motives: to gain glory for France and to win freedom for suppressed nationalities. It was the conflict between the selfishness and the altruism, the realism and the idealism, inherent in these aims that accounts for much of the fateful vacillation in Napoleon's policy. The vacillation first manifested itself in his dealings with Italy.

Italy After 1848

As a result of the abortive revolutions of 1848, unification under the leadership of the kingdom of Piedmont-Sardinia had emerged as the most feasible scheme for Italy. The king of Piedmont, Victor Emmanuel II, had been unique in not revoking the liberal constitution granted during the revolution. He did not relent, furthermore, in his hostile policy toward Austria. Turin, the capital of Piedmont, soon became a haven for Italian patriots from all over the peninsula trying to escape the persecutions of their reactionary, pro-Austrian rulers.

The man who realized the unique position of Piedmont and used it to bring about the unification of Italy was Count Camillo di Cavour. At the age of forty, in 1850, Cavour was appointed minister of agriculture and commerce, and in 1852 he became prime minister. Cavour at first was not so much interested in uniting the whole of Italy as he was in extending the power of Piedmont in the north. This, he realized, could be done only against the opposition and at the expense of Austria. To prepare for a showdown with Austria thus became one of his major concerns.

Before Austria could be tackled, however, several things were needed. The first was to create sympathy for the "Italian Question" outside Italy. This was done by having Piedmontese troops participate in the Crimean War and by having the Italian problem discussed by the powers at the Paris Peace Conference. A second prerequisite for a successful war against Austria was the military and economic strengthening of

A Paris boulevard (1860). Detail of one part of a stereographic pair on glass, showing the results of Napoleon III's "urban renewal" program.

Count Camillo di Cavour (1810–61).

Piedmont. Cavour did his best to improve the armed forces and to further the building of railroads, of whose strategic importance he was very much aware. In a number of commercial treaties, Cavour integrated the economy of Piedmont with that of western Europe. He also fostered legislation improving the structure of business corporations, credit institutions, and cooperative societies. These economic measures alone entitle Cavour to a place of honor in his country's history.

Cavour and Napoleon III

The third requirement for Piedmont to be able to move against Austria was outside military aid. To get such aid, Cavour looked to Napoleon III. The French emperor had always held a lingering affection for Italy. To aid Italian unification not only appealed to his idealism but it also would strengthen the prestige of France and of himself. It was

considerations like these that led to a super-secret meeting at Plombières in 1858 at which Napoleon promised Cavour his aid in a war between Piedmont and Austria. If victorious, Piedmont would form an enlarged kingdom of Upper Italy, and the whole peninsula was then to be united in a loose federation with the pope as president. France was to be rewarded for its help with the Piedmontese regions of Nice and Savoy. The Plombières agreement did not call for an Italy united under Piedmont.

While trying to find a pretext for war with Austria, the two conspirators continued their preparations. As rumors of an impending war in Italy grew more persistent, the other powers began to show concern. Austria was the least worried. The Austrians were used to recurrent rumors of an Italian war and refused to take them seriously. England and Prussia, on the other hand, were less confident. The former, in the spring of 1859, proposed the evacuation of Austrian troops from the peninsula and the creation of an Italian federation. This was such an appealing scheme that Napoleon began to show signs of trying to back out of his agreement with Piedmont. At this point, when Cavour's carefully laid plans seemed about to fail, the Austrian emperor, Francis Joseph, forced a showdown by demanding that Piedmont demobilize its forces. When Piedmont turned down this ultimatum, Austrian troops, on April 29, 1859, invaded Piedmont. France thereupon joined its ally in the war against Austria.

The War of 1859

Had the Austrians moved quickly, they might have won the war. But by wasting time, they allowed the French to move their forces into Italy. After six weeks of bloody fighting, the French and Italian armies had won two indecisive victories at Magenta and Solferino and had driven the Austrians out of Lombardy. The next obvious step was the liberation of Venetia.

At this point, in July 1859, Napoleon surprised his ally and the world by concluding an armistice with Francis Joseph at Villafranca. There were several reasons

THE UNIFICATION OF ITALY   1859–70

Piedmont-Sardinia on the eve of war in 1859

Acquired in 1859 through war with Austria

Additions in 1860

Addition in 1866

Addition in 1870

SAVOY

LOMBARDY

PIEDMONT

Magenta
Milan
Solferino
Custozza

VENETIA

Venice

To France 1860

Turin

Po R.

PARMA

NICE

Genoa

MODENA

ROMAGNA

Villafranca

KINGDOM OF SARDINIA

LUCCA

Florence

TUSCANY

MARCHES

ADRIATIC SEA

CORSICA

UMBRIA

PAPAL STATES

Tiber R.

Rome
ROME

Naples

TYRRHENIAN SEA

SARDINIA

KINGDOM OF THE TWO SICILIES

Palermo

Messina

MILES
0   300

for Napoleon's sudden defection: he apparently had been shocked by the bloodshed at Magenta and Solferino; the Austrian army was by no means beaten; there was dissatisfaction among many Frenchmen with a war against another Catholic power; and there was some fear that Prussia might come to Austria's aid. Under the terms of the Villafranca agreement, Napoleon broke his promise that Piedmont should get both Lombardy and Venetia. Austria merely surrendered Lombardy, which Napoleon then offered to Victor Emmanuel. The king, much to Cavour's consternation, accepted.

The First Phase of Italian Unification

Villafranca, however, turned out to be a blessing in disguise for the Italians. Up to this point the war had been waged chiefly for the enlargement of Piedmont. Now suddenly it became a national war for Italian unification. At the start of the war, some of the small states in northern and central Italy had revolted and driven out their rulers. The prospect of their return now led the populace of these regions to raise an army and to proclaim their union with Piedmont. Cavour, in January 1860, asked Napoleon's consent to Piedmont's annexation of the central Italian states. Napoleon agreed, in return for the surrender of Nice and Savoy, which he had been promised at Plombières but which he had forfeited at Villafranca. In March 1860, plebiscites in Parma, Modena, Romagna, and Tuscany confirmed the union of central Italy with Piedmont.

The next act in the drama of unification was dominated not by Cavour but by a man who was his opposite in all respects—a romantic, a republican, a superb military leader, but a complete political amateur—Giuseppe Garibaldi. In May 1860, Garibaldi assembled an expeditionary force at Genoa. Its task was to help complete the liberation of the Kingdom of the Two Sicilies, where an uprising against the reactionary Bourbon regime was under way. Garibaldi's expedition was a huge success. Aided by the local population, his small force of "Redshirts" defeated an army twenty

times its size. By August Sicily was in Garibaldi's hands, and he was ready to cross to the mainland.

Garibaldi's success, however, raised a number of problems. His growing popularity threatened to displace Victor Emmanuel as the leader of a united Italy. Garibaldi might give in to the urgings of Mazzini and surrender the southern half of the peninsula to republicanism; or else he might move against Rome, to complete the unification of Italy. Such a move might lead to a conflict with France, which still considered itself the protector of the papacy. To avert such a crisis, Cavour convinced Napoleon that the only way to stop Garibaldi was for Victor Emmanuel to meet him on the way. Promising to respect the independence of Rome itself, the Piedmontese army now invaded the Papal States, defeated the papal forces, and after bypassing Rome came face to face with Garibaldi's band not far from Naples. The situation was tense. But Garibaldi was too much of a patriot to let selfish ambitions interfere with his hope for a united Italy. Instead, he voluntarily submitted to Victor Emmanuel, thus completing the first phase of Italian unification.

The Kingdom of Italy

The Kingdom of Italy was proclaimed in March 1861. Two months later, Cavour succumbed to an attack of typhoid fever and died, just as his country needed him most. The unification of Italy was by no means completed. Venetia did not become part of the kingdom until after another Austrian defeat, this time by Prussia in 1866; and Rome remained in papal hands until 1870. Other difficulties beset the new state. Not all Italians were happy with the results of unification. The followers of Mazzini would have preferred a republic to a monarchy, and even many monarchists would rather have seen a loosely federated union than the centralized monarchy that resulted from the "conquest" of the peninsula by Piedmont. Regionalism and particularism also interfered with the integration of the eight or more separate states. Tensions between the prosperous north and the poverty-ridden south were especially

Giuseppe Garibaldi (1807–82).

Victor Emmanuel II, king of Italy (1849–78).

marked. The illiteracy of the Italian masses, furthermore, made the extension of democracy a slow process, and Italy's parliamentary regime soon became known for its corruption. The wars of unification imposed staggering financial burdens, and taxes now were higher than ever before. At the same time, lack of coal and iron prevented large-scale industrialization, which might have relieved Italy's economic plight. Yet despite these shortcomings, the new Italy considered itself one of the great powers and tried to imitate the wealthier nations by maintaining an army and navy far beyond its means.

Much of the discontent and disillusionment in Italy after unification was blamed on Cavour's hurried policy. But we must remember that the unification of Italy had not really been his goal at the start. Much of his policy was determined by the other two makers of Italy, Napoleon III and Garibaldi, and by the forces of nationalism, which he could not control. Where we may find fault with Cavour is in the devious methods he employed to achieve his aims. But such *Realpolitik*, as it came to be called, was not considered out of place by an age that gloried in nationalism and worshiped success. Much the same spirit that animated Cavour was to guide Bismarck in his German policy. And just as Cavour had started out in the hope of enlarging Piedmont but ended by creating the Kingdom of Italy, so Bismarck began working for a greater Prussia and wound up with a German Reich.

AUSTRO-PRUSSIAN RIVALRY

The most striking similarity between the unification of Italy and that of Germany was Austria's involvement in both. Austria's defeats in 1859 and 1866 were due in large measure to internal weakness caused by political disunity. Nationalism, which proved a boon to Cavour and Bismarck, was a source of infinite trouble to Francis Joseph and the many capable Austrian ministers who tried to find some way of keeping their empire from falling to pieces.

Francis Joseph I (1830–1916), emperor of Austria and king of Hungary.

Nationalism in the Austrian Empire

Prince Schwarzenberg, who had succeeded Metternich in 1848, had given Austria a constitution early in 1849. While calling for a high degree of centralization, it had recognized at least some local and provincial privileges. These mild concessions to the spirit of nationalism, however, were only temporary. Beginning in 1850, all but the centralizing tendencies of the constitution were ignored. Schwarzenberg died in 1852, but his policies were continued. Petty officials, most of them German, directed the affairs of provinces whose language they did not speak and whose customs they ignored. Yet instead of counteracting the centrifugal tendencies of nationalism, this system merely increased the tension between the German ruling caste and the subject peoples.

Austria's defeat at the hands of France and Piedmont in 1859 once again brought home the need for reform. As a result, the excessive centralization of the preceding decade now gave way to some degree of provincial autonomy. In 1861 a new constitution established a central legislature, the *Reichsrat*, made up of delegates from the various regional diets. But the new system, like all earlier ones, had serious flaws. Since the German element was still guaranteed a majority, some of the other nationalities, especially the Hungarians (or Magyars), refused to attend the meetings of the *Reichsrat*. It soon became clear that another effort at solving the nationalities problem had failed. In September 1865 Francis Joseph suspended the constitution of 1861.

At this point the war with Prussia intervened, leaving Austria still weaker and less able to resist the demands of the Hungarian nationalists. As a result of extended negotiations between Austrian and Hungarian leaders, a compromise, or *Ausgleich*, was finally reached in 1867. Under the new arrangement a Dual Monarchy was established, with Francis Joseph serving both as emperor of Austria and king of Hungary. Except in such fields as finance, foreign affairs, and war, where joint ministries were set up, the two parts of the monarchy now were entirely autonomous. Yet since neither the Germans nor the Hungarians held a majority in either half of the Dual Monarchy, the *Ausgleich* did not solve the nationalities problem. Subsequent efforts to recognize the Slavic regions by establishing a Triple Monarchy were defeated by opposition from Germans and Hungarians alike. This continued oppression of Slavic nationalism constituted a major threat to the existence of Austria-Hungary and to the peace of Europe.

Prussia After 1850

Prussia presented quite a different picture from Austria. In administrative efficiency, financial soundness, and military strength, Prussia after 1850 was far superior to its Austrian rival. Except for a small Polish minority in the eastern provinces, its population was homogeneous. And while in Austria industrialization had hardly begun, Prussia during the 1850s began to take its place among the leading industrial powers of the Continent.

Like Austria, Prussia had been granted a constitution in 1849. Since it provided for universal suffrage, it had a deceptively democratic appearance. But by dividing the electorate into three classes, according to the taxes each voter paid, the Prussian constitution made certain that the wealthiest citizens controlled a majority in the lower house of the *Landtag*. With this constitutional arrangement it was not surprising that Prussia continued to be one of the most reactionary states in Germany. In 1857 King Frederick William IV was succeeded by his brother, Prince William, first as regent and in 1861 as king. William was sixty-two years old and an arch-conservative. Having spent most of his life in the army, he had little experience in government. It was due to William's concern over the shortcomings of Prussia's military establishment that Prussia, in 1860, entered upon one of the most serious domestic crises in its history.

Despite a considerable increase in population, Prussia's armed forces in 1860 were still essentially what they had been in 1814. When William tried to correct this situation, however, he ran into opposition from the liberal majority in the *Landtag*, which, under the constitution, had to authorize the necessary funds and which objected to some of the details of the government's reform proposals. By 1862 king and parliament had become deadlocked over the issue. At this point William decided to recall his ambassador to Paris, Otto von Bismarck, and charge him with carrying on the fight with the *Landtag*.

Bismarck and the Constitutional Conflict

The man who was soon to direct the affairs of Germany as first chancellor of the German Reich was then forty-seven years old. He came from an old Prussian family of noble landowners, or Junkers. During the revolution of 1848 he had proved himself a devoted royalist. As a reward he had been appointed Prussia's representative to the Frankfurt Diet during the 1850s and later ambassador to St. Petersburg and Paris. In these various assignments he had shown outstanding ability as a diplomat and as a manipulator of men. But he was also known as a fighter. It was this combination that had recommended him to William I.

Bismarck first tried to mediate the conflict between king and parliament. When this proved impossible, he carried out the proposed army reforms without parliamentary approval. The conflict was never resolved but was ultimately overshadowed by more spectacular events. Two wars, in 1864 and 1866, not only gave proof of the excellence of Prussia's reformed army but so aroused the patriotism of the *Landtag* delegates that they were ready to forget their liberal principles. When, during the war with Austria in 1866, Bismarck asked parliament for retroactive assent to the unauthorized expenditures of the previous years, the majority of delegates supported him.

The Prussian constitutional conflict had thus been "solved." But in the process, Prussian and German liberalism had suffered a serious defeat. Liberals in Germany henceforth were split in two factions—a larger one that continued to support Bismarck, putting nationalism

Prince Otto von Bismarck (1815–98).

above liberalism, and a smaller faction that stuck to its liberal principles. This split within German liberalism was never healed. It was the most fateful legacy of the period of German unification.

Rivalry Between Austria and Prussia

Bismarck did not really plan the unification of Germany; it developed more or less accidentally out of Prussia's desire to assert itself against Austria's claims for supremacy in German affairs. The rivalry between Austria and Prussia was of long standing—it went back at least to the days of Frederick the Great and Maria Theresa in the eighteenth century (see p. 507). During most of the intervening period, Prussia had been quite ready to recognize Austria's traditional leadership. The most recent manifestation of Prussia's subjection to Austria had occurred in 1850, when Austria had prevented a scheme advanced by Frederick William IV for a union of German princes under Prussian leadership.

Bismarck, as Prussia's delegate to the Frankfurt Diet, did not object to Austria's leadership in German affairs so long as Austria, in return, recognized Prussia's preeminence in northern Germany. Only after Bismarck realized Austria's unwillingness to cooperate did he decide that the interest of Prussia demanded that Austria be excluded from Germany. Before Prussia could assume leadership in Germany, however, it had to make sure of the good will, or at least the acquiescence, of the great powers. The Italian national movement had enjoyed the sympathy of almost everyone outside Austria, but few people in western Europe wanted to see a Germany united under Prussian auspices. During the Crimean War, Austria had tried to induce Prussia to join in aiding the western powers, but Prussia had remained friendly toward Russia. This was the basis for a close friendship between Prussia and Russia that was to remain a constant element in international affairs for the next few decades.

The first outward sign of Prussia's emancipation from Austrian tutelage came during the Italian war of 1859. Austria at the time fully expected Prussia to be its ally against Piedmont and France. Prussia was ready to comply, but asked to be put in charge of its own and whatever other German forces might be raised. Austria, still filled with its own importance, refused this understandable request. Prussia's neutrality during the war won the gratitude of both France and Italy. Austria's defeat, on the other hand,

---

Principles of "Realpolitik"

The state is by nature a realistic politician, if only by virtue of the conditions of its existence, and has therefore always had to suffer being treated as a criminal by political idealists and visionaries. . . . In contrast to the politics of the state, the politics of the people is most susceptible to idealism and fantastication. The causes of this difference are obvious. On the one hand we have the school of political life and the consciousness of responsibility, on the other hand inexperience and yielding to intellectual or emotional whim with little or no thought for the consequences. . . .

For the state, in contrast to the individual, self-preservation is the supreme law. The state must survive at any price; it cannot go into the poorhouse, it cannot beg, it cannot commit suicide; in short, it must take wherever it can find the essentials of life.

Politics, in so far as they are not in the hands of the community, are a mandate which carries responsibility toward the constituency as well as toward the moral law, two responsibilities which need to be weighed against one another.

The right of the politician to sacrifice the welfare of the state to his personal scruples of conscience may be undeniable in simple matters or those of secondary significance, but it may be extremely doubtful in difficult and important cases.

The clash of duties, which the individual can as a rule easily avoid, occurs so often, so unavoidably, and so fatefully in the life of the state that politics is often a matter of choice between two moral evils.

Finally, there occur historic necessities and political acts of nature before which the state and the people resign themselves irresistibly and passively, and to which, therefore, the ethical criterion of human conduct is quite inapplicable. . . .

From A. L. von Rochau, *Grundsätze der Realpolitik* (1869), as quoted in W. M. Simon, *Germany in the Age of Bismarck* (New York: Barnes and Noble, 1968), pp. 133–34.

clearly showed how much its claim to leadership was based on past prestige rather than present power.

By the end of the 1850s most German liberals were expecting Prussia to take the lead in unifying Germany. The constitutional struggle over the reform of the Prussian army, however, put a temporary damper on their enthusiasm. At the same time, the Austrian constitution of 1861 seemed to indicate more liberal tendencies in the Habsburg Empire. It thus encouraged the Catholic and traditionalist forces, especially in southern Germany, who hoped for a united Germany under Austrian leadership. To take advantage of this shift in opinion, Austria convened a congress in 1863 to consider the reform of the German Confederation in the direction of greater national unity. But Bismarck urged his king to boycott the congress. Without Prussia, the Frankfurt meeting was doomed to failure.

The Schleswig-Holstein Question and the War with Denmark

The final showdown between Austria and Prussia grew out of their involvement with the two northern German duchies of Schleswig and Holstein. The Schleswig-Holstein question is famous for its intricacy, and its details need not concern us here. The duchies, largely German but partly Danish, had long been held in personal union by the king of Denmark. In an age of rising nationalism, however, this indeterminate status became increasingly difficult to maintain. The issue had already led to a brief war between Danes and Germans in 1848, in which Denmark had been defeated. The problem became acute again in 1863, when Denmark tried to annex Schleswig. This time both Austria and Prussia rushed to the defense. Both wanted to pose as defenders of German unity, but Prussia also wanted to expand its power in northern Germany.

The war itself was brief and the Danes suffered a crushing defeat. Under the Peace of Vienna in 1864 Denmark surrendered Schleswig and Holstein to Austria and Prussia. In this joint possession of the duchies lay the seeds of the

war between Austria and Prussia two years later. Austria and most of the German states wanted the duchies to go to a German claimant, the Duke of Augustenburg; but Bismarck wanted the duchies for Prussia. In 1865 the victors reached a temporary compromise in the Convention of Gastein, under which Prussia was to administer Schleswig and Austria Holstein, while the future of the duchies was to remain a joint responsibility. But as Austria continued to encourage the aspirations of the Duke of Augustenburg, and as Prussia proceeded to make itself at home in Schleswig, it became clear that compromise was impossible.

The War of 1866

In the fall of 1865, Bismarck met Napoleon III at Biarritz to sound him out on France's attitude toward a possible war between Prussia and Austria. The meeting suggests a certain parallel to the Plombières meeting of Cavour and Napoleon, except that Bismarck was not asking for French aid; all he wanted was a promise of neutrality. This Napoleon gave, hinting at some unspecified compensations for France. Bismarck agreed. In the spring of 1866, Prussia concluded an alliance with Italy, to which Napoleon also gave his blessing. The remaining great powers did not present much of a problem. Since England had stood by while Denmark was defeated, Bismarck felt that it would not intervene to save Austria. And Russia's friendship for Prussia and its antagonism toward Austria left little doubt where it would stand.

With the diplomatic spadework done, Bismarck's next task was to find a cause for war with Austria that would rally the rest of Germany to Prussia's side. This was not easy, since most of the German princes sided with Austria on the future of Schleswig-Holstein. When Bismarck finally used Prussia's differences with Austria over the duchies as an excuse to order Prussian troops into Holstein, the remaining members of the German Confederation joined the Austrian side. The war of 1866 was thus not only a war of Prussia against Austria but against most of the rest of Germany as well.

A cartoon depicting the nature of the European balance of power.

There was little enthusiasm in either camp at the start. Austria was deeply divided and poorly prepared and was handicapped by having to fight on two fronts, Italy and Germany. The Prussians, on the other hand, were in excellent military form, equipped with the latest weapons and led by a master-strategist, Count Helmuth von Moltke. The war was over in a few weeks. It was decided almost entirely by one major battle, near Königgrätz and Sadowa, in Bohemia, in which the Austrians were defeated, though not annihilated.

The final peace treaty was signed at Prague in August 1866. Chiefly because of Bismarck's insistence, the settlement was remarkably lenient. Bismarck realized that the rest of the powers, especially France, would not stand for a punitive peace. Austria consented to the dissolution of the German Confederation and recognized the various territorial gains Prussia had made in the north, including Schleswig-Holstein. In a separate settlement Austria surrendered Venetia, which went to Italy. As for Austria's German allies, most of the northern ones were annexed by Prussia, while the southern ones had to pay indemnities and conclude military alliances with Prussia. Prussia thus consolidated its holdings in the north and assumed indirect control over the rest of Germany.

THE UNIFICATION OF GERMANY

The war of 1866 had been waged for the aggrandizement of Prussia. But in the minds of most Germans it soon appeared as a deliberate stage in the unification of Germany. During the winter of 1866/67, delegates from the states that were left in northern Germany after the peace settlement met in Berlin to form a North German Confederation. The plan had originated with Bismarck, whose aim was to establish Prussia's preponderance over the whole region north of the Main River.

THE UNIFICATION OF GERMANY   1866–71

Prussia to 1866

Annexed to Prussia in 1866

Areas joining Prussia in 1867 to form the North German Confederation

Areas added to the North German Confederation in 1871 to form the German Empire

0   MILES   100

The North German Confederation

The constitution of the North German Confederation established a federal system under which the central government controlled foreign and military affairs. The executive was vested in the king of Prussia as president, assisted by a chancellor—Bismarck. An upper house, or *Bundesrat*, consisted of delegates from the various member states. The lower house, or *Reichstag*, was made up of deputies elected by universal manhood suffrage. Most of the power was vested in the upper house, in which Prussian influence prevailed. There was no ministerial responsibility, since the only minister was the chancellor, and he was responsible only to the president, or king.

The main significance of the North German Confederation's constitution was that it served as a basis for the constitution of the German Empire after 1871. Just as it assured the domination of Prussia in northern Germany after 1867, so after 1871 it perpetuated Prussia's domination over the rest of Germany. How far Bismarck actually foresaw developments beyond 1867 is hard to say. He never was a German nationalist—his major concern was with the power and security of Prussia. Nor was there much desire among the rulers of southern Germany to submit to the king of Prussia. The state of affairs that existed in 1867, therefore, could have lasted for a long time had it not been for the unfortunate machinations of Napoleon III. Like his uncle, Napoleon served as the involuntary agent of German nationalism.

Bismarck and Napoleon III

Napoleon's readiness at Biarritz to let Prussia settle accounts with Austria had been due to his underestimation of Prussian strength. Thinking Prussia and Austria evenly matched, he had expected to throw French power into the balance at the crucial moment. Austria's defeat at Sadowa, therefore, had come as a shock. Together with France's fiasco in Mexico (see p. 628), the defeat of Austria was built up by Napoleon's domestic opponents as a major French defeat. The only way to save French prestige was through some kind of territorial compensations such as France had received during the unification of Italy.

Napoleon should have pressed his demands for compensations while the fate of Austria still hung in the balance. Once Prussia had won, Bismarck was no longer ready to make concessions. On the contrary, Napoleon's demands served Bismarck to good effect in furthering his own policy. He used Napoleon's bid for territories in the west or south of Germany to cement ties with the southern German states as the best possible protection against French designs; and he later used Napoleon's request for Prussian support in the acquisition of Belgium to incriminate France in the eyes of Great Britain. In a third attempt to gain territorial compensation, Napoleon tried to buy the Duchy of Luxembourg. Bismarck at first approved of the deal but later changed his mind.

Napoleon III, faced with mounting criticism at home and frustrated in his efforts to gather laurels abroad, gradually realized that an armed showdown with Prussia might be inevitable. To prepare himself, he began casting about for allies. But neither Austria nor Italy had any desire to become involved in a war between France and Prussia. Even so, Napoleon assumed that in case of a war with Prussia he could count on the aid of one or both of the Catholic powers.

The War of 1870

The immediate cause of the war between France and Prussia was the offer of the Spanish throne, temporarily vacated by revolution, to a Hohenzollern prince, distantly related to the king of Prussia. Bismarck was instrumental in having the prince accept the Spanish offer; yet when France protested the Spanish candidacy, the Prussian government urged the prince to abandon the project. But this did not satisfy the French, who demanded an apology from King William and a promise that the candidacy would not be renewed. This unreasonable demand was made in a famous interview between the French ambassador and the king at the watering place of Ems, an interview that William cut short. When news of this incident reached Berlin, Bismarck edited the report in such a way to make it look as though France had suffered a major diplomatic defeat. It was this edited "Ems dispatch" that led France to declare war on Prussia. In this case Bismarck had foreseen the results, and to that extent he may be held responsible for the war of 1870. Yet his action was merely the latest in a whole series of mutual recriminations, and most historians now agree that responsibility for the war must be shared by both sides.

Events in the early summer of 1870 had moved so quickly that all of Europe was taken by surprise. France's precipitate action lost whatever sympathy it had enjoyed among the other powers. England maintained the aloofness it had shown ever since the Crimean War. Russia continued its policy of benevolent neutrality toward Prussia. Italy was preoccupied with completing its unification by taking the city of Rome. And Austria would prove dangerous only if Prussia ran into difficulties. But there was little chance of that. In numbers, leadership, and morale, Prussia's forces were far superior to those of France. The participation of southern German contingents made this a national German war. The French army fought valiantly, but the quality and morale of its leadership was low. The fact that Napoleon III, worn out by a lingering illness, assumed personal command did not help matters.

The war itself was decided in a series of bloody battles. The climax came on September 2, with Napoleon's capitulation at Sedan. But the fighting continued for several more months, and the city of Paris, where a republic had been proclaimed, did not surrender until the end of January 1871. A temporary armistice was concluded on January 28, pending the election of a representative assembly. The National Assembly chose the liberal monarchist Adolphe Thiers as chief executive. The first task of the new government was to negotiate a final settlement with Bismarck.

The Results of the War

The peace signed at Frankfurt on May 10, 1871, was a harsh one. France had to pay an indemnity of 5 billion francs, and the country was to remain occupied until the indemnity had been paid. In addition, France had to cede Alsace and part of Lorraine, which, for the most part, it had taken from the Holy Roman Empire in the seventeenth century. The inhabitants of Alsace spoke German, but they were pro-French and anti-Prussian in feeling. To take so large a slice of territory in an age of ardent nationalism was a dangerous move. The issue of France's "lost provinces" remained an insuperable obstacle to closer Franco-German relations.

The signing of the peace did not end France's troubles. The new National Assembly had a majority of monarchists, so that the survival of the republic de-

---

Napoleon III Surrenders at Sedan

September 2, 1870

[Napoleon's aide-de-camp] approached His Majesty and, with a few words, handed him Napoleon's letter. The King opened it and read the short message written by the Emperor himself: "My dear Brother, not having been able to die amidst my troops, nothing remains for me but to surrender my sword into Your Majesty's hands. I remain, Your Majesty's good Brother, Napoleon. Sedan, 1 Sept. 1870." . . . Then the King first discussed with Count Bismarck, General Moltke, and myself the content of the letter he wished to send to Napoleon. . . . The letter, then written by His Majesty himself, ran as follows: "My dear Brother. While regretting the circumstances in which we meet, I accept Your Majesty's sword, and I ask that you would kindly appoint one of your officers, provided with your full powers, to negotiate the conditions for the capitulation of the army which has fought so bravely under your orders. For my part, I have designated General von Moltke for this purpose. I remain, Your Majesty's good Brother, William.—In front of Sedan, 1 September 1870." . . . [Next day, the two men met.] . . . The interview may have lasted for a good quarter of an hour, after which the King and Napoleon by his side stepped back into the reception hall, where the tall, commanding figure of our King appeared wonderfully exalted beside the small, very thick-set figure of the Emperor. When Napoleon saw me, he shook hands with me; heavy tears ran down his cheeks, which he wiped away with his hand, as he mentioned, with the utmost gratitude for both the words and the manner, the way in which His Majesty had just expressed himself. I told him that it was only natural to meet the unfortunate above all with compassion.

From the War Diary of the Prussian Crown Prince, as quoted in H. N. Weill, *European Diplomatic History, 1815–1914* (Jericho, N.Y.: Exposition Press, 1972), pp. 204–05.

pended on the continued split among the three monarchist factions—Bourbon, Orléanist, and Bonapartist. The republican minority had its main support in the city of Paris. It was here, in March 1871, that fear of a monarchist revival, indignation over a humiliating peace, and general misery resulting from the recent siege of the city led to a violent uprising. The Paris Commune, as the government of the insurgents was called, lasted until the end of May. Its aims, on the whole, were moderate. But the Commune also included some socialists. This fact, plus some of the excesses committed during the fighting against the troops of the National Assembly, did much to reawaken middle-class fear of a "red peril," of which the Commune remained the symbol. After their defeat in the final "Bloody Week" of May, thousands of Communards were executed, imprisoned, or deported. The issue of republic against monarchy continued to hang in the balance for some time.

While the siege of Paris was still under way, another important event had taken place. On January 18, 1871, in the Hall of Mirrors in the palace at Versailles, King William of Prussia was proclaimed German emperor. This ceremony was the climax of long negotiations between Bismarck and the rulers of southern Germany. There had been much hesitation among these Catholic and more liberal states to submit to a confederation dominated by Protestant and reactionary Prussia. Many conservative Prussians were equally hesitant, fearing that Prussia might lose its identity in the larger empire. Even Bismarck, the architect of unification, was not motivated by national enthusiasm. But by fulfilling the German people's dream for unity, he hoped to increase the power and prestige of his beloved Prussia.

The Franco-German War not only completed the unification of Germany; it ended the long struggle for Italian unity. After a plebiscite in October 1870, Rome was annexed to Italy and became Italy's capital. A subsequent effort to mollify the papacy by a generous Law of Papal Guarantees was turned down by the pope, who henceforth considered himself "the prisoner of the Vatican." This state of affairs remained unchanged until 1929, when the signing of the Lateran Treaty put an end to the feud.

The year 1871, like the year 1815, was a landmark in European history. Both years saw the end of a major war, and

French battery in front of Belfort (Alsace), which capitulated to the Germans on February 13, 1871, after a siege of 108 days.

Animated French map of Europe in 1870. A caption with it explains: "England, isolated, swears with rage and almost forgets Ireland, whom she holds on a leash. Spain frets, propped up by Portugal. France repulses the invasion of Prussia, who reaches with one hand for Holland and the other for Austria. Italy, also, says to Bismarck: 'Take your feet away from there.' Corsica and Sardinia, a regular urchin who laughs at it all. Denmark, who has lost his legs in Holstein, hopes to regain them. European Turkey yawns and wakes up. Asiatic Turkey inhales the smoke of her water pipe. Sweden leaps like a panther, and Russia resembles a bugbear out to fill his basket."

both initiated a long period of peace among the major powers. But this is about as far as the parallel goes. Relations among states in 1815 and after had still been conducted according to certain general rules. But the cynical diplomacy of Cavour, Napoleon III, and Bismarck had changed this. From now on, suspicion rather than trust characterized international dealings, and, though there was to be no major war for forty-three years, the threat of war was almost always present.

In 1815 the balance of power had been revived along traditional lines, but by 1871 an entirely new balance had emerged. Austria, Russia, Great Britain, and France had been the leading powers at Vienna, with Prussia lagging far behind and with Italy a mere "geographical expression." By 1871 that order had been thoroughly revised. Both Austria and France now were overshadowed by a Prussianized Germany, and even Italy demanded recognition as a great power. England and Russia continued in their former status; but while at Vienna they had taken an active part in shaping the affairs of the Continent, the balance of 1871 had been brought about without their participation. Here, perhaps, lies the major difference between 1815 and

1871. When Napoleon I had upset the balance of power, the Concert of Europe met at the Congress of Vienna to restore it. There was no such concert in 1871, and hence there was no congress. The Concert of Europe had gone to pieces over the Crimean War. Both Great Britain and Russia had kept out of the subsequent wars of Italian and German unification. It was the passivity of these peripheral powers, as much as the activities of Cavour, Bismarck, and Napoleon III, that helped to bring about the changed European balance of 1871.

ENGLAND'S "VICTORIAN COMPROMISE"

England had always maintained a certain isolation from the Continent, and it had added reason to do so after the middle of the nineteenth century. The British people did not remain immune from the virus of nationalism. But the Crimean War had brought home the futility of military involvement. And besides, it had brought defeat to Russia, whose advances in the eastern Mediterranean had presented the only real threat to British commerce.

| 1714 | 1727 | 1760 | | 1820 | 1830 | 1837 | | 1901 | 1910 | Edward VIII (abdicated) ↓ 1936 | 1952 |

| George I | George II | George III | Geo. IV | Wm. IV | Victoria | Ed-ward VII | George V | George VI | Eliz. II |

The ''Workshop of the World''

The twenty years after 1850 were the most prosperous in British history. While wars elsewhere helped retard economic development, Britain's industry and commerce experienced an unprecedented boom. This was the heyday of free trade, a policy from which Britain, as the most advanced industrial nation, profited most. The change in shipbuilding from wood to iron, furthermore, opened up a wholly new field for expansion. By 1870, Britain's carrying trade enjoyed a virtual monopoly. While British engineers were building railroads the world over, Britain's surplus capital sought outlets for investment on the Continent and overseas. Between 1854 and 1870, England's foreign holdings more than doubled.

Though Britain was reluctant to become involved in European politics, it showed no such hesitation overseas. (The next chapter has more to say on British colonial policy.) While in some parts of the British Empire, such as Canada and Australia, the basis for self-government was being laid, elsewhere, notably in India, Britain tightened its reins. In 1859 the rule of the East India Company was taken over by the British government. Commercial expansion in China, begun in the 1840s, made rapid advances in the late 1850s. The new Suez Canal, built by French interests, soon became a major artery for British commerce.

The Second Reform Bill

Britain's prosperity did not do away with political discontent. There had been no major political reforms since 1832. The Tories, now officially called Conservatives, had reluctantly acquiesced in the new conditions created by the Great Reform Bill; and the Whigs, now called Liberals, while favoring reforms in other fields, also considered the Reform Bill

EUROPE IN 1871

Caricature of William Gladstone in 1869, by "Ape" (Carlo Pellegrini).

This growth could not help but create a demand for further extension of the franchise. By the 1860s the need for reform could no longer be ignored. Both parties at the time had leaders ready to take charge of the contest over parliamentary reform. Since 1852 the Conservative Benjamin Disraeli and the Liberal William Gladstone had played important roles in cabinets of their respective parties. In 1866 Gladstone introduced a moderate reform bill that was promptly defeated by the Conservatives. An even more radical bill introduced the next year by Disraeli was passed, largely with Liberal support. The Second Reform Bill of 1867, by giving the vote to urban workers, doubled the number of voters. It did not introduce universal suffrage, but it did provide the majority of adult British males with a voice in their government.

Gladstone's First "Great Ministry"

The agitation surrounding the Second Reform Bill had ended the Victorian Compromise. Both Conservatives and Liberals now tightened their organizations and became parties in the modern sense. When the elections of 1868 returned a Liberal majority, Gladstone formed his first "great ministry." Just as the Bill of 1832 had been followed by a long series of domestic reforms, so the years after 1867 saw many overdue measures enacted. Notable among them was the Education Act of 1870, which, at long last, relieved a situation in which almost half of Britain's children had received no schooling.

One problem concerned Gladstone above all others—the problem of Ireland. That unhappy country, vastly overpopulated, had long been on the verge of starvation. Migration to the United States relieved some of the pressure but also added to unrest. The Fenian Brotherhood, founded in New York in 1858, was responsible for many acts of violence in England and Ireland. Gladstone considered the solution of the Irish problem his major mission. Its roots were partly religious, partly economic. To solve Ireland's religious grievances, the Disestablishment Act of 1869 freed Irish Catholics from having to support the Anglican

French satirical drawing of England's Irish problem. Queen Victoria, touring the island, is shielded from seeing unpleasant sights.

final. The aims of the two parties had thus become almost indistinguishable. Neither the aristocracy nor the middle class was dominant. Government proceeded by compromise.

Meanwhile, as a result of advancing industrialization, Britain's middle and working classes were growing rapidly.

Church. To improve land tenure, the Land Act of 1870 curtailed the power of absentee landlords to evict their tenants without compensation. But since the Land Act did not heed Ireland's demands for the "three F's"—fair rent, fixity of tenure, and free sale—it was only a half-measure.

Like most of Gladstone's reforms, his Irish policy violated many vested interests and contributed to his defeat in 1874. There were other causes of discontent. Though elected by working-class votes, Gladstone had done little to improve the status of the laborer. Prosperity, meanwhile, had begun to level off, and from 1873 on depression elsewhere made itself felt in Britain as well. Finally, Gladstone's foreign policy—peaceful, sensible, but unexciting—lacked popular support. With Disraeli, who succeeded him in 1874 and who combined social legislation at home with an active imperial policy abroad, a new chapter in British history began.

RUSSIA: REACTION AND REFORM

The second great power on the periphery of Europe, tsarist Russia, pursued its own peculiar course through most of the nineteenth century. The westernization of Russia that had begun during the eighteenth century continued, but very slowly. Because of its vast size and the multiplicity of its backward peoples, Russia faced a number of problems not shared by any of the other great powers. To establish political control in the face of such obstacles required a regime of strict autocracy. The will of the tsar was law. His decrees were translated into action by a huge bureaucracy whose openness to bribery helped somewhat to soften the harshness of tsarist rule. Russia's government has been aptly described as "despotism tempered by corruption."

Aside from autocracy, there were other institutions peculiar to the tsarist empire. Although in western Europe the nobility had lost much of its power, Russia's aristocracy continued to enjoy its traditional privileges. Besides owning al-most all the land, the nobles were exempt from taxation and from military service. There was as yet no middle class to speak of, except in the few larger towns. The majority of the tsar's subjects, more than 95 percent, were peasants, and most of them were still serfs. Serfdom in Russia was much more burdensome than it had been in western Europe. Even the legally free peasants, who by 1833 constituted about a third of the population, were kept in a decidedly inferior position. Occasionally, when the misery of the Russian masses became too much to bear, they sought relief in local uprisings. There had been more than five hundred such mutinies during the rule of Nicholas I (1825–55). Nicholas actually had introduced some measures aimed at alleviating the worst abuses of serfdom, but to go to the root of the evil and to liberate the serfs would have meant taking land away from the nobility; even the autocratic tsars did not dare do that. Instead, Nicholas continued to preach the principles dearest to his reactionary heart—obedience to autocracy, adherence to the traditional Orthodox religion, and patriotic faith in the virtues of Russian nationality.

"Westerners" versus "Slavophils"

The obstacles that the tsarist government put in the way of education and the restriction it imposed on western ideas helped to keep down the numbers of the Russian "intelligentsia"—that is, those few people whose intellectual interests set them apart from the majority of the people. Still, by the middle of the nineteenth century this group had grown numerous enough to make its influence felt. There were two clearly defined factions among Russian intellectuals—the "Westerners" and the "Slavophils." The Westerners saw their country as essentially a part of western civilization, merely lagging behind but able eventually to catch up. The Slavophils, on the other hand, held that the difference between Russia and the West was not one of degree but of kind. They pointed to the peculiar foundations of Russian civilization—Byzantine, Slavic, and Greek-Orthodox as compared with the Roman, Germanic, and Catholic roots of western civilization. And they believed that each nation should live according to its own traditions rather than try to imitate the institutions and practices of other countries. These theoretical differences between Westerners and Slavophils also determined their attitudes toward current problems. While the Westerners favored constitutional government, rationalism, and industrial progress, the Slavophils saw the salvation of Russia in benevolent autocracy, Orthodox Christianity, and the reform of Russia's predominantly agrarian society. This eastern-versus-western orientation henceforth remained a permanent characteristic of Russian political and social philosophy.

The most important political developments during the regime of Nicholas I were in foreign affairs. One of the main aims of Russian policy continued to be the domination, direct or indirect, over the disintegrating Ottoman Empire.

Western opposition to Russia's Turkish aspirations had finally led to the Crimean War. More than any previous event, this conflict had shown the inefficiency, corruption, and poor leadership of the tsarist regime. Nicholas had died during the war. His successor, Alexander II (1855–81), was far less reactionary. Though he had little understanding of social and economic problems, he was impressed by the clamor for reform that had set in after the Crimean defeat. The most widespread demand of the reformers was for the emancipation of the serfs.

The Emancipation of the Serfs

Alexander II realized that the alternative to abolishing serfdom from above might ultimately be revolution from below. He therefore initiated a careful study of the situation that finally, in March 1861, led to the Emancipation Edict. Its immediate effects, however, were far from happy. It was of little use for the Russian serf to gain his freedom without at the same time obtaining sufficient land to make a living. Yet to deprive the nobility of its labor force and most of its land would have placed the burden of emancipation entirely on that class. The solution finally arrived at was a compromise that satisfied no one. The peasants were given almost half the land, not in direct ownership but in large holdings administered by the village community, the *mir*. The *mir* in turn apportioned land use among the village households. The landowners were compensated by the government; but the redemption money that the government paid to the nobles had to be repaid over a period of forty-nine years by each village community.

Emancipation thus freed the individual peasant from servitude to his noble master but subjected him to the communal control of his village. It substituted a new "peasant problem" for the old problem of serfdom. To be freed from the redemption payments and the tutelage of the *mir*, and to get hold of the land still in the hands of the nobility—these remained burning issues for the Russian peasantry into the twentieth century.

Serfdom

Few realize what serfdom was in reality. There is a dim conception that the conditions which it created were very bad; but those conditions, as they affected human beings bodily and mentally, are not generally understood. It is amazing, indeed, to see how quickly an institution and its social consequences are forgotten when the institution has ceased to exist, and with what rapidity men and things change. I will try to recall the conditions of serfdom by telling, not what I heard but what I saw . . . :

Father . . . calls in Makár, the piano-tuner and sub-butler, and reminds him of all his recent sins. . . . Of a sudden there is a lull in the storm. My father takes a seat at the table and writes a note. "Take Makár with this note to the police station, and let a hundred lashes with the birch rod be given him."

Terror and absolute muteness reign in the house. The clock strikes four, and we all go down to dinner. . . . "Where is Makár?" our stepmother asks. "Call him in." Makár does not appear, and the order is repeated. He enters at last, pale, with a distorted face, ashamed, his eyes cast down. . . . Tears suffocate me, and immediately after dinner is over I run out, catch Makár in the dark passage, and try to kiss his hand; but he tears it away, and says, either as a reproach or as a question, "Let me alone; you, too, when you are grown up, will you not be just the same?"

From Prince Peter Kropotkin, *Memoirs of a Revolutionist* (Boston: Houghton Mifflin, 1899), pp. 49–51.

Reform, Radicalism, and Reaction

The liberation of the serfs, while the most spectacular of Alexander's acts, was not the only effort he made to strengthen his regime through timely reforms. In 1863 he granted universities a greater degree of academic freedom. In 1864 he reformed the Russian judicial system along western lines. The same year Alexander introduced a measure of local and regional self-government through elected assemblies, or *zemstvos*. The hope of the reformers that this development might eventually culminate in a national assembly was disappointed. But even so, the *zemstvos* provided some opportunity for public discussion and the development of civic responsibility, both hitherto unknown in Russia.

The more changes Alexander introduced, the more hopes he aroused. One of the results of his policy had been to give an impetus to various reform movements among the intelligentsia, whose aims and agitation became ever more radical. Western socialism had been slow to gain a hold in Russia, where industry was still in its infancy. Consequently, Russian socialists like Alexander Herzen tried to appeal to the Russian peasant, whose village community already exhibited many of the collective features cherished by socialists. In the 1860s it became the fashion for members of the intelligentsia to go out and live among the peasants in the hope of arousing them from their apathy and urging them into starting a revolution. This "go-to-the-people" movement (*Narodniki*), however, failed because the peasants were too backward and the authorities too vigilant. In their opposition to everything their government stood for, the younger members of the intelligentsia now began to refer to themselves as "nihilists," believers in nothing. Most of them vented their anger over the existing system merely by expounding radical ideas and by disregarding conventional manners and mores. During the 1870s, however, some of the nihilists fell under the influence of Mikhail Bakunin and his philosophy of anarchism (see p. 591). In 1879 this terrorist faction formed a secret society, "The Will of the People," whose aim was to overthrow the government by direct action and assassination.

Frightened by these manifestations of radicalism, Alexander II reverted to a policy of renewed reaction. Yet by reverting to repression, he merely helped to strengthen the revolutionary forces he hoped to combat. This fact was brought home to him in several attempts on his life, and in 1880 he tried once again to return to his initial policy of reform. But by then it was too late. Alexander II was killed by a terrorist bomb in 1881.

THE PRIMACY OF FOREIGN POLICY

During the two decades after 1850 foreign policy in most of Europe overshadowed domestic policy. There were few discernible trends in domestic affairs. Industrialization continued, but its progress was still uneven. Democracy made gains in some countries (notably England), but it suffered reversals in others (notably Germany). Some important reforms helped ease tension—the Emancipation Edict in Russia, the *Ausgleich* between Austria and Hungary, the Second Reform Bill in England. But for each issue resolved, others arose elsewhere—the conflict between monarchism and republicanism in France, the defeat of

Alexander II (*ca.* 1876).

Alexander Herzen (1812–70), Russian writer and socialist whose journal, *Kolokol* (the *Bell*), published in exile, was widely read in Russia, even though it had been banned.

liberalism in Germany, the tension between north and south in Italy, to mention but a few.

The most significant event in the "era of unification" was the emergence of Germany as a great power. From 1871 to 1945 the influence of that belatedly unified nation made itself felt in every major international crisis and in the history of every country. Compared with German unification, the unification of Italy today seems of minor importance, though it did not appear so at the time. Of much greater consequence was the tragic fate of the Second French Empire. Its defeat at the hands of Prussia sowed some of the seeds that brought forth the great wars of our century. But these events were far off in 1871. At the time it seemed as though the Continent at long last had found the stability that statesmen before 1850 had tried so hard to achieve. The future was to show the precariousness of the new balance of power.

Suggestions for Further Reading

Note: Asterisk denotes a book available in paperback edition.

General Most of the general works cited after Chapter 24 also cover this later period. An admirably comprehensive view may be gained from R. C. Binkley, *Realism and Nationalism, 1852–1871** (1935), and, more recently, from E. J. Hobsbawm, *The Age of Capitalism, 1848–1875* (1976). The international affairs of Europe are covered in A. J. P. Taylor, *The Struggle for Mastery in Europe, 1848–1918** (1954).

The Eastern Question The disintegration of the Ottoman Empire is treated authoritatively in J. A. R. Marriott, *The Eastern Question in European Diplomacy* (1926), and more briefly in M. S. Anderson, *The Eastern Question** (1966). On the background of the Crimean War, see E. Horvath, *Origins of the Crimean War* (1937); H. W. V. Temperley, *England and the Near East: The Crimea* (1936); G. B. Henderson, *Crimean War Diplomacy and Other Historical Essays* (1947); D. Hopwood, *The Russian Presence in Syria and Palestine, 1843–1914* (1969); and P. W. Schröder, *Austria, Great Britain, and the Crimean War: The Destruction of the European Concert* (1973). W. E. Mosse, *The Rise and Fall of the Crimean System, 1855–1871* (1967), takes a new look at the larger issues connected with the war. The war itself is vividly portrayed in N. Bentley, ed., *William H. Russell's Despatches from the Crimea, 1854–1856* (1967). The Crimean War also provides a somber background for two fine books by C. Woodham-Smith: *Florence Nightingale, 1820–1910** (1951) and *The Reason Why** (1953). The best account of Rumanian independence is still T. W. Riker, *The Making of Roumania* (1931).

The Second French Empire The most thorough studies of Napoleon III's early career are both by F. A. Simpson, *The Rise of Louis Napoleon* (1950) and *Louis Napoleon and the Recovery of France, 1848–1856*, 3rd ed. (1951). The political history of the Empire is covered in O. Aubry, *The Second Empire* (1940), and in J. M. Thompson, *Louis Napoleon and the Second Empire* (1955). A. Guérard, *Reflections on the Napoleonic Legend* (1924), traces the Napoleonic heritage of the emperor. The same author, in his *Napoleon III** (1943), draws a sympathetic picture of a man whom others have called a "herald of fascism." A collection of contrasting interpretations of Napoleon III may be found in B. D. Gooch, ed., *Napoleon III: Man of Destiny— Enlightened Statesman or Proto-Fascist?** (1963). N. N. Barker, *Distaff Diplomacy: The Empress Eugénie and the Foreign Policy of the Second Empire* (1967), deals with the influence of the wife of Napoleon III. Among more specialized studies of the Empire, the following are of interest: T. Zeldin, *The Political System of Napoleon III* (1958); F. C. Palm, *England and Napoleon III: A Study in the Rise of a Utopian Dictator* (1948); L. M. Case, *French Opinion on War and Diplomacy During the Second Empire* (1953); L. M. Case and W. F. Spencer, *The United States and France: Civil War Diplomacy* (1970); C. W. Hallberg, *Franz Joseph and Napoleon III, 1852–1864: A Study of Austro-French Relations* (1955); and D. S. Pinckney, *Napoleon III and the Reconstruction of Paris* (1958). R. L. Williams, *Gaslight and Shadow: The World of Napoleon III** (1957), conveys some of the glamour and excitement of one of the most brilliant periods in French history. The same author's *The French Revolution of 1870–1871** (1969), deals with the end of the Empire. E. S. Mason, *The Paris Commune* (1968), is a balanced account. The best books in English on Gambetta are J. P. T. Bury, *Gambetta and the National Defense* (1936) and *Gambetta and the Making of the Third Republic* (1973).

The Unification of Italy

The dramatic events of these crucial years are best studied through the lives of the main participants, including Napoleon III. A. J. Whyte, *The Political Life and Letters of Cavour, 1848–1861* (1930), and W. R. Thayer, *The Life and Times of Cavour,* 2 vols. (1914), are standard works. The same holds true for the classic accounts of Garibaldi's colorful exploits in G. M. Trevelyan, *Garibaldi and the Thousand* (1911) and *Garibaldi and the Making of Italy* (1911). More recent are the excellent studies by D. Mack Smith: *Cavour and Garibaldi, 1860: A Study in Political Conflict* (1954); *Garibaldi* (1956); and *Victor Emmanuel, Cavour, and the Risorgimento* (1971). For a good brief account, see D. Beales, *The Risorgimento and the Unification of Italy* (1971). The best biographies of Mazzini are B. King, *The Life of Mazzini* (1902), and G. O. Griffith, *Mazzini: Prophet of Modern Europe* (1932). The role of Napoleon III in the unification of Italy is treated in most of the works on the Second Empire cited above, as well as in L. M. Case, *Franco-Italian Relations, 1860–1865* (1932), and in J. W. Bush, *Venetia Redeemed: Franco-Italian Relations, 1864–1866* (1967). On British policy, see D. E. D. Beales, *England and Italy, 1859–1860* (1961).

The Unification of Germany

The most recent comprehensive account in English of the events culminating in 1871 is O. Pflanze, *Bismarck and the Development of Germany: The Period of Unification, 1815–1871* (1963). T. S. Hamerow, *The Social Foundation of German Unification, 1858–1871* (1969), supplies the domestic background. See also, H. Boehme, *The Foundations of the German Empire* (1973). The Prussian constitutional conflict is the subject of E. N. Anderson, *The Social and Political Conflict in Prussia* (1954). On the war with Denmark, L. D. Steefel, *The Schleswig-Holstein Question* (1932), remains standard. For an understanding of Austro-Prussian rivalry, H. Friedjung, *The Struggle for Supremacy in Germany, 1859–1866* (1897, 1935), is still important. See also C. W. Clark, *Franz Joseph and Bismarck: The Diplomacy of Austria Before the War of 1866* (1934), and E. A. Pottinger, *Napoleon III and the German Crisis, 1865–1866* (1966). Subsequent Austrian developments are covered in A. J. May, *The Hapsburg Monarchy, 1867–1914* (1951), and in F. R. Bridge, *From Sadowa to Sarajevo* (1972). On the war of 1866, see G. Craig, *The Battle of Königgrätz: Prussia's Victory over Austria, 1866* (1964). On the outbreak of the Franco-Prussian War, see L. D. Steefel, *Bismarck, the Hohenzollern Candidacy, and the Origins of the Franco-Prussian War* (1962). R. Millman, *British Foreign Policy and the Coming of the Franco-Prussian War* (1965), is useful. There are many biographies of Bismarck, none of them wholly satisfactory. E. Eyck, *Bismarck and the German Empire** (1950), is an abbreviation of a much longer German work; A. J. P. Taylor, *Bismarck: The Man and the Statesman** (1955), is more readable but less sound. A. Palmer, *Bismarck* (1976), makes pleasant and profitable reading. The international repercussions of German unification are admirably clarified in W. E. Mosse, *The European Powers and the German Question, 1848–1871* (1958). On the war between France and Prussia, see M. E. Howard, *The Franco-Prussian War** (1961).

England

Both A. Briggs, *The Age of Improvement, 1783–1867* (1959), and G. Kitson-Clark, *The Making of Victorian England* (1962), contain authoritative accounts of the mid-Victorian era. See also, G. F. A. Best, *Mid-Victorian Britain* (1972). E. Longford, *Victoria R. I.** (1964), is based on the queen's personal archives. British foreign policy and its chief maker are vividly presented in D. Southgate, *"The Most English Minister": The Policies and Politics of Palmerston* (1966). H. C. F. Bell, *Lord Palmerston,* 2 vols. (1936), is the best biography. On Gladstone see P. Magnus, *Gladstone: A Biography* (1955). For a brilliant survey of social and intellectual life, see G. M. Young, *Victorian England: Portrait of an Age** (1936). Good monographs on important domestic developments are J. H. Hanham, *Elections and Party Management: Politics in the Time of Disraeli and Gladstone* (1959), and F. B. Smith, *The Making of the Second Reform Bill* (1966). On the Irish question, see the excellent book by G. Dangerfield, *The Damnable Question* (1976).

Russia

The history of Russia is covered in M. T. Florinsky, *Russia: A History and an Interpretation,* Vol. II (1953); H. Seton-Watson, *The Russian Empire, 1801–1917* (1967); and R. Pipes, *Russia under the Old Regime* (1975). J. H. Billington, *The Icon and the Axe* (1966), is a comprehensive synthesis of Russian culture. A. Herzen, *My Past and Thoughts,* 6 vols. (1924–27), is a graphic contemporary account by one of Russia's leading intellectuals. On the crucial problem of serfdom, see G. T. Robinson, *Rural Russia Under the Old Regime* (1949), and T. Emmons, *The Russian Landed Gentry and the Peasant Emancipation of 1861* (1968). D. M. Wallace, *Russia** (1912), is still valuable for an understanding of the Russian people. The following discuss two basic trends of Russian life and thought: H. Kohn, *Pan-Slavism: Its History and Ideology** (1953), and N. V. Riasinovsky, *Russia and the West in the Teaching of the Slavophiles* (1953). On the latter, see also the pioneering study by A. Walicki, *The Slavophile Controversy* (1975). D. R. Brower, *Training the Nihilists* (1975), dissects the intelligentsia. S. Graham, *Tsar of Freedom: The Life and Reign of Alexander II* (1935), deals sympathetically with a tragic figure. W. E. Mosse, *Alexander II and the Modernization of Russia** (1958), is a brief survey.

27 Europe and the World in the Nineteenth Century

From the Age of Discovery until the nineteenth century the world leadership of Europe had remained virtually unchallenged. As European nations established overseas commercial or colonial contacts, the ultimate conquest of the globe by western civilization appeared inevitable. But there had also been signs of a reverse trend, as some regions seemed to grow restive under Europe tutelage. The United States had been the first European overseas possession to gain independence, and there were soon to be similar movements for independence in the other regions where Europeans had settled. Despite the continued ascendancy of Europe during the nineteenth century, therefore, there were already some indications that the days of European supremacy were drawing to a close.

This chapter deals only with the major spheres of European expansion— North and South America, the British Empire, and Asia. The African continent was not opened up to European penetration until the end of the nineteenth century, and the resulting rivalry among the powers there will be more profitably discussed in a later chapter. The United States will command far more attention than any of the other regions, mainly because America remains to this day the most important overseas extension of European civilization.

THE UNITED STATES BECOMES A GREAT POWER

At the beginning of the nineteenth century, the United States was still a second-class power, playing only a minor role in international affairs. A century later, it had become the decisive arbiter in the greatest war Europe and the world had ever seen. The involvement of this newcomer in world affairs was a slow and gradual process. Through most of the nineteenth century America remained politically isolated, so much so that "isolationism" became a term commonly applied to American foreign policy.

America and Europe

In the Monroe Doctrine of 1823, America had warned Europe to desist from any further colonization in the Western Hemisphere. On several occasions during the nineteenth century, notably during the 1830s and 1840s, the United States became involved with its neighbors to the north and south over territorial issues. But these localized conflicts had no effect on the European balance of power. Even the international repercussions of the American Civil War did not lead to European intervention. It was only at the close of the nineteenth century, in the war with Spain, that America once again went to war with a European power.

Despite the political isolation in which the United States shaped its destiny, cultural relations between the new republic and the old continent remained close, though America at first was a recipient rather than a contributor in this cultural exchange. In the 1830s and 1840s, foreign travelers still commented on the backwardness and boorishness of American manners and customs. But there were also some friendlier critics, like the young Frenchman Alexis de Tocqueville, whose *Democracy in America* (1835–40) predicted correctly the leading role that the United States would some day play in world affairs.

America had shared the European vogue of Romanticism, and some of Europe's early socialists had tried out their utopian experiments on American soil. By the middle of the nineteenth century, American writers like Irving, Cooper, Longfellow, and Poe drew foreign attention to American literature, and the monumental works of the historians Prescott, Parkman, Bancroft, and Motley did the same for American historiography. There were other fields in which American influence made itself felt. The pioneering efforts of American reformers in advocating women's rights, pacifism, and temperance evoked responses overseas; and the gradual adoption in Europe of universal male suffrage and free public education profited greatly from the American example. In technical inventions America already showed signs of

Opposite: The reception held on the occasion of the arrival of a new British governor in East Africa as depicted by an African artist.

At 8.45' A.M. Friday May 24th 1844 this sentence was transmitted from Baltimore, being the first sentence sent and indited by Miss Annie G. Ellsworth. Sam F B Morse, Superintendent of Electro Magnetic Telegraphs —

W h a t h a t h G o D w r o u g h t

America led the way in invention of better means of communication. Above: the tape on which the first telegraph message was received in Baltimore on May 24, 1844. Samuel F. B. Morse had tapped out "What hath God wrought?" from Washington. Below: Alexander Graham Bell's invention—the telephone (1876).

the genius that was ultimately to make it the leading industrial nation of the world. The cultural exchange between Europe and the United States thus became less one-sided as time went on. Better means of communication also played their part. By the 1860s, the steamship had begun to compete successfully with the sailing vessel, and the laying of a transatlantic cable in 1858 speeded the exchange of news and ideas.

The Westward Movement

In its domestic development the United States faced many of the same social and economic problems that confronted the nations of Europe. But since America was a new nation, unencumbered by feudal traditions and endowed with a rich and virtually empty continent, it grew into something radically different from Europe. Within one century the territory of the United States increased

more than fourfold. To assimilate and integrate these new lands proved to be America's foremost political problem, and its final accomplishment contributed to the origins of a bloody civil war. Yet the abundance of fertile lands also helped to relieve economic and social pressures that might have had similarly violent repercussions. The result of America's territorial expansion was a superpower marked by vast size, advantageous location, wide variety of climate, and great wealth of natural resources.

Immigration

The territorial growth of the United States was closely related to the phenomenal growth of its population. From less than 4 million in 1790, the population shot up to over 60 million in the course of a hundred years. Much of this increase was due to the ceaseless stream of European immigrants, totaling more than 35 million between 1815 and 1914. Many of them still came to escape political or religious persecution, but there was also the attraction of the seemingly unlimited economic opportunities of the New World. The constant supply of cheap labor provided by immigration was a boon to America's growing economy. The rapid Americanization of these new citizens was aided by the fact that the United States had no privileged classes, no established church, and no military caste. American society had its sectional and occupational groupings, but they were not as rigid as the European hierarchies. Economic opportunity for all, an open society in which ability and hard work brought success—these were the ingredients of the "American dream," if not always the American reality.

Early Industrialization

Like most European countries, the United States in the first part of the nineteenth century remained predomi-

De Tocqueville on Russia and America   1835

There are at the present time two great nations in the world, which started from different points, but seem to tend towards the same end. I allude to the Russians and the Americans. . . . All other nations seem to have nearly reached their natural limits, and they have only to maintain their power; but these are still in the act of growth. . . . These alone are proceeding with ease and celerity along a path to which no limit can be perceived. The American struggles against the obstacles that nature opposes to him; the adversaries of the Russian are men. The former combats the wilderness and savage life; the latter, civilization with all its arms. The conquests of the American are therefore gained by the plowshare; those of the Russian by the sword. The Anglo-American relies upon personal interest to accomplish his ends and gives free scope to the unguided strength and common sense of the people; the Russian centers all the authority of society in a single arm. The principal instrument of the former is freedom; of the latter, servitude. Their starting-point is different and their courses are not the same; yet each of them seems marked out by the will of Heaven to sway the destinies of half the globe.

From Alexis de Tocqueville, *Democracy in America* (New York: Knopf, 1953), Vol. I, p. 434.

Immigrants at Ellis Island,
New York City (*ca.* 1912).

nantly agrarian. It was the abundance of land that attracted land-hungry Europeans. But as in Europe, the vast increase of population required additional economic outlets, and these were provided by industry. By the middle of the nineteenth century the eastern states had thriving industries. At the same time, the opening up of western territories provided an ever-expanding market. Full-scale industrialization did not take hold until after the Civil War. Prior to 1860, however, many of the social effects of industrialization that were seen in Europe had already made themselves felt. Labor conditions in American factories on the whole were better than those in Europe. During the first half of the nineteenth century there were the beginnings of American labor unions, but a labor movement in the modern sense, in America as in Europe, did not develop until later.

In its economic philosophy, America shared the faith of European liberals in freedom from state control. The American Revolution had been fought against the mercantilist restrictions imposed by the mother country. Once these restrictions had been removed, there remained few obstacles to free enterprise. A philosophy of laissez faire thus came to permeate the economic life of the United States. There was only one field in which American industry not only tolerated but demanded government control, and that was tariff legislation. With the world's largest free-trade area within their own borders, American manufacturers were eager to keep foreign competitors out.

America After 1815

The revolutionary turmoil in Europe after 1815 had its parallel in the unrest that prevailed in the United States during the 1820s. The source of this unrest was economic and social. As America's population increased, and as the new territories acquired with the purchase of Louisiana (1803) and Florida (1819) filled up with new settlers, a number of differ-

Above: Andrew Jackson (1767–1845), by Thomas Sully. Right: Jackson's campaign poster in 1828.

Jackson Forever!
The Hero of Two Wars and of Orleans!
The Man of the People!
HE WHO COULD NOT BARTER NOR BARGAIN FOR THE
PRESIDENCY!

Who, although "*A Military Chieftain*," valued the purity of Elections and of the Electors, MORE than the Office of PRESIDENT itself! Although the greatest in the gift of his countrymen, and the highest in point of dignity of any in the world,

BECAUSE
It should be derived from the
PEOPLE!

No Gag Laws! No Black Cockades! No Reign of Terror! No Standing Army or Navy Officers, when under the pay of Government, to browbeat, or

KNOCK DOWN

Old Revolutionary Characters, or our Representatives while in the discharge of their duty. To the Polls then, and vote for those who will support

OLD HICKORY
AND THE ELECTORAL LAW.

ences arose between the established interests in the East and the new forces on the frontier. Another source of unrest arose among the new workers of the East, most of them recent immigrants with little bargaining power and no social standing. Thanks to the growth of the democratic process after the Revolution, this discontent was able to express itself at the ballot box.

Democracy in the United States had been slow to reach all levels of society, and it was not until the late 1820s that male suffrage had been adopted in the majority of states. Largely as a result of this increased democratization, Andrew Jackson was elected president in 1828. More than any of his predecessors, Jackson could claim to be the people's choice. He was the first westerner to win the highest office, a popular hero of the War of 1812, and, most important, a man who had risen from poverty by his own efforts. The road from log cabin to White House henceforth became part of the American dream.

The "Age of Jackson"

The "Age of Jackson" was a period of major change in American life, more so even than the 1830s were in western Europe. The democratization of political life continued with the adoption of the patronage, or "spoils system," and with the

practice of having presidential candidates nominated by national conventions rather than by a handful of party leaders. Closest to Jackson's heart was the further development of the West. In a number of treaties concluded with Indian tribes, the federal government won title to millions of acres of virgin land. These were sold at auction at low cost, after free land for schools, roads, a state university, and other public purposes had been set aside. Jackson's opposition to eastern financial interests, furthermore, made him the advocate of state banks, whose lavish granting of credit helped develop the West.

With the opening of the West, sectional rivalry became one of the major issues in American politics. Not only the West, but the South as well, found itself at odds with the North, especially over tariffs. The South, depending on cotton exports, favored free trade, while the North demanded high tariffs to protect its infant industries. Finding itself more and more overshadowed by the North, the South used the proposal of a high tariff in 1828 as an occasion for raising the vital question of "states' rights." The relationship between state and federal governments had been an issue in American politics since the early days of the Republic. The Constitution of 1787 had considerably widened the power of the central government over what it had been under the Articles of Confederation, and the policy since then had been to carry this centralization further.

But there was also strong sentiment against this tendency. Critics of centralization took the view that the Constitution was primarily a compact among sovereign states, and that the states had the right to nullify an act of Congress if it violated the terms of that compact. It was this idea of nullification that was used by Jackson's vice president, John C. Calhoun, a southerner, to fight the "tariff of abominations." In the ensuing crisis Jackson broke with Calhoun and defended the sovereignty of the Union against the advocates of states' rights. A final showdown was averted by the compromise tariff of 1833. But this did not remove the underlying conflict between federal power and state sovereignty.

John C. Calhoun (1782–1850), by Charles Bird King.

Expansionism of the 1840s

In foreign affairs the Jacksonian period was uneventful. As more and more settlers began moving westward, however, it was inevitable that tensions would develop with the British in the north and the Mexicans in the south over rival claims to western territories. These intermittent conflicts came to a head and were settled during the 1840s. American-British economic relations were so advantageous that it was in the interest of both to avoid a major crisis over the American-Canadian frontier. By the Webster-Ashburton Treaty (1842), therefore, the northeastern boundary was adjusted to mutual satisfaction. A similar compromise was reached for the Northwest in the Oregon Treaty (1846), which fixed Oregon's northern boundary along the forty-ninth parallel.

Relations with America's southern neighbor, Mexico, were considerably more stormy. The main controversy here arose over Texas. The influx of American settlers into this Mexican border region had begun in 1821. Because of constant difficulties with Mexican authorities, the American settlers first demanded autonomy and then, in 1836, proclaimed their independence. The next logical step, admission of Texas to the Union in 1845, led to war with Mexico. As a result of the Mexican War (1846–48), Mexico relinquished its claims to Texas. Mexico also ceded California and New Mexico in return for $15 million. Six years later, with the Gadsden Purchase, America acquired another slice of Mexican territory.

The settlement with Mexico, together with the Oregon Treaty, gave the United States an extended frontage on the Pacific. The implications of this development for American foreign policy were to become evident only gradually. For the time being, the most pressing need of the vast regions of the new West was for settlers to substantiate America's claims. In a fitting climax to a decade of expansion, gold was discovered in the Sacramento Valley in 1848. The resulting gold rush profited only a few of the many thousands who streamed to California from all over the world. But these "forty-niners" helped to increase the population of California more than fourfold in a single decade.

The Slavery Issue

The expansionism of the 1840s also aggravated the long-standing sectional conflict between proslavery and antislavery forces. What has been said about the democratic nature of American society did not apply to the large number of black slaves in the South or even to free blacks in the North. While almost everywhere in the world slavery was being

Slavery

AN APOLOGIST'S VIEW

The negro slaves of the South are the happiest, and, in some sense, the freest people in the world. The children and the aged and infirm work not at all, and yet have all the comforts and necessaries of life provided for them. They enjoy liberty, because they are oppressed neither by care nor labor. The women do little hard work, and are protected from the despotism of their husbands by their masters. The negro men and stout boys work, on the average, in good weather, not more than nine hours a day. . . . Besides, they have their Sabbaths and holidays. White men, with so much of license and liberty, would die of ennui; but negroes luxuriate in corporeal and mental repose. With their faces upturned to the sun, they can sleep at any hour; and quiet sleep is the greatest of human enjoyments. . . . The free laborer must work or starve. He is more of a slave than the negro, because he works longer and harder for less allowance than the slave, and has no holiday, because the cares of life with him begin when its labors end. He has no liberty, and not a single right.

AN ABOLITIONIST'S VIEW

The slaves in the United States are treated with barbarous inhumanity . . . they are overworked, underfed, wretchedly clad and lodged, and have insufficient sleep . . . they are often made to wear round their necks iron collars armed with prongs, to drag heavy chains and weights at their feet while working in the field . . . they are often kept confined in the stocks day and night for weeks together, made to wear gags in their mouths for hours or days, have some of their front teeth torn out or broken off, that they may be easily detected when they run away . . . they are frequently flogged with terrible severity, have red pepper rubbed into their lacerated flesh, and hot brine, spirits of turpentine, etc., poured over the gashes to increase the torture . . . they are often stripped naked, their backs and limbs cut with knives, bruised and mangled by scores and hundreds of blows with the paddle, and terribly torn by the claws of cats, drawn over them by their tormentors.

From George Fitzhugh, *Cannibals All!* (1857); from Theodore Dwight Weld, *Slavery As It Is* (1839).

Insignia of the Third United States Colored Troops.

abolished, it was gaining a new lease on life in the American South. In a nation dedicated to a belief in equality, there now arose an aristocracy of wealthy plantation owners whose belief in their own superiority and the inferiority of the black race was not unlike the racist ideologies that already existed in Europe and became more widespread during the later nineteenth century.

The main concern of southern politicians in the first half of the nineteenth century was to prevent antislavery legislation. This could be done only if an even balance between slave and free states was maintained. Such a balance in the past had been maintained by compromise. But compromise became increasingly difficult as more and more territories were added to the Union. With the petition of California in 1849 for admission as a free state, the issue reached a critical stage. If granted, the admission would upset the existing balance between slave and free states. After prolonged debates, differences were once more patched up. The Compromise of 1850 called for the admission of California as a free state, but it left the question of whether the two new territories of New Mexico and Utah were ultimately to be admitted as free or slave states up to

their own decisions. It was this introduction of state option, or popular sovereignty, that injected a new and disturbing element into the slavery controversy.

Beginning in the mid-1850s a series of tragic events and incidents drove the opposing factions on the issue of the expansion of slavery still further apart. The rivalry between proslavery and antislavery forces over whether Kansas was to be a free or slave state soon plunged that territory into a miniature civil war. The Supreme Court's Dred Scott decision (1857), which ruled that slaves were property and thus could not become free by moving to a free state, deeply antagonized the North. On the other hand, an attempt by the abolitionist John Brown to lead slaves in a raid on the arsenal at Harper's Ferry (1859) aroused the specter of a slave revolt in the South. The presidential campaign of 1860 was dominated by the slavery issue. The Democrats were divided into a southern, proslavery wing and a northern faction holding to the compromising policy of popular sovereignty. The Republicans, on the other hand, stood united against any further extension of slavery.

The Republican candidate, Abraham Lincoln, was chosen as president by an electorate divided along sectional lines.

THE SLAVERY ISSUE   1861

Repeatedly in previous years the South had talked of secession as a last resort in defending its way of life. Calhoun, the defender of states' rights, had suggested that if compromise proved impossible the states should "agree to separate and part in peace." It was South Carolina, the home of the "great nullifier," that now replied to Lincoln's election by passing its Ordinance of Secession. One after another, most of the slave states seceded from the Union and formed the Confederate States of America. In his inaugural address Lincoln strongly rejected the right of secession and vowed to maintain the Union. But he also left the door open for possible reconciliation. The issue of peace or war hung in the balance for a while longer. It was decided on April 12, 1861, when Confederate forces opened fire on the federal garrison at Fort Sumter in Charleston Harbor.

The American Civil War

The American Civil War was fought initially to preserve and protect the Union. To that extent it belongs among the great wars of national unification that were being waged in Europe at the same time. The Civil War was expected to be a brief conflict in which the immense advantages of the North would prove decisive. But the South put up a valiant fight, and in the early part of the war won some brilliant victories. Nobody would have predicted that the war would last four years and would turn into one of the most costly military ventures known up to that time.

Union troops in the Civil War stringing telegraph wires on the battlefield.

Garrison of South Carolina Confederate troops (1861).

Among the political developments of the war the most important was Lincoln's Emancipation Proclamation, a promise of freedom to come. The extension of northern war aims to include the abolition of slavery changed the war from a mere political struggle to an ideological crusade. This change was brought about more by the pressure of circumstances than by actual design. Lincoln himself would have preferred a more gradual and voluntary process of emancipation.

The granting of freedom to black Americans inevitably raised the closely related question of granting them equality as well. The abolitionist minority had never made any distinction between the two. But it took endless debates and several years before the country as a whole was ready to implement the gift of freedom with the guarantee of equality. This was done in several constitutional amendments and civil-rights acts. Beginning in the 1870s, however, the United States Supreme Court interpreted this postwar legislation in a way that violated its spirit, if not its letter, and that kept America's blacks in a position of inferiority for decades to come.

Europe and the Civil War

The Emancipation Proclamation made a very strong impression in Europe. The European powers had watched America's westward movement in the early part of the century with disapproval. During the Mexican War, Great Britain actually considered joint intervention with France on behalf of Mexico, and during the 1850s these two powers helped to discourage American plans for the acquisition of Cuba from Spain. The outbreak of the Civil War led official European circles to hope that America would be permanently weakened by the secession of the southern states. Both the British and the French governments were decidedly cool toward the North. As far as Britain was concerned, the fact that its industry depended on southern cotton played its part. When a northern warship removed two Confederate commissioners from the British steamer *Trent* in 1861, a major crisis was averted only by America's readiness to give in to British pro-

tests and release the commissioners. Great Britain, on the other hand, had to heed the protests of the North against permitting southern privateers to be outfitted and to operate from British ports.

American relations with France became strained when Napoleon III tried to bolster his position at home by establishing a puppet regime in Mexico. In 1863 French troops occupied Mexico City, and the following year Archduke Maximilian of Austria was proclaimed Emperor of Mexico. This was in open violation of the Monroe Doctrine, but the United States was too preoccupied to make any protest. Once the Civil War was over, however, it demanded the withdrawal of French troops (1866). Left without support, Maximilian could not last long. He was executed by a Mexican firing squad in 1867.

Not all the governments of Europe hoped to profit from America's domestic tragedy. The Prussian government was favorably disposed toward the North and wished to see the Union preserved as a counterweight to Britain's maritime supremacy. Russia took a similar attitude. The Russians had given up their settlements in California in 1844, and American fears that the tsarist government would take advantage of the Civil War to extend its sphere of influence southward from Alaska proved groundless. Russia sold Alaska, its last remaining colony in North America, to the United States in 1867 for a mere $7.2 million. The same year America also occupied the Midway Islands, thus signifying its new interest in the Pacific area.

The most wholehearted support of the northern cause during the Civil War came from the rank and file of Europe's population. To the Germans and Italians the war appeared as a struggle for national unity, and to people everywhere the Civil War was another phase in the universal fight for freedom and independence that had been waged in Europe ever since the French Revolution. Even before Lincoln's Emancipation Proclamation, most Europeans saw the American war entirely in terms of liberating the southern slaves. The victory of the North was widely hailed as a triumph of democracy, and some historians feel that it

Archduke Maximilian of Austria, emperor of Mexico (1864–67).

contributed to the liberalization of the British and French governments after 1865.

Reconstruction in the South

America's reputation for liberalism and tolerance, however, was considerably tarnished by the Reconstruction period following the Civil War. The assassination of Lincoln had aroused worldwide indignation and sorrow, and the absence of his moderating influence was keenly felt in the American government's efforts to deal with a recalcitrant South. In an attempt to overcome southern resistance to the political and social emancipation of southern blacks, the Reconstruction Acts of 1867 and 1868 placed the South under military rule, from which it could escape only after drafting new constitutions that accepted the constitutional amendments and civil rights legislation passed since the end of the war.

Added to the political tension were economic problems. The South emerged from the war with many of its cities destroyed, its economy disrupted, and one of its major economic assets, slavery, gone. The influx of northern "carpetbaggers," intent on making personal or political profit out of southern misfortune, kept alive the bitterness generated by war. The distinctive way of life on which southerners had prided themselves was gone forever; but the ideals on which it had rested remained alive. The slow process by which southern blacks were once again disenfranchised and, by a series of "Jim Crow" laws, segregated as well, did not really gain momentum until the 1890s. Its cumulative effect was to perpetuate sectionalism by creating a "solid South" dominated by the Democratic Party and dedicated to keeping the black "in his place."

Economic Growth

While America was trying to heal the wounds of war during the last decades of the nineteenth century, it was also trying to fill in its remaining "open spaces" and to realize its great industrial potentialities. Both these developments were aided

A poster of 1874 advising farmers of "the greatest invention of the age"— barbed wire.

by the continued influx of millions of immigrants. Of considerable help in attracting new citizens and in aiding American farmers were the Homestead Act of 1862 and successive land laws, as well as the easy access provided to the West by the construction of transcontinental railroads. The first such line was completed in 1869. American agriculture already had profited from mechanization. The invention of barbed wire in 1873 made possible the fencing in of vast areas for cattle-raising, and the introduction of the refrigerator car proved a boon to the meat-packing industry. As a result of these and other improvements, western farming took on some of the characteristics of an industry, producing on a large scale for distant markets.

Even more important than the growth of America's agriculture after the Civil War was the expansion of its industries. Government procurement of war materials even at the cost of heavy federal deficits had caused an industrial boom, which continued once the war was over. Between 1860 and 1900 the amount of capital invested in American industry increased more than tenfold, and the export of manufactured articles by 1900 was four times what it had been in 1860. By 1890 the United States had emerged as the world's leader in the production of steel and pig iron, and with close to two hundred thousand miles of railroads in 1900 America had more mileage than the whole of Europe. America also excelled in mass-production methods based on standardization, interchangeable parts, and, ultimately, the assembly line.

Government Regulation of Business

As often happens in rapidly expanding economies, America suffered a series of economic crises, of which the Panics of 1873 and 1893 were the most significant. Both had their parallels overseas, and the withdrawal of European capital from American industry in each case precipitated matters. To modify the effects of competition, American heavy industry after 1873 began to combine its resources in order to meliorate the cost of competition, to fix prices, and to control markets. The first of these "trusts" was the Standard Oil Company of John D. Rockefeller (1879). But since these large organizations evoked strong public protests, Congress in 1890 enacted the Sherman Antitrust Law, a gesture, at least, toward remedy. Its enforcement was sufficiently lax, however, to permit the continued concentration of control in industry and banking.

There were other occasions when the federal government had to intervene in order to curb the excesses of unrestricted competition. Contrary to the practice in Europe, where governments had taken an active hand in the construction and operation of railroads, American lines were built through private initiative, aided by lavish grants of public lands. To realize maximum profits, American railroads charged exorbitant rates where there was no competing carrier. There had been various earlier proposals for federal regulation of the railroads, but not until 1887 was the Interstate Commerce Act passed. The new law was chiefly concerned with rates, and to enforce its provisions it created an Interstate Commerce Commission that at first, however, was not very effective.

There was one field in which American business did not mind governmental intervention. Protective tariffs had been a major concern of industrialists during the early nineteenth century. Southern opposition to protectionism, together with Britain's abolition of the Corn Laws in 1846, had brought a brief interval of free trade. But the economic and financial demands of the Civil War reversed the trend. Beginning in 1861 America entered upon a new era of protectionism. Its high point came with the Dingley Tariff Act of 1897, which made the United States the most protectionist country in the world.

The unprecedented industrial expansion of the years after the Civil War gave an air of opulence and optimism to the "Gilded Age." Not all Americans, however, shared in the rise from rags to riches. The South in particular was slow to recover from its defeat and adjust to a world in which cotton was no longer king. The Panic of 1873, moreover, by causing price cuts among farmers and wage cuts among workers, bred widespread discontent. As a result, the 1870s saw the first serious efforts among these potentially powerful groups to assert their influence in national affairs.

Labor and Farm Unrest

There had been a growing awareness among American workers that they might improve their status by combining their small local unions into a more powerful national organization. The first such body to wield any real influence, the Knights of Labor, was founded in 1869. At its height, it had more than seven hundred thousand members. In 1886 a wave of strikes culminated in the Haymarket Square riot in Chicago, in which several policemen were killed. The Knights of Labor, though not directly involved, were nevertheless blamed. There were other reasons for their decline, notably the growing strength of a new national movement, the American Federation of Labor. The A. F. of L. was to be the spearhead of the American labor movement for the next half-century.

Workers' attempts at organization, however, did not at first materially improve their condition. With large numbers of impoverished immigrants swelling the labor market, working conditions continued to be harsh, hours long, and wages low. Repeated strikes, in which hired strikebreakers fought with strikers, further widened the gap between capital

Poster announcing the opening of the Union Pacific Railroad after the railroad had been joined from the Atlantic to the Pacific.

and labor. After the Pullman strike of 1894, the Supreme Court ruled that the Sherman Antitrust Act applied to labor unions if they obstructed interstate commerce. It was only after the turn of the century that American workers began to get a "square deal," in large part because of the efforts of their own unions, but also because of the intervention of a more sympathetic government.

Another large body of Americans who felt their interests neglected in a nation that was becoming rapidly industrialized were the farmers. In 1867 the National Grange of the Patrons of Husbandry had been formed, chiefly as a social organization, but also as a platform for agrarian discontent. The main grievance of farmers was the unfair practices of railways. The Interstate Commerce Act (1887) sought to improve the situation, but its initial effectiveness was limited. Suffering increasingly from protectionism abroad and falling prices at home, America's farmers during the 1880s formed regional groupings that ultimately grew into the National Farmers' Alliance and Industrial Union. Its purpose was to aid farmers by cooperative ventures and by bringing pressure against eastern industrial and banking interests who were held responsible for much of the farmer's plight. The climax of the farmers' discontent came with the formation of the People's Party in 1891. The Populists, profiting from the unrest among workers as well, soon emerged as a powerful third force in national politics. Their demands included currency reform, a graduated income tax, and government ownership of the railroads. A particular issue long close to farmers' hearts was the free and unlimited coinage of silver, from which they expected an upturn of farm prices. When the Democratic Party in 1896 adopted some of the Populist platform, including "free silver," the new party joined forces with the Democrats, thus making the latter the spokesmen of agrarian and labor interests.

Foreign Policy After the Civil War

There were few noteworthy events in American foreign policy between the Civil War and the end of the century. In 1889 America signed a treaty with Germany and Great Britain that established tripartite control over the island of Samoa in the South Pacific. The following year Congress adopted a sweeping naval program, calling for a fleet that would place the United States among the world's leading naval powers. Various plans during the 1890s for an American-controlled canal across Central America failed to materialize, as did attempts to annex Hawaii. The islands did not become American until the Spanish-American War in 1898.

Closer to home, the United States improved relations with the nations of the Western Hemisphere. In 1889 the first Pan-American Conference was held in Washington. In 1895, during a border dispute between Venezuela and British Guiana, Secretary of State Olney reaffirmed the principles of the Monroe Doctrine in strong and belligerent tones. A few years later, in 1898, the United States caught the expansionist fever that was driving the European powers into imperialist ventures. From then on American foreign policy became more and more involved with the rivalries of the other great powers. The days of American isolation were almost over.

American Culture

In cultural matters the United States during the second half of the nineteenth century continued to share in the leading trends of Europe. American painters still went to study in Paris; American scholars were trained at foreign universities; and America's symphony orchestras and opera companies depended almost entirely on European talent. But there was some evidence of a native American culture, making up in freshness and originality for what it lacked in refinement. The writings of Walt Whitman and Mark Twain, the paintings of Winslow Homer and Thomas Eakins, the compositions of Edward MacDowell, and the functional architecture of Louis Sullivan all had an unmistakably American flavor. The most original and influential of America's intellectual contributions during the late nineteenth century was the philosophy

Mark Twain (1835–1910), American humorist of the "Gilded Age" in front of his boyhood home in Hannibal, Missouri.

of pragmatism. Its beginnings went back to the early 1870s, but it only attracted general attention with the writing of William James at the turn of the century. In the popular mind pragmatism justified America's preoccupation with practical pursuits and gave moral sanction to the fierce struggle for material success.

Most Americans were proud of this success. Yet there were some critical voices. In a period of progress and prosperity, both seemingly the result of laissez faire, the American journalist Henry George wrote his *Progress and Poverty* (1879), which challenged the free enterprise system. Thorstein Veblen, in *The Theory of the Leisure Class* (1899), examined the role of the consumer in the economy of his day and found that such materialistic considerations as "conspicuous consumption" and "conspicuous waste" were exerting an unhealthy influence on the existing price structure. Social criticism also found expression in the novels of Edward Bellamy, Theodore Dreiser, and Frank Norris. All these

writers had considerable influence in Europe, where concern over the effects of unrestrained economic liberalism had long agitated socialists and social critics. In the realm of ideas, as in politics and economics, America at the end of the nineteenth century was making its influence felt far beyond its frontiers.

LATIN AMERICA: AN AGE OF DICTATORS

When Latin America won its independence from Spain and Portugal in the early nineteenth century, the region comprised nine sovereign states, most important among them Argentina, Brazil, Chile, Mexico, and Peru. By 1850 several of these states had divided, and their number had grown to seventeen; on the eve of the First World War there were twenty independent Latin American nations. These countries had certain things in common. With the exception of Brazil (where Portuguese was spoken), they were Spanish in culture and language; they were all predominantly Catholic; and the majority of their people were Indians, with white minorities that grew larger as more and more immigrants arrived from the Latin countries of Europe. Economically, Latin America throughout the nineteenth century remained predominantly agrarian and backward. Industrialization did not take hold until after the turn of the century, and then only slowly.

One other characteristic all Latin American countries shared was political instability. Lack of political experience, together with economic difficulties and sectional conflicts, brought an endless succession of dictators. Few countries produced any outstanding leaders comparable to Simón Bolívar (1783–1830), hero of the wars of liberation against Spain. Mexico was an exception, with Santa Anna (1828–55), Benito Juárez (1855–72), and Porfirio Díaz (1877–1911) all gaining fame chiefly through their efforts to resist foreign encroachment.

The weakness and confusion of Latin America seemed to invite such encroach-

Walt Whitman: The American Genius

The genius of the United States is not best or most in its executives or legislatures, nor in its ambassadors or authors or colleges or churches or parlors, nor even in its newspapers or inventors . . . but always most in the common people. Their manners, speech, dress, friendships—the freshness and candor of their physiognomy—the picturesque looseness of their carriage . . . their deathless attachment to freedom—their aversion to anything indecorous or soft or mean—the practical acknowledgment of the citizens of one state by the citizens of all other states—the fierceness of their roused resentment—their curiosity and welcome of novelty—their self-esteem and wonderful sympathy—their susceptibility to a slight—the air they have of persons who never knew how it felt to stand in the presence of superiors—the fluency of their speech—their delight in music, the sure symptom of manly tenderness and native elegance of soul . . . their good temper and openhandedness—the terrible significance of their elections—the President's taking off his hat to them not they to him—these too are unrhymed poetry. It awaits the gigantic and generous treatment worthy of it.

From Walt Whitman, Preface to *Leaves of Grass*, 1855.

ment. The United States, through its Monroe Doctrine, tried to forestall outside intervention. But it was chiefly Britain's support of American policy, combined with a temporary lull in overseas expansion, that kept Europe from challenging the Monroe Doctrine during the first half of the nineteenth century. When the first such challenge was delivered, during the Mexican venture of Napoleon III, the United States was strong enough to take a firm stand. Meanwhile Washington had embarked on its own course of expansion at the expense of Mexico in the 1840s. This first phase of American imperialism was followed by a second round fifty years later (see p. 685). Except for this transitory intervention on the part of the United States, however, Latin America remained free from outside interference. Isolation had its political advantages, but it retarded the economic development of a potentially prosperous region.

THE BRITISH EMPIRE: FROM COLONIES TO DOMINIONS

Prior to 1800 only the American continents had attracted any substantial number of European settlers. Elsewhere, European influence had remained chiefly commercial. It was only during the course of the nineteenth century that Asia, Africa, Australia, and New Zealand were colonized by Europeans. In this process of Europeanization, Great Britain led the way. As the nineteenth century opened, it still had vast holdings on the North American continent and in India. In addition, it had taken the first steps toward opening up Australia and had established claims to New Zealand.

The Empire After 1815

Despite these large possessions, England's colonial enthusiasm after 1815 was at a low ebb. The loss of the American colonies was partly responsible. With the decline of mercantilism, furthermore, the possession of colonies as sources of raw materials and possible markets had lost much of its meaning, since free trade enabled every nation to trade wherever it chose. By 1830 a number of British people were advocating the release of most of the remaining colonies from the control of the mother country. These proposals never got very far, however, mainly because of the agitation of a handful of men usually called the Colonial Reformers. Chief among them were Edward Gibbon Wakefield and the Earl of Durham. Wakefield, in his *Letter from Sidney* (1829), had laid down a plan for the systematic colonization of regions suitable for white settlement. Many of his ideas were subsequently carried out in Australia and New Zealand.

Lord Durham (1792–1840), governor of Canada from 1837 to 1840.

Canada: The First Dominion

Of still greater significance than Wakefield's activities were the proposals made by Lord Durham in his *Report on the Affairs of British North America* in 1839. Canada had been a source of trouble ever since it was taken over from the French in 1763. Its original French settlers resented the influx of large numbers of Britishers, especially after the American Revolution, and efforts to separate the two nationalities by the Canada Act of 1791 had not eased tensions. Discontent with British rule in both Upper and Lower Canada after 1815 had culminated in a brief uprising in 1837. To restore order, Lord Durham was made governor of Canada, and it was on the basis of his first-hand experience that he wrote his famous *Report*. In it he suggested that Upper Canada (Ontario) and Lower Canada (Quebec) be reunited and given responsible self-government. Durham's proposals were incorporated in the Union Act of 1840.

This new arrangement, noted for its granting of self-government, still did not solve the differences between French and British settlers. After long debates among the provincial leaders of Canada, a new federal constitution, the British North America Act, was finally adopted by Britain's Parliament in 1867. Ontario and Quebec were once more separated, and together with the provinces of New Brunswick and Nova Scotia were united in the Dominion of Canada. From the start the Dominion had complete control over its internal affairs, and as time went on it became more and more independent in external matters as well.

Australia, New Zealand, and the Union of South Africa

The evolution of dominion status for Canada was a landmark in the history of the British Empire. A former colony had been set free and yet had remained loyal to the mother country. The first step had thus been taken on the road toward what later came to be known as the British Commonwealth. The practice followed in Canada was in time applied to other British settlements overseas. Australia's various states were granted self-government beginning in 1850 and were given dominion status as the Commonwealth of Australia in 1901. In New Zealand, self-government began in 1876 and dominion status was achieved in 1907. Finally, in South Africa various of the smaller territories were joined together in the Union of South Africa in 1910. This completed the list of Britain's original dominions.

The four self-governing dominions thus established were not by any means fully sovereign and independent states. In their foreign affairs in particular, they were still under the control of Great Britain. But such dependence was not felt as a burden. When war broke out in 1914, England did not have to bring pressure to bear on its dominions to join the fight against the Central Powers. The bond of common ideals and institutions had created a community of interest that stood the test of war.

India Under the East India Company

The change from colonies to dominions happened only in those regions that had substantial numbers of white settlers. Elsewhere traditional colonialism continued. This was particularly true in the most valuable of England's possessions, India. As a result of the Seven Years' War, England in 1763 had become the dominant European power in that part of the world. Britain's interests in India, since 1600, had been represented by the East India Company. This was a joint stock company that enjoyed a monopoly of trade and operated with little interference from the British government. Primarily concerned with making profits for its investors, the company systematically exploited the natives.

In time the East India Company's policy began to run into criticism at home, forcing the government to impose restrictions on the company's activities. The Regulation Act of 1773 provided for a governor general appointed by the crown, and the India Act of 1784 placed the company's political activities under the supervision of a Board of Control in London. Later measures restricted and ultimately abolished the East India Company's trade monopoly. The general tendency before the middle of the nineteenth century was to transfer more and more of the company's functions and powers to the British government.

The event that brought the company's rule in India to an end was the In-

Walter Bagehot on the Superiority of Englishmen   1869

Let us consider in what a village of English colonists is superior to a tribe of Australian natives who roam about them. Indisputably in one, and that a main sense, they are superior. They can beat the Australians in war when they like; they can take from them anything they like, and kill any of them they choose. . . . Nor is this all. Indisputably in the English village there are more means of happiness, a greater accumulation of the instruments of enjoyment, than in the Australian tribe. The English have all manner of books, utensils, and machines which the others do not use, value, or understand. . . . I think that the plainer and agreed-on superiorities of the Englishmen are these: first, that they have a greater command over the powers of nature upon the whole. . . . Secondly, that this power is not external only; it is also internal. The English not only possess better machines for moving nature, but are themselves better machines. . . . Thirdly, civilized man not only has greater powers over nature, but knows better how to use them, and by better I here mean better for the health and comfort of his present body and mind. . . . No doubt there will remain people like the aged savage who in his old age went back to his savage tribe and said that he had "tried civilization for forty years, and it was not worth the trouble." But we need not take account of the mistaken ideas of unfit men and beaten races.

From Walter Bagehot, *Physics and Politics* (New York: Knopf, 1948), pp. 214–16.

dian Mutiny of 1857. Britain's policy in India during the first half of the nineteenth century, especially under such able governor generals as Lord William Bentinck and the Earl of Dalhousie, had begun to be much more beneficial. India's finances had been overhauled, a system of western education had been introduced, and Indians had been given some participation in their government. Despite these and other improvements, however, there remained a great deal of discontent and unrest. Princes and landlords who had lost their former influence, orthodox Moslems and Hindus who feared the spread of Christianity, intellectuals who objected to the westernization of Indian culture, and the people at large who lived in acute misery—all

these elements combined to bring about the "Great Mutiny" that was staged in 1857.

The revolt started over a minor incident among the sepoys—the native soldiers who made up the bulk of England's armed forces in India. The mutiny was poorly organized and short-lived, but its violence cast a long shadow on Anglo-Indian relations. The British public blamed the East India Company for most of the conditions that helped bring on the rebellion. In 1858, therefore, Parliament took over all the company's duties and obligations. The governor general now became a viceroy, and the place of the old Board of Control was taken by a secretary of state for India within the British cabinet.

HE BRITISH EMPIRE   Nineteenth century

HER MOST GRACIOUS MAJESTY.

Our Queen and our Empress
Is greater and wiser
Than all foreign monarchs,
Including "der Kaiser."

British imperialism: cartoon and verse from *Pictures for Little Englanders,* a children's book published in the late nineteenth century.

British Rule in India

With the assumption of full control by the British government, the history of India entered a new phase. Under the Indian Councils Act of 1861, the viceroy was assisted by legislative and executive councils that included some Indian representation. But the viceroy retained the veto power. It was thus native participation rather than self-government that prevailed in India. Britain's efforts, moreover, to cope with the major problems of a rapidly growing population living in dismal poverty were only partly successful. The Indian farmer, paying exorbitant rents to his landlord and working small plots of exhausted soil, was subject to periodic famines. Industrialization, which might have absorbed much of the surplus population, was discouraged for fear that it might compete with industry back home.

Despite these shortcomings, British rule of India proved a vast improvement over what had existed under the East India Company. With the growth of a native middle class, demands for political and social reforms became more vociferous. In 1886 the most important native political party, the National Congress, held its first meeting. At the start the Congress demanded only moderate reforms. But as time went on it became more radical, and by 1907 there was a faction asking for complete independence. To encourage the moderates within the Congress, the British in 1909 made further concessions toward representative government. For the time being these improvements seemed to satisfy India's demands. When war broke out in 1914, India, like the dominions, rallied to the side of the mother country.

The "New Imperialism"

The lack of interest in colonial expansion, which had prevailed in England during the first half of the nineteenth century, came to an end after 1870. The man who helped rekindle the interest of his countrymen in the far-flung possessions of their empire was Benjamin Disraeli. In 1875 he quietly bought a substantial interest in the Suez Canal Company, thus starting Britain's involvement in Egypt. The following year Disraeli had Parliament confer the title of Empress of India on Queen Victoria.

The revival of imperialist sentiment was not confined to England. Almost all the major and some of the minor powers of Europe now started competing for the still unclaimed regions of the world. The reasons for this sudden wave of "new imperialism" were partly political and largely economic (see p. 643). The rivalries resulting from this scramble for overseas possessions were a major factor in the mounting international tension leading up to the First World War. The main spheres of expansion were the newly explored continent of Africa and the ancient empire of China.

CHINA AND THE GREAT POWERS

Contacts between China and the western world in the past had been limited. Some commercial relations had developed with Dutch, Portuguese, and British traders, and in the eighteenth century Jesuit missionaries had been welcomed at the court of the Manchu dynasty. Beginning in 1757, however, the Chinese government, antagonized by the conduct of some of the European traders, had closed all its ports except Canton. Henceforth all business had to be transacted there and under narrowly prescribed rules. These irksome restrictions generated most of the tension that ultimately led to the Opium War of 1839.

The Opium War

Various efforts in the early nineteenth century, especially on the part of the British government, to have additional ports opened to foreign trade were unsuccessful. An added source of trouble between Britain and China was the flourishing trade in opium that had developed during the eighteenth century. There were few commodities China was ready to buy from the outside world, and opium was one of them. The Chinese government had long been alarmed by the flourishing trade in opium and had vainly tried to stop it. In 1839 it moved to confiscate and destroy the vast quantities of the drug stored in Canton. It was this action that started the Opium War with Great Britain.

After three years of intermittent fighting, the Chinese were forced to agree to Britain's terms as laid down in the Treaty of Nanking (1842). Under its provisions, four ports in addition to Canton were opened to British traders, and Britain was given the island of Hong Kong as a base. In subsequent treaties, France and the United States received additional concessions that came to be shared by all powers alike. Most important among these was the principle of "extraterritoriality," which placed all foreigners in China under the jurisdiction of their own consular courts.

The "first treaty settlement," as these various Chinese concessions came to be called, was a landmark in that country's history. As more and more "treaty ports" were added in the course of the century, many of them inland cities, the Chinese Empire was gradually opened up by foreign traders and missionaries, with far-reaching effects on China's economy and society. The first effects of this sudden contact between two very different civilizations were felt in one of the most violent crises in China's history, the Taiping Rebellion (1850–64).

The Taiping Rebellion

The underlying cause of the rebellion was the inefficiency and corruption of the Manchu government and the weakness it had shown in its dealings with the western powers. There had been mounting discontent with a system that exploited the masses of the people for the good of a small ruling clique. With the death of the emperor in 1850, various local manifestations of unrest came together in a general rebellion. In its ideology, the Taiping Rebellion was influenced by Christianity. Its leader was a religious mystic, Hung Hsiu-ch'üan. Its main appeal to the Chinese peasant lay in its abolition of the high land rent.

The Taiping rebels, though antiforeign, nevertheless hoped to gain the support of the European powers in their struggle against the Manchu regime. Tensions between China and the western powers had continued into the 1850s; and as the British and French continued to insist on their treaty rights, a new series of conflicts broke out. The Chinese government thus found itself at war with domestic as well as foreign elements. Had these two opponents joined forces, they could easily have overthrown the Manchu dynasty. As it turned out, however, the European powers, aided by the Taiping rebels, first defeated the Chinese government and then helped the government defeat the Taiping rebels.

After the fall of Canton and the occupation of Tientsin in 1858, Peking was once more ready to come to terms with the powers. Under the Treaties of Tientsin, China opened several more treaty ports, agreed to the establishment of foreign legations at Peking, and permitted foreigners to move freely throughout the country. In addition, the Yangtze River was opened to foreign navigation and the opium trade was legalized. When the Chinese failed to honor these obligations, the French and British briefly resumed

A French caricature of the causes of the Opium War. The Englishman, backed by troops, is telling China: "You must buy our poison. We want you to deaden yourself so completely that we'll be able to take all the tea we want to drink with our beefsteak."

hostilities. The climax came with the storming of Peking and the burning of the emperor's summer palace. Under a new convention signed in 1860, China had to make further concessions. Simultaneously the Russians, taking advantage of China's embarrassment, secured for themselves a large slice of territory north of the Amur River, as well as along the Pacific. Here they founded the port of Vladivostok (1860), thus gaining a long-desired naval outlet.

Once peace had been made, the Manchu government could turn its full force against the Taiping rebels. In this it had the support of the foreign powers.

This western attitude has been rightly criticized. The Taiping rebels certainly were far more enlightened and progressive than the reactionary clique that surrounded the Manchu court. Yet the powers were mainly concerned with the preservation of their privileges, which the rebels intended to abolish. Western policy was motivated by self-interest rather than a desire to reform China.

The suppression of the Taiping Rebellion ushered in a period of comparative peace in Chinese affairs. Some efforts were made by the government to modernize China while maintaining its Confucian tradition, but these were not very successful. Beginning in 1877 China established its first diplomatic missions abroad. The telegraph meanwhile helped to bridge the country's vast distances, but the first railroad was not opened until 1888. The great powers did little to further China's reforming efforts. Some Chinese students studied abroad, and Protestant missionaries continued to bring western ideas to China. But frequent incidents in which Chinese crowds attacked foreigners served as convenient excuses for further foreign encroachment. France strengthened its influence over Indochina in 1884, and Britain's protectorate in Burma was recognized by China in 1886. These regions in the past had been tributaries of China.

The Sino-Japanese War

China's first major international conflict after 1860, however, was not with a western power but with an eastern rival, the empire of Japan. Japan had been far more successful than China in adapting to western ways. And the Japanese did not overlook the revelation of China's weakness in its dealings with the European powers. The area over which the two came to blows in 1894 was Korea, the section of the mainland closest to Japan. Korea had long been a tributary of China, but it had also seen gradual encroachment by Japan. It was this encroachment that finally led to war.

The Sino-Japanese War (1894–95) was won by Japan despite Chinese superiority in manpower and naval strength. Under the Treaty of Shimonoseki (1895), China had to recognize the independence of Korea and cede to Japan the island of Formosa, the Pescadores Islands, and the Liaotung Peninsula. The European powers, with the exception of England, were much alarmed by Japan's obtaining a foothold on the Chinese mainland. Russia in particular did not want the Japanese in the Liaotung Peninsula. Russia was joined by France, with whom it had recently concluded an alliance, and by Germany, who was eager to get on better terms with Russia, in putting pressure on Japan to forgo annexation of the peninsula. Japan had little choice but to give in.

German cartoon showing the western nations lining up to take their slice of China (1900).

The Japanese got even with Russia ten years later (see p. 642).

The Scramble for Foreign Concessions

China's defeat by Japan came just when the rivalry among the great powers for overseas territory had reached a new height. The weakness of China now served as the occasion for an imperialist feast the likes of which the world had rarely seen. Between 1896 and 1898, all the major European powers imposed upon China spheres of influence, trading rights, railway concessions, naval stations, mining rights, and whatever other forms of direct and indirect control western imperialists could devise. Russia got Port Arthur on the very same Liaotung Peninsula from which it had just ousted Japan; Germany acquired special rights on the Shantung Peninsula; the British secured a naval base at Weihaiwei; and the French obtained a lease of Kwangchow Bay. The United States, preoccupied with its own venture into imperialism during the Spanish-American War, merely issued a warning to the powers not to interfere with existing treaty ports and other interests in China. This "Open Door" (that is, equal economic opportunity for everyone) note of 1899 had little immediate effect, but it expressed an important principle of future American foreign policy for the Far East.

Reform and Reaction

At the height of the foreign encroachments in 1898, the imperial government made a belated attempt at reform. The short-lived "hundred days

Tz'ŭ Hsi (1854–1908), the dowager empress of China who resisted foreign encroachment by encouraging the abortive Boxer Rebellion. Shortly after her death the Manchu dynasty came to an end.

of reform," as this effort was called, was inspired and directed by K'ang Yu-wei, China's last great Confucian scholar. He hoped to create a constitutional monarchy, improve the civil service, reform the educational system, and introduce some western technology. The reformers had the support of the emperor, Kuang-hsü, but they were opposed by the established political and military hierarchy, which looked for leadership to the dowager empress, Tz'ŭ Hsi. This remarkable woman had long been the center of resistance to all reforms. Discovering in the fall of 1898 that she was about to be arrested, she decided to strike first. She imprisoned the emperor and suppressed the reform movement. Until her death in 1908, the dowager empress ruled supreme.

The victory of reaction in China was aided by a military uprising at the turn of the century, directed primarily against foreigners. The "Fists of Righteous Harmony," or "Boxers," as these antiforeign elements were called, were chiefly active in the north of China. As more and more foreigners were attacked and the foreign legations in Peking put under siege, the great powers decided to strike back. An international expeditionary force descended on China, took Tientsin, and sacked Peking. Only the rivalry among the powers prevented the outright partitioning of the country. Instead, China had to pay a huge indemnity.

China's repeated defeats at the hands of the West had given ample proof that western civilization, at least in its material aspects, was superior to that of the East. As demands for reform within China became stronger, the Manchu dynasty was forced into some half-hearted attempts to liberalize the government. In 1908 a draft constitution was published, calling for the election of a national parliament after nine years. Before it could go into effect, however, the Manchu regime was overthrown.

The Revolution of 1911

The leader of the revolution was a Chinese doctor, Sun Yat-sen, generally considered the founder of modern China. His movement—the Kuomintang, or Na-

tional People's Party, as it was ultimately called—aimed to reform China and to free it from foreign encroachment. Its program consisted of three main points: national independence, democracy, and social justice. Prior to 1911 Sun's organization engineered some abortive local uprisings. To overthrow the Manchu dynasty, however, added support was needed. This was supplied by some of the provincial governors and military leaders who had long been at odds with the central government. Outstanding among these military figures was Yüan Shih-k'ai, a follower of the dowager empress, who had lost his position when the empress died in 1908. In 1911 the government asked Yüan to help put down a local uprising of Sun Yat-sen's followers at Hankow. Instead, Yüan helped depose the last Manchu emperor. It was this combination of forces that brought about the initial victory of the Revolution. In return for his support, Yüan was made president of the new Chinese Republic.

The main problem facing China after 1911 was how to reconcile the diverse elements in its government. In 1912 a provisional constitution called for a parliamentary government. But meanwhile Yüan Shih-k'ai was trying to extend his own power in the hope of ultimately founding a new dynasty. In 1914 Yüan embarked on a brief period of personal government. He died in 1916. With him China lost a leader who might have prevented the general anarchy and civil war that prevailed throughout the country for the next ten years. China's efforts to set its own house in order had failed.

THE EMERGENCE OF MODERN JAPAN

China's contacts with the West had proved disastrous; Japan's experience was far more fortunate. In the first half of the seventeenth century, Japan had been virtually closed to western influence. It was not until the middle of the nineteenth century that internal weakness and outside pressure brought about the reopening of the island empire. Japan at the time was still being ruled—as it had been for centuries—by the emperor's commander in chief, or shogun. This essentially feudal system, however, was proving increasingly inefficient, and there was fear that unless Japan modernized its ways, it might suffer the fate of China and become a victim of western exploitation.

The Opening Up of Japan

Japan was reopened to the outside world, suddenly and dramatically, through the efforts of the American commodore Matthew Perry. His request in 1853, backed by an imposing fleet of steam warships, that commercial relations be established between the United States and Japan could not be refused, given Japan's military backwardness. In the resulting Treaty of Kanagawa (1854) the first Japanese ports were opened to foreign trade. Commercial and other agreements followed, not only with America but with other nations as well. The long period of Japan's seclusion, thanks to American initiative, had been ended.

Japan, however, did not become a victim but rather a competitor of the western powers in the colonization of the Far East. This it did by a policy of determined modernization and westernization. Japan's rapid transition from feudalism to industrialism did not come about without a major domestic upheaval. The sudden influx of foreigners caused deep resentment among many Japanese. While the shogun was forced by circumstances to collaborate with the western powers, the emperor and his advisers advocated resistance. The struggle between these two factions was decided in 1867, with the victory of the imperial supporters and the resignation of the last shogun. In 1868 the Meiji emperor assumed direct control over the nation, moving his capital from Kyoto to Edo, now renamed Tokyo.

The Meiji Period

The Meiji period (1868–1912) saw the emergence of Japan as a modern great power. The outstanding developments during the last decades of the nineteenth century were the abolition of feudalism and the industrialization of Japan. In 1871 an imperial decree abolished the large feudal fiefs and inaugurated a more highly centralized government along western lines. As the power of the old privileged families declined, so did the importance of their retainers, the samurai. When in 1876, the members of this traditional warrior class were forbidden to wear their two swords, the sign of their privileged status, they revolted. The Satsuma Rebellion (1877), involving some two hundred thousand men, was crushed by troops armed with modern weapons. With it the last resistance of feudal forces came to an end.

The modernization of Japan was most rapid and thorough in the industrial field. Industrialization had to start virtually from scratch, but the imperial government from the beginning took a hand in founding and running essential industries. When financial difficulties after 1880 forced the government to sell its enterprises, they were bought by a few wealthy families, the *zaibatsu*, who from then on dominated the economic life of Japan. The influence of the state over economic affairs, however, continued to be close, and the spirit of laissez faire, so prominent in the West, never gained a comparable hold in Japan.

The modernization of Japan affected every aspect of its life. Together with universal military service, universal education helped to transform illiterate peasants into trained and obedient workers. Buddhism was deemphasized and Christianity was tolerated. There was also renewed interest in the ancient native religion of Japan, the cult of Shinto.

Two views of Commodore Matthew Perry. Above: Japanese representation printed shortly after his mission to Japan in 1853. Below: daguerrotype by Mathew Brady.

With its veneration of the emperor as the Son of Heaven, Shintoism provided a religious basis for Japan's new nationalism. In its efforts to catch up with the West, Japan borrowed freely wherever it could find the institutions best suited to its needs. Its legal system was modernized along French lines, and its financial organization was borrowed from the United States. British officers helped build a new navy, and the new Japanese constitution followed a Prussian model.

One of the main concerns of the Meiji period was the creation of some form of representative government. The emperor had promised a deliberative assembly in his "Charter Oath" of 1868. But it was not until 1884 that the drafting of a Japanese constitution was begun. As promulgated in 1889, the constitution established an Imperial Diet of two houses. The lower house was elected under a restricted franchise that gave the vote to less than half a million Japanese. There was no ministerial responsibility. The emperor could issue decrees with the force of laws, and he could declare war. The Japanese constitution thus did not really affect the traditional power structure. Still, the introduction of parliamentary practices gave some voice and

experience to the rising middle class, and the Japanese people gained more political influence than they had ever had before.

Despite its preoccupation with domestic reform, Japan also was able to carry on an active and successful foreign policy. Industrialization called for raw materials and markets, and a growing population called for living space. As early as 1874 Japan sent an expedition to Formosa. In 1876 Japan started the long rivalry with China over Korea that led to the Sino-Japanese War (1894–95). Japan's victory in that war, as we have seen, caused the tension with Russia that in turn led to a still more important war ten years later.

The Russo-Japanese War

The rivalry between Japan and Russia in the Far East went back to the middle of the nineteenth century. At that time Russia began extending its influence over the portion of China facing the Sea of Japan. By the end of the century, the only region opposite Japan still free from Russian domination was Korea. Japan continued to assert its interests in Korea after its victory over China in 1895. At the same time, however, the tsarist empire was stepping up its activities there. In 1902 Japan concluded an alliance with Great Britain, which had long opposed Russia's expansion in Asia. Japan thus was assured of the friendship of another major power with interests in the Far East.

The Russo-Japanese War, long in the making, broke out in 1904. Japan had definite strategic advantages, but even so the world was little prepared for the resounding defeat inflicted on the Russians. After eighteen months of fighting, the mediation of President Theodore Roosevelt ended the war. The treaty of peace signed at Portsmouth, New Hampshire (1905), completed the emergence of Japan as a major power. Its interests in Korea were now recognized. In addition, Japan received control over the Liaotung Peninsula, together with some Russian railroad concessions in southern Manchuria. Russia also ceded to Japan the southern half of the island of Sakhalin.

Theodore Roosevelt with the Russian and Japanese representatives to the peace negotiations in Portsmouth, New Hampshire, that ended the Russo-Japanese War (1905). Left to right: Sergius Witte, Baron Rosen, Roosevelt, Baron Komura, and Baron Takahira.

Japan's victory over Russia marked a turning point in relations between Europe and Asia. For the first time in modern history, one of the so-called backward nations had defeated one of the major powers of the West. The effects of this event were felt in an upsurge of nationalism among the nations of Asia, the ultimate repercussions of which have lasted into our own day.

AN EVALUATION OF WESTERN IMPERIALISM

The growth of the United States into a major power, the transformation of the British Empire into a worldwide Commonwealth, the opening up of China, and the westernization of Japan—all these were manifestations of the vast influence that western civilization had gained in the course of a single century. One region became almost wholly subservient to western domination during the latter part of the nineteenth century—the continent of Africa (see p. 679).

Much of this expansion of western civilization had taken place in the last decades of the nineteenth century. In an age of ardent nationalism, it was considered a point of honor for any great power to raise its flag over as large an area of the globe as possible. At a time, furthermore, when unprecedented industrial growth created an urgent need for raw materials, markets, and outlets for surplus capital and population, colonies and foreign concessions seemed to provide a ready solution to economic problems. Finally, a civilization that considered itself superior to all others could easily convince itself that its members had a civilizing mission and should assume what Rudyard Kipling called "the white man's burden."

The various motives for imperialist expansion have come in for a good deal of criticism. There can be no doubt about the sincerity with which most western imperialists believed in the advantages that the spread of their civilization would bring to the rest of the world. It was only after the bitter experiences of the twentieth century, when the cause of western imperialism suffered one reversal after another, that this belief began to be shaken. Politically, western domination of colonial regions merely seemed to awaken among the subjected peoples a consciousness of their own national interests and a desire for independence. While this in itself may be a positive achievement, it certainly was not what the imperialists of the last century had envisaged. Economically, the advantages derived from imperialism were limited to small groups within the mother countries. As time went on it became clear that the most advantageous policy in the long run was the economic development rather than the exploitation of backward areas. Such development, however, was slow and expensive, and its ultimate effect was to emancipate rather than subdue colonial areas.

About the civilizing effects of the spread of western civilization, there are divided opinions. There is no need to point out the many advantages that have

Christian missionary in India (*ca.* 1900).

J. A. Hobson on Imperialism 1902

Thus do the industrial and financial forces of Imperialism, operating through the party, the press, the church, the school, mould public opinion and public policy by the false idealization of those primitive lusts of struggle, domination and acquisitiveness, which have survived throughout the eras of peaceful industrial order, and whose stimulation is needed once again for the work of imperial aggression, expansion, and the forceful exploitation of lower races. For these business politicians biology and sociology weave thin convenient theories of a race struggle for the subjugation of the inferior peoples, in order that we, the Anglo-Saxon, may take their lands and live upon their labours; while economics buttresses the argument by representing our work in conquering and ruling them as our share in the division of labour among nations, and history devises reasons why the lessons of past empire do not apply to ours, while social ethics paints the motive of "imperialism" as the desire to bear the "burden" of educating and elevating races of "children." Thus are the "cultured" or semi-cultured classes indoctrinated with the intellectual and moral grandeur of Imperialism. For the masses there is a cruder appeal to hero-worship and sensational glory, adventure and the sporting spirit: current history falsified in coarse flaring colours, for the direct stimulation of the combative instincts. . . . Imperialism is a depraved choice of national life, imposed by self-seeking interests which appeal to the lusts of quantitative acquisitiveness and of forceful domination surviving in a nation from early centuries of animal struggle for existence.

From J. A. Hobson, *Imperialism: A Study* (Ann Arbor, Mich.: Ann Arbor Paperbacks, 1965), pp. 221–22, 368.

come to the rest of the world from its contacts with the West. In the field of medicine alone, the lives of millions of people have been saved by western scientists, and the slow but steady rise in the living standards of even the most backward regions would have been impossible without western aid and examples. The fault that has been found with the westernization of the world has been chiefly in the methods employed by western imperialists. Until quite recently the advantages that western civilization brought to many parts of the world were largely incidental to the primarily selfish aims and ambitions of the more advanced nations. The white man's burden, it has been said, has rested heavily on the shoulders of the black, brown, and yellow men who were subjugated by him. Only in our own day have we come to recognize and to correct some of the mistakes made by western imperialism in the past.

Suggestions for Further Reading

Note: Asterisk denotes a book available in paperback edition.

General

Because of its wide range, there are no general works covering the whole subject matter of this chapter. D. K. Fieldhouse, *The Colonial Empires* (1966), and *Colonialism, 1870–1945: An Introduction* (1981) are useful surveys, as is S. L. Easton, *The Rise and Fall of Western Colonialism** (1964). P. T. Moon, *Imperialism and World Politics* (1926), is still a standard work on the expansion of Europe. K. S. Latourette, *A History of the Expansion of Christianity*, Vols. V and VI (1945), deals with an important aspect of Europe's spreading influence. Good general works on East Asia are E. O. Reischauer and A. M. Craig, *A History of East Asian Civilization*, Vol. II: *East Asia: The Modern Transformation* (1965), and C. Schirokauer, *Modern China and Japan: A Brief History** (1982). C. E. Carrington, *The British Overseas* (1950), deals with British colonization. The motives of modern imperialism are treated in numerous books, among them the classics by J. A. Hobson, *Imperialism: A Study** (1902), and N. Lenin, *Imperialism: The Highest State of Capitalism** (1916). More recent studies and critiques of imperialism are J. A. Schumpeter, *Imperialism and Social Classes** (1955), and E. M. Winslow, *The Pattern of Imperialism* (1948). See also A. P. Thornton, *Doctrines of Imperialism** (1965), and R. Koebner and H. D. Smith, *Imperialism: The Story and Significance of a Political Word, 1840–1960* (1964). The effect of imperialism on the colonial peoples is the subject of F. Fanon, *The Wretched of the Earth** (1969). D. O. Mannoni, *Prospero and Caliban: The Psychology of Colonization* (1956), is unique and provocative. On the spread of Europe's economic influence, see W. Woodruff, *Impact of Western Man: A Study of Europe's Role in the World Economy, 1750–1960* (1967).

The United States

The vast literature on American history during the nineteenth century makes any selection of representative titles difficult. An excellent introduction to the subject are the relevant chapters in J. M. Blum, et al., *The National Experience: A History of the United States*, 5th ed. (1981), written by experts and containing detailed bibliographies. S. E. Morison, *History of the United States* (1965), is considered the master's masterpiece. On the pre-Jacksonian period, see G. Dangerfield, *The Era of Good Feelings** (1952) and *The Awakening of American Nationalism** (1965). The westward movement is discussed in R. G. Athearn, *America Moves West* (1964), and R. A. Billington, *Westward Expansion* (1967). W. E. Washburn, *The Indian in America* (1975), is the best survey of a controversial subject. Among studies on slavery, K. M. Stampp, *The Peculiar Institution** (1956), and E. D. Genovese, *The Political Economy of Slavery* (1965) and *Roll, Jordan, Roll: The World the Slaves Made* (1974), stand out. Industrial development is treated in D. C. North, *The Economic Growth of the United States, 1790–1860** (1961). On the Age of Jackson, see J. C. Curtis, *Andrew Jackson and the Search for Vindication* (1976), and C. M. Wiltse, *The New Nation, 1800–1845** (1961). A. Nevins, *Ordeal of the Union*, 2 vols. (1947), and J. G. Randall and D. Donald, *The Civil War and Reconstruction* (1961), are representative works on the Civil War and its background. The aftermath of the war is treated in K. M. Stampp, *The Era of Reconstruction* (1965), and in C. V. Woodward, *Origins of the New South, 1877–1913** (1951). The following are recommended for their insights into various phases of American thought and society: R. Hofstadter, *The American Political Tradition** (1955); L. Hartz, *The Liberal Tradition in America** (1955); and C. Rossiter, *Conservatism in America** (1955). On relations between the United States and Europe, see J. B. Brebner, *North Atlantic Triangle: The Interplay of Canada, the United States, and Great Britain* (1945), and H. Koht, *The American Spirit in Europe: A Survey of Transatlantic Influences* (1949).

America's search for overseas territory is comprehensively covered in C. S. Campbell, *The Transformation of American Foreign Relations, 1865–1900* (1976).

Latin America   One of the best recent histories of Latin America is J. F. Rippy, *Latin America: A Modern History* (1958). Other good standard works are D. G. Munro, *The Latin American Republics* (1950); H. Herring, *A History of Latin America* (1955); and W. L. Schurz, *The New World: The Civilization of Latin America* (1954). F. Tannenbaum, *Ten Keys to Latin America* (1962), deals with the broader aspects and issues of Latin American life, as does C. Véliz, *The Centralist Tradition of Latin America* (1980). The following cover specific subjects: J. L. Mecham, *Church and State in Latin America* (1934); W. C. Gordon, *The Economy of Latin America* (1950); R. Crawford, *A Century of Latin American Thought*, rev. ed. (1966); and G. Arciniegas, *Latin America: A Cultural History* (1967). On hemispheric relations, see D. Perkins, *A History of the Monroe Doctrine*, rev. ed. (1955); S. F. Bemis, *The Latin American Policy of the United States* (1943); J. L. Mecham, *A Survey of United States—Latin American Relations* (1965); and W. H. Calcott, *The Western Hemisphere: Its Influence on United States Policies to the End of World War II* (1968).

The British Empire   The most comprehensive work on the subject is J. H. Rose et al., eds., *The Cambridge History of the British Empire*, 7 vols. (1929–40). For the period of the "new imperialism," see C. J. Lowe, *The Reluctant Imperialists: British Foreign Policy, 1878–1902* (1967). Two good recent books are B. Porter, *The Lion's Share: A Short History of British Imperialism, 1850–1970* (1976), and R. Hyam, *Britain's Imperial Century, 1815–1914* (1976). The four original dominions are treated individually in J. M. S. Careless, *Canada: A Story of Challenge* (1953); M. Clark, *A Short History of Australia*, rev. ed. (1969); K. Sinclair, *A Short History of New Zealand* (1961); and C. W. de Kiewiet, *A History of South Africa: Social and Economic* (1941). Good brief histories of India are W. H. Moreland and A. C. Chatterjee, *A Short History of India* (1957), and P. Spear, *India: A Modern History* (1961). Britain's role in India is evaluated in P. Woodruff, *The Men Who Ruled India*, 2 vols. (1954); R. P. Mansani, *Britain in India* (1961); M. Bearce, *British Attitudes Towards India* (1961); and E. J. Thompson and G. T. Garratt, *Rise and Fulfilment of British Rule in India* (1934). A key event in Indian history is the subject of T. R. Metcalf, *The Aftermath of Revolt: India, 1857–1870* (1964).

China   I. C. Y. Hsu, *The Rise of Modern China* (1983) is a solid, reliable survey. Volumes 10 (1800–70) and 11 (1870–1911) of the *Cambridge History of China* edited by J. K. Fairbank are major works of synthesis. J. B. Grieder, *Intellectuals and the State in Modern China: A Narrative History* (1981) provides a good introduction to its subject. P. Kuhn, *Rebellion and Its Enemies in Late Imperial China* (1970) is an important treatment of a major subject. M. C. Wright, ed., *China in Revolution: The First Phase, 1900–1913** (1968) is a valuable collection. C. Wilbur, *Sun Yat-sen: Frustrated Patriot* (1977) is a judicious study of "the father of the Chinese Revolution." For diplomatic history see I. C. Y. Hsu, *China's Entrance into the Family of Nations: The Diplomatic Phase, 1858–1890* (1956) and J. C. Thompson, Jr., *American–East Asian Relations: A Survey* (1972), which emphasizes bibliography. J. K. Fairbank, *The United States and China* (1979) is an exceptionally well written broad survey.

Japan   J. W. Hall, *Japan from Pre-History to Modern Times* (1970), and W. G. Beasley, *The Modern History of Japan* (1981), are good introductions. See also A. Tiedemann, ed., *An Introduction to Japanese Civilization* (1974). Special aspects of Japanese history and culture are treated in W. W. Lockwood, ed., *The State and Economic Enterprise in Japan* (1968); M. B. Jansen, ed., *Changing Japanese Attitudes Toward Modernization* (1965); R. E. Ward, ed., *Political Development in Modern Japan* (1968), and D. H. Shively, ed., *Tradition and Modernization in Japanese Culture* (1971). G. B. Sansom, *The Western World and Japan: A Study in the Interaction of European and Asiatic Cultures* (1950), discusses the rest of Asia as well as Japan. Japanese relations with the United States are treated in P. J. Treat, *Diplomatic Relations Between the United States and Japan, 1853–1905*, 3 vols. (1938–63); R. A. Esthus, *Theodore Roosevelt and Japan** (1967); and R. S. Schwantes, *Japanese and Americans: A Century of Cultural Relations* (1955). Important, though not always accurate, is R. Benedict, *The Chrysanthemum and the Sword: Patterns of Japanese Culture* (1946).

28 Europe 1870–1914: Promise and Pessimism

The last decades of the nineteenth century in Europe were puzzling years. On the one hand, with economic prosperity at home, with peace abroad, and with rapid advances in all fields of scientific research, the belief in progress that had prevailed since the Enlightenment seemed happily confirmed. But on the other hand, from a later vantage point and with the knowledge of what happened in 1914, the period looks different. Despite rising prosperity, there were several periods of depression, and many Europeans continued to live in poverty. Peace on the European continent was bought at the price of subjugating colonial peoples overseas and suppressing national minorities at home. The preeminence of science, with its stress on material values, makes the pre-1914 period appear in retrospect as a crass and materialistic age. An air of optimism and apprehension, therefore, of promise and pessimism prevailed during the half-century before the First World War.

This chapter is primarily concerned with domestic affairs. Developments in various parts of Europe differed, but certain political, economic, and social trends were common to most countries. In politics, Europe after 1870 witnessed the further spread of constitutional and democratic government, often accompanied by unrest. In economics, most countries shared in the unprecedented industrial upheaval that is sometimes referred to as the "Second Industrial Revolution." In the social sphere, the labor movement and its doctrine of socialism came to play an increasingly important role in the affairs of almost all nations, causing fear and frustration among the established order.

THE GROWTH OF DEMOCRACY

To have true democracy, all adult citizens must have a voice in deciding how they are to be governed. In this sense, no country in 1870, and only two or three in 1914, could be called democratic. The main concern during the intervening period was with winning democracy for men only; and here much progress was made. By 1914 most of the countries in Europe had universal manhood suffrage and several had parliamentary government. But the degree and effectiveness of this male democracy varied. In England some 20 percent of adult males still could not vote. In France and Italy universal manhood suffrage existed, but parliamentary government functioned poorly. Germany, too, had universal manhood suffrage; but since the chancellor was not responsible to parliament, democracy hardly existed. In Austria-Hungary the main obstacle to democratic government was the perennial problem of nationalities. In Russia the franchise in 1914 was still limited, and the National Assembly, or *Duma*, had merely advisory functions.

Women's Rights

The only countries in 1914 where women were allowed to vote were Norway, New Zealand, Australia, and some parts of the American West, and it was in the United States that agitation for women's rights had its earliest start. In Europe the main efforts were centered in England and to a lesser extent in Germany. We have already seen John Stuart Mill's pioneering agitation on behalf of equality for women (see p. 580). By the end of the century, various women's suffrage societies had grown up in England and on the Continent, and in 1903 Emmeline Pankhurst launched her activist Women's Social and Political Union. The efforts of these determined "suffragettes" to gain political rights for women were met by staunch male and also some female opposition. Queen Victoria, herself an example of the equal, if not superior, ability of women, was highly critical of "this mad, wicked folly of 'women's rights' with all its attendant horrors." Outside the political arena, women were gradually being freed from the legal restrictions that had kept them the virtual wards of their husbands or fathers. As more and more women started careers of their own, they also gained economic independence. But most of the professions were still closed to women in an age that disapproved and made fun of the "emancipated woman" and adhered to the male slogan that "woman's place is in the home," be it as mother or as domestic servant.

Opposite: Eastman Johnson, *The Hatch Family* (1871).

Women's labor parade, New York City (1912).

Democracy and Education

One profession in which women did gain considerable influence was elementary education. The success of democracy depended to no small extent on an informed electorate. Consequently the spread of democracy was accompanied almost everywhere by determined efforts to improve education. In England the Education Act of 1870 and subsequent acts made instruction free and compulsory. In Germany, already known for its advanced school system, further progress was made, especially in technical training. The main concern of the French Third Republic was to make instruction compulsory and nonsectarian. Both aims were accomplished by the so-called "Ferry Laws" (after Jules Ferry) in the early 1880s.

The need for education was especially acute in countries with high illiteracy rates. To improve the status of some 68 percent of its population who could not read or write, the Italian government in 1877 made education compulsory. But this act became effective only after 1911, when the central government took over the financial support of local schools. While all other countries, including the smaller ones, made deliberate efforts to stamp out ignorance, the tsarist government of Russia tried to discourage lower-class education on the grounds that it would "draw people away from the environment to which they belong."

The growth of democracy and general education between 1870 and 1914 did not necessarily bring the many blessings that liberals in particular had expected. Some earlier writers on democracy, like de Tocqueville and Mill, had already warned against imposing the standards of the majority on society as a whole. Such criticism continued in the late nineteenth century. To Henry Adams, democracy was one of the lower forms of government. The Englishman Walter Bagehot warned that the voice of the people might easily turn out to be the voice of the Devil. And the German philosopher Friedrich Nietzsche criticized parliamentary government as a means "whereby cattle become masters." How justified these warnings would turn out to be in some countries was not realized until after the First World War.

THE "SECOND INDUSTRIAL REVOLUTION"

The second general trend shared by most of Europe in the late nineteenth century was unparalleled industrial growth. The growth rate differed from country to country, of course, and was slower during the so-called "Great Depression" between 1873 and 1895, than it was before and after. This "Second Industrial Revolution" had certain unique characteristics. New sources of power—electricity and oil—competed with steam and coal in driving more intricate machinery. Refined techniques of steel production and the discovery of methods to use lower-grade ores made steel available in greater quantities and at a lower price. Synthetic products, notably dyes produced from coal tars, became the foundation of whole new industries; and the introduction of dynamite by the Swedish chemist Alfred Nobel in 1867 had repercussions in the military as well as the industrial field.

There were many other novel features of industrialism at the end of the century. New means of communication and transportation helped to speed up business transactions; new methods of pro-

Evidence of the growth of advertising—a London bus at the turn of the century.

motion boosted sales; a vast increase in the supply of liquid capital aided economic growth; and the rapid expansion of many enterprises led to new forms of industrial organization. All these innovations helped to increase the industrial output of Europe beyond anything ever known. The Second Industrial Revolution was mainly a quantitative phenomenon. The total production of the western world, including the United States, more than tripled between 1870 and 1914.

Social Effects

This increased industrialization accentuated earlier trends in society. The population of Europe, except in France, continued to grow dramatically, and the shift from rural to urban life continued. By 1900 from one-third to one-half of the population in the more highly industrialized countries lived in large cities. As industries expanded, agriculture declined. Through mechanization and chemical fertilizers, farmers were able to achieve remarkable increases in crop yields. But even so, Europe would have gone hungry had it not been for the expanding agricultural economies of Russia, the Americas, and Australia.

Industrialization continued to affect people's lives in other ways. The invention of labor-saving devices and the mass production of consumer goods helped to make life easier and more comfortable. Central heating, the use of gas and electricity, ready-made clothing, and the perfection of canning and refrigeration were only a few of the conveniences now enjoyed by most of the population.

But mechanization and mass production also had their negative sides. Some critics began to worry that the influence that machines gained over man might in time make him the slave rather than the master of his inventions. Mass production tended to standardize and cheapen public taste. It also led to overproduction. To stimulate sales, advertising steadily gained in importance. The production of cheap paper from wood pulp in the 1880s and the resulting growth of popular journalism proved a boon to advertisers. Yet some people deplored the money spent by manufacturers to make people

buy at higher cost goods that they did not really need or want. Industrialization at best was a mixed blessing.

"Big Business"

One of the characteristics of industrial development after 1870 was the substitution of "big business" for the smaller factories that had prevailed earlier. As enterprises became fewer, larger, and more competitive, producers formed combinations to control production, distribution, and price levels. The "trusts" of the United States, the "amalgamations" of Great Britain, and the "cartels" of Germany, differed in specifics but were alike in their efforts to establish some control over the production and distribution of goods. Opponents of this industrial concentration claimed that it tended to create monopolies that kept prices at artificially high levels. In response to such criticism, the United States in 1890 prohibited the formation of trusts, but it was the only major country to do so.

The period of "monopolistic capitalism," as the decades after 1870 are called, was also the heyday of the great industrialists—the Carnegies, Rockefellers, Krupps, Nobels, and others. The huge economic power of these "tycoons" could not help but give them political influence as well. But business leaders did not use their wealth only for their own ends. The ruthlessness that had characterized business during the early days of industrialization was gradually mitigated by signs of social consciousness on the part of some leading capitalists. One of the best examples of this humanitarian attitude was the steel magnate Andrew Carnegie. In his book *The Gospel of Wealth* (1900), Carnegie insisted that wealth was a public trust, not to be handed on within a single family but to be returned to the community from which it had been derived. To practice what he preached, Carnegie gave more than $300 million to worthy causes in the United States and Great Britain. There were also humanitarian capitalists in Europe, where the Nobel Prizes and the Rhodes Scholarships commemorate two highly successful businessmen.

PIG-IRON PRODUCTION 1860-1910

UNITED KINGDOM ———
GERMANY • • • • •
RUSSIA ━━━

metric tons (in millions)

COAL PRODUCTION 1860-1910

UNITED KINGDOM ———
GERMANY • • • • •
RUSSIA ━━━

metric tons (in millions)

Sidney (1859–1947) and Beatrice Webb (1858–1943), English Fabian socialists.

THE RISE OF THE WORKING CLASS

A third general trend during the period after 1870 was the increasing influence of the working class and its socialist philosophy. Much of the improvement in the worker's condition was due to the political power of the various socialist parties and to the economic power of the labor unions. As a result, the status of the European worker by 1914 had been raised far above what it had been in 1870.

New Varieties of Socialism

The basic aims and ideas of modern socialism as derived from Karl Marx and Friedrich Engels have been discussed (see pp. 587–90). Marx had predicted an increasing concentration of capital, balanced by a growing impoverishment of the masses, leading eventually to the collapse of capitalism. Events during the late nineteenth century, however, failed to bear out Marx's predictions. While much capital was concentrated in a few hands, there was a corresponding diffusion of ownership by means of joint stock companies. And while workers still suffered from some of the hardships that had marked the First Industrial Revolution, their condition steadily improved. By the end of the century it became clear that

Marx's prediction had to be adjusted to changed circumstances. The result of this adjustment in Marxian doctrine is called "revisionist," or "evolutionary," socialism.

The leading theorist of revisionism was the German socialist Eduard Bernstein. Bernstein had spent some time in England, where he came in contact with a non-Marxian brand of socialism advocated by a group of intellectuals, among them Sidney and Beatrice Webb, H. G. Wells, and George Bernard Shaw. Their socialism was called "Fabianism" after the Roman general Fabius, who preferred to defeat his enemies by gradually exhausting rather than by directly attacking them. The Fabian Socialists opposed violent revolution and sought instead to achieve socialization by way of gradual reform. Bernstein, on his return to Germany in the 1890s, began to expound his own revised version of Marxian socialism. In his *Evolutionary Socialism* (1899), Bernstein advocated that instead of waging a revolutionary struggle against the middle class, the working class should collaborate with any group, proletarian or bourgeois, that would help improve the workers' condition.

The revisionist ideas of Bernstein caused a major stir in Marxist circles. Orthodox Marxists denounced revisionism and reaffirmed their faith in the validity of all Marx's teachings. One of the most determined defenders of pure Marxism, the Russian Vladimir Ilyich Ulyanov, better known by his pseudonym, N. Lenin, held that collaboration with capitalism would help to perpetuate a system that would become more and more oppressive to the working class. Only a revolution could overthrow this system, and it was up to a minority within the proletariat, to prepare the way for revolution by keeping alive the idea of class struggle. Except in eastern Europe, this revolutionary brand of "Leninism" found few followers before the First World War.

Another form of violent protest arising at the turn of the century was syndicalism. Its main exponent was the Frenchman Georges Sorel, whose *Reflections on Violence* (1908) popularized his social philosophy. Like anarchism (see

p. 591), syndicalism saw the state as an instrument of oppression and advocated its abolition. Instead, the trade unions (*syndicat* is the French word for "union"), should seize control of a socialist society. To achieve their aim, the syndicalists advocated various means of industrial sabotage, culminating in a general strike. Syndicalism flourished most in Italy, Spain, and France; it also influenced the Industrial Workers of the World (IWW) in the United States.

International Socialism

Marxism was envisaged by its founder as an international movement, and Marx had been instrumental in founding the International Workingmen's Association in 1864. But the First International, as it was called, was not very successful. Marx's domineering manner, his controversy with Bakunin, who was among the leaders of the International, and the excesses of the Paris Commune in 1871, which were falsely blamed on the socialists, combined to bring about the gradual decline of the First International and its demise in 1876.

With the rise of socialist parties in most major countries during the next decade, however, a Second International was formed in 1889. From the start it was beset by internal differences, especially on the issue of revisionism. As time went on, moreover, it became obvious that the national loyalties of most socialists were stronger than their feelings of international solidarity. The Second International opposed war as a means of settling international disputes; but when the test came in 1914 the ideals of international socialism quickly gave way to the stronger appeal of national patriotism.

The Growth of Labor Unions

In addition to setting up their own political parties, workers tried to improve their lot through the formation of labor unions. In the early part of the nineteenth century, unions had made little progress anywhere except in Great Britain, and even there their activities remained restricted. This situation improved markedly after 1870. In England,

Headquarters of the First International, in a Paris back street.

in a series of legislative acts in 1874 and 1875, unions were given permission to strike and to engage in peaceful picketing. The most important advance in the history of British organized labor came as a result of the famous London dock strike of 1889. The first major strike among unskilled workers, this event marked the extension of union activity

Leninism

1902

I assert: [(1)] That no movement can be durable without a stable organization of leaders to maintain continuity; (2) that the more widely the masses are spontaneously drawn into the struggle and form the basis of the movement, the more necessary it is to have such an organization and the more stable must it be (for it is much easier then for demagogues to sidetrack the more backward sections of the masses); (3) that the organization must consist chiefly of persons engaged in revolutionary activities as a profession; (4) that in a country with an autocratic government, the more we *restrict* the membership of this organization to persons who are engaged in revolution as a profession and who have been professionally trained in the art of combating the political police, the more difficult will it be to catch the organization; and (5) the *wider* will be the circle of men and women of the working class or of other classes of society able to join the movement and perform active work in it.

From N. Lenin, "What Is to Be Done?" in *Selected Works* (London: Lawrence and Wishart, 1936), Vol. II, pp. 138–39.

beyond the skilled groups that in the past had made up union membership.

On the Continent the labor movement was slower in gaining momentum. In France, the bloody events of the Paris Commune of 1871 (see p. 611) cast a shadow on any kind of labor activity, and it was not until 1884 that the Waldeck-Rousseau Law granted full legal status to unions and allowed them to form larger federations. The decisive step in this direction came in 1895, when the General Confederation of Labor (CGT) was organized along syndicalist lines.

In Germany, where the labor movement was closely allied with socialism, it was adversely affected by the antisocialist measures of Bismarck. It thus did not really gain momentum until after 1890. Under the Imperial Industrial Code, German workers were permitted to strike, but an unfriendly government and hostile courts restricted the activities of organized labor wherever possible. In the less industrialized countries of Italy, Austria-Hungary, and Russia, trade unionism played a minor role. In Italy the labor movement was split into several factions, the largest of which, the socialist General Italian Federation of Labor, was founded in 1907. Socialist unions also predominated in Austria, though there was hardly any organized labor in agrarian Hungary. Russia had no real labor unions until after 1905, and even then they did not wield much influence.

The "Welfare State"

The agitation of European workers for political, economic, and social reforms did much to make their governments adopt programs of social legislation designed to help the lower classes. Such intervention by the state was a radical departure from the laissez-faire philosophy of early-nineteenth-century liberalism. The idea that the state should concern itself with the well-being of its citizens and become a "welfare state" found acceptance among politicians both in England and on the Continent. The social legislation resulting from this new attitude was so far-reaching that it has been referred to as "state socialism." Its chief purpose was to satisfy those grievances of the working class that did not interfere with the preservation of the capitalist system.

Similar motives were behind various appeals of the Christian churches, notably the Catholic Church, for collaboration rather than conflict between employers and workers. Christian Socialism was nothing new, but it gained significance as the teachings of Marx began to compete with and to undermine the influence of Christianity among workers. The leading pronouncement on Christian social policy was made by Pope Leo XIII in his encyclical *Rerum novarum* in 1891, in which he condemned socialist attacks on private property and the Marxian concept of class struggle and suggested that the state aid its poorer citizens and that employers and workers settle their differences in a spirit of Christian brotherhood.

So much for the general trends—political, economic, and social—that prevailed in Europe between 1870 and 1914. As we now turn to a discussion of the domestic affairs of the major powers, we shall find these trends much in evidence.

ENGLAND: "MOTHER OF DEMOCRACY"

England after 1870 continued along the road of gradual political and social reform. The long reign of Queen Victoria reached its halfway mark in 1869. Gladstone's "great ministry" came to an end in 1874. For the next six years Disraeli, Earl of Beaconsfield after 1876, conducted a policy noted chiefly for its successes abroad. Between 1880 and 1895, Liberal and Conservative governments alternated, with Gladstone heading three more ministries and Lord Salisbury serving as his Conservative counterpart. The last two decades before 1914 were equally divided between the two major parties, the Conservatives remaining in power until 1905 and the Liberals leading thereafter. Generally speaking, the Liberals were more active in domestic affairs, where Gladstone's reforming zeal found its successor after the turn of the century in the dynamic David Lloyd George. The Conservatives, on the other

Benjamin Disraeli, British Conservative prime minister, shown around 1870, before his first ministry.

hand, were more concerned with foreign affairs, especially England's overseas interests. Lord Salisbury personally assumed the post of foreign minister in his three cabinets, and he was ably seconded by Joseph Chamberlain as colonial secretary.

The problem that overshadowed all others was still Ireland. Gladstone sought once again to remedy some of the worst abuses of Irish land tenure in the Land Act of 1881. He failed, however, chiefly because of resistance from Ireland's Nationalists. Under the leadership of Charles Parnell, the Nationalists demanded political rather than economic reforms. Gladstone hoped to satisfy Irish demands by two Home Rule Bills, but he was defeated both times. Subsequent Land Purchase Acts, under Conservative sponsorship and aimed at helping Irish tenants buy their land, somewhat counteracted the agitation of Irish nationalism. The Irish question became acute once more in 1912, when the Liberals introduced a third Home Rule Bill, which did not become law until September 1914. By that time war had broken out, and home rule had to be postponed.

England's ability to resist any really serious crises, except for the perennial Irish question, was largely due to the peaceful adjustments it continued to make to the demands for democratic reform. The franchise that had been granted to urban workers in the Reform Act of 1867 was extended to rural laborers under the Franchise Act of 1884. A Redistribution Bill in 1885 established uniform electoral districts, and the Parliament Bill of 1911 abolished the veto power of the House of Lords over money bills. Democracy (for men only) had made considerable progress in Britain by 1914, leaving only some 20 percent of the male population without a vote.

Economic Developments

Economically, the picture in England looked somewhat less bright. Prior to 1870, British industry had enjoyed undisputed leadership, and despite the repeal of the Corn Laws in 1846 British agriculture had been able to hold its own. This situation gradually changed as Ger-

Gladstone giving a "whistle-stop" speech (1885). His practice of making political speeches from trains was said to have horrified Queen Victoria.

Victoria's "Golden Jubilee"

Queen Victoria made her historic progress through London on June 22nd, 1887, in brilliant sunshine. As if to put a seal on the legend of "Queen's Weather," the sun came out from a dull sky as the first guns in Hyde Park announced that she had left the Palace, having previously touched an electric button which telegraphed her Jubilee Message round the Empire: "From my heart I thank my beloved people. May God bless them!"

Queen Victoria's account of her reception by London was by no means exaggerated. "No one ever, I believe, has met with such an ovation as was given me, passing through those six miles of streets . . . the crowds were quite indescribable, and their enthusiasm truly marvellous and deeply touching. The cheering was quite deafening, and every face seemed to be filled with real joy."

London's sense of its own greatness, as the metropolis of a far-flung Empire, vied with a poignantly personal affection for the venerable figure who was both a living and a symbolic mother. "Our Hearts Thy Throne," declared a triumphal arch at Paddington; the Bank of England declaimed: "She Wrought Her People Lasting Good." "Go it, old girl!" called an ecstatic voice from the crowd. . . .

Nothing went wrong. Gradually she relaxed in her carriage . . . tears of happiness filled her eyes and sometimes rolled down her cheeks, whereupon the Princess of Wales would lean forward and gently press her hand. . . . She was incomparably the best Queen the world had got and more than one foreign nation, still struggling under the rule of tyranny, self-indulgence or fatuity, wished she were theirs.

From Elizabeth Longford, *Victoria R. I.* (London: Weidenfeld and Nicolson, 1964), pp. 688–90.

many and the United States became England's chief industrial rivals, and as the influx of cheap agricultural products from overseas caused a rapid decline in British farming. Germany and America had overtaken England in the basic iron and steel industries by 1914, and England's share of the world's total trade fell from 23 percent in 1876 to 15 percent in 1913.

Much of this relative decline in England's economic leadership was inevitable, of course, as nations that had once been Britain's customers began to supply their own needs and claim their own share of world trade. But there were other causes for the slowdown in England's economic growth. Scientific and technical education lagged behind that of other nations, notably Germany. England was slow in modernizing its industrial equipment and adopting new methods, and it failed to realize the importance of effective salesmanship. Furthermore, while tariff walls were being erected everywhere else to protect industry and agriculture, Britain clung to its policy of free trade, despite efforts, notably by Joseph Chamberlain at the turn of the century, to change to protectionism.

Labor and Social Reform

Even though its economic leadership was declining, Britain was still the most prosperous nation of the world. This prosperity was shared by the British worker, who was far better off than the workers in most continental countries. Great Britain was the only major European country in which Marxian socialism did not gain any large following. In 1881 an organization advocating Marxist principles was founded, but its advocacy of violence had little attraction for the British workingman. The Fabian Society, founded in 1883, appealed chiefly to middle-class intellectuals. What political influence the British working class exerted before 1914 came chiefly from the British Labour Party. Its origins went back to the early 1890s, but its official beginning dates from 1900, when several groups, including trade unions and Fabians, joined forces behind the Labour Representation Committee. In the general election of 1906, the Labour Party won twenty-nine seats in Parliament. Its program called for the gradual socialization of key industries and utilities, very much along Fabian lines.

Another avenue through which British labor improved its status was union activity. The London dock strike of 1889 was successful, but there were occasional reverses, such as the Taff Vale decision of 1901 and the Osborne Judgment of 1909, both handed down by the House of Lords. Under the Taff Vale decision, labor unions were to be liable for damages resulting from strikes, while the Osborne Judgment made it illegal for unions to pay stipends to Labour members of Parliament. Both restrictions were subsequently removed under pressure from the Labour Party.

While the workers were helping themselves, the government also did its share through welfare legislation. There had already been examples of such legislation earlier in the century, especially the several factory acts. Factory legislation was now extended by other acts—in 1878, 1901, and 1908—and a minimum-wage law was passed in 1912. Social insurance was initiated, first against accidents (1880), then against old age (1909), and finally against sickness and unemployment (1911). To finance these expensive measures, the Liberal government of Lloyd George in 1909 introduced a "People's Budget," which shifted the main tax burden to the rich. It was passed only over the stiff opposition of the House of Lords, whose powers, as we have seen, were subsequently curtailed.

As the result of an enlightened policy at home and a strong position abroad, England in 1914 was at the height of its power. Yet there were some danger signals in Ireland and India; Britain's economy was going "soft"; and its political system needed further reforms. Some pessimists wondered if the country would be able to cope with these issues in the future, as it had always been able to in the past.

FRANCE: REPUBLIC IN CRISIS

Britain's steady progress toward political and social democracy had no parallel on the Continent. The French Third Republic, after stormy beginnings, developed a system of government that, while more democratic, was far less stable than that of Great Britain. The French presidency was largely a ceremonial office. The cabinet was responsible to a bicameral legislature, the lower body of which, the Chamber of Deputies, was elected by universal male suffrage. Instead of clearly defined political parties, France had a large number of loosely organized factions, each headed by some outstanding political figure. This feature made the formation of workable majorities extremely difficult and led to a long series of coalition cabinets, more than fifty during the forty years before the First World War.

English cartoon of General Georges Boulanger as Napoleon Bonaparte (1889), a parody of the famous painting of Napoleon by Jacques Louis David, *The First Consul Crossing the Alps.*

Republicans versus Monarchists

One of the main reasons for the erratic course of French politics after 1870 was antirepublicanism. On several occasions in the early years of the Republic, the various royalist factions had come dangerously close to resurrecting the monarchy. But the Third Republic survived, partly because of the lack of unity among its enemies. It was not until 1879 that the French government became wholly republican in its legislative and executive branches.

But the republican elements were no more united than their enemies. A radical faction, led since Gambetta's death in 1882 by Georges Clemenceau, was deeply anticlerical and interested chiefly in revenge against Germany. The moderate republicans, on the other hand, were willing to compromise on domestic and foreign issues. Their chief figure, Jules Ferry, emerged as France's leading statesman in the last decades of the century. During most of the 1880s, radicals and moderates managed to cooperate in launching the Republic on a successful course at home and abroad. Despite their many achievements, however, widespread opposition persisted. Beginning in

1886 this opposition rallied around the recently appointed minister of war, General Georges Boulanger. By early 1889 the popularity of the dashing general was such that he might easily have led a successful *coup* against the Republic, had not his courage failed him at the crucial moment.

As it turned out, the Boulanger affair helped to strengthen the Republic by drawing the radical and moderate republicans more closely together. But this gain was soon lost again in the so-called Panama Scandal, in which a number of radical republican deputies were found to have accepted large bribes from the corrupt and bankrupt Panama Canal Company. The dust of this affair had still not quite settled when the Third Republic was shaken by an even more serious crisis, the Dreyfus case.

In the fall of 1894, Captain Alfred Dreyfus, a Jew, was accused of having betrayed military secrets to the Germans and was condemned to life imprisonment on Devil's Island. Despite clear evidence of his innocence, it took five years before he was fully vindicated. During this time, the reactionary right—monarchists, Catholics, and the army, together with a handful of anti-Semites—denounced any attempt to clear Dreyfus as an attack on the honor of the nation and the discipline of the army. The radical left, spearheading the defense of Dreyfus, cleared its reputation of the blemish incurred in the Panama Scandal. The Dreyfus case was an extended duel between the two factions that had fought each other since the founding of the Third Republic. While its outcome was a victory of republicanism, the struggle itself testified to the continued strength of the forces of reaction.

The most immediate result of the Dreyfus affair was a shift from moderate to radical republicanism. After winning the elections of 1902, the Radicals formed their first ministry and at long last were able to carry out their own program. Their most drastic measures were directed against the Catholic Church. A bill for the separation of church and state brought to an end the Concordat of 1801, whereby the state had paid the salaries of the clergy and had participated in the selection of priests. The Church, henceforth, was to be entirely on its own. In social reform the Radicals were less successful. With the emergence of socialism in France at the turn of the century, radi-

calism found a powerful rival with far more sweeping social and economic aims.

Economic Developments

France, which had enjoyed considerable prosperity before 1870, was set back by the Franco-Prussian War and was slow to profit from the Second Industrial Revolution. The losses in manpower and material, Germany's demand for a heavy indemnity, and especially the surrender of the valuable industrial region of Alsace-Lorraine, severely retarded French industrial growth. The majority of the French, moreover, were still engaged in agriculture, and protective tariffs, such as the Méline Tariff of 1892, mainly aided the farmers. What industry there was consisted largely of small establishments, and only a few industries were affected by the trend toward industrial concentration. French foreign trade almost doubled between 1870 and 1914. But since the commerce of its competitors increased at a much greater rate, France found itself demoted from second to fourth place in world trade. There was one activity in which France led the rest of the world: the amount of French money invested abroad during the thirty years before 1914 rose from 13 to 44 billion francs. These foreign loans were a valuable source of national income, and they were used as an effective instrument to facilitate French foreign policy.

Socialism and Social Reform

Since France was less industrialized than some other nations, its working class was smaller and French socialism never gained the influence it did elsewhere, especially in Germany. Socialism in France, furthermore, had received a serious setback in the Paris Commune from which it did not recover until the early 1880s. Like socialists in most other countries, the French were split into moderate and radical factions. The revolutionary group, led by Jules Guesde, and the moderates, led by Jean Jaurès, did not join forces until 1905, when they formed the United Socialist Party. Again like most other socialist parties, the French socialist party was revolutionary in the-

Captain Alfred Dreyfus in 1899 passing between a "guard of dishonor," soldiers whose backs are turned to him. The reactionary military faction arranged for this practice in order to discredit and humiliate Dreyfus.

ory but evolutionary in practice. Between 1906 and 1914, its membership in the Chamber of Deputies nearly doubled.

In the realm of social reform, France lagged behind England. A factory law of 1874, amended by subsequent acts, fixed the minimum working age for children at thirteen, restricted working hours for adults to twelve hours, and introduced various other health and sanitation measures. Social insurance did not begin until the end of the century. Accident insurance was introduced in 1898, and old-age pensions were started in 1910. There was no protection against unemployment, and health insurance was left to private initiative under state supervision.

Even though the French working class was not as numerous as its counterparts in England and Germany, the government's failure to solve some of the economic and social problems of the worker caused constant domestic unrest during the years just before 1914. At the same time, the Third Republic continued to be attacked from the right. Royalism and an intense brand of nationalism were kept alive by a few wealthy reactionaries in the *Action Française* of Charles Maurras and Léon Daudet. Yet the majority of the French seemed to approve the programs of reform at home and peace abroad, which brought resounding victory for the Radicals and Socialists in the elections of 1914. French pacifism, while admirable, came at a most inopportune time, just when Europe was getting ready for a major war. France, on the eve of the First World War, was still a nation divided on many vital issues.

GERMANY: EMPIRE TRIUMPHANT

The new German *Reich* presented a spectacle of success and supreme self-confidence. Had its industrial growth been paralleled by political reforms, Germany might easily have rivaled England as the most progressive nation in Europe. But repeated demands of liberals and socialists for the reform of the Prussian three-class franchise and for the introduction of parliamentary government in the Empire were of no avail. The *Reichstag*, to be sure, was elected by manhood suffrage. But the main direction of policy continued to rest with the chancellor (who was appointed by and responsible to the emperor) and the Federal Council, or *Bundesrat*, in which Prussia held a controlling position. Even so, the German electorate might have made its influence felt more decisively had it not been split into five or six major parties, each of which differed in political and economic aims and none of which ever won a majority.

Repression at Home— Aggression Abroad

During its first twenty years, the German Empire was ruled by the strong hand of Bismarck. The "iron chancellor's" claim to fame rests on his foreign rather than his domestic policy. During the 1870s Bismarck antagonized large sections of the German people by his fierce struggle against the Catholic Church. The so-called *Kulturkampf* (conflict of cultures; that is, German and Catholic), while appealing to liberal anticlericalism, failed in its major objective—to prevent the rise of political Catholicism. The Catholic Center Party emerged from its persecution as a potent factor in German politics. Bismarck's attempt, during the 1880s, to prevent the rise of a strong Socialist Party was equally unsuccessful. By enlisting liberal support in his fight against Catholics and socialists, Bismarck perpetuated the political disunity of the German people and contributed further to the decline of German liberalism.

Bismarck had no worthy successor. The unceremonious manner in which the great chancellor was dismissed by William II in 1890 was indicative of the young emperor's desire to be his own chancellor. But William II was utterly unsuited for such a role. Erratic, unstable, and given to rash utterances, especially on matters of foreign policy, the kaiser launched Germany on an expansionist *Weltpolitik* (world policy) that soon lost it the international trust it had gained under Bismarck. More than in any other country, issues of foreign policy played a dominant role in Germany.

Jean Jaurès (1859–1914) at a socialist party rally in 1913.

William II, emperor of Germany and king of Prussia (1888–1918), in the uniform of the Death's Head Hussars.

The army, long powerful in Prussian affairs, remained one of the cornerstones of the empire. Except for its budget, which the *Reichstag* had to grant for several years in advance, it remained entirely free from civilian control.

Within the *Reichstag* there was very little chance for any effective opposition. The alliance between prominent industrialists and landowners, initiated under Bismarck, assured the government of a workable parliamentary majority. Both groups profited from tariff protectionism, and both were opposed to lower-class demands for political and social democracy. Against this coalition between the industrialist National Liberals and the agrarian Conservatives, the Socialist opposition and the occasionally critical Center and Progressive parties could do very little. On a few occasions, notably during the "Daily Telegraph Affair" in 1908, when William II made some irresponsible statements on Anglo-German relations, it seemed as though public indignation might check the kaiser's erratic rule. But the discipline so deeply instilled in every German, and the economic prosperity the nation enjoyed, kept the public from taking any drastic steps.

Economic Developments

The immediate effect of Germany's unification in 1871 had been a short-lived economic boom, which had come to a sudden halt in the worldwide depression of 1873. It was only during the last two decades of the century that Germany began to show its great economic power. Much of Germany's economic success can be attributed to the protective policy that Bismarck initiated in 1879. Germany was not the first nation to abandon free trade, but it was Germany's step that ushered in a period of tariff rivalry among the major powers and thus injected a strong element of nationalism into economic relations.

Germany's rapid economic growth was due in large measure to the development of its domestic market—its population increased from 41 million to 67 million between 1871 and 1914—but German competition was also felt abroad. The main pillars of German prosperity were coal and iron, concentrated in Alsace-Lorraine, the Saar, Upper Silesia, and particularly the Ruhr area, where the firms of Krupp, Thyssen, and Stinnes built their huge industrial empires. Germans took the lead in other pursuits as well, especially the electrical and chemical industries. By 1914 Germany's merchant marine was second only to that of Great Britain, although the British commercial fleet was still more than three times as large as that of Germany.

Socialism and Social Reform

The main critics of German domestic and foreign policy were the Social Democrats. Theirs was the largest and most

---

Kaiser Wilhelm II

Every society, it is sometimes said, gets the ruler it deserves. This is true in part, but only in part, for Wilhelmine Germany. Kaiser Wilhelm II was certainly more representative of his age than Bismarck or Hitler were of theirs. And yet the Second Reich was unlucky in the man fate chose to rule it. He was deformed from birth, his left arm hanging six inches shorter than his right and incapable of movement. . . . His upbringing at the hands of the Calvinist Hinzpeter was severe. He hated his English Liberal mother, and despised his father for permitting her to dominate him. Although inwardly he may have been plagued by a sense of insecurity, his public utterances and actions stressed his own importance to a disturbing degree. He intervened in ship-design, archaeology, music, painting and theatre production with the same self-assurance that characterized his military and political moves. Much of his thinking was tinged with a brutal racialism which most people would now associate with a later period in German history. . . . He warned new recruits that they would have to shoot down their own fathers and brothers if he ordered them to. . . . His strongest language he reserved for the deputies of the Reichstag. They were "scoundrels without a fatherland" who were behaving "more and more like pigs.". . . It is no exaggeration to say that contending with the Kaiser was a major preoccupation of Germany's leading statesmen from Bismarck's fall until the outbreak of the First World War.

From J. C. G. Röhl, *Germany Without Bismarck: The Crisis of Government in the Second Reich, 1890–1900* (London: Batsford, 1967), pp. 27–29.

influential socialist party in Europe. The origins of the party went back to the 1860s, but it did not become a political force until 1875. At that time a non-Marxian faction, organized by Ferdinand Lassalle in 1864, and a Marxian faction, led by Wilhelm Liebknecht and August Bebel, united to form the Social Democratic Party (SPD). Despite severe restrictions and the persecution of its members by the Bismarckian government, the numbers of the SPD steadily increased, until by 1912 it had become the largest party in the *Reichstag*. Its program, first formulated at Gotha in 1875 and revised at Erfurt in 1891, while strictly "orthodox" in tone, nevertheless included a number of "revisionist" demands for specific reforms.

The agitation of the SPD was directed against the political and social rather than the economic inequities of the empire. The phenomenal economic growth of the country could not help but be reflected in a rising standard of living for the workers. The German government, furthermore, through extensive programs of social reform, tried to alleviate the hardships inherent in massive industrialization. In 1878 factory inspection was made compulsory, and in 1891 an Imperial Industrial Code introduced the usual sanitary and safety provisions and regulated working hours for women and children. Germany's pioneering efforts were in the field of social legislation. In a calculated effort to divert German workers from socialism, Bismarck, between 1883 and 1889, introduced far-reaching measures for health, accident, and old-age insurance. These served as models for similar legislation in other countries, notably England.

The German Empire in 1914 was an anomaly among European powers—economically one of the most advanced, yet politically one of the most backward. The majority of Germans, though not happy about their political impotence, took comfort in their economic achievements. They might criticize their government's domestic policy, but most Germans saw little wrong with a foreign policy that demanded "a place in the sun" for Germany.

Bertha von Suttner (1843–1914), Austrian writer, whose pacifist novel, *Lay Down Your Arms* (1892), inspired Alfred Nobel to establish the Nobel Peace Prize. In 1905 she became the first woman recipient of the prize.

AUSTRIA-HUNGARY: THE RAMSHACKLE EMPIRE

The Austro-Hungarian Empire, since the *Ausgleich* of 1867, had been virtually divided into two separate states. Both Austria and Hungary were constitutional monarchies, but their governments were far from democratic. Various attempts before 1914 to improve this situation were complicated by the problem of nationalities. After 1873 the Austrian lower house, or *Reichsrat*, was elected by a complicated four-class franchise, which gave disproportionate influence to the upper classes and the German minority among the population. This system, with some minor changes, lasted until 1907. By that time agitation among the various subject nationalities could no longer be ignored. The electoral law of 1907 at long last granted universal manhood suffrage. But the return of a large majority of non-German delegates led to such constant wrangling in the *Reichsrat* that the orderly conduct of democratic government became impossible and rule by decree remained the order of the day. In Hungary the situation was still more hopeless. Here the upper crust of Magyar landowners completely dominated both houses of parliament. The rising protest of Hungary's various subject nationalities brought some slight electoral reforms, but Hungary in 1914 remained essentially a feudal state dominated by a Magyar aristocracy.

Conflict of Nationalities

The overriding problem of Austria-Hungary continued to be its many nationalities. In Austria the Czechs were the main problem. The Poles of Galicia formed a compact group that was relatively well treated and enjoyed cultural autonomy. The Czechs, on the other hand, were closely intermingled with Germans. Attempts to introduce Czech, together with German, as the official languages of Bohemia were met by German opposition. Meanwhile, the "Young Czechs," led by Thomas Masaryk, fought for the rights of their own people.

While Austria made at least some concessions to its minorities, Hungary followed a strict policy of Magyarization. The major problem in Hungary was created by the Croats, who looked to Serbia for the lead in forming a Yugoslav—that is, South Slav—federation. The situation was complicated by the fact that the region of Bosnia-Herzegovina, since 1878 under Austrian administration, was also inhabited by Southern Slavs. The heir to the Austro-Hungarian crowns, Archduke Francis Ferdinand, was known to favor reforms that would give the Slavic element within the Dual Monarchy equal rights with Germans and Magyars. Neither Hungary nor Serbia liked such schemes. The Hungarians wanted to continue lording it over their Slavs, and the Serbs hoped to attract the Southern Slavs away from Austria-Hungary.

Economic Developments

Even though there was considerable industrialization in the Austrian half of the empire, the country as a whole remained predominantly agrarian. As such it suffered increasingly from the competition of the larger agrarian economies of Russia, the United States, and Australia. A high tariff policy, though it protected agriculture, kept living costs high, which in turn made for high wages and prevented Austrian industries from successfully competing abroad. Even so, there was some economic progress. It would have been greater had the economic interdependence between Austria and Hungary been better utilized. As it was, industrial Austria and agrarian Hungary pursued separate and often contradictory economic policies.

Socialism and Social Reform

Socialism in Austria did not become a factor to be reckoned with until the end of the century. In 1889, Victor Adler, the most prominent Austrian socialist, unified various socialist factions behind the Austrian Social Democratic Party. Socialist agitation, in part, was responsible for the introduction of universal male suffrage in Austria in 1907. This development, in turn, helped the party to grow. The program of the Austrian socialists was revisionist, and their main support came from the working-class population of Vienna. Their major weakness was national diversity: by 1911 the party had split into German, Czech, and Polish factions. There was no socialist movement to speak of in Hungary.

The Austrian government also took a hand in improving the workers' lot. A

Emperor Francis Joseph (center) relaxing with guests at the wedding party of his grandnephew and eventual successor, Archduke Karl Franz Joseph (1911).

system of factory inspection was set up in 1883, and an Industrial Code in 1907 set the minimum working age at twelve, provided for an eleven-hour working day, and introduced safety and sanitation standards for factories.

The economic and social problems of the Austro-Hungarian Empire in 1914 were still overshadowed by its nationalities problem. Every possible solution to this problem had been proposed, and a few had been tried. Since each proposal left one or another of the many nationality groups dissatisfied, a policy of repression always prevailed. The result of this negative policy was the assassination of Francis Ferdinand at Sarajevo on June 28, 1914.

Francesco Crispi (1819–1901), prime minister of Italy (1887–91, 1893–96).

ITALY: GREAT POWER BY COURTESY

In Italy, economic backwardness and widespread illiteracy retarded the growth of democracy. The Italian constitution, the *Statuto*, which Piedmont had adopted in 1848, still limited the franchise in 1870 to a mere 2.5 percent of the population. Property qualifications and the voting age were gradually lowered, however, and virtually all adult males were permitted to vote by 1914. But this extension of the franchise was a mixed blessing. By giving the vote to the illiterate poor, it enabled a handful of ambitious politicians to manipulate elections and to make Italy's parliament a pliable instrument of their policy. The practice of "transformism"—that is, of avoiding parliamentary opposition by giving the most powerful critics a share in the government, proved a serious obstacle to the growth of democracy in Italy.

Political Instability

Despite marked economic improvements, Italy remained a poor and struggling country. A great power by courtesy more than through actual strength, Italy's frantic efforts to live up to a glorious past led it into military ventures it could ill afford. The conservative forces that had brought about the country's unification remained in power until 1876. Regional opposition to extreme centralization and widespread discontent with heavy taxation then shifted the power to the more liberal factions. From 1887 to 1891 and from 1893 to 1896, the experienced Francesco Crispi as prime minister provided firm leadership. His attempts to divert the people's attention from discontent at home through colonial ventures abroad suffered a dismal defeat at the hands of Ethiopia in the battle of Adua (1896). The end of the century saw a rising tide of labor unrest, bread riots, and street fighting. In 1900 King Humbert fell victim to an anarchist assassin and was succeeded by the more liberal Victor Emmanuel III.

During the last years before the war, Italy, under the capable but unprincipled Giovanni Giolitti (1842–1928) at long last made some headway in the solution of its worst economic difficulties. Giolitti also managed to effect a partial reconciliation between the Italian government and the Catholic Church. The pope continued to consider himself "the prisoner of the Vatican," but in 1905 he did lift the ban against the participation of Catholics in political affairs.

Giovanni Giolitti (1842–1928). Five times prime minister of Italy (1892–93, 1903–05, 1906–09, 1911–14, 1920–21).

Economic Developments

Most of Italy's troubles were due to its poverty. Italy was still primarily an agrarian nation. Yet Italy's soil was too poor and its agricultural methods too backward to support its rapidly growing population. The mounting population pressure could be relieved only through large-scale emigration and increased industrialization. The latter was hampered by lack of essential raw materials and shortage of capital. Attempts at protectionism, furthermore, tended to affect Italy's exports, and it was only with the conclusion of a series of commercial treaties in the 1890s that the economy picked up. With the help of hydroelectric power, Italy gradually developed its own textile industry and gained world leadership in the production of silk. But despite these improvements, and despite almost a doubling of its foreign commerce between 1900 and 1910, Italy's balance of trade continued to be unfavorable and Italy depended heavily on foreign loans.

Socialism and Social Reform

As almost everywhere else in Europe, industrialization in Italy brought in its wake the rise of socialism. The first socialist party in Italy was organized in 1891. It, too, had its initial difficulties over revisionism, and it was not until 1911 that the radical, "orthodox" element won the upper hand. The Italian socialist party did not gain any mass following until after 1900. Many Italian workers were attracted by the more violent programs of anarchism and syndicalism. The first major general strike in Italy took place in 1904. It failed for lack of popular support.

The Italian government tried to cope with the social effects of industrialization by factory acts and social legislation. Accident and old-age insurance were introduced in 1898. But the basic causes of trouble—poverty and illiteracy—could not be erased overnight. Meanwhile the Italian people, inexperienced in the ways of democracy, fell more and more under the influence of extremists of the right or left—the right calling for glorious ventures abroad, the left opposing war and demanding reforms at home. Thus divided, Italy was in no condition to enter a major war in 1914.

RUSSIA: STRONGHOLD OF AUTOCRACY

Tsarist Russia, to the bitter end, remained the most autocratic among European states. The brief flurry of reforms under Alexander II (1855–81) during the 1860s had soon given way again to Russia's traditional policy of repression. The reign of Alexander II came to a violent end in 1881, when he was assassinated by members of the terrorist "Will of the People." His son, Alexander III (1881–94), was a reactionary and a Slavophile, not unlike Nicholas I. For well over a quarter-century Alexander III and his son and successor, Nicholas II (1894–1917), followed a policy of darkest reaction. Aided by Vyacheslav Plehve, director of the state police and later minister of the interior, and by Constantine Pobedonostsev, who as "Procurator of the Holy Synod" was the highest official in the Russian Orthodox Church and one of the most powerful men in Russia, the principles of orthodoxy, autocracy, and nationality once again became the watchwords of Russian policy. Catholics in Poland and Protestants in the Baltic provinces were persecuted; the powers of local and provincial zemstvos (councils), established under Alexander II, were curtailed; popular education was discouraged; and nationalism in Finland, Poland, the Ukraine, and elsewhere was suppressed. A particularly shocking feature of Russian policy was its persecution of the Jews. There were hardly any positive achievements during this period of unrelieved repression, except the economic reforms of Count Witte.

Economic Developments

Russia was the last major European power to feel the impact of industrialization. The government's main concern prior to 1890 had been the improvement of farming methods and the cultivation of new lands. Russia's agricultural exports between 1860 and 1900 increased almost fourfold, despite rising tariff barriers. Beginning in the 1890s, Russia also embarked on a program of industrialization, chiefly under the direction of its minister of finance and commerce, Count Sergei Witte (1849–1915). By introducing the gold standard in 1897, Witte made investment in Russian industry more attractive to outsiders. The construction of the Trans-Siberian Railway, begun in 1891, helped open up the country's rich mineral resources. As a result, Russia by 1900 held fourth place among the world's iron producers and second place in the production of oil. The opposition of agrarian interests to Witte's industrial policy, however, led to his retirement in 1903. Together with an economic depression and the Russian defeat in the war with Japan (1904–05), Witte's departure helped to slow down Russia's industrial development. Lack of capital, the educational backwardness of the Russian workers, and their continued subjection to the village community were chiefly responsible for Russia's failure to realize its tremendous economic potentialities.

Socialism and Social Reform

Because of the government's vigilance toward all manifestations of social and political protest, socialism in Russia was slow to take hold. It was not until 1891 that the first Marxian socialist party was organized by Georgi V. Plekhanov. The activity of the Social Democratic Party was largely confined to underground agitation. At a party congress in London in 1903, Russia's socialists split into two groups. The Mensheviks (or minority), under Julius Martov, advocated a gradual evolution to democracy and socialism, while the Bolsheviks (or majority), under Lenin, followed the more radical, "Leninist" line. The two factions (despite their name, the Bolsheviks were actually in the minority) also differed on the question of how their party should be organized. Besides Marxian socialism there was also an organization of agrarian socialists in Russia, the Socialist Revolutionaries. Their program harked back to the ideas of Alexander Herzen and to the populist "go-to-the-people" movement (see p. 617). To achieve their goals, the Socialist Revolutionaries advocated terrorism and assassination.

Increased industrialization in Russia brought the usual hardships for the working class. With an ample supply of manpower from landless peasants, wages remained low and the Russian worker had to slave long hours to eke out a meager existence. The government, in time, did regulate the employment of women and children and introduced maximum working-hours. But without a corresponding increase in wages, these restrictions merely tended to lower the total income of workers' families. Moreover, to voice discontent through labor unions was prohibited by law. Even so, unrest among the workers gave rise to frequent strikes of increasing violence.

The Revolution of 1905

The workers were not the only class that was restless. There were the masses of landless peasants; there was opposition among national minorities against the government's policy of Russification; and there was growing agitation among liberal members of the middle class, who demanded constitutional government. As economic depression was worsening the lot of the workers, the Russo-Japanese War upset the rural economy by drafting

"Bloody Sunday" (January 22, 1905). A procession of workers is fired on by tsarist troops on its way to the Winter Palace; 70 people were killed and 240 wounded.

The march on the Winter Palace on "Bloody Sunday" in 1905 was organized by the priest Georgy Gapon.

peasants. With the tide of war turning against Russia, tension finally erupted in revolution. The Revolution of 1905 began on January 22, "Bloody Sunday," when a peaceful protest march was fired on by tsarist troops. A general strike soon crippled the major industrial centers, peasants rose against their landlords, and mutinies broke out in the army and navy. In October the Social Democrats and the Socialist Revolutionaries set up a Soviet (or Council) of Workers' Delegates in St. Petersburg.

By that time, however, the revolution had run its course. Tsar Nicholas finally gave in and made a number of political concessions. The "October Manifesto" of 1905 guaranteed individual freedoms and called for the election of a National Assembly, or *Duma*, by almost universal male suffrage. But the promises made by Nicholas under duress were soon forgotten. It took three elections, each under a more restrictive franchise, before a *Duma* was finally elected that satisfied the tsar's wish for an advisory rather than a legislative body. Meanwhile the government had taken savage reprisals, executing an estimated fifteen thousand and arresting many times that number. Even so, Russia for the first time in its history now had an elected national assembly that could at least serve as a training-ground in parliamentary procedures. The democratic spirit thus penetrated, if ever so slightly, the last stronghold of autocracy.

Repression and Reform

The outstanding figure of the last decade before the war was Peter Stolypin, chief minister until 1911. A conservative monarchist, he nevertheless believed in a limited degree of representative government. He worked harmoniously with the moderate faction within the third *Duma*, the "Octobrists," who in contrast to the more liberal "Cadets" (constitutional democrats) were satisfied with a mere consultative role. Stolypin's policy combined repression with reform. On the one hand, he bore down hard on all revolutionary activities by Social Democrats and Socialist Revolutionaries. Their leaders were arrested, driven into exile (as were Lenin and Trotsky), or sent to Siberia (as was Stalin). These negative measures, however, were supplemented by far-reaching reforms. Realizing the desire of Russia's peasants for land of their own, and aware of the support that could be gained from a large class of small farmers, Stolypin started to divide the communal holdings of the villages, distributing the land among the individual members of the *mir*. This was a slow and complicated process, and by 1917 only about one-tenth of Russia's peasants had become independent farmers. Nevertheless, it was a farsighted move, and it might have saved the tsarist regime if land reform had been completed in time.

Stolypin's reformist policy was opposed not only by the advocates of revolution, for whom it did not go far and fast enough, but also by the forces of reaction. The latter again gained the upper hand when Stolypin was assassinated in 1911. Nicholas II was a weak and vacillating monarch, firmly committed to the autocratic beliefs of his father and deeply under the influence of his German wife. The Tsarina Alexandra had fallen under the spell of an evil and ignorant "holy man," Gregory Rasputin. This power-hungry Siberian peasant gained such influence over the imperial family that he became the real power in Russia. Reaction coupled with corruption and inefficiency led to a gradual paralysis of Russia's government, making it doubly vulnerable to any major crisis. Such a crisis arose with the First World War.

THE "CULT OF SCIENCE"

After our survey of the political, economic, and social developments in the major powers between 1870 and 1914, there remains to be considered the intellectual and cultural trends of these years. Their outstanding characteristic may be seen as an overriding interest and belief in science. There had been interest in science before; but it was only in the second half of the nineteenth century that a veritable "cult of science" developed. Science offered a positive alternative to the seemingly futile idealism and Romanticism of the early nineteenth century. Scientific research, in the past the domain of a few scientists and gentleman scholars, now became the concern of large numbers of people, especially as the application of science to industry gave an incentive for new inventions. "Pure" science continued to be of fundamental importance. But "applied" science—the "marriage of science and technology" so characteristic of the Second Industrial Revolution—now took precedence in the minds of most people. A virtually endless series of scientific inventions seemed to provide tangible evidence of man's ability to unlock the secrets of nature. If support was needed for the optimistic belief in unlimited progress, science provided it.

Materialism and Positivism

The growing concern with the material aspects of civilization was also reflected in late-nineteenth-century thought. A few basic scientific discoveries served as a foundation for an essentially materialistic philosophy that appealed to the educated middle class. An early exponent of this philosophy was the German philosopher Ludwig Feuerbach (1804–72). More influential, however, was the German physician Ludwig Büchner (1824–99), whose book *Force and Matter* (1855) went through twenty-one editions and was translated into all major languages. Proclaiming the eternity of force (that is, energy) and matter, Büchner concluded that it was "impossible that the world can have been created. How could anything be created that cannot be annihilated?" Another influential figure was the German biologist Ernst Haeckel (1834–1919), whose most famous book, *The Riddle of the Universe at the Close of the Nineteenth Century* (1899), became an international best-seller. Haeckel's "monistic philosophy" was entirely concerned with the material world, emphasizing not merely the eternity of matter and energy but insisting that even the human mind and soul had their material, physical substance. As for the riddles of the universe, Haeckel de-

clared with the optimism typical of his age that all but one of them had been solved; and the remaining one, "what the pious believer called Creator or God," was not worth troubling with, since there was no means of investigating it.

More lasting in its effect than materialism was another philosophy concerned with the impact of modern science on society—positivism. It had been worked out in the first half of the nineteenth century by the Frenchman Auguste Comte (1798–1857), but its influence was not felt until later. According to Comte, man had passed through two well-defined phases, the theological and the metaphysical, and had now entered a third phase, the scientific, or positive. In this last phase man no longer concerned himself with ultimate causes, as he had during the metaphysical stage, but was satisfied with the material world and with whatever he might learn from observing it. Here was a philosophy that accepted science as its only guide and authority and for that reason was eminently suited to the late nineteenth century.

THE DARWINIAN REVOLUTION

The development that had the most revolutionary impact on western thought and society in the nineteenth century occurred in biology. It concerns the theory of evolution set forth by the British scientist Charles Darwin (1809–82). The idea of evolution was nothing new. Both in the general sense of a gradual development of human society from simple to more complex institutions, and in the more narrow biological sense that all organisms had evolved out of more elementary forms, the concept of evolution had earlier roots. Darwin's major contribution was to provide a scientific basis for what had previously been a mere hypothesis.

Darwinism

Darwin was influenced by the writings of the geologist Charles Lyell (1797–1875) and by Thomas Robert Mal-

A Russian political cartoon, "The Russian Ruling House," shows Nicholas II and Alexandra manipulated by the dominating Rasputin.

Charles Darwin (1809–82) at the age of forty-five, five years before the publication of *Origin of Species*.

Darwin's main idea—that all existing forms of life have evolved out of earlier and simpler forms—remains valid to this day. Only his explanation of the actual process of evolution has been challenged. The idea of the inheritance of acquired characteristics had been pretty well shaken by the end of the nineteenth century. Darwin's concept of evolution as a cumulative result of many minute changes, furthermore, has given way to the view that evolution proceeds by way of larger and more sudden "mutations." These modifications came later, however, and thus could not affect the revolutionary impact of Darwin's theories when they were first announced.

The Impact of Darwinism

To an age that worshiped science, the thought that man was just as much subject to the logic of science as was everything else in nature held a great fascination. Underlying much of Darwin's work was the idea of progress, an idea dear to the nineteenth century. The gentle and retiring scientist himself took little part in the excitement and controversy stirred up by the doctrine that bore his name. The popularization of Darwin's thought was due chiefly to the efforts of other men, especially his friend Thomas Huxley (1825–95). The application of the evolutionary concept to every aspect of human society, from physics to ethics, was carried out by another admirer of Darwin, Herbert Spencer (1820–1903). Spencer's ten-volume *Synthetic Philosophy*, published between 1860 and 1896, was hailed at the time as a brilliant synthesis of all existing scientific knowledge. Today it has been practically forgotten.

Of all Darwin's new ideas, the concept of life as a struggle for existence had particular appeal. The philosophy of laissez faire, with its emphasis on competition, had long been hailed as the root of economic success. Darwinism seemed to give scientific sanction to this belief in laissez faire. Big business, according to John D. Rockefeller, was "merely a survival of the fittest . . . the working out of a law of nature and a law of God." But not only the capitalists derived great

thus' *Essay on the Principle of Population.* Lyell, in his *Principles of Geology* (1830), had restated an earlier thesis that the earth's physical appearance was the result of the same geological processes still active today. This idea of gradual changes brought about by natural causes Darwin applied to the world of organisms. In searching for an explanation of organic evolution, Darwin was impressed by Malthus' account of the intense competition among mankind for the means of subsistence.

The essence of Darwinism is stated in the full title of his basic work: *On the Origin of Species by Means of Natural Selection, or the Preservation of Favoured Races in the Struggle for Life* (1859). His theory was subsequently applied to the human species in *The Descent of Man* (1871). According to Darwin, life is a constant "struggle for existence." In this struggle only the fittest survive. This survival of the fittest was due to certain favorable variations within the given organism that aided in its competitive struggle with other organisms. These variations, handed on to subsequent generations, would in time evolve an entirely new species. This "natural selection," Darwin suggested, was further aided by "sexual selection"—the mutual attraction and consequent mating of the fittest members of a species to bring forth the fittest offspring. Darwin also accepted the notion that certain "acquired characteristics"— the long neck of the giraffe, for example—may be inherited.

comfort from Darwin. His emphasis on the importance of environment for the improvement of man also gave hope to the socialists in their demands for social and economic reform. More than ten years before Darwin published his *Origin of Species*, Karl Marx, the "Darwin of the social sciences," had already sketched the evolution of society through a series of struggles among social classes.

The emphasis on struggle as a necessary condition for progress, however, was a narrow and one-sided interpretation of Darwinism, not shared by its author. In his *Descent of Man*, Darwin had emphasized that a feeling of sympathy and coherence, social and moral qualities, were needed for the advancement of society. But to the majority of people the struggle for existence assumed the validity of a natural law, a law, moreover, that applied not just to relations among individuals but to relations among groups.

"Social Darwinism"

Herbert Spencer was one of the first to apply the theory of evolution to groups and states. The classical statement of what came to be called "Social Darwinism" was made by the English political scientist Walter Bagehot (1826–77) in his book *Physics and Politics: Thoughts on the Application of the Principles of Natural Selection and Inheritance to Political Science* (1872). According to Bagehot, in the struggle for existence among groups, "the majority of the groups which win and conquer are better than the majority of those which fail and perish." In other words, among nations as among individuals, the strongest survive and the strongest, for that reason, are the best. Needless to say, this restatement of the well-known maxim that "might makes right" had little to do with Darwin's original theory.

To a generation that had recently experienced several major wars and that was actively engaged in numerous expeditions against colonial peoples overseas, Social Darwinism, with its glorification of war, came as a welcome rationalization. "The grandeur of war," Heinrich von Treitschke, one of Germany's most pop-

Darwin testing the speed of an elephant tortoise in the Galápagos Islands during his voyage on the surveying ship *Beagle* (1831–36). This journey provided most of the observations for his theory of evolution. Drawing by Meredith Nugent.

ular historians, told his students, "lies in the utter annihilation of puny man in the great conception of the state. . . . In war the chaff is winnowed from the wheat." The influence of Social Darwinism may also be seen in the injection of racialism into politics. If being victorious meant being better, what was more natural than to view the triumph of one nation or race over another as a sign of the victor's inherent superiority? Among the earliest writers on racialism was the French count Arthur de Gobineau (1816–82). His *Essay on the Inequality of the Human Races* (1853–55) proclaimed the superiority of the white race and distinguished within that race between the superior Germanic "Aryans" and the inferior Slavs and Jews. Gobineau's doctrine found its main echo in Germany. But the idea of white, specifically Anglo-Saxon, superiority was also popular in England and America.

The "Warfare of Science with Theology"

The most violent repercussions of Darwinism were felt in the religious field. It was part of a larger conflict, the "warfare of science with theology." The religious revival during the Age of Romanticism had soon given way to a noticeable decline in religious interest. As the state took over the functions of social welfare and education, and as the material benefits of industrialization spread among the lower classes, the need for the churches declined. The tendency of the churches, furthermore, to favor the political status quo antagonized many liberals, and political anticlericalism became an important issue. Finally, there was the appeal that nationalism, socialism, and materialism came to have for many people. Both socialism and materialism were avowed enemies of religion.

The most important reason for the decline in religious interest was the effect modern science had on Christianity. Many scientific discoveries, especially in geology and biology, contradicted Christian beliefs, and scientific inquiry, when applied to Christianity itself, produced some disturbing results. Scholars studying the origins of the Bible, for instance, discovered that most of its books had been written long after the events and that few biblical writings existed as they had originally been written. Other scholars, concerned with the study of comparative religion, detected striking similarities between Christianity and other religions. They found that there were few differences in dogma and ritual between early Christianity and some of the many mystery cults that had flourished in the eastern Mediterranean at the time of Christ. Christianity, it seemed, was merely the one among many similar religions that had survived.

These discoveries became more widely known when they were used in modern accounts of the life of Christ. A German scholar, David Friedrich Strauss, (1808–74), as early as 1835 had written a *Life of Jesus* that denied the divinity of Christ. Less scholarly and more popular was the *Life of Jesus* (1863) by the French writer Ernest Renan (1823–92). Both works recognized Christ as a superior human being, but they denied that he had performed miracles or had risen from the dead.

Darwin on Man's Moral Qualities

The development of the moral qualities is a more interesting problem. The foundation lies in the social instincts. . . . A moral being is one who is capable of reflecting on his past actions and their motives—approving of some and disapproving of others; and the fact that man is the one being who certainly deserves this designation, is the greatest of all distinctions between him and the lower animals. But in the fourth chapter I have endeavoured to show that the moral sense follows, firstly, from the enduring and ever-present nature of the social instincts; secondly, from man's appreciation of the approbation and disapprobation of his fellows; and thirdly, from the high activity of his mental faculties, with past impressions extremely vivid; and in these latter respects he differs from the lower animals. . . .

Social animals are impelled partly by a wish to aid the members of their community in a general manner, but more commonly to perform certain definite actions. Man is impelled by the same general wish to aid his fellows. . . . The moral nature of man has reached its present standard, partly through the advancement of his reasoning powers and consequently of a just public opinion, but especially from his sympathies having been rendered more tender and widely diffused through the effects of habit, example, instruction, and reflection. It is not improbable that after long practice virtuous tendencies may be inherited. With the more civilized races, the conviction of the existence of an all-seeing Deity has had a potent influence on the advance of morality. . . . Nevertheless the first foundation or origin of the moral sense lies in the social instincts, including sympathy; and these instincts no doubt were primarily gained, as in the case of the lower animals, through natural selection.

From Charles Darwin, *The Descent of Man*, rev. ed. (New York: Appleton, 1886), pp. 610–12.

Darwinism and Religion

Still more drastic in their effect on the faithful were the findings of Darwin. Not only did Darwin and Lyell challenge the biblical view of creation, but by making humans a part of general evolution, Darwin deprived them of the unique position they had hitherto occupied. Why, one might ask, should man alone of all creatures possess an immortal soul, and at what stage of his evolution was he endowed with it?

The Catholic Church, because it was more tightly organized and in its doctrine placed less exclusive emphasis on the Bible, was able to take a firmer and more consistent stand in this controversy than the various Protestant churches. In 1864 Pope Pius IX issued "A Syllabus of the Principal Errors of Our Times," which condemned most of the new political, economic, and scientific tendencies. Six years later a general Church council, in an effort to strengthen the pope's position, proclaimed the dogma of papal infallibility. The pope henceforth was to be infallible in all statements he made *ex cathedra*—that is, officially—on matters of faith and morals. The new dogma ran into some opposition among Catholics, and it also contributed to the struggle between Church and state in Germany, Italy, and France.

The succession of the more conciliatory Leo XIII to the papacy in 1878 helped pacify matters. Leo was able to make peace with the German and, to a lesser extent, the French governments, and in the social and economic sphere, he tried to steer a middle course between capitalism and socialism. In science, Leo did not oppose discoveries that did not affect Catholic doctrine. Only on the subject of evolution did the papacy persist in its rigid opposition. Some Catholics had begun searching for ways to reconcile the contradictions between science and theology. This "modernism," as such attempted compromise was called, was considered a heresy by the Church. Only after the First World War did the Church gradually take a more tolerant view.

In contrast to Catholicism, Protestant (and to some extent Jewish) doctrine and ritual were almost entirely based on the Bible. The effect of scientific discoveries at variance with biblical statements, therefore, was felt more deeply. The fact, furthermore, that Protestantism was split into almost three hundred sects made any uniform stand in the warfare between science and theology very difficult. At the same time, however, Protestant emphasis on the freedom of the individual to work out his own relations with God made it possible for many Protestants to reach their own compromise between faith and reason. A minority of Protestants, called "Fundamentalists," less influential in Europe than in the United States, continued to cling to a literal interpretation of the Bible and insisted on the validity of the account of creation as given in the Book of Genesis.

Despite the confusion it caused not only among Christians but among Jews, the conflict between science and theology did not seriously interfere with the progress of science. The world in 1914 was still viewed as an intricate mechanism whose secrets would gradually yield to scientific inquiry. Only a handful of scientists realized that new developments—the discovery of X-rays (1895), the isolation of radium (1898), and, most important, the formulation of the theory of relativity (1905)—had opened up an infinite number of new mysteries and had brought the world to the threshold of another scientific revolution.

ART IN THE AGE OF SCIENCE

The cult of science that dominated the intellectual climate at the end of the nineteenth century also had its devotees in art and literature. It is difficult in dealing with any period, especially one as diverse as the one described in this chapter, to single out those artistic trends that most clearly reflect the spirit of the age. To call the early nineteenth century an Age of Romanticism and the late nineteenth century an Age of Realism is very much an oversimplification. There were Romanticists and Realists in both these "ages," and some artists combined the characteristics of both periods in their work.

Still, there were noticeable differences between the two periods. The Romantic artist had preferred an ideal world of his imagination to the real world in which he lived. He had set his concept of natural beauty against the ugliness of early industrialism. And he had escaped from a harsh present to a more rosy past. Before the middle of the nineteenth century, however, some artists had already begun to be interested in the world as it was, not as they felt it ought to be. This shift from Romanticism to Realism was most evident in literature; it was less pronounced in painting, and there were hardly any signs of it in music.

Realism and Naturalism

The novel now became the favorite medium in literature. Most of the great novels of the nineteenth century—from those of Dickens and Thackeray in Eng-

Henri de Toulouse Lautrec (1864–1901) at work in the garden of his Montmartre studio in Paris.

land to those of Balzac and Flaubert in France, Fontane in Germany, and Turgenev and Tolstoy in Russia—fall into the category of social novels. Not only did these authors describe the society in which they lived; they dwelled on the problems of that society. Literature was becoming increasingly a form of social criticism.

The shift toward Realism reached its climax in the late nineteenth century in a literary movement called Naturalism. Naturalism represented the conscious effort of some writers to apply scientific principles to art. Naturalistic writers like Émile Zola in France, Henrik Ibsen in Norway, and Gerhart Hauptmann in Germany were not interested so much in beauty as they were in truth. To get at truth they discarded subjective intuition and strove to describe objectively what they had learned from study and observation. The Naturalist was much impressed with the discoveries of modern science, especially in biology and such new fields as sociology and psychology. He felt it was one of his chief functions to call attention to existing evils and abuses. If this meant focusing his artistic efforts on the seamy side of life, he did so,

hoping that by serving as diagnostician of society's illness he might help cure it.

Impressionism

The change from Romanticism to Realism was less pronounced in painting than in literature, although some new trends did appear. In the past artists had been concerned with the unusual and beautiful, but now they turned more to ordinary and often ugly everyday subjects heretofore considered unworthy of their attention—farmers, laborers, and urban scenes.

The real innovation in nineteenth-century painting, however, was not so much in subject matter as in technique. As Naturalism did to literature, so Impressionism applied scientific principles to painting. Influenced by scientific discoveries about the composition of light, painters like Camille Pissarro (1830–1903), Claude Monet (1840–1926), and Auguste Renoir (1841–1919) used short strokes of pure color to depict nature in its ever-changing moods, not as it appeared to the logical mind but as it "impressed" the eye in viewing a whole scene rather than a series of specific objects. An Impressionist painting, examined at close range, thus appears as a maze of colored dabs that, viewed from a distance, merge into recognizable objects with the vibrant quality imparted by light.

In trying to find the scientific temper of the late nineteenth century reflected in literature and art, however, one must guard against oversimplification. A relationship between art and science certainly existed. But it would be wrong to assume that the majority of people at the time were aware of this relationship. The average person had little use for Naturalistic novels or plays or Impressionist paintings. He liked pictures that "told a story," preferably a sentimental one. And he liked second-rate novels of love and adventure by authors long since forgotten.

Friedrich Nietzsche (1844–1900).

Symbolism

If these cultural interests of the average person expressed an unconscious desire to escape the realities of the present, a similar tendency may be noted among a few highly sensitive writers. They deplored their generation's preoccupation with material values, and far from singing the praises of the industrial age, they spoke out against its dirt and vulgarity. Earlier in the century, the Englishmen Matthew Arnold (1822–88) and John Ruskin (1819–1900) had lamented the materialism and loss of esthetic values resulting from industrialization. Their complaints were echoed later by their compatriot William Morris (1834–96), who would have preferred to withdraw from the machine age with its cheapening of taste and return to the simplicity and dignity of the Middle Ages.

There was a note of romanticism and escapism in this longing for beauty in an age of slums and soot. Naturalism had little use for beauty; to the Naturalist, art had to serve a purpose and preach a message. In protest against this arid view, a group of French writers at the end of the century proclaimed that art was sufficient unto itself—"art for art's sake." Art to these neo-Romantic, or Symbolist, poets—Stéphane Mallarmé (1842–98), Paul Verlaine (1844–96), and others—was

not for everyone but only for the select few to whom it spoke in "symbols," using words not so much for their meaning but for the images and analogies they conveyed, often by sound alone. Symbolism, like Romanticism before, was deeply subjective and thus difficult to define. It is significant as an indication that there were people before 1914 who did not find all things perfect in a society that gloried in its material achievements and accepted the struggle for wealth as a sign of progress.

The Symbolists were not alone in their criticism. The most outspoken critic of the generation before 1914 was the German philosopher Friedrich Nietzsche (1844–1900). In a series of beautifully written, epigrammatic books in the 1880s, Nietzsche attacked almost everything his age held sacred—democracy, socialism, nationalism, racialism, imperialism, militarism, materialism, intellectualism, and especially Christianity. Little understood by his contemporaries and much misunderstood since, Nietzsche's influence was felt more after than before the First World War. Few people today would agree with his wholesale condemnation of his age. Yet in striking out, Nietzsche could not help but hit on many of the weaknesses we have since come to recognize in an age characterized above all by smugness and misplaced self-confidence.

Suggestions for Further Reading

Note: Asterisk denotes a book available in paperback edition.

General Two good broadly conceived works that treat European civilization as an entity are C. J. H. Hayes, *A Generation of Materialism, 1871–1900** (1941), and O. J. Hale, *The Great Illusion, 1900–1914** (1971). National events are well covered in R. C. K. Ensor, *England, 1870–1914* (1936); D. W. Brogan, *The Development of Modern France, 1870–1939*, Vol. I, rev. ed. (1966); K. S. Pinson, *Modern Germany, Its History and Civilization*, 2nd ed. (1966); D. Mack Smith, *Italy: A Modern History* (1959); A. J. May, *The Hapsburg Monarchy, 1867–1914* (1951); and H. Seton-Watson, *The Decline of Imperial Russia, 1855–1914** (1952).

The Growth of Democracy The progress of political and social democracy is treated in A. Rosenberg, *Democracy and Socialism* (1939). On social thought, see G. Masur, *Prophets of Yesterday: Studies in European Culture, 1890–1914** (1961), and H. S. Hughes, *Consciousness and Society: The Reorientation of Social Thought, 1850–1930** (1958). Other relevant works are J. Bowle, *Politics and Opinion in the Nineteenth Century** (1954); C. Moraze, *The Triumph of the Middle Classes* (1966); and C. Cipolla, *Literacy and Development in the West** (1969). Problems of parliamentary government in western Europe are discussed in É. Halévy, *History of the English People in the Nineteenth Century,** Vols. V and VI (1936), and D. Thomson, *Democracy in France Since 1870,** 4th ed. (1964). The peculiar situation in Germany is analyzed in A. Gerschenkron, *Bread and Democracy in Germany* (1943). Habsburg attempts to cope with the nationalities problem are disentangled in O. Jászi, *The Dissolution of the Habsburg Monarchy** (1929), and with emphasis on individual national groups in R. A. Kann, *The Multinational Empire*, 2 vols. (1950). The halfhearted efforts at political reform in Russia are discussed in G. Fischer, *Russian Liberalism from Gentry to Intelligentsia* (1958), and B. Pares, *The Fall of the Russian Monarchy* (1939). Women's efforts for equal rights are the subject of W. L. O'Neill, *Woman Movement: Feminism in the United States and in England* (1969), and D. Mitchell, *The Fighting Pankhursts: A Study in Tenacity* (1967). L. A. Tilly and J. W. Scott, *Women, Work, and Family* (1978), deals mainly with France. See also, R. J. Evans, *The Feminist Movement in Germany, 1894–1933* (1976).

The "Second Industrial Revolution" Several of the books mentioned in the reading list for Chapter 25 also cover this later period. D. Landes, *The Unbound Prometheus: Technological Change and Industrial Development in Western Europe from 1750 to the Present* (1969), is a major recent contribution. Additional treatments for the leading industrial countries are A. L. Levine, *Industrial Retardation in Britain, 1880–1914* (1967); W. W. Rostow, *The British Economy in the Nineteenth Century* (1948); G. Palmade, *French Capitalism in the Nineteenth Century* (1972); and G. Stolper, K. Häuser, and K. Borchardt, *The German Economy—1870 to the Present* (1967). M. S. Miller, *The Economic Development of Russia, 1905–1914* (1926), is more detailed, and W. L. Blackwell, *The Industrialization of Russia: An Historical Perspective** (1970), covers a longer period. On European economic expansion overseas, see H. Feis, *Europe, the World's Banker, 1870–1914** (1930).

The Rise of the Working Class A brief introduction to European radicalism is D. Caute, *The Left in Europe Since 1789** (1966). On evolutionary socialism, see P. Gay, *The Dilemma of Democratic Socialism: Eduard Bernstein's Challenge to Marx** (1952), and A. M. McBriar, *Fabian Socialism and English Politics, 1884–1918** (1962). The best book on socialism in Germany is C. Schorske, *German Social Democracy, 1905–1917** (1955). For France, see A. Noland, *The Founding of the French Socialist Party, 1893–1905* (1956), and H. Goldberg, *Life of Jean Jaurès* (1962). Good surveys of international socialism are J. Joll, *The Second International, 1889–1914** (1955), and M. Beer, *Fifty Years of International Socialism* (1937). On the growth of organized labor, see W. A. McConagha, *The Development of the Labor Movement in Great Britain, France, and Germany* (1942); H. Pelling, *The Origins of the Labour Party, 1880–1900*, 2nd ed. (1964); and J. W. Scott, *The Glassworkers of Carmaux* (1974). Social legislation before 1914 is covered in K. de Schweinitz, *England's Road to Social Security* (1943), and W. H. Dawson, *Social Insurance in Germany, 1883–1911* (1912). The influence of individual reformers in England is discussed in H. Ausubel, *In Hard Times: Reformers Among the Late Victorians* (1960), and M. Richter, *The Politics of Conscience: T. H. Green and His Age* (1964). On the role of the churches in the field of social reform, see D. O. W. Wagner, *Church of England and Social Reform Since 1854* (1930); J. N. Moody, ed., *Church and Society: Catholic Social and Political Thought and Movements, 1789–1950* (1953); K. S. Inglis, *Churches and the Working Class in Victorian England* (1963); and J. McManners, *Church and State in France, 1870–1914* (1972).

Domestic Affairs of the Major Powers Much of this subject is covered in the works already cited. An interesting way of supplementing the more general accounts is through biographies. Among the standard lives of the great, L. Strachey, *Queen Victoria** (1921), is a classic, though E. Longford, *Victoria R. I.** (1964), is more reliable. R. Blake, *Disraeli* (1967), and E. J. Feuchtwanger, *Gladstone* (1975), are more readable than earlier standard accounts. Two great French leaders are commemorated in G. Bruun, *Clemenceau** (1943), and G. Wright, *Raymond Poincaré and the French Presidency* (1942). On the continental monarchs, see M. Balfour, *The Kaiser and His Times* (1964), and I. V. Hull, *The Entourage of Kaiser Wilhelm II 1888–1918* (1982). J. Redlich, *Emperor Francis Joseph* (1929), lacks color; and neither Nicholas II of Russia nor the kings of Italy have been found worthy of major scholarly biographies.

B. D. Wolfe, *Three Who Made a Revolution** (1955), tells about the future rulers of Russia—Lenin, Trotsky, and Stalin—before their rise to power. The nineteenth-century background of Russia's revolutionary movement is described in E. Lampert, *Studies in Rebellion* (1957) and *Sons Against Fathers* (1965). See also A. Yarmolinsky, *Road to Revolution* (1957). T. H. von Laue, *Sergei Witte and the Industrialization of Russia* (1963), is important for Russian economic history. R. E. Johnson, *Peasant and Proletarian: The Working Class in Moscow in the Late Nineteenth Century* (1979), is an original work.

Significant monographs on German history include P. G. J. Pulzer, *The Rise of Political Anti-Semitism in Germany and Austria** (1964); J. C. G. Röhl, *Germany Without Bismarck: The Crisis of Government in the Second Reich, 1890–1900* (1967); M. Kitchen, *The German Officer Corps, 1890–1914* (1968); G. Roth, *Social Democrats in Imperial Germany* (1963); and F. Stern, *The Politics of Cultural Despair** (1965). For a balanced view of the most crucial event in French politics, see D. Johnson, *France and the Dreyfus Affair* (1967). Other phases of French politics are treated in E. Weber, *Action Française* (1962) and *Peasants into Frenchmen: The Modernization of Rural France, 1870–1914* (1976); M. Curtis, *Three Against the Third Republic* (1959), which deals with Sorel, Barrès, and Maurras; and R. Byrnes, *Anti-Semitism in Modern France* (1950). R. D. Anderson, *France, 1870–1914: Politics and Society* (1977), is brief and has an excellent bibliography. Britain on the eve of the First World War is the subject of C. Cross, *The Liberals in Power, 1905–1914* (1963), and G. Dangerfield, *The Strange Death of Liberal England** (1961). See also C. Holmes, *Anti-Semitism in British Society, 1876–1939* (1979). The Italian scene is described in J. A. Thayer, *Italy and the Great War: Politics and Culture, 1890–1915* (1964), and in C. Seton-Watson, *Italy from Liberalism to Fascism, 1870–1925* (1967).

Intellectual History The general works by J. H. Randall, *The Making of the Modern Mind* (1926, 1940), and C. Brinton, *Ideas and Men** (1950), have good chapters on the intellectual life of the late nineteenth century. E. Weber, *Paths to the Present: Aspects of European Thought from Romanticism to Existentialism** (1960), contains unusual selections of readings. See also O. Chadwick, *The Secularization of the European Mind in the Nineteenth Century* (1976). On the history of science, see A. E. E. McKenzie, *The Major Achievements of Science,* 2 vols. (1960), and W. C. Dampier, *A Shorter History of Science** (1957). The all-pervasive influence of Darwin is shown in P. B. Sears, *Charles Darwin: The Naturalist as a Cultural Force* (1950), and J. C. Greene, *The Death of Adam: Evolution and Its Impact on Western Thought* (1959). On the contemporary impact of Darwinism, see W. Irvine, *Apes, Angels, and Victorians* (1955). J. Barzun, *Darwin, Marx, Wagner** (1958), stresses similarities in three outwardly different contemporaries. The wide appeal of Social Darwinism is shown in R. Hofstadter, *Social Darwinism in American Thought** (1955). W. Kaufmann, *Nietzsche: Philosopher, Psychologist, Antichrist** (1956), is a leading interpretation of the most influential philosopher of the period. R. Hayman, *Nietzsche: A Critical Life* (1980), is faithful and balanced.

The classic study on the literature of the nineteenth century is G. Brandes, *Main Currents in Nineteenth-Century Literature,* 6 vols. (1923). Briefer and more pertinent is E. Wilson, *Axel's Castle: A Study in the Imaginative Literature of 1870–1930** (1958). For the impact of science on literature, see M. Nicolson, *Science and Imagination* (1956). The beautifully illustrated volume by R. Raynal, *The Nineteenth Century: New Sources of Emotion from Goya to Gauguin* (1951), shows the transition from traditional to modern art. T. Shapiro, *Painters and Politics: The European Avante-Garde and Society, 1900–1925* (1976), is a pioneering work. See also F. Mathey, *The World of the Impressionists* (1961). H. Leichtentritt, *Music, History, and Ideas* (1938), and C. Gray, *History of Music* (1947), discuss musical trends. On "popular culture," see R. Williams, *Culture and Society, 1780–1950** (1958), and B. Rosenberg and D. M. White, eds., *Mass Culture** (1959).

The Struggle for a European Equilibrium 1871-1914

The diplomatic history of Europe and the world between 1871 and 1914 must be viewed in the context of the political, economic, and cultural trends noted in the preceding chapter. The spirit of competition that pervaded relations among individuals and classes had its parallel in the political and economic rivalry among nations. Many international crises arose directly out of domestic tensions. Had the internal affairs of the powers before 1914 been more harmonious, international affairs might possibly have been more peaceful.

Our view of international relations after 1870 is conditioned by knowledge of what happened in 1914. Most historians agree that, while some of the immediate causes that brought about war in 1914 could have been avoided, its real causes were deeply rooted. To understand how deeply, we must remember the far-reaching effects that the unification of Italy and Germany had had on the European balance of power. Two regions that heretofore had been mere pawns in international affairs suddenly emerged as great powers. The political and territorial framework of the Continent thus lost much of its former elasticity. The only region in Europe where major changes

were still possible was the Balkan Peninsula. Austria-Hungary, now excluded from German and Italian affairs, claimed the Balkans as its natural sphere of influence. Since Russia and, less strongly, Italy made the same claim, the Balkans became the scene of recurrent international crises.

Another source of international tension was the growing colonial rivalry among the powers. With opportunities for territorial expansion on the Continent restricted, and with expanding economies clamoring for markets and raw materials, colonial conflicts injected an element of perennial friction into international affairs. An added cause for tension was nationalism. As long as members of one nationality were subjected to domination by another, as was the case in Austria-Hungary, Turkey, Russia, and, to a lesser extent, Germany and Great Britain, the peace of Europe remained precarious at best.

THE AGE OF BISMARCK, 1871–90

Despite the unsettling effects of Italian and German unification, Europe at first managed to adjust peacefully to the changed situation. The chief credit for the relative stability that prevailed for the two decades after 1871 belongs to Prince Bismarck. The fundamental aim of the German chancellor was the consolidation of the new German *Reich*. For this he needed peace. Bismarck considered Germany a "satiated" power, with no further territorial ambitions. The main threat to its security was France's desire for revenge. To keep France isolated, therefore, became the guiding principle of Bismarck's foreign policy.

The basic moderation of the German chancellor's aims and the consummate skill of his diplomacy rightly command respect. They show that *Realpolitik* need not necessarily rely on "blood and iron" but can use with equal effect peaceful pressure and persuasion. Yet in merely trying to maintain existing conditions and ignoring those forces that were straining against the status quo—notably nationalism and imperialism—Bismarck showed the same blindness that had characterized Metternich before him.

William II and George V at Potsdam (1913); this was the last meeting of the cousins before the outbreak of the First World War.

Admirable as the Bismarckian system was, it was to fall to pieces as soon as the masterful guidance of its creator was removed.

The "Three Emperors' League"

The first of Bismarck's many international agreements was concluded in 1872 among Germany, Austria, and Russia. The *Dreikaiserbund* tried to revive the collaboration that had existed in the days of the "Holy Alliance." But the feeling of solidarity that had animated the three conservative powers in the days of Metternich had since given way to mutual rivalries. Russia, in particular, had never forgiven Austria its "ingratitude" during the Crimean War, and it now resented the leadership that Germany assumed within the new Three Emperors' League. A first sign of disagreement between Germany and Russia appeared during the so-called "war-in-sight" crisis of 1875, when rumors that Germany was planning a preventive war against France brought protests from England and Russia. Bismarck's role in fomenting the crisis is not quite clear, though there is no evidence that he was seriously considering war against France. Russia's action, therefore, seemed unnecessarily meddlesome, especially in view of its traditional friendship with Prussia. The monarchical front had shown itself far from solid.

The Russo-Turkish War and the Congress of Berlin

A far more serious rift within the Three Emperors' League developed out of Russia's ambitions in the Balkans. The inefficiency and corruption of the disintegrating Ottoman Empire had invited intervention several times before, most recently during the Crimean War. In 1875 new revolts against Turkish misrule broke out in the Balkans. The Turks acted with their usual ferocity in putting down these nationalist uprisings and would have held the upper hand if Russia, in the spring of 1877, had not joined the insurgents. It did so after making sure of Austrian neutrality and recognizing in return Austria's right to occupy the Turkish provinces of Bosnia and Herzegovina. In addition, Russia promised not to support the formation of any large Balkan state.

The Russo-Turkish War, after some reversals, ended in Russian victory. In a treaty signed at San Stefano in March 1878, several of Turkey's subject nationalities were granted independence. Among them was to be a large Bulgarian state, which Russia was to occupy for several years. In addition, Russia was to get some territorial compensations. This startling increase of Russian influence in the Balkans deeply alarmed the other great powers. Their pressure induced Russia finally to agree to submit the settlement to an international conference at Berlin in June 1878.

Most of the important decisions of the Congress of Berlin were actually reached in preliminary agreements, which the Congress then confirmed. The proposed Greater Bulgaria was divided into three parts, leaving only a small Bulgarian state; Serbia, Montenegro, and Rumania were granted full independence; Austria was given the right to occupy and administer Bosnia and Her-

Bismarck

PRO

Bismarck is generally described in the textbooks as the first *Realpolitiker*; but unfortunately so much has been written about *Realpolitik* that its meaning has become obscure and mixed up with blood and iron and incitement to war by the malicious revision of royal telegrams. . . . It may be permissible to suggest that the essence of Bismarck's realism was his recognition of the limitations of his craft, and that it was this, coupled with the passion and the responsibility that he brought to his vocation, that made him a great statesman.

CON

Himself always plotting combinations against others, Bismarck was convinced that all the world was plotting combinations against him and lived in a half-mad imaginary world in which every statesman was as subtle and calculating, as ruthless and assiduous as he was himself. . . . At bottom he was a barbarian of genius, mastering in the highest degree the mechanical and intellectual side of civilization, altogether untouched by its spirit.

From Gordon A. Craig, *From Bismarck to Adenauer: Aspects of German Statecraft* (Baltimore: Johns Hopkins University Press, 1958), p. 28; from A. J. P. Taylor, *The Course of German History* (New York: Coward-McCann, 1946), pp. 95–96.

zegovina; and England was given control over the island of Cyprus. Russia rightly felt that it had been cheated out of its victory. While England and Austria made substantial gains, Russia had to be satisfied with a small addition to Bessarabia and some gains in the Caucasus. The Russians blamed their defeat on Bismarck, who, they held, had violated his self-styled role as "honest broker" by favoring the interests of Russia's adversaries. The Congress of Berlin provoked a serious crisis in the relations between Germany and Russia and ended the Three Emperors' League.

The Austro-German Alliance

The breakup of the Three Emperors' League forced Bismarck to find a substitute. This he did in a secret alliance with Austria. The Dual Alliance of 1879 was the climax of Germany's *rapprochement* with Austria that had been Bismarck's concern since 1866. The alliance was renewed periodically and remained in force until 1918. Its provisions were purely defensive, calling for mutual aid if either member was attacked by Russia. Bismarck has been criticized for tying Germany's fate to the ramshackle Dual Monarchy. But he did not necessarily envisage the alliance as permanent, and he thought Germany strong enough to keep Austria's ambitions in the Balkans in check so as to avoid a showdown with Russia. Nor did the union with Austria mean that Germany was ready to sever relations with Russia altogether. Bismarck expected that Russia, unable for ideological reasons to draw closer to republican France, and separated from England by rivalries in Asia, would feel sufficiently isolated to desire a renewal of its former ties with Germany. Bismarck's assumption proved correct.

The Second "Three Emperors' League"

Russia would have preferred a treaty with Germany alone, but Bismarck insisted that Austria be included as well. A new Three Emperors' League was finally concluded in 1881. It provided that in case one of the members became in-

THE TREATY OF SAN STEFANO   1878

THE CONGRESS OF BERLIN   1878

volved in war with a fourth power, the other two would remain neutral. In this way Bismarck relieved his fear that Russia might join France in a war against Germany. The most important provisions of the treaty dealt with the Balkans: any territorial changes in that region henceforth were to require the consent of all three powers; Austria reserved its right to annex Bosnia and Herzegovina at a time of its own choosing; and Russia's wish for the eventual union of Bulgaria and

Eastern Roumelia (one of the regions separated from Greater Bulgaria at Berlin) was recognized. By dividing the Balkans into spheres of influence, the three powers seemed finally to have brought the Balkan problem under control. The new arrangement, however, overlooked the national aspirations of the Balkan peoples themselves.

The Triple Alliance

Before the Balkan question became acute once more in 1885, Bismarck had further extended his diplomatic network with the Triple Alliance of Germany, Austria, and Italy in 1882. The initiative this time came from the Italians. Italy for some time had hoped to enhance its status as a great power by occupying the Turkish region of Tunis in North Africa. It was deeply distressed, therefore, when the French took Tunis in 1881. To strengthen its diplomatic position for the future, Italy sought closer ties with Austria and Germany. Like the rest of Bismarck's treaties, the Triple Alliance was primarily defensive. Bismarck never took it very seriously, except for the fact that it contributed to the diplomatic isolation of France.

The years immediately after 1882 mark the high point of Bismarck's influence in Europe. French nationalism appeared to have been successfully diverted into colonial channels in North Africa; the situation in the Balkans appeared under control; and Austria's position had been strengthened by a secret treaty with Serbia in 1881 that made Austria the protector of its small neighbor. In 1883 Rumania concluded an alliance with Austria, to which Germany adhered later. The treaty was chiefly directed against Russian ambitions in the Balkans, where a new crisis flared up in 1885.

The Reinsurance Treaty

This latest Balkan crisis was touched off by an upsurge of Bulgarian nationalism in Eastern Roumelia, leading to the reunion of that region with Bulgaria. During the ensuing wrangle the Three Emperors' League met its final fate. For some time Russian nationalists, resenting German support of Austria in the Balkans, had demanded that Russia seek the friendship of France. Bismarck's worst fears seemed about to come true. But the tsarist government was reluctant to cut its connections with Berlin. Russia, therefore, proposed to the Germans that they enter into an agreement without Austria. The upshot was the so-called Reinsurance Treaty of 1887, which provided for benevolent neutrality in case either partner became involved in war, unless Germany attacked France or Russia attacked Austria. The Reinsurance Treaty also recognized Russia's interests in Bulgaria and the Turkish Straits.

This last of Bismarck's major treaties has been both hailed as a diplomatic masterpiece and condemned as an act of duplicity. It certainly did run counter to the spirit, if not the letter, of the Dual Alliance. But while Bismarck encouraged Russia's Balkan ambitions, he at the same time put an obstacle in the way of these ambitions by sponsoring the so-called Mediterranean Agreements between England, Italy, and Austria. Signed also in 1887, these agreements called for the maintenance of the status quo in the Mediterranean, including the Balkans. Any assurances Bismarck had given to Russia about Bulgaria and the Straits were thus successfully neutralized.

In making a fair appraisal of Bismarck's diplomacy, it is necessary to go beyond a mere comparison of treaty texts and consider the motives behind his treaties. These invariably were to maintain peace. Bismarck hoped to achieve this aim by isolating France and balancing the rest of the powers so that any unilateral disturbance of the peace would automatically result in a hostile coalition against the aggressor. Seen in this light, Bismarck's policy was less crafty than it appeared when the world first learned about the Reinsurance Treaty after the chancellor's retirement. A valid criticism of Bismarck's policy is that it was far too complicated to be successful in the long run and that it rested more on the attitudes of Europe's statesmen than on the sentiments of their peoples. Such disregard of public opinion became increasingly difficult in an age of democracy and nationalism.

FROM EUROPEAN
TO WORLD POLITICS

One of the most important trends in international affairs after Bismarck was the growing involvement of Europe in world affairs. This development, as we have seen, had started much earlier, of course; but it was only at the end of the nineteenth century that events in Europe and overseas became so intricately interwoven that the histories of Europe and the world could no longer be treated separately.

The "New Imperialism"

The expansion of European influence in the late nineteenth century is often called the "new imperialism," to distinguish it from earlier phases of overseas expansion. Its motives were similar to those found earlier in the century, although they now operated with far greater intensity. Imperialism in the past had been chiefly limited in its appeal to the upper classes. Now suddenly it became of vital concern to everyone. More than any other movement, the new imperialism expressed the general climate of the period before 1914. Aggressive nationalism, ruthless economic competition, the restless struggle for success, all found an outlet in the scramble for overseas colonies and concessions, protectorates and spheres of influence. Here was an opportunity for men of daring and initiative to suffer hardships in distant lands not merely to advance their own fortunes but also, as they never tired telling the world, to undertake a "civilizing mission" for the good of mankind.

England continued to lead in the new imperialism as it had in the old. After a period of declining interest in overseas expansion, Britain resumed its imperialist course after 1870. By 1914 it controlled one-fifth of the world's land and one-fourth of its population. The second largest colonial empire in 1914, that of France, had been acquired almost entirely during the nineteenth century. In its expansion into North Africa, France became involved first with Italy over Tunis, then with England over Egypt and the Sudan, and finally, after the turn of the century, with Germany over Morocco. Germany, prior to 1880, had no overseas possessions, and Bismarck was slow to enter the colonial race. When he finally did, beginning in 1884, it was in part to enhance Germany's bargaining position in Europe. It was William II who launched Germany in earnest on a course of *Weltpolitik,* in pursuit of which it provoked several international crises. Similar friction was caused by Italy's belated claims to colonies. Russia confined its expansion to adjacent areas in Asia. The only major power refraining from colonial expansion was Austria-Hungary.

THE CONQUEST OF AFRICA

The most spectacular expansion of European influence after 1870 took place in Africa. In order to simplify the involved story of the scramble for African territory, events in the northern, central, and southern regions will be discussed separately. But it must be remembered that many of these developments actually happened simultaneously.

North Africa

The Mediterranean coast of Africa, since the seventh century, had been under the influence of Moslem civilization; since the early sixteenth century, it had been under the direct or indirect rule of the Ottoman Empire. France gained its first foothold in North Africa with the acquisition of Algiers in 1830. In the course of the century France extended its sphere of influence inland, and in time Algeria was declared an integral part of France. The next major move came with the establishment of a French protectorate over Algeria's eastern neighbor, Tunis, in 1881. Subsequently France began extending its influence westward over the sultanate of Morocco. The situation here was complicated by the fact that several other powers, notably Germany, also had economic interests in that region. A French protectorate over Morocco was thus not won until 1911, and

Algerian officer in the French army (1886).

The Sphinx is neck-high in sand and British soldiers in this photograph taken in 1882, after the bombardment of Alexandria.

The influence of African art on European art. Above: wood doll from Ghana (late nineteenth century); below: Amedeo Modigliani, *Head* (ca. 1913).

then only after two major international crises (see pp. 689, 691).

Egypt, the Sudan, and Tripoli

While France was establishing itself in the western half of North Africa, Britain was doing the same in Egypt and the Sudan. Egypt in 1870 was still nominally part of the Turkish Empire. Its gradual subjugation to foreign control was due to reckless borrowing of foreign money at prohibitive interest rates. When, in 1876, the Egyptian government suspended interest payments on some of its foreign obligations, Britain and France, the leading creditors, established a dual control over Egypt's finances. The subsequent rise in taxes infuriated the Egyptian taxpayer. To counteract a rising tide of Egyptian nationalism, Britain occupied Egypt in 1882. As a result, Anglo-French dual control over Egypt came to an end.

France, needless to say, resented its exclusion from Egypt and on every occasion tried to put obstacles in England's way. Tension between the two powers was aggravated by their rivalry over the Sudan. This Egyptian dependency had won temporary independence in 1885. But when France and Belgium began advancing toward the Sudan from central Africa, British and Egyptian forces in 1896 started to retake the region. The climax of their expedition came in 1898, when British and French forces met at Fashoda on the Upper Nile. As both Britain and France laid claim to the

Sudan, war seemed imminent. But the French government, troubled by the Dreyfus affair at home and inferior in naval strength, finally gave in and left England in control. In 1899 Egypt and England established joint control over what came to be known as the Anglo-Egyptian Sudan.

One stretch of land along the Mediterranean had not as yet come under foreign control—the region of Tripoli between Egypt and Tunis. It was of little value, consisting largely of desert. But in an age when overseas expansion was a matter of prestige, even so poor a prize seemed worth taking. After making certain of French support by recognizing France's claims in Morocco, Italy in 1911 and 1912 waged war against Turkey and annexed Tripoli. The Italian colony of Libya, as it was called, was one of the least lucrative of imperialist ventures. But it was a source of great pride to the Italians.

Central Africa

Very little of central Africa had been explored before the second half of the nineteenth century. Among the most famous explorers of the region were David Livingstone and Henry Morton Stanley. Livingstone, a Scottish missionary, spent almost thirty years in Africa. When he failed to return from his third and last major expedition in 1871, Stanley, a British-born American journalist, was sent to find him. Stanley's successful search for Livingstone gave him a taste for exploration that made him the leading explorer of the Congo region. After vainly seeking to interest the British in his plans for opening up the Congo, Stanley found a sponsor in King Leopold II of Belgium. Leopold's claims to the Congo Free State were recognized by an international conference at Berlin in 1885. For the next twenty years a policy of the most ruthless colonial exploitation made a vast fortune for Leopold's various personal enterprises in the Congo. Only after these brutal methods were revealed was control over the region transferred to the Belgian state in 1908.

The practice whereby enterprising individuals staked out claims that were later protected by their governments was also used to great advantage by the Germans. Beginning in 1884 the German government took over the rights that various German merchants and explorers had staked out over large parts of southwest, central, and east Africa. The British tried to discourage these German moves. When this attempt proved fruitless, they moved quickly to stake out their own claims for the interior of the continent. France, meanwhile, extended its holdings in central and west Africa and in 1896 proclaimed possession of the island of Madagascar. Italy acquired Eritrea and Somaliland at the southern end of the Red Sea in 1890. Italy's attempts to extend its holdings inland into Abyssinia were stopped by Ethiopian forces in the battle of Adua (1896).

South Africa

Some of the most valuable colonial prizes were to be found in the southern part of the African continent. Britain had acquired the Dutch Cape Colony there in 1806. As a result of tension between the

IMPERIALISM IN AFRICA   1884 and 1914

ASIA IN 1880

new British immigrants and the original Dutch settlers, or Boers, the latter, beginning in the 1830s, had moved northward and founded two new Dutch colonies, the Orange Free State and the Transvaal. Britain recognized the independence of these republics in 1852. With the subsequent discovery of diamonds and gold in these regions, however, the inhabitants of the Cape Colony began to call for an extension of British sovereignty over the Orange Free State and the Transvaal.

The leading advocate of Britain's South African interests in the late nineteenth century was Cecil Rhodes. A typical "empire builder," Rhodes owned extensive interests in South Africa's diamond and gold fields. He became prime minister of the Cape Colony in

1890. Meanwhile a new discovery of gold in the Transvaal in 1886 had touched off a veritable British invasion into the region. To discourage this foreign influx, the president of the Transvaal, Paul Krüger, placed heavy restrictions on British immigrants. One of the more spectacular incidents in the growing tension between Britons and Boers was the abortive Jameson Raid at the turn of the year 1895/96, an attempt by one of Rhodes's associates to start a revolution among the British minority in the Transvaal. An ill-advised and well-publicized telegram from the German kaiser congratulating Krüger on his defeat of the plot cast a deep shadow on Anglo-German relations at the time.

Finally, in 1899, tension between the Boers and the British led to war. It took

ASIA IN 1914

THE NEW IMPERIALISM IN ASIA AND THE PACIFIC

The sudden outburst of imperialism after 1880 also affected Asia and the Pacific. In contrast to Africa, large parts of this region had been under European domination for some time. Developments in

Britain two and a half years to defeat the tenacious Boers. Not until 1902 did the Boers lay down their arms, and then only on the promise of very lenient peace terms. As a result of this leniency, the issues of the past were quickly forgotten. When the Union of South Africa was formed in 1910, a former Boer general became the first prime minister of this newest self-governing dominion.

India and China have already been discussed (see pp. 634–40); we shall now turn to the rest of the Asian continent and to the Pacific islands.

Russia in Asia

One of the principal powers with interests in Asia was Russia. Its advances there took three main directions: to the southwest into the Near East—the Ottoman Empire and especially the region around the entrance to the Black Sea; to the Far East—Siberia and the adjacent coastal regions of China; and to the Middle East—Afghanistan and Persia. Foremost among Russia's aims in the Near and Far East was to find outlets to the sea and ice-free harbors that would enable it to escape its landlocked position. Attempts to do so in the Near East, as we have seen, were met by resistance from the other great powers, notably England. Whenever it met with a setback, as in 1878, Russia shifted its attention from west to east, from Europe to Asia.

Russian expansion into Siberia had proceeded slowly but steadily for more than three centuries. It was greatly facilitated by the acquisition of a section of China's coast along the Sea of Japan in 1860 and the founding of the Pacific port of Vladivostok. Russia's aim was to expand southward across the Amur River into Manchuria and then into Korea. But its plans were foiled by the conflicting interests of Japan. As a result of the Russo-Japanese War, Russia's territorial position in the Far East in 1905 was substantially what it had been fifty years earlier. Its failures in the Far East in part explain Russia's renewed interest in the affairs of Europe and the Near East during the last decade before the First World War.

Anglo-Russian Rivalry

In the third sphere of Russian expansion, the Middle East and central Asia,

Russia made considerable progress during the nineteenth century. By 1880 the whole region north of Persia and Afghanistan had become Russian. This extension of Russian power was watched with growing apprehension by Great Britain, which feared that Russia's advance was ultimately directed at India. The mountainous country of Afghanistan served as a buffer against a possible invasion of India from the northwest. In 1879 England had overthrown the pro-Russian ruler of Afghanistan and had occupied most of the country. But British-Russian rivalry continued. It was not resolved until 1907, when Russia finally recognized England's predominant position in Afghanistan.

Another scene of Anglo-Russian rivalry was Persia. The contest here was primarily economic, with both Russian and British interests seeking concessions. But England also feared that Persia might serve as another approach to India. Differences in Persia, as in Afghanistan, were negotiated by the Anglo-Russian Entente in 1907 (see p. 689).

This encroachment of the great powers on hitherto sovereign states was typical of much of European imperialism in Asia. The gradual subjection of China to foreign tutelage during the second half of the nineteenth century was an example. Another example was Siam. The French, after extending their protectorate over Indochina during the 1880s, turned their attention westward. Here they came in conflict with the English, who were interested in Siam because it bordered on Burma, which Britain had taken in 1852. After a certain amount of controversy, Siam in 1896 was made into a neutral buffer state between Burma and Indochina.

The Pacific

The most valuable islands of the Pacific were taken long before 1870. The rivalry of the powers over the few remaining small islands was a sign of how intense the imperialist urge had become. The main contestants in the Pacific were England and Germany, with the United States and France intervening occasionally. It is unnecessary to enumerate all

President McKinley and the Philippines

I have been criticized a good deal about the Philippines, but I don't deserve it. The truth is, I didn't want the Philippines, and when they came to us, as a gift from the gods, I did not know what to do with them. . . . I walked the floor of the White House night after night until midnight; and I am not ashamed to tell you, gentlemen, that I went down on my knees and prayed Almighty God for light and guidance. And one night late it came to me this way—I don't know how it was, but it came: (1) That we could not give them back to Spain—that would be cowardly and dishonorable; (2) that we could not turn them over to France or Germany—that would be bad business and discreditable; (3) that we could not leave them to govern themselves—they were unfit for self-government . . . and (4) that there was nothing left for us to do but to take them all, and to educate the Philippinos, and uplift and civilize and Christianize them, and, by God's grace, do the very best we could by them, as our fellow men for whom Christ also died. And then I went to bed, and went to sleep, and slept soundly, and next morning I sent for the chief engineer of the War Department (our map-maker), and told him to put the Philippines on the map of the United States.

William McKinley, as quoted in G. A. Malcolm and M. M. Kalaw, *Philippine Government* (Manila: Associated Publishers, 1923), pp. 65–66.

the bits and pieces of land picked up by these powers. The most important, besides America's annexation of the Philippines, was the acquisition of eastern New Guinea by England and Germany in 1884. The most serious crisis arose over the Samoan Islands, which were claimed by Britain, Germany, and the United States. After ten years of intermittent dispute, the islands were divided in 1899 between the United States and Germany, with England receiving compensations in the Solomons.

THE UNITED STATES AS A GREAT POWER

Developments in the United States during the period before 1914 were remarkably similar to developments in Europe. In the purely political sphere, there was less need for further democratization than there was in some European countries, although the agitation of the Populists in the 1890s and of the Progressive Party in 1912 showed that many Americans felt their interests were neglected under the two-party system. In the economic sphere, the United States shared fully in the industrial expansion that took place in Europe, and by 1914 America led the world in the production of coal, iron, and petroleum.

In trying to cope with the social and economic problems resulting from rapid industrialization, the activities of both the labor unions and the government, in America as in Europe, brought a marked improvement of the worker's status. The efforts of Theodore Roosevelt (1901–1909), to secure a "square deal" for the workingman, and his attempts at "trust busting," helped to bridge the gap between capital and labor. Despite the opposition of many Americans to governmental intervention in economic affairs, the United States showed the same tendency toward becoming a "welfare state" that prevailed in most European countries. In the one field in which American business had welcomed government interference—tariff legislation—the trend by 1914 was in the direction of lower tariffs. This was seen by some as a sign that American industry had come of age and was ready to compete with foreign imports on the home market.

The Spanish-American War

America at the end of the nineteenth century thus shared most of the major trends of Europe. This was nowhere more evident than in foreign affairs. Agitation during the 1890s to annex Hawaii and to construct a canal across Central America ran parallel to European expansionism during the same period. Under the administration of Grover Cleveland, such expansionist sentiments were kept under control. His successor, William McKinley, however, was less able to resist the pressures of American nationalism. One of the main subjects of agitation at the time was Cuba, where a revolt against Spanish rule had started in 1895. American sentiment sided with the Cuban rebels and demanded that the United States go to their aid. When the U.S.S. *Maine* mysteriously exploded in Havana harbor in early 1898, the clamor for war became too strong to be resisted any longer.

The Spanish-American War was the first war between the United States and a European power since 1814. The United

American forces landing at a Cuban port in 1898, during the Spanish-American War.

Cartoon of Theodore Roosevelt "walking softly and carrying a big stick" as he tows American ships through the Caribbean.

States had little difficulty winning the "splendid little war" against Spain. In the peace treaty signed at Paris in December 1898, the United States obtained Puerto Rico, the Philippines, and Guam. Cuba received its independence, though the Platt Amendment, adopted by Congress in 1901, made it a virtual American protectorate.

America made its influence felt in the Far East and elsewhere in other ways as well. In 1898 the United States finally annexed Hawaii and in the following year divided the Samoan Islands with Germany. Also in 1899, Secretary of State John Hay proclaimed the "Open Door" policy, which called for equal opportunity in China for all powers, and in 1900 an American contingent participated in a joint expedition of the powers to put down the Boxer Rebellion in China (see p. 640). The United States also sent delegates to the First Hague Peace Conference in 1899, at which a Permanent Court of International Arbitration was created; and in 1905 President Roosevelt helped settle the Russo-Japanese War in the Treaty of Portsmouth.

The United States and Latin America

America's first and foremost concern, however, was with affairs closer to home.

Theodore Roosevelt in particular had long favored an active American policy in Central America. The Hay-Pauncefote Treaty of 1901 secured British consent for the construction of an American canal across the isthmus. In 1903 Panama, in a revolt sponsored by American interests, seceded from Colombia, and the United States was able to acquire the necessary land for its canal. The Panama Canal was opened shortly after the outbreak of war in 1914.

One of the chief dangers to peace in Latin America came from the loans that European investors in search of large profits had granted to the dictators of that region. Failures to meet payments invariably led to foreign intervention and threatened violations of the Monroe Doctrine. In 1902, Germany, Italy, and Great Britain sent warships to force Venezuela to pay its debts. Two years later another group of powers moved against the Dominican Republic. As a warning, and to forestall European intervention, President Roosevelt, in 1904, proclaimed a Corollary to the Monroe Doctrine. It gave the United States the exclusive right to exercise international police power in the Western Hemisphere. In line with its new policy, America sent marines to Cuba in 1906 and to Nicaragua in 1912.

The motive for America's intervention on these occasions was not merely to maintain order but also to protect its own financial interests. This "dollar diplomacy," as its opponents called it, caused much resentment in the countries concerned and among the other great powers. America's policy, its Latin American neighbors charged, despite idealistic pronouncements, was every bit as imperialistic as that of the European powers.

THE FORMATION OF THE TRIPLE ENTENTE 1890–1907

The events outside Europe discussed in the preceding pages provide the background for the diplomatic realignment of Europe after 1890 and the succession of international crises that culminated in the First World War.

The Franco-Russian Alliance

When Bismarck was dismissed in 1890, his complicated diplomatic system did not long survive. To start with, William II followed the advice of some of Bismarck's more timid underlings and refused to renew the Reinsurance Treaty with Russia. The cutting of Bismarck's "wire to St. Petersburg" did not by itself make the subsequent rapprochement between Russia and France inevitable. Only when Germany continued to show deliberate coolness toward its former friend while drawing closer to England did Russia begin to listen to French suggestions for a better understanding. The Anglo-German Heligoland-Zanzibar Agreement of 1890, by which Germany surrendered large claims in East Africa to England in return for the small strategic island of Heligoland in the North Sea, was generally interpreted as a sign of German eagerness to oblige England. At the same time, a tariff war was impairing Russo-German commercial relations, and an increase in Germany's armed forces was seen as preparation for a possible war on two fronts. Germany's policy toward Russia, it seemed, was undergoing a complete reorientation.

Even so, Russia was slow to respond to France's overtures. The main obstacle was the differences between their autocratic and republican systems of government. It took four years of deliberations before a final agreement was reached. On January 4, 1894, France and Russia signed a secret military convention that amounted to an alliance. It was designed as a counterpart to the Triple Alliance between Germany, Austria, and Italy. Like the latter, the Franco-Russian alliance was defensive. It protected France against an attack by Germany, or by Italy supported by Germany; and it protected Russia against an attack by Germany, or by Austria supported by Germany.

By the middle of the 1890s, therefore, two sets of European alliances existed. This did not mean, however, that the Continent had been split in two. There were many subsequent occasions when Russia cooperated with Germany and Austria, or when Germany cooperated with Russia and France. International rivalries for the next decade shifted almost entirely to regions outside Europe. Both French and Russian interests in many parts of the world conflicted with those of Great Britain; and Germany, unable to tie England as closely to its side as it wished, now frequently joined the two in opposing British aims. Faced by the discomforting possibility of a continental alliance against it, Britain, rather than Germany, had cause to be alarmed by the new alignment of powers.

Britain's Colonial Rivalries

The regions over which Britain came into conflict with one or several of the continental powers during the 1890s were chiefly the Near and Far East, the Sudan, and South Africa. In the Near East the source of trouble, as usual, was the disintegrating Ottoman Empire. Beginning in 1894 a series of Armenian uprisings against Turkish repression were put down with the massacre of thousands of Armenians. England tried repeatedly to intervene, and Lord Salisbury on two occasions suggested plans for partitioning the Ottoman Empire. But rival interests among the powers and suspicion of British motives prevented what might have been a final solution of the troubles of the Near East. The situation was further complicated in 1897 by an insurrection against Turkey on Crete in favor of union with Greece. In the resulting war between Greece and Turkey, the British supported Greece, but the rest of the powers prevented any aid from reaching Greece. The Turks were victorious, although the powers succeeded in obtaining autonomy for Crete.

While Britain thus found itself at cross-purposes with the rest of Europe in the Near East, Germany took advantage of the various crises in that region to advance its own economic interests. The main instrument of its push to the southeast was to be a Berlin-to-Baghdad railway, for which the sultan granted a concession in 1899. In 1898, Emperor William, on a visit to Damascus, proclaimed himself the friend of the world's 300 million Moslems. Germany appeared well on the way toward replacing England as the protector of Turkey.

In this German cartoon, Queen Victoria is flattened by the Boer leader, Paul Krüger, as the South African imperialist Cecil Rhodes looks on with dismay.

In the Far East the first serious differences between England and the three continental powers came as a result of the Sino-Japanese War in 1895 (see p. 639). When Russia, Germany, and France asked British participation in forcing Japan to give up most of the territory it had taken from China, Britain refused. In the subsequent scramble for concessions from China, France, Germany, and especially Russia gained at the expense of England's hitherto unchallenged dominance there.

All the time that Britain was losing ground in the Near and Far East, its situation in Africa was even more serious. First there was the trouble with Germany over the kaiser's "Krüger telegram" (see p. 682); then came the showdown with France over the Sudan; and finally, in 1899 the Boer War broke out. During that war Britain was without a single friend, and it is surprising that Russian proposals for a continental coalition in favor of the Boers did not materialize. The plan failed because of Germany's insistence that the three powers first guarantee one another's own territories in Europe. This would have meant French renunciation of Alsace-Lorraine.

In view of England's many predicaments, it is understandable that it should look for some way out of its no longer splendid isolation. The obvious choice for a possible ally, considering Britain's many points of friction with France and Russia, was Germany. So in 1898 England began to sound out Germany on a closer understanding.

Britain Abandons Isolation

The Anglo-German negotiations failed. And the main reason for the failure was the reluctance of the Germans to abandon what they considered an unusually favorable position between the Franco-Russian and British camps. Overestimating Britain's eagerness to come to an understanding and underestimating Britain's ability to find friends elsewhere, Germany's foreign secretary, Bernhard von Bülow, and his chief adviser, Baron Friedrich von Holstein, made demands on England that it was unwilling to meet. Britain was primarily interested in enlisting German support against further Russian encroachment in the Far East. Germany, on the other hand, was chiefly worried about a war between Russia and Austria in which Germany might become involved and for which it wanted British aid. Britain, however, refused to extend its commitments to eastern Europe, where, as a naval power, it could not be of much use.

When Anglo-German negotiations finally broke down in 1901, England turned elsewhere. In 1902 it concluded an alliance with Japan. This did nothing to end England's isolation in Europe, but it fulfilled a main purpose—to stop Russia's advance in the Far East. Two years later Japan took advantage of this situation and in the Russo-Japanese War destroyed Russian sea power in the Pacific (see p. 642). In this way Japan emerged as the dominant power in the Far East.

Before the showdown between Russia and Japan, England had already taken a step in Europe to escape its isolation—*rapprochement* with France. England had long been irked by its dependence on Germany, which the latter used on every possible occasion to wring concessions from the British. By settling its long-standing differences with France, Britain not only hoped to find support against Germany but also to allay once and for all its fear of a continental alliance against it. France also felt a need for new friends. Its alliance with Russia had proved disappointing, especially during the Fashoda crisis, when the Russians had refused to back up their ally (see p. 680). After Fashoda, France had turned its attention once more to the Continent. The aim of its nationalistic foreign minister, Théophile Delcassé, was to strengthen France's position by improving its relations with powers other than Germany. He had taken a first step in this direction in 1902 by concluding a secret agreement with Italy. In return for French support of Italian ambitions in North Africa, the Italians promised to support French aims in Morocco, and to remain neutral in case France became involved in a defensive war, even if France "as the result of a direct provocation" should find it necessary to declare such a war itself.

A far greater achievement of Delcassé, however, was the Entente Cordiale between France and England. The Anglo-French agreement of 1904 settled the main colonial differences that had disturbed relations between the two countries, especially in Africa. Most important was France's recognition of British interests in Egypt and Britain's recognition of French interests in Morocco. The agreement was merely a "friendly understanding." It was not an alliance, and it need never have assumed the character of one had it not been for the careless actions of Germany.

The First Moroccan Crisis

Germany, which was understandably alarmed by the agreement between France and Britain, decided to test the strength of the Entente. In March 1905 William II, on a visit to Tangier in Spanish Morocco, proclaimed Germany's continued support of Moroccan independence and served notice that Germany, too, had an interest in Morocco. The ensuing crisis forced the resignation of Delcassé, and Germany seemed ready to go to war. Franco-German differences were finally brought before an international conference at Algeciras (1906). Here the independence of Morocco was reaffirmed; but in settling specific questions of Moroccan internal administration, the majority of the powers supported the French. Only Austria-Hungary stood by its German ally. Germany's attempt to split the Anglo-French Entente had backfired.

Actually, the first Moroccan crisis brought the French and British still closer together by inaugurating conversations between French and British military and naval authorities concerning possible cooperation in case of war. These conversations continued intermittently until 1914. Beginning in 1912, furthermore, the British navy concentrated its forces in the North Sea, permitting the French to shift their own warships to the Mediterranean. England thus assumed at least a moral obligation for protecting France's northern coast in case of war. The Entente Cordiale, in spirit if not in fact, had been transformed into a virtual alliance.

PRE-FIRST WORLD WAR ALLIANCES AND ALIGNMENTS

●●●●●●	Austro-German Alliance, 1879
———	Triple Alliance, 1882
– – –	Franco-Russian Alliance, 1894
ꟷꟷꟷ	Triple Entente, 1904/07
▮▮▮▮▮▮	Franco-Italian Agreement, 1902
▬▬▬	Russian-Serbian Friendship
⦚⦚⦚⦚	Russian Push to Constantinople
+ + +	Turkish-German Alliance, 1914
●●●●●●	Anglo-Japanese Alliance, 1902
▰▰▰▰	Balkan League

The Triple Entente

England's close affiliation with France quite naturally raised the question of its relations with France's ally Russia. As a result of Russia's war with Japan, the threat of Russian predominance in China had been removed, and there was now no reason why England should not try to settle its colonial differences with Russia as it had with France. This was done in the Anglo-Russian Entente of 1907, which settled the long-standing rivalries of the two powers in Afghanistan, Persia, and Tibet.

The formation of the Triple Entente, as the agreements of 1904 and 1907 together are called, amounted to a diplomatic revolution. A situation that only a few years earlier Germany had considered impossible had now come to pass: England had settled its differences with France and Russia, and the Triple Alliance had found its match in the Triple Entente. The latter was no more aggressive in its initial intent than the Triple Alliance had originally been. But as areas for compromise outside Europe became fewer with the annexation of the remaining colonial spoils, the scene of international rivalries once more shifted to Europe and especially to the Balkans. In the past, Russia's ambitions in this area had been held in check by the rest of the powers. Now it could count on French and British support against Germany and Austria. Germany, on the other hand, left with only Austria as a reliable friend, could no longer restrain Austria's Balkan policy as it had in the past. Any change in the status quo of the Balkans, therefore, was sure to lead to a major crisis.

THE MOUNTING CRISIS 1908–13

This brings us to the last fateful years before 1914, when growing international tension, at least in retrospect, appears as a fitting prelude to an inevitable showdown.

Revolution in Turkey and the Bosnian Crisis

The Balkans once again became the scene of international complications in 1908 when a revolution broke out in the Ottoman Empire. Turkey's ruler since 1876, Abdul-Hamid II, had never lived up to his repeated promises of reform. Opposition to the sultan's corrupt and decadent regime centered in a group of liberal patriots, the "Young Turks." Their aim was to reform Turkey along the lines of a liberal constitution that had been granted in 1876 but had been completely disregarded afterward. The revolutionaries had a large following among the Turkish army, and the government's resistance to the uprising in 1908 soon collapsed. The Young Turks, however, though liberal in some respects, were extremely nationalistic in their dealings with Turkey's many national and religious minorities. Persecution of Greek Orthodox Christians and efforts to assimilate Turkey's subject peoples soon led to further disruption of the empire: Bulgaria proclaimed its independence in 1908; Crete completed its union with Greece in 1912; and Albania, after a series of bloody uprisings, finally gained its independence from the Ottoman Empire in 1913.

The most important event connected with the Turkish revolution, in its effects on relations among the great powers, was Austria's annexation of Bosnia and Herzegovina in 1908. There had been no serious tension between Austria and Russia over the Balkans for some twenty

Abdul-Hamid II, known as "Abdul the Damned" for his cunning and cruelty, was chiefly responsible for the continued backwardness and corruption of the Ottoman Empire during his long rule (1876–1909).

years. But this peaceful situation changed after 1905, as Russia once again turned its attention from the Far to the Near East. Russia's foreign minister, Alexander Izvolsky, was an unusually ambitious man, and he found a kindred spirit in his Austrian colleague, Count Alois Aehrenthal. Russia had long hoped to lift the closure of the Turkish Straits to Russian warships; Austria, for its part, had been looking forward to annexing Bosnia and Herzegovina, which it had been administering since 1878. Encouraged by the Turkish revolution, Izvolsky and Aehrenthal met at the latter's castle of Buchlau in September 1908 and there pledged mutual support for their respective aims.

The Bosnian crisis was precipitated when shortly after the Buchlau Agreement Austria went ahead and proclaimed the annexation of Bosnia and Herzegovina without waiting for Russia to act in the Straits. Russia, thereupon, backed by France and England, demanded that Austria's action be brought before an international conference. Germany, on the other hand, supported Austria in opposing a conference unless the annexation of Bosnia-Herzegovina was recognized beforehand. The situation was made more serious because Serbia also had hoped one day to take Bosnia-Herzegovina. Encouraged by Pan-Slav propaganda emanating from Russia, Serbia now demanded compensation from Austria. Since Russia, however, was in no position to fight a war at this time, it had to bring pressure on Serbia to recognize the *fait accompli* in Bosnia and Herzegovina. This the Serbs did under protest.

The Bosnian crisis left a legacy of tension that lasted until the First World War. Both Russia and Serbia had been humiliated. To prevent the recurrence of such a defeat, Russia now began to prepare in earnest for the showdown that seemed inevitable, while Serbia stepped up its agitation among Austria's southern Slavs. Austria had been the real culprit in the affair. But even it would have had to back down if it had not had the support of Germany. The fact that such support had been given only reluctantly was not known to the rest of the world. Italy, finally, was hurt not to have been consulted by Austria about the annexation of Bosnia and Herzegovina and not to have received compensations, both of which it felt entitled to under the Triple Alliance. In October 1909 Italy entered into a secret understanding with Russia, the Racconigi Agreement, in which it promised to support Russia's interests in the Straits, while Russia agreed to back Italy's designs in Tripoli. Italy thus had taken another step away from the Triple Alliance.

The Second Moroccan Crisis

Europe had barely recovered from the Bosnian affair when another crisis arose, this time in North Africa. Despite the Act of Algeciras of 1906, friction in Morocco between French and German interests had continued. When native disturbances in Morocco in 1911 led to the intervention of French troops, Germany protested against what it considered a violation of Moroccan independence. To make up for France's increased influence in Morocco, Germany now claimed compensations elsewhere. And to give weight to its demands, it sent a German gunboat, the *Panther*, to the Moroccan port of Agadir, ostensibly to protect German lives and interests. For the most part it was British intervention that finally forced Germany to modify its claims and settle the crisis. But meanwhile Europe

had once again been brought to the brink of war.

Anglo-German Naval Rivalry

England, throughout the crisis, suspected that Germany's real aim was to secure a naval base in Morocco, which would have posed a threat to Britain's base at Gibraltar. Anglo-German naval rivalry had by now become a matter of deep concern to the British. Naval expansion was closely related to imperialism. A powerful fleet was considered necessary to protect overseas possessions, and overseas possessions in turn were needed as naval bases and coaling stations. The most influential exponent of this new "navalism" was an American, Captain Alfred T. Mahan, whose writings, especially *The Influence of Sea Power upon History* (1890), were carefully studied in England and Germany.

As a precaution against the naval increases of the rest of the world, England in 1889 had adopted a "two-power standard," which called for a British fleet 10 percent stronger than the combined naval forces of the two next-strongest powers. The most serious challenge to Britain's naval power came from Germany. Beginning in 1898, Germany entered on a course of naval expansion that, by 1914, had made it the second-strongest naval power in the world. Germany's

THE DISSOLUTION OF THE OTTOMAN EMPIRE   to 1914

secretary of the navy, Admiral Alfred von Tirpitz, knew that he could not possibly expect to catch up with the British. He tried to build a navy strong enough that no other country would dare risk getting into a fight with Germany. The German navy, he claimed, was built not so much for a possible showdown with England as for reasons of prestige.

It was difficult for England to see matters in quite the same light. The British felt that Germany, primarily a land power, did not really need a navy, especially since it already had a powerful army. If the Germans went to the great expense of building a navy, this could only mean that they expected some day to challenge Britain's naval supremacy. Again and again, notably in 1908 and 1912, Great Britain urged Germany to slow down its naval construction, offering in return to support German colonial aspirations. But William II and Tirpitz saw these efforts merely as a confirmation of their "risk theory" and looked forward to the day when England would be forced to seek an agreement on Germany's terms. More than any other issue, this naval race was responsible for the growing tension between Germany and England during the last decade before the war.

The Balkan Wars

The Moroccan crisis of 1911—besides further strengthening the Anglo-French Entente—also helped to start a series of small wars aimed at the further disruption of the Ottoman Empire. The first of

these broke out in the fall of 1911, when Italy, encouraged by France's success in Morocco, decided to embark on the annexation of Tripoli. Since Italy had carefully secured the prior consent of all the great powers, its war with Turkey of 1911 to 1912 did not by itself cause any major crisis. As we have seen, it brought Italy its long-coveted North African colony. The Tripolitanian War, however, encouraged several small Balkan states to move against Turkey and thus to reopen the Balkan question.

The chief motive behind the First Balkan War (1912) was the desire of Bulgaria, Serbia, and Greece to gain further concessions at the expense of Turkey. Together with Montenegro, these countries had formed a Balkan League in early 1912. Taking advantage of the war over Tripoli, they invaded the Ottoman Empire in October of that year. Turkey was decisively defeated, and under the Treaty of London (May 1913) it lost all its European possessions except the region adjacent to the Straits.

The peace was less than a month old when a Second Balkan War broke out, this time among the victors over the distribution of the spoils. Under arrangements made before the first war, Serbia was to receive an outlet to the Adriatic in Albania. This met with Austrian and Italian protests, however. As compensation for its loss, Serbia now demanded some of the territory that Bulgaria had received in Macedonia; and when the Bulgarians refused, war ensued between Bulgaria on the one hand and Serbia, Greece, Montenegro, Rumania, and Turkey on the other. Against such an overwhelming coalition, the Bulgarians proved powerless. In the Treaty of Bucharest (August 1913), Bulgaria kept only a small part of Macedonia, the Greeks and Serbs taking the rest.

The Balkan Wars caused deep anxiety among the great powers. A Conference of Ambassadors was convened in London to deal with the Balkan problem, notably the controversy between Austria and Serbia over the latter's aspirations in Albania. As in the past, Russia backed Serbia. Germany, on the other hand, served as a brake on Austria's desire to intervene against Serbia. Since England and

Turkish infantry during the First Balkan War (1912).

Italy also favored the independence of Albania, Russia finally withdrew its support from Serbia and peace was preserved. In the course of events, however, Austria and Russia, together with their allies, had again come close to war. Serbia had suffered another defeat, for which it blamed Austria and for which even its gains in Macedonia could not be consolation enough. Serbia's outraged nationalism sought revenge a year later in the assassination of the Austrian Archduke Francis Ferdinand at Sarajevo.

THE OUTBREAK OF THE GREAT WAR

In discussing the origins of the First World War, historians distinguish between underlying and immediate causes. In the first category belong all those factors that contributed to the acute state of international tension before 1914: nationalism, territorial disputes, economic competition, and imperialist rivalries. Some of the tension has also been blamed on the secret diplomacy of the powers, which led to secret alliances that involved nations in conflicts not of their making. But it has also been held that there was not enough secret diplomacy, that a "summit" meeting of Europe's leading statesmen in the summer of 1914, away from the clamor of their nationalistic press, might have resolved the differences that instead led to war. There had been many instances in the past when such joint action on the part of the Concert of Europe had proved effective. By 1914, however, the feeling of European solidarity that had animated the great powers in the days of Metternich and even Bismarck had everywhere given way to the powerful and divisive force of nationalism. The absence of any effective international agency to preserve peace did much to bring about the catastrophe of 1914.

The story of why and how the war came about has been told many times and in great detail. But to this day there are still wide differences among historians in the evaluation of the available evidence. It is quite possible that a different action by one or another of the

statesmen in the summer of 1914 might have once more prevented a general war. Yet it seems unlikely that such a war could have been postponed much longer. If ever there was a time that seemed ripe for war, it was the summer of 1914.

Sarajevo

As we turn from the underlying to the immediate causes of the war, the most important was the assassination of Austrian Archduke Francis Ferdinand at the Bosnian capital of Sarajevo, on June 28, 1914.

The assassination of the archduke and his wife was carried out by an Austro-Bosnian citizen of Serb nationality, Gavrilo Princip. The crime had been planned and its execution aided by a secret society of Serb nationalists, the "Black Hand." The archduke had been chosen as victim because he was known to favor reconciling the southern Slav element in the Dual Monarchy, a policy that interfered with the aspirations of Serb nationalism, which hoped for the ultimate union of all southern Slavs under Serbian rule. There is no evidence that the Serbian government had any hand in the plot itself; but Serbia's prime minister, Nicholas Pashitch, had general knowledge of it. Austria, taking for granted that the Serbian government was involved, decided once and for all to settle accounts with Serbia. This it hoped to do in a localized war. But Austria's foreign minister, Count Leopold von

Archduke Francis Ferdinand of Austria and his wife at Sarajevo on June 28, 1914, about to enter the automobile that carried them to their deaths.

The arrest of the assassin.

England Goes to War

August 4, 1914

It was 11 o'clock at night—12 by German time—when the ultimatum expired. The windows of the Admiralty were thrown wide open in the warm night air. Under the roof from which Nelson had received his orders were gathered a small group of Admirals and Captains and a cluster of clerks, pencil in hand, waiting. Along the Mall from the direction of the Palace the sound of an immense concourse singing "God save the King" floated in. On this deep wave there broke the chimes of Big Ben; and, as the first stroke of the hour boomed out, a rustle of movement swept across the room. The war telegram, which meant "Commence hostilities against Germany," was flashed to the ships and establishments under the White Ensign all over the world.

I walked across the Horse Guards Parade to the Cabinet room and reported to the Prime Minister and the Ministers who were assembled there that the deed was done.

From Winston S. Churchill, *The World Crisis, 1911–1918* (New York: Scribner's, 1931), p. 128. [Churchill at the time was First Lord of the Admiralty.]

Berchtold, did not seem averse to a larger war if it was necessary to achieve Austria's aim.

European reaction to the assassination at first was one of deep shock and genuine sympathy for Austria. In indignation over the horrible crime, Germany gave Austria that fateful promise to "stand behind it as an ally and friend" in anything the Austrian government should decide to do. As it became clear, however, that Austria intended to use the Sarajevo incident to punish Serbia, the powers became alarmed. Russia warned the Austrians that it "would not be indifferent to any effort to humiliate Serbia." At the same time, France's president, Raymond Poincaré, assured the Russians of French support in any action they took on behalf of Serbia. By the middle of July, it was clear that Austria, backed by Germany, was ready to move against Serbia, and that Russia, backed by France, was equally ready to protect Serbia.

The Eve of War

The situation thus far was serious, but it was not as yet critical. It became so when Austria, on July 23, presented a stiff ultimatum to Serbia. The latter's reply, while not wholly complying, nevertheless was favorable enough to justify further negotiations. Instead, Austria broke off diplomatic relations and on July 28 declared war on Serbia. Germany had little choice but to live up to its earlier "blank check" and to support Austria. By doing so, the Germans hoped to discourage Russia from helping Serbia and thus to localize the Austro-Serbian conflict. But the Germans were also ready to stand by Austria if the conflict should develop into a general war.

The decision whether the war was to be a local or a general one rested primarily with Russia. Germany's action throughout the crisis had given the impression, not unjustifiably, that far from trying to discourage Austria, the German government was actually urging it on into the showdown with Serbia. Since an Austrian victory over Serbia would be tantamount to a Russian defeat, Russian military authorities now began calling for mobilization. The question was: should such mobilization be partial, against Austria-Hungary only, or should it be general, against Germany as well? Plans for a partial mobilization had been abandoned some time ago and in any case would have entailed considerable disadvantages in case general mobilization should become necessary later on. But a general mobilization, it was understood, would make a European war inevitable. The internal debate over this issue went on for several days. Only when the tsar finally became convinced, on July 30, that efforts to restrain Austria were futile, was the decision made to go ahead with a general mobilization.

The Outbreak of War

Germany's chief of staff, General Helmuth von Moltke, nephew of the great Moltke of Bismarckian times, was worried by reports from Russia. He therefore urged Austria, behind his government's back, to mobilize against Russia, promising unconditional German support. Austria ordered general mobilization on July 31, thus killing any chance for last-minute peace efforts. The same day Germany sent Russia an ultimatum demanding that the latter cease its preparations for war. When the tsar's government replied that this was impossible, Germany, on August 1, mobilized its own forces and a few hours later declared war on Russia. France, meanwhile, had also begun military preparations. To a German inquiry about its attitude in a Russo-German war, France replied that it would "act in accordance with its interests." On August 3, Germany declared war on France.

The reason for Germany's haste in declaring war lay in the plans that its general staff had worked out for a war on two fronts. The basic idea of the "Schlieffen Plan"—named after its originator, Count Alfred von Schlieffen, who had been chief of the general staff from 1891 to 1906—was for Germany's main forces to turn west, deliver an annihilating blow against France, and then turn east against the slowly mobilizing Russians. To succeed with its plan, Germany not only needed to mobilize as quickly as possible, but it also had to invade France at its most vulnerable spot, the northeastern frontier between France and Belgium. The Schlieffen Plan, in other words, called for German violation of Belgian neutrality, which, together with the rest of Europe, the Germans had guaranteed in 1839.

Germany's invasion of Belgium on August 3 brought England into the war the next day. Great Britain has subsequently been reproached for not making its position in the crisis clear enough from the start, the argument being that if it had come off the fence earlier, it would have deterred the Austrians from going to war against Serbia. Through the Entente Cordiale, especially its secret military and naval understandings, England was deeply committed to France. On the other hand, there had been a marked improvement in Anglo-German relations in the early months of 1914; and England's Entente with Russia had never been very popular. For reasons of its own security, Britain could not possibly afford to stand idly by while Germany won victories over France and Russia that would make it the dominant power on the Continent. But to get the British pub-lic to approve involvement in the war, some event was needed to dramatize the German danger. Such an event was Germany's violation of Belgian neutrality. Almost overnight it helped to convert Britain's indecisive neutrality into determined belligerency.

"War Guilt"

A word remains to be said about the question of "war guilt," a subject of controversy to the present day. Most historians agree that Germany, Austria, and Russia bear a major share of the responsibility. England clearly belongs at the other extreme, its errors being chiefly of omission; and France stands somewhere in between. This much is certain: no one power alone was responsible for the war, and none of the great powers was entirely free from responsibility. Many Europeans actually welcomed the war as a

THE UNEXECUTED SCHLIEFFEN PLAN Pre-1914

The Schlieffen Plan: A Critique

It was a conception of Napoleonic boldness, and there were encouraging precedents in Napoleon's early career for counting on the decisive effect of arriving in the enemy's rear with the bulk of one's forces. . . . But Schlieffen failed to take due account of a great difference between the conditions of Napoleonic times and his own—the advent of the railway. While his troops would have to march on their own feet round the circumference of the circle, the French would be able to switch troops by rail across the chord of the circle. That was all the worse handicap because his prospects mainly depended on the time factor. The handicap was further increased because his troops would be likely to find their advance hampered by a succession of demolished bridges, while their food and ammunition supply would be restricted until they could rebuild the rail tracks and rail bridges through Belgium and Northern France. The great scythe-sweep which Schlieffen planned was a manoeuvre that had been possible in Napoleonic times. It would again become possible in the next generation—when air-power could paralyze the defending side's attempt to switch its forces, while the development of mechanized forces greatly accelerated the speed of encircling moves, and extended their range. But Schlieffen's plan had a very poor chance of decisive success at the time it was conceived.

B. H. Liddell Hart, from Foreword to G. Ritter, *The Schlieffen Plan: Critique of a Myth* (Horsham, Eng.: Riband Books, 1956), pp. 6–7.

relief from the almost unbearable tension that had preceded it. Yet most of the leading statesmen, when faced with the certainty of war, were overcome by fear and desperation. It was as though they had a foreboding that the war they had failed to avert would be far more terrible than they could imagine, and that the world they had known would never be the same again.

Suggestions for Further Reading

Note: Asterisk denotes a book available in paperback edition.

General

Among the major studies on the diplomatic background of the First World War, L. Albertini, *The Origins of the War of 1914*, 3 vols. (1952–57), is generally considered the best. A. J. P. Taylor, *The Struggle for Mastery in Europe, 1848–1918** (1954), is shorter and less objective. J. Remak, *The Origins of World War I, 1871–1914** (1967), is the briefest and most readable account. L. Lafore, *The Long Fuse** (1965), emphasizes the disintegration of Austria-Hungary as a cause of war. Monographs on the foreign policy of individual powers are F. R. Bridge, *Great Britain and Austria-Hungary, 1906–1914* (1972); M. Foot, *British Foreign Policy Since 1898* (1956); J. A. S. Grenville, *Lord Salisbury and Foreign Policy: The Close of the Nineteenth Century* (1964); C. Howard, *Splendid Isolation* (1967); C. J. Lowe and F. Marzari, *Italian Foreign Policy 1870–1914* (1975); and I. Geiss, *German Foreign Policy 1871–1914** (1976).

The Age of Bismarck

The leading book in English is still W. L. Langer, *European Alliances and Alignments,* 2nd ed. (1950). The Near Eastern crisis of the 1870s is discussed in R. Millman, *Britain and the Eastern Question 1875–1878* (1979), and its outcome in W. N. Medlicott, *The Congress of Berlin and After* (1938). For the formation of Bismarck's system of alliances, see A. C. Coolidge, *The Origins of the Triple Alliance* (1926), and N. D. Bagdasarian, *The Austro-German Rapprochement, 1870–1879* (1976). P. B. Mitchell, *The Bismarckian Policy of Conciliation with France* (1935), rounds out the picture in the West. Germany's first colonial ventures are described in M. E. Townsend, *The Origins of Modern German Colonization, 1871–1885* (1921), and in A. J. P. Taylor, *Germany's First Bid for Colonies** (1938). The closing years of Bismarck's career are studied critically in G. F. Kennan, *The Decline of Bismarck's European Order: Franco-Russian Relations 1875–1890** (1979). The chancellor's dismissal is dealt with in K. F. Nowak, *Kaiser and Chancellor* (1930). G. A. Craig, *From Bismarck to Adenauer: Aspects of German Statecraft** (1958), offers a sympathetic appraisal of Bismarck the diplomat.

Imperialism in Africa and Asia

Some of the works cited in the suggested reading list in Chapter 27 are also relevant here. The authoritative work on the imperialist rivalries of the great powers is W. L. Langer, *The Diplomacy of Imperialism, 1890–1902,* 2nd ed., 2 vols. (1951). The colonization of Africa is covered in R. Robinson and J. Gallagher, *Africa and the Victorians** (1961); E. A. Walker, *A History of Southern Africa* (1957); R. L. Tignor, *Modernization and British Colonial Rule in Egypt, 1882–1914* (1966); P. Gifford and W. R. Louis, eds., *Britain and Germany in Africa* (1967); and H. R. Rudin, *Germans in the Cameroons, 1884–1914* (1938). See also N. Ascherson, *The King Incorporated: Leopold II of the Belgians* (1963), and J. Duffy, *Portuguese Africa* (1959). On the Far East, G. P. Hudson, *The Far East in World Politics* (1939), is the best brief book. See also J. T. Pratt, *The Expansion of Europe in the Far East* (1947); P. Joseph, *Foreign Diplomacy in China, 1894–1900* (1928); and D. and P. Warner, *The Tide at Sunrise: A History of the Russo-Japanese War, 1904–1905* (1974). For the economic penetration of the Middle East, see S. N. Fisher, *The Middle East* (1959), and W. I. Shorrock, *French Imperialism in the Middle East* (1976). Financial imperialism is treated in H. Feis, *Europe, the World's Banker, 1870–1914** (1930), and E. Staley, *War and the Private Investor* (1935). Good general treatments of the colonial policy of some of the great powers include M. Beloff, *Imperial Sunset: Britain's Liberal Empire, 1897–1921* (1969); D. K. Fieldhouse, *Economics and Empire, 1830–1914* (1973); H. Brunschwig, *Myths and Realities of French Colonialism, 1871–1914* (1966); and W. D. Smith, *The German Colonial Empire* (1978). The following monographs are based on fresh archival sources: A. White, *The Diplomacy of the Russo-Japanese War* (1964); G. N. Sanderson, *England, Europe and the Upper Nile, 1882–1899* (1965); C. C. Eldridge, *England's Mission: The Imperial Idea in the Age of Gladstone and Disraeli, 1868–1880* (1974); R. G. Brown, *Fashoda Reconsidered* (1970); P. Thomas, *The Boer War* (1979); and I. H. Nish, *The Anglo-Japanese Alliance: The Diplomacy of Two Island Empires, 1894–1907* (1966).

The United States as a Great Power

America's share in the scramble for overseas possessions is treated in A. K. Weinberg, *Manifest Destiny* (1935); J. W. Pratt, *America's Colonial Experiment* (1950); and H. K. Beale, *Theodore Roosevelt and the Rise of America to World Power* * (1956). The best books on the Spanish-American War are J. W. Pratt, *Expansionists of 1898* * (1936); F. B. Freidel, *Splendid Little War* * (1958); and H. W. Morgan, *America's Road to Empire: The War with Spain and Overseas Expansion* * (1965). Other phases of American foreign policy are dealt with in E. H. Zabriskie, *American-Russian Rivalry in the Far East* (1946); P. M. Kennedy, *The Samoan Tangle: A Study in Anglo-German-American Relations, 1878–1900* (1974); H. Sprout and M. Sprout, *The Rise of American Naval Power, 1776–1918* (1939); C. D. Davis, *The United States and the Second Hague Peace Conference* (1976); and R. H. Heindel, *The American Impact on Great Britain, 1898–1914* (1940). The influence of the military is treated in R. D. Challener, *Admirals, Generals, and American Foreign Policy, 1898–1914* (1973). For a seasoned diplomat's analysis of America's involvement in world affairs since 1898, see G. F. Kennan, *American Diplomacy, 1900–1950* * (1951).

The Formation of the Triple Entente

W. L. Langer, *The Franco-Russian Alliance, 1890–1894* (1929), is another authoritative study by this distinguished diplomatic historian. On the formation of the Entente, see J. J. Mathews, *Egypt and the Formation of the Anglo-French Entente of 1904* (1939); P. J. V. Rolo, *The Entente Cordiale* (1969); G. Monger, *The End of Isolation: British Foreign Policy, 1900–1907* (1963); C. Andrew, *Théophile Delcassé and the Making of the Entente Cordiale* (1969); and R. P. Churchill, *The Anglo-Russian Convention of 1907* (1939). Also still relevant is E. N. Anderson, *The First Moroccan Crisis* (1930). S. R. Williamson, *The Politics of Grand Strategy: Britain and France Prepare for War, 1904–1914* (1969), deals with the military conversations growing out of the Entente Cordiale. There is no satisfactory general work on Anglo-German relations during this period, but the following discuss various aspects of the problem: R. J. Sontag, *Germany and England: Background of Conflict, 1848–1894* * (1938); R. J. S. Hoffman, *Great Britain and the German Trade Rivalry, 1875–1914* (1933); and P. R. Anderson, *The Background of Anti-English Feeling in Germany, 1890–1902* (1939). The influence of sea power on diplomacy is treated in E. L. Woodward, *Great Britain and the German Navy* (1935), and A. J. Marder, *The Anatomy of British Sea Power* (1940) and *From the Dreadnought to Scapa Flow: The Royal Navy in the Fisher Era, 1904–1919*, 3 vols. (1961–66). See also P. G. Halpern, *The Mediterranean Naval Situation, 1908–1914* (1971). A good deal of diplomatic history can be found in N. Rich, *Friedrich von Holstein: Politics and Diplomacy in the Era of Bismarck and William II*, 2 vols. (1965).

The Mounting Crisis

The events of the last decade before the war are summarized in D. E. Lee, *Europe's Crucial Years: The Diplomatic Background of World War I, 1902–1914* (1974). The policy of two of the major powers is brilliantly discussed in V. R. Berghahn, *Germany and the Approach of War in 1914* (1973), and Z. Steiner, *Britain and the Origins of the First World War* (1977). On individual phases of the mounting crisis, see B. E. Schmitt, *The Annexation of Bosnia* (1937); I. Barlow, *The Agadir Crisis* (1940); W. C. Askew, *Europe and Italy's Acquisition of Libya, 1911–1912* (1942); E. C. Helmreich, *The Diplomacy of the Balkan Wars* (1938); P. Padfield, *The Great Naval Race: The Anglo-German Naval Rivalry, 1900–1914* (1974); A. Rossos, *Russia and the Balkans: Inter-Balkan Rivalries and Russian Foreign Policy 1908–1914* (1981); and R. J. Crampton, *The Hollow Detente: Anglo-German Relations in the Balkans, 1911–1914* (1981). See also, R. J. B. Bosworth, *Italy, the Least of the Great Powers: Italian Foreign Policy Before the First World War* (1979). The influence of public opinion on foreign policy during the prewar era is explored in O. J. Hale, *Publicity and Diplomacy* (1940), and E. M. Carroll, *Germany and the Great Powers, 1866–1914: A Study in Public Opinion and Foreign Policy* (1939) and *French Public Opinion and Foreign Affairs, 1870–1914* (1930).

The Outbreak of War

V. Dedijer, *The Road to Sarajevo* (1966), is the last word on this subject. The assassination of the Austrian archduke is dramatically told in J. Remak, *Sarajevo* * (1959). Although the crisis thus set in motion has been more carefully studied than any comparable event in history, historians still do not agree on who was responsible for the war. S. B. Fay, *The Origins of the World War*, * 2 vols. (1932), puts the major blame on Serbia and Russia. B. E. Schmitt, *The Coming of the War, 1914*, 2 vols. (1930), is more severe toward Germany and Austria. The German case is presented in E. Brandenburg, *From Bismarck to the World War: A History of German Foreign Policy, 1870–1914* (1927), and the French position is stated in P. Renouvin, *The Immediate Origins of the War* (1928). More recently, two German historians have placed the major blame on their own nation: F. Fischer, *Germany's Aims in the First World War* * (1967) and *War of Illusions* (1974), and I. Geiss, ed., *July 1914: The Outbreak of the First World War* * (1968). Their works have touched off a major controversy among historians, which is summarized in F. Fischer, *World Power or Decline* * (1974).

30 War, Revolution, and Peace, 1914–1929

The "Great War," as it was called at the time, only gradually turned into a "World War." It was not the first worldwide conflict, but it was the largest. Before the war ended in November 1918, 49 million men had been mobilized in the "Allied" camp, against 25 million among the "Central Powers." More than any previous conflict, this war involved everyone, not only soldiers. The First World War was a truly "total war." The war lasted much longer than anyone had thought a modern war could, and it brought far more sweeping changes than anyone would have thought possible. Traditional empires collapsed and new nations arose from the wreckage. The New World, hitherto of little significance in European affairs, suddenly emerged as decisive to an Allied victory. Europe, which in the past had always settled its own affairs, apparently was unable to do so any longer.

The Great War was part of a transitional phase in modern history and will be treated as such here. There was no clear-cut end to the war—certainly not the peace settlements of 1919 to 1920. The problems that the statesmen at Paris wrestled with then continued to plague Europe and the world for at least a decade thereafter. It took a new series of crises, touched off by the Great Depression of 1929 and culminating in another World War, to complete the transition from nineteenth to twentieth century.

THE COMPARATIVE STRENGTH OF THE POWERS

Despite differences in numbers, the actual military strength of the Allies and the Central Powers at the start of the war was evenly balanced. The impressive size of the Allied armies was due chiefly to the ill-trained and poorly equipped Russian army. Germany's forces, on the other hand, were the best in the world. France and Britain matched the Germans in numbers, but the Germans excelled in the quality and quantity of their equipment. The Austrian army was weakened by its large Slav contingent. But since the main showdown was expected in the West, this handicap did not seem serious.

The Central Powers had other advantages, aside from their superior strength on land. Command of the interior lines of communication enabled them to shift their forces rapidly from one theater of war to another. The Allies, on the other hand, were widely separated; Russia in particular, with the closing of the Baltic and Black Seas, was cut off from much-needed aid. German industry, furthermore, was more readily converted to war production than the industries of its opponents. The Central Powers had more than enough coal and iron, and territories seized on the western front increased their resources. In their supplies of foodstuffs, however, Austria and Germany fell seriously short of their needs.

Had the war been as brief as most wars of the nineteenth century, Germany and Austria might have won it. But as the fighting dragged on, Allied inherent superiority made itself felt. Their manpower was greater; their industrial potential was superior; and, thanks to Great Britain, the Allies enjoyed naval supremacy. By keeping the sea lanes open, the British navy assured the uninterrupted flow of men and material; and by clamping a tight blockade on Central Europe, Britain aggravated Germany's and Austria's food problems.

Each side tried to strengthen its position further by seeking additional partners. Since the Allies usually had more to offer, they were more successful in this contest. At the end of the war, thirty "Allied and Associated Powers" were ranged against the Central Powers—Germany, Austria-Hungary, Turkey, and Bulgaria.

The most important additions to the Allied camp, aside from the United States, were Japan, Italy, Rumania, and Greece. Japan's entry into the war in August 1914 proved to be a most profitable move. Without delay the Japanese seized Germany's holdings in China's Shantung Province and occupied Germany's Pacific islands north of the equator. Italy did not join the war until 1915. It had refused to honor the Triple Alliance, claiming that its terms did not apply. To balance possible Austrian gains in the Balkans, moreover, the Italians had demanded territorial concessions from

Opposite: British soldiers blinded by poison gas during the German spring offensive (1918).

British soldiers "go over the top" to attack German lines.

Austria. The Austrians agreed to some of Italy's demands, but the Allies were able to offer more. By the secret Treaty of London in April 1915, they promised Italy not only the Austrian regions inhabited by Italians but also considerable territory along the eastern Adriatic and in Asia Minor and Africa. Having received these promises, the Italians declared war against Austria-Hungary in May 1915, and against Germany in August 1916. At that time, Rumania also joined the Allies, and Greece followed in June 1917. In both these cases the pressure of military events and the hope for territorial gains were decisive.

German Zeppelin attacking Antwerp in 1914. Painting by W. Moralt.

The only two countries that joined the Central Powers were Turkey and Bulgaria. The Ottoman Empire had long maintained close economic ties with Germany, and its army had been trained by German officers. In August 1914 Turkey concluded an alliance with Germany; three months later a Turkish naval squadron bombarded Russia's Black Sea ports; and in early November 1914 the Allies declared war on the Ottoman Empire. As for Bulgaria, it had been wooed by both sides. But the Central Powers were able to promise more, and in October 1915 Bulgaria joined the Germans and Austrians in a major drive against Serbia.

THE GREAT STALEMATE 1914–16

Both sides had prepared plans for a brief offensive war. In its grand simplicity, however, the German Schlieffen Plan promised a far quicker decision than France's Plan XVII, which called for an invasion of Alsace-Lorraine.

1914: Stalemate

From the start of hostilities on the western front, Germany held the initiative. After one month of fighting, German forces had advanced to within twenty-five miles of Paris. In early September 1914, however, the German drive was halted at the river Marne. The battle of the Marne was one of the decisive events of the war, since it dashed Germany's hope for an early victory. The battle was followed by a series of engagements in which each side hoped to outflank the other, and in the course of which the front was gradually extended to the sea. By November 1914 the fighting in the West had changed from a war of movement to a war of position. Until the spring of 1918 the western front, except for an occasional thrust of a few miles in one direction or the other, remained unchanged.

With the bulk of Germany's forces tied down in the West, Russia was able to score some unexpected successes in the East. In mid-August 1914 two Russian armies invaded East Prussia and within a few days overran almost half of Germany's easternmost province. At the height of danger, the kaiser recalled from retirement General Paul von Hindenburg, a specialist on conditions in the East, and appointed as Hindenburg's chief of staff the younger and more capable Erich Ludendorff. These men soon reversed the situation on the eastern front. In two major battles, at Tannenberg and the Masurian Lakes, Russia lost close to 250,000 men. Russia's reversals in the north were balanced by successes in the southeast against Austria. In a sweeping campaign under Russia's commander in chief, Grand Duke Nicholas, Russian forces in September took most of Galicia and advanced to the Carpathian frontier of Hungary.

In the East, as in the West, the end of 1914 found the Allied and Central Powers locked in a stalemate. But since Germany had failed to deliver a knockout blow in the West and appeared to be stalled in the East, the advantage was felt to lie with the Allies. In addition, British naval superiority had been responsible for the sinking of a German naval squadron off the coast of South America and for the seizure of most of the colonies that had belonged to Germany.

1915: Allied Reverses

With the British attack on the Gallipoli Peninsula and the entry of Italy into the war on their side in the spring of

THE FIRST WORLD WAR 1914–18

Central Powers

Land occupied by Central Powers at their height

Allied Powers

MILES 0 300

Advertisement placed by Germany in American newspapers to warn neutral travelers of the risks of crossing the Atlantic in the British vessel *Lusitania*.

The Sinking of the *Lusitania*

The full horror of the sinking of the *Lusitania* has now been revealed; and it has stirred the people of this country more deeply than even the poison clouds, or any other of the wanton and murderous acts committed by the Germans. . . . By thousands of dastardly crimes the Germans have demonstrated that they are determined to wage this war under conditions of cold-blooded and deliberate murder and outrage, of destruction and brutality, such as the world has never known. . . . Never before, since the world began, has there been witnessed the spectacle of a whole race, numbering many millions, scientifically organised for the objects of wholesale murder and devastation. . . . It is universally seen now that the Germans are a nation apart, that their civilisation is a mere veneer, that they have fallen immeasurably lower than their tribal forbears, and that their calculated and organised barbarity is without precedent in history. Nations, we perceive, can sink to unprecedented depths. No nation has ever fallen so low in infamy. . . .

From an editorial in *The Times* (London), May 10, 1915.

1915, the Allies began to dream of victory. But these dreams proved premature. The Italians proved of little use, and the Gallipoli attack failed. Had it succeeded, Turkey would have been seriously weakened and the Black Sea opened to Allied shipping. Instead, the Straits remained closed for the rest of the war.

The most serious Allied reverses during 1915 were on the eastern front and in the Balkans. In the spring and summer, German forces in the north and combined Austro-German forces in the south advanced in a series of offensives that cost the Russians Poland, Lithuania, and Courland, drove them out of Galicia, and lost them almost a million men. All of central and eastern Europe was now in German and Austrian hands. In October the Central Powers turned against Serbia; and in November they moved into Montenegro and Albania.

By the beginning of 1916 the tide of war on land seemed definitely to have turned against the Allies. Even on the high seas the Germans were able to make some gains. To counteract Britain's blockade, the German government, in early 1915, imposed a submarine blockade against the British Isles. The first phase of German submarine warfare came to a head with the sinking of the British liner *Lusitania* in May 1915. The loss of 139 American passengers caused a serious crisis in American-German relations. It was settled only after Germany promised to restrict its submarine tactics.

1916: Stalemate Again

Since time was clearly on the side of the Allies, it seemed imperative to the Germans to force a major showdown. In February 1916, therefore, they launched an all-out offensive against the French stronghold of Verdun. The battle of Verdun was the most famous battle of the war. It lasted more than four months and caused more than seven hundred thousand casualties; yet it ended undecided. Its chief hero on the French side was General Henri Philippe Pétain. Like Hindenburg after the battle of Tannenberg, Pétain became the idol of his people. Both men were to play fateful roles in later years. The battle of Verdun was followed by an Allied counteroffensive along the Somme River. But the battle of the Somme, like that of Verdun, failed to force a final decision in the West.

Events elsewhere during 1916 were equally indecisive. In June, Russian forces under General Alexei Brusilov started a major drive against the Austrian line and within a few weeks had taken most of eastern Galicia. These successes brought Rumania into the war. But its participation only made matters worse for the Allies. In late September, Austro-German forces invaded Rumania, and by January 1917 most of that country's rich resources were in the hands of the Central Powers. In the East as in the West, the outcome of the war continued to hang in the balance.

The year 1916 also saw the one great naval battle of the war between Germany and Britain. The German navy, to have a chance of success, had to fight in its home waters. On several occasions the Germans went out into the North Sea, hoping to entice the British into battle. It was on one of these sallies that the two fleets made contact off the coast of Jutland in May 1916. The battle of Jutland was costly and indecisive. The British lost more naval tonnage than the Germans, but they could better afford to. The German fleet henceforth remained safely at home.

By the end of 1916 a stalemate had been reached on all fronts, and victory for either side seemed far away. Meanwhile losses and material costs of the war had been staggering, and the strain of war had begun to tell on the home fronts as well as on the battlefields.

THE HOME FRONTS

People everywhere had greeted the outbreak of war with enthusiastic demonstrations of national unity. Each side believed that it was fighting a "just war." In addition, the war was expected to be short. The Germans hoped to be in Paris before the summer was over, and the French were looking forward to Christmas in Berlin. When instead the war dragged on with no end in sight, enthusiasm gave way to depression.

One of the important conditions for victory was effective leadership. Both England and France found outstanding civilian leaders—the British in David Lloyd George, and the French in Georges Clemenceau. In Germany, Austria, and Russia, on the other hand, where the monarch was both chief executive and symbol of national unity, much depended on the leadership he provided. In none of the three countries did the ruler measure up to expectations. William II had neither the ability nor the energy to cope with the problems of a total war. As he gradually faded into the background, his role was taken over by Hindenburg and Ludendorff. In Austria, Francis Joseph was too old and his grandnephew Charles, who succeeded him in 1916, was too inexperienced to keep the crumbling empire together. The saddest figure among Europe's monarchs was Nicholas II of Russia. In 1915 he assumed personal command of his armed forces, leaving the government in the hands of his wife and her sinister adviser, Rasputin.

Total War

The demands of total war presented many new and difficult problems. All the powers experienced periodic munitions

Nicholas II with Grand Duke Nicholas, commander in chief of the Russian armies until 1915.

shortages. Labor was scarce. Women were employed in growing numbers, and Germany "recruited" workers from Belgium. Except for the Russians, who were almost completely isolated, the Allies were able to supplement their domestic production of food and war materials with overseas imports. The Central Powers, on the other hand, cut off by the blockade, were chiefly dependent on their own resources. The Germans tackled the problem with customary efficiency, devising scores of ersatz, or substitute, products and perfecting new processes to obtain scarce materials. Austria-Hungary was far less successful in these respects. Its difficulties were made worse by continuous economic feuds between Austria and Hungary.

The most serious shortages of the Central Powers were in food and clothing. Germany began rationing in 1915. Shortages of labor and transportation reduced the coal supply, adding the misery of cold to hunger. Faced with these hardships, many Germans, especially among the working class, hoped for a speedy end to the war, even without victory.

War Aims and Peace Proposals

Neither side ever stated its war aims openly, except in the most general terms.

German women working in a government munitions factory during the war.

Secretly, however, the Allies had agreed on a distribution of spoils: Russia was to get most of the Polish regions under German and Austrian rule, as well as control over the Turkish Straits; France was promised the left bank of the Rhine; England was allotted the German colonies; and Italy was to have parts of Austria and territories elsewhere. In supplementary agreements most of the Ottoman Empire was divided into Russian, Italian, French, and British spheres of interest.

The war aims of the Central Powers called for the "liberation" of the Poles and the Baltic peoples from Russian domination, the setting up of small satellite states under German and Austrian control, and the annexation of some regions outright. In the West, Germany hoped for additional regions rich in iron ore from France and political and economic control over Belgium. There were also ambitious schemes for a central European federation under German leadership, a *Mitteleuropa,* and for a compact central African colony.

In view of these far-reaching Allied and German war aims, it is not surprising that efforts to reach a compromise peace proved fruitless. The Central Powers took the first official step in December 1916, informing President Wilson that they were ready to enter into peace negotiations. Wilson thereupon asked both sides to state their terms. But this the Germans refused to do. There were other peace moves, notably one inaugurated by Pope Benedict XV in August 1917. All these efforts failed. Both sides wanted peace, but neither side wanted it badly enough to make any real concessions.

Women in Wartime

In industry as a whole the total employment of women and girls over ten as between 1914 and 1918 increased by about 800,000, from 2,179,000 to 2,971,000. . . . It is in these arid statistics that we traverse a central theme in the sociology of women's employment in the twentieth century. . . . The growth of large-scale industry and bureaucracy would undoubtedly have brought this development eventually, but it was the war, in creating simultaneously a proliferation of Government committees and departments *and* a shortage of men, which brought a sudden and irreversible advance in the economic and social power of a category of women employees which extended from sprigs of the aristocracy to daughters of the proletariat. . . .

Given the rigidities of the Edwardian class structure, there are difficulties in the way of summing up the consequences of the war for women as an entire sex. In the business, medical and military functions . . . the women concerned were very largely women of the middle and upper classes. Yet the major section of these women had been in pre-war years a depressed class, tied to the apron-strings of their mothers or chaperons, or to the purse-strings of their fathers or husbands. Now that they were earning on their own account, they had economic independence; now that they were working away from home, in some cases far from home, they had social independence.

Obviously, then, women of all classes shared in a similar kind of emancipation. The suffragette movement before the war had . . . aimed simply at the same limited franchise for some women as was enjoyed by some men. The Women's Movement from 1915 onwards is a more unified movement than ever it had been previously.

From A. Marwick, *The Deluge: British Society and the First World War* (New York: Norton, 1970), pp. 91–94.

THE UNITED STATES ENTERS THE WAR

The United States at first had made every effort to remain neutral. Isolationism was still a strong force; and although there were many Anglophiles in the East, there were also large numbers of German-Americans in the Middle West. America's abandonment of neutrality had several causes. Effective Allied propaganda was one. Another was the growing financial involvement of many Americans in the Allied cause. But more important than either of these factors was Germany's resumption of unrestricted submarine warfare early in 1917.

Unrestricted Submarine Warfare

Germany decided to step up the submarine campaign after its peace move of December 1916 had failed. Germany's civilian authorities opposed unrestricted submarine warfare, fearing that it might bring America into the war. But the real power now lay with the military. With time on the Allied side, Hindenburg and Ludendorff felt that only drastic submarine action could win the war. They realized that this might lead to American intervention, but they thought England would be defeated long before such intervention would become effective.

Unrestricted submarine war began on February 1, 1917. America broke off diplomatic relations with Germany on February 3. As German submarines began sinking American ships, public opinion became more and more interventionist. The publication of the intercepted "Zimmermann Telegram," a note sent by Germany's foreign secretary urging Mexico to make war on the United States, did the rest. On April 6, 1917, Congress declared war on Germany.

THE RUSSIAN REVOLUTION

America's entrance into the war was made more urgent by changes in Russia that weakened the Allied cause. Events there had long been pointing toward a major domestic upheaval. At first the Russian people had loyally supported their government's war effort. But the sufferings of war soon dampened their spirit. With insufficient arms and a chronic shortage of munitions, the army lost more than a million men during the first year of the war. While the armies lacked essential materials, the civilian population suffered from food shortages, despite Russia's agrarian economy. The blame for all these ills was rightly placed on the inefficiency and corruption of the government. The elected assembly, the *Duma*, repeatedly urged the adoption of reforms; but the tsar continued to meet discontent with repression.

The Background of the Revolution

Repression alternating with reform had been the policy for decades. There had been an earlier revolution in 1905, but it had brought few changes (see pp. 663–64). To understand the sudden collapse of the tsarist regime in 1917, we must go back to 1861 and the emancipation of the serfs by Alexander II (see p. 616). The peasants liberated at the time provided the manpower for the belated industrialization of Russia. The resulting proletariat, uprooted and subject to the hardships of too rapid industrialization, provided a fertile breeding ground for revolution. By 1914 industrial workers made up less than 20 percent of the total population, but they were concentrated in the larger cities. It was here that the revolution started; but it found a ready echo in the countryside, where the mass of the peasants were leading a marginal existence, only a few of the more enterprising among them, the *kulaks*, having profited from the emancipation.

The "February Revolution" and Provisional Government

The overthrow of the tsarist regime was the climax of a gradually mounting wave of popular protest. By 1917 more than a million soldiers had deserted; in the cities, food shortages led to strikes and riots; and in the countryside, landless peasants began to seize the land of their noble landlords. In early March street demonstrations broke out in Petrograd (the name given to St. Petersburg at the beginning of the war). In the past the government had always been able to use the army against such disturbances. But the troops now fraternized with the rioters. From the capital, insurrection spread to the provinces. On March 12—or February 27 in the Russian calendar, hence the term "February Revolution"—the *Duma* established a Provisional Government under a liberal aristocrat, Prince George Lvov. Three days later, Nicholas II abdicated. He and his family were later murdered by the Bolsheviks in the summer of 1918.

The new Provisional Government was faced with problems for which it was unprepared. To meet the discontent of the masses some reforms were introduced, but these did not go far enough. The situation was complicated by the existence of a rival for political power, the Petrograd Soviet (Council) of Workers' and Soldiers' Deputies, consisting of Socialist Revolutionaries, Mensheviks, and some Bolsheviks.

The Provisional Government's main difficulty arose from its desire to continue the war. In July the new minister of war, Alexander Kerensky, launched a futile offensive against the Austrians. Its failure led to further riots in Petrograd. To restore order, Kerensky, on July 25, replaced Prince Lvov as prime minister. To strengthen his position, Kerensky appointed as commander in chief Gen-

Alexander Kerensky studying a map (November 1917). Kerensky took over the supreme command of the Russian forces.

Bolshevik propaganda poster: the tired Russian soldier.

eral Lavr Kornilov, who was popular with the army's rank and file. Kornilov succeeded in restoring some discipline but was unable to halt a German offensive. When there were signs that Kornilov wanted to make himself military dictator, he was arrested, and on September 14 Kerensky himself assumed supreme command of the army.

The revolution, meanwhile, which thus far had been free from terrorism, became increasingly violent, as workers sacked stores, peasants burned manor houses, and soldiers killed their officers. Revolution among the non-Russian nationalities in the borderlands, furthermore, threatened the unity of the country. Finally, the Petrograd Soviet, which until then had tolerated the Provisional Government, was gradually falling under the control of its most radical faction, the Bolsheviks.

The "October Revolution"

The exiled Bolshevik leaders—Lenin, Trotsky, Stalin, and others—had returned from abroad or from Siberia after the February Revolution. Their immedi-

ate aim was to gain control of the soviets in Petrograd and elsewhere. At first they only commanded a small minority within the Petrograd Soviet. Lenin advanced his radical program—immediate peace, seizure of land by the peasants and of factories by the workers—against the do-nothing policy of the Mensheviks and the Socialist Revolutionaries. Constantly reiterating this program, the Bolsheviks gradually increased their following within the Soviet and without. By September the Bolsheviks controlled the soviets in Petrograd, Moscow, and several other cities.

The only way for the Bolsheviks to gain control of the government was to use force. When Kerensky got wind of the Bolshevik plot and ordered the arrest of their leaders, Bolshevik forces began occupying strategic points in Petrograd on November 6. The main fighting took place around the Winter Palace, seat of the Provisional Government. On November 7 Kerensky took flight. The same afternoon an All-Russian Congress of Soviets convened. The majority of its delegates were Bolsheviks. As a first move they formed a new executive, the Council of People's Commissars, with Lenin as Chairman, Trotsky as Foreign Commissar, and Stalin as Commissar for National Minorities.

The "October Revolution"—so named because November 7 was October 25 old-style—was only the first stage on the road to a Bolshevik victory; a long drawn-out civil war was yet to follow. The followers of Lenin still numbered only a small percentage of the Russian people. When the constituent assembly was elected in late November, less than one-fourth of the delegates were Bolsheviks. But this was to be the first and last free election in Russia. When the assembly met for the first time in January 1918, it was dispersed by Bolshevik forces.

The Treaty of Brest-Litovsk

The most important immediate result of the October Revolution was to end the war on the eastern front. On December 5, 1917, the Bolsheviks concluded an armistice with Germany, and on December 22 peace negotiations began at Brest-

Litovsk. The Bolsheviks wanted "a just, democratic peace without annexations or indemnities." But the Germans were in no mood to forgo their advantages. At one point the Russians broke off negotiations, whereupon the Germans resumed their advance. On March 3, 1918, the Russians gave in and accepted Germany's terms.

Under the Treaty of Brest-Litovsk, Russia was to lose a quarter of its European territory, a third of its population, more than half of its coal and iron, and a third of its industry. The treaty was later invalidated because of the Allied victory in the West. But, for the moment, the Central Powers were freed from the burden of a two-front war and won access to the vast economic resources of eastern Europe. Their position was further strengthened by a peace treaty forced on Rumania at Bucharest on March 5, 1918, under which Germany received a ninety-year lease on that country's oil wells. The triumph of German expansionist aims served to warn the Allies of what to expect in the event of a German victory.

CONTINUED STALEMATE IN THE WEST, 1917

With the Central Powers victorious in the East, the Allies more than ever depended on aid from the United States. A first small contingent of American troops under General John J. Pershing had landed in France as early as June 1917. But it was not until spring of 1918 that American units took any real part in the fighting. America's main contribution was material aid. To meet the submarine danger, a vast shipbuilding program was initiated. Unrestricted submarine warfare at first was a serious threat to the Allied cause. But in time various ways of countering the submarine menace were devised, notably the convoy system.

While the Allies were holding their own at sea, the Central Powers were successfully resisting Allied attempts to force a decision on land. The campaigns on the western front in 1917 were among the bloodiest in the whole war. Yet the lessons of Verdun and the Somme still

Lenin in 1919.

held true—a decision on the western front was impossible. The Central Powers, meanwhile, scored one of their greatest victories on the Italian front. The battle of Caporetto in October 1917 cost Italy close to half a million men. Only French and British reinforcements averted a greater disaster.

Lenin

November 7, 1917

It was just 8:40 when a thundering wave of cheers announced the entrance of the presidium, with Lenin—great Lenin—among them. A short, stocky figure, with a big head set down in his shoulders, bald and bulging. Little eyes, a snubbish nose, wide, generous mouth, and heavy chin; clean-shaven now, but already beginning to bristle with the well-known beard of his past and future. Dressed in shabby clothes, his trousers much too long for him. Unimpressive, to be the idol of a mob, loved and revered as perhaps few leaders in history have been. A strange popular leader—a leader purely by virtue of intellect; colourless, humourless, uncompromising and detached, without picturesque idiosyncrasies—but with the power of explaining profound ideas in simple terms, of analysing a concrete situation. And combined with shrewdness, the greatest intellectual audacity.

From John Reed, *Ten Days That Shook the World* (New York: International Publishers, 1919), p. 125.

The Decline of Civilian Morale

Continuous heavy losses at the front and deprivations at home caused a serious decline in civilian morale. The British, suffering least, bore up best. The French, on the other hand, experienced a major military and political crisis. In May 1917 the senseless bloodshed in the West led to open mutiny among troops. The French home front, too, was becoming more and more defeatist. In Italy, shortages of food and coal brought on a series of strikes. It was only the disaster of Caporetto that made people rally to the support of the government, realizing that the future of their country was at stake.

The Central Powers underwent similar crises. In Germany, differences between civilian and military leaders caused the resignation of Chancellor Theobald von Bethmann Hollweg and the assumption of virtually dictatorial control by Hindenburg and Ludendorff. In Austria the war gave new momentum to the separatist tendencies of the empire's many nationalities. The Czechs and the Yugoslavs set up organizations abroad to work for Allied recognition of their cause, and Polish, Czech, and Yugoslav prisoners in Allied hands were formed into national legions to fight against their homeland.

The general weariness that affected all the belligerents after three years of war quite naturally gave rise to further peace efforts. Like all the earlier attempts, however, they failed, since neither side was ready to make the necessary concessions. The Bolsheviks published the secret treaties revealing Allied war aims, and western statesmen made highly idealistic pronouncements to counteract these revelations. In January 1918 President Wilson, in an effort to dissociate America from agreements to which it had not been a party, stated his famous Fourteen Points as the basis for a just peace. Briefly stated, they were:

(1) "Open covenants of peace" and an end to secret diplomacy; (2) freedom of the seas in peace and war; (3) "the removal . . . of all economic barriers and the establishment of an equality of trade conditions"; (4) the reduction of armaments "to the lowest point consistent with domestic safety"; (5) the "impartial adjustment of all colonial claims"; (6) the "evacuation of all Russian territory" and an attitude of "intelligent and unselfish sympathy" toward Russia; (7) the evacuation and restoration of Belgium; (8) the freeing of the invaded portions of France and the restoration to it of Alsace-Lorraine; (9) the "readjustment of the frontier of Italy . . . along clearly recognizable lines of nationality"; (10) "the freest opportunity of autonomous development" for the peoples of Austria-Hungary; (11) the evacuation and restoration of Rumania, Serbia, and Montenegro; (12) autonomy for the non-Turkish nationalities of the Ottoman Empire and the permanent opening of the Dardanelles to all nations; (13) the creation of an independent Poland, including "the territories inhabited by indisputably Polish populations," and assurance to Poland of "a free and secure access to the sea"; and (14) the formation of "a general association of nations . . . for the purpose of affording mutual guarantees of political independence and territorial integrity to great and small states alike."

The Fourteen Points were to play an important role in the later negotiations for an armistice and peace, but for the time being they had little effect. The only way to get peace, was to win the war. With time running against it, Germany, in the spring of 1918, decided to make an all-out bid for victory.

THE COLLAPSE OF THE CENTRAL POWERS

Ludendorff's plan for a large-scale spring offensive had some chance of success. The Germans were able to move large numbers of troops from the East. The Allies, on the other hand, were still suffering from the heavy losses of their 1917 offensives, and reinforcements from America were only just beginning to arrive in sufficient numbers.

The Last Offensives

The gigantic "Emperor's Battle" was launched in March 1918. At first it was overwhelmingly successful. Within three months the Germans once again stood on the Marne, only fifty miles from Paris.

But despite brilliant victories, they failed to breach the Allied front. On July 15, when the Germans mounted their last major drive, in the vicinity of Reims, the Allied front was held largely with the aid of American forces.

On July 18, the Allies began their counteroffensive. Ludendorff at first was able to withdraw his forces in good order. But on August 8, the German army suffered its "black day." Using for the first time large numbers of tanks, the British advanced almost eight miles. From here on the Allies never gave the Germans a moment's rest. By the end of September the German army had lost a million men in six months. Morale was low and desertions mounted. Germany's allies, moreover, were showing signs of imminent collapse. On October 4, finally, Germany and Austria appealed to President Wilson for an armistice based on the Fourteen Points.

Chaos in Central Europe

By the time prearmistice negotiations were completed a month later, all the Central Powers had collapsed. The first to give up was Bulgaria. The Bulgarian lines were broken in late September, and before the month was out the government had sued for an armistice. Next came Turkey. During the last year of the war, British forces had steadily advanced from the Persian Gulf into Mesopotamia and from Egypt into Palestine and Syria. With Bulgaria out of the war, Turkey was threatened from the north as well. On October 30 it concluded an armistice.

The Austro-Hungarian Empire, meanwhile, was falling to pieces. On October 21, 1918, the Czechoslovaks declared their independence, and a week later the Yugoslavs followed suit. On November 1, Hungary established an independent government. Ten days later, Emperor Charles renounced his throne, and by the middle of November both Austria and Hungary had proclaimed republics.

In Germany the government had reformed itself, in the hope of obtaining more favorable armistice terms. But the Allies would have no dealings with the kaiser. On November 3 mutiny broke

British tanks at Amiens in 1918. In the final months of the war the Allies effectively used large numbers of tanks under a smoke screen as a cover for advancing infantry.

out among German sailors at Kiel. Within days the revolt spread through most of northern Germany. On November 7 revolution broke out in Munich and the king of Bavaria abdicated. On November 9, finally, revolution in Berlin overthrew the monarchy and a German Republic was proclaimed.

The Allies, meanwhile, had agreed to accept the Fourteen Points as a basis for an armistice. Under its provisions Germany had to withdraw its forces beyond the Rhine; it had to renounce the treaties of Brest-Litovsk and Bucharest; and it had to surrender large quantities of strategic materials. The terms were designed to make any resumption of hostilities impossible. Fighting was officially ended on November 11.

The war that was to have been over in four months had lasted more than four years. At its height it had involved some thirty-four nations. It had killed close to 10 million soldiers, wounded twice that number, and caused close to a million civilian deaths. It had brought revolution to central and eastern Europe and had swept away the last remnants of autocratic monarchism. The war's initial purpose—to determine the future of Serbia—had long since given way to far bigger aims. Germany had dreamed of hegemony in Europe and perhaps the world. The Allies had hoped to avert that German threat and in the process to round out their own possessions. Only the United States was seeking nothing. The Peace Conference was to show whether America's idealism would prevail against the hardheaded nationalism of its European allies.

THE PARIS PEACE CONFERENCE

The Peace Conference opened on January 18, 1919. All the belligerents were present, except the Central Powers and Russia; this was to be a peace dictated by the victors. As in most major peace conferences, the important decisions were made by the great powers who had contributed most to winning the war. The peace was thus made by a handful of men, the "Big Four": Wilson, Lloyd George, Clemenceau, and Orlando.

The star of the conference was Woodrow Wilson, a figure of hope to Europeans. The favorite aim of the American president was to set up a League of Nations. But his position had been weakened by the return of a Republican majority in the recent congressional elections. Great Britain was represented by its prime minister, David Lloyd George, the mercurial Welsh politician. Although his views on the peace were fairly moderate, he had recently won an election on the promise of a harsh peace. The most impressive figure of the conference was France's premier, Georges Clemenceau. He hated the Germans, and his foremost aim was to protect France by weakening its former enemy in every possible way. Italy's representative, Prime Minister Vittorio Orlando, played only a minor role.

Problems of Peacemaking

The problems before the Paris conference were without precedent. The last comparable meeting had been held at Vienna a century earlier. But while the Congress of Vienna had been concerned only with reordering the affairs of Europe, the problems before the Paris conference ranged over the whole world. The Allies as well as the Central Powers had accepted the Fourteen Points as a basis for peace, but many of Wilson's principles differed from the provisions of the Allies' secret treaties. Other complications arose from the many foreign and domestic disturbances that occurred while the conference was in session, the popular clamor in the Allied countries for a speedy settlement, and the physical and nervous strain under which the delegates labored. It is not surprising that the peace they made was not perfect.

So long as the victors agreed among themselves, negotiations at Paris went smoothly. But there were several questions on which they did not see eye to eye. The most important were Germany's colonies, the Rhineland, reparations, Fiume, and the Shantung Peninsula.

The Allies agreed that Germany's colonies should not be returned, but they did not agree on what to do with them. France, Japan, and Great Britain and its dominions wanted to annex Germany's holdings. President Wilson, on the other hand, felt that this would violate his Fourteen Points. The impasse was finally resolved by the adoption of the "Mandate Principle," which provided that the German colonies as well as a large part of the Ottoman Empire were to be placed under foreign control, subject to supervision by the League of Nations. Germany later attacked this solution as a violation of Wilson's Fourteen Points.

The crisis over the future of the Rhineland almost broke up the conference. The French demanded that the left bank of the Rhine be made into an autonomous buffer state for reasons of security. Such an arrangement, however, ran counter to Wilson's principles. The compromise arrived at after long and acrimonious debate called for the permanent demilitarization of the Rhineland and its occupation by Allied forces for fifteen years. In addition, the territory of

Woodrow Wilson and French President Raymond Poincaré wave to Parisians on Wilson's arrival in Paris for the Peace Conference.

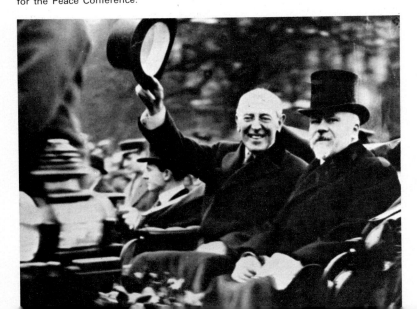

the Saar was to remain under League administration for fifteen years, and France was given the region's coal mines. Finally, Great Britain and the United States promised France an alliance against possible German aggression.

In the discussion of reparations, an argument arose over the extent to which Germany was to make good damages done to the civilian population of the Allies. Wilson finally gave way to the pressure of his European colleagues and agreed that this should include pensions to victims of war and allowances to their families. To justify so vast a claim, the Allies affirmed that German aggression had been responsible for starting the war. The controversial issue of "war guilt" was thus injected into the peace treaty.

The crisis over Fiume arose from Italy's demand that it be given the Adriatic port in place of the Dalmation coast, which it had been promised in the Treaty of London but which had been incorporated into Yugoslavia. When Prime Minister Orlando finally left Paris in protest, the united Allied front showed its first open rift. Italy felt that it had been cheated out of its just reward.

The issue of Shantung involved Japan and China. China had entered the war on the Allied side in 1917. Japan's claim to succeed to Germany's former rights in the Shantung Peninsula clearly conflicted with China's own rights and with Wilson's principles. But the president had only just managed to resist French demands in the Rhineland, and the Fiume crisis was still at its height. So he gave in to Japan's demands. The Shantung solution was a serious defeat for the American president, and it lost the United States the traditional friendship of China.

While the negotiations at Paris were in their final stages, the German delegation arrived at Versailles. The Germans were handed a draft of the treaty on May 7 and were given fifteen days in which to present their written observations. These resulted in only a few minor changes. The Germans, therefore, charged that this was a dictated settlement. The signing of the treaty took place on June 28, 1919, at Versailles, five years to the day

Germany Unrepentant   May 7, 1919

Germany's foreign minister, Count Brockdorff-Rantzau, denied Allied charges of German "war guilt" in a speech at the Peace Conference at Versailles.

Gentlemen, we are deeply impressed with the great mission that has brought us here to give to the world forthwith a lasting peace. . . . We know the intensity of the hatred which meets us, and we have heard the victors' passionate demand that as the vanquished we shall be made to pay, and as the guilty we shall be punished.

The demand is made that we shall acknowledge that we alone are guilty of having caused the war. Such a confession in my mouth would be a lie. We are far from seeking to escape from any responsibility for this World War, and for its having been waged as it has . . . but we with all emphasis deny that the people of Germany, who were convinced that they were waging a war of defense, should be burdened with the sole guilt of that war. . . .

Public opinion in every enemy country is echoing the crimes Germany is said to have committed in the war. Here, too, we are ready to admit that unjust things have been done. . . . But in the manner of waging war, Germany was not the only one that erred. . . . Crimes in war may not be excusable, but they are committed in the struggle for victory, when we think only of maintaining our national existence, and are in such passion as makes the conscience of peoples blunt. The hundreds of thousands of noncombatants who have perished since November 11, because of the blockade, were destroyed coolly and deliberately after our opponents had won a certain and assured victory. Remember that, when you speak of guilt and atonement. . . .

From A. Luckau, *The German Delegation at the Paris Peace Conference* (New York: Columbia University Press, 1941), pp. 220–21.

after the assassination of the Austrian archduke at Sarajevo.

THE TREATY OF VERSAILLES

The peace treaty with Germany contained territorial, military, and economic clauses. It also called for the punishment of "war criminals," including the kaiser. Under the territorial terms of the treaty, Germany had to surrender 13 percent of its prewar area and population. This meant a loss of more than 15 percent of its coal, close to 50 percent of its iron,

The Disillusionment of Peace

We came to Paris confident that the new order was about to be established; we left it convinced that the new order had merely fouled the old. We arrived as fervent apprentices in the school of President Wilson: we left as renegades. I wish to suggest in this chapter (and without bitterness), that this unhappy diminution of standard was very largely the fault (or one might say with greater fairness 'the misfortune') of democratic diplomacy.

We arrived determined that a Peace of justice and wisdom should be negotiated: we left it, conscious that the Treaties imposed upon our enemies were neither just nor wise. To those who desire to measure for themselves the width of the gulf which sundered intention from practice I should recommend a perusal of the several Notes addressed to the Supreme Council by the German Delegation at Versailles. . . . It is impossible to read the German criticism without deriving the impression that the Paris Peace Conference was guilty of disguising an Imperialistic peace under the surplice of Wilsonism, that seldom in the history of man has such vindictiveness cloaked itself in such unctuous sophistry. Hypocrisy was the predominant and unescapable result. Yet was this hypocrisy wholly conscious, wholly deliberate? I do not think so. . . . We did not realise what we were doing. We did not realise how far we were drifting from our original basis. We were exhausted and overworked.

From Harold Nicolson, *Peacemaking, 1919* (New York: Harcourt Brace Jovanovich, 1933), pp. 187–88.

Clemenceau, Wilson, and Lloyd George leaving the palace at Versailles after signing the peace treaty with Germany.

and 19 percent of its iron and steel industry. Besides giving up its colonies, Germany also had to recognize the independence of Austria. This last provision was to prevent a possible *Anschluss*, or union, for which there was much sentiment in both countries.

The military clauses of the treaty called for the reduction of Germany's army to one hundred thousand volunteers. The German navy was limited to six battleships of ten thousand tons and a few smaller ships. Germany was to have no offensive weapons—submarines, aircraft, tanks, or heavy artillery—and its general staff was to be dissolved. To supervise German disarmament, an Allied Military Control Commission was appointed.

In the economic field, the precise amount of reparations to be paid by Germany was left for a Reparations Commission to decide. In the meantime France was to receive large amounts of coal to make up for the wanton destruction of its coal mines by Germany's retreating armies, and Britain was given quantities of ships to compensate for the losses suffered from submarine warfare. German foreign assets of some $7 billion were confiscated; its rivers were internationalized; its patents were seized; and it was prohibited from raising tariffs above their prewar level. In short, everything possible was done to avert the threat of a renascent and vengeful Germany. The treaty was no worse than the treaties of Brest-Litovsk and Bucharest, which Germany had imposed on Russia and Rumania. Nor was it very much better.

THE TREATIES WITH GERMANY'S ALLIES

The supplementary treaties with the smaller Central Powers were signed in 1919 and 1920. The Treaty of St. Germain with Austria was almost as harsh as that of Versailles. It called for the surrender of large territories to Czechoslovakia, Poland, Yugoslavia, and Italy. Not counting Hungary, the prewar area of the former empire was cut to less than one-third and its population to one-fifth. In addition, Austria's army was limited to thirty thousand men. It also had to pay large reparations and agree not to become part of Germany.

Hungary signed its own treaty. Because of a brief communist interregnum under Bela Kun, Hungary did not sign the Treaty of Trianon until the middle of 1920. Its territorial provisions were the most severe of all the postwar treaties. After ceding lands to all its neighbors, Hungary was left with little more than a quarter of its former territory and a third of its population. It also had to pay reparations and reduce its army.

Bulgaria, in the Treaty of Neuilly, lost the outlet to the Aegean it had gained in 1913, agreed to reparations, and had to cut its armed forces.

Turkey concluded two peace treaties, one at Sèvres in 1920 and a later one at Lausanne in 1923. The first, which called for a virtual partition of the country, was superseded by the later agreement. In the interim, a revolt of Turkish nationalists under Mustapha Kemal Pasha had completed the revolution begun by the Young Turks in 1908 and overthrown the regime of the sultan. The Allies had favored the dismemberment of Turkey and in 1919 supported the invasion of Asia Minor by Greek forces. But Turkish resistance under Mustapha Kemal finally convinced the powers that their aim was unattainable. The Allies, therefore, revised the earlier peace settlement. Under the Treaty of Lausanne, signed in 1923, Turkey gave up everything except Asia Minor and a small foothold in Europe. It did not have to pay any reparations, and the "capitulations"—rights and privileges granted centuries ago to foreign powers—were abolished. The Straits were demilitarized and opened to ships of all nations in time of peace. Alone among all the defeated countries, Turkey had thus been able to enforce a radical change in an initially harsh peace settlement. In October 1923 it was proclaimed a republic, with Mustapha Kemal "Atatürk" as first president.

THE AFTERMATH OF WAR

As might be expected, the defeated countries, foremost among them Germany, were deeply opposed to the postwar settlement. They attacked it not only as too harsh but also as unjust, since it violated Wilson's Fourteen Points. In its attempt to sort out the hopelessly intermingled peoples of central Europe, for instance, the principle of self-determination was often ignored. In countries like Poland, Czechoslovakia, and Rumania, from one-fourth to one-third of the population consisted of alien minorities, mostly Germans or Hungarians. The problem of national minorities, a source of much unrest before 1914, had not been solved by the war.

The situation looked more hopeful with respect to another prewar problem: the war, outwardly at least, had brought the victory of democracy. Popular governments replaced autocratic monarchies

Mustapha Kemal Pasha "Atatürk" (1881–1938), the first president of Turkey (1923–38).

THE PEACE SETTLEMENTS IN EUROPE   1919–20

Territories lost by:

Germany

Bulgaria

Austria-Hungary

Russia

Plebiscite areas

Demilitarized Rhineland zone of Allied occupation

NATIONAL MINORITIES IN CENTRAL EUROPE 1919

Legend:
- Polish
- German
- Russian
- Serbian
- Croatian
- Slovenian
- Bosnian
- Macedonian
- Bulgarian
- Hungarian
- Rumanian
- Albanian
- Czechoslovakian

MILES 0 200

Revolutionaries drive through the streets of Budapest, January 1919, in a demonstration preceding the Communist takeover in March.

countries carried a blemish that only time and success could erase. The tense and tumultuous atmosphere of postwar Europe, however, was not conducive to the peaceful consolidation of democracy. The chaos left behind by war and revolution soon proved too much for the new and inexperienced parliamentary governments of central and eastern Europe. In their place there emerged new kinds of dictatorial and totalitarian regimes, better suited, it seemed, to cope with the emergencies of a world in crisis (see Chapter 31).

The first of these authoritarian systems arose in Russia during the 1920s. The victory of communism in that powerful Eurasian country brought an entirely new and disturbing element into international affairs. The founding of the Third Communist International ("Comintern") in 1919 by Lenin's lieutenant, Grigori Zinoviev, seemed to confirm the western fear that communism was not content to confine its influence to one country. Short-lived communist regimes in Hungary and Bavaria at the end of the war showed that communism profited from domestic disorder. After several attempts to engineer communist risings in Germany, Lenin finally decided to concentrate his efforts first on the communization of his own country. But the threat of communist Russia continued to frighten the statesmen of Europe until it was overshadowed in the 1930s by the more immediate threat posed by Nazi Germany.

The tripartite division of Europe into victors, vanquished, and the Soviet Union was the cause of much international unrest. To remedy this situation the Allies had created the League of Nations. Here was something entirely new, a parliament of nations in which international problems could be discussed and solved. That was how the founders of the League had envisaged its mission. But events soon proved otherwise. When the League opened its first session at Geneva in 1921, several of the great powers were missing: Germany was not admitted until 1926, the Soviet Union became a member eight years later, and the United States never joined.

in central and eastern Europe and Turkey. But since the political changes in countries like Germany, Austria, and Hungary were closely associated with military defeat, democracy in these

The failure of the United States to ratify the Treaty of Versailles, which included the Covenant of the League of Nations, showed that Americans were not yet ready to assume the role they were to play later as the world's most powerful nation. America's absence from the League could not help but have unfortunate results. In an assembly dominated by the European victors, the United States would have served as an impartial arbiter. The League of Nations had many shortcomings; but none was as crucial as the void left by America's refusal to become a member.

THE LEAGUE OF NATIONS AND COLLECTIVE SECURITY

The general purpose of the League was "to promote international cooperation and to achieve international peace and security." It was founded on the concept of collective security, under which peace was to be maintained by an organized community of nations rather than by an uncertain "Concert of Europe." The specific tasks of the League were: to work for international disarmament; to prevent war by arbitration of international disputes; to apply sanctions against aggressors; and to register and revise international agreements. In very few of these tasks was the League successful.

Disarmament

The Treaty of Versailles had stated that the disarmament of Germany was intended "to render possible the initiation of a general limitation of the armaments of all nations." But general disarmament was tackled most hesitantly. Only in 1926 did a Preparatory Commission begin discussions of a Disarmament Conference, and the Conference itself did not meet until 1932. Its deliberations at that time proved entirely fruitless.

There were several causes for this failure. Shortly after the war, the Allied Military Control Commission began to report a long series of German violations of the Versailles disarmament provisions. Most important were secret contacts between the new German *Reichswehr* and the Russian Red Army. These German violations were alarming enough to keep the Allies from reducing their own military forces. Another reason for Allied failure to disarm was the difficulty of finding a valid basis for determining a nation's military power. Geographic location, manpower, industrial development, and raw materials, it was felt, were far more significant factors than the actual size of armies. In most of these factors Germany and the Soviet Union excelled, and general disarmament would have been greatly to their advantage.

Arbitration of International Disputes

The second task of the League was to arbitrate international disputes. Members promised to bring any dispute "suitable for submission to arbitration" before the League Council. Any decision by the Council had to be "unanimously agreed to by the members thereof." The League was able to settle a number of international conflicts. Of some thirty cases submitted during the 1920s, the majority were arbitrated. The League was most effective in settling disputes between small powers. As soon as a major power was involved, however, the League proved quite powerless. In the "Corfu incident" of 1923, for instance, when Italy bombarded and occupied the Greek island of Corfu in retaliation for the murder of some Italians, the Italian government refused to acknowledge the League's competency.

Sanctions Against Aggression

The League's procedure for dealing with military aggression was laid down in Article 16 of the Covenant. As major punishment it provided for economic sanctions. To be effective, this policy needed the cooperation of all the great powers. But since two or more of them usually were outside the League, the application of economic sanctions proved impossible. This became evident at the time of Japan's invasion of China in 1931 and Italy's war against Abyssinia in 1935. Article 16 also provided for military sanctions, but these were left entirely to individual members. The League itself maintained no armed forces.

Treaty Revision

The registration and publication of international agreements, called for under Article 18 of the Covenant, was intended to prevent "secret diplomacy." Even so, most serious diplomatic negotiations after the war still went on behind closed doors, and the fear of secret treaties persisted. More significant than the publication of treaties was the provision made in Article 19 of the Covenant for the revision of existing treaties. Had the powers availed themselves of this opportunity, Europe and the world might have been spared the Second World War.

Clearly the League of Nations suffered from many weaknesses. Most of these could have been eliminated. But since each power was primarily concerned with its own selfish aims, the hopeful experiment of the League turned out a failure. Only in fields that involved none of the vital interests of the great powers did the League score any gains. The League's Mandate Commission was able to improve the standard of colonial administration. The International Labor Organization, affiliated with the League, did much to raise the status of workers. Various other League agencies concerned themselves with matters of health, the illicit drug traffic, the international arms

trade, and so forth. These agencies set important precedents for the far-reaching activities of the United Nations today.

THE "WAR AFTER THE WAR," 1919–23

For several years after the Peace Conference, Europe underwent so many major and minor international crises that people wondered if the war had really ended. Until the fall of 1919, the Allies intervened against the Bolshevik regime in Russia. Poland fought with Lithuania over the town of Vilna, with Czechoslovakia over the region of Teschen, and with Russia over its eastern frontiers. Polish and German irregular forces fought over Upper Silesia in 1922. Intermittent conflicts between Italy and Yugoslavia over Fiume lasted until 1924. The Greeks invaded Turkey between 1919 and 1922 and almost came to blows with Italy in 1923. Austria and Hungary clashed over the Burgenland region in 1921. And in 1923 Germany's default in reparation payments led to the invasion of its key industrial region, the Ruhr, by French and Belgian troops. These were only the more noteworthy among an unending series of international incidents during the early postwar period.

The French Search for Security

The greatest danger to peace was Germany's desire to escape the restrictions of Versailles. This worried the French in particular. The alliance between France and the Anglo-Saxon powers failed to materialize when America withdrew from the peace settlement. Since Germany was still superior in human and industrial resources, the French felt that their security demanded the strictest fulfillment of the peace terms. But this insistence on fulfillment caused a growing rift between France and Great Britain. To Britain, Germany was no longer a serious economic and naval rival; and since Germany had been one of England's best customers before the war, Britain wanted it to get back on its

Will it work?—a cartoon portraying League of Nations sanctions against Italy as a robotlike contraption constructed by League members. The sanctions against Italy for its invasion of Ethiopia in 1935 did not work.

Will It Work?

feet. Moreover, England felt that a healthy Germany was the best protection against the westward spread of communism. When France invaded the Ruhr in 1923, therefore, Britain expressed its disapproval. It had no desire to see the French assume hegemony over the Continent.

The loss of British support forced France to look elsewhere for security. With Russia disqualified by communism and Italy dissatisfied with the peace settlement, only the smaller "succession states" of central Europe were left. In 1921 France concluded an alliance with Poland, in 1926 with Rumania, and in 1927 with Yugoslavia. In addition, Rumania, Yugoslavia, and Czechoslovakia organized the "Little Entente." All these countries were interested in maintaining the status quo, which was being threatened by the revisionist agitation not only of Germany but of Hungary and Russia as well. As an attempt to isolate Germany, however, the French system failed, as the two outcasts of Europe—Germany and Russia—drew together.

The Russo-German Rapprochement

Common economic and military interests, after a few years, led to a political rapprochement between Germans and Russians. The first outward sign was a treaty of friendship concluded at Rapallo in April 1922. The world was startled and disturbed by what it suspected of being a military alliance. But the Treaty of Rapallo was merely a promise of cooperation between the two partners, important chiefly because it helped Germany escape its diplomatic isolation. There were people in both Germany and Russia who hoped that the treaty would develop into something more. But this hope was never fulfilled. Economically the two countries were complementary, and both stood to gain from mutual trade. But ideological differences made such an exchange difficult. Despite some later economic and neutrality agreements, Russo-German relations throughout the 1920s remained decidedly cool.

The Ruhr Occupation

The French occupation of the Ruhr in 1923 marked a turning point in the history of postwar Europe. Deprived of its major industrial region, Germany was thrown into an economic crisis, which was made more serious by the passive resistance the people of the Ruhr put up against the French. Financial pressures helped to escalate an already severe German inflation. By refusing to mine the coal France hoped to get from the Ruhr, the resisters in the Ruhr contributed to French economic difficulties as well. The German government, which feared for the nation's existence, finally ended the Ruhr struggle. There were communist disturbances in central Germany and separatist uprisings in the Rhineland. In Bavaria an unknown ex-corporal, Adolf Hitler, was preparing to make his first try for power.

The Ruhr episode taught an important lesson to both French and Germans: rigid insistence on the fulfillment of the Versailles Treaty on the one hand, and stubborn resistance against such fulfillment on the other, helped neither side. Both, it seemed, had to give way if chaos was to be averted. For the next six years a group of dedicated statesmen devoted their efforts to bringing about such a compromise.

THE "ERA OF LOCARNO" 1924–29

The year 1924 saw important political changes in both France and England. In France the rightist cabinet of Raymond Poincaré, known for his vengeful attitude toward Germany, was replaced by a left-wing coalition in which Aristide Briand was foreign minister. In England the Labour Party had a brief inning but soon gave way to a Conservative government with Austen Chamberlain as foreign secretary. In Germany the direction of foreign policy after the Ruhr crisis was in the hands of Gustav Stresemann. Together, Briand, Chamberlain, and Stresemann brought Europe a brief respite from fear and uncertainty.

A trainload of coal on its way to France during the occupation of the Ruhr in 1923.

			Peace Settlements				
1914	1918	1919	1920	1923	1924		192

First World War	"War After the War"	French Occupation of Ruhr	"Era of Locarno"

The Locarno Pact

Europe's return to stability after 1924 was chiefly due to a more efficient handling of the reparations problem. Without these economic developments, the rapprochement between Germany and the western powers would hardly have come about. The first political result of this rapprochement was the Locarno Pact.

Under the terms of the Treaty of Versailles, the Allies were to begin withdrawing their forces from the Rhineland in 1925. But because of German disarmament violations, the Allies refused to leave. Stresemann realized that the basic reason for this refusal was France's fear of Germany. To dispel this fear he now proposed a treaty by which not only France and Germany, but also England, Italy, and Belgium would guarantee the status quo in western Europe. Such a treaty was signed at Locarno in October 1925.

To a world torn for more than a decade by international strife, the Locarno Pact came as a harbinger of a new age. "We are citizens each of his own country," Stresemann said at Locarno, "but we are also citizens of Europe." This seeming conversion of Stresemann from a rabid German nationalist into a "good European" commanded the admiration of his contemporaries. But Stresemann was every bit as eager to abolish the restrictions of Versailles as were his nationalist compatriots. Where he differed was in his realization that the revision of Versailles could not be achieved by force but only through patient negotiation.

The rapprochement between Germany and the West, meanwhile, worried the Soviet Union. Despite Russia's resumption of diplomatic relations with France and Britain in 1924, it had remained an outsider in international affairs. England in particular resented the activities of the Comintern, and in 1927 once again severed its connections with the Soviets. What Russia feared most was that Germany, as a member of the League, might be obligated to participate in sanctions against the Soviet Union. To quiet these fears Stresemann, at Locarno, had obtained a modification of Article 16 of the League Covenant, allowing Germany to abstain from participating in any sanctions that endangered its own security. When this still did not satisfy the Russians, Germany in April 1926 signed a treaty of neutrality with them. Some saw this Treaty of Berlin as an attempt on Germany's part to play a double game between the East and the West. But there is no doubt that Stresemann's foremost concern was always for closer relations between Germany and the West.

The Kellogg-Briand Pact

The efforts of the powers to guarantee Europe's security by treaties that would bolster the collective security system of the League climaxed in the signing of the Pact of Paris, or Kellogg-Briand

German Foreign Minister Dr. Gustav Stresemann addressing the League of Nations for the last time, September 9, 1929, shortly before his death.

Pact, in 1928. Its sixty-two signatories, which included the United States, promised "to renounce war as an instrument of national policy." Nothing was more characteristic of the spirit of hopefulness that pervaded the world after Locarno than this attempt to banish war simply by signing a treaty.

THE ECONOMIC CONSEQUENCES OF THE WAR

The economic consequences of the war were even more serious than its political aftermath. The territorial losses by themselves caused a major economic shock among the defeated powers. The Allies added to their distress by making seemingly limitless demands for reparations. But the victors, too, found the going far from easy. In the West, French and Belgian industrial regions had been devastated. In eastern Europe, lack of seed, fertilizers, and agricultural implements resulted in a marked decline of farm production. All the powers, England in particular, had lost important foreign markets. And a general return to protective tariffs retarded recovery everywhere.

The effects of the postwar economic crisis were felt in many ways. Five years after the war Europe's total industrial production was still at only two-thirds of its prewar level. Unemployment, never much of a problem in the past, now assumed alarming proportions. Another repercussion was felt in financial matters. All the major countries of Europe suffered from severe inflation. In Germany and Austria, inflation led to total devaluation of the currency.

The Reparations Problem

Much of the responsibility for Europe's economic difficulties rested with the peacemakers of 1919. In their efforts to solve the Continent's political problems, they often ignored the economic effects of their decisions. A member of the British peace delegation, the economist John Maynard Keynes, called attention to these oversights in his book *The*

Economic Consequences of the Peace (1920), a sweeping indictment of the Versailles settlement on economic grounds. The most troublesome part of the treaty turned out to be reparations. In order to pay the large sums called for, the defeated nations needed surplus capital. This they could gain only through increased exports. But such exports competed with the products of the nations who hoped to profit from reparations. The transfer of large amounts of capital, furthermore, had unsettling effects on

---

The Kellogg-Briand Pact

Secretary of State Frank B. Kellogg came to Paris with a bouquet of white lilies in one hand and in the other a pen to sign a pact. He was a little old man who looked like a little old woman who resembles a little old man. . . . Stresemann came too; this was the first time a German foreign minister had visited Paris since the Franco-Prussian War of 1871. But he was gravely ill, and when he went to pay his respects to Prime Minister Poincaré, a doctor waited in the anteroom. After an hour the doctor sent a written message to Poincaré beseeching him to order Stresemann home to bed.

The Kellogg-Briand Pact was signed on August 27, 1928, at the Quai d'Orsay in the Salle de l'Horloge, amid an orgy of marbles, velvets, silks, all exquisitely blended, spiced with silver and gold. . . . The scenery must have been pleasing to Richelieu's ghost; but this was an American affair. . . . Now for the first time I saw Hollywood intrude into the plush-carpeted sanctum of a Foreign Office . . . platoons of sweating technicians in shirtsleeves installed 35-millimeter film howitzers that spied down upon the horseshoe table where "those guys" (as I learned engineers refer to ministers) would perform. As the statesmen entered the room (Poincaré stumbling over the cables), the klieg lights exploded in a pink glow, and all the eighteenth-century Venetian luster of crystal and candles was snuffed out by the crude and sober floodlight of twentieth-century technology.

The pact was signed by fifteen nations, with a heavy gold fountain pen especially manufactured for the occasion. It bore the inscription: "If you want peace, prepare for peace." Kellogg took up the pen with trembling hand, but it was too heavy for the old man, and a French secretary had to help him affix his name.

The Kellogg-Briand Pact has been ineffective in practice every time it has been invoked. . . . It was not a pact, after all, so much as a declaration against sin.

From Emerey Kelen, *Peace in Their Time* (New York: Knopf, 1963), pp. 168–69.

Runaway inflation in Germany. Above: a 2 billion mark note; below: marks being baled as waste paper.

the economies of debtors and creditors alike. It was easy, in other words, to ask for huge reparations, but it was difficult to devise methods of paying them.

The reparations problem was further complicated by the mutual indebtedness of the victors. The easiest way out would have been the cancellation of all inter-Allied debts. This solution was rejected by the United States, who would have ended up paying for the whole war.

The main source of reparations was Germany. The total amount of Germany's obligations was settled at $32 billion in 1921. From the start Germany fell behind in its payments. The French, who were to receive more than half of the reparations, were adamant in their demands for prompt payment. The climax of France's insistence on fulfillment came with the invasion of the Ruhr in 1923.

The Dawes Plan and the Young Plan

America had already suggested that the reparations issue be studied by an international committee of experts. With the failure of the Ruhr venture, such a body was appointed late in 1923. It worked out a plan, named after its chairman, the American financier Charles G. Dawes, which went into effect in September 1924. Under the Dawes Plan, Germany was to pay gradually rising amounts that were to reach a "standard annuity" in 1929. The Plan worked well. But, more than was realized, Germany's ability to pay depended on the influx of foreign loans, especially from the United States. This flow continued until 1929, when American investors began to speculate at home. Since at the same time Germany's yearly payments under the Dawes Plan were about to reach the "standard annuity," and since no time limit had been set on such payments, it seemed a good time to reconsider the whole reparations question.

Meetings between German and foreign experts during 1929 finally led to the Young Plan, named after the American expert Owen D. Young. But the Young Plan never went into effect. As the Great Depression spread from the United States to Europe, Germany ceased its payments altogether. At a final conference in Lausanne in 1932, Germany was relieved of any future obligations. Opinions differ on the total amount of reparations actually paid by Germany. A likely estimate puts it at $6 billion. This was not only far less than originally demanded, but in return Germany had received a far larger amount in foreign loans. The reparations settlements clearly had been a failure.

EUROPEAN RECOVERY

American capital played an important role in the economic life of Europe. Most of America's loans were private and short-term. Their repayment was made difficult by the American government's tariff policy. Instead of helping foreign debtors to meet their obligations through increased exports, the United States surrounded itself with high tariff walls. This policy soon provoked a worldwide wave of protectionism. Insistent warnings by economists against such shortsightedness finally led the League of Nations to call a World Economic Conference in 1927. In their final report, the delegates urged their governments to lower tariffs as soon as possible. Before this advice was taken, the Great Depression began. Not least among its causes was protectionism.

Except for its warning on tariffs, however, the World Economic Conference was optimistic. France had rebuilt its destroyed regions, had modernized its industry, and had stabilized its currency. Germany had recovered from the shock of inflation and with the aid of foreign loans had improved its industries so that once again it was the industrial leader of Europe. England's recovery was slowed by adherence to the gold standard, antiquated production methods, and the higher living standard of its workers. In Italy, the Fascist government of Benito Mussolini successfully raised food production. Even in Russia the "New Economic Policy," with its partial return to capitalist practices, brought gradual economic improvement.

But this apparent economic recovery also had its weak points. It was chiefly restricted to industry. Agriculture continued to suffer from overproduction and foreign competition. The resulting decline of rural buying power reacted upon industry. Some producers, tempted by American loans and the example of American mass-production methods, expanded far beyond the need of their markets. When, after the American crash in October 1929, American loans ceased and old loans were recalled, Europe's economy, deprived of this financial infusion, collapsed.

Within one decade, Europe had thus come full cycle from despair through hope and back to despair. In the early 1920s it had seemed that the German

Oswald Spengler had been right in his best seller *The Decline of the West* (1918), which predicted the impending doom of Western civilization. But then in the mid-1920s a "silver lining" had appeared on the horizon. The optimism of the "Era of Locarno" may appear unjustified in retrospect. But to contemporaries the decrease of international tension, the economic recovery, and the general air of well-being and stability seemed quite real. They were seen as proof that Europe at long last had found the peace it had been looking for. One may rightly wonder what would have happened if the recovery had lasted for another decade. In any attempt to find the causes of the unhappy events of the 1930s and 1940s, the Great Depression looms large.

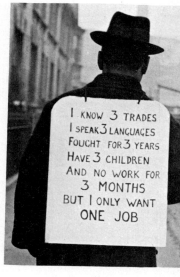

Unemployment in Britain in 1930 afflicted all levels of society.

Suggestions for Further Reading

Note: Asterisk denotes a book available in paperback edition.

General
There are many volumes covering world history since 1914. One of the most interesting and original is C. Quigley, *Tragedy and Hope: A History of the World in Our Time* (1966). Other recommended books are F. P. Chambers, *This Age of Conflict: The Western World—1914 to the Present*, 3rd ed. (1962), and, for the years between the two World Wars, R. J. Sontag, *A Broken World, 1919–1939** (1971). D. Thomson, ed., *The Era of Violence, 1898–1945* (1960), Vol. XII in the *New Cambridge Modern History* series, includes contributions by noted specialists on every facet of European and world history. The declining influence of Europe in world affairs is the theme of a small volume by H. Holborn, *The Political Collapse of Europe** (1954). R. Aron, *The Century of Total War** (1955), is a thoughtful analysis of world events in the twentieth century, and G. Barraclough, *An Introduction to Contemporary History** (1964), presents a stimulating discussion of modern issues.

The First World War
The military side of the war is told in B. H. Liddell Hart, *The War in Outline** (1936), and C. Falls, *The Great War, 1914–1918** (1936). M. Ferro, *The Great War, 1914–1918* (1973), and G. Hardach, *The First World War, 1914–1918* (1977), are more recent treatments. On the home fronts, see J. Williams, *The Other Battleground: The Home Fronts—Britain, France nd Germany, 1914–1918* (1972); G. D. Feldman, *Army, Industry, and Labor, 1914–1918* (1966), which deals with Germany, A. J. May, *The Passing of the Hapsburg Monarchy*, 2 vols. (1966); A. Fontaine, *French Industry During the War* (1962); E. L. Woodward, *Great Britain and the War of 1914–1918** (1967); and A. Marwick, *The Deluge: British Society and the First World War** (1970). The diplomatic history of the war years is covered in Z. A. B. Zeman, *The Gentlemen Negotiators: A Diplomatic History of the First World War* (1971). The problem of war aims is treated in F. Fischer, *Germany's Aims in the First World War** (1967); H. W. Gatzke, *Germany's Drive to the West** (1950); and W. R. Louis, *Great Britain and Germany's Lost Colonies, 1914–1919* (1967). America's involvement in the war is discussed in A. S. Link, *Wilson the Diplomatist** (1957), and E. R. May, *The World War and American Isolation* (1959). For a briefer assessment, see D. M. Smith, *The Great Departure: The United States and World War I** (1964). The following are important monographs on various aspects of the war: J. C. King, *Generals and Politicians: Conflict Between France's High Command, Parliament and Government, 1914–1918* (1951); P. Guinn, *British Strategy and Politics, 1914 to 1918* (1965); M. C. Siney, *The Allied Blockade of Germany, 1914–1916* (1957); and T. Ashworth, *Trench Warfare, 1914–1918: The Live and Let Live System* (1980). For a more vivid impression of the war, the following are highly recommended: B. W. Tuchman, *The Guns of August**

(1962); L. Wolff, *In Flanders Fields: The 1917 Campaign** (1958); and A. J. P. Taylor, *The First World War: An Illustrated History* (1963).

The Russian Revolution

W. H. Chamberlain, *The Russian Revolution, 1917–1921*, 2 vols. (1952), is a standard work. E. H. Carr, *A History of Soviet Russia: The Bolshevik Revolution, 1917–1923,** 3 vols. (1950–53), is scholarly but controversial. Tsuyoshi Hasegawa, *The February Revolution: Petrograd, 1917* (1981), is an important study. Other recent studies include R. V. Daniels, *The Russian Revolution** (1972); A. Rabinowitch, *The Bolsheviks Come to Power* (1976); and J. L. H. Keep, *The Russian Revolution: A Study in Mass Mobilization* (1976). The background of the Revolution is treated authoritatively in A. B. Ulam, *The Bolsheviks: The Intellectual and Political History of the Triumph of Communism in Russia* (1965). The peace negotiations between Russia and the Central Powers are described by J. W. Wheeler-Bennett, *Brest-Litovsk: The Forgotten Peace, March 1918** (1939), and R. Debo, *Revolution and Survival: The Foreign Policy of Soviet Russia, 1917–1918* (1979). Allied intervention is dealt with in G. F. Kennan, *Russia Leaves the War** (1956) and *The Decision to Intervene** (1958), and R. H. Ullman, *Anglo-Soviet Relations, 1917–1921,** 3 vols. (1961–73). See also S. White, *Britain and the Bolshevik Revolution* (1979). On developments among Russia's national minorities, see R. Pipes, *The Formation of the Soviet Union: Communism and Nationalism, 1917–1923* (1954). O. H. Radkey, *Agrarian Foes of Bolshevism* (1958), deals with the Socialist Revolutionaries during the Revolution. Several participants have provided their own version of events: L. Trotsky, *The History of the Russian Revolution*, 3 vols. (1932); V. M. Chernov, *The Great Russian Revolution* (1936); N. N. Sukhanov, *The Russian Revolution 1917: A Personal Record* (1955); A. F. Kerensky, *The Kerensky Memoirs* (1966); and P T. Wrangel, *The Memoirs of General Wrangel* (1929). A vivid eyewitness account by a young American communist is J. Reed, *Ten Days That Shook the World** (1919).

Revolution in Central Europe

The last days of the war are treated in H. R. Rudin, *Armistice, 1918* (1944); F. Maurice, *The Armistices of 1918* (1943); and K. F. Nowak, *The Collapse of Central Europe* (1924). On the overthrow of the Hohenzollern and Habsburg dynasties, see A. J. Ryder, *The German Revolution of 1918* (1967); Z. A. B. Zeman, *The Break-Up of the Habsburg Empire, 1914–1918* (1961); and F. L. Carsten, *Revolution in Central Europe, 1918–1919* (1972). Both A. Rosenberg, *The Birth of the German Republic, 1871–1918** (1931), and O. Jászi, *The Dissolution of the Habsburg Monarchy** (1929), put events in their respective countries into historical perspective. H. Seton-Watson, *Eastern Europe Between the Wars, 1918–1941,** rev. ed. (1962); J. Rothschild, *East Central Europe Between the Two World Wars* (1974); and S. Borsody, *The Tragedy of Central Europe** (1960), deal with the problems of the small succession states.

The Peace Treaties

The standard history of the Peace Conference is H. W. V. Temperley, *A History of the Peace Conference of Paris*, 6 vols. (1920–24). A. J. Mayer, *Politics and Diplomacy of Peacemaking** (1967), emphasizes the peacemakers' fear of communism, as does J. M. Thompson, *Russia, Bolshevism, and the Versailles Peace* (1966). H. Nicholson, *Peacemaking, 1919** (1933), vividly captures the atmosphere of the negotiations. M. L. Dockrill and D. Goold, *Peace without Promise: Britain and the Peace Conferences 1919–1923* (1981) presents a convenient synthesis. The following deal with inter-Allied relations before and during the Peace Conference: H. I. Nelson, *Land and Power: British and Allied Policy on Germany's Frontiers, 1916–1919* (1963); S. P. Tillman, *Anglo-American Relations at the Paris Peace Conference of 1919* (1961); and A. J. Mayer, *Political Origins of the New Diplomacy, 1917–1918** (1959). The classic indictment of the Versailles settlement is J. M. Keynes, *The Economic Consequences of the Peace* (1920). It is challenged in E. Mantoux, *The Carthaginian Peace, or the Economic Consequences of Mr. Keynes** (1946). P. Birdsall, *Versailles Twenty Years After* (1941), is a judicious reappraisal of the treaty. See also R. B. McCallum, *Public Opinion and the Last Peace* (1944). On the peace settlements with Austria, Hungary, and Turkey, see N. Almond and R. H. Lutz, *The Treaty of St. Germain* (1939); F. Deak, *Hungary at the Paris Peace Conference* (1942); and P. C. Helmreich, *From Paris to Sèvres: The Partition of the Ottoman Empire at the Peace Conference of 1919–1920* (1974). America's part in the negotiations is reassessed in T. A. Bailey, *Wilson and the Peacemakers* (1947). See also V. S. Mamatey, *The United States and East Central Europe, 1914–1918* (1957).

The Aftermath of War

There is no satisfactory general work in English on international relations between the two wars, although E. H. Carr, *International Relations Between the Two World Wars, 1919–1939** (1947), is an admirable summary. S. Marks, *The Illusion of Peace: International Relations, 1918–1933** (1976), covers a shorter period. See also D. P. Silverman, *Reconstructing Europe after the Great War* (1982). H. W. Gatzke, ed., *European Diplomacy Between Two Wars, 1919–1939** (1972), is a collection of articles on various aspects of postwar European diplomacy. On British foreign policy, see F. S. Northedge, *The Troubled Giant: Britain Among the Great Powers, 1916–1939* (1946), and W. N. Medlicott, *British Foreign Policy Since Versailles, 1919–1963,** rev. ed. (1968). Differences between the western powers are treated in A. Wolfers, *Britain and France Between Two Wars** (1940), and W. M. Jordan, *Great Britain, France, and the German Problem, 1918–1939* (1943). See also K. L. Nelson, *Victors Divided: America and the Allies in Germany, 1918–1923* (1976). Russo-German relations are covered in K. Rosenbaum, *Community of Fate: German-Soviet Relations, 1922–1928* (1965), and H. Dyck, *Weimar Germany and Soviet Russia, 1926–1933* (1966). Germany's relations with the western powers are the subject of J. Jacobson, *Locarno Diplomacy: Germany and the West, 1925–1929* (1972). German agitation over "war guilt" is criticized by L. Fraser, *Germany Between Two Wars: A Study of Propaganda and War Guilt* (1944). On Germany's attempts to evade the disarmament restrictions of Versailles, see H. W. Gatzke, *Stresemann and the Rearmament of Germany** (1954), and E. W. Bennett, *German Rearmament and the West, 1932–1933* (1979). The reparations problem is surveyed in the book by E. Mantoux cited in the section above, and in M. Trachtenberg, *Reparations in World Politics* (1980). See also D. H. Aldcroft, *From Versailles to Wall Street: The International Economy in the 1920's* (1976). S. A. Schuker, *The End of French Predominance in Europe: The Financial Crisis of 1924 and the Adoption of the Dawes Plan* (1976), is an admirable book. The standard history of the League of Nations is F. P. Walters, *A History of the League of Nations,* 2 vols. (1952). See also G. Scott, *The Rise and Fall of the League of Nations* (1973). G. A. Craig and F. Gilbert, eds., *The Diplomats, 1919–1939** (1953), is a collection of lively essays on the making and makers of interwar diplomacy.

31 Democracy in Crisis

Before 1914 the countries of Europe, despite national differences, still had much in common. What feeling of European unity there had been then was gone by 1919. The Continent was now divided into victors and vanquished, "have" and "have-not" nations. Among the latter were not only the countries that had lost the war but countries, like Italy and Russia, that felt dissatisfied with the peace settlements. It was in these "revisionist" powers that a new type of totalitarian government arose, dividing Europe into democracies and dictatorships.

Another change was the decline of the Continent's central role in world affairs. As the United States gradually emerged from its isolation, and as regions that hitherto had been dominated by Europe began to play a role of their own, Europe's longstanding predominance faded. World politics gradually overshadowed European politics.

THE AFTERMATH OF WAR 1919–29

One of the major war aims of the western powers had been the triumph of democracy over autocracy. This aim seemed to have been achieved. But the war left so many unsolved problems that even traditional democracies like France and England, found it difficult to adjust to changed circumstances. It is not surprising, therefore, that some of the new democratic nations found it hard to cope with the aftermath of war and that their democracy turned out to be short-lived.

Stability in Great Britain

Among the western powers, Great Britain enjoyed by far the most stable domestic development. Democracy became complete when Britain's franchise was extended to all adults in two further reform acts in 1918 and 1928. But while women were thus at long last granted political rights, the economic advantages they had gained during the war were soon again curtailed. Transition from war to peace was made easier by the continuation of Lloyd George's coalition cabinet and by a brief industrial boom. Beginning in 1920, however, England entered an extended economic crisis. Its effect was to shift power from the Liberals, first toward the Conservatives and later to Labour.

During most of the 1920s Britain was ruled by the Conservatives, who tried vainly to tackle the perennial problems of a large deficit and widespread unemployment. In the elections of 1929 Labour finally won its first major victory. But the solution of England's economic difficulties had to wait until after the Great Depression.

Despite its unsettled economy, Britain had no serious domestic disturbances. There was some unrest among the workers, and in 1926 trouble in the coal

British Women in Industry

During the War women passed rapidly into trades hitherto considered unsuitable for them. . . . Because of this increase in numbers, as well as owing to the efficiency shown by women in every type of occupation, the Women's Employment Committee foresaw an extension of openings for women not only in industry, but in the higher branches of commerce, and believed that employers would gladly continue to use them after the War in the work formerly done by men in shops, such as managing, buying and travelling. . . . These sanguine hopes were doomed to disappointment. The War had certainly given the world an object lesson in woman's achievement, but men in general showed a disturbing tendency to be appalled rather than encouraged by this demonstration of unexpected ability. . . . While employers were quite ready to offer "equal pay by results" in trades to which women were not well adapted, they were most opposed to it in such industries as engineering and aircraft wood-working, in the light processes of which women notoriously excelled men. . . . By the autumn of 1919 three-quarters of a million of the women employed at the time of the Armistice had been dismissed, and the position of women in general could "certainly not be described as enviable."

From V. Brittain, *Women's Work in Modern England* (London: Noel Douglas, 1928), pp. 8–15, as quoted in W. C. Langsam, ed., *Documents and Readings in the History of Europe Since 1918* (New York: Lippincott, 1951), pp. 275–77.

mines led to a general strike. But there was no violence. The Labour Party, though accused of being "soft" on communism, was always moderate in its program and policy; and the Conservatives, though eager to curb the power of the labor unions, were sincerely concerned about the workingman's welfare. The government's policy of maintaining a stable currency was detrimental to British trade, since it hampered competition on the world market. But it also saved Britain's middle class from the demoralizing effects of inflation that were felt in most continental countries.

Instability in France

France led a far more hectic existence. It was worse off economically, having suffered greater losses in money and in manpower than Britain. Moreover, the French electoral system of proportional representation aggravated the factionalism of French politics and caused great instability. There were more than forty

Opposite: Delegates to the Second Hague Conference were caught napping by Erich Salomon, whom Aristide Briand called "the king of the indiscreets."

A Nazi coalition poster of 1924 addressing an anti-Semitic appeal to the "exploited" working class in Germany.

different cabinets during the interwar period. For the first five years after the war France was governed by a "national bloc" with Raymond Poincaré as the leading figure. In 1924 the Ruhr fiasco brought to power a "cartel of the left," under Édouard Herriot and Aristide Briand.

The most urgent task before the French government was the reconstruction of the devastated regions. Since Germany, until 1924, remained behind in its reparations, France had to pay for this reconstruction. Attempts to increase taxation ran into opposition from the right. Only the threat of runaway inflation finally led to drastic action. In 1926 a cabinet of "national union" under Poincaré was able to stabilize the currency and put France on the road to recovery. With reconstruction completed and German reparations coming in regularly, France's economy improved rapidly. By 1928 the budget began to show a surplus, unemployment had vanished, and increased wages together with social legislation gave the lower classes a greater share than before in the nation's economy. France seemed well on the way toward resolving the longstanding conflicts between its rich and its poor.

The Weimar Republic

The new German republic was from the beginning plagued by disunity and disorder. In 1919 a constituent assembly at Weimar had drawn up an admirably democratic constitution. One of its less happy features, however, was proportional representation, which contributed greatly to political instability. During the fourteen years of its existence, the Weimar Republic saw more than twenty different cabinets. The heavy legacy of war required a government that had the full support of its citizens. Throughout most of its brief life, the Weimar Republic failed to win such support.

The most loyal friends of the republic were the workers who had suffered most from political discrimination under the empire. The German working class, however, was no longer united. It had been split before and during the revolution of 1918 into a moderate majority of Social Democrats and a radical minority of communists. On several occasions between 1919 and 1923 the latter threatened to overthrow the republic.

Most of the bourgeois parties of the Weimar Republic professed loyalty to the new regime, although the parties of the right were hostile to it. This hostility was nourished by nationalist propaganda, which blamed the republic both for Germany's defeat and for signing the *Diktat* of Versailles. Soon after the war, rabidly nationalistic groups of "free corps" and veterans' organizations embarked on a series of uprisings against the hated republic.

Considering the many attacks from every direction, it is surprising that the Weimar Republic was able to survive. In the early 1920s the antirepublican parties of the right were able to attract almost 30 percent of the vote. The most critical year in the postwar decade was 1923, when the French invasion of the Ruhr, antirepublican risings on the right and left, and the total devaluation of the currency threatened the country's very existence. But as Germany's economy improved after 1924, the prorepublican parties made significant gains. Had this recovery lasted longer, the Germans might yet have become reconciled to their new republic.

The New Nations of Eastern Europe

If democracy found the going rough in Germany, it faced even greater difficulties in eastern Europe. Most of the states in this area had gained their independence as a result of the war, and most of them faced similar problems. With the exception of Austria and Czechoslovakia, their economy was predominantly agrarian, and the division of large estates among the peasantry had long been a major issue. Where such land reform was carried out successfully, as in the Baltic states, the rise of independent small proprietors contributed greatly to political stability. In Poland and Hungary, on the other hand, where reform was obstructed by the landed aristocracy, domestic peace remained precarious.

Economic recovery in eastern Europe was slow. Widespread illiteracy, antiquated agricultural methods, and lack of capital funds for industrialization were the main obstacles. Efforts at economic collaboration ran into strong nationalist opposition. Nationalism in eastern Europe was intensified by the problem of minorities. Almost all the new nations included large numbers of foreign nationals.

All the new states started out with parliamentary governments. But this democratic trend was soon reversed. The first to change was Hungary. After a brief communist interlude under Bela Kun in 1919, conservative forces restored order under Admiral Nicholas Horthy, who founded Europe's first postwar dictatorship of the right. In Poland the rise of authoritarian rule came with Marshal Joseph Pilsudski's seizure of power in 1926. Elsewhere "strong men" suspended constitutions and silenced political opposition. None of these regimes was as totalitarian as the communist dictatorship in Russia or the fascist dictatorship in Italy. It was only after Hitler's rise in the 1930s that fascism gained control over most of central Europe (see Chapter 32).

Of the few countries in eastern Europe where democracy took hold after the war, the most important were Czechoslovakia and Austria. Czechoslovakia, ably led by Thomas Masaryk and Eduard Beneš, was generally considered the model among the new democracies. Czechoslovakia's major problem was the desire for greater autonomy among its numerous minorities. Especially troublesome were the 3 million Germans living in the Sudeten region.

Austria, since the war, had only Germans within its borders. But even so the new republic was deeply divided along social and economic lines between the urban, industrialized, and radical workers of Vienna, and the rural, agrarian, and conservative peasants of the prov-inces. Economically, Austria suffered greatly from the consequences of partition. In 1922 the situation became so serious that the League had to grant substantial loans for Austrian reconstruction. By 1926 Austria seemed to be out of danger. But the real cause of Austria's difficulties—the loss of its economic hinterland—had not been solved. As the least viable among the new states of Europe, Austria was the first to feel the effects of the Great Depression.

German Inflation

The prewar value of the German mark was twenty-five cents. When I first went to Munich at the end of 1921, I already could get about a hundred marks for a dollar. A year later I was getting about sixty-five hundred marks for the dollar. Then, in January 1923, French armies marched into Germany's richest industrial region, the Ruhr, and the German Government decided to finance passive resistance to such foreign military occupation. . . . and for this purpose printed enormous additional amounts of paper money. A month after the occupation of the Ruhr, I was getting more than forty thousand marks for a dollar, and the bottom of the money market began to drop out completely. By August a dollar was buying millions, in September billions, in October trillions of marks. A sad cartoon appeared in a Munich paper showing a little girl sitting beside two huge bundles of paper money, crying pitifully. A passerby was saying: "Why are you crying, little girl?" She answered: "someone stole the leather straps off my money!" I occasionally played a dollar limit poker game for German marks. When we began that game, the limit was one hundred marks; in October 1923, one trillion marks. It was quite a thrill to raise a trillion.

Finally, that month, the German Government virtually repudiated its enormous public debt by introducing a new unit of value called the rentenmark. . . . This meant that every German who had sacrificed and saved to provide for his old age and for his family was ruined.

From Robert Murphy, *Diplomat Among Warriors* (New York: Doubleday, 1964), pp. 37–38.

THE UNITED STATES AND EUROPE

The recovery of Europe, though uneven, seemed well under way by 1929. It would have come earlier, had the United States been more aware of its new responsibilities as the world's leading economic power. But America preferred to keep aloof from European affairs.

Isolationism and Nationalism

Most Europeans considered this isolationism extremely selfish. America, after all, had suffered much less from the war than Europe had and had gained from the war economically, not merely by supplying the Allies but by penetrating into regions formerly controlled by European commerce. The least America could do was to forget the loans it had made to its allies during the war. But this the United States refused to do.

There were other sources of friction between the United States and its wartime friends. The French resented America's refusal, together with Britain, to guarantee French security; the British were alarmed by America's growing commercial and naval competition; and neither France nor Britain welcomed the evident rapprochement between the United States and Germany. A further cause for concern was America's obvious intent of isolating itself not only politically but economically, by adopting some of the highest tariffs in its history.

America's isolationism had its domestic roots in a growing nationalist opposition to "foreign" and "radical" influences. The Ku Klux Klan soon after the war claimed wide support for its persecution of racial and religious minorities; fear of radical elements in the early 1920s caused a "red scare" that led to several thousand arrests; and, most important, restrictions on immigration severely limited immigrants from less desirable regions.

American International Involvement

But despite isolationism, America's humanitarian conscience and its economic interests could not help but lead to renewed involvement in international affairs. Right after the war, various relief organizations had dispensed millions of dollars' worth of supplies wherever they were most needed, even in the Soviet Union. Beginning in 1924 American experts took the lead in tackling the reparations problem. With the return of economic stability, American investors during the next five years lent vast amounts to various European countries, especially Germany.

In the political sphere America shared the general hope for peace and security. The warm reception of the Pact of Paris for the "outlawry of war" seemed a hopeful sign that America had outgrown its isolationism. But in other respects the country remained aloof. Even though many Americans had come to favor the League of Nations, the government refused to participate in any except the League's cultural and social work.

America was also concerned about disarmament, not so much on land as on sea. The rising influence of Japan and the large increase in Japanese naval expenditure made some limitation of naval forces seem highly desirable. Agreement on this point was reached at a naval conference in Washington in 1921 and 1922. It called for a ten-year naval holiday, the scrapping of large numbers of ships, and a fixed ratio for the capital ships of the major powers. Simultaneous political agreements guaranteed the status quo in the Pacific, reaffirmed the "Open Door" policy for China, and ended the Anglo-Japanese alliance of 1902. Subsequent

New members (kneeling in front) being sworn into the Ku Klux Klan in Maryland (1922).

efforts to extend the naval agreement to small ships did not succeed until 1930. But because Japan, France, and Italy remained dissatisfied with the results, these attempts at naval limitation were only partly successful.

AMERICA DURING THE "ROARING TWENTIES"

Economically the United States, like Europe, found adjustment to peacetime conditions far from easy. The sudden cancellation of government contracts deeply upset the economy. As European industries resumed production, furthermore, United States exports declined. Attempts to cut costs by lowering wages met with strong opposition from the workers, and once the wartime ban on strikes was lifted, labor unrest revived.

Return to "Normalcy"

In domestic as in foreign affairs, the American people were looking back with nostalgia to the peace and prosperity they had known before the war. The man who promised a return to such "normalcy" was the Republican Warren G. Harding, who was elected president by a large majority in 1920. It was under Harding's administration that America entered on the era of hectic prosperity for which the 1920s are best remembered. The heyday of the "Roaring Twenties" came under Calvin Coolidge.

The Republican administration's overriding concern was with aiding the American business community. High tariffs, the repeal of the excess-profits tax, the lowering of taxes on corporations and on high incomes, injunctions against strikes—all these measures directly or indirectly benefited big business. America's phenomenal economic growth was also due to the ample capital resources and growing investments that were available from a broader segment of society. Big business, it seemed, was becoming everybody's business.

It was not quite everybody's, though. Neither the worker nor the farmer was

President Calvin Coolidge at work on his Vermont farm (ca. 1925).

getting his due share of prosperity. Labor had suffered from the postwar depression and from the hysteria that equated union protest with communism. As a result, union membership during the 1920s declined from its wartime high. Even so, most workers in time benefited from the nation's rising economy through almost full employment and better wages.

The stepchild of the American boom was the farmer. As a result of the war, America's farm output by 1919 had more than doubled. Then, as foreign demand decreased and surpluses accumulated, prices dropped. The government tried to help farmers by additional credit facilities and cooperatives, but the Republican administration shrank from direct subsidies. Protective tariffs, furthermore, led foreign countries to retaliate by cutting down their imports of American grain.

The "Jazz Age"

There was an air of frenzy about America's pursuit of business and pleasure during the "Jazz Age" of the 1920s. As is common in periods of rapid economic boom, America had its share of private and public corruption. The Eighteenth Amendment introducing prohibition in 1920, invited violation of the law by the average citizen. The "speakeasy" and the "bootlegger" became part of American life, and "racketeering" was a common form of crime.

These were the features that made the deepest impression abroad. Europeans professed to be shocked by the "materialism" of their *nouveau riche* American cousins. But Europe did not remain immune to American influences. American products and production methods found ready imitators abroad, and American styles and American jazz had their admirers among the young. For the first time in history Europe showed signs of becoming Americanized.

The American people themselves seemed well satisfied with their country's apparently endless prosperity. In 1928 they voted overwhelmingly for another Republican president, Herbert Hoover. Some developments, however, should have caused alarm. Already before 1929 expansion in some basic areas had begun to slow down. Commodity prices had declined and agricultural prices continued to fall. These signs of recession were obscured by a continuing boom on the stock market. Here prices were bid up by speculators, to levels far out of proportion to actual values. In mid-September 1929, stock prices showed some decline. Failures of speculative companies in London later in the month caused some tremors on Wall Street, but still no panic. The collapse of the stock market came suddenly, on October 23. The next day, "Black Thursday," American investors

Cab Calloway with his band (1936).

sold close to 20 million shares at a total loss of $40 billion. The Great Depression was on its way.

THE GREAT DEPRESSION

"Business cycles"—that is, alternating phases of prosperity and depression—were a recognized feature of modern capitalism. But there had never been a depression quite so severe as the one following the American stock market crash. The basic cause of the depression was the world's failure to solve the economic problems inherited from the First World War. Industrial expansion continued full force after the war and soon led to overproduction. Beginning in 1924 a brief recovery set in, but it was artificial. As neither farmers nor workers really shared in the economic rise, purchasing power failed to keep up with production. In countries like Germany and Austria, furthermore, industrial expansion was largely stimulated by foreign loans. As these credits dried up, recovery ceased and the economy of these nations collapsed.

This, however, did not happen until the spring of 1931. In the meantime the situation in central Europe had become serious enough to demand radical remedies. One solution proposed in early 1931 was for an Austro-German customs union. But this proposal met with strong opposition from the French, who regarded it as a first step toward an eventual political *Anschluss*. To put pressure on the Austrians, France began to withdraw its short-term credits. In May 1931 Austria's largest bank collapsed. This is generally seen as the beginning of the European phase of the Great Depression. In July German banks suspended payments. In September the British government abandoned the gold standard. As other nations followed Britain's example, the only major European power to cling to the gold standard was France. Here the depression was not felt until 1932.

Effects of the Depression

It is difficult to convey the staggering economic blow that the world suffered in

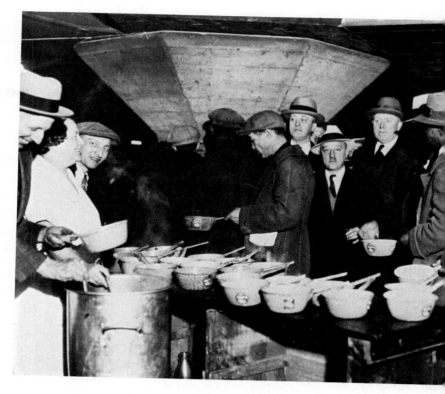

Soup kitchen in New York City during the Great Depression (1931).

the brief span of three or four years. World industrial production declined more than one-third, prices dropped more than one-half, and more than 30 million people lost their jobs. Some countries, especially Germany, were harder hit than others. In the United States, industrial production and national income by 1933 had decreased more than one-half, and the unemployment figure was estimated at 14 million.

Because of the worldwide scope of the depression, any attempt to counteract it demanded cooperation among all the major powers. As debtor nations began to default, President Hoover in 1931 initiated a year's moratorium on all reparations and war debts. But this proved to be only a stopgap. A year later an economic conference at Lausanne all but buried the troublesome problem of intergovernmental debts. A World Economic Conference in London in 1933 sought to stabilize currencies. It failed when America refused to adopt its proposals.

International efforts to pull the world

President-elect Roosevelt greets President Hoover on the way to the Inauguration (March 4, 1933).

political leadership was imperative. In countries like Germany and the succession states of central Europe, democratic governments were no longer able to provide such leadership. As authoritarian regimes gained the upper hand, these nations were lost to the democratic cause. But even among the western democracies the crisis of the 1930s called for firm guidance. The need for leadership was felt particularly strongly in the United States.

The United States: The "New Deal"

The Hoover administration, unwilling to interfere with free enterprise, had done too little to help relieve the economic crisis. Discontent with Republican half-measures was chiefly responsible for the Democratic sweep in the elections of 1932. For more than twelve years thereafter, the United States was guided by Franklin D. Roosevelt. The new president met the most difficult domestic and foreign emergencies with a boldness and confidence that earned him the admiration of the majority of Americans.

Some of Roosevelt's measures were intended for immediate relief, but many others remain in effect to the present day. Republicans charged that government interference with free enterprise tended to corrupt America's pioneering spirit of self-reliance. In taxing the rich and aiding the poor, America certainly went far toward repudiating its traditional faith in laissez faire. But the rising standard of living tended to hasten rather than retard the growth of American business; and if the "New Deal" entailed staggering financial burdens, the nation as a whole seemed willing and able to bear them.

out of its economic slump thus were either too little or too late. In the meantime governments everywhere reverted to the same practices that had helped to bring on the depression in the first place. As America raised its tariffs to unprecedented heights, the rest of the powers followed suit, with even Britain abandoning its traditional policy of free trade in 1932. These and other restrictive measures hindered the revival of international trade.

THE DEMOCRACIES ON THE EVE OF THE SECOND WORLD WAR

The Great Depression belonged to both world wars—its roots went back to the First, and its effects contributed to the Second. While governments were still trying to repair the damages of the upheaval of 1929, clouds were already gathering for the far greater catastrophe of 1939. In this mounting crisis, resolute

Great Britain: Slow Recovery

The most successful holding action against the depression in Europe was waged in Great Britain. To rally parliamentary support, Ramsay MacDonald in 1931 transformed his Labour cabinet into a national coalition government. Subsequent elections returned overwhelming

Conservative majorities, and in 1935 Stanley Baldwin took over as prime minister. He was succeeded two years later by Neville Chamberlain. As might be expected from a predominantly Conservative regime, Britain sought to solve its economic problems by retrenchment rather than reform. Taxes were raised, government expenditures cut, and interest rates lowered. The devaluation of the pound stimulated exports. The Imperial Duties Bill of 1932 introduced protectionism. The overall effect of these measures was a modest but steady recovery.

There were few important domestic events during the 1930s. King Edward VIII abdicated in 1936 to marry an untitled divorcée. Economic improvement helped to keep labor unrest at a minimum. Britain's main concern was with developments abroad, where Italy and Germany had started on the course of aggression that was to culminate in the Second World War.

France: A House Divided

In contrast to England and the United States, the French Third Republic during the 1930s was shaken to its very foundations. France until 1932 was an island of prosperity in a sea of economic misery. But when disaster came it struck swiftly. By 1935 French industrial production had fallen almost one-third, exports were declining rapidly, and capital was fleeing the country at an alarming rate. Things looked up briefly after the government devalued the franc in 1936, but the rise in domestic prices soon neutralized any advantage.

It was not so much the severity of the economic crisis as the inability of the French government to cope with it that accounts for the political chaos that ended with the fall of France in 1940. The Third Republic had been deeply divided from the start. Workers and petty employees were virtual outcasts from French society, while the right-leaning wealthy classes and peasants had little enthusiasm for the Republic. The war had temporarily drawn the nation together, and once the difficult postwar transition had been made, French do-

Ramsay MacDonald and Stanley Baldwin at a press conference in 1931, during their national coalition government.

Roosevelt's New Deal

In our day these economic truths have become accepted as self-evident. . . :

The right to a useful and remunerative job in the industries or shops or farms or mines of the nation;

The right to earn enough to provide adequate food and clothing and recreation;

The right of every farmer to raise and sell his products at a return which will give him and his family a decent living;

The right of every businessman, large or small, to trade in an atmosphere of freedom from unfair competition and domination by monopolies at home or abroad;

The right of every family to a decent home;

The right to adequate protection from the economic fears of old age, sickness, accident and unemployment;

The right to a good education.

All of these rights spell security. . . . For unless there is security here at home there cannot be lasting peace in the world.

From President Franklin D. Roosevelt, message to Congress, January 11, 1944.

mestic tensions seemed to have eased. But at this most critical point, the depression intervened, reopening wounds that had only just begun to heal.

Discontent flared up with sudden violence during the Stavisky scandal in early 1934. Rumors that an unsavory promoter, Alexander Stavisky, had enjoyed support in high places, touched off a major riot among rightists in Paris. Many of the rioters were members of various fascist leagues, right-wing and royalist organizations, which in aims and tactics were similar to Hitler's storm troopers and Mussolini's Black Shirts. Fascism, like communism, was apt to strike any country weakened by internal discord.

The government's efforts to rally the country behind a cabinet of national union proved fruitless. In 1936 the parties of the left—Radical Socialists, Socialists, and Communists, alarmed over the fascist threat, buried their longstanding differences. Their "Popular Front" won a decisive popular victory in the subsequent elections.

For almost two years various leftist coalitions, in which the Socialist Léon Blum was the leading figure, tried to halt the disintegration of the Republic. Blum introduced more far-reaching reforms, especially for the workers, than any government since the war. But to succeed,

Blum's social reforms needed the cooperation of businessmen and bankers. And that cooperation was not forthcoming. There were other obstacles to recovery, notably the unsettled state of international affairs, which called for costly rearmament. But the basic reason for Blum's failure was that he was too radical for the right and not radical enough for the left.

While the Germans were preparing to fight the world, the French were fighting one another. Successive waves of "sit-down" strikes—a French innovation—and a rigidly enforced forty-hour week slowed down industry when it should have been working overtime. In April 1938 a shift to the right brought Édouard Daladier to the premiership, with far-reaching powers to rule by decree. But Daladier could not do what abler men before him had failed to do: heal the breach between right and left, bourgeoisie and workers, capitalists and socialists, rich and poor. It was a deeply divided France that went to war in September 1939.

THE TWILIGHT OF IMPERIALISM

This discussion of events between the two world wars has dealt thus far only with Europe and the United States. But there were important developments elsewhere in the world that affected especially those countries that had colonial possessions. Beginning with the First World War, western imperialism entered a period of slow but steady decline. The war itself had weakened the great powers and had aroused a feeling of nationalism among the colonial peoples. Just as the desire for independence among European nations had made for international unrest during the nineteenth century, so colonial nationalism was a major cause of international tension in the twentieth.

The Mandate System

The powers had shown signs of a more enlightened attitude toward colonies at the Paris Peace Conference, when

The Stavisky riots of early February 1934, in which thousands of persons were injured and a number killed.

they adopted the mandate system. The former German colonies and certain territories taken from Turkey were to be administered by mandatory powers responsible to the League. In theory this was a worthy innovation. But in practice the former German colonies became almost indistinguishable from the mandatory powers' own colonies; and of the more advanced Turkish regions that were promised ultimate independence, only Iraq became a sovereign state. Transjordan, under British tutelage like Iraq, was considered too weak to stand on its own feet. The French mandates, Syria and Lebanon, made some progress toward self-government, but the constitutions granted these countries assured French control.

A special case among Turkey's former possessions was the British mandate of Palestine. The root of the trouble in that area was the conflicting national aspirations of Arabs and Jews. Nationalism among the Jews went back to the Zionist Organization, founded by Theodor Herzl in 1897 to provide a home for the Jews in Palestine. In 1917 the British government, in the so-called Balfour Declaration, had backed these Zionist aspirations. Both Arabs and Jews at first seemed ready to cooperate in joint plans for the future of Palestine. But as more and more Jews migrated to Palestine, the Arabs feared that the Jews would emerge as the dominant faction. In 1929 the first major riots broke out among Arabs and Jews. With the advent of Hitler in 1933, Palestine became a refuge for thousands of Jews and immigration increased manyfold. The result was further violence between Arabs and Jews. On the eve of the Second World War, the future of Palestine was still far from settled.

The British Commonwealth

The mandate system was not the only innovation in colonial administration after the First World War. There were also important changes within the British Empire. During the nineteenth century those regions of the empire inhabited chiefly by white settlers had gradually changed from colonies into self-govern-

Theodor Herzl in 1904.

ing dominions. This emancipation from British influence continued after the war. At the Peace Conference, on matters concerning their own interests, the dominions had shown considerable independence. When they refused to follow Britain's lead on several other occasions

The Balfour Declaration   November 2, 1917

Foreign Office
November 2nd, 1917

Dear Lord Rothschild,

I have much pleasure in conveying to you, on behalf of His Majesty's Government, the following declaration of sympathy with Jewish Zionist aspirations which has been submitted to, and approved by, the Cabinet.

"His Majesty's Government view with favour the establishment in Palestine of a National Home for the Jewish people, and will use their best endeavours to facilitate the achievement of this object, it being clearly understood that nothing shall be done which may prejudice the civil and religious rights of existing non-Jewish communities in Palestine, or the rights and political status enjoyed by Jews in any other country."

I should be grateful if you would bring this declaration to the knowledge of the Zionist Federation.

Yours sincerely,
(Signed) ARTHUR JAMES BALFOUR.

Quoted in L. Stein, *Zionism* (London: Ernest Benn, 1925), p. 377.

during the 1920s, it became clear that the relationship needed clarification. This was achieved at the Imperial Conference of 1926. The formula agreed on stated that Great Britain and the dominions were to be completely equal in status, united only through common allegiance to the crown. The British Commonwealth of Nations thus established was officially launched by the Statute of Westminster in 1931. The dominions became fully sovereign states, bound to the mother country merely by ties of blood, sentiment, and economic self-interest.

Even so tenuous a relationship, however, was too much for one member of the Commonwealth—Ireland. Efforts to extend home rule to that unhappy island had been interrupted by the outbreak of war in 1914. During the war, the anti-British Easter Rebellion of 1916, spearheaded by the Republican Sinn Fein movement, had been put down with undue severity. From that point on, Sinn Fein became the most dynamic force in Irish politics. In 1921 Britain set up the Irish Free State, which held dominion status and thus shared in the transition from Empire to Commonwealth. Yet in the midst of this hopeful development the depression came, and with it a resurgence of radicalism. In the elections of 1932 the Republicans gained a majority, and their leader, Eamon De Valera, became president. During the next few years Ireland severed most of its connections with Great Britain. A new constitution in 1937 completely ignored crown and Commonwealth.

India

Another part of the British Empire that was clamoring for independence was India. Like the dominions, India had stood by Great Britain during the war. As a reward for this support, India expected to be given self-government. A new Government of India Act in 1919, however, still fell far short of home rule. The extremists in the National Congress Party, therefore, refused to cooperate. The new leader of the Congress Party was Mohandas K. Gandhi. Gandhi had supported the British during the First World War, only to become their most

persistent foe thereafter. The keynote of his policy was "noncooperation," or passive resistance.

England entered into many fruitless conferences and proposals to try to solve the Indian problem. Since all of them fell short of granting at least dominion status, the National Congress turned them down. The claim of the Congress Party that it represented all of India was denied by the Moslem League of Mohammed Ali Jinnah. This religious split was India's most burning problem. But there were others—economic crises, natural catastrophes, riots, strikes, and famines—all of them adding to the country's extreme instability. When war began in 1939, India's entrance into the family of Commonwealth nations seemed as far away as it had been twenty years earlier.

Colonial Nationalism

The colonial nationalism that caused so much trouble in India was felt elsewhere in the British Empire and in the overseas possessions of the other powers. Britain's protectorate over Egypt was officially terminated in 1922, but continued British control over the Sudan and the Suez Canal gave the Egyptian nationalist "Wafd" party ample cause for agitation. France, in theory at least, had for some time granted French citizenship and representation in the French parliament to some of its colonies. But French centralized rule discouraged the growth of colonial self-government. In advanced regions like North Africa and Indochina, native nationalists rebelled against Frenchification and demanded a voice in running their own affairs. Similarly, in the Netherlands East Indies a swiftly growing nationalist movement opposed the paternalistic rule of the Dutch.

The End of American Colonialism

One country that was in earnest about abandoning its imperialist practices was the United States. America had only one real colony, the Philippines. After repeatedly promising independence to the islands, Congress in 1934

Mohandas Gandhi arriving at an Indian conference in London (1931).

provided for American withdrawal after a transition period of ten years. In 1946 the Philippines became a sovereign nation. In Latin America, American "dollar diplomacy" continued briefly after the First World War. But in time the United States adopted a more benevolent "good neighbor policy," especially in economic matters. In 1930 the Clark Memorandum abandoned the Roosevelt Corollary to the Monroe Doctrine, which had been used in the past to excuse United States intervention in Latin America.

THE FAR EAST: PRELUDE TO WAR

Almost everywhere in the world, colonialism after the First World War found itself on the defensive against native nationalism. The only region where imperialism still thrived was in the Far East. Between the two world wars, Japan embarked on a wholly new phase of expansion, mainly at the expense of China. During the war the Chinese Republic had already felt the threat of its powerful neighbor: the Twenty-one Demands of 1915 had established a Japanese sphere of influence over the mainland opposite Japan; and Chinese efforts at the Peace Conference to enlist Allied support in regaining the Shantung Peninsula had proved in vain. Only when the powers realized that Japanese expansion might threaten their own interests did they become alarmed. The Washington Conference of 1921 to 1922, reaffirmed the "Open Door" principle and promised to respect China's integrity and independence.

China Under the Kuomintang

China's domestic affairs, since the death of General Yüan in 1916, had been chaotic, with powerful warlords ruling various provinces. The only group that held any promise for the future was the Chinese Nationalist Party, or Kuomintang. But although its leader, Sun Yat-sen, was elected president in 1921, his influence was restricted to a small region around Canton. His program of freeing China from outside influences needed foreign help. Since he had been rebuffed by the West in the past, Sun Yat-sen in 1923 turned to the Russians for aid.

The Soviet Union welcomed the Chinese Republic not only as an ally against Japan but also as a possible convert to communism. A small Chinese Communist Party had been founded in 1921. As a result of its collaboration with the Soviet Union, the Kuomintang became a mass movement. To provide the trained military forces necessary to unite China, a military academy was founded under the direction of an able young officer and ardent follower of Sun Yat-sen, Chiang Kai-shek. Sun Yat-sen himself died in 1925 and to this day remains the saint and symbol of the struggle for Chinese unity.

The campaign against the northern warlords was led by Chiang Kai-shek in 1926. By 1929 the Nationalist government controlled the whole country from its headquarters at Nanking. But except for the lower Yangtze region, its control was at best nominal. In the west and north the provincial warlords maintained their power; and to the south, in Kiangsi and Fukien provinces, the Chinese Communists under Mao Zedong and Chu Teh were busy organizing the landless peasants in opposition to the Nanking regime. The breach between Chiang Kai-shek and the Communists had come in 1927 when Chiang, in a bloody purge, had freed himself from Russian and Communist influence. Here were the seeds of the domestic conflict that was to have such serious consequences after the Second World War.

In the meantime the Nationalist regime had begun to tackle the many problems it had inherited from the past. The western powers assisted by making a few concessions, although most of these did not go far enough. In 1929 Chiang Kai-shek terminated unilaterally the obnoxious treaties granting extraterritoriality to western nations. Railroad construction, a uniform currency, legal reform, and an income tax all tried to help overcome the country's regionalism and backwardness. But the failure of the Nationalist government to introduce an

Chiang Kai-shek (above) succeeded Sun Yat-sen to the leadership of the Kuomintang in 1925 and led the Nationalist government in Nanking. Mao Zedong (below) led the Communist faction in southern China in opposition to the Nationalists.

effective agrarian program left the Chinese masses discontented and open to communist agitation. Added to domestic discord and disunity was the constant threat of Japanese intervention.

Moderation in Japan

Japan, in contrast to China, had fared well during the First World War. The country had profited economically from the increased demand for Japanese goods; it had gained territorially from the seizure of German colonies; and it had established a veiled protectorate over part of China. Any desire for further expansion was checked by Allied resistance at the Washington Conference of 1921 to 1922. A terrible earthquake in 1923, furthermore, tied down the nation's energies. The 1920s were taken up chiefly with domestic developments, and the outward westernization of Japan continued. In 1925 universal manhood suffrage was introduced. Apathy among the voters, however, together with the limited powers of the Diet, retarded further democratic growth.

The comparative moderation of Japan's policy was especially apparent in the country's relations with China. In 1922 Shantung was returned to China, with Japan retaining only its commercial privileges. A number of moderate Japanese premiers recognized China's right to organize its own affairs and did not hinder the Kuomintang's policies so long as they did not affect Japan's interests. Only when Chiang Kai-shek's move into northern China threatened Japan's sphere of interest in Manchuria were Japanese troops once more sent to Shantung. As late as 1930, however, Japan still recognized China's tariff autonomy; and in October of that year the government, over the violent protests of Japanese patriots, ratified the London Naval Treaty, which further limited naval construction. But this was the end of the era of moderation. The depression began to hit Japan with disastrous results. The need for cuts in military spending particularly alarmed the militarists, who now came to the fore again, advocating their own brand of totalitarianism. In 1931 they urged Japan into the invasion of Manchuria, which touched off a sequence of events that ended in the Second World War.

AN AGE OF UNCERTAINTY

Before we turn from the democracies to the dictatorships during the "long armistice" between 1919 and 1939, we must briefly consider the intellectual climate of these critical years. The war and its aftermath had shaken many traditional beliefs and had disappointed many expectations. National self-determination and democracy, it seemed, did not necessarily solve Europe's political problems; nor did rugged individualism and laissez faire provide the answer to the world's economic ills. The hope that human reason would solve the few remaining "riddles of the universe" was being undermined by new scientific discoveries, and the widely held belief in progress seemed open to serious question. As a result of growing doubts about hitherto accepted values, the prevailing attitude during the postwar era was one of uneasiness and uncertainty.

Material Progress

Not everyone, of course, was equally sensitive to these changes. The majority of people, once they had overcome the hardships of war, were ready to enjoy the spectacular achievements that science had in store for them. Material progress certainly seemed as promising as ever. Not only were there such new "miracles" as the radio and the talking picture, but constant improvements in production made these and earlier inventions, like the automobile, available to the average person. The veritable avalanche of labor-saving devices that combined to make up a "high standard of living" did not necessarily make life richer, but they certainly made it easier.

Other technological and scientific achievements also changed everyday life. Improvements in transportation virtually eliminated distance as a barrier. The Old World and the New, up until then days

"Miracles" of the 1900s: a 1932 Ford motor car; an automatic two-slice toaster, manufactured in 1928, that rang a bell when the toast was ready and automatically turned off the current; and an "easily wheeled" Vortex vacuum cleaner, ca. 1920.

apart, became separated only by hours. Some of the most spectacular developments took place in medicine. A concentrated attack—through research, public hygiene, and improvements in nutrition—brought some of the most deadly diseases under control. This accomplishment in turn lengthened the average lifespan in the more advanced countries from less than fifty years in 1900 to almost sixty-five years by 1939. Modern science and industry thus continued to fulfill their promise of enabling people to live both better and longer.

Critics of Mass Culture

But material progress was not without its drawbacks. The growth of population now was seen more as a threat to cultural values than to the world's food supply. The Spanish philosopher José Ortega y Gasset, in his book *The Revolt of the Masses* (1932), warned that the increase in human beings was so rapid that it was no longer possible to educate people in the traditions of their culture. As a result, the gap between the cultured few and the superficially educated many was wider than ever and becoming more so. And since it was the masses who exerted political and economic power, their low standards would henceforth predominate.

Other voices were raised against the dangers of a civilization that envisaged progress entirely in material terms. One of the most perceptive critics was the British novelist Aldous Huxley, who, in his satirical novel *Brave New World* (1932), predicted many later "triumphs" of human ingenuity, from tranquillizer pills to brainwashing. The picture Huxley

painted was of a well-adjusted society whose members were scientifically conditioned to whatever status they occupied, existing like animals on a well-tended experimental farm. Man as a slave to his technological inventions, as a mere cipher in a collectivist society, as a rootless, lonely, and lost being in a world of bewildering complexity—such were the subjects that increasingly occupied social critics, novelists, and poets.

The "Behavioral Sciences"

The study of man, both as an individual and as a member of society, had for some time past been the task of the social sciences. This term had at first been used only for the traditional sub-

Another "miracle" of the 1920s: a radio broadcast (featuring operatic soprano Dame Nellie Melba).

Sigmund Freud on the occasion of his only trip to the United States (September 1909).

jects: history, political science, and economics. But in time the field had been widened to include the new "behavioral sciences": psychology, sociology, and cultural anthropology.

The beginnings of modern psychology are associated with Sigmund Freud, a Viennese doctor who began formulating his theories at the turn of the century. There had been psychologists before him. Men like the German Wilhelm Wundt and the American William James had tried to discover the organic roots of human behavior, assuming that the brain, like any other organ, performed purely biological functions. Freud's approach was radically different. Basic to his teachings was the idea that human behavior is directed by subconscious instincts, or "drives," of which the most important is the sexual impulse. These drives are inhibited, usually in early childhood, and such inhibition leads to various degrees of frustration, which in turn may cause serious neuroses. In an effort to cure his patients, Freud developed a technique called "psychoanaly-

sis," which consisted of an extended and deep probing of the patient's mind to get at its subconscious layers. The purpose of such probing was to make the patient understand the conflicts that caused his abnormal behavior and by such understanding remove the causes of his mental disturbance.

Freud was not the only pioneer in modern psychology; there were others. All of them tried to discover what made people act the way they did. Far from increasing man's self-confidence, modern psychology merely added to his feeling of bewilderment and uncertainty. Ever since the Age of Enlightenment man had gloried in the belief that he was a wholly intelligent and rational being. Now suddenly he was faced with the realization that he was subject to dark instincts and drives, and that it was these forces rather than his intellect that determined his behavior.

The second of the behavioral sciences, sociology, originated in the nineteenth century with men like Auguste Comte, Karl Marx, and Herbert Spencer. But here, too, the twentieth century introduced new methods and provided new insights. One of the most important modern sociologists was the Italian Vilfredo Pareto, whose *Mind and Society* was originally published in English in 1916. Pareto accepted the findings of the psychologists that men were swayed by emotion rather than guided by reason. The ideals or rationalizations that social groups set up were to him mere fronts, or "derivations," that screened the basic irrational motives, or "residues," that really moved people. Pareto held that any clever leader or any elite capable of seeing through this human self-deception could use the basic aims of their fellow men to gain supremacy and to establish an authoritarian system in which the masses would obey slogans that appealed to their inner instincts. Pareto thus seemed to provide a "scientific" explanation of fascist totalitarianism. His analysis, if correct, held little hope for a rationally ordered, democratic society.

The third behavioral science, cultural anthropology, likewise tried to explain human behavior. By studying primitive tribes, chiefly American Indians and the

The Freudian Revolution

Freud's extraordinary achievement was to show us, in scientific terms, the primacy of natural desire, the secret wishes we proclaim in our dreams, the mixture of love and shame and jealousy in our relations to our parents, the child as father to the man, the deeply buried instincts that make us natural beings and that go back to the forgotten struggles of the human race. Until Freud, novelists and dramatists had never dared to think that science would back up their belief that personal passion is a stronger force in people's lives than socially accepted morality. Thanks to Freud, these insights now form a widely shared body of knowledge.

In short, Freud had the ability, such as is given to very few individuals, to introduce a wholly new factor into human knowledge; to impress it upon people's minds as something for which there was evidence. He revealed a part of reality that many people before him had guessed at, but which no one before him was able to describe as systematically and convincingly as he did. In the same way that one associates the discovery of certain fundamentals with Copernicus, Newton, Darwin, Einstein, so one identifies many of one's deepest motivations with Freud. His name is no longer the name of a man; like "Darwin," it is now synonymous with a part of nature.

From Alfred Kazin, "The Freudian Revolution Analyzed," *The New York Times Magazine*, May 6, 1956.

natives of Pacific islands, anthropologists like Ruth Benedict and Margaret Mead hoped to determine what role environment played in shaping culture. One of their discoveries was that differences between cultures were due to environmental influences rather than to inherent biological factors and that there was no basis for the belief in "superior" and "inferior" races. It was one thing, however, to study a small primitive tribe and another to apply the same techniques to larger and more complex societies. But some promising beginnings were made. Students in the field of "human relations," through detailed case studies, were able to gather valuable data on small segments of their own society, in the hope of determining what motivated its members.

Spengler and Toynbee

Most social scientists were concerned with the present rather than the past. But even historians dealing with past events often did so to gain a better understanding of the present. Some of them, notably the German Oswald Spengler and the Englishman Arnold Toynbee, studied the rise and fall of past civilizations in order to predict the future of their own civilization. In the past, history had usually been viewed as a linear process, moving onward and upward toward some faraway goal. These historians presented a different view, according to which history seemed to repeat itself. Civilizations, they held, had always risen and fallen in cycles or curves—from birth to death, from spring to winter, from morning to night. These grandiose views of history tried to supply at least some answer to men's anxious questions about where their civilization was going.

Oswald Spengler's *The Decline of the West* (1918) was written during the First World War. The author compared some twenty past "cultures," tracing each through identical phases down to a final phase that Spengler called "civilization." Europe, according to Spengler, was in the midst of this final phase. And like all earlier cultures, European culture would soon disintegrate and collapse. Historical

scholars, to be sure, warned that this "morphology of cultures" was far too sweeping, based on incomplete or incorrect evidence. Yet it could not be denied that in his comparative study Spengler had uncovered many suggestive parallels, and in his predictions of things to come he seemed to be remarkably correct.

It was largely due to Spengler's inspiration that the historian Arnold Toynbee embarked on his own monumental work, *A Study of History* (1934–54). Like Spengler, Toynbee assumed that there are parallel phases in the development of major civilizations. The birth of a civilization Toynbee saw in man's successful "response" to a "challenge," usually supplied by geography or climate. The growth of a civilization consists in man's gradually solving his physical problems, thus freeing his energies for more elevated intellectual and spiritual pursuits. Not every member of society shares in this process. It is, rather, a creative minority that takes the lead and makes its views prevail over the passive majority. The breakdown of a civilization, according to Toynbee, occurs when this minority can no longer muster enough creative force to meet a particular challenge. Europe, Toynbee said, was in the midst of this final phase, which he called the "Time of Troubles." He thus arrived at substantially the same prognosis as Spengler of what the future held in store. But unlike Spengler, Toynbee held out some hope for western civilization, if it learned from the mistakes of the past.

The "New Physics"

While the social sciences were giving little comfort in an age of uncertainty, the natural sciences for some time past had been demolishing the simple, rational, and mechanistic view of nature that had prevailed since the days of Newton. Physical science in the late nineteenth century still viewed the universe substantially in Newtonian terms. Before the end of the century, however, the findings of scientists like Wilhelm Konrad Roentgen, Pierre and Marie Curie, Ernest Rutherford, and Max Planck had already raised doubts concerning those hypothe-

Margaret Mead visiting a school in New Guinea.

Marie Curie in her laboratory (1906).

Albert Einstein in Berlin (1920).

ses. They made it clear that a major new explanation, a whole new system of physics and mathematics, was needed to supply the answers to questions on which Newton had been silent. Such a new system appeared in 1905 when the young German physicist Albert Einstein advanced his "theory of relativity."

According to Einstein's theory, time and space were not absolute, as Newton had assumed, but relative to the observer. Later he included gravitation and motion in his calculations. Mass in Einstein's universe was thus a variable. The mass of a body depended on its rate of motion; its mass increased as its velocity increased, with the speed of light as the theoretical limit. It was the velocity of light, therefore, rather than time and space, that now emerged as absolute in the "new physics."

A further radical departure from accepted theory was Enstein's assumption of the equivalence of mass and energy. Experiments in nuclear physics already had shown that the dividing line between mass and energy was far from clear, and that matter slowly disintegrated into energy by way of radiation. The amount of matter thus lost was infinitesimal compared with the resulting energy. Einstein expressed this relationship between mass and energy in his famous formula $E = mc^2$, in which E is energy, m is mass, and c is the velocity of light. This formula implied that if a process were devised by which matter could suddenly be transformed into energy, only a small amount of matter would be required to produce a vast quantity of energy. A practical demonstration of the validity of Einstein's formula came with the first atomic explosion in 1945.

These and other revolutionary developments in science did not immediately affect the outlook of the average person. But as scientists began speaking of the "limitations of science," admitting that they no longer knew all the answers, some of their feeling of uncertainty could not help but enter general consciousness. Instead of living in a rational world with few remaining riddles, man, in the words of the British astronomer Sir Arthur Eddington, was faced by a universe in which "something unknown is doing, we don't know what." A mysterious world

(as the physicists said it was), inhabited by irrational man (as the psychologists said he was), caught in a civilization predestined for decay and disintegration (as Spengler and Toynbee said our civilization was)—all these factors made the future appear a dismal prospect indeed.

New Cultural Trends

The uncertainty of the age was also reflected in its literature and art. Social criticism among writers was nothing new. But while the Naturalists of the late nineteenth century had hoped to bring about much-needed reforms by their attacks upon society, there was little such hope behind the criticism of the postwar era. Its common denominator was disillusionment—as seen in T. S. Eliot's *The Waste Land* (1922), Thomas Mann's *Magic Mountain* (1924), Theodore Dreiser's *An American Tragedy* (1925), and Sinclair Lewis' *Main Street* (1920). Some of the greatest literature of the years between the wars was escapist—the poetry of Rainer Maria Rilke, Marcel Proust's *Remembrance of Things Past* (1913–27), and Thomas Wolfe's *Look Homeward, Angel* (1929).

Though deeply tinged with disillusionment, postwar literature was also immensely creative. The insights of modern psychology proved a boon to writers in their quest for an understanding of human nature. Every writer, consciously or unconsciously, came under the influence of modern psychology, and especially of Freud. The Irishman James Joyce, in his novel *Ulysses* (1922), introduced a method known as "stream-of-consciousness." The search into the subconscious, so typical of Joyce, also motivated dramatists like the Italian Luigi Pirandello and the American Eugene O'Neill. One of the effects of Freudian psychology was to call attention to the role of sex as a force in man's life. As a result, sexual matters were now written about with far more candor than earlier generations would have thought permissible. Still, a book as outspoken on the subject as *Lady Chatterley's Lover* (1928), by the Englishman D. H. Lawrence, could not be published, except in expurgated form, until over thirty years later.

The mixture of uncertainty and creativity that characterized literature between the two wars also prevailed in painting. Most artists still dealt with recognizable subjects, but more and more of them rebelled against the Realism and Impressionism of the prewar era. Instead, painters like Paul Klee, Vassily Kandinsky, Pablo Picasso, and Ernst Ludwig Kirchner expressed on canvas their inner feelings and impulses, often in styles that reflected the chaotic world in which they lived. These "Expressionists" in time became so abstract that it was impossible any longer to recognize in them common aims and interests. Each artist had become a law unto himself.

This same creative uncertainty and search for new means of expression had its parallel in modern music. Some composers—Jan Sibelius, Sergei Rachmaninoff, Richard Strauss, and Ralph Vaughan Williams—continued to use traditional methods, inspired by the heritage of their various cultural backgrounds. But others—Arnold Schönberg, Arthur Honegger, Béla Bartók, and Paul Hindemith—departed from familiar forms and in some cases, by adopting new scales and chords, developed a wholly new musical idiom.

Because so much modern art and music was highly individualistic, it appealed to only a few. Modern architecture had a somewhat wider following. Most architecture in the nineteenth century had been a mere imitation or a mixture of earlier styles. New building materials, steel and concrete, had been developed; but the inherent possibilities of these materials had been ignored by all but a few pioneers, such as the Americans Louis Sullivan and Frank Lloyd Wright. All this changed after the First World War. Architects became increasingly concerned with the function as well as the appearance of their buildings and by striving for simplicity and utility were able to produce structures of great beauty. The doctrine of "functionalism" found its European exponents in Le Corbusier, Walter Gropius, and Ludwig Mies van der Rohe. It took some time, however, before the general public abandoned its preference for traditional and more ornate styles in favor of contemporary simplicity.

Pablo Picasso, *Woman* (study for *Guernica,* 1937).

Anti-Intellectualism

It is difficult to gauge correctly the temper of a period as brief as the twenty years between the two world wars. Many of its accomplishments, especially in science, were impressive. But there was a puzzling paradox behind this extension of human knowledge. The more man found out about the world, the more he realized how little he had known before. From a feeling of supreme self-importance at the end of the nineteenth century, man's view of himself was pushed to the opposite extreme: he felt uncertain and insignificant, a creature of instinct, no longer able to shape his own destiny.

It is not surprising that this uncertainty should turn many people against the rationalist philosophy that had prevailed for the past two hundred years. There had been a similar revolt against reason a century before. And like Romanticism then, antirationalism now sprang from the disillusionment that followed a seemingly futile war. Modern anti-intellectualism, as it is called, took several forms. It brought a revived interest in religion, even among scientists, who had not long ago been ardent defenders of materialism. But far larger numbers turned elsewhere for guidance. There were many reasons for the sudden rise of totalitarianism after the First World War. Not the least among them was that it provided its followers with simple beliefs in an age of bewildering uncertainty.

Suggestions for Further Reading

Note: Asterisk denotes a book available in paperback edition.

Great Britain and France A. J. P. Taylor, *English History, 1914–1945* (1965), and C. L. Mowat, *Britain Between the Wars* (1955), are the best general books on the subject. R. Graves and A. Hodge, *The Long Weekend: A Social History of Great Britain, 1918–1939** (1940), re-creates the moods and manners of British society during the period. The same is done for the British "establishment" in H. Nicolson, *Diaries and Letters*, 3 vols. (1966–68). There are some excellent biographies of the leading political figures: K. Morgan, *David Lloyd George: Welsh Radical as World Statesman* (1963); R. Blake, *The Unknown Prime Minister: The Life and Times of Andrew Bonar Law* (1955); G. M. Young, *Stanley Baldwin* (1952); G. E. Elton, *The Life of James Ramsay MacDonald* (1939); K. Feiling, *The Life of Neville Chamberlain* (1946); and H. Nicolson, *King George V* (1952). C. R. Attlee, *The Labour Party in Perspective* (1949), is a review of the party's development between the wars by its leader. C. F. Brand, *The British Labour Party: A Short History* (1964), is a useful survey. The best introduction to French postwar history is D. W. Brogan, *France Under the Republic** (1940). N. Greene, *From Versailles to Vichy: The Third French Republic, 1919–1940** (1970), is a brief survey, and A. Werth, *The Twilight of France, 1933–1940* (1942), describes the mounting crisis on the eve of the Second World War. D. Thomson, *Democracy in France** (1964), is helpful for understanding French politics. For biographies of major politicians, see: G. Bruun, *Clemenceau** (1943); G. Wright, *Raymond Poincaré and the French Presidency* (1942); V. Thompson, *Briand: Man of Peace* (1930); and J. Colton, *Léon Blum: Humanist in Politics* (1966). An excellent comparative study is C. S. Maier, *Recasting Bourgeois Europe: Stabilization in France, Germany, and Italy in the Decade after World War I* (1975).

Germany The most complete history of the Weimar Republic in English is E. Eyck, *A History of the Weimar Republic,** 2 vols. (1962). A. J. Nicholls, *Weimar and the Rise of Hitler** (1968), is a competent briefer treatment. On the dissolution of the Republic, see A. Brecht, *Prelude to Silence: The End of the German Republic* (1944), and the collection of essays by German scholars entitled *Path to Dictatorship, 1918–1933** (1966). The two leading personalities of the period are discussed in H. Turner, *Stresemann and the Politics of the Weimar Republic* (1963), and A. Dorpalen, *Hindenburg and the Weimar Republic* (1964). F. L. Carsten, *The Reichswehr and Politics, 1918 to 1933* (1966), and G. Post, *The Civil-Military Fabric of Weimar Foreign Policy* (1973), deal with a significant phase of the Republic's history.

The Small Powers Good general surveys are: H. Seton-Watson, *Eastern Europe Between the Wars, 1918–1941,** rev. ed. (1962); R. L. Wolff, *The Balkans in Our Times* (1956); and B. A. Arneson, *The Democratic Monarchies of Scandinavia* (1939). On individual countries, see M. MacDonald, *The Republic of Austria, 1918–1934* (1946); H. Roos, *A History of Modern Poland* (1966); C. A. Macartney, *October Fifteenth: A History of Modern Hungary, 1929–1945*, 2 vols. (1957); and R. W. Seton-Watson, *A History of the Czechs and Slovaks* (1943).

The United States Two very good studies of the pre-Roosevelt era are A. M. Schlesinger, Jr., *The Crisis of the Old Order, 1919–1933* (1957), and W. E. Leuchtenburg, *The Perils of Prosperity, 1914–1932** (1958); see also G. W. Hawley, *The Great War and the Search for a Modern Order: A History of the American People and their Institutions, 1917–1933** (1979). On America's relations with Europe, see M. P. Leffler, *The Elusive Quest: America's Pursuit of European Stability and French Security, 1919–1933* (1979). The Roosevelt years are covered in several excellent works: A. M. Schlesinger, Jr., *The Coming of the New Deal** (1959) and *The Politics of Upheaval* (1960); D. W. Brogan, *The Era of Franklin D. Roosevelt* (1951); W. E. Leuchtenburg, *Franklin D. Roosevelt and the New Deal, 1932–1940* (1936); and J. M. Burns, *Roosevelt: The Lion and The Fox** (1956). E. F. Goldman, *Rendezvous with Destiny: A History of American Reform** (1952), and R. Hofstadter, *The Age of Reform** (1955), deal with the American liberal and progressive movements. F. L. Allen, *Only Yesterday** (1940) and *The Big Change** (1952), are lively social histories of the period. Among memoirs and biographies of New Dealers, the following stand out: R. E. Sherwood, *Roosevelt and Hopkins** (1948); J. M. Blum, *From the Morgenthau Diaries*, 3 vols. (1959–67); R. G. Tugwell, *The Democratic Roosevelt* (1957); and E. Roosevelt, *This I Remember** (1949).

The Great Depression J. S. Davis, *The World Between the Wars, 1919–1939: An Economist's View* (1975), puts the world economic crisis in its long-range perspective. The crisis itself is studied in J. K. Galbraith, *The Great

Crash, 1929* (1955). See also C. P. Kindleberger, *The World in Depression 1929–1939** (1973). A. J. H. Latham, *The Depression and the Developing World, 1914–1939* (1981), is a useful survey. H. W. Arndt, *The Economic Lessons of the Nineteen-Thirties* (1944), is an attempt to learn from the past. A major aspect of the international repercussions of the financial crisis is the subject of E. W. Bennett, *Germany and the Diplomacy of the Financial Crisis, 1931* (1962).

The Twilight of Imperialism Typical of western disillusionment with imperialism are the books by G. Clark, *The Balance Sheets of Imperialism* (1936) and *A Place in the Sun* (1936). The changes in the British Empire and Commonwealth are discussed in K. Robinson, *The Dilemma of Trusteeship: Aspects of British Colonial Policy Between the Wars* (1965). H. Mukerjee, *India Struggles for Freedom* (1948), traces the long road to Indian independence. Earlier stages on this road are related in M. K. Gandhi, *Autobiography** (1948), and in two autobiographical works by J. Nehru, *Toward Freedom** (1941) and *Glimpses of World History** (1942). On events in the Far East, see A. Iriye, *After Imperialism: The Search for a New Order in the Far East, 1921–1931** (1965); R. Gould, *China in the Sun* (1946); and S. Chen and P. S. R. Payne, *Sun Yat-sen: A Portrait* (1946). The situation in the Middle East is discussed in G. Antonius, *The Arab Awakening: The Story of the Arab National Movement* (1939); and the first stirrings of unrest in Africa are treated in R. L. Buell, *The Native Problem in Africa* (1928). See also W. E. B. DuBois, *The World and Africa* (1947).

Intellectual History Books dealing with the intellectual ferment of the "age of uncertainty" are legion. H. S. Hughes, *Consciousness and Society: The Reorientation of European Social Thought, 1890–1930** (1958), is a fine general study. J. Barzun, *The House of Intellect** (1959), covers the more recent period. See also the stimulating comparative Study by R. Wohl, *The Generation of 1914* (1979). Other attempts to see the crisis of our civilization in historical perspective are R. Niebuhr, *The Irony of American History** (1952), and R. Williams, *Culture and Society* (1958). J. Ortega y Gassett, *The Revolt of the Masses** (1932), is a classic criticism of our mass society. The modern trend toward conformity is analyzed in W. H. Whyte, *The Organization Man** (1956); V. O. Packard, *The Status Seekers** (1959); and A. C. Valentine, *The Age of Conformity* (1954). Other dangers to democratic freedom are pointed out by F. A. Hayek, *The Road to Serfdom** (1944), and K. R. Popper, *The Open Society and Its Enemies** (1950).

The basic work on Freud and psychoanalysis is E. Jones, *The Life and Work of Sigmund Freud,** 3 vols. (1953–57). See also G. Costigan, *Sigmund Freud: A Short Biography* (1965). The wide impact of Freudianism is treated in P. Reiff, *Freud: The Mind of the Moralist** (1959), and F. J. Hoffmann, *Freudianism and the Literary Mind** (1957). D. E. Stannard, *Shrinking History: On Freud and the Failure of Psychohistory* (1981), deals with the impact of Freud on historical writing.

New trends in the social and behavioral sciences are exemplified in T. Parsons, *The Structure of Social Action* (1949); E. Fromm, *Escape from Freedom** (1941); C. Kluckhohn, *Mirror for Man** (1949); B. L. Cline, *The Questioners* (1965); and in the studies of American society by D. Riesman, *The Lonely Crowd** (1953) and *Individualism Reconsidered** (1955). See also the essays by noted social scientists in R. Linton, ed., *The Science of Man in the World Crisis* (1945). For the influence of science on society, see B. Barber, *Science and the Social Order** (1952); B. F. Skinner, *Science and Social Behavior** (1956); J. Russell, *Science and Modern Life* (1955); and W. Esslinger, *Politics and Science* (1955).

The "prophets of doom" are evaluated in H. S. Hughes, *Oswald Spengler: A Critical Estimate** (1952), and K. Winetrout, *Arnold Toynbee: The Ecumenical Vision* (1975). On the scientific revolution of our century, see L. Infeld, *Albert Einstein** (1950); L. Barnett, *The Universe and Dr. Einstein** (1952); W. Heisenberg, *The Physicist's Conception of Nature* (1958); and M. Planck, *Scientific Autobiography and Other Papers* (1949).

Modern literature is covered in M. Colum, *From These Roots: The Ideas That Have Made Modern Literature* (1944), and C. Mauriac, *The New Literature* (1959). On modern art, see E. Langui, ed., *Fifty Years of Modern Art** (1959); W. Haftmann, *Painting in the Twentieth Century,* 2 vols. (1965); and J. Joedicke, *A History of Modern Architecture* (1959). P. Collaer, *A History of Modern Music** (1961), is an introduction to the subject. See also J. Willett, *Art and Politics in the Weimar Period: The New Sobriety, 1917–1933* (1979).

32 The Rise of Totalitarianism

The Communist and Fascist regimes that arose between the two world wars have been variously described as autocratic, authoritarian, dictatorial, and totalitarian. These terms are not synonymous. There had been autocratic and authoritarian regimes in the past, most recently in tsarist Russia and imperial Germany; and there have been dictatorships from ancient times to the present. But none of these deserved to be called totalitarian. What we mean by a totalitarian regime is a regime in which a determined minority, by use or threat of force, imposes its will on the total life of a society. The aims of this ruling clique are usually rooted in some all-embracing ideology. The origins of these totalitarian ideologies go back at least to the nineteenth century, with the appearance of the two creeds that contributed most to totalitarianism: socialism and nationalism. Their growth and spread were aided by industrialism, which gave birth to the mass society in which totalitarianism thrives, and which provided the technical means whereby total domination by a ruling clique was made possible.

There were many ideological differences between the totalitarianism of the right and the left—fascism and communism. Communism owed much of its success to the fervor that Marxian socialism inspired among its followers. There was no room for nationalism in Marxism, although nationalism in time became an ingredient of communism. Fascist ideology, by comparison, was less coherent. A mixture of warmed-over nineteenth-century "isms"—Romanticism, Social Darwinism, racialism, militarism, and so forth—its outstanding characteristic was nationalism. Fascism, too, professed a belief in socialism, but it was an extreme form of state socialism from above rather than the Marxian concept of popular socialism from below.

Despite these ideological differences, fascism and communism were alike in many ways. Both exercised the most minute control over the life of every individual; both ruled through a mixture of propaganda and terror; both segregated and persecuted their opponents in concentration and slave-labor camps; and both sought to extend their power abroad through force or subversion. Why should totalitarian regimes have arisen at the time and in the countries they did? The circumstances differed from country to country, but there were also certain similarities. Totalitarianism arose only in nations with little or no democratic tradition. Most of them had undergone lengthy domestic crises caused by the First World War or the Great Depression. In all cases a resolute minority, posing as saviors, initiated changes amounting to a revolution. And as a rule this minority was headed by a leader with great demagogic gifts.

COMMUNISM IN CRISIS 1917–28

It took several years for communism to gain full control in Russia. The initial difficulties faced by the new Soviet Republic were so severe that its survival seems almost miraculous.

"War Communism" and Civil War

The Bolsheviks began by totally eradicating the tsarist past. In what was called "War Communism" the nation's economy was socialized, where necessary through terror. But to Lenin, revolution in Russia was merely the prelude to world revolution; and he saw the spread of the latter as necessary to guarantee the success of the former. In March 1919, the Soviet-controlled Third Communist International (Comintern) was founded as a permanent agency dedicated to inciting world revolution.

But these Bolshevik attempts to communize Russia and the world simultaneously turned out to be premature. "War Communism," instead of bringing relief, actually brought further misery. Opposition to the new regime was helped by Allied intervention. Its chief motive was to revive Russian resistance against Germany. The Germans, still in control of much of Russia, encouraged separatist movements in the Ukraine and along the Baltic. And to complete the troubles of the Bolsheviks, the Allies imposed a tight naval blockade.

Opposite: Hitler and Mussolini in Rome in May 1938, following the firm establishment of the Rome-Berlin Axis and Hitler's Austrian *Anschluss*.

747

Russian poster published around 1920. It illustrates suffering during the grain famine; the caption reads: "HELP."

Leon Trotsky in France after his expulsion from the Soviet Union in 1929 by Stalin.

As the antirevolutionary White armies converged on the Soviet heart of Russia, the sphere of Bolshevik influence shrank to the region around Moscow and Petrograd. Yet the Bolsheviks were able to hold their own. The main reason for their survival was the disunity and dispersion of their opponents. Allied intervention was at best half-hearted. The White armies lacked popular support, and the fact that they enjoyed Allied help further weakened their cause. The White armies, furthermore, operated on widely separated fronts and under divided leadership. For all these various reasons, the White armies were no match for the newly created Red army. By the beginning of 1920, the Bolsheviks had defeated all the White forces except those in southern Russia under General Wrangel.

At this point a new danger arose. The Poles, who wanted to extend their frontier eastward beyond the boundary assigned to them at the Peace Conference, now joined forces with Wrangel in a concerted drive against the Red army. This was no longer a civil but a national war, and the Russian people rushed to the defense. In a brilliant counterattack, the Polish army was driven back to the gates of Warsaw. Here, in August 1920, the Red army was halted and thrown back. Under the subsequent Peace of Riga, Poland advanced its borders some 150 miles eastward into regions inhabited chiefly by Russians.

Lenin's "New Economic Policy"

The end of civil and foreign war did not relieve Russia's misery. Droughts and crop failures in 1920 and 1921 brought one of the worst famines in its history. The desperate situation called for drastic measures. In March 1921, therefore, Lenin initiated his "New Economic Policy," or NEP, which called for a radical departure from "War Communism" and a partial return to capitalist practices. Lenin's policy was justified by its results. In the seven years of NEP, agriculture and industry returned to their 1913 levels. As a result, most Russians were able to get at least the food and clothing they needed and to enjoy a slight rise in wages and standard of living.

The modification of Soviet policy at home had repercussions abroad. The failure of communist uprisings in central Europe had shown that world revolution was not as imminent as the communists had hoped. And with Russia's recovery depending heavily on foreign trade and capital, the Soviets were eager to resume normal relations with the rest of the world. In this aim the New Economic Policy proved helpful, since it was interpreted abroad as a sign that the Bolsheviks had learned the error of their ways. There was no reason, therefore, why foreign interests should not avail themselves of Russia's vast market and resources. Economic rapprochement between Russia and the West began in 1921. By 1925 diplomatic recognition had been granted the Soviet Union by all major powers except the United States.

But despite such hopeful beginnings, relations between Russia and the West never became very close. The major obstacle was the well-founded suspicion that the Soviets had not really abandoned their aim of world revolution.

Lenin did not live to see the results of his New Economic Policy. In 1922 he suffered a stroke, and in 1924, at the age of fifty-three, he died. He had been a remarkable man, with a great mind and superior talents as an agitator and organizer. With a rare mixture of fanaticism and realism, he had always known how to adjust his policy to changed circumstances. Without his leadership it is doubtful that Russia's revolution would have succeeded.

Stalin versus Trotsky

Lenin's death brought into the open a struggle for power that had been going on for some time. The two contenders were Trotsky and Stalin. In their aims they were not unlike: both looked forward to the ultimate victory of world communism. Where they differed was in their methods. Trotsky believed that Bolshevik Russia could not survive unless the rest of the world became communist too. Russia, therefore, should concentrate on fomenting revolutions elsewhere. Stalin, on the other hand, wanted to concentrate first on "socialism in one country"—and only then pursue the spread of communism elsewhere.

In the struggle between Trotsky and Stalin, their personalities and tactics turned out to be decisive. Both men had served the revolution well. But while Trotsky's importance as Commissar of War declined once victory had been won, Stalin's influence continued to grow. He won his most important position in 1922, when he became general secretary of the Communist Party. This gave him control over the entire party apparatus. Trotsky's doctrine of "permanent revolution," meanwhile, found little response in a nation exhausted by foreign and civil war. And while Trotsky's aloof manner offended his comrades, Stalin was careful to make friends with such "Old Bolshe-viks" as Leo Kamenev, the party's chief ideologist, and Grigori Zinoviev, the head of the Comintern.

In 1925 Stalin's policy of conciliation and cunning succeeded in forcing Trotsky to resign from the Ministry of War. Soon thereafter, Kamenev and Zinoviev quarreled with Stalin and joined Trotsky in opposition. But Stalin proved the stronger. Allying himself with two other Old Bolsheviks, Alexei Rykov and Niko-lai Bukharin, he had the "Trotskyites" expelled from the party. Trotsky was banished, first to Siberia and after 1929 abroad. He was assassinated in Mexico in 1940. In the meantime Stalin, in 1929, had ousted Rykov and Bukharin. With the last potential rivals out of the way, Stalin had emerged supreme.

COMMUNISM TRIUMPHANT 1928–41

The Soviet government was a highly complex system. It received its final form under the "Stalin Constitution" of 1936. The Soviet Union was a federation of states, whose number increased from four in 1922 to sixteen in 1941. Each state retained cultural autonomy but was under the strict political control of the Supreme Soviet in Moscow. That body consisted of two chambers, the Soviet of the Union and the Soviet of Nationalities. When they were not in session, their functions were exercised by a Presidium

Joseph Stalin (1879–1953) in 1919.

of some twenty-seven members. More important, however, was the Council of People's Commissars, appointed by the Supreme Soviet.

Actual power rested in the hands of only a few people. But a multiplicity of local, regional, and provincial soviets,

Lenin's Testament

1922–23

Comrade Stalin, having become general secretary, has concentrated enormous power in his hands, and I am not sure that he always knows how to use that power with sufficient caution. On the other hand, Comrade Trotsky . . . is distinguished not only by his exceptional ability—personally, he is, to be sure, the most able man in the present Central Committee—but also by his too far-reaching self-confidence and a disposition to be far too much attracted by the purely administrative side of affairs. . . . Stalin is too rude, and this fault, entirely supportable in relation to us Communists, becomes insupportable in the office of general secretary. Therefore I propose to the comrades to find a way to remove Stalin from that position and appoint to it another man who in all respects differs from Stalin only in superiority—namely, more patient, more loyal, more polite, and more attentive to comrades, less capricious, et cetera. This circumstance may seem an insignificant trifle, but I think that from the point of view of preventing a split and from the point of view of the relations between Stalin and Trotsky, which I discussed above, it is not a trifle, or it is such a trifle as may acquire a decisive significance.

N. Lenin, as quoted in David Shub, *Lenin* (New York: Doubleday, 1966), pp. 434–35.

A Soviet poster, "Knowledge breaks the chains of slavery," used in a campaign against illiteracy.

ЗНАНИЕ
РАЗОРВЕТ ЦЕПИ РАБСТВА·

Harvest time on a collective farm in the Ukraine in the 1920s. A propaganda newspaper, *The Collective Farmer*, is being printed on the back of the truck for distribution to the peasants.

together with the Supreme Soviet, gave at least an appearance of representative government. Other features of the Russian constitution did the same. Franchise was universal, and a bill of rights guaranteed all kinds of rights and freedoms.

But these rights had to be exercised "in the interests of the working people." And the agency that interpreted these interests was the Communist Party.

The Communist Party

The membership of the Russian Communist Party in 1918 was estimated at two hundred thousand. Ten years later, it had increased to over 1 million. But while it continued to grow, it never became a mass party. Its function was rather to serve as an elite, "the vanguard of the working class." Undeviating faith in Marxian doctrine as interpreted by the party's leaders, together with blind obedience to orders from above—these were the basic demands made of all party members. Party organization resembled the structure of the Soviet state, from "cells" at the bottom to the All-Union Party Congress at the top. The Congress selected the Central Committee as the chief policy-making organ, and the Central Committee in turn delegated power to the Politburo, the party's highest authority.

The obedience and self-abnegation demanded by party membership was highly rewarded by the Soviet state. All the leading positions in the bureaucracy went to party members, and they alone could hold political office. The upshot of this system was the growth of a new ruling caste of Communist functionaries. With the Communist Party as the dominant force in Soviet life, control of the party ensured domination of the state. Stalin owed his absolute power to his leading role in the Communist Party rather than to any governmental position. And beginning in 1928 he used this absolute power to carry the Communist revolution to its final triumph.

The Five-Year Plans

In order to survive in a hostile world of capitalist powers, Stalin felt the Soviet Union had to realize as rapidly as possible its inherent economic power. He hoped to achieve this goal in three Five-Year Plans. Their aim was the large-scale

ВИЗНА РЕДАКЦИЯ
ЖАШКІВЩИНИ РАЙГАЗЕТИ НА ЖНІВАХ КОЛГО

development of basic industries and the increase of agricultural production through collective farming.

The first Five-Year Plan was launched in 1928. Even if one discounts Communist propaganda, the achievements of Stalin's policy were impressive. Between 1928 and 1940 Russia's industrial output grew more than sevenfold. On the eve of the Second World War, the Soviet Union had become one of the world's leading industrial powers.

Collectivization was less successful. Agriculture in Russia was hampered by small holdings and antiquated methods. The solution was seen in large-scale farming and mechanization. But the conservative Russian peasant was opposed to any drastic changes and resorted to passive resistance. To break this opposition, the authorities used force. Executions and deportations, added to the severe famine of 1932 to 1933, caused the death of some 4 million people. But even strong-arm methods did not bring the desired results. While by 1940 most of Russia's land had been converted into collective farms, the problems of Russian agriculture had by no means been solved.

Stalin's Five-Year Plans completed the victory of communism in Russia. But that victory was won at the price of untold sacrifices on the part of the Russian people. Even so, the lot of the average Russian gradually improved. Free medical care and other social services, together with full employment, provided the Russian worker with security at the expense of freedom. At the same time, some of the changes introduced after the revolution were now abandoned. The family, at first deemphasized, now again became the basic unit of society. Education became less progressive but more universal. Religion, once persecuted, was at least tolerated. One of the most surprising reversals of the Stalinist era was

the renewed veneration of Russia's past. This new Russian nationalism turned for inspiration to the great events of Russian history, thus ignoring Marx's admonition that the proletariat had no fatherland.

The Sabotage and Treason Trials

Although communism under Stalin gained a firm hold in Russia, there were nevertheless frequent signs of internal unrest. Among the manifestations of such unrest were the so-called sabotage trials of 1928 to 1933 and the treason trials of 1934 to 1938. The sabotage trials

Collectivization

Hot dry winds had blighted some of the crops in 1932, and there had been a good deal of neglect in cultivation, as a result of apathy and discouragement. The huge weed crop choked out much of the grain, and in some cases a considerable part of the crop remained unharvested. Still it was the general testimony of the peasants that they could have pulled through if the local authorities had not swooped down with heavy requisitions. The last reserves of grain, which had been buried in the ground by the desperate peasants, were dug up and confiscated. A man named Sheboldaev, with a reputation in "liquidating" kulaks in the lower Volga district, was made President of the North Caucasus, where the passive resistance was doubtless stiffer than in other sections of the country, because a considerable part of the population consisted of Cossacks, who had enjoyed a higher standard of living than the mass of the peasants before the Revolution and who had mostly fought on the side of the Whites during the civil war. Under Sheboldaev's orders whole communities, such as Poltavskaya, in the Western Kuban, were deported *en masse* to the frozen regions of the north in the dead of winter. Other villages which did not fill out the grain quotas that were demanded from them were "blockaded," in the sense that no city products were allowed to reach them. Local officials who protested against the pitiless repression were deposed, arrested, in a few cases shot.

From W. H. Chamberlin, *Russia's Iron Age* (Boston: Little, Brown, 1934), pp. 85–86.

involved Russian and foreign engineers who were accused of sabotaging Russia's industrial efforts. These trials were staged probably to hide or excuse the many instances of waste and inefficiency revealed during the early years of the Five-Year Plans.

The same explanation did not hold for the treason trials. These amounted to a major purge of thousands of leading Soviet figures. The reason given for the Great Purge was an alleged plot by Hitler and Trotsky directed at Stalin. In January 1935 Zinoviev and Kamenev were accused of conspiracy, imprisoned, and condemned to death, together with fourteen other "Trotskyites," in 1936. Many others followed, including Rykov and Bukharin. In 1937 the purge spread to the Red army and throughout the entire Soviet hierarchy. Tens of thousands were arrested, executed, or exiled.

Foreign observers were bewildered by this spectacle of the revolution "devouring its children." The Great Purge was generally seen as a sign of Russian weakness. The significance of the fact that the Soviet state was strong enough to survive so tremendous a bloodletting was overlooked at the time. That there was opposition in Russia cannot be doubted. In spreading his net as wide as he did, some historians feel, Stalin destroyed any possible danger of a future conspiracy. Such drastic action may well have assured the survival of the Soviet Union in the Second World War.

Russia and the West

Prominent in Stalin's repressive policy was the fear of possible intervention from abroad. The memory of such intervention during the revolution was never forgotten. Outwardly, Russia's relations with the West improved during the 1930s. The Soviet Union was the only major power not affected by the Great Depression, and the Russian market offered commercial opportunities that existed nowhere else. The rising threats of Nazi Germany in Europe and of Japan in Asia established a further bond between the Soviet Union and the democracies. In 1933 the United States finally recognized the Soviet Union; the following year Russia was admitted to the League of Nations; and in 1935 the Soviets joined France and Czechoslovakia in military agreements against Germany. But despite this apparent rapprochement, Russia continued to distrust the West and the West continued to distrust Russia. This mutual suspicion had tragic consequences on the eve of the Second World War.

THE FASCIST REVOLUTION IN ITALY

The rise of fascism was in part a reaction to the real or imaginary threat of communism. But even without such a threat, conditions in Italy after the First World War made major changes imperative. The Italian people had been divided about intervention in the war. But once the nation joined the Allies, hopes for territorial rewards ran high. Such expectations were bitterly disappointed, and

---

Khrushchev on the Great Purge

Stalin originated the concept "enemy of the people." This term automatically rendered it unnecessary that the ideological errors of a man or men engaged in a controversy be proven; this term made possible the usage of the most cruel repression, violating all norms of revolutionary legality, against anyone who in any way disagreed with Stalin, against those who had bad reputations. This concept "enemy of the people" actually eliminated the possibility of any kind of ideological fight or the making of one's views known on this or that issue, even those of a practical character. In the main, and in actuality, the one proof of guilt used, against all norms of current legal science, was the "confession" of the accused himself, and, as subsequent probing proved, "confessions" were acquired through physical pressures against the accused. This led to glaring violations of revolutionary legality and to the fact that many entirely innocent persons, who in the past had defended the party line, became victims.

From *The Crimes of the Stalin Era: Special Report to the 20th Congress of the Communist Party of the Soviet Union* by Nikita S. Khrushchev, ed. by Boris I. Nicolaevsky (New York: The New Leader, 1956).

popular discontent was heightened by postwar economic problems. Riots and strikes, together with a sharp increase in the Socialist vote, made Italy's propertied elements fear that a communist revolution was at hand. Various democratic governments tried to cope with this hopeless situation but with little success. Parliamentary democracy had never worked well in Italy. Here, then, was a situation in which some able and unscrupulous demagogue could promise a solution to Italy's problems. The man who saw and seized this opportunity was Benito Mussolini.

Benito Mussolini

Mussolini was Italian fascism personified, and the movement would have been unthinkable without him. Born in 1883, son of a Socialist blacksmith, Mussolini himself had become a Socialist in his youth. In 1912 he had become editor of *Avanti*, Italy's leading Socialist newspaper. When war broke out, he was still a pacifist. But he soon changed and advocated Italian intervention on the Allied side. This was the first of many radical reversals in the life of this accomplished opportunist.

Mussolini's first *Fasci di Combattimento*, or "groups of combat," were formed in the spring of 1919. These groups were initially made up of discontented veterans. The number of these "Black Shirts" rapidly increased from a few hundred to many thousands. Their aims were mostly negative: they were against the monarchy, the Church, the Socialists, and the capitalists. In the elections of 1919 the Fascists failed to get a single seat. But two years later they won thirty-five. Capitalizing on the fears of the middle class by posing as the defender of law, order, and property, Mussolini was able to seize power in the fall of 1922.

Mussolini (in suit in center) with Fascist followers in 1922 during the famous "March on Rome."

The "March on Rome"

Mussolini's boast of having saved Italy from a communist revolution was false. That danger, if it ever existed, had run its course by 1922. Meanwhile, the Black Shirts were waging a virtual civil war against Socialists and labor unions, and Mussolini was mending his fences in preparation for his *coup*. First he changed his revolutionary movement into a regular political party. Then he proclaimed his loyalty to the monarchy and the Church. And finally he made certain that the army would not oppose him. When everything was ready, in October 1922, Mussolini mobilized his Black Shirts for a dramatic "March on Rome." But King Victor Emmanuel had been well prepared and gave way easily. On October 29, 1922, Mussolini was invited to form a new government.

The change from democratic to totalitarian rule in Italy took several years. Mussolini was given full emergency powers for only one year. He used these powers to tighten Fascist control. A new electoral law in 1923 provided that any party that gained a plurality of votes would automatically receive two-thirds of the parliamentary seats. Even so, opposition in the Chamber continued. In June 1924 one of Mussolini's most fearless critics, the Socialist leader Giacomo Matteotti, was kidnapped, "taken for a ride," and murdered. At first it seemed as though popular indignation would sweep the Fascists from power. Mussolini promised severe punishment of the guilty. But when he realized how little united his opponents were, he reversed his course. A new secret police, the OVRA, was founded, and in a wave of arrests, enemies of the state were brought before a special tribunal and sentenced to prison or exile. Non-Fascist members of the cabinet were dismissed, and Mussolini was given power to rule by decree. In 1926 all opposition parties were outlawed. The Matteotti affair, far from bringing about the fall of Fascism, served to cap its victory.

The Fascist State

Like communism, Italian fascism created its own system of government. Political power, in Mussolini's "corporative state," was vested in some thirteen "syndicates." These confederations, which included both workers and employers, were initially organized to regulate labor conditions. Strikes and lockouts were declared illegal, and the final word in labor disputes rested with the government. Beginning in 1928 this corporate system was made the basis of Italy's political organization. Under a new electoral law, the syndicates drew up a list of candidates for the Chamber of Deputies. Their final selection, however, rested with the Fascist Grand Council, a body of some twenty party leaders appointed by Mussolini. As under communism, the party thus wielded complete political control. Parliament, under this new system, lost most of its former functions. In 1938 even the outward forms of democracy disappeared when the Chamber of Deputies was replaced by a new Chamber of Fasces and Corporations. Since all its members were appointed, there was no longer any need for elections.

The Fascist Party, like its Communist counterpart, considered itself a ruling elite. Its membership in 1934 was about 1.5 million. Its leader, or *Duce*, was Mussolini. Fascist youth organizations took care of indoctrinating the young. The press, radio, and movies were under strict censorship, and every facet of intellectual and artistic life was made to fit the party mold. Only in his relations with the Church did Mussolini show leniency. One of his major achievements was the Lateran Treaty of 1929, which settled the long-standing feud between the Italian government and the papacy.

The major efforts of Mussolini's policy at home were aimed at improving Italy's economy. Reduction of government spending, suppression of strikes, and increased taxation brought some financial stability. Italy also shared in the

---

The Fascist Decalogue   1938

1. Remember that those who fell for the revolution and for the empire march at the head of your columns.
2. Your comrade is your brother. He lives with you, thinks with you, and is at your side in the battle.
3. Service to Italy can be rendered at all times, in all places, and by every means. It can be paid with toil and also with blood.
4. The enemy of Fascism is your enemy. Give him no quarter.
5. Discipline is the sunshine of armies. It prepares and illuminates the victory.
6. He who advances to the attack with decision has victory already in his grasp.
7. Conscious and complete obedience is the virtue of the Legionary.
8. There do not exist things important and things unimportant. There is only duty.
9. The Fascist revolution has depended in the past and still depends on the bayonets of its Legionaries.
10. Mussolini is always right.

From M. Oakeshott, *The Social and Political Doctrines of Contemporary Europe* (Cambridge: Cambridge University Press, 1949), pp. 180–81.

general economic recovery of the late 1920s. The Great Depression, however, undid these gains. Even though the Italian government by then had assumed far-reaching control over economic affairs, its policy was far less successful than Russia's planned economy under the Five-Year Plans. Not only was Mussolini less ruthless than Stalin, but Italy lacked the Soviet Union's vast natural resources. Beginning in 1935, furthermore, Mussolini embarked on a costly war, the burden of which was borne by the Italian people.

One sure way of diverting domestic discontent was through a strong and successful foreign policy. Mussolini first tried this remedy in 1923, with the bombardment of the Greek island of Corfu. But foreign protests dampened his enthusiasm, and for the next ten years, Mussolini was careful not to appear too aggressive. Italy concluded treaties of friendship with a number of countries, especially those that, like Austria and Hungary, shared its opposition to the peace treaties. In 1924 Yugoslavia, in return for concessions elsewhere, agreed to Italy's annexation of Fiume. Mussolini's restoration of domestic order, meanwhile, endeared him to foreign visitors; his opposition to communism made him appear the ally of anti-Communists everywhere; and his improved relations with the Church won him Catholic support. As a result, the new Italy and its leader commanded considerable respect abroad, at least until 1935. Only then did the world begin to realize the danger that fascism posed to world peace.

Fascist Ideology

When Mussolini founded his movement he had, by his own admission, "no specific doctrinal plan." In his formative years, Mussolini had come under the influence of a variety of writers from Machiavelli to Pareto, including Nietzsche, Sorel, and even Marx. Fascism also had its own philosophers, men like Giovanni Gentile and Alfredo Rocco. But one looks in vain for an exposition of fascist doctrine as clear as that provided for communism by Marx. Fascism was a dynamic movement, devoted to action rather than thought. Its motto was "Believe, Obey, Fight." "Believe" covered a wide range of romantic ideals, from the glories of Rome to modern nationalism. "Obey" meant subjection to the authority of the state and the *Duce*. To "fight" was the noblest aim of all. War alone, Mussolini said, "puts the stamp of nobility upon the people who have the courage to meet it." This belief in war for war's sake was the essence of Italian fascism.

THE RISE OF NATIONAL SOCIALISM IN GERMANY

Mussolini's success in Italy was observed with keen interest in Germany, where a movement akin to Italian fascism had been active since the early 1920s. Its leader was an obscure Austrian rabble-rouser, Adolf Hitler, the moving spirit behind the National Socialist German Workers' Party (NSDAP). The brown-shirted members of the party—or "Nazis," as their opponents called them—were similar to Mussolini's first Black Shirts. Most of them were disgruntled war veterans. Like their Italian counterparts, they hoped to seize power by a *coup d'état.* But their Munich *Putsch* in November 1923 had failed. For the next few years Adolf Hitler all but disappeared from the public eye.

Adolf Hitler and His Aims

The man who was soon to determine the fate of the world was not taken very seriously at first. Born in 1889, the son of an Austrian customs official, Hitler had gone into politics after the First World War, in which he had fought as a German soldier. Considering his background and haphazard education, Hitler's subsequent rise to power was remarkable. Circumstances played their part, but even they needed a master. The *Führer*, or leader, of the Nazi Party was neither physically nor intellectually impressive. Yet he had certain qualities and abilities that enabled him to subject to his power first a whole people and ultimately a whole continent. There can be no doubt that Germany's past and the characteristics of its people help to explain the rise of Hitler. But of equal if not greater significance were the evil genius of Hitler himself and the specific circumstances in the early 1930s that made his victory possible.

As far as Hitler's aims were concerned, National Socialism, in contrast to Italian fascism, had a detailed, though internally contradictory, program. Its twenty-five points offered something to everyone. They were, of course, never completely implemented, and provisions that might scare off prospective support-ers were explained away. Yet with its pan-German nationalism, its anti-Semitism, and its opposition to democracy, it clearly foreshadowed future Nazi policy. A still more important prediction of things to come was given in Hitler's autobiography, *Mein Kampf* (*My Battle*), which he began in 1924. Besides Judaism and Marxism, bolshevism now emerged as a major target, and Russia was singled out as the chief victim of future German expansion.

Hitler's Rise to Power

Before Germany had found time to recover from the results of a lost war and a runaway inflation, it was plunged once more into a major economic crisis—the Great Depression. With millions of unemployed, political extremism flourished. Between 1928 and 1932 Nazi delegates in the *Reichstag* rose from 12 to 230, and Communists from 54 to 89. This radicalization made orderly government impossible. Democracy, which never had taken firm hold in Germany, broke down. Economic and political chaos, the threat of communism, and constant nationalist agitation against the Peace Treaty—these were the elements that helped prepare the ground for the rise of dictatorship in Germany, just as they had done ten years earlier in Italy.

Hitler's assumption of power was through perfectly legal means. Like Mussolini, he was asked—on January 30, 1933—to form a coalition government. The men who helped Hitler gain power—the aged President von Hindenburg and his political advisers—felt confident that they would be able to use the Nazi movement to achieve their own ends: the establishment of a conservative and authoritarian regime. They failed to realize that Hitler was not a man to let himself be used.

To strengthen his position, Hitler first dissolved the *Reichstag*. Shortly before the new elections, the *Reichstag* building went up in flames, an event Hitler blamed on the Communists. But despite the intimidation of political opponents, only 44 percent of the German people voted National Socialist. As a next step, Hitler manipulated the *Reichstag* into

Adolf Hitler

Hitler cannot be confined within a simple formula. For my part I knew three facets of his personality, each corresponding to a like facet in his nature.

His first aspect was one of pallor; his jumbled complexion and vague globular eyes, lost in a dream, lent him an absent, faraway air, the troubled and troubling face of a medium or somnambulist.

The second aspect was animated, colored, swept away by passion. His nostrils would twitch, his eyes dart lightning; he was all violence, impatience of control, lust for domination, abomination of his antagonists, cynical boldness, with a fierce energy ready at no provocation to pull down the universe about his ears. Then his "storm and assault" face was the face of a lunatic.

Hitler's third aspect was that of a naïve, rustic man, dull, vulgar, easily amused, laughing boisterously as he slapped his thigh; a commonplace face without any distinguishing mark, a face like thousands of other faces spread over the face of the earth. . . .

These alternate states of excitement and depression, these fits mentioned by his familiars, ranged from the most devastating fury to the plaintive moanings of a wounded beast. Because of them, psychiatrists have considered him a "cyclothimic"; others see in him the typical paranoiac. This much is certain: he was no normal being. He was, rather, a morbid personality, a quasi-madman, a character out of the pages of Dostoevski, a man "possessed."

From André François-Poncet, *The Fateful Years: Memoirs of a French Ambassador in Berlin, 1931–1938*, trans. by J. LeClerq (New York: Harcourt Brace Jovanovich, 1949), pp. 289–91.

President von Hindenburg
in 1933. Visible directly
behind him is Adolf Hitler
next to a heavily decorated
Hermann Göring.

passing an Enabling Act that gave the government dictatorial powers for four years. These powers were then used to prohibit political parties. By July 1933 the National Socialists had become the only legal party. When President Hindenburg died in August 1934, Hitler combined the office of president with that of chancellor, assuming the title of *Führer und Reichskanzler*, leader and chancellor. The transition from democracy to dictatorship was complete.

NATIONAL SOCIALISM IN POWER

Other than assuming supreme power, Hitler did not introduce any formal constitutional changes. The *Reichstag* continued to meet, though infrequently, to endorse all measures put before it. There were no more elections, but occasionally the German people were asked in a plebiscite to support an act of the *Führer*'s. Needless to say, they always did so by a rousing majority. The organization of the civil service was maintained, though it was purged of Jews and political opponents. The legal system was overhauled, and traditional concepts of law were abandoned in favor of a new kind of justice that elevated the welfare of the people and the state above the rights of the individual. To ferret out enemies of the state, a secret police, the Gestapo, was given sweeping powers.

Nazism at Home

As was the case in other totalitarian states, the Nazi Party controlled every

Hitler speaks.

aspect of German life. Most of Hitler's lieutenants were rewarded with leading positions in the government. But some of his old comrades failed to get what they expected. And others felt that Hitler had broken his word by not carrying out the more radical promises of the early Nazi program. To forestall any "second revolution" on the part of these malcontents, Hitler, on June 30, 1934, instituted a major "Blood Purge." In a lightening move the *Führer* had several hundred of his possible opponents executed.

With the government and the party now under his firm control, there remained only one sphere in which the *Führer* did not wield complete authority. The armed forces had sworn personal allegiance to him after Hindenburg's death, and Hitler's renunciation of disarmament in March 1935 had further enhanced his standing with the army. But it was not until 1938, after a thoroughgoing purge of the army's top echelons, that the *Führer* felt he had a force on which he could fully rely. Henceforth Hitler himself was to wield personal command of all Germany's armed forces.

The same process of *Gleichschaltung*, or "coordination," that was carried out in government, party, and army, was extended to every other phase of German life. In many of his innovations, Hitler consciously imitated Mussolini. This was true not only of the symbols and ceremonies of the "Third Reich" but of many of its policies. Like Mussolini, Hitler tried to make his country's economy strong and self-sufficient. Public works, rearmament, and military conscription completely eradicated unemployment. In 1934 the *Führer* launched the first of two Four-Year Plans to prepare Germany's economy for war. To finance such costly ventures, huge funds were raised through increased taxation, special levies, and rigid control of prices and profits.

The main sufferer of this policy of "guns instead of butter" was the German worker. His wages were low and his hours long. A German "Labor Front" took the place of the former unions. Strikes were forbidden, and all labor relations were controlled by the state. The farmer fared somewhat better. He was given various kinds of subsidies and was protected against foreclosure. Food production increased, although Germany did not become self-sufficient. One of Hitler's aims was a large and healthy rural population. In Nazi mythology "blood and soil" were considered the source of a nation's strength. Artists and writers, regimented like everyone else, were called upon to glorify the "nobility of labor," and Nazi propaganda urged each and every German to place the welfare of the community before the good of the individual.

The majority of Germans readily complied with this appeal. Not that the German people were all ardent Nazis. The Nazi Party, like its counterparts in Russia and Italy, considered itself an elite, and its membership was restricted. The average German welcomed what he considered the "positive" features of the Nazi regime, and he secretly grumbled about the things he did not like. There was some active opposition—the thousands of prisoners in the concentration camps testified to that. But they were only a minority. Before the outbreak of the Second World War, Hitler's many admirers abroad praised him, like Mussolini, for the miraculous improvements he had brought about, and in particular for the firm stand he had taken against communism.

Anti-Semitism

One aspect of Nazi policy, however, stirred deep concern among observers abroad, and that was the persecution of the Jews. Anti-Semitism had been one of Hitler's earliest obsessions, and it was the aim that he pursued most persistently and ruthlessly to the bitter end. The first measures against Germany's Jews—1 percent of the population—were taken shortly after the Nazis came to power. In April 1933 all Jews were excluded from the civil service. Soon thereafter the Jews were excluded from universities, and lawyers and doctors were barred from practice. The next major step came with the "Nuremberg Laws" of 1935, which deprived Jews of their citizenship and forbade their marriage to non-Jews. As a result of this "cold pogrom," many Jews went into exile. But worse was yet to come. In November 1938 the assassination of a German diplomat in Paris by a young Polish Jew was made the occasion for a "spontaneous" demonstration against the Jews, in which many lost their properties and their lives.

The intensification of Jewish persecution in 1938 was merely another sign that Hitler was getting ready for war. Most of Germany's domestic policies since 1933 had been geared to that purpose, no matter how ardently the *Führer* might proclaim his peaceful intentions. Hitler's ultimate aim was a "New Order" for Europe, under which the German people would expand into the unlimited *Lebensraum* (living space) of the East and rule over the "inferior" Slavic peoples of that region. The unbounded ambition of Hitler's megalomania plunged the world into the most frightful war it had ever seen.

THE SPREAD OF AUTHORITARIANISM

One of the dangers of totalitarianism was its tendency to spread to nations that had been weakened by economic crises and political unrest. The rise of communism was generally considered the greater threat, and many a dictatorship of the right gained power against a real or imaginary communist menace. The Soviet Union tried its best, with the aid of the Comintern, to help Communist parties abroad. But its attempts at fomenting leftist plots in central Europe and in the Far East remained unsuccessful. Nowhere outside the Soviet Union did communism gain a decisive victory during the interwar period.

Authoritarianism in Europe

Efforts to set up rightist dictatorships, on the other hand, proved more successful. We have already seen the rise of strong men in most of the smaller nations of central Europe during the aftermath of the First World War. Similar regimes

Nazi picket during the boycott of Jewish-owned shops in 1933. The placard reads: "Germans! Strike back! Don't buy from Jews!"

arose in Spain and Portugal. In some countries—Yugoslavia, Albania, Bulgaria, Greece, and Rumania—kings turned into dictators. In others—Hungary, Poland, and Spain—power was wielded by an alliance of military and agrarian groups. In still others—Austria and Portugal—authority rested with parties supported by the Catholic Church. As in the case of Russia, Italy, and Germany, all these small nations lacked a strong democratic tradition. Their new regimes were authoritarian rather than totalitarian. In some instances Germany and Italy tried to aid the rise of such authoritarian regimes. In Austria a Nazi *Putsch* in July 1934 failed, and Nazi victory was postponed until the *Anschluss* four years later. In Spain, on the other hand, General Francisco Franco defeated the republican government with the help of Italy and Germany. Like communism, fascism had followers in the democracies as well. But with the exception of France, these native Fascist parties never posed a serious threat. It was only during the Second World War that the Fascist "Fifth Column" became a real danger.

Japanese Fascism

In one nation outside Europe—Japan—economic crisis, rabid nationalism, and the failure of democracy gave rise to a totalitarian regime. The impact of the Great Depression on that heavily industrialized nation had increased the smoldering discontent with the government's inefficiency at home and moderation abroad. The opposition in Japan was centered in the army, particularly among its junior officers. Their aims were expressed in the writings of a young radical, Ikki Kita, who opposed the big industrialists and their political allies and advocated an almost socialist program: restriction of private property, nationalization of industries, and virtual abolition of parliamentary government. With the empire thus revolutionized, he envisaged Japan taking the lead in a crusade against western imperialism and ultimately extending its influence throughout Asia.

The military clique itself had no clear program of action other than to gain control of the government. This they hoped to achieve through terror, mainly by assassinating moderate politicians. Early in 1936 these activities culminated in a mutiny and the murder of several high officials. The army high command took countermeasures and executed the ringleaders. But at the same time the government made a number of concessions that assured the domination of the military in national affairs. In November 1936 Japan joined Germany and Italy in a treaty against communism, the Anti-Comintern Pact. Fascism had thus founded its own "International."

Japanese fascism differed in several respects from its European counterparts. It was not a well-organized movement under a single leader but rather a small pressure group; and it did not attempt to change the existing system of government but rather to dominate it. Yet in its demands for the submission of the individual to the state, and in its veneration of tradition as embodied in the person of the emperor, Japan's militarism showed definite fascist traits. Most pronounced was the similarity of the foreign policies of the three Fascist powers. Each sought solution of domestic difficulties through foreign expansion; each based the right to such expansion on claims of inherent superiority; and each looked to a special sphere of influence beyond its frontiers.

In the case of Japan that sphere was the mainland of China.

THE MARCH OF FASCIST AGGRESSION, 1931–37

The series of international crises that culminated in the outbreak of the Second World War began as far back as 1931 in the Far East.

Japan Against China

Japan, for some time past, had been trying to gain control over Manchuria, China's border province in the northeast. In September 1931 the Japanese army, using a minor incident along the South Manchurian Railway as an excuse, invaded the region. Local Chinese forces proved no match for the aggressors, and within a few months most of Manchuria had come under Japanese domination. In 1932 the Japanese renamed their conquest Manchukuo and declared it a protectorate of Japan.

The Chinese government meanwhile protested to the League of Nations against this Japanese act of force. The League appointed a special commission of inquiry, and its report condemned Japan's aggression and proposed the establishment of an autonomous Manchuria. This was as far as the powers were prepared to go. Under the League Covenant they should have taken more drastic action. But China seemed far away and sanctions might prove costly at a time when the world was in the throes of depression.

Hitler Against Versailles

The moral of the Manchurian story was that if an aggressor acted quickly, nobody would stop him. This lesson was not lost on Adolf Hitler. In a series of dramatic moves between 1933 and 1936, he freed Germany from the most onerous restrictions of the Peace Treaty. In October 1933 the Germans withdrew from the Disarmament Conference and the League of Nations. In January 1935 the Saar region voted to return to Germany. Two months later Hitler denounced the disarmament clauses of the Versailles Treaty.

In order to forestall any opposition to his unilateral policy, Hitler stressed at every step Germany's peaceful intentions. In January 1934 he signed a non-aggression pact with Poland. In 1935 Hitler quieted Britain's fears of German rearmament by concluding an Anglo-German naval agreement. The British thereby acquiesced in the *Führer's* violation of the Treaty of Versailles and added to France's feeling of insecurity. It is hardly surprising, then, that France should have sought help elsewhere. In May 1935 it concluded an alliance with the Soviet Union. But this merely gave Hitler the pretext for his next major *coup.*

On March 7, 1936, Hitler ordered the German army to march into the demilitarized Rhineland. It was his most daring move to date. Had he been forced to back down at this crucial point, the future would doubtless have been far different. But again nothing happened. The French were afraid to act without the British. The British criticized Germany's act, but the general feeling was that the Germans merely did what any people would have done under the circumstances—namely, to establish mastery over their own territory. The implications of Hitler's action were overlooked. Should Germany want to move quickly, as it had done in 1914 and was to do again in 1940, there was no longer any protective zone to save the Lowlands from German invasion.

Mussolini Against Ethiopia

One reason why Hitler was able to get away with his daring move was that it coincided with a serious crisis elsewhere. On October 3, 1935, an Italian army had invaded Ethiopia, or Abyssinia, in northeastern Africa. This isolated and backward region had escaped the scramble for colonies among the European powers before 1914. Once before, in 1896, Italy had tried to invade Ethiopia but had been repulsed. This humiliation was never forgotten. Mussolini now hoped to

Former British Prime Minister David Lloyd George visiting Hitler at Berchtesgaden.

Hitler's Visitors

Lloyd George visited Hitler in September 1936, discussed world affairs, and came away convinced that Hitler was a reasonable man with acceptable aims and no desire whatsoever to plunge Europe into war. Conservatives, Liberals, and Socialists alike sought out the Führer, and were mesmerized by him. Even Arnold Toynbee was reported to have been won over at his interview to a belief in Hitler's genuine desire for peace in Europe "and close friendship with England." George Lansbury, a pacifist, and earlier leader of the Labour Party, was convinced after their personal encounter that Hitler "will *not* go to war unless pushed into it by others." Lord Allen of Hurwood told the *Daily Telegraph* on his return from Germany that "I watched him with the utmost vigilance throughout our lengthy conversation, and I am convinced he genuinely desires peace." Halifax recorded after his own visit to Berchtesgaden: "He struck me as very sincere, and as believing everything he said." But all Hitler did at these meetings was to repeat to each visitor the same dreary monologue about the insults of Versailles, the need for German unity on an ethnic basis, the evils of communism which he as a German could appreciate more than they could, the stubbornness of the Czechs, the pugnacity of the Poles, and the long-suffering innocence of the Germans. . . . But . . . when Lord Allen of Hurwood, with greater courage than most of his fellow-visitors, raised the issue of Jewish persecution, Hitler had nothing to say.

From Martin Gilbert, *The Roots of Appeasement* (London: Weidenfeld and Nicolson, 1966), pp. 164–65.

Ethiopian chiefs in the Ethiopian War (1935–36).

ETHIOPIA (ABYSSINIA)   1934

join Ethiopia with the existing Italian colonies of Eritrea and Somaliland into a sizable imperium. Italy's forces were too powerful for the antiquated forces of Emperor Haile Selassie. On May 9, 1936, Mussolini proclaimed the annexation of Ethiopia. Meanwhile the League of Nations had not been idle. After declaring Italy an aggressor, it had imposed economic sanctions. But such a program, to be effective, had to be airtight. With several major powers outside the League, it could not be. Still, it might have been possible to stop the Italians if oil had been included in the list of embargoes. But the fear that oil sanctions might lead to a general war made both France and England hesitate to take such a step. The French, who looked on Italy as a possible ally against Germany, did not wish to endanger their relations with Mussolini. The British feared that their navy would have to bear the major brunt of a possible conflict. Without the support of its two leading members, the League was powerless to act.

Once again the western powers, instead of supporting collective security, had preferred to buy peace by making concessions at someone else's expense. But such concessions merely whetted the appetites of the dictators. Prior to this time, relations between Hitler and Mussolini had not been very close. Hitler's designs on Austria worried Mussolini, who was himself interested in the Danube region. But with the conquest of Ethiopia, Italy's energies had found an outlet elsewhere, and Germany's friendly attitude during the conflict had paved the way for closer collaboration. On October 25, 1936, the two powers concluded a formal agreement to coordinate their foreign policies. This "Rome-Berlin Axis" was later joined by Japan.

War in Spain

The significance of the Axis became evident in connection with the Spanish Civil War. Spain had become a republic in 1931, but the traditionally pro-monarchist forces—clergy, army, and aristocracy—still wielded considerable power. The Republican regime had been unable to cope with the economic consequences of the Great Depression. In 1936, a "Popular Front" of Republicans, Socialists, Syndicalists, and Communists, had won a major election victory. But this Republican success merely hastened the inevitable clash between Nationalists and Republicans. In July 1936 army units in Spanish Morocco, led by General Francisco Franco, rebelled against the Republic. The Spanish Civil War had begun.

Had the Spaniards been left alone, the war would hardly have become the major tragedy it turned out to be. But Hitler and Mussolini favored Franco's Nationalists and sent men and materials to their aid. The Russians in turn gave support to the Republican, or Loyalist, side. But the Communists alone were incapable of matching the aid supplied by the Fascists. To assure the survival of the Republicans, the help of the democracies was needed.

England and France were no more willing to risk a general war over Spain than they had been over Manchuria or Ethiopia. Public opinion supported the Republicans, and foreign volunteers fought in the International Brigades on the Republican side. But the governments were more cautious. In September 1936 a Nonintervention Committee met in London. But the committee could not prevent German and Italian "volunteers" from fighting on Franco's side. In an effort at neutrality, President Roosevelt invoked the Neutrality Act of 1935, prohibiting the export of arms and munitions to both sides. But this move hurt mainly the Loyalists, since Franco continued to receive supplies from Germany and Italy.

The Spanish Civil War lasted for almost three years and caused more than two hundred thousand deaths. By the time the last Republican forces surrendered in March 1939, events in Spain had long been overshadowed by more important developments elsewhere. But Hitler's policy of bloodless expansion in central Europe was doubtless aided by the diversion provided by the slow death of democracy in Spain.

THE ROAD TO WAR

Except for the war in Spain, the international situation at the beginning of 1937

Barcelona after bombardment by Franco's forces (July 1936).

Emblem of the International Brigades, which served in the Republican army in the Spanish Civil War.

seemed hopeful. But this impression was mistaken. The preceding years had been crucial for the new German *Wehrmacht*, when determined outside resistance might still have put a stop to Hitler's plans. From now on the balance of military power began to turn more and more in Germany's favor. In June 1937 Hitler issued the first directive to prepare for a future war. Five months later he met with his top advisers to present an outline of his strategy. First Germany would seek control over Austria and Czechoslovakia. Then it would be ready to pursue its major aim of eastward expansion to win the living space that the German people required.

War in the Far East

While Hitler was making his plans in Europe, warfare had again broken out in the Far East. In July 1937 a minor incident near Peking touched off an undeclared war between China and Japan that lasted until 1945. By the end of 1938 the Japanese were in control of most of northern China. Farther south, Japan had seized the city of Canton and surrounding territory. In March 1938 the Japanese set up a "Reformed Government of the Republic of China" at Nanking.

The government of Chiang Kai-shek, meanwhile, had taken refuge in Szechwan province. The Chinese armies, while superior in numbers, were woefully short of equipment. To fight the invaders more effectively, Chiang Kai-shek and the Chinese Communists agreed to bury their differences. A "scorched earth" policy and guerrilla warfare on the part of the Chinese kept the Japanese from consolidating their gains. But despite the determined resistance of the Chinese, their ultimate survival depended on outside aid.

Chinese protests to the League of Nations brought little more than verbal condemnation of Japanese aggression. The French feared that resistance to

Japanese troops breaking through the Great Wall in northern China (1937).

Japan might lead to a Japanese attack on French Indochina. And Britain hoped that by appeasing Japan it might keep its commercial interests in China. The United States, too, was careful at first not to antagonize Japan. Only when it became clear that the "Open Door" policy was being threatened did the United States begin to aid the Chinese. The Soviet Union was the only major power that supported the Chinese from the start.

The Austrian Anschluss

Beginning in the spring of 1938, attention was diverted from Asia to Europe. Hitler's first victim was Austria. Union with Austria, or *Anschluss*, had always been a major Nazi aim. The fail-

ure of a Nazi *Putsch* in 1934 did not end the Nazi conspiracy. In January 1938 the Austrian government uncovered another Nazi plot. To remove the tension resulting from this latest incident, Austria's chancellor, Kurt von Schuschnigg, went to see Hitler at Berchtesgaden in February. But instead he was presented with a set of demands that would have made Austria a virtual German protectorate. Refusal to accept, Hitler made clear, would lead to a German invasion of Austria.

Faced with this ultimatum, Schuschnigg in March decided to make one final attempt to save his country by appealing to the Austrian people in a plebiscite. Hitler's reaction was swift. Once more threatening invasion, he forced Schuschnigg to resign. On March 11, an Austrian Nazi, Artur Seyss-Inquart, be-

Hitler's victory parade through Vienna, Austria (March 14, 1938).

NORWAY

SWEDEN

FINLAND

Leningrad
PURGES, 1934-37

NORTH SEA

ESTONIA

LATVIA

Moscow

DENMARK

BALTIC SEA

MEMEL
1939

LITHUANIA

NAZI-SOVIET TREATY, 1939

GREAT BRITAIN

Danzig
1939

EAST PRUSSIA

POLISH CORRIDOR

U. S. S. R.

London

ANGLO-GERMAN NAVAL AGREEMENT, 1935

Berlin

GERMAN-POLISH TREATY OF Warsaw

NETH.

BURNING OF REICHSTAG, 1933

FRIENDSHIP AND NONAGGRESSION, 1934

POLAND

BELGIUM

RHINELAND

Godesberg

1936

GERMANY

1938

SUDETENLAND

Prague

1939

1939

LUXEMBOURG

NUREMBERG LAWS, 1935

CZECHOSLOVAKIA

SAAR PLEBISCITE, 1935

1938

MUNICH CONFERENCE, 1938

Berchtesgaden

Vienna

FRANCE

SWITZ.

NAZI PUTSCH, 1934

AUSTRIA

HUNGARY

RUMANIA

ROME-BERLIN AXIS, 1936

YUGOSLAVIA

BLACK SEA

SPANISH CIVIL WAR, 1936-39

BULGARIA

CORSICA

I T A L Y

1939

ALBANIA

TURKEY

BALEARIC IS.

SARDINIA

Rome

GREECE

INVASION OF ETHIOPIA, 1935

Germany in 1930

German acquisitions, 1930-39

German allies in 1939

MILES
0   200

SICILY

CRETE

MEDITERRANEAN   SEA

came chancellor; on March 12, German troops crossed the Austrian frontier; and on March 13, Austria was incorporated into the Greater German Reich.

The ultimate success of this latest act of aggression again depended on the attitude of the other powers. As on earlier occasions, there were loud protests but no action. The French were in the midst

of one of their innumerable governmental crises and looked to the British to take the lead. But Britain, while deploring Hitler's methods, saw nothing wrong with an Austro-German *Anschluss*, so long as both peoples wanted it. And Italy, although long a champion of Austrian independence, was by now in the German camp. There was also the hope that Hitler would be satisfied, now that his dearest wish had been fulfilled. The *Führer* did his best to confirm that hope by making his usual promises of peaceful intentions. The Soviet Union came forth with suggestions for a collective stand, warning that Czechoslovakia was next on Hitler's list; but the western powers refused.

The Conquest of Czechoslovakia

The pretext for Germany's intervention in Czechoslovakia was the German minority in the Czech border regions. The 3 million Sudeten Germans had long been a source of trouble to the Czech government, especially since Hitler's rise to power. Beginning in 1936 their leader, Konrad Henlein, had begun to collaborate secretly with the Nazis; and as Germany's power increased, the demands of the Sudeten Germans became louder. In April 1938, after the fall of Austria, Henlein demanded complete autonomy for the Sudetenland, and Nazi propaganda quickly seconded this demand. The climax of Germany's campaign against the Czech government of President Eduard Beneš came with Hitler's address to the annual party congress at Nuremberg on September 12, 1938, in which he threatened German intervention on behalf of the Sudeten Germans.

The German army had been spending the summer of 1938 preparing for the invasion of Czechoslovakia. The French and British, meanwhile, had been trying desperately to effect a compromise on the Sudenten problem. But the Czechs proved adamant, trusting in their own military strength and that of their French and Russian allies. When Hitler's speech intensified riots in the Sudetenland, the Czech government proclaimed martial law. War, it seemed, was imminent. It was narrowly averted by the action of Britain's prime minister, Neville Chamberlain, who now initiated a series of last-minute conferences with Hitler that sealed the fate of Czechoslovakia.

At their first meeting in Berchtesgaden, Hitler seemed to be satisfied with "self-determination" for the Sudeten region. But when Chamberlain returned to Germany a week later for a second meeting, at Godesberg, the *Führer* upped his demands. He now asked for the immediate surrender of the Sudetenland. This the Czechs declared unacceptable. But their protests were ignored at the final meeting in Munich on September 29–30. Hitler and Chamberlain, together with Mussolini and French Premier Édouard Daladier, now agreed on the Godesberg terms. In a separate agree-

Chamberlain on His Trip to Munich

The events of the next 48 hours entailed terrific physical and mental exertions. I was up the night before till after 2 A.M. preparing my speech. Then came the early rising and the scenes at the aerodrome, and the long flight to Munich. The rest of that day, till after 2 o'clock next morning, was one prolonged nightmare, and I have only gradually been able since then to sort out my impressions.

Hitler's appearance and manner when I saw him appeared to show that the storm signals were up, though he gave me the double handshake that he reserves for specially friendly demonstration. Yet these appearances were deceptive. His opening sentences, when we gathered round for our conference, were so moderate and reasonable, that I felt instant relief.

Mussolini's attitude all through was extremely quiet and reserved. He seemed to be cowed by Hitler, but undoubtedly he was most anxious for a peaceful settlement. . . . His manner to me was more than friendly; he listened with the utmost attention to all I said, and expressed the strong hope that I would visit him early in Italy, where I should receive a very warm welcome. . . .

I asked Hitler about 1 in the morning, while we were waiting for the draftsmen, whether he would care to see me for another talk. He jumped at the idea, and asked me to come to his private flat . . . I had a very friendly and pleasant talk. . . . At the end I pulled out the declaration, which I had prepared beforehand, and asked if he would sign it. As the interpreter translated the words into German, Hitler frequently ejaculated "*ja, ja,*" and at the end he said "yes, I will certainly sign it; when shall we do it?" I said "now," and we went at once to the writing-table, and put our signatures to the two copies which I had brought with me.

From a letter from Neville Chamberlain to his sisters, October 2, 1938, as quoted in Sir Keith Feiling, *The Life of Neville Chamberlain* (London: Macmillan, 1946), pp. 375–77.

ment, Great Britain and Germany promised to renounce war in settling their national differences. "Peace for our time," as Chamberlain hopefully put it, seemed to have been assured.

The first reaction, when the Munich decisions were announced, was one of relief that war had been averted. But it was not long before criticism started. Deprived of its fortifications and most of its heavy industries, which were located in the Sudetenland, Czechoslovakia was now at Germany's mercy. The Russians, to be sure, had insisted that they would stand by their treaty obligations. But the strength of the Red army was not rated very high, and there was always the fear that the Soviet Union might try to embroil the West in a war with Hitler. The French, in betraying their Czech ally, bore a major share of the responsibility for Czechoslovakia's defeat. But how could they have acted without the support of Great Britain? And the British were neither morally nor materially ready for war. Appeasement, ever since

Munich, has been an ugly word. But the purchase of peace at the expense of smaller or weaker nations had been going on for some time. The basic cause of the Czech disaster was the failure of the democracies all through the 1930's to understand Hitler's true aims. Even at Munich these aims were not yet fully understood. It took one more of Hitler's moves to bring home the futility of appeasement.

On the eve of Munich Hitler had promised that the Sudetenland would be his last territorial claim. But even before the year was out he issued directives for the final liquidation of Czechoslovakia. On March 15, 1939, German army units crossed the Czech border, and the next day Hitler proclaimed a German protectorate over the Czech regions of Bohemia and Moravia. Slovakia was to become an "independent" German satellite.

This final dismemberment of Czechoslovakia was an important turning point. Up to then the desire to unite all German-speaking peoples had seemed

Prime Minister Neville Chamberlain signs the Munich Pact (September 30, 1938).

Sullen Czechs watch German troops enter Prague (March 15, 1939).

to be the motive of Hitler's expansionist policy. Now suddenly the world recognized his real aim: to gain living space and to subjugate foreign peoples. It was this latest act of Hitler's that brought about a decisive change in the attitude of the western democracies. On March 31, 1939, Great Britain promised the Poles all possible support in defending their independence. And in April both England and France gave similar assurances to Rumania and Greece. What the western powers did not know was that on April 3, 1939, a secret directive had been issued to the German army ordering preparations for war against Poland any time after September 1, 1939.

The Eve of the Second World War

That Hitler should turn against Poland next was hardly surprising. Of all the territorial provisions of Versailles, the loss of the Polish corridor and the city of Danzig had been the most resented by Germany.

The world had still not recovered from the dismemberment of Czechoslovakia when the Fascist powers made two more quick moves. On March 21, 1939, Lithuania, in compliance with Hitler's demands, returned to Germany the small territory of Memel; and on April 8, 1939, Mussolini sent his troops to occupy the Kingdom of Albania, which since 1927 had been a virtual Italian protectorate. A month later, Germany and Italy converted their Axis into a full-fledged alliance, the "Pact of Steel."

In late May 1939 Hitler informed his generals that war with Poland was inevitable. On August 22 he held another of his briefing conferences. The *Führer* expressed the hope that France and Britain might decide not to fight. Not that he feared their intervention. The western powers, he said, were completely unprepared. As a final surprise, Hitler then told his generals about the Nazi-Soviet Pact, being signed in Moscow at that moment. He further declared "A few weeks from now I shall, on the common German-Russian border, shake hands with Stalin and carry out with him a redistribution of the world."

The Nazi-Soviet Pact

The role of Russia in a future war had concerned Germany and the western powers for some time. Since April 1939 Russia had been negotiating with both sides. But France and Britain were unable to overcome their fundamental distrust of the Russians; and they had little faith in the Red army, especially after the recent purges. Still more significant, the western powers were unwilling to concede to Russia the predominance in eastern Europe that Stalin demanded. The Germans, on the other hand, had no hesitation in making concessions in the East if it meant gaining a free hand in the West. The Russo-German talks did not enter their decisive phase until mid-August. From then on events moved swiftly. On August 23 the two powers signed a nonaggression pact. Its most weighty part was a secret protocol that divided eastern and southeastern Europe into respective spheres of Russian and German influence.

The advantages of the Russian pact for Germany were obvious: it saved the *Wehrmacht*, once Poland had been disposed of, from having to fight on two fronts. Russia's motives were less clear. According to Stalin, the Soviet Union had long been afraid that the West was trying to turn Nazi aggression against communism. But it has also been argued that Stalin, by supporting Hitler, hoped to embroil Germany in a war with the western powers, allowing Russia to emerge as the decisive factor in the international balance of power.

With the signing of the Nazi-Soviet pact, the stage was set for the outbreak of war. It was still not clear whether the French and British would keep their word and come to Poland's aid. Negotiations for a last-minute compromise continued, and Hitler at one point postponed the start of hostilities to allow the West one more try at appeasement. But the lessons of the last few years had at long last been learned. On September 3, 1939, two days after the German invasion of Poland, England and France declared war on Germany. The Second World War had begun.

Reading of the proclamation of war at the Royal Exchange in London.

Suggestions for Further Reading

Note: Asterisk denotes a book available in paperback edition.

General H. Arendt, *The Origins of Totalitarianism** (1951), and E. Fromm, *Escape from Freedom** (1941), are seminal works on the subject of totalitarianism. C. J. Friedrich and Z. K. Brzezinski, *Totalitarian Dictatorship and Autocracy,* rev. ed. (1965), provides a general theory of the phenomenon. See also C. W. Cassinelli, *Total Revolution: A Comparative Study of Germany under Hitler, the Soviet Union under Stalin, and China under Mao* (1976). The development of communist thought from Marx to Stalin is surveyed in R. N. Carew-Hunt, *The Theory and Practice of Communism** (1963), and B. D. Wolfe, *Marxism: One Hundred Years in the Life of a Doctrine* (1965). Other important books on communism are J. Braunthal, *History of the International,* 2 vols. (1967); R. V. Daniels, *The Nature of Communism** (1962); and M. M. Drachkovitch, ed., *Marxism in the Modern World* (1965). Life under communism is described from personal experience by W. Leonhard, *Child of the Revolution** (1967), and C. Milosz, *The Captive Mind** (1953). M. Fainsod, *Smolensk under Soviet Rule** (1963), is based on unique Russian sources. G. Orwell, *1984** (1949), presents a perceptive fictionalized account. The Fascist brand of totalitarianism is dealt with historically in F. L. Carsten, *The Rise of Fascism** (1967), and ideologically in E. Nolte, *Three Faces of Fascism** (1966). See also H. A. Turner, ed., *Reappraisals of Fascism** (1975), and R. De Felice, *The Interpretations of Fascism* (1977).

Communist Russia E. H. Carr, *The Russian Revolution: From Lenin to Stalin* (1979), is a synopsis of the distinguished scholar's ten-volume *A History of Soviet Russia* (1950–75). Another good brief history is D. W. Treadgold, *Twentieth Century Russia* (1959). F. B. Randall, *Stalin's Russia: An Historical Reconsideration* (1965), is factual and objective. H. Schwartz, *Russia's Soviet Economy* (1954), is a good introduction. S. Swianiewicz, *Forced Labor and Economic Development: An Enquiry into the Experience of Soviet Industrialization* (1965), is more specialized. M. Fainsod, *How Russia Is Ruled* (1963), discusses the constitution and functioning of Soviet government. L. B. Schapiro, *The Communist Party of the Soviet Union** (1960), is the standard work on the subject. Soviet foreign policy before the Second World War is treated in L. Fischer's two books, *The Soviets in World Affairs** (1951) and *Russia's Road from Peace to War* (1969), as well as in M. Beloff, *The Foreign Policy of Soviet Russia, 1929–1941,* 2 vols. (1947–49). The best and most recent general account is A. B. Ulam, *Expansion and Coexistence: The History of Soviet Foreign Policy, 1917–1973** (1974). The following are good monographs on various aspects of Soviet history and society: J. Erickson, *The Soviet High Command* (1962); L. D. Gerson, *The Secret Police in Lenin's Russia* (1976); R. Conquest, *The Great Terror: Stalin's Purge of the Thirties* (1968); C. Brandt, *Stalin's Failure in China, 1924–1927* (1958); D. J. Dallin and B. I. Nicolaevsky, *Forced Labor in the Soviet Union* (1947); L. B. Schapiro, *The Origins of the Communist Autocracy** (1955); and L. Kochan, ed., *The Jews in Soviet Russia since 1917* (1970). The best biographies of the Communist leaders are L. Fischer, *Lenin* (1965), and I. Deutscher, *Trotsky,* 3 vols. (1954–65) and *Stalin: A Political Biography** (1949). See also R. Wistrich, *Trotsky: Fate of a Revolutionary* (1979), and R. Hingley, *Joseph Stalin: Man and Legend* (1974).

Fascist Italy E. Wiskemann, *Fascism in Italy: Its Development and Influence** (1969), is a good brief introduction. The early years of Fascist rule are discussed in A. Rossi, *The Rise of Italian Fascism, 1918–1922* (1938). G. Salvemini, *Under the Axe of Fascism* (1936) and *Prelude to World War II* (1954), are authoritative studies of Italian domestic and foreign policy by a leading anti-Fascist Italian historian. Other good accounts are H. Finer, *Mussolini's Italy** (1935); E. R. Tannenbaum, *The Fascist Experience: Italian Society and Culture, 1922–1945* (1972); and C. Seton-Watson, *Italy from Liberalism to Fascism* (1967). The structure of Mussolini's government is treated in H. Steiner, *Government in Fascist Italy* (1938), and W. Ebenstein, *Fascist Italy* (1939). On foreign policy, see A. Cassels, *Mussolini's Early Diplomacy* (1970), and D. M. Smith, *Mussolini's Roman Empire* (1976). Biographies of Mussolini are I. Kirkpatrick, *Mussolini: Study of a Demagogue* (1964), and D. M. Smith, *Mussolini* (1982). The resistance to Mussolini is dealt with in C. F. Delzell, *Mussolini's Enemies* (1961). M. Michaelis, *Mussolini and the Jews* (1978), deals judiciously with a controversial subject.

Nazi Germany The best general work on the subject is K. D. Bracher, *The German Dictatorship: The Origins, Structure, and Effects of National Socialism** (1970). Among the many books dealing with the roots of nazism, G. L. Mosse, *The Crisis of German Ideology: Intellectual Origins of the Third Reich** (1964); F. Stern, *The Politics of Cultural Despair** (1961); and H. Rauschning, *The Revolution of Nihilism* (1939), are the most revealing. W. L. Shirer, *The Rise and Fall of the Third Reich** (1960), is by a noted journalist. For a briefer and more balanced account, see H. Mau and H. Krausnick, *German History, 1933–1945** (1953). The best biography of Hitler is still A. Bullock, *Hitler: A Study in Tyranny** (1964). For a more recent treatment, see J. C. Fest, *Hitler** (1974). On Hitler's early years, B. F. Smith, *Adolph Hitler: His Family, Childhood and Youth** (1967), sheds much new light. Hitler's aims are stated in A. Hitler, *Mein Kampf** (1939), and more openly in *Hitler's Secret Conversations, 1941–1944* (1953). See also *Hitler's Secret Book** (1961). The early events of Nazi Germany are examined in W. S. Allen, *The Nazi Seizure of Power** (1965). P. Ayçoberry, *The Nazi Question: An Essay on the Interpretations of National Socialism, 1922–1975* (1981), is brilliant historiography.

The domestic affairs of Germany under Hitler are treated in R. Grunberger, *A Social History of the Third Reich* (1971), and its government is discussed in W. Ebenstein, *The Nazi State* (1943). The fateful role of the army in German politics before and during the Hitler years is described in J. W. Wheeler-Bennett, *The Nemesis of Power: The German Army in Politics, 1918–1945** (1953), and R. J. O'Neill, *The German Army and the Nazi Party* (1966). The best books on the SS are H. Höhne, *The Order of the Death's Head* (1969), and H. Buchheim et al., *Anatomy of the SS-State* (1968). On the treatment of the Jews, see G. Reitlinger, *The Final Solution** (1953), and R. Hilberg, *The Destruction of the European Jews* (1961). E. Kogon, *The Theory and Practice of Hell** (1958), is the best book on the concentration camps. Other important works on various phases of Nazi rule are: D. Schoenbaum, *Hitler's Social Revolution, 1933–1939** (1967); E. K. Bramsted, *Goebbels and National Socialist Propaganda, 1925–1945* (1965); G. Lewy, *The Catholic Church and Nazi Germany** (1964); P. H. Merkl, *Political Violence Under the Swastika** (1975); J. Stephenson, *The Nazi Organization of Women* (1981); B. A. Carroll, *Design for Total War: Arms and Economics in the Third Reich* (1968); and A. Schweitzer, *Big Business in the Third Reich* (1964). J. C. Fest, *The Face of the Third Reich** (1969), presents vivid portraits of some of Hitler's lieutenants. On the various resistance efforts against Hitler, see P. Hoffmann, *The History of the German Resistance, 1933–1945* (1976), and G. van Roon, *German Resistance to Hitler* (1971). The final act of the Nazi nightmare is dramatically told in H. R. Trevor-Roper, *The Last Days of Hitler** (1947).

The Road to War   A. J. P. Taylor, *The Origins of the Second World War** (1961), is stimulating but totally unreliable. G. Weinberg, *The Foreign Policy of Hitler's Germany: Diplomatic Revolution in Europe, 1933–1936* (1971), and *Starting World War II, 1937–1939* (1980), are dull but reliable. K. Hildebrand, *The Foreign Policy of the Third Reich** (1973), is brief, but excellent. See also D. E. Kaiser, *Economic Diplomacy and the Origins of the Second World War: Germany, Britain, France, and Eastern Europe, 1930–1939** (1980). Several books discuss Germany's relations with individual countries during the Nazi era: M. Toscano, *The Origins of the Pact of Steel* (1967); E. Wiskemann, *Czechs and Germans* (1938); C. A. Micaud, *The French Right and Nazi Germany, 1933–1939* (1943); J. E. McSherry, *Stalin, Hitler, and Europe* (1968); and E. Presseisen, *Germany and Japan* (1958). Relations between military planning and foreign policy are the subject of E. M. Robertson, *Hitler's Pre-War Policy and Military Plans, 1933–1939* (1963), and D. C. Watt, *Too Serious a Business: European Armed Forces and the Approach to the Second World War* (1975). The following works dealing with British foreign policy in the 1930s are all severely critical of appeasement: M. Gilbert, *The Roots of Appeasement** (1966); M. George, *The Hollow Men: An Examination of British Foreign Policy between the Years 1933 and 1939* (1967); and W. R. Rock, *Appeasement on Trial: British Foreign Policy and Its Critics* (1966). On French foreign policy, see A. Adamthwaite, *France and the Coming of the Second World War* (1977), and R. J. Young, *In Command of France: French Foreign Policy and Military Planning, 1933–1940* (1978). American diplomacy in the late 1930s is analyzed in detail by W. L. Langer and S. E. Gleason, *The Challenge to Isolation, 1937–1940** (1952). See also C. A. Macdonald *The United States, Britain, and Appeasement, 1936–1939* (1981). On United States–German relations, see A. A. Offner, *American Appeasement: United States Foreign Policy and Germany** (1969), and J. V. Compton, *The Swastika and the Eagle: Hitler, the United States, and the Origins of World War II* (1967). The major crises fomented by Hitler are discussed in J. Gehl, *Austria, Germany, and the Anschluss, 1931–1938* (1963); J. W. Wheeler-Bennett, *Munich** (1964); and H. Noguères, *Munich: "Peace for Our Time"* (1965). The best books on the Civil War in Spain are G. Jackson, *The Spanish Republic and the Civil War, 1931–1939* (1965), and H. Thomas, *The Spanish Civil War** (1961). The diplomacy of the Ethiopian War, is covered in G. W. Baer, *The Coming of the Italian-Ethiopian War* (1967), and A. Del Boca, *The Ethiopian War, 1935–1941* (1969). See also J. Coverdale, *Mussolini and Franco: Italian Intervention in the Spanish Civil War* (1975). The best brief accounts of the events preceding the outbreak of the Second World War are C. Thorne, *The Approach of War, 1938–1939** (1967), and R. Douglas, *The Advent of War, 1939–1940* (1978).

33 The Second World War and Its Aftermath 1939–1950

The Second World War, in its origins and events, was quite different from the First. While the question of responsibility for the First World War has caused much controversy, there can be no doubt that the major responsibility for the Second rests heavily on one country, Germany, and on one man, Adolf Hitler. Still, it might be argued that Hitler would never have been able to go to war if the western Allies had stopped him in time. To that extent England and France, too, may bear some responsibility. As for the Soviet Union, its pact with Hitler made the war well-nigh inevitable.

The war of 1939, far more than the war of 1914, was a world war. Japan had been fighting China intermittently for more than eight years, and before long the conflict was to spread to other parts of Asia and to Africa. The earlier war had been largely a war of position. The Second World War was one of almost constant movement. New weapons were chiefly responsible for the greater speed and mobility of the war. The airplane in particular revolutionized warfare on land and sea. Its use against civilian targets, furthermore, eradicated all differences between the fighting and the home fronts. The Second World War was a truly total war.

THE AXIS TRIUMPHANT 1939–42

Since he had prepared his war for some time, Hitler at first enjoyed all the advantages of the aggressor. He expected the war to be short. Even though England and France had entered the war, he did not believe they would fight.

Blitzkrieg in Poland

Germany's forces crossed the Polish border on September 1, 1939. Everything went according to plan. The Poles were no match for the crack Nazi troops, and the fighting lasted less than four weeks. The Germans obviously had lost none of their skill at making war.

The world was stunned by Germany's rapid success. The Russians were hardly ready to avail themselves of the spoils that had fallen to them as a result of their recent deal with Hitler. At the end of September 1939 a treaty of partition was signed between the Reich and the Soviet Union. Under its provisions Poland was wiped off the map, Germany taking the western and Russia the eastern half. This operation completed, Germany and Russia announced that there was no longer any reason for Britain and France to continue the war.

War at Sea

This appeal for ending the war was directed primarily at France. The French were neither enthusiastic nor confident about the war. The French army had dutifully occupied the fortified Maginot Line along France's eastern frontier, but there it sat and waited in the "phony war." The British for their part expected a German air attack at any minute. But so long as Hitler thought that Chamberlain might be made to give up the fight, the German air force remained grounded. It was at sea that England felt the first effects of the war. On September 17 the aircraft carrier *Courageous* was torpedoed off Ireland, and in mid-October a German submarine sank the battleship *Royal Oak.* It was not until December 1939 that the British scored their first naval victory, against the German battleship *Admiral Graf Spee* off the coast of South America.

The Russo-Finnish War

The next aggressive act in Europe did not come, as was expected, in the West, but in the East. And this time it was the Russians who took the initiative. No sooner had the Soviets shared in the Polish loot than they pressured the small republics of Estonia, Latvia, and Lithuania to sign "mutual assistance" pacts that allowed the Red army to occupy strategic bases. In June 1940, these states officially became members of the Soviet Union. The only country to resist Russian pressure was Finland. So on November 30, 1939, Russia renounced a seven-year nonaggression pact with Finland and crossed the Finnish border. The Finns were finally beaten, in March 1940; but

Opposite: Four-engine United States Air Force heavy bombers overpower the single-engine German fighter planes.

in the meantime the Russian armies suffered serious losses and showed themselves woefully unprepared. In protest against Russia's attack on Finland, the League of Nations expelled the Soviet Union from membership. But attention was soon diverted away from Finland as the Germans embarked on a second round of aggression against the small nations on their periphery.

Germany Turns North and West

Norway and the Low Countries were of great strategic importance. Possession of Norway would give German submarines a wider radius of action. The Low Countries, besides providing a protective glacis for Germany's industrial heart, the Ruhr, would offer the necessary base for operations against France and England. Reports that Britain might occupy Norway made Hitler decide to move. Operations began on April 9, 1940. Simultaneously with their invasion of Norway, the Germans occupied Denmark. The main fighting in Norway took only a few days. Some pockets of resistance held out until early June, but by that time the Germans had already turned their attention elsewhere.

Hitler's delight after learning of the fall of France in 1940.

The war in the West was launched on May 10, 1940. It was one of the most breathtaking and frightening military performances ever witnessed. It took the Germans less than a week to overrun the Netherlands and little over two weeks to defeat the Belgian, French, and British forces in Belgium. The remains of the Allied armies were evacuated to England from Dunkirk. The Allied cause had suffered a resounding defeat.

On the day the Lowlands were invaded, Chamberlain resigned. He was succeeded by Winston Churchill, sixty-five years old and already famous, although his greatest contributions still lay ahead.

The Fall of France

There was no one to do for France what Churchill did for England. The man who was pushed into the limelight in the hope that he would unite the French people was Marshal Henri Philippe Pétain. Once before, in 1916, he had been the symbol of his country's resistance in time of national emergency. But in 1940 the old marshal was less concerned with continuing the war than with making peace. France, he felt, had been betrayed by its radical left and deserted by its British allies. Why not try and save what could be by collaborating with Hitler?

As the German armies reached the Channel coast in late May 1940, Hitler was faced with a major decision: should he invade England, or should he complete the conquest of France? He decided to do the latter, perhaps because he was still hoping to reach a compromise with the British. There is no need to go into the melancholy details of the "Fall of France." When the French were at their lowest and German victory was beyond a doubt, Italian troops invaded southeastern France. Mussolini had stayed out of the war thus far, claiming that he was not ready for it. But the collapse of France was too good an opportunity to miss.

The official French surrender took place on June 22, 1940, at Compiègne. Under the terms of the armistice Germany occupied three-fifths of France, including its entire Atlantic coast. There were no final territorial provisions; these were to await a later peace conference. The unoccupied, southern part of France chose as its capital the town of Vichy. Besides Pétain, the leaders of the Vichy government included Pierre Laval and Admiral Jean Darlan.

The Battle of Britain

With France out of the war, Great Britain now stood alone. Its most immediate fear was of a German invasion. But Hitler lacked the necessary naval power to launch his "Operation Sea Lion," and besides, he never gave up hope that England would capitulate without fighting to the finish. To break down British resistance, the German *Luftwaffe*, in July 1940, embarked on an all-out air offensive. The Battle of Britain lasted through the rest of the year. Several times the British reached the limits of their reserves in planes and pilots. But they did not give in. Meanwhile, halfhearted preparations for "Operation Sea Lion" continued. But a successful invasion of England required control of the sea and air, which the Germans never achieved. In the fall of 1940, invasion plans were postponed and Hitler decided to strike elsewhere.

War in North Africa and the Balkans

An empire as large as that of Britain was vulnerable in many places. The British possession most coveted by Hitler was Gibraltar. To take this strongly fortified gateway to the Mediterranean, however, the *Führer* needed the support of Franco's Spain, which he failed to get. Another important British region was Egypt. The task of ousting the British from there was given to the Italians. In September 1940 an Italian army invaded Egypt from Libya. It was stopped by a far smaller British force, which drove the Italians back into Libya. A major Axis defeat was avoided only by the intervention of the German *Afrikakorps* under General Erwin Rommel. By early April 1941 the Axis forces were once again on Egyptian soil.

The Italians, meanwhile, had become involved in another venture. In October 1940 Italian troops crossed from Albania into Greece. After some minor gains, they were soon pushed back again. Once more the Germans had to intervene and thus open another major front. Bulgaria and Hungary were already on the side of the Axis. Yugoslavia was quickly overrun by German, Bulgarian, and Hungarian troops. Greece was defeated and occupied. In the spring of 1941 it seemed that Germany was looking still farther afield toward the Middle East. But before the *Führer*'s schemes went very far, he became occupied with more important objectives in eastern Europe. Combined British and Free French forces were able, therefore, to keep the upper hand in the strategically vital eastern Mediterranean.

There were some other hopeful developments in the spring of 1941, while Britain was still fighting with its back to

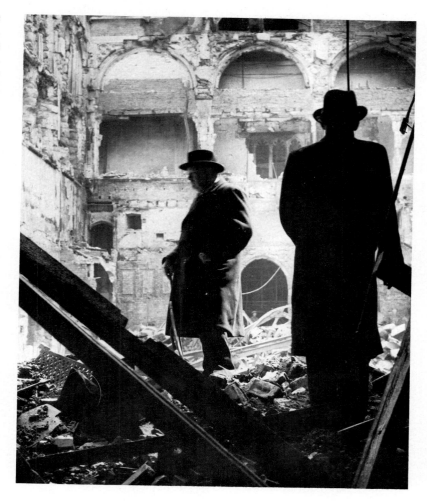

Prime Minister Winston Churchill inspecting ruins of the House of Commons following bombing by the German *Luftwaffe* in 1940.

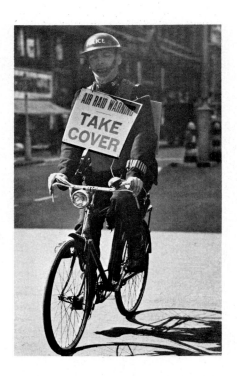

A policeman cycles through London to warn of an air raid.

the wall. The United States was constantly increasing its aid to Great Britain, and ultimate American involvement in the war appeared a definite possibility. The British navy, meanwhile, won a major victory when it sank the German superbattleship *Bismarck* on May 27. And, most important, there were persistent rumors that relations between Germany and Russia were rapidly deteriorating.

HITLER'S RUSSIAN GAMBLE

Russo-German relations since the outbreak of the war had been far from smooth. Two totalitarian countries, each bent on expansion, could not avoid for long getting in each other's way. To be sure, the two partners maintained a mutually beneficial economic exchange. But on the political front Russo-German interests were far less complementary. Hitler was disturbed by Russia's expansion along the Baltic, and Stalin was taken aback by Hitler's unexpected successes in the West. More serious still were Russo-German differences over the Balkans, where no clear line of demarcation

German soldier in battle.

had been worked out. Efforts to clarify these and other matters were made in November 1940 at a conference in Berlin. But the attempt failed, partly because of Russia's far-reaching demands for the control of eastern and southeastern Europe, partly because Hitler had already decided to attack the Soviet Union.

The German Invasion of Russia

There were obvious reasons for Hitler's Russian gamble: he wanted *Lebensraum*, and he hated communism. But there was still another reason why he decided to strike at Russia. To defeat Russia while it was still weak from the Finnish War was the best way of inducing Britain to surrender. The first preparations for the invasion of Russia were made as early as July 1940. The final directives were issued the following December. The *Wehrmacht* struck on June 22, 1941.

The German armies at first were disastrously successful, taking hundreds of thousands of Russian prisoners. But the Russians seemed to have inexhaustible manpower. Opposition to Stalin's ruthless regime disappeared in the face of foreign aggression. One of Hitler's gravest errors was not to have posed to the Russian people as liberator from communist oppression. Instead, the *Führer* ordered Russian prisoners to be herded into vast camps where they died of starvation, or else had them transported to Germany as slave labor.

The Russian war overnight closed the gap between the East and West. Great Britain now offered Stalin an alliance, and the Americans included the Soviets in their program of Lend-Lease. The Germans, meanwhile, were encountering unforeseen difficulties. Winter came unusually early in 1941, and the German army was not prepared for it. When Germany's commanders wanted to halt their advance, Hitler relieved them and took charge himself. The Germans suffered terrible hardships, but they continued their advance. In the fall of 1942 Hitler's generals once again urged him to shorten his lines, but the *Führer* remained unyielding. Since August, large German

Russian soldiers pursuing remnants of the German Sixth Army in the battle of Stalingrad (1943).

Churchill on the German Invasion of Russia

Hitler is a monster of wickedness, insatiable in his lust for blood and plunder. Not content with having all of Europe under his heel or else terrorized into various forms of abject submission, he must now carry his work of butchery and desolation among the vast multitudes of Russia and Asia. The terrible military machine which we and the rest of the civilized world so foolishly, so supinely, so insensately, allowed the Nazi gangsters to build up, year by year, from almost nothing—the machine cannot stand idle lest it rust, or fall to pieces. It must be in continual motion, grinding up human lives and trampling down the homes and the rights of hundreds of millions of men.

Moreover, it must be fed, not only with human flesh but with oil. So now this bloodthirsty guttersnipe must launch his mechanized armies upon new fields of slaughter, pillage and devastation. Poor as are the Russian peasants, workmen and soldiers, he must steal from them their daily bread. He must devour their harvests. He must rob them of the oil which drives their plows, and thus produce a famine without example in human history, and even the carnage and ruin which his victory, should he gain it—he has not gained it yet—will bring upon the Russian people will itself be only a stepping-stone to the attempt to plunge the 400,000,000 or 500,000,000 who live in China and the 350,000,000 who live in India into the bottomless pit of human degradation over which the diabolic emblem of the swastika flaunts itself. . . .

The Nazi regime is indistinguishable from the worst features of Communism. . . . No one has been a more consistent opponent of Communism than I have for the last twenty-five years. I will unsay no words that I have spoken about it. But all this fades away before the spectacle which is now unfolding. The past with its crimes, its follies and its tragedies flashes away.

From a speech by Winston Churchill, June 22, 1941, as quoted in *The New York Times,* June 23, 1941.

The New Order

The following is from a confidential address given by Heinrich Himmler to his SS officers on October 4, 1943.

What happens to a Russian, to a Czech, does not interest me in the slightest. What the nations can offer in the way of good blood of our type we will take, if necessary by kidnaping their children and raising them here with us. Whether nations live in prosperity or starve to death like cattle interests me only in so far as we need them as slaves to our *Kultur;* otherwise it is of no interest to me. Whether 10,000 Russian females fall down from exhaustion while digging an antitank ditch interests me only in so far as the antitank ditch for Germany is finished.

From *Nazi Conspiracy and Aggression* (Washington, D.C.: Government Printing Office, 1946), Vol. IV, p. 559.

The "Final Solution"

The first train arrived . . . 45 freightcars with 6,700 people, of which 1,450 were already dead on arrival. . . . A large loudspeaker blares instructions: Undress completely, take off artificial limbs, glasses, etc. Hand in all valuables. Shoes to be tied together (for the clothing collection) . . . Women and girls to the barber, who cuts off their hair in two or three strokes and stuffs it into potato sacks. . . .

Then the line starts moving. . . . At the corner a strapping SS-man announces in a pastoral voice: Nothing will happen to you! Just breathe deeply inside the chambers, that stretches the lungs; this inhalation is necessary against the illnesses and epidemics. When asked what would happen to them, he replies: Well, of course the men will have to work, build houses and roads, but the women won't have to work. If they want to they can help in the household or the kitchen. For a few of these unfortunates a small glimmer of hope which suffices to have them take the few steps to the chambers without resistance—the majority knows what is ahead, the stench tells their fate. . . .

The wooden doors are opened. . . . Inside the chambers, the dead stand closely pressed together, like pillars of stone. . . . Even in death one recognizes the families. They still hold hands, so they have to be torn apart to get the chambers ready for their next occupants. The corpses are thrown out—wet with sweat and urine, covered with excrement, menstrual blood. Children's bodies fly through the air. . . . Two dozen workers use hooks to pry open mouths to look for gold. . . . Others search genitals and anuses for gold, diamonds and valuables. Wirth [an SS-guard] motions to me: Just lift this can of gold teeth, this is only from yesterday and the day before! . . .

From an eyewitness account of mass gassings, in *Vierteljahrshefte für Zeitgeschichte* (1953), Vol. I, pp. 190–91.

forces had laid siege to Stalingrad on the lower Volga. A German victory at Stalingrad would have given Germany control over the rich oil fields of the Caucasus. But instead of ejecting the Russians from Stalingrad, the Germans were caught in a Russian counteroffensive and suffered a major defeat by February 1943.

The battle of Stalingrad was not the first Nazi defeat. The western allies were simultaneously advancing and winning in North Africa. But the disaster in Russia was a decisive event. In a gradually mounting offensive, the Russians began to push Hitler's armies back across the plains of eastern Europe. It took almost two more years before the fighting reached German soil. Meanwhile the expansion of Japan in the Far East had also been halted in the winter of 1942/43, and the Japanese were being driven back to their home bases. By the spring of 1943, fascist aggression had overextended itself, and the tide of the war began to turn.

HITLER'S "NEW ORDER"

There was never any master plan for Hitler's "New Order," since the future depended on the final outcome of the war. Few of the territories under German domination were annexed outright, although the degree to which some of them were being Germanized left no doubt about their ultimate fate. The war had done its share in decreasing the population of eastern Europe. In addition, more than 7 million foreign workers were forced to work in German factories. Into the areas thus vacated, ethnic Germans, mostly from outside the Reich, were sent as pioneers of Hitler's Germanization policy.

But Hitler was not content merely with taking land away from other peoples. The most frightful deed committed in the name of his "New Order" was the willful extermination of from 6 to 8 million people, most of them Jews. Wherever the German armies went, the elite SS (*Schutzstaffel*, protective force), followed to see that the party's racial policies were carried out. At first there was merely persecution of the Jews, and in this the local populations often participated. But in time more drastic measures were adopted. Hitler's "Final Solution" called for nothing less than the complete extermination of all Jews. This was carried out by means of gas chambers in special extermination camps, such as Auschwitz. There were several such camps, not only for the extermination of Jews but for the "mercy killing" of the incurably ill and insane, and for the liquidation of political prisoners.

These were only the more gruesome acts committed by the Nazis. Additional millions were kept in concentration, slave-labor, and prisoner-of-war camps, where many died more "natural" deaths of starvation. A great many Germans were involved in these crimes; yet after the war no one would admit having known what went on behind the barbed wire of these camps.

AMERICA ENTERS THE WAR

America's involvement in the war was a gradual process. The government had followed a policy of neutrality during the various acts of German and Italian aggression prior to the war. The question was whether this attitude could be maintained. As one country after another fell victim to the Axis powers, America's role in the war became of crucial importance. Axis domination of western Europe and North Africa would have posed a serious threat to the United States itself.

Benevolent Neutrality

On November 4, 1939, Congress had passed a revised Neutrality Act that lifted the embargo on all implements of war and put all trade on a "cash and carry" basis. This move tended to favor the country with the largest funds and the strongest navy, Great Britain. But Britain's enormous need for material aid made its dollar credits dwindle rapidly. The two governments tried to overcome this difficulty in several ways. One was the "destroyer deal" of 1940, when the United States gave Britain some fifty ships in return for a lease of certain British-held naval bases in the Western Hemisphere. Another way for America to

help was through the Lend-Lease Act of 1941. It gave the president power to provide goods and services to any nation whose defense was considered vital to the United States.

There were other signs that America was getting off the fence. But in August 1941, Congress extended the Selective Service Act of the preceding September only by the slimmest margin. The American people, it seemed, were perfectly willing to go to any limit in helping the Allied cause so long as they did not become involved in the war themselves. It took the Japanese attack on Pearl Harbor to push the United States across the line from nonintervention to belligerency.

War with Japan

The United States, for some forty years past, had stood in the way of Japan's major aim: to dominate China and to control the trading area of southeastern Asia and the neighboring Pacific. Since the start of the Sino-Japanese War in 1937, Washington had been concerned about Japan's violations of the "open door" policy in China. To put pressure on the Japanese, the United States, in July 1939, ended its thirty-year-old commercial treaty with Japan and subsequently imposed an embargo on certain strategic goods. By the middle of 1941 the embargo was seriously affecting the Japanese. Tokyo's demand for the cessation of United States restrictions were met with American counterdemands for Japan's withdrawal from China. As far back as January 1941 the Japanese government had begun to prepare for an armed showdown.

When the Japanese air force staged its attack against Pearl Harbor, on December 7, 1941, it caught the American forces entirely unprepared. The United States suffered one of the greatest defeats in its history. Yet the catastrophe of Pearl Harbor had one good effect—it cut short the debate between isolationists and interventionists. As Italy and Germany declared war on the United States, the American people rallied wholeheartedly behind the war effort of their government.

Pearl Harbor, December 7, 1941.

THE DEFEAT OF THE AXIS   1942–45

Axis Powers at the outbreak of war

Greatest area of Axis military power

Allies

→ Heaviest Allied bombing

---- Inside limit of U-boat operations

SINKING OF THE BISMARCK

THE DEFEAT OF THE AXIS

The European Allies were worried at first that America's involvement in the Pacific would prevent it from continuing its aid to Europe. The Russians in particular kept up a nagging insistence on the immediate opening of a second front on the Continent. Before such an operation could be thought of, however, large numbers of American troops had to be shipped overseas, and that was possible only after the threat of Germany's submarine fleet had been overcome. The final victory over the submarine menace was due in part to the convoy system and to improved methods of detecting submarines. But the victory at sea could not have been won without the "battle of the shipyards," in which American workers built ships faster than the Germans could sink them.

The Invasion of North Africa

The first involvement of American ground forces in the war against the European Axis took place in North Africa. On November 8, 1942, an Anglo-American force, commanded by General Dwight D. Eisenhower, landed at Casablanca in French Morocco and at various points in Algeria. Allied intervention in North Africa was made easier by the collaboration of the French forces stationed there. The leading French representative in Morocco and Algeria at the time was Admiral Darlan. His cooperation helped keep Allied losses during the landing to a minimum, although the fact that Darlan was profascist caused some embarrassment. The North African campaign ended on May 13, 1943, with the Allied capture of Tunis and Bizerte.

In the meantime, the German people were also feeling the effects of American intervention nearer home. Almost daily, large fleets of United States and British planes penetrated the antiaircraft defenses of the Reich, bombing industrial centers and strategic objectives. The much-advertised *Luftwaffe* of Reichsmarshal Göring, which had earlier failed to bomb the British into submission, now proved equally ineffective in defending German soil.

The Allied Invasion of Italy

Having won North Africa, the Allies next aimed for control of the rest of the Mediterranean. The invasion of Sicily and southern Italy was launched in the summer of 1943. Resistance in Sicily collapsed in mid-August, and on September 2 British and American troops landed on the Italian mainland. The campaign in Italy, which lasted until the end of the war, played a vital part in the final victory, since it helped tie down large German forces that might otherwise have been used on Hitler's two other fronts. But the Italian war also caused one of the first major crises between the Anglo-Saxon powers and their Russian ally.

Stalin had long been annoyed with the West for not opening what he considered a real second front. The invasion of Italy gave new cause for such annoyance. During the Sicilian campaign in July 1943, a number of high officials within the Italian Fascist Party staged a *coup d'état* and forced Mussolini to resign. The new Italian government under Marshal Pietro Badoglio asked the Allies for an armistice. The agreement with Badoglio further aroused the suspicion of Stalin. What he feared was that the West might conclude a separate peace without the Russians.

"Operation Overlord"

The delay in opening a second front in the north was partly due to differences within the western camp on where the attack against Hitler's "Fortress Europe" should be launched. Some British experts favored the Balkans, expecting fewer losses from striking there. President Roosevelt and his advisers, on the other hand, saw France as the more suitable terrain for a second front, and the American view prevailed.

The final decision for the invasion of France, "Operation Overlord," was made at a conference of the "Big Three" at Teheran in December 1943. The supreme command was entrusted to General Eisenhower; the scene of the landing was to be the coast of Normandy; and D-Day was set for early June 1944. Since the Germans had expected the invasion nearer Calais, the Allies were able to

The end of Mussolini. He and his mistress were executed by Italian partisans in Milan (April 29, 1945).

establish a firm beachhead. After three months of fighting, the Allies had driven the Germans out of northwestern France. On August 15 a second amphibious operation landed on the French Mediterranean coast and within a month made contact with the main invasion forces in the north. In mid-September the first American forces crossed the German frontier. Here they were halted by the fortified German "Westwall."

The German *Wehrmacht*, although on the run, was still far from beaten. During the week before Christmas 1944, Hitler staged his last big offensive of the war. Under cover of fog and snow in the difficult terrain of the Ardennes, eight German armored divisions drove a deep salient into the Allied lines. This "Battle of the Bulge" proved to be a costly failure for the Germans, but for a brief moment it seemed to threaten the Allied victory in the West.

Germany Invaded from East and West

The Russians, meanwhile, had been pressing slowly but steadily westward. By the end of January 1945 the Red army stood on the Oder River, less than a hundred miles from Berlin. These were terrible months for the Germans, who now felt what it was like to be the victims of invasion. Since the fortunes of war had begun to turn, sporadic German opposition to Hitler had gathered sufficient strength for a final attempt to rid the country of its tyrant. But the plot of July 20, 1944, miscarried, and the *Führer* took horrible vengeance. Thousands of decent men and women, who might have played a leading role in the postwar reconstruction of Germany, were put to death. The rest of the German people were urged on into suicidal resistance, especially since the Allied demand for "unconditional surrender" seemed to leave no alternative.

Early in 1945 the Allies stood poised for the final phase of the European war. The invasion of the Rhineland was launched on February 8, 1945. From here on events happened with lightning speed. By the end of March the Rhine had been crossed; by the middle of April the Ruhr district had been taken; and on April 25 the first American and Russian patrols met on the Elbe River. On April 30, while the Russians were fighting their way into the center of Berlin, Adolf Hitler committed suicide. On May 7, 1945, at the headquarters of General Eisenhower at Reims, a German military delegation signed the terms of Germany's unconditional surrender. May 8, 1945, was officially proclaimed V-E Day, victory day in Europe.

THE WAR IN THE PACIFIC

The war against Japan was primarily a naval war in which the United States carried the major burden. Considering America's losses at Pearl Harbor and its heavy commitment in Europe, the victory in the Pacific was a great achievement. This was particularly true considering the extent of Japanese expansion. A few days after Pearl Harbor, the Japanese overran America's outposts at Guam and Wake Island. Early in 1942, they invaded the Philippines. The Dutch East Indies, the Malay Peninsula, and Burma went next. By May 1942 the whole area east of India and north of Australia, except for the southern part of New Guinea, had fallen into Japanese hands.

D-Day: the invasion of Normandy, June 6, 1944.

American Naval Victories

It was the Japanese attempt to force the Allies out of New Guinea and to gain a base for the invasion of Australia that triggered the first major naval battle between United States and Japanese forces. The battle of the Coral Sea in May 1942 brought heavy American losses, but it kept the Japanese from their objective. A still more decisive naval battle a month later at Midway Island brought a resounding Japanese defeat. For the first time America held a slight naval edge in the Pacific. The Japanese achieved some last successes when they occupied Attu and Kiska in the Aleutian Islands. But with the landing of United States marines in the Solomon Islands in August 1942, Japanese expansion was halted, and soon the tide began to turn.

The Turn of the Tide

In 1942 United States naval supremacy was established in the Pacific; the next year brought the first breaks through the outer perimeter of Japan's defenses. Beginning with the battle of Guadalcanal, one after another of Japan's island outposts were retaken in some of the war's bloodiest fighting. Places most Americans had never heard of—Tarawa, Makin, Eniwetok, Iwo Jima, Okinawa— now suddenly became headlines. Meanwhile, United States submarines were taking a heavy toll of Japanese shipping, and the Japanese islands were put under a blockade. In June 1944 American superfortresses began their first bombing raids on Japan. In October 1944 United States forces under General Douglas MacArthur began their reconquest of the Philippines. And in Burma, British imperial forces under Lord Louis Mountbatten, supported by Americans and Chinese, were rounding up the Japanese invaders.

The End of the War

The climax of the war in the Pacific came on October 21–22, 1944, with the battle of Leyte Gulf in the Philippine Sea, one of the biggest naval battles ever fought. Japanese losses were such that their navy henceforth was no longer a factor in the war. As Allied successes in Europe mounted, more and more strength could be diverted to the Pacific theater. In the spring of 1945 America's commanders in the Pacific were asked to prepare plans for the invasion of Japan. But while these preparations were still under way, on July 16, 1945, the first atomic bomb was successfully exploded at Los Alamos, New Mexico. The atomic

The Naming of the Second World War

10 September 1945

The President
The White House

Dear Mr. President:

President Wilson, under date of July 31, 1919, addressed a letter to Secretary of War Baker which read, in part, as follows: "It is hard to find a satisfactory 'official' name for the war, but the best, I think, that has been suggested is 'The World War,' and I hope that your judgment will concur. . . ."

As a matter of simplicity and to insure uniform terminology, it is recommended that "World War II" be the officially designated name for the present war covering all theaters and the entire period of hostilities.

The term "World War II" has been used in at least seven public laws to designate this period of hostilities. Analysis of publications and radio programs indicates that this term has been accepted by common usage.

If this recommendation is approved it is further recommended that the title "World War II" be published in the *Federal Register* as the official name of the present war.

Respectfully yours,
Henry L. Stimson
Secretary of War

James Forrestal
Secretary of the Navy
Approved: September 11, 1945
Harry S. Truman

From U.S., Department of State, *Bulletin*, Vol. XIII (Washington, D.C.: Government Printing Office, 1945), pp. 427–28.

bombing of Hiroshima and Nagasaki on August 6 and 9 led to the surrender of Japan on August 14, 1945 (V-J Day), and to the end of the Second World War.

The decision to use this terrible new weapon was not easy. Should not efforts be made to lay siege to Japan first? But President Truman and his advisers felt that an early surrender of Japan without invasion was most unlikely. And an invasion of Japan, it was estimated, would cost more than a million Allied casualties and at least again that many Japanese. It was thought preferable, therefore, to bring the war to a quick, though horrible, end: 78,000 people were killed at Hiroshima and 50,000 at Nagasaki. The Atomic Age had begun.

THE SEARCH FOR PEACE

Considering the tremendous political upheaval resulting from the Second World War, it is surprising how little advance thought had been given to the

problem of peace. There had been some general pronouncements, especially the Atlantic Charter, which President Roosevelt and Prime Minister Churchill had issued in August 1941. But this idealistic blueprint for the future, which aimed at a world free from want and fear, was drawn up before the harsh realities of the postwar situation were known. Several conferences during the war—between Roosevelt and Churchill at Casablanca and Quebec, and among the two western leaders and Stalin at Teheran—had dealt primarily with immediate military matters and only incidentally with long-range political questions. Only in the final months of the war did the larger issues of the future become the subject of top-level discussions. These took place at two conferences at Yalta and Potsdam, in February and July 1945.

The Yalta Conference

To understand the concessions made at Yalta to the Soviet Union, we must remember that Russia was still an ally of the West and that the expansionist aims of communism were not yet understood. Some of Stalin's claims, furthermore, in the Baltic, in Poland, and in the Balkans, had already been recognized, at least by implication. And the fact that all these regions were already occupied by Red armies gave added strength to Soviet arguments. Most important, finally, was the conviction of western military leaders that Russia's continued contribution to the common war effort was essential to ensure an early victory.

The main issues discussed at Yalta dealt with the future of Germany, Poland, the Far East, and the United Nations. On Germany, the meeting achieved very little. The only firm agreement dealt with the postwar division of the country into four occupation zones, including a French one.

A great deal of time at Yalta was spent in trying to determine the future frontiers of Poland and to agree on the composition of its government. On both points the Russians scored a major success. Poland's border was moved west-

Hiroshima

At about 0815 there was a blinding flash. Some described it as brighter than the sun, others likened it to a magnesium flash. Following the flash there was a blast of heat and wind. The large majority of people within 3000 feet of ground zero were killed immediately. Within a radius of about 7000 feet almost every Japanese house collapsed. Beyond this range and up to 15,000-20,000 feet many of them collapsed and others received serious structural damage. Persons in the open were burned on exposed surfaces, and within 3000–5000 feet many were burned to death while others received severe burns through their clothes. . . . The people appeared stunned by the catastrophe and rushed about as jungle animals suddenly released from a cage. Some few apparently attempted to help others from the wreckage, particularly members of their family or friends. Others assisted those who were unable to walk alone. However, many of the injured were left trapped beneath collapsed buildings as people fled by them in the streets. Pandemonium reigned as the uninjured and slightly injured fled the city in fearful panic.

From "The Effects of Atomic Bombs on Health and Medical Services in Hiroshima and Nagasaki," *The United States Strategic Bombing Survey* (Washington, D.C.: Government Printing Office, 1947), p. 3.

ward to the Curzon Line, where it had been fixed briefly after the First World War. Russia thus received almost 47 percent of Poland's prewar territory. The powers agreed, however, that Poland should receive compensations in the north and west. The new provisional government of Poland, meanwhile, was to be drawn chiefly from the Soviet-sponsored Committee of National Liberation rather than from the Polish government-in-exile, which the western powers favored; but to make sure that Poland was ruled democratically, "free and unfettered elections" were to be held.

The Far Eastern decisions made at Yalta caused little difficulty at the time, although they came in for much criticism later. In return for Stalin's promise to participate in the Pacific war, the Soviet Union was granted large concessions at the expense of both China and Japan.

Most of these reversed Russia's losses in the Russo-Japanese War of 1904–1905 (see p. 642).

The problem that most concerned the American delegation at Yalta was to get Russian and British agreement to final plans for a United Nations organization. Most of the details for such an organization had already been worked out, except for two important points: the extent of the great powers' veto in the Security Council and the number of seats each was to hold in the UN Assembly. Both points were satisfactorily settled, a fact that greatly contributed to the success of the conference in American eyes. There was some hard bargaining at Yalta, but on the whole the atmosphere was friendly. It remained to be seen whether the powers could carry over their wartime unity of purpose into their postwar search for peace.

The official symbol of the United Nations.

The Yalta Conference. Churchill, Roosevelt, and Stalin sit for a formal picture-taking session with their advisers. Roosevelt clearly shows the strain of their meeting. He was to die two months later, on April 12, 1945.

The United Nations

The first problem tackled after Yalta was the drafting of a charter for the United Nations. This was done at the San Francisco Conference in the spring of 1945. The United Nations owes much to its predecessor, the League of Nations.

Like the League, the UN, at least at the start, was entirely dominated by the great powers. The most important agency of the UN is the Security Council, five of whose seats were assigned to the United States, Great Britain, the Soviet Union, France, and Nationalist China. (The latter's place was taken by Communist China in 1972.) Since each of these powers had an absolute veto, the effectiveness of the UN was seriously hampered. The chief task of the Council was to maintain peace and security. Like the Council of the League of Nations, it could recommend peaceful arbitration or measures short of war, such as economic sanctions. But unlike the League, the Security Council could also take "such actions by air, sea, or land forces as may be necessary to maintain or restore international peace."

The Potsdam Conference

While the San Francisco Conference was still in session, the end of the war in Europe called for another top-level meeting to settle the future of Germany. Russia's unilateral actions in eastern Europe, notably in Rumania and Poland, had already called forth repeated western protests. When the powers assembled at Potsdam in July 1945, therefore, the cordiality that had prevailed at Yalta had given way to coldness. The United States, after President Roosevelt's death in April 1945, was represented by President Harry S Truman; and Great Britain, after Churchill's defeat at the polls, was represented by Prime Minister Clement Attlee. This left Stalin as the only original member of the Big Three.

The main differences at Potsdam arose over the eastern borders of Germany and over German reparations. As compensation for the territories it had lost to Russia at Yalta, Poland had occupied about one-fifth of Germany, east of the Oder and Neisse rivers. Against Stalin's insistence that these lands become permanently Polish, the western powers at Potsdam won a postponement of any final decision until a later peace conference. As for German reparations, the

Soviet Union held on to the high demands it had made at Yalta. But the West got Stalin to agree that Germany was to be left with sufficient resources to support itself and that the country was to be treated "as a single economic unit." Here were several causes for subsequent friction.

During the closing days of the Potsdam Conference attention shifted to the Far East, where the war with Japan was drawing to a close. The Soviet Union entered the war at the last minute by invading Manchuria. When the fighting stopped, Russia took possession of the rights and territories it had been promised at Yalta. The United States claimed control over Japan itself. Korea was divided into Russian and American zones. Here was another potential source of conflict.

The launching of the United Nations, as seen by the British magazine *Punch*.

Peace with the Axis Satellites

With the war finally over, peace negotiations could begin. The peace conference of the twenty-one nations that had fought against the Axis met in Paris in July 1946. The peace treaties with Italy, Rumania, Hungary, Bulgaria, and Finland were signed in February 1947. Italy was let off remarkably easily. It lost some territory to France, Yugoslavia, and Greece; its colonies were put under the trusteeship of the UN; and Italy had to pay reparations. The settlements with the rest of the powers were similar. Since, with the exception of Finland, these countries were already under Russian domination, the details of the peace terms are not very important. The Soviet Union in each case was the main beneficiary, getting the major share of reparations and extensive territories. Some of these territories—the Baltic states, eastern Poland, and Bessarabia—had formerly belonged to tsarist Russia; but the Baltic states between the wars had been independent, and Bessarabia had belonged to Rumania. Stalin's aim, it seemed, was to restore Russia's borders as they had been before the advent of communism.

THE PROBLEM OF GERMANY

The signing of the Paris treaties ended peacemaking for the time being. Treaties with Japan and Austria were not signed until several years later, and there has as yet been no peace treaty with Germany. It was over the issue of Germany that the East and West had their first real falling-out.

Germany, at Potsdam, lost about one-fourth of the territory it had held in 1937. But it still had almost 70 million people, and its industrial resources were considerable. The former Reich, therefore, would continue to be a vital factor in world affairs. Beginning in 1946, Russia and the West tried to reach an agreement on the future of Germany. But it soon became clear that they did not see eye to eye on many crucial points. What each side hoped was to create a united Germany in its own image. And when this proved impossible, the East and West reorganized their respective zones, eventually creating a divided Germany.

The Division of Germany

The first disagreements arose over economic matters. The division of Germany into occupation zones proved a

TERRITORIAL ADJUSTMENTS AFTER THE SECOND WORLD WAR   1945

The boundaries shown on this map date from the beginning of Second World War

0   MILES   200

Axis nations after Second World War

Lands that changed hands after Second World War

economically. West Germany's economy was then given considerable American aid. The result was a miraculous turn for the better. By 1950 the industrial output of West Germany had again reached its 1936 level.

While the West was integrating its two-thirds of Germany into the economy of western Europe, the Russians began the thorough "sovietization" of their eastern zone. These diverging policies could not help but lead to partition. From 1948 to 1949, the Soviet Union tried to force the West out of the former German capital by imposing a blockade on the Allied sectors of Berlin. But a gigantic western airlift foiled Russia's scheme. In May 1949 a West German Parliamentary Council adopted a constitution for the Federal Republic of Germany, with Bonn as capital and with Konrad Adenauer as its first chancellor. In East Germany a Communist-dominated German Democratic Republic was founded in October 1949. By 1950 the struggle between East and West over Germany had resulted in the political division of the country, each part refusing to recognize the other and claiming to speak for the whole.

THE BEGINNING OF THE COLD WAR

As with most other wars, the origins and causes of the "Cold War" have been a subject of controversy. Most western historians still agree that the major responsibility for the Cold War lay with the Soviet Union's attempt to use the chaos of the postwar world to further its own expansionist and ideological aims. In the late 1960s, however, some "revisionist" historians in the United States began to see their own country's desire for economic predominance as having caused the Cold War by forcing the Soviets into communizing eastern Europe for reasons of self-protection.

The Spread of Communism

The communization of eastern Europe was gradual. At first some outward show of democracy was maintained, with

serious obstacle to economic recovery. But western proposals for economic unification were met by Russian counter-proposals for political unity first. Since it had been agreed at Potsdam that Germany was to be treated "as a single economic unit," the western powers, in December 1946, merged their zones

The Berlin airlift (June 1948–May 1949).

"popular front" governments and "free" elections. But gradually the non-Communist members were ousted and coalition governments were transformed into "people's democracies." By 1947 this policy was causing deep concern in the West. Poland, Rumania, Yugoslavia, Albania, and Bulgaria all had either Communist or pro-Communist regimes, and the trend in Czechoslovakia and Hungary was in the same direction. The only way to halt this creeping expansion of communism, it was felt, was to meet force with force. The occasion to proclaim such a policy of "containment" came in the spring of 1947, when Russia tried to extend its influence near the entrance to the Black Sea.

The Truman Doctrine and the Marshall Plan

In Greece, a small communist minority, supported by communists in neighboring countries, was waging a civil war against the government. The British, after the war, had supplied the Greek monarchy with financial and military aid. But Britain had serious economic problems at home, and it was also supporting Turkey's resistance to Soviet demands. In the spring of 1947, Britain announced that it could no longer give aid to Greece and Turkey. At this point the United States took over. In a message to Congress on March 12, 1947, President Truman called for American support to "free peoples who are resisting attempted subjugation by armed minorities or by outside pressures." A comprehensive scheme for American aid to Europe was announced three months later by Secretary of State George C. Marshall. By fighting the economic and social conditions that gave rise to communism, the United States hoped to contain it.

The Cominform and the Molotov Plan

The Truman Doctrine and the Marshall Plan opened a wholly new phase in United States foreign policy. America had broken with its isolationist past and had assumed the leadership of the free world. The significance of this break was not lost on the Soviet Union. To tighten its control over eastern Europe, the Soviet Union had already concluded mutual assistance pacts with most of its satellites. In order to coordinate the efforts of European communism, the Russians, in

1947, founded the Communist Information Bureau (Cominform), as successor to the Comintern, which had been dissolved in 1943. In the economic field, finally, the Russians announced their "Molotov Plan" as counterpart to the Marshall Plan.

The Communist Coup in Czechoslovakia

While East and West were consolidating their positions, the Russians scored another victory in the Cold War. Among the occupied nations of eastern Europe, Czechoslovakia alone had been able to maintain some democratic freedoms. But these were gradually undermined by the infiltration of native Communists with Russian backing. By February 1948 the country was ripe for a *coup d'état*. In March, Foreign Minister Jan Masaryk, a friend of the West, was killed in a fall from his office window; and in June, President Beneš gave way to Communist leader Klement Gottwald. Except for Finland, all the countries of eastern Europe were now under Communist rule.

The North Atlantic Treaty

The Communist seizure of Czechoslovakia dramatized the need for military as well as economic integration of the West. Great Britain and France had already concluded a treaty of alliance at Dunkirk in 1947. As an additional safeguard, in 1948 they asked the Benelux countries—Belgium, the Netherlands, and Luxembourg—to join them in the Brussels Treaty. But the nations of western Europe realized that effective resistance to Russia required the help of the United States. So on April 4, 1949, the United States joined the members of the Brussels Treaty, together with Italy, Portugal, Denmark, Iceland, Norway, and Canada, in the North Atlantic Treaty. These twelve powers were joined later by Greece and Turkey (1951) and by West Germany (1955). The gist of the treaty was contained in Article 5, which stated that "an armed attack against one or more" of its signatories "shall be considered an attack against them all." A North Atlantic Council was set up to direct the formation of the North Atlantic Treaty Organization (NATO).

THE UNITED NATIONS IN THE COLD WAR

The growing tension between the East and West was also felt within the United Nations. As long as one of the major powers, through its veto in the Security Council, could prevent joint action, the effectiveness of the UN was limited.

The *Coup d'État* in Prague

Letter from President Beneš to the Presidium of the Communist Party:

. . . **You know my sincerely democratic creed. I cannot but stay faithful to that creed even at this moment because democracy, according to my belief, is the only reliable and durable basis for a decent and dignified human life.**

I insist on parliamentary democracy and parliamentary government as it limits democracy. I state I know very well it is necessary to social and economic content. I built my political work on these principles and cannot—without betraying myself—act otherwise. . . .

◊   ◊   ◊

Reply by the Presidium of the Communist Party:

The Presidium of the Central Committee of the Communist Party acknowledged your letter dated February 24 and states again that it cannot enter into negotiations with the present leadership of the National Socialist, People's and Slovak Democratic Parties. . . .

Massive people's manifestations during the last few days clearly have shown our working people denounce, with complete unity and with indignation, the policy of these parties and ask the creation of a government in which all honest progressive patriots devoted to the republic and the people are represented. . . .

Being convinced that only such a highly constitutional and parliamentary process can guarantee the peaceful development of the republic and [that] at the same time it corresponds to the ideas of a complete majority of the working people, the Presidium of the Central Committee hopes firmly after careful considerations that you will recognize the correctness of its conclusions and will agree with its proposals.

From H. L. Trefousse, *The Cold War—A Book of Documents* (New York: Putnam, 1965), pp. 109–12.

Only when international disputes did not involve the interests of a major power could the United Nations make its influence felt. It was thus possible to stop the fighting between Dutch and native forces in Indonesia and between India and Pakistan over Kashmir. In trying to keep Russia from meddling in the affairs of Iran, however, or in calling a halt to the civil war in Greece, United States aid was more important than UN pressure. The United Nations did score one major success before 1950: the founding of the state of Israel. But this was possible only because both the Soviet Union and the United States supported it.

The Founding of Israel

There had already been intermittent clashes between Arabs and Jews in Palestine before the Second World War. After the war when the British found it increasingly difficult to keep peace within their mandate, they decided to withdraw. At this point, in 1948, the UN stepped in, hoping to bring about a peaceful partition of Palestine. The Jews proclaimed the independent state of Israel, which was recognized by the United States and the Soviet Union. But the Arabs, who opposed this solution, resisted. In the ensuing war the Israeli forces proved superior. UN efforts for an armistice finally succeeded in 1949. But peace remained precarious and full-scale war was resumed in 1956.

Other UN Activities

The United Nations had other tasks besides settling international disputes. In some of these economic, social, and cultural activities, the UN was highly successful. In December 1948 the General Assembly adopted an ambitious program of technical assistance for underdeveloped areas, for which the United States provided much of the necessary money.

More important than the economic and social problems, however, was the need for some regulation of international armaments. Here the United Nations made little headway. The main concern was over the control of atomic weapons.

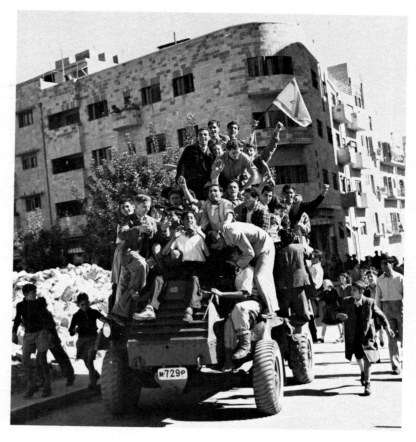

Celebrating the partition of Palestine and waving the flag of their new nation, happy Israelis crowd onto an armored British patrol car in Jerusalem.

In 1946 America proposed the establishment of an International Atomic Development Authority to which the United States would transfer its atomic knowledge and facilities. Since America still had a monopoly in the atomic field, this proposal was most generous. But the Soviet Union vetoed the American proposal, objecting in particular to its provisions for inspection. In July 1949, after three years of fruitless debate, the UN Atomic Energy Commission adjourned. Two months later, Russia announced the first successful explosion of its own atomic bomb.

THE COLD WAR IN THE FAR EAST

The most momentous changes after 1945 occurred outside Europe. The emancipation of former colonial regions from foreign rule transformed the hitherto passive masses of Asia and Africa into active participants in international affairs. The most important change of the postwar period was the emergence of the "People's Republic of China" as a major force in the global balance of power.

Postwar Japan

Because of its dominant role in the occupation of Japan, America's policy prevailed. Since Japan's governmental machinery was left intact, the transition from war to peace went more smoothly in Japan than in Germany. A democratic constitution, in May 1947, transferred sovereignty from the emperor to the people. The Japanese army and navy had already been dissolved, patriotic organizations were banned, and education was reformed along democratic lines. In the economic sphere, the changes were less drastic. Plans to break up the large in-

dustrial and financial combinations of the *zaibatsu*, the great family trusts of Japan, were abandoned when such dismantling was found to interfere with Japan's recovery. Most of the large holdings of absentee landlords, on the other hand, were divided among tenant farmers.

By 1951 the occupation of Japan had accomplished most of its aims and the time had come for a peace settlement. Peace with Japan was signed at San Francisco on September 8, 1951. The treaty was generous, restoring full Japanese sovereignty but permitting the United States to maintain military bases in Japan. America and Japan also concluded a defense agreement that ultimately became an alliance.

Communist Victory in China

While events in Japan were going largely according to American wishes,

THE FAR EAST SINCE THE SECOND WORLD WAR

Revolution 1911		1916		1921		1929	First Communist Republic Set Up 1931		1945	Communist Victory 1949

Rule of General Yüan	Chaos	China United by the Nationalists	Nationalists Nominally in Control	Civil War

developments on the Chinese mainland were taking a different turn. The end of the war found most of China still divided between the government forces of Chiang Kai-shek and the Communist armies of Mao Zedong. Chiang had the backing of Chinese business and banking interests, while Mao's program of land reform brought him the support of the landless masses. Both sides now began a fight for the regions held until recently by Japan. In this contest the Communists proved more successful. By the end of 1948 most of northern China was in Communist hands.

The United States had given large amounts of financial and military aid to Chiang Kai-shek. But as the Nationalist government failed to introduce much-needed reforms, United States aid was curtailed and finally cut off. In the spring of 1949, Chiang Kai-shek began to withdraw his forces to the island of Formosa. By early 1950 the whole Chinese mainland was in Communist hands. On October 1, 1949, the People's Republic of China was officially proclaimed at Peking, with Mao Zedong as president. The Soviet Union immediately recognized the new regime, whereas the United States continued to recognize the Nationalist government of Chiang Kai-shek.

The East–West Conflict over Korea

The victory of communism in China radically changed the balance of power between East and West. The effects of this change were felt almost immediately, as events in Korea transformed the Cold War in that country into an armed conflict. The Korean peninsula had been divided into American and Russian zones of occupation. Just as in Germany, this partition gradually brought about two quite different regimes. In 1948, elections in the United States-occupied southern part of Korea resulted in the founding of the Republic of Korea, with Dr. Syngman Rhee as president. The Russians thereupon sponsored their own Communist-dominated northern People's Democratic Republic, under the presidency of veteran Communist Kim Il Sung.

Late in 1948 the Soviet Union and the United States began to withdraw their troops from North and South Korea. A UN commission remained behind, trying to prevent a possible conflict between the two parts of Korea. Its efforts, however, proved in vain. On June 25, 1950, North Korean forces crossed the thirty-eighth parallel to "liberate" South Korea. Since Russia at the time was boycotting the Security Council, the United Nations could act without being hindered by a Soviet veto. When North Korea refused to halt its aggression, the Security Council asked the members of the UN to go to the aid of South Korea. The United States had already intervened and was soon joined by small contingents from other countries. For the first time, the United Nations had gone to war. The Cold War had turned hot.

Suggestions for Further Reading

Note: Asterisk denotes a book available in paperback edition.

General   The most monumental account of the Second World War is W. S. Churchill, *The Second World War,** 6 vols. (1948–53). An admirably comprehensive treatment is G. Wright, *The Ordeal of Total War, 1939–1945** (1968). Among general military accounts, the following stand out: J. F. C. Fuller, *The Second World War, 1939–45* (1949); P. Young, *World War, 1939–1945* (1966); and B. H. Liddell Hart,

*History of the Second World War** (1970). J. Lukacs, *The Last European War: September 1939/December 1941* (1976), successfully recaptures the atmosphere of the war at the fronts and at home. K. Anderson, *Wartime Women: Sex Roles, Family Relations, and the Status of Women During World War II* (1981), ably deals with a complex subject.

The War: Military and Naval The most detailed coverage of the major engagements may be found in the multivolume series dealing with America's armed forces in the Second World War: Office of the Chief of Military History, *United States Army in World War II*, 70 vols. (1947–69); S. E. Morison, *History of United States Naval Operations in World War II*, 14 vols. (1947–60); and W. F. Craven and J. L. Cate, *The Army Air Forces in World War II*, 7 vols. (1948–53). Phases of the war are treated in M. Bloch, *Strange Defeat* (1949), on the fall of France; A. Johnson, *Norway: Her Invasion and Occupation* (1948); M. Knox, *Mussolini Unleashed 1939–1941: Politics and Strategy in Fascist Italy's Last War* (1982); A. Clark, *Barbarossa: The Russian-German Conflict, 1941–1945** (1965); and K. Wierzynski, *The Forgotten Battlefield: The Story of Finland* (1944). On the maritime war, J. Creswell, *Sea Warfare, 1939–1945*, rev. ed. (1967), and S. W. Roskill, *The War at Sea, 1939–1945*, 3 vols. (1954–61), are excellent. For some of the war's more dramatic stories, see R. Grenfell, *The Bismarck Episode* (1949); D. Young, *Rommel: The Desert Fox** (1950); C. V. Woodward, *The Battle for Leyte Gulf** (1947); W. Ansel, *Hitler Confronts England* (1960); C. Ryan, *The Longest Day** (1959), on the Allied invasion of Normandy; and J. Hersey, *Hiroshima** (1946). Saburō Ienaga, *The Pacific War* (1978), is a thoughtful overview by a Japanese historian. Most of the war's leading military figures have written their memoirs. Of special interest are D. D. Eisenhower, *Crusade in Europe** (1948); Viscount Montgomery, *Memoirs* (1958); C. de Gaulle, *War Memoirs,** 3 vols. (1960); M. Weygand, *Recalled to Service* (1952); J. Stilwell, *The Stilwell Papers* (1948); and J. Wainwright, *General Wainwright's Story* (1946). For the German side, see B. H. Liddell Hart, *The German Generals Talk** (1948); H. Guderian, *Panzer Leader* (1952); and E. von Manstein, *Lost Victories* (1958). M. Cooper, *The German Army, 1933–1945* (1978), is highly critical. The best book on the final phase of the European war is R. F. Weigly, *Eisenhower's Lieutenants: The Campaign of France and Germany, 1944–1945* (1981).

The War: Political and Economic J. L. Snell, *Illusion and Necessity: The Diplomacy of Global War** (1963), is a concise and readable introduction. The gradual involvement of the United States in the war is treated in W. L. Langer and S. E. Gleason, *The Undeclared War, 1940–1941** (1953), and more briefly in R. A. Divine, *The Reluctant Belligerent: American Entry into World War II** (1965). The best account of the diplomatic background of the war with Japan is H. Feis, *The Road to Pearl Harbor** (1950). For highly critical views of Roosevelt's foreign policy, see C. C. Tansill, *Back Door to War* (1952); G. Kolko, *The Politics of War: The World and United States Foreign Policy, 1943–1945* (1968); and B. M. Russett, *No Clear and Present Danger: A Skeptical View of the United States Entry into World War II* (1972).

R. E. Sherwood, *Roosevelt and Hopkins** (1948); E. L. Stimson, *On Active Service in Peace and War* (1948); R. Murphy, *Diplomat Among Warriors** (1964); and W. D. Leahy, *I Was There* (1950), give valuable insights into American policy making.

The sordid story of the Vichy regime is brilliantly told in R. O. Paxton, *Vichy France: Old Guard and New Order, 1940–1944* (1973). See also B. M. Gordon, *Collaborationism in France during the Second World War* (1980). E. L. Woodward, *British Foreign Policy in the Second World War* (1962), is the standard work. The relations among the Allies are reviewed in H. Feis, *Churchill, Roosevelt, Stalin** (1957), and M. Viorst, *Hostile Allies: FDR and Charles de Gaulle* (1965). See also A. W. De Porte, *De Gaulle's Foreign Policy, 1944–1946* (1968). On Russia's foreign policy, see V. Mastny, *Russia's Road to the Cold War: Diplomacy, Warfare and the Politics of Communism, 1941–1945* (1979). The Soviet Union's harsh wartime experiences are related in A. Werth, *Russia at War** (1964), and H. Salisbury, *900 Days: The Siege of Leningrad** (1969).

Explanations of Hitler's fateful decision to invade Russia are provided in A. Rossi, *The Russo-German Alliance* (1951), and G. L. Weinberg, *Germany and the Soviet Union, 1939–1941* (1954). Hitler's attitude toward the United States is analyzed in A. Frye, *Nazi Germany and the American Hemisphere, 1933–1941* (1967); S. Friedländer, *Prelude to Downfall: Hitler and the United States, 1939–1941* (1967); and J. V. Compton, *The Swastika and the Eagle* (1967). Relations within the Axis are dealt with by F. W. Deakin, *The Brutal Friendship: Mussolini, Hitler and the Fall of Italian Fascism,** 2 vols. (1966). J. M. Meskill, *Hitler and Japan: The Hollow Alliance* (1966), tells a story of failure. See also M. D. Fenyo, *Hitler, Horthy, and Hungary: German-Hungarian Relations, 1941–1944* (1972). Spain's role in the war is the subject of H. Feis, *The Spanish Story: Franco and the Nations at War** (1948), and C. B. Burdick, *Germany's Military Strategy and Spain in World War II* (1968). On Japan's wartime policy, see F. C. Jones, *Japan's New Order in East Asia: Its Rise and Fall, 1937–1945* (1954).

On the economic aspects of the war, see D. M. Nelson, *Arsenal for Democracy* (1946), and D. L. Gordon and R. Dangerfield, *The Hidden Weapon: The Story of Economic Warfare* (1947). Germany's economic war effort is treated in A. S. Milward, *The German Economy at War* (1965), and B. A. Carroll, *Design for Total War: Arms and Economics in the Third Reich* (1968).

Hitler's "New Order"

N. Rich, *Hitler's War Aims*, 2 vols. (1973–74), deals competently with a complicated subject. See also A. Toynbee, ed., *Hitler's Europe* (1954), and J. T. Gross, *Polish Society under German Occupation* (1979). A. S. Milward, *The New Order and the French Economy* (1971), is an able monograph. A. Dallin, *German Rule in Russia, 1941–1945* (1957), is excellent. The large-scale popular migrations during the war are treated in E. M. Kulischer, *Europe on the Move: War and Population Changes, 1917–1947* (1948). On German use of slave labor, see E. M. Homze, *Foreign Labor in Nazi Germany* (1967). L. Poliakov, *Harvest of Hate* (1954), and G. Reitlinger, *The Final Solution** (1953), deal with the extermination of the European Jews. W. Laqueur, *The Terrible Secret* (1980), and M. Gilbert, *Auschwitz and the Allies* (1981), are highly critical of the Allies. On the concentration camps, see R. Hoess, *Commandant of Auschwitz** (1959); B. Naumann, *Auschwitz* (1966); and Lord Russell of Liverpool, *The Scourge of the Swastika: A Short History of Nazi War Crimes** (1954). Resistance to the "New Order" is ably surveyed in H. Michel, *The Shadow War: European Resistance, 1939–1945* (1972). See also J. D. Wilkinson, *The Intellectual Resistance in Europe* (1981).

The Search for Peace

The plans made during the war for a postwar settlement are discussed in R. Opie et al., *The Search for Peace Settlements* (1951), and more briefly in W. L. Neumann, *Making the Peace, 1941–1945* (1950). See also T. A. Wilson, *The First Summit: Roosevelt and Churchill at Placentia Bay, 1941* (1970), which deals with the "Atlantic Charter"; J. L. Snell, *Wartime Origins of the East–West Dilemma over Germany* (1956); and E. F. Penrose, *Economic Planning for the Peace* (1953). The conferences at Yalta and Potsdam are described by some of the leading participants: E. R. Stettinius, *Roosevelt and the Russians* (1949); H. S. Truman, *Memoirs*, Vol. I: *Year of Decisions** (1955); J. F. Byrnes, *Speaking Frankly* (1947); and W. S. Churchill, *Triumph and Tragedy** (1953). The best studies of the two conferences are D. S. Clemens, *Yalta* (1970), and H. Feis, *Between War and Peace: The Potsdam Conference** (1960). On the peace with Japan, see F. S. Dunn, *Peace-Making and the Settlement with Japan* (1963).

The Cold War

The best general account of the early postwar years is D. Yergin, *Shattered Peace: The Origins of the Cold War and the National Security State* (1977). See also H. Feis, *From Trust to Terror: The Onset of the Cold War, 1945–1950* (1970); L. E. Davis, *The Cold War Begins: Soviet-American Conflict over Eastern Europe* (1974); and J. L. Gaddis, *The United States and the Origins of the Cold War, 1941–1947* (1972). The "revisionist" position is stated in G. Kolko and J. Kolko, *The Limits of Power: The World and United States Foreign Policy, 1945–1954** (1972); W. A. Williams, *The Tragedy of American Diplomacy** (1972); and D. Horowitz, *The Free World Colossus* (1971). Their findings are criticized by R. J. Maddox, *The New Left and the Origins of the Cold War* (1973). On events in Germany, see A. Grosser, *The Colossus Again: Western Germany from Defeat to Rearmament* (1955); H. Zink, *The United States in Germany, 1944–1955* (1957); L. D. Clay, *Decision in Germany* (1950); and J. P. Nettl, *The Eastern Zone and Soviet Policy in Germany, 1945–1950* (1951). Austria is treated in W. B. Bader, *Austria Between East and West, 1945–1955* (1966). H. Seton-Watson, *The East European Revolution* (1951), and M. Mc-Cauley, ed., *Communist Power in Europe, 1944–1949* (1977), treat the victory of communism in that area. The Communist seizure of individual countries is told in S. Mikolajczyk, *The Rape of Poland* (1950); H. Ripka, *Czechoslovakia Enslaved* (1950); and for Hungary in F. Nagy, *The Struggle Behind the Iron Curtain* (1948). Developments in the Far East are analyzed by H. Feis, *The China Tangle** (1953) and *Contest over Japan* (1967). See also R. Swearingen, *The Soviet Union and Postwar Japan* (1978). S. E. Ambrose, *The Rise to Globalism: American Foreign Policy since 1938** (1971), is a first-rate survey. For the early years of the United Nations, see C. M. Eichelberger, *UN: The First Ten Years* (1955). T. P. Ireland, *Creating the Entangling Alliance* (1981), deals with the origins of NATO. J. Kimche and D. Kimche, *A Clash of Destinies: The Arab-Jewish War and the Founding of the State of Israel* (1960), and E. Berger, *The Covenant and the Sword: Arab-Israeli Relations, 1946–1956* (1965), deal with postwar events in the Middle East. W. O. McCagg, Jr., *Stalin Embattled, 1943–1948* (1978), discusses the Soviet Union's involvement in the Cold War, and G. Herken, *The Winning Weapon: The Atomic Bomb in the Cold War, 1945–1950* (1980), deals with a key issue in that war.

34 From Cold War to Coexistence

In the past a war like the one in Korea might easily have sparked a third world war. That the conflict remained localized was in large measure due to the deterrent effect of the atomic bomb. With both the United States and Russia accumulating large stockpiles of nuclear weapons, the fear that some incident or accident might upset the precarious "balance of terror" became a dominant factor in world affairs. Gradually the perennial crises of the Cold War gave way to a state of coexistence between the Communist and non-Communist worlds.

The years since 1950 have seen other significant changes. In its early phases, the Cold War was primarily a conflict between two superpowers, the United States and the Soviet Union. Europe, which in the past had occupied the center of the stage, seemed to have been relegated to a mere supporting role. Since then, however, the Continent has staged a remarkable comeback. At the same time, the rise of the former colonial and underdeveloped regions, especially China, to independence and influence has injected a wholly new element, sometimes referred to as a "third world," into the world's balance of power.

Other, nonpolitical, issues today have suddenly become far more urgent than they were in the past. Foremost among them is the "population explosion." Demographers estimate that by the end of this century 6 billion people will be alive, almost twice as many as in 1975. Scientists claim that the development of existing resources, especially atomic energy, could provide ample livelihood for these vast masses. But much wealth and energy continue to be diverted to nonproductive military uses. It seems that the alternatives faced by mankind today are either to risk, through a nuclear arms race, the possible extermination of all life on earth, or to ensure, through peaceful effort, a good life for all.

THE DECLINE AND RISE OF WESTERN EUROPE

The decline of Europe's role in world affairs had already set in during the First World War, when only the intervention of the United States had enabled the Allies to win. For a brief span between the two wars, a semblance of the old European system of great powers was resurrected. But the Second World War brought the preeminence of Europe definitely to an end.

The postwar problems facing the nations of Europe were alike in many ways. All the major powers of western Europe suffered territorial losses, either in Europe or overseas, and several of them were threatened by communism from without or within. The one concern shared by all countries was to recover from the economic effects of the war. In trying to cope with these problems, the nations of free Europe were forced to modify their economic and political nationalism and to attempt some measure of economic, if not political, union. European recovery was retarded by the fact that the Continent continued to be divided into Communist and non-Communist spheres. But in time the gulf that the Cold War had created between the two halves of Europe grew narrower. As both eastern and western Europe recovered from the war and as relations between the two improved, the reunion of the European continent again appeared possible.

Great Britain: From World Empire to European Power

Great Britain after the Second World War had to cope with two related problems: the need for economic recovery and the loss of most of its empire. In 1945 the British electorate for the first time returned a Labour majority. Under the leadership of Clement Attlee, the government embarked on a program that was denounced as socialist by the Conservatives under Winston Churchill. Most of the enterprises that were nationalized, however—railroads, airlines, utilities, coal mines, and the Bank of England—remained so even after the Conservatives returned to power in 1951. The most far-reaching measures introduced by the Labour government were the various Social Welfare Acts that aimed at equality of opportunity for all citizens.

The tendency of these measures to

Opposite: President Richard Nixon and Premier Chou En-lai exchange toasts in Peking in 1972.

make British society more egalitarian was enhanced by the drastic program of austerity by which the government hoped to balance the budget and regain Britain's former position in world trade. Under Conservative rule from 1951 to 1964, the country experienced a temporary economic recovery. In 1964, however, dissatisfaction with a weak foreign policy and renewed economic stagnation once more brought a Labour victory. The second Labour cabinet was no more successful in overcoming Britain's economic paralysis than the first had been. When foreign loans, heavy taxation, and reduced government spending failed to improve matters, the government of Prime Minister Harold Wilson in 1967 devalued the pound, in the hope of thus solving Britain's perennial trade deficit. But this and other drastic measures failed to improve the country's economic malaise. In 1970 the Conservatives under Edward Heath won another chance to cope with the nation's rising inflation and unemployment. To economic unrest and strikes now were added bloody riots and bombings in Northern Ireland. In 1974 it became Labour's turn again. But neither party was able to halt the spiraling inflation, chiefly caused by union demands.

One of the initial causes of Britain's depression was the rapid shrinking of its empire after the war. Wherever colonial peoples became restive and demanded independence, British interests were usually involved. Most of the resulting new states remained within the Commonwealth of Nations. But the ties of this elusive organization grew weaker over the years, partly because of the racial policies pursued by countries like South Africa and Rhodesia. Within less than a generation, the once mighty British Empire virtually melted away.

One possible way of improving its position was for Britain to draw closer to the continental nations that had joined forces in the European Economic Community, or Common Market. But the island kingdom was reluctant to do so, for fear that such economic rapprochement might conflict with its Commonwealth ties. It was not until 1963 that Britain applied for membership in the Common Market. At that time it was barred by the veto of Charles de Gaulle, who asserted that the British were not ready to assume the full obligations of membership. Ten years later Britain finally joined the European Economic Community, hoping to share in that organization's economic prosperity.

Economic difficulties—high inflation and rising unemployment—continued to be Britain's major problem. In 1979 the Conservatives under Margaret Thatcher once again gained control. The first woman prime minister was a firm believer in free enterprise and laissez faire. But as in most other industrialized nations, social services continued to require high taxation and retard economic growth. In addition, intermittent violence between Catholics and Protestants in Northern Ireland put a constant strain on Britain's finances. In 1982, a showdown with Argentina over the Falkland Islands, while bringing an upsurge of national unity, further added to the country's

Queen Elizabeth II with heads of state and representatives of the Commonwealth nations at Buckingham Palace in 1977.

Fall of France 1940	Provisional Government Under de Gaulle		1958	
Vichy Government		Fourth Republic		Fifth Republic

1945 1946

economic ills and reminded the British people of how little was left of their once-mighty empire.

France: Search for Lost Grandeur

In France political instability at home and continued colonial wars abroad slowed down postwar economic recovery. To make a clear break with the past, the French in 1946 gave themselves a new constitution. But the Fourth Republic was little different from the Third. As old enmities persisted and new ones arose, the traditional bickering among numerous small parties and interest groups again dominated the political scene. The chief beneficiaries of this confusion were the French Communists, who until 1958 made up the largest party in the National Assembly. Only in foreign policy did the new republic show some consistency.

France, like Great Britain, found it difficult at first to regain its economic health. Financial problems were staggering, and their solution required heavy taxation and a stable currency. But reluctant taxpayers, creeping inflation, and incessant strikes counteracted the beneficent effects of American Marshall Plan aid. It was not until President de Gaulle began to dominate the national scene in the late 1950s that a broad austerity program, combined with careful economic planning, put France back on the road to prosperity.

France, again like Britain, also faced the rapid dissolution of its colonial empire. In 1946 the Fourth Republic tried to maintain some control over its overseas holdings by founding the French Union. This federation, however, was far too centralized to satisfy the more developed territories, and a number of them—Syria, Lebanon, Morocco, and Tunisia—demanded, and were given, their independence. Indochina and Algeria won independence only after drawn-out and costly fighting. In 1958 the French Union was transformed into the French Community, which included France proper, its few remaining overseas possessions, and most of the new African nations that formerly made up French Equatorial and West Africa. The Community was a loose federation whose main significance lay in whatever prestige it held for the former mother country of a once great empire.

Prestige was the main concern of the man who assumed direction of French affairs in 1958. Charles de Gaulle, leader of the Free French forces in the Second World War, had served briefly as provisional president in 1945 but had retired before the domestic confusion that reigned at that time. He was recalled in 1958 at the height of the national crisis caused by the war in Algeria. Under de Gaulle's direction a new constitution was adopted that, in an attempt to ensure greater political stability, vastly increased the power of the president. In December 1958 General de Gaulle was elected first president of the Fifth Republic.

From 1958 until his retirement in 1969, the general's towering figure dominated the French scene. De Gaulle's most important achievement was the solution of the Algerian problem. In 1962 an agreement between French and Arab representatives, endorsed by the French electorate, gave Algeria its independence. Elsewhere, in Europe and overseas, de Gaulle's main ambition was to recapture some of France's past "grandeur." To strengthen his country's position in Europe, de Gaulle maintained close ties with West Germany and cemented relations with the communist powers, notably the Soviet Union. To counteract Anglo-Saxon influence, he took France out of NATO, preferring instead to rely on an independent French nuclear force, and he barred Britain from membership in the Common Market. Along similar lines, de Gaulle drew closer to Communist China, criticized American involvement in Vietnam, and even encouraged separatist sentiment among French Canadians. Supporters of the French presi-

Charles de Gaulle, then prime minister of France, campaigning in overseas France on behalf of his constitutional proposals in 1958. In December of that year he was elected president.

France and West Germany united in the opening of a new waterway on the Moselle River in 1962. Among the dignitaries on board were Charles de Gaulle, Heinrich Lübke, president of the Federal Republic of Germany, and the Grand Duchess Charlotte of Luxembourg.

dent defended his obstructionist policies as a reassertion not merely of French influence but of European influence as well against the United States. His critics, however, charged that when the general said Europe, he meant France; and when he said France, he meant de Gaulle.

In France itself, de Gaulle's preoccupation with foreign concerns at the expense of domestic ones gave rise to a wave of discontent, especially among workers and students, that almost led to revolution in May 1968. When some of his reform proposals were defeated in a national referendum the following year, de Gaulle resigned.

De Gaulle's successor was one of his close associates, Georges Pompidou. The new president's major concern was with domestic affairs; he tried to improve France's economy by overcoming its antiquated production methods and to ease France's rapid transition into a highly industrialized and urban society. In foreign affairs, Pompidou at long last welcomed Great Britain into the Common Market. When Pompidou died in 1974, Valéry Giscard d'Estaing continued along a road of domestic reforms, fiscal austerity, and long-range economic planning. Abroad he maintained de Gaulle's self-assertive and independent stand.

Meanwhile, gains in local elections by the parties of the left showed that many Frenchmen remained critical of their government's policy. This discontent came to a head in the elections of 1981, which gave a resounding victory to Socialist leader François Mitterand. The inclusion of some Communists in his new cabinet worried France's allies, but Mitterand's subsequent policies firmly endorsed the defense of western Europe against the Soviet Union. His domestic program of job-creation, nationalization of major industries, and taxation of the rich ran into parliamentary opposition and did little to improve France's economy. Relations between France and West Germany under Mitterand continued to be close.

West Germany: The "German Federal Republic"

The most spectacular rise from rubble to riches in postwar Europe occurred in West Germany. The partition of the former Reich in 1949 as a result of the Cold War has already been discussed (see p. 788). During the 1950s the western Federal Republic experienced a veritable "economic miracle." In contrast to the nationalization measures adopted by Great Britain and, to a lesser extent, France, Germany followed a more traditional policy of laissez faire. With a favorable balance of trade, a freely convertible currency, and hardly any unemployment, Germany's "free-market economy" aroused the admiration and envy of its neighbors.

Politically, developments in West Germany were remarkably steady, especially compared with the turbulent years after the First World War. The constitution of the Federal Republic was framed to avoid some of the mistakes of the Weimar Republic. The country was fortunate in having as its first chancellor Konrad Adenauer, a conservative opponent of nazism and a sincere friend of the West. The "old man" virtually dominated German politics from 1949 until his retirement in 1963 at age eighty-seven. His successor, Ludwig Erhard, popular as the author of the "economic miracle," was a man of lesser political stature. In 1966 the middle-of-the-road Christian Democratic Union (CDU), which hitherto had dominated the government, had to share power with the moderately leftist Social Democratic Party (SPD), with Kurt Georg Kiesinger of the CDU as chancellor and Willy Brandt of the SPD as foreign minister. The shift toward the Social Democrats continued in 1969, when Willy Brandt became chancellor in a coalition of the SPD with the small, liberal Free Democratic Party (FDP). Brandt resigned the chancellorship over a domestic issue in 1973 and was succeeded by the equally able Helmut Schmidt.

Next to economic development, the two most vital issues before the West German government in the 1950s and 1960s were reunification and rearmament. To reunite not only East and West Germany but also the region beyond the Oder-Neisse line (occupied by Poland in 1945) was the fervent wish of every German. Repeated proposals of the western powers to achieve German unity through free general elections invariably met with Soviet opposition. Meanwhile the West German Federal Republic refused to recognize the East German Democratic Republic, in order to keep alive the idea of a united Germany. But in time, and as each section of Germany developed along widely divergent lines, a growing number of Germans became reconciled to the thought that they might not live to see their country reunited. As long as Adenauer was in control, however, any open acquiescence in the partition of Germany was out of the question.

This situation changed with the advent of Willy Brandt. As foreign minister, Brandt had stated his intention of bringing about a détente with the communist world, while at the same time maintaining close relations with the West. Once he was chancellor, he proceeded to carry out his design. As first steps he signed treaties with the Soviet Union and Poland in 1970 that called for mutual renunciation of the use of force and the establishment of normal relations. The agreement with Poland also included West Germany's recognition of the Oder-Neisse line as the German-Polish frontier. Of still greater significance was a treaty in 1972 between East and West Germany that recognized the existence of two sovereign German states and provided for closer collaboration between them. To round out this policy of rapprochement with the communist world, the Brandt government also resumed economic relations with a number of East European states and established diplomatic ties with Communist China. Despite much criticism from his political opponents, Brandt's *Ostpolitik* (eastern policy) had the support of the majority of West Germans, as was shown by his election victory in 1972.

Brandt's policy also helped to dispel whatever apprehension had arisen over German rearmament. The creation of a West German army caused considerable debate in the 1950s. As the Russians at the time began training a German military force in East Germany, the western powers decided to permit the limited rearmament of West Germany. Under an agreement ratified in 1955, West Germany was to contribute a maximum of five hundred thousand men to the common defense of the West under NATO. In return, the Federal Republic was granted complete sovereignty.

There was some fear, both in Germany and outside, that rearmament would cause a revival of German militarism and nationalism. But such fears proved groundless. Relations between Germany and its "traditional enemy" France were better than they had ever been, leading to a treaty of friendship in 1963. Collaboration with the Anglo-Saxon powers was close, and Brandt's *Ostpolitik* gave further proof of West Germany's peaceful intentions. In its domestic policy, furthermore, West Germany showed that it had made a clean break with the Nazi past. There were a few incidents of neonazism, and in the late 1960s a right-wing group, the National Democratic Party, gained some ground in local elections; but the majority of Germans disapproved of these activities. In the mid-1970s, a new type of leftist radicalism emerged in Germany, spearheaded by a small terrorist group whose anarchist violence was reminiscent of the "nihilists" of tsarist Russia (see p. 617). Their acts of terror against government and business leaders led the government to curtail the generous civil rights guaranteed by the Bonn constitution. The fear that such measures would lead to a revival of authoritarianism, however, proved groundless.

West Germany had thus emerged as the strongest nation in Europe (other than the Soviet Union) and America's most valued ally. There were some differences between the two partners, however, and chancellor Schmidt frequently criticized his American counterparts for being inconsistent in their foreign and short-sighted in their domestic policies. As West Germany's economy began to slow down and share the fate of some of its industrial competitors, balancing the budget became increasingly difficult and many Germans seemed to feel that it was time for a change. This took place in 1982, when the coalition between Socialists and Free Democrats broke apart, chiefly over domestic issues. As a result of general elections in 1983, a new coalition of Christian Democrats (CDU/CSU)

Helmut Kohl campaigning before the West German general election of 1983.

and Free Democrats won a safe majority, ensuring continued stability, especially in foreign affairs, under the chancellorship of Helmut Kohl, leader of the CDU.

Italy: Least of the Great Powers

Italy emerged from the Second World War with its already backward economy in a dismal state. After a slow start, however, the nation staged a remarkable recovery. By 1965 Italy's industrial production had increased fourfold, and the nation's per capita income had doubled. With economic improvement came a period of political stability. The new Italian republic was launched successfully in 1946 under the capable leadership of Alcide de Gasperi and his Christian Democratic Party. But with the onset of the Cold War, the government came under increasing attacks from a strong Communist Party on the left and a grow-

ing neofascist movement on the right. Only when the Christian Democrats, beginning in 1962, started to ally themselves with the moderate Socialists on their left did some measure of political calm return.

Even so, the fact that one out of every three Italians continued to vote Communist showed that all was far from well. While there was prosperity, poverty persisted, especially in the agricultural south. Even in the north real wages did not keep up with the general rise in the economy, and the distribution of income remained uneven. In the late 1960s, economic discontent led to numerous strikes, which, in turn, aggravated the economic crisis. In addition, the center-left coalition broke apart, as Christian Democrats and Socialists differed over the controversial divorce law of 1970 and other issues. Meanwhile, the Communists remained the country's second-largest party, and the neofascist Italian Social movement doubled its forces in the elections of 1972. From here on, Italy was governed by frequently changing minority coalitions that were still dominated by the Christian Democrats. The elections of 1976 brought further Communist gains, and Italy, like France, faced the possibility of having to let the Communists share in its government. In 1978 a wave of attacks by a small band of terrorists, the Red Brigades, against prominent political and business leaders was climaxed by the abduction and murder of a former Christian Democratic premier, Aldo Moro. The resulting grief and anger, shared by the Communists, did much to reunite the deeply divided Italian nation.

Italy could ill afford to lose one of its ablest leaders. Its ailing economy, burdened by excessive social services, high unemployment, and astronomical inflation, led to continued instability. By 1980, Italy had had more than forty governments since the Second World War. The polarization between the Communist left and the neofascist right, furthermore, made viable coalitions difficult. The situation was exacerbated by continued terrorism, by scandals in high places (which included President Giovanni Leoni), and by the disastrous earthquake of 1980. Among the leading

Toward a "European Consciousness"?

The adjective "European," which a century ago was understood only by a small minority, and which even in the early twentieth century was accepted perhaps only by the aristocracy, by the high bourgeoisie and by certain intellectuals, today has become an accepted adjective, a designation, a self-ascribed characteristic for the majority of the populations even in Central and Eastern Europe. To many a peasant in the Danube Valley the adjective "European" even twenty or thirty years ago meant either nothing at all or something that was vaguely and suspiciously alien. This is no longer so. Despite Communist political rule and regimentation, life for large masses of people in Warsaw and Belgrade and Budapest and Bucharest has now more in common with life in Berne and Brussels and Paris than it had fifty or one hundred years ago, and this is true of people in Lisbon, Madrid, Palermo, Athens. It is, let me repeat, by no means clear whether the increasing standardization of certain forms of life will, within Europe, lead to a further, and decisive, phase in the development of a European consciousness. That ten thousand Bulgarians watch television or that tens of thousands in Budapest experience their first traffic jam is unimportant. What is important, for our purposes, is to recognize that the collapse of the European state system did not mean the end of European history; that, indeed, we are facing two countervailing historical developments: decline—definite decline—of the European state system on the one hand; rise—vague rise—of a European consciousness on the other.

From John Lukacs, *Decline and Rise of Europe* (Garden City, N.Y.: Doubleday, 1965), pp. 169–70.

industrial nations of the West, Italy was clearly the last and the least.

The Quest for European Unity

Given the similarity of their problems, especially in the economic field, it was only natural that western European nations should try to devise means for common action. The Marshall Plan had shown that lasting recovery could be won only through economic cooperation; and the Brussels Pact, besides calling for a military alliance, had also stressed the need for collaboration in economic, social, and cultural affairs (see p. 790). The first major instance of such collaboration was the Schuman Plan, which established the European Coal and Steel Community (ECSC). In 1952 France, Germany, the Benelux countries, and Italy agreed to merge their resources of coal and steel in a common western European market. By 1957 enough progress had been achieved to make it possible to extend the common market to other goods through the European Economic Community (EEC).

The European Economic Community is not a closed organization; any country can apply for membership. The admission of Great Britain was delayed until 1973, at which time Ireland and Denmark also joined. The next candidates—Greece, Spain, and Portugal—applied in 1977, and Greece joined in 1981. Representing more than 270 million people, the EEC is the most important and powerful trade area in the world.

Plans for European political union were less successful. Prospects looked bright in 1949, when the Council of Europe was founded at Strasbourg. But it remained a purely consultative body, and the hope for a United States of Europe did not materialize. As Europe recovered economically and as the threat of Soviet expansion subsided, national differences once again came to the fore. Yet despite these disappointments, the general trend toward European unity was unmistakable. The European powers realized that the only way they could wield any real influence was by joining forces and forgetting the divisive issues of the past. At their periodic summit meetings, the leaders of the European Community in-creasingly not only dealt with economic issues, but discussed and took a stand on matters of common political concern, such as the defense of western Europe or the support of Great Britain in the Falkland Islands crisis.

THE AMERICAS

To the rest of the world the United States in 1945 appeared as a country of unbelievable wealth, untouched by the hardships of war. But to Americans the picture looked quite different. Price controls, wage controls, real or artificially induced shortages of essential goods, incessant waves of strikes, and signs of widespread corruption—these were some of the problems faced by the American people after the war. The Democratic administration's attempts to deal with the situation by further legislation found little support. It seemed that the country was tired of government controls and of a social service state that to most Republicans smacked of socialism.

The Truman Era

President Truman was reelected in 1948 chiefly because of his foreign policy: the Truman Doctrine, the Marshall Plan, and the Berlin airlift. At the time, these measures were applauded by a majority of Americans. Isolationism, of course, did not vanish overnight. But the fact that a Republican administration after 1952 continued substantially the same foreign policy showed that the shift from isolationism was a matter not so much of choice as of necessity.

One aspect of American involvement abroad that was not universally popular was the foreign-aid program. During the first fifteen years after the war, United States economic and military aid amounted to more than $75 billion. Much of it was given in a spirit of genuine helpfulness. But foreign aid was also an important weapon in the Cold War, especially after 1955, when the Soviet Union began stepping up its own foreign-aid program.

In American domestic affairs, one of the major issues at the time was the fear of Communist infiltration. This fear

A unique photograph of the four men who occupied the American presidency between 1945 and 1968—Kennedy, Johnson, Eisenhower, and Truman. The occasion was the funeral of House Speaker Sam Rayburn in 1961.

John F. Kennedy (1917–63) brought a vigorous approach to the presidency.

reached its climax during the Korean War. Chiefly because of the agitation of Wisconsin's Senator Joseph McCarthy, the American public in the early 1950s was led to believe that its government had allowed Communists to get into key positions in the State Department and the army. These unfounded accusations created a climate of fear and suspicion and did much to harm the reputations of innocent people.

The reality of the Communist threat abroad, meanwhile, was brought home by events in Korea. As the war there bogged down in a bloody stalemate, critics of the administration demanded an escalation of the war, including the bombing of Communist bases in China. Foremost among these critics was America's commander in chief in Korea, General Douglas MacArthur. When efforts to silence him failed, President Truman, in April 1951, relieved the general of his command. The ensuing crisis was the most serious the United States had faced since 1945. Together with a mounting wave of government scandals and continued suspicion of Communist influence in the government, the Korean War was a major cause of the defeat of the Democrats in the election of 1952.

The Eisenhower Years

The victories of the Republican candidate, Dwight D. Eisenhower, in 1952 and 1956 were as much personal as partisan. He enhanced his popularity by concluding a Korean armistice in 1953. During his two administrations, bipartisan majorities in Congress collaborated to produce much valuable social legislation. The nation's economy continued to flourish, except in the agricultural sector, where overproduction posed a serious problem. The administration's attempts to reduce price supports and to return to a free market in agricultural products incurred the opposition of farm groups; this opposition was one of the reasons for the overwhelming congressional victory of the Democrats in 1958. Other reasons were the temporary economic recession of that year and the antagonism that the Republican administration had aroused among organized labor.

A major issue that came to the fore during the Eisenhower administration was desegregation. In *Brown v. Board of Education of Topeka* (1954), the United States Supreme Court ruled that American blacks had the right to attend the same schools as whites. Desegregation proceeded smoothly in most states, but in the Deep South every possible means was used to prevent it. From 1957 to 1958 President Eisenhower had to send federal troops to enforce desegregation in Little Rock, Arkansas. This was only the beginning of a drawn-out crisis, as blacks began to demand that desegregation be extended to other fields. The resistance of die-hard "white supremacists" to these demands did much to tarnish America's image abroad.

From Kennedy to Johnson

The victory of John F. Kennedy in 1960 injected a fresh note into American politics. His administration got off to a promising start when Congress approved a series of social-service measures chiefly designed to aid the poor. When the president began to tackle the touchy subject of civil rights, however, he lost the support of southern Democrats and his domestic program came to a halt. Some improvement in the status of blacks was made under pressure of nonviolent protests directed by able black leaders. But as police in the South met peaceful demonstrations with violence, the situation became increasingly explosive. Much of President Kennedy's attention was taken up with crises in foreign affairs. In his efforts to counter Communist threats in Southeast Asia, Cuba, and Berlin, the president generally found the support that Congress withheld from his domestic program.

President Kennedy was assassinated on November 22, 1963. A major political crisis was avoided because of the firm manner in which his successor, Lyndon B. Johnson, took charge. Where Kennedy had labored in vain against congressional opposition, Johnson, a former majority leader in the Senate, was able to achieve some notable successes. By 1964 the new president had gained sufficient popular support to win a landslide victory.

From then on, however, President Johnson found the going more and more difficult. Civil rights had become the key issue in domestic politics. The Civil Rights Act of 1964 was the most sweeping legislation of its kind ever enacted. But its provisions were still disregarded in many parts of the South. Meanwhile black protests spread to the North, where the demand was for greater equality in employment, housing, and education. Demonstrations that hitherto had been orderly now became increasingly violent, as bloody riots swept through major American cities and as advocates of "black power" preached the use of force. To cope with the economic roots of black discontent, the Johnson administration stepped up the antipoverty programs initiated under Kennedy. But while the "war on poverty" called for vast amounts of money, more and more funds were being diverted to another kind of war.

The war in Vietnam, in which the United States had become increasingly involved after 1961, proved the most divisive issue in American politics during the last two years of the Johnson administration. As "hawks" (advocating victory through war) ranged against "doves" (favoring American withdrawal), many young Americans chose to go to prison or abroad rather than to fight an "unjust" war. The cause of reform suffered a major loss with the assassination, in June 1968, of Senator Robert F. Kennedy, a leading Democratic contender for the presidency. Racial unrest, meanwhile, had flared up anew after the murder that April of the Reverend Dr. Martin Luther King, Jr., an outstanding figure in the nonviolent civil-rights movement. It was a deeply disturbed and divided nation that gave the Republican candidate, Richard M. Nixon, a narrow victory in November 1968.

The Nixon Administrations

The war in Vietnam continued to be the major cause of tension in American politics. The withdrawal of American forces beginning in 1972 and the subsequent start of armistice negotiations were largely responsible for President Nixon's reelection the same year by an overwhelming majority. An uneasy armistice was finally concluded in early 1973. Meanwhile the president and his dynamic secretary of state, Henry Kissinger, had embarked on new ventures elsewhere by paying visits to the Soviet Union and Communist China, thus easing tensions with the Russians and establishing first contacts with the mainland Chinese.

In his domestic affairs, President Nixon had a less fortunate hand. Most problems had already plagued previous administrations; but some of them worsened as time went on. One of these was crime. "Law and order," a key issue in the 1972 elections, was part of a larger question—the rapid decay of American cities into breeding grounds of crime, often connected with drug addiction. Another growing concern was protection of the environment against pollution by individuals and industries. Unrest among blacks decreased somewhat, as some of their demands were being met. There remained, however, the controversial issue of "busing" white or black students outside their school districts to achieve a better racial balance. Many of these problems called for official intervention. But such intervention was opposed by an administration that tried to halt the increasing role of government in the life of the individual.

Intervention could not be avoided, however, in the economic sphere. To slow the country's rising inflation, the Nixon administration, beginning in 1971, imposed wage and price controls, measures never before initiated in time of peace. To improve America's growing trade deficit, the dollar was officially devalued by a total of 17 percent in 1972 and 1973. And to curtail government spending at home, President Nixon refused to spend some funds appropriated by Congress for purposes he considered wasteful. This action did not endear him to the legislature, and confrontations be-

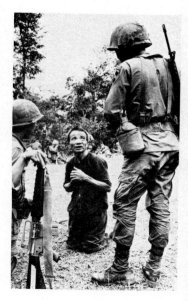

American versus Vietcong: a struggle that lasted more than a decade.

The Reverend Dr. Martin Luther King (1929–68) at civil-rights rally in Washington, D.C., August 28, 1963: "I have a dream. . . ."

A beleaguered president tries to regain the nation's confidence in 1973 in a televised address concerning the events of the Watergate Affair.

tween the White House and Capitol Hill were frequent.

Far more disquieting than any of these issues, however, was the "Watergate Affair," in which leading members of the president's staff were found to have been involved in illegal acts against the Democratic Party during the 1972 campaign. As judicial and Senate hearings uncovered a sordid story of intrigue and attempted cover-up, the question arose as to whether President Nixon had any part in these events. The president denied any such involvement. As more and more incriminating evidence came to light, however, and as Congressional impeachment hearings got under way in early 1974, Nixon, on August 9, decided to resign rather than face further charges and revelations. He was the first president ever thus to leave office.

From Ford to Carter

The new president, Gerald Ford, had been appointed vice president by Nixon when Spiro Agnew had resigned after being found guilty of income tax evasion. The fact that Ford had not been elected was a disadvantage, though his amicable manner made him many friends. His popularity suffered, however, when he first granted a general pardon to Nixon and somewhat later a limited amnesty to draft evaders during the Vietnam War. To ensure continuity in foreign policy, Ford retained Secretary of State Kissinger, who tended to overshadow the president. In domestic affairs, economic issues and the effects of the energy crisis continued to loom large. Also, the nightmare of Watergate was not easily forgotten.

The race for the presidency in 1976 was the closest in recent times. The winner, Democrat James Earl ("Jimmy") Carter, was a dark horse, who owed most of his victory to his own efforts. President Carter's proposals for tax reform, reduced government spending, and legislation to deal with long-term energy requirements were innovative and addressed to the nation's most urgent needs. In an effort to correct the "imperial" image of the presidency, Carter affected a more folksy style, which did not always enhance his popularity. To many

Americans, the peanut farmer from Plains, Georgia, seemed to lack sufficient experience for his high office, especially in military and foreign affairs, where the Panama Canal Treaty and the decision to halt development of the neutron bomb met with widespread criticism.

From Carter to Reagan

Carter was defeated by Ronald Reagan in 1980, due partly to ineptitude, partly to circumstances beyond his control. The president's failure to cope with "stagflation" (an economy suffering simultaneously from stagnation and inflation) was no worse than the futile efforts of national leaders elsewhere or, for that matter, of his successor. Nor can Carter be blamed for the seizure of American hostages by Iran, although his bumbling attempts at their liberation, including the abortive raid in April 1980, contributed to his defeat. The Carter years in retrospect did bring some positive achievements: the Camp David accords between Israel and Egypt, the Panama Canal Treaty, the stress on human rights—for minorities and women at home and for political dissidents abroad.

Ronald Reagan won by a sizeable majority. Personal charm and skill as a politician, as shown in his public debate with Carter, played their part. His promise to balance the budget by reducing government spending and to stimulate production through tax cuts was appealing, but it was also inconsistent. After some initial successes, he ran into serious congressional opposition. Similar contradictions characterized Reagan's foreign policy, where efforts at détente conflicted with stepped-up military preparedness against the Soviet Union. This uncertainty in foreign policy caused great uneasiness among America's allies and led to the resignation of Secretary of State Alexander Haig in 1982.

The United States and Its Neighbors

Since the contest between communism and capitalism was a global one, the maintenance of harmony within the Western Hemisphere was of major concern to every administration after 1945.

Relations with America's northern neighbor were, on the whole, cordial. Because of its tremendous economic growth, Canada ranked as one of the world's leading industrial powers. United States capital played an important part in this expansion, and the resulting American influence caused some resentment among Canadian nationalists. Military relations between the two countries were close, both within NATO and without. Continued membership in the (British) Commonwealth saved Canada from becoming too dependent on its powerful neighbor, although ties with Great Britain grew noticeably weaker. Canadian politics was dominated by the Liberal Party, led until 1957 by Mackenzie King, thereafter until 1968 by Lester Pearson, and since then by Pierre Elliott Trudeau. One of the most burning domestic issues continued to be the division between French- and English-speaking Canadians. Separatism in the predominantly French province of Quebec was successfully resisted by Trudeau, a French Canadian himself, who favored bilingualism and greater autonomy, but opposed independence.

Relations between the United States and its southern neighbors were more complicated. The twenty republics of Latin America differed widely in size and significance, and the absence of a strong democratic tradition made many of them prone to authoritarian regimes of the right or left. The most pressing problem of the whole area was its alarming rise in population. Latin America had great economic potentialities, but financial and technical assistance were needed to develop them. The United States was expected to supply this aid. Prior to 1960 little such aid found its way to Latin America. Subsequently, a number of ambitious development schemes were launched, notably the Alliance for Progress, proclaimed by President Kennedy in 1961. But the results of such schemes were disappointing. Besides looking to the United States for help, the nations of Latin America increasingly looked to one another. The Latin American Free Trade Association (LAFTA), set up in 1960, called for the creation of a common market for all of Latin America, but its progress has been slow. More successful in fostering economic cooperation were various subregional groups, especially the Central American Common Market.

The United States was concerned with building a united military front against the threat of communism in the Western Hemisphere. In 1947 the Latin American nations and the United States signed the Rio Treaty, which called for mutual assistance in case of war. Subsequent agreements arranged for the exchange of United States arms against strategic raw materials. The most important agency of inter-American cooperation was the Organization of American States (OAS), founded in 1948. It originally included all nations of the Western Hemisphere except Canada, but Cuba was excluded (though not formally expelled) in 1962. The Charter of the OAS proclaimed the equality of its members and laid down the principle of nonintervention in their external and internal affairs. The OAS proved of great value as a stabilizing influence.

The main threat to the security of the Western Hemisphere in the eyes of the United States was Fidel Castro's Cuba. The United States initially hailed the victory of Castro's rebel forces in 1959, but his close relations with Communist China and the Soviet Union led the United States to break off relations with Cuba and make various attempts to overthrow the Castro regime.

The United States was also involved in a number of other Latin American crises, notably in Chile and Panama. In Chile, the United States was accused of having engineered the violent overthrow of President Salvador Allende Gossens, a Marxist, by a military junta in 1973, a charge that subsequently was proved correct. In Panama, perennial demonstrations against American control of the Panama Canal finally led to the signing of a treaty by presidents Carter and Torrijos in 1977, by which the waterway would come under Panamanian control by the end of the century.

Under the Reagan administration, the main trouble spot in Central America was El Salvador. Here leftist guerillas, aided by Nicaragua and ultimately by Cuba, waged war against a military and civilian junta supported by the United States. On this as on many earlier occa-

Nikita Khrushchev delivers an angry diatribe during a United Nations debate in 1960.

Leonid Brezhnev showing journalists in Moscow his official portrait.

sions, conservative Americans viewed popular unrest in ideological terms—attacking demands for economic reform as socialism, and equating socialism with communism.

THE COMMUNIST WORLD

For almost two decades after 1945, while the Cold War lasted, the Communist world appeared to be a monolithic bloc dominated by Moscow. It took the rest of the world some time to realize how much this Soviet predominance depended on one man. In retrospect, the death of Joseph Stalin on March 5, 1953, was a major event in world history. It spelled the end of an era, not only for Russian communism but for world communism as well.

Russia Under Khrushchev

The main features of the Stalinist era, which reached its height after 1945, have already been discussed (see pp. 749–52). To repair the staggering damages of the war, two Five-Year Plans called for a new round of industrialization and collectivization. Simultaneously, strictest orthodoxy remained the keynote of Soviet political and cultural life. The slightest deviation from Stalinist-Marxist theory brought imprisonment, slave labor, or death. In a famous speech before the twentieth Party Congress in 1956, Khrushchev charged that Stalin, "a very distrustful man, sickly suspicious," had planned even to liquidate his most intimate political associates.

Stalin's reign of terror came to a sudden end with his death. For the first four years or so after Stalin's death, "collective leadership" was instituted. But it was only a matter of time before one of the most determined members of the group, Nikita S. Khrushchev, emerged as the recognized leader of the Soviet Union. As Stalin had done a generation earlier, Khrushchev used his key position as Secretary of the Central Committee of the Communist Party to rid himself of his associates. The only novelty was that his rivals were not killed but merely ousted—an example of the "new look" in Soviet policy.

Khrushchev, a career party functionary, never achieved the absolute power that Stalin had wielded before him. Russia under Stalin had undergone not only an economic but a social revolution. From a nation of illiterate peasants, the Soviet Union had become a nation of educated workers. Although the basic Marxist concept of state ownership of the means of production remained in force, the concept of a classless society had been far from realized. Instead, a substantial upper class had grown up: the party elite, the top echelons of the vast political and economic bureaucracy, managerial personnel, technical experts, scientists, and the like. The Soviet Union, in other words, had become a far more complex society than it had been. To run such a nation by regimentation based on terror was no longer possible.

The most dramatic change in the life of the average Russian came with the retreat from terror after Stalin's death. This did not mean that there were no longer any political prisoners. But it did mean that the number of punishable political crimes became smaller than it had been under Stalin. Henceforth it was possible to criticize certain aspects of the regime without risking execution.

The liberalization of Soviet life was felt in other ways. In factories and on collective farms discipline was relaxed. Consumer goods became more plentiful, and the housing shortage was reduced. Education was broadened to admit more students to secondary schools and universities. With the easing of travel restrictions, the Russian people for the first time came in contact with the outside world. In Russian art and literature, the orthodox emphasis on "socialist realism" gave way to some modern trends. Initially, outside observers saw these changes as signs that Russia had abandoned its unbending opposition to the West. But Soviet leaders made no secret of the fact that the "new look" was merely a change in methods and that their aim remained what it had always been: the overthrow of capitalism.

Russia Under Brezhnev

The return to virtual one-man rule under Khrushchev was suddenly reversed in 1964, when the Russian leader was purged by his party's Central Committee and his double role as premier and party secretary was divided between Alexei N. Kosygin and Leonid I. Brezhnev. The main reasons for Khrushchev's dismissal appeared to be domestic, notably his failure to live up to his boastful economic promises, although foreign reversals, such as the Cuban missile crisis, also played their part. For a while the trend seemed once again to be toward collective leadership. But like Khrushchev (and Stalin) before him, Brezhnev, as General Secretary of the Communist Party, gradually emerged as the key figure in Soviet affairs. Continuity in foreign policy was assured by the presence of veteran Foreign Minister Andrei A. Gromyko. In 1977 Brezhnev assumed the additional position of President of the Supreme Soviet, or head of state, replacing Nikolai V. Podgorny and making one-man rule still more visible. A new constitution, meanwhile, attempted to project a more liberal image of the Soviet state by stressing individual rights; but like Stalin's effort in 1936, it was seen by western observers as mere window dressing.

Economic growth in the Soviet Union continued during the 1960s and 1970s at a slower rate than predicted, especially in the agrarian sector, where dependence on American grain imports gave the United States a limited means of exerting diplomatic pressure. With increased material gain came signs of spiritual unrest. The younger generation in particular, the "grandchildren of the revolution," seemed less and less willing to accept the intellectual restrictions of a totalitarian regime. The reaction of the post-Khrushchev regime to manifestations of dissent was twofold. On the one hand, critical writers like Alexander Solzhenitsyn and Andrei Sinyavsky, advocates of civil liberties like Yosif Brodsky and Andrei Sakharov, and various na-

tional dissidents in the Ukraine and Lithuania were arrested and in some cases forced to emigrate. But at the same time the government also tried to counter discontent by economic concessions, raising the living standard of the average Soviet citizen. The general tendency, however, was in the direction of repression rather than reform, leading some foreign observers to speak of a return to Stalinism.

From Brezhnev to Andropov

Brezhnev, whose health had been failing for some time, died in 1982. He was succeeded as General Secretary of the Communist Party's Central Committee by Yuri Andropov, for many years head of the secret police, or KGB. The Politburo regained a degree of collective leadership, but Andropov was clearly more than merely first among equals. In his domestic policy he aimed at overcoming Russia's economic stagnation, and in foreign affairs he continued Brezhnev's policy of drawing closer to China and resisting American efforts at arms control and nuclear disarmament.

Yuri Andropov confers with Andrei Gromyko during Kremlin celebrations of the 113th anniversary of Lenin's birth.

Western hopes for major changes in Russia's foreign policy remained unfulfilled.

Unrest Among the Satellites

The effects of the post-Stalin "thaw" were also felt among the satellite nations of eastern Europe. The first defection from the Soviet bloc had occurred as early as 1948, when Marshal Tito of Yugoslavia, preferring "Titoism" to "Stalinism," had struck out on his own. By 1956, Stalin's successors had made peace with Tito and had acknowledged that there were "various roads to socialism." But the satellites were not satisfied with mere promises of greater independence. In the fall of 1956, revolts against Soviet domination broke out first in Poland and later in Hungary. Both revolts were motivated by ardent nationalist sentiments. In addition, the Hungarian uprising was strongly anti-Communist. For that reason the Hungarian revolution was brutally suppressed by Russian intervention, while Poland's Communists, under Wladyslaw Gomulka, were given greater autonomy from Russian control.

For the next ten or twelve years, there were no further attempts to resist Russian domination. The nations of eastern Europe were enjoying far greater freedom of action than they had ever had under Stalin. From mere satellites they were gradually becoming junior partners of the Soviet Union. In 1961 growing tension between Russia and Albania over the latter's continued adherence to Stalinism led to an open break. In 1964 Rumania declared its virtual independence from Soviet influence and, like Yugoslavia before, drew closer to the West. The most dramatic change, however, occurred in Czechoslovakia, where, as a result of a peaceful revolution in the spring of 1968, the country briefly regained many democratic freedoms. The Soviet Union's armed intervention in Czechoslovakia against the regime of Alexander Dubček emphasized the threat that these liberalizing tendencies posed to Russia's leadership in the Communist world.

Crisis in Poland

The country that posed the greatest threat to that leadership was Poland. There had been periodic unrest, chiefly among Polish workers, most recently in 1970 and 1976. The main causes had been economic—food shortages and rising prices—but in time grievances had become more general, demanding individual freedoms and popular participation in governmental decisions. As intellectuals and other dissidents made common cause with the workers, their protest gained momentum. The latest crisis was touched off by a massive strike among shipyard workers at Gdansk in August 1980. Major violence was avoided when the government granted most of the strikers' demands, especially for an independent union, "Solidarity," headed by Lech Walesa.

But this was only the beginning of what took on all the earmarks of a revolution. Farmers now also demanded their own independent union, while workers asked for further liberalization of Communist rule. Sporadic strikes, meanwhile, stalemated the economy and food shortages caused riots. Next to Poland itself, the country most deeply concerned over these developments was the Soviet Union. Using economic aid and the threat of military intervention, the Russians tried to contain a movement that might spread to other parts of their empire. As opposition to Russia's influence in Polish affairs became more open, Poland's new prime minister, General Wojcieck Jaruzelski, imposed martial law, leading to the arrest of thousands of dissidents, including Walesa. From the start, the West had supported Poland's fight for freedom, now also backed by the Catholic Church of Poland and its most illustrious son, Pope John Paul II.

Hungarians burning Communist books during the uprising in 1956.

There was also sympathy among the people, if not the governments, of the other satellites. Brezhnev's and Andropov's threats of repression, on the other hand, found firm support from their strongest and most loyal European ally, Erich Honecker, head of the (East) German Democratic Republic.

"Socialist Pluralism"

Despite Russia's efforts to maintain its leadership over world communism, the unity that once had prevailed among Communist states and parties had thus given way to diversity. At a Communist world conference in 1976, the Communist parties of western Europe proclaimed their own brand of "Euro-communism," asserting their allegiance to democratic principles and their readiness to join in parliamentary governments. Instead of a monolithic Communist bloc directed from Moscow, there now existed a plurality of socialist states.

The most important split within the Communist camp developed between Moscow and Peking. While Stalin was alive, the potentially powerful People's Republic of China had not contested Russia's claim to leadership. But after 1953 the Chinese gradually began to assert themselves. At first it seemed as though China's influence was to be on the side of moderation. Beginning in 1957, however, and especially after 1963, Peking showed signs of a new, hard line. The Sino-Soviet dispute was first and foremost ideological, each side accusing the other of deviating from true "Marxism-Leninism." Following the principles of Mao Zedong's "great proletarian cultural revolution," China's radical ideologists preached "liberation" of peoples everywhere through "armed struggle" rather than through peaceful competition, as advocated by Moscow. Since Mao Zedong's death in 1976, and especially with the rise to predominance of Deng Xiaoping, China's policy has become less ideological and more pragmatic, emphasizing its role as a member of the third world rather than the Communist bloc. The general effect of this shift presents a further step on the road to "socialist pluralism."

FROM COLD WAR TO COEXISTENCE

While Russia's leadership in a Communist World was thus becoming a thing of the past, America's leadership in the Free World was likewise undergoing a change. As Western Europe in particular became once again a factor in world affairs, the role of the United States within the Western alliance became more and more one of first among equals. As a result of these changes, the most clearly discernible trend in international relations during the 1960s and 1970s was the gradual shift away from the angry confrontation of East and West in the Cold War to an equally competitive but more peaceful state of coexistence. The Cold War had developed as the result of a gradually mounting crisis; the state of peaceful coexistence came only after a decade of intermittent sparring during the 1950s, in which each side felt out the strength of the other.

The Korean War

The years immediately after 1950 brought to a climax the international tension that had been building up since 1945. In the fall of 1950, United Nations forces fought their way into North Korea, close to the borders of Red China. But when victory seemed almost in sight, the Chinese Communists intervened and drove the UN armies back into South Korea. By the spring of 1951, the front had become stabilized once more along the thirty-eighth parallel, and there it substantially remained during the stalemate that lasted for two years. Armistice negotiations were begun in 1951 but were not completed until 1953. The Korean armistice merely established an uneasy truce in which North Korean troops continued to face South Korean and American forces across a demilitarized zone.

Escalation in Both Camps

One of the effects of the Korean conflict was a substantial buildup of western military strength. The United States increased its military expenditures fivefold,

General Douglas MacArthur waves to New York City crowds during a ticker-tape parade in his honor after he had returned from Korea in 1951.

doubled its armed forces, and extended its network of military bases abroad. It was during the Korean War that NATO perfected its organization and increased its membership by adding Greece and Turkey. At the same time plans were laid for including West Germany in the western alliance. In 1952, furthermore, the United States exploded its first hydrogen bomb, thus regaining the nuclear lead it had held before the Soviet atomic explosion in 1949.

The change from a Democratic to a Republican administration in Washington in 1953 brought to the fore a man who seemed determined to use America's military strength not merely to contain but to challenge communism. Until his death in 1959, Secretary of State John Foster Dulles was the leading political strategist in the western camp. But his policy of "massive retaliation" and "brinkmanship" did not always have the support of America's friends, nor did it have the desired effect of scaring the Russians into making political concessions.

More decisive than the changing of the guard in Washington were the events touched off by Stalin's death in 1953. While the new Soviet rulers were consolidating their position at home, they adopted a more conciliatory policy abroad. At the same time, however, the Russian government announced its first successful testing of a hydrogen bomb. And while the West was rallying its forces behind NATO, the Soviets were lining up their eastern satellites behind the Warsaw Pact of 1955.

The Search for Coexistence

The first sign that Russia might be willing to negotiate East–West differences was seen in the Korean armistice, which would have been impossible without Soviet acquiescence. In January 1954 the foreign ministers of the Big Four nations (United States, Britain, France, and the Soviet Union) resumed their talks in Berlin after an interval of several years. In April the Geneva Conference on Far Eastern Affairs, with Communist China attending, temporarily divided Vietnam, where the French had recently been de-feated by the Vietminh Communist insurgents. Elections for the whole of Vietnam were to be held in 1956, but these never took place.

The culmination of the initial search for coexistence came with the Geneva Summit conference of 1955. This was the first time since Potsdam, ten years earlier, that the Big Four heads of state had assembled. On the eve of the meeting, the Russians agreed to an Austrian peace treaty, another hopeful sign of growing Soviet moderation. Relations at Geneva were cordial, though the results of the conference were disappointing. On none of the major issues—German reunification, European security, and disarmament—was any understanding reached. The only positive achievement was an agreement on cultural exchanges between East and West.

Continuation of the Cold War

While the "spirit of Geneva" appeared to have dissipated some of the suspicions of the Cold War, events in the Middle East soon showed that war to be far from over. President Nasser's nationalization of the Suez Canal in the summer of 1956 (see p. 832) was seen as a victory for Nasser and his backers in the Communist camp. The Soviet Union's reputation as a champion of anticolonialism, however, was immediately tarnished by its brutal intervention against the uprising in Hungary. Both the Suez crisis and the Hungarian revolution might easily have led to a major showdown had it not been for the fear of a nuclear war.

The year 1957 was relatively peaceful. America's proclamation of the Eisenhower Doctrine served notice that the nation was ready to oppose the spread of Soviet influence in the Middle East. In the Soviet Union, meanwhile, Khrushchev emerged as the supreme leader of communism. The most spectacular event of the year, however, was the successful launching of Russia's first earth satellite, *Sputnik I*. This development proved that the Russians possessed rockets powerful enough to launch a nuclear attack on the United States. The balance of power in the Cold War had apparently shifted in Russia's favor.

To the Brink of War

For the next five years the initiative in international affairs largely rested with the Soviet Union. The United States launched its first satellite, *Explorer I*, in 1958. But the Russians maintained their lead by placing heavier satellites in orbit. Continued Communist attempts to stir up trouble in the Middle East were foiled by American and British landings of troops in Lebanon and Jordan in 1958. Next came a crisis in the Far East, where Chinese Communist attacks on the off-shore islands of Quemoy and Matsu were halted only because America stood firmly by its Nationalist Chinese ally. In November 1958 the Soviet Union reopened the German question by once again challenging the western position in Berlin.

While East–West relations were thus being kept in a state of latent tension, there were feelers from both sides for a second try at summit diplomacy. But the conference finally scheduled for 1960 never materialized. On the eve of the Paris meeting the Russians shot down an American U-2 intelligence plane flying over the Soviet Union. Eisenhower's refusal to make amends for this incident led to Khrushchev's withdrawal from the conference before it started.

There was much concern in the West over the increasingly aggressive Soviet stance in foreign affairs. Aside from trying to scare the United States into making concessions, Russia's policy was also influenced by the growing rift between Moscow and Peking. Much of the conflict between Russia and China was over the allegiance of unaligned countries. It was to reassert his claim to leadership over world communism that Khrushchev delivered his boastful threats of "burying capitalism."

The advent of the Kennedy administration in 1961 at first seemed to bring a slight lessening of East–West tension. The new president was faced by a perplexing array of foreign problems. In April 1961 the ill-fated Bay of Pigs invasion of Cuba—undertaken by anti-Castro refugees with American backing—was quickly suppressed by Castro's forces. In South Vietnam, meanwhile, Vietcong guerrillas, supported by Communist North Vietnam, were stepping up their "war of liberation." A similar war was going on between the Communist Pathet Lao and the government forces in Laos. The most serious problem Kennedy inherited, however, was the continued Russian demand for western withdrawal from Berlin.

Kennedy and Khrushchev had a brief impromptu but courteous meeting at Vienna in June 1961. But shortly after the Vienna meeting the Russians increased their agitation over Berlin, threatening to sign a peace treaty with the East Germans that would give the latter control over access to West Berlin. Only Kennedy's obvious determination to go to war rather than give in made Khrushchev finally back down. To stop the stream of refugees from East Germany into West Berlin, the Communists built the Berlin Wall, which henceforth made East Germany a virtual prison.

On the Brink of War   1962

Sunday, October 28, was a shining autumn day. At nine in the morning Khrushchev's answer began to come in. By the fifth sentence it was clear that he had thrown in his hand. Work would stop on the sites; the arms "which you described as offensive" would be crated and returned to the Soviet Union; negotiations would start at the UN. Then, no doubt to placate Castro, Khrushchev asked the United States to discontinue flights over Cuba. . . . Looking ahead, he said, "We should like to continue the exchange of views on the prohibition of atomic and thermonuclear weapons, general disarmament, and other problems relating to the relaxation of international tension." It was all over, and barely in time. If word had not come that Sunday, if work had continued on the bases, the United States would have had no real choice but to take action against Cuba the next week. No one could discern what lay darkly beyond an air strike or invasion, what measures and countermeasures, actions and reactions, might have driven the hapless world to the ghastly consummation. The President saw more penetratingly into the mists and terrors of the future than anyone else. A few weeks later he said, "If we had invaded Cuba . . . I am sure the Soviets would have acted. They would have to, just as we would have to. I think there are certain compulsions on any major power." . . . When Kennedy received Khrushchev's reply that golden October morning, he showed profound relief. Later he said, "This is the night to go to the theater, like Abraham Lincoln."

From Arthur M. Schlesinger, Jr., *A Thousand Days: John F. Kennedy in the White House* (Boston: Houghton Mifflin, 1965), p. 830.

Citizens of West Berlin wave to friends and relatives on the other side of the Berlin Wall.

There were other signs that negotiations might replace confrontations in East–West relations. In July 1962 a foreign ministers' conference in Geneva agreed on the formal neutralization of Laos. This, it was hoped, would calm the situation in Southeast Asia. But at the same time the Russians were involved in secret activities in Cuba that soon brought the United States and the Soviet Union to the very brink of war.

The Cuban crisis gained momentum during the summer of 1962 as Washington learned about Russia's stepped-up military support for Castro. In September a Soviet-Cuban security treaty was announced. In October the United States gained proof that the Soviets had supplied Cuba with missiles capable of delivering nuclear warheads and that launching sites were under construction in Cuba. President Kennedy imposed a strict blockade on further arms shipments to Cuba and demanded that all Soviet offensive weapons be withdrawn and all missile bases dismantled. Faced with pressure from the United Nations and American threats of retaliation, Khrushchev backed down. The most serious confrontation of the Cold War was over.

East–West Détente

The Cuban crisis, surprisingly, ushered in the first genuine détente in the East–West conflict. To reduce the risk of accidental war, Washington and Moscow in early 1963 established a "hot line" of direct communication. In early July 1963 the two powers, together with Great Britain, signed a Nuclear Test Ban Treaty outlawing all but underground tests. There were other agreements on minor issues. The relaxation of tension, moreover, did not end with Kennedy's death and Khrushchev's fall from power. In the summer of 1967, at the height of the Middle Eastern crisis, President Johnson and Premier Kosygin held a businesslike conference at Glassboro, New Jersey, which helped lessen the international strain.

The détente between Moscow and Washington did not at first resolve any of the major issues of the Cold War. The most serious crisis in the late 1960s was

the drawn-out war in Vietnam. The United States poured several hundred thousand men and billions of dollars into a conflict that was in some ways similar to the war in Korea. Just as in that earlier war, the United States perceived the People's Republic of China as the ultimate threat. But while at the time of Korea the Soviet Union, in its role as leader of world communism, had been instrumental in helping end the war, such mediation was difficult now that Moscow's leadership was being challenged by Peking.

But even the Vietnam War did not seriously alter the climate of coexistence. One of the more hopeful results of that climate was the Nuclear Non-Proliferation Treaty of 1968, which tried to halt the spread of nuclear weapons. It was not only the fear of nuclear war that made peaceful coexistence appear preferable to warlike confrontation. Another factor was the loosening of ties within the eastern and western camps and the emergence of the uncommitted and underdeveloped nations as a "third force" in world affairs. The trend toward "polycentrism," or many-centeredness, was also evident in the United Nations, where the new countries of Asia and Africa increasingly challenged the predominance of the superpowers.

The most dramatic moves toward a more pragmatic, nonideological foreign policy came in the 1970s. Most of the important events have already been noted: West Germany's improved relations with eastern Europe; President Nixon's historic visits to Moscow and Peking; and the many instances of improved relations between other Communist and non-Communist countries. In 1972, a four-power treaty on Berlin removed another perennial source of friction by guaranteeing access to and easing communications within the city. American withdrawal from South Vietnam, while not ending the troubles, helped to ease tensions in that part of the world.

But while an improved international climate thus helped solve or at least defuse some explosive issues, others continued and new ones arose. Arab-Israeli differences in the Near East and black-white confrontations in southern Africa remained a constant threat to peace in both areas, though neither led to major East-West confrontations, as earlier such crises had done. In an effort to limit the arms race, the United States and the Soviet Union in 1972 had concluded a first Strategic Arms Limitation Treaty (SALT I); but efforts at further SALT-talks in 1977 and 1978 made slow progress. By that time a new issue had arisen in American-Russian relations, as President Carter began to criticize the Soviet Union and other regimes for violating the basic human rights guaranteed by the Helsinki Accords of 1975. Some Americans, pointing to the continued buildup of Russia's military forces, criticized détente for letting down America's guard; but others welcomed the feeling of relief that normalization of East-West relations had brought.

DÉTENTE OR DISASTER: THE NUCLEAR QUESTION

By the early 1980s, détente was still only a hope. There were no violent confrontations between the Soviet Union and the United States, but there were still many areas of disagreement. It was only the fear of nuclear war that prevented these differences from escalating into war.

In this latest phase of antagonistic coexistence, the Russians seemed to be the more aggressive. Their invasion of Afghanistan in 1979 to aid a pro-Soviet regime and their refusal to withdraw, were seen as signs that the Russians might have the military superiority some critics of détente feared. Russia's un-friendly attitude during the Iranian hostage crisis, moreover, and its support of a hard line over Poland put further obstacles on the way to détente. As in most crises, actions on one side brought on reactions from the other, thus escalating tension. American counter-measures, the temporary embargo on grain shipments to the Soviet Union or the boycott of the Moscow Olympics, by sowing dissent between the United States and its allies, merely proved counterproductive. There was much verbal recrimination between the two governments; but there were also frequent frank, businesslike, and serious talks between their foreign ministers.

Because the contest by now had become lethal. The issue that loomed largest between the two super-powers was the nuclear arms race. Both sides controlled the most advanced nuclear weapons and the most perfected means of delivering them. The contest had become one of quantity rather than quality. The United States, fearing that the Russians held the advantage in this race, aimed to catch up. It is unnecessary to go into the technical details of the countless proposals and counter-proposals for mutual arms reduction that prevented the implementation of strategic arms limitations talks (SALT II). The rivalry between the United States and the Soviet Union had reached a stage where the alternative was between détente and disaster.

It was at this point that a new element entered the debate. Hitherto the public at large had been passive spectators in the sparring between the nuclear giants. This now changed, as sporadic antinuclear demonstrations grew into well organized popular protests, attracting hundreds of thousands. This spontaneous fear of war was more visible and vocal in the West, but there were signs that it existed in the East as well. Whether it would affect the decisions of the world's leaders remained to be seen.

Competitive Coexistence

Even though there is a real danger of spontaneous or accidental nuclear war even in an age of coexistence, we should not lose sight of the positive effects which the competitive rivalry between capitalism and communism has had.

When the Organization of Petroleum Exporting Countries (OPEC) imposed its oil embargo in 1973–1974, the effects were felt the world over, especially in the highly industrialized nations of the West. Much of the economic malaise since then has been due to this epoch-making decision. Because of its great potential as the leading energy source, nuclear power has become the main substitute for oil and thus a major factor not only in the military but in the economic competition between capitalism and communism.

With efforts being concentrated on

nuclear armaments, much less has been done to develop the peaceful possibilities of the atom. America's Atoms for Peace Program of 1953 was helpful in sponsoring atomic research among friendly nations, and Russia gave similar support to its allies. To bridge the gap between the two camps, an International Atomic Energy Agency with headquarters in Vienna was established under UN auspices in 1957. One of its main purposes was to aid atomic projects in less developed countries. In the same year the nations of the European Economic Community set up their own European Atomic Energy Community (Euratom) to promote peaceful atomic research and development.

The greatest progress in peaceful nuclear development has been in the generation of electric power. By 1983, the United States was still leading the rest of the world in nuclear power capacity, far in advance of its nearest competitors— Great Britain, the Soviet Union, Japan, France, West Germany, and Canada. This spread of peaceful uses of the atom was hampered, however, by fears on the part of the leading nuclear powers that atomic equipment supplied to other nations might ultimately be used to produce nuclear weapons. Another delaying factor was the often violent protests by environmentalist groups against possible dangers from radiation. It may be some time before atomic power is generally accepted as a fact of life.

THE CONQUEST OF SPACE

The harnessing of nuclear power certainly *is* a new fact of life, setting us apart from all earlier generations. We now have the means of vastly improving or totally destroying our civilization.

An equal alternative for good or evil has been given us by the conquest of outer space. Mankind's first probes into extraterrestrial regions are still so recent that they are hardly a subject for the historian. Yet the year 1957, when the first man-made object went into orbit around the earth, may some day take its place alongside that other memorable date, 1492, when Europe discovered a whole new world beyond the horizon of the old.

The conquest of outer space began in earnest on October 4, 1957, when the Soviet Union sent its first *Sputnik* into orbit. The United States launched its first *Explorer* on January 31, 1958. Russia's most spectacular feat came on April 12, 1961, when history's first "cosmonaut," Yuri Gagarin, went into orbit around the earth. America did not put its first "astronaut," John H. Glenn, into orbit until February 20, 1962. From then on the two superpowers were engaged in a veritable race for outer space (see color map "Exploration in Space"). While bigger and more sophisticated space vehicles were carrying teams of astronauts on more extended orbital flights, unmanned satellites made their first landings on the moon. America's greatest triumph came on July 20, 1969, when astronaut Neil A. Armstrong became the first man to set foot on the moon. Subsequent lunar landings brought back a wealth of scientific information. Meanwhile, the United States and the Soviet Union were extending their unmanned space probes to Mercury, Venus, Mars, Jupiter, and beyond. In 1975 two Soviet spacecraft softlanded on Venus, and in 1976 America's *Viking I* set down on Mars, sending back remarkably clear photographs. By the year 2000, it is predicted, man will have visited that planet.

The implications of these extraordinary advances are far-reaching indeed. Within the foreseeable future, we are told, large numbers of satellites will be orbiting the earth, serving as way-stations to the moon and the planets. America's successful development of a reusable "space shuttle" makes the transport of people and materials to outer space easier and cheaper. The next step will be the development of large "sailing ships," spacecraft powered by radiation from the sun, to carry passengers on a three-year round trip to Mars. To the ordinary person, these and other schemes, such as giant space ships accommodating thousands of people and relieving population pressure on earth, still belong in the realm of science fiction. But they are being seriously advanced by leading scientists, who claim that the only obstacle to their realization is their truly astronomical cost.

For the time being, the main concern is with developments closer to home, in the space immediately surrounding the earth. It is here that space research has had important scientific, economic, and military results. Satellites are now being used for communication, meteorology, large-scale surveying, and reconnaissance. The military potential and danger of satellites are obvious. The nation that controls outer space will control the world. In 1966 the United States and the Soviet Union agreed to limit their space exploration to peaceful uses and to ban

weapons of mass destruction from outer space. But as each side suspects the other of developing military space vehicles and "hunter-killer" satellites to interfere with communications, the fear of an arms race in space persists.

The exploration of outer space thus diverted the attention of the main contenders, at least temporarily, from their rivalry on earth. Yet without that rivalry, the probes into extraterrestrial regions, and the tremendous discoveries thus gained, would have been unthinkable. In the long run these discoveries may overshadow anything happening on this planet. Here, at least, is one positive result of competitive coexistence.

Suggestions for Further Reading

Note: Asterisk denotes a book available in paperback edition.

General To gain a wider perspective on the events in this chapter, see G. Lichtheim, *Europe in the Twentieth Century* (1972). One of the best works on the Cold War is D. Yergin, *Shattered Peace: The Origins of the Cold War and the National Security State* (1977). A. Fontaine, *History of the Cold War,** 2 vols. (1968–69), is lively and informative. The works by D. F. Fleming, *The Cold War and Its Origins, 1917–1960*, 2 vols. (1961), and by G. Kolko and J. Kolko, *The Limits of Power: The World and United States Foreign Policy, 1945–1954** (1972), are "revisionist," that is, highly critical of American foreign policy. The best books on Soviet foreign policy are A. B. Ulam, *Expansion and Coexistence: The History of Soviet Foreign Policy, 1917–1973** (1974) and *The Rivals: America and Russia Since World War II** (1972). A. Z. Rubinstein, *Soviet Foreign Policy Since World War II* (1981), is comprehensive and readable.

The Decline and Rise of Europe The most reflective book on this theme is J. L. Lukacs, *Decline and Rise of Europe** (1965). W. Laqueur, *Europe Since Hitler** (1970), is admirably comprehensive. M. Crouzet, *The European Renaissance Since 1945** (1971), presents a French view. On Europe's economic recovery, see C. P. Kindleberger, *Europe's Postwar Growth* (1967), and M. M. Postan, *An Economic History of Western Europe* (1967). The following books deal with individual countries: F. Boyd, *British Politics in Transition** (1964); A. Sampson, *The New Anatomy of Britain* (1973); P. Williams, *French Politicians and Elections, 1951–1968* (1970); P. G. Cerny, *The Politics of Grandeur: Ideological Aspects of De Gaulle's Foreign Policy* (1980); A. Grosser, *Germany in Our Time* (1971); D. P. Conradt, *The German Polity** (1978); and N. Kogan, *A Political History of Postwar Italy* (1966). On the search for European unity, see R. Mayne, *The Community of Europe* (1963); and P. Scalingi, *The European Parliament: The Three-Decade Search for a United Europe* (1980). Europe's relations with the superpowers, are treated in A. Grosser, *The Western Alliance: European–American Relations Since 1945* (1980); and A. W. DePorte, *Europe Between the Superpowers: The Enduring Balance* (1979). See also R. McGeehan, *The German Rearmament Question: American Diplomacy and European Defense After World War II* (1971). On Germany's relations with the United States, see R. Morgan, *The United States and West Germany 1945–1973* (1975); and H. W. Gatzke, *Germany and the United States: A "Special Relationship"?* (1980). The role of France within the western community is the subject of M. M. Harrison, *The Reluctant Ally: France and Atlantic Security* (1981).

The Americas R. Polenberg, *One Nation Divisible: Class, Race, and Ethnicity in the United States Since 1938* (1980) is an excellent general history of American society. The best study of the Truman Administration is A. L. Hamby, *Beyond the New Deal: Harry S. Truman and American Liberalism* (1973). For the Eisenhower years, see H. Parmet, *Eisenhower: The Necessary President* (1972). Kennedy is treated sympathetically in A. M. Schlesinger, *A Thousand Days: John F. Kennedy in the White House** (1965). D. Kearns, *Lyndon Johnson and the American Dream** (1976) is a good biography. G. Wills, *Nixon Agonistes** (1970) is critical. For the Watergate story, see C. Bernstein and R. Woodward, *All the President's Men** (1974). Presidents since then still await their scholarly biographers. But see C. Mollenhoff, *The Man Who Pardoned Nixon* (1976); J. E. Carter, *Why Not the Best?* (1975); and F. F. Piven and R. A. Cloward, *The New Class War: Reagan's Attack on the Welfare State and its Consequences** (1982). Earlier works on America's economy include J. K. Galbraith, *The Affluent Society** (1969), and W. H. Heller, *New Dimensions of Political Economy* (1966). The problems of blacks and poverty are discussed in A. Lewis, *Portrait of a Decade** (1964); J. W. Silver, *Mississippi: The Closed Society** (1966); and M. Harrington, *The Other America: Poverty in the United States* (1963). See also C. Carson, *In Struggle: SNCC and the Black Awakening of the 1960's* (1981). The Vietnam War is surveyed thoroughly and judiciously in G. C. Herring, *America's Longest War: The United States and Vietnam, 1950–1975* (1979).

The growing importance of Canada is treated in N. L. Nicolson, *Canada in the American Community** (1963), and G. M. Craig, *The United States and Canada* (1968). On Latin America, see S. Clissold, *Latin America: New World, Third World* (1972), and L. D. Langley, *The United States and the Caribbean, 1900–1970* (1980). E. R. Wolf and E. C. Hansen, *The Human Condition in Latin America* (1972), deals with various aspects of Latin American society past and present. One of the best books on the changes in Cuba is T. Draper, *Castroism: Theory and Practice* (1965). M. Halperin, *The Taming of Fidel Castro* (1981), is critical and disillusioned. A. MacEwan, *Revolution and Economic Development in Cuba* (1981), is a positive assessment.

The Communist World
Many of the books cited for Chapters 32 and 33 are also relevant to this later phase of communism. For works on more recent events, see S. Bialer, *Stalin's Successors: Leadership, Stability, and Change in the Soviet Union* (1980); R. Conquest, *Russia After Khrushchev* (1965); and A. B. Ulam, *The New Face of Soviet Totalitarianism* (1965). On the Soviet economy, see T. Dunmore, *The Stalinist Command Economy: The Soviet State Apparatus and Economic Policy, 1945–53* (1980), and H. Schwartz, *The Soviet Economy Since Stalin* (1965). J. F. Hough and M. Fainsod, *How the Soviet Union Is Governed* (1979) is the revised version of a classic work. Criticism of the regime is treated in P. Reddaway, ed., *Uncensored Russia: Protest and Dissent in the Soviet Union* (1972). There are several general studies of Russia's satellites: Z. K. Brzezinski, *The Soviet Bloc: Unity and Conflict** (1967); J. F. Brown, *The New Eastern Europe* (1967); and S. Fischer-Galati, *Eastern Europe in the Sixties** (1963). On Yugoslavia, see D. Wilson, *Tito's Yugoslavia* (1979), and M. Djilas, *Tito: The Story from the Inside* (1980), by a former aide of the Yugoslav leader. Two major crises among the satellites are discussed in J. Valenta, *Soviet Intervention in Czechoslovakia, 1968** (1981), and D. Singer, *The Road to Gdansk: Poland and the USSR* (1981). The split between the Soviet Union and Communist China is analyzed in J. Gittings, *Survey of the Sino–Soviet Dispute* (1968), and D. W. Treadgold, *Soviet and Chinese Communism: Similarities and Differences* (1967). "Socialist pluralism" is treated in W. Leonhard, *Three Faces of Communism* (1974), and V. V. Aspaturian et al., eds., *Eurocommunism Between East and West* (1980).

From Cold War to Coexistence
Most of the general works mentioned above also deal with this subject. The following is a selection of individual studies on the major international crises of the last three decades: D. Rees, *Korea: The Limited War* (1964); H. Thomas, *The Suez Affair* (1967); J. Radvány, *Hungary and the Superpowers* (1972); J. E. Smith, *The Defense of Berlin* (1963); H. B. Johnson, *The Bay of Pigs* (1964); A. Abel, *The Missile Crisis* (1966); E. R. F. Sheehan, *The Arabs, Israelis, and Kissinger: A Secret History of American Diplomacy in the Middle East* (1976). American foreign policy is the subject of R. A. Divine, *Eisenhower and the Cold War* (1981); R. Hilsman, *To Move a Nation* (1967), on Kennedy's foreign policy; and P. L. Geyelin, *Lyndon B. Johnson and the World* (1966). On the new international situation of the 1970s, see A. Buchan, *The End of the Postwar Era* (1975), and G. W. Ball, *Diplomacy for a Crowded World: An American Foreign Policy* (1976), by a seasoned American diplomat. C. Sterling, *The Terror Network: The Secret War of International Terrorism* (1981), tries to make sense of a puzzling subject. On the SALT agreements, see J. Newhouse, *Cold Dawn: The Story of SALT* (1973), and M. Willrich and J. B. Rhinelander, eds., *SALT: The Moscow Agreements and Beyond** (1974).

Détente or Disaster: The Nuclear Question
R. Calder, *Living with the Atom* (1962), and H. P. Metzger, *The Atomic Establishment* (1972), are general treatments. There has been much concern over the dangers of atomic energy: R. E. Webb, *The Accident Hazards of Nuclear Power Plants** (1976); and R. S. Lewis, *The Nuclear-Power Rebellion: Citizens vs. the Atomic Industrial Establishment* (1972). See also M. C. Olsen, *Unacceptable Risk: The Nuclear Power*

*Controversy** (1976). The military results of the nuclear revolution have given rise to a large literature. H. Kahn, *On Thermonuclear War* (1960), is a controversial classic. E. L. M. Burns, *Megamurder* (1967), paints a fearful picture. R. Rapoport, *The Great American Bomb Machine* (1971), deals with America's nuclear arsenal. M. Mandelbaum, *The Nuclear Question: The United States and Nuclear Weapons, 1946–1976* (1979), presents some original insights. Nuclear disarmament is discussed by A. Myrdal, *The Game of Disarmament: How the United States and Russia Run the Arms Race* (1977); and its urgency is stressed in W. Epstein, *The Last Chance: Nuclear Proliferation and Arms Control* (1976).

The Conquest of Space L. B. Taylor, *For All Mankind: America's Space Programs of the 1970's and Beyond* (1974), is a good general introduction. The more distant space probes are treated in M. R. Sharpe, *Satellites and Probes: The Development of Unmanned Space Flight* (1970), and J. Strong, *Search for the Solar System: The Role of Unmanned Interplanetary Probes* (1973). Y. Gagarin and V. Lebedev, *Survival in Space* (1969), relates the experiences of Russia's first cosmonaut. America's major achievements in space are the subject of D. Thomas, ed., *Moon: Man's Greatest Adventure* (1970), and M. Caidin, *Destination Mars* (1972). M. Kinsley, *Outer Space and Inner Sanctums: Government, Business, and Satellite Communication* (1976), deals with the commercial uses of space satellites. The possibility of human residence in space is discussed in T. A. Heppenheimer, *Colonies in Space** (1977), and G. K. O'Neill, *The High Frontier: Human Colonies in Space* (1977). See also W. S. Bainbridge, *The Spaceflight Revolution: A Sociological Study* (1976).

35 The "Third World"

The title of this chapter needs an explanation. The term "third world" originated with China's Mao Zedong. The Communist leader divided the nations of the world into three groups: a first world of the superpowers (the United States and the Soviet Union); a second world of the developed non-superpowers (Western Europe and Japan); and a third and largest world of underdeveloped countries. Historians have objected to these categories as too sweeping, vague, and patronizing. Yet, despite its Communist origin, the term "third world" has found wide currency and most people know what is meant by it. That is the reason why we use it here, even though we are aware of its shortcomings.

One of the most revolutionary developments since the Second World War was the liberation of the world's former colonial territories. This independence movement, already begun in the years between the two world wars, was hastened by two factors: the weakening of the mother countries in the Second World War and the subsequent rivalry between the free and Communist worlds. Although the various native revolts differed from country to country, they all had one thing in common—intense opposition to any form of colonialism. Some of the new nations took sides in the Cold War, but most of them preferred a "neutralist" stand. For them the most urgent need was economic and technical assistance. At first, most of this aid came from the United States. But in time the other industrialized nations of the West, as well as the Soviet Union and Communist China, began to set up foreign aid programs and compete for the allegiance of these uncommitted regions.

THE END OF COLONIALISM IN SOUTH ASIA

The first major additions to the nations of the third world came with the partition of the subcontinent of India in 1947 into the independent states of India and Pakistan. Although both were republics, they continued as members of the (British) Commonwealth. India was predomi-

nantly Hindu and Pakistan mostly Moslem. In the process of separating the two religions, many bloody riots broke out. India and Pakistan also clashed repeatedly over the northern state of Kashmir, to which both laid claim. In addition, there were intermittent border incidents between India and Communist China.

India

The Republic of India was by far the more important of the two states. The new nation suffered a tragic loss in 1948, when its political leader, Mohandas K. Gandhi, was assassinated by a religious fanatic. The task of guiding India through its formative years fell to Gandhi's disciple, Jawaharlal Nehru, leader of the ruling Congress Party. India's main problems were economic. The only way to support its huge population was through long-range development of the country's abundant natural resources with outside aid. India's dependence on such aid from all sides, together with its closeness to the centers of communism and its recent experience with western imperialism, led to a neutralist stand on most international issues. With Nehru's death in 1964, domestic affairs became less stable, especially under his daughter, Indira Gandhi, who became prime minister in 1966. Whatever economic growth the country experienced was neutralized by its high birthrate, despite costly birth-control programs. Periodic famines, epidemics, and riots between Hindus and Moslems, together with a renewed Indo-Pakistani clash in 1971, led to a permanent state of crisis.

In 1971, India veered away from its nonalignment by signing a treaty of friendship with the Soviet Union. This was followed two years later by an economic and trade agreement. In 1974, the world was startled by the explosion of a nuclear device, showing that India was ready to join the nuclear club. Meanwhile Prime Minister Indira Gandhi, who had been accused of illegal activities in connection with her reelection, became increasingly authoritarian by declaring a state of emergency, arresting political opponents, and suspending civil liberties.

Opposite: The opening session of the Seventh Non-Aligned Summit in New Delhi, March 1983. Prime Minister Indira Gandhi of India (left) takes over the chair from President Fidel Castro of Cuba (center).

Mohandas K. Gandhi and his disciple and eventual successor, Jawaharlal Nehru, in 1946.

Indira Gandhi, prime minister of India from 1966 to 1977, and since 1980.

With Mrs. Gandhi's electoral defeat in 1977, constitutional government was restored.

The departure of Prime Minister Gandhi from the national scene, however, was only temporary. Her successor, Morarji R. Desai, was initially quite successful, especially abroad, where he drew close to the United States under President Carter. But economic problems at home and disarray within his own Janata Party, cut short his tenure, and in 1980 Mrs. Gandhi staged a spectacular comeback. Since then, India's affairs have again been dominated by that determined woman. There have been continued problems—bureaucratic inefficiency and corruption, party strife, social unrest, and regional violence. But India's economy has been on the upswing, despite the energy crisis and continued rise in population. Mrs. Gandhi has tried to steer a middle course between the superpowers, leaning now in one, now in the other direction, especially on the issue of Afghanistan. As the dominant power on the South Asian subcontinent, India stands on the threshold between the third and second worlds. Having a population of 700 million, ranking as the tenth industrial nation, and maintaining the world's fourth largest army, the one-time British colony is now a power to be reckoned with.

Pakistan

In contrast to India, popular government in the Islamic Republic of Pakistan was much slower in taking root. Like India, Pakistan suffered a serious loss in 1948, when its outstanding leader, Mohammed Ali Jinnah, died. The country's economy was mainly agricultural, and trade with India, its natural market, suffered from political tensions. Economic difficulties in turn led to political instability. When democracy was no longer able to cope with bureaucratic inefficiency and corruption, the head of Pakistan's armed forces, General Ayub Khan, took over and ruled as virtual dictator from 1958 to 1969. Pakistan's foreign policy, at first firmly prowestern, became increasingly neutralist during the 1960s in an effort to attract aid and trade from both sides.

One of Pakistan's major difficulties derived from the fact that it consisted of two regions, separated by a thousand

THE WEALTH—AND POVERTY—OF THE THIRD WORLD

SELECTED COUNTRIES	BALANCE OF PAYMENTS* (in millions of dollars)	GNP PER CAPITA (in dollars, 1978)	DAILY CALORIE SUPPLY PER CAPITA (as percent of requirement, 1977)	AVERAGE ANNUAL POPULATION GROWTH (in percent, 1970–78)
LOW-INCOME COUNTRIES				
Bangladesh	−302	90	78	2.7
Ethiopia	−98	120	75	2.5
Somalia	−63	130	88	2.3
India	915	180	91	2.0
Sierra Leone	−96	210	93	2.5
Zaire	88	210	104	2.7
Pakistan	−550	230	99	3.1
Tanzania	−442	230	89	3.0
Afghanistan	38	240	110	2.2
Haiti	−39	260	93	1.7
Uganda	−129	280	91	2.9
Sudan	−54	320	93	2.6
Kenya	−474	330	88	3.3
Senegal	−114	340	95	2.6
Indonesia	−773	360	105	1.8
MIDDLE-INCOME COUNTRIES				
Egypt	−540	390	109	2.2
Ghana	32	390	86	3.0
Southern Yemen	−20	420	81	1.9
Zambia	−191	474	88	3.0
Thailand	−1,098	490	105	2.7
Philippines	−991	510	97	2.7
El Salvador	−230	660	90	2.9
Ivory Coast	−533	840	105	5.6
Colombia	305	850	102	2.3
Ecuador	−54	880	92	3.3
Guatemala	−192	910	98	2.9
Tunisia	−411	950	112	2.0
Malaysia	284	1,090	117	2.7
South Korea	−455	1,160	119	1.9
Turkey	−1,121	1,200	115	2.5
Algeria	−2,977	1,260	99	3.2
Mexico	−896	1,290	114	3.3
Taiwan	1,979	1,400	120	2.0
Chile	−659	1,410	109	1.7
South Africa	2,010	1,480	116	2.7
Brazil	−5,310	1,570	107	2.8
Argentina	2,512	1,910	126	1.3
Portugal	−337	1,990	126	1.0
Venezuela	−4,973	2,910	99	3.3
Israel	−732	3,500	122	2.7
CAPITAL-SURPLUS OIL-EXPORTERS				
Iraq	1,209 (1977)	1,860	89	3.3
Iran	5,370 (1977)	2,160 (1977)	130	2.9
Libya	1,024	6,910	126	4.1
Saudi Arabia	12,793	7,690	88	3.5

*Current account balance before interest payment on external debt.
Source: World Bank data.

miles of Indian territory. Relations between the two regions were far from smooth; the more numerous and poverty-stricken Bengalis of East Pakistan felt exploited by the affluent and influential Punjabis of West Pakistan. The only bond between the two peoples was their common Moslem religion. Differences between East and West Pakistan came to a head in 1971, when civil war broke out between Bengali and government forces. The Bengalis were first defeated but then, after intervention by India, West Pakistan was defeated. East Pakistan now seceded, taking the name of Bangladesh. In 1972 the new nation signed a treaty of friendship with India, and in 1974 it was recognized by (West) Pakistan. The latter was now headed under a new democratic constitution by Prime Minister Zulfikar Ali Bhutto, who valiantly tried to cope with Pakistan's economic backwardness. In 1977, Bhutto was ousted by the army, whose chief of staff, General Mohammad Zia ul-Haq, proclaimed martial law to help overcome the country's political and economic problems.

Colonial Nationalism

The West, having sown its own national wild oats in the past, is now sometimes inclined to look with a combination of dismay and superior wisdom on the upstart countries which assert an allegedly anachronistic desire to follow the same course. . . . However great the disenchantment of Europe with nationalism, the colonial nationalist is little likely to be persuaded by an argument so easily identifiable with the interest of the West in maintaining some facsimile of its older relationships in a world swiftly sliding out of its grasp. . . . Even if it be conceded that nationalism fails to furnish the foundations for an acceptable world order and has outlived its usefulness for the advanced, thoroughly "nationalized," countries of the West . . . it has by no means exhausted its contribution to the development of the non-Western peoples. Nationalism . . . has a chronology of its own derived not from the calendar but from the stages of the gradually spreading impact of the revolution which originated in Western Europe. . . . One can plausibly argue that in the different but related stages of the cycle in which Asia and Africa are now engaged nationalism intrudes itself not only with an aura of inevitability but also as the bearer of positive goods.

From Rupert Emerson, *From Empire to Nation: The Rise to Self-Assertion of Asian and African Peoples* (Cambridge, Mass.: Harvard University Press, 1960), p. 379.

The regime of General Zia, which was intended to be only temporary, remained in power into the 1980s. Its main problem was to find a viable form of representative government. Zia, who assumed the office of president in 1978, instituted a number of Islamic reforms, which led to increased Islamization of Pakistan's legal and political system. These reforms included barbaric criminal punishments, resulting in numerous violations of human rights. The most spectacular was the execution in 1979 of former premier Ali Bhutto for the murder of a political opponent. Under a new provisional constitution of 1981, an appointive Federal Council was set up to give at least the appearance of popular participation in government. Economically, Pakistan has fared better under President Zia's rule. Much of this improvement was due to foreign aid, especially from the United States. America views Pakistan as a potential supporter in its conflicts with Iran and with the Soviet Union over Afghanistan. Still, Pakistan tries to follow a course of nonalignment. Relations between Pakistan and India continued to be watchful, although both sides have made efforts to allay tension. Pakistan's main problems continued to be domestic—with political repression leading to protests of increasing violence and the continuation of military dictatorship.

Bangladesh

Compared with India and Pakistan, the People's Republic of Bangladesh played only a minor role in the affairs of South Asia. The first ten years following its independence in 1971 were characterized by political and economic instability. The leading figure during this period was General Ziaur Rahman, who ruled under martial law since 1975 and became president in 1977. Elections in 1978 and 1979 further aided transition to civilian rule. When Ziaur was assassinated in 1981, Vice President Abdus Sattar succeeded him, as provided by the constitution. But in 1982 the army once again interfered, with General Hossein Mohammad Ershad declaring himself chief martial administrator. Instability continued.

Economically, Bangladesh is very

poor, depending on continuous foreign aid to maintain its rapidly increasing population of 90 million. In its foreign policy, Bangladesh belongs to the non-aligned bloc, active in trying to find ways for the rich nations to share their resources with the poor. Its closest ties are with Communist China and India. Relations with the Soviet Union, initially close, have become less so, especially after the government of Bangladesh criticized the Soviet invasion of Afghanistan.

Afghanistan

The Democratic Republic of Afghanistan is one of the least developed countries in the world. It deserves mention here chiefly as the latest scene of Soviet aggression. Russia's efforts to gain influence over Afghanistan go back to the early nineteenth century. After the First World War, the kingdom of Afghanistan still retained its sovereignty, and during the 1920s it maintained cordial relations with the Soviet Union. After a dormant period, when Russia was preoccupied with events in Europe, the Soviets again turned their attention to Afghanistan in the mid-1950s by establishing economic and military ties. In 1973, a coup of military officers, influenced by Russia, overthrew the monarchy and set up a leftist government. Subsequent coups in 1978 and 1979, openly directed by the Soviets, brought in more pliable Marxist leaders. The last, Babrak Karmal, was installed as president by a Soviet invasion force in 1979.

Why did the Soviets thus openly abandon détente? One reason was to challenge American influence in the Indian Ocean, while the United States was involved with Iran; in addition, Afghanistan had large natural resources; and finally, Russia's drive was merely the latest phase in its century-old encroachment on Afghanistan. Soviet involvement, however, did not achieve its purpose. Widespread popular resistance to the Marxist government of Babrak Karmal necessitated the deployment of large numbers of Soviet troops. At the same time, the Soviet Union was accused of aggression by most of the rest of the world and was asked to withdraw its forces.

THE EMERGENCE OF COMMUNIST CHINA

The most significant development in the emergence of a third world was the return of China as major factor in world affairs. The People's Republic of China was founded in 1949 (see p. 792). Its government at that time was closely modeled on that of the Soviet Union. As in Russia, all power in China rested with the Communist Party and its leader, Mao Zedong. Under the constitution of 1954, the main task of the state was "to bring about, step by step, the socialist industrialization of the country," a goal that was to be achieved in several Five-Year Plans. As was the case in other underdeveloped nations, the rapid increase in China's production resulted in some impressive achievements. Symbolic of the country's scientific and technical achievements was the detonation of its first atomic bomb in 1964, followed by a hydrogen bomb in 1967.

The Mao Zedong Era

In the long run, only through industrialization could China solve its most pressing problem of too many people and too little land. With an estimated yearly population growth of more than 16 million, the 1-billion mark would be reached by 1990. Yet the backbone of the Chinese economy was still agriculture, and the government tried by every possible means to boost agricultural production. The second Five-Year Plan of 1958 called for a "great leap forward" in both agriculture and industry. The population was organized in gigantic "people's communes" including as many as one hundred thousand persons and embracing both farms and factories.

However, the "great leap" not only failed to reach its goals, it actually brought a decline in production. The cause for this failure was seen in the continued moderation of many leading officials. To purge Chinese communism of these "revisionist" elements, another sweeping revolutionary movement was initiated in the 1960s, the "great proletarian cultural revolution." Spearheaded by younger members of the party, the

Mao Zedong with steel workers (1959).

Celebration of National Day in China, October 2, 1966. The statue of Mao Zedong is being carried by the paraders.

China's regimented society—a teacher directs a group of school children to sweep sidewalks in Peking.

Poster of Hua Guofeng in Canton urges the Chinese to "March Victoriously Forward Under the Leadership of Chairman Hua."

"Maoist" revolution repudiated traditional cultural values, emphasized collectivization and austerity, and elevated the figure of Mao Zedong to unprecedented heights of personal adulation. Through indoctrination, brainwashing, and terror China hoped to produce the most regimented society the world had ever seen. At first, these drastic measures aggravated rather than solved China's economic problems. But eventually the discipline and industry of the Chinese people did achieve new high levels of production and made China a major economic power.

As a result of these achievements, the pace of China's development became less hectic. In 1976 Mao Zedong died, and his more radical followers, including his widow, were purged in favor of a more moderate faction, headed by the new Chairman of the Communist Party, Hua Guofeng.

China under Deng Xiaoping

The leading figure in China's domestic and foreign affairs since then has been Deputy Premier Deng Xiaoping. Temporarily ousted under Mao, he was rehabilitated in 1977 and soon became active in party reform, economic liberalization, and the improvement of China's relations with the West, especially the United States. In 1980, one of his supporters, Zhao Ziyang, an economic planner, replaced Hua Guofeng as Premier, and in 1981, Hua's position as Chairman was taken over by Hu Yaobang. These new leaders followed a more pragmatic and flexible policy, free from the ideological restrictions of Maoism. In 1978, a new constitution emphasized civil rights, and at subsequent party meetings Mao's "cultural revolution" was severely criticized. A further outlet for popular dissent, however, the "democracy wall," where individuals could proclaim their views without censorship, was soon again curbed.

China's foremost concern continued to be with economic modernization. Under a new ten-year plan, agriculture was further improved through mechanization, stepped-up fertilizer production, and experimentation with high-yield seeds. Various incentives to peasants and communes resulted in overall food increases, but continued population growth prevented a simultaneous rise in per capita consumption. In the industrial area, the new plan called for a doubling of annual steel production, substantial increases in coal mining (China ranks third among the world's producers), and the further exploration of oil resources, a valuable export commodity. Another major source for exports is the country's growing textile industry. Despite spectacular growth, China's economy still depends on foreign investments and technical assistance. The shift toward liberalization at home thus also called for a parallel liberalization of China's policy abroad.

China's Foreign Policy

In foreign affairs, Communist China was at first deeply anti-American. The two countries were on opposite sides in the Korean War and in most other conflicts in Asia. Washington's support of the Chinese Nationalists on Taiwan, its alliance with Japan, and its refusal to recognize Peking were major targets for Communist attacks. This situation changed dramatically in 1972, when the United States, having abandoned its opposition to Communist China's membership in the United Nations, reciprocated Chinese feelers for normalization of relations, and President Nixon visited Peking. Full diplomatic relations between the two countries were not established until 1979, after the United States had abrogated its defense treaty with Taiwan. The following year, when the Sino-Soviet alliance of 1950 ran out, it was not renewed.

Relations between China and the Soviet Union, initially very close, had become increasingly hostile. In 1969 the two countries had actually waged a brief border war. Ten years later, when China invaded Vietnam and the Soviets invaded Afghanistan, each protested the aggression of the other. China's global strategy was to seek a "united front" with the second and third worlds, as well as with the United States, against the Soviet Union. In 1978 China and Japan concluded a treaty of peace and friendship, and economic relations with Japan and western Europe were very active.

During the 1950s and 1960s in its dealings with third world nations, China had alternated between kindness and threats. There were repeated clashes along the borders with India, Burma, and Nepal, and Tibetan resistance to communization was ruthlessly suppressed. As relations with the Soviet Union worsened, China's attitude toward the third world came to be guided by national rather than ideological motives; it supported noncommunist countries, like Pakistan and Egypt, that opposed the Soviet Union and opposed Communist countries, like Vietnam and Cuba, that supported the Russians. Given its economic potential and its anti-Soviet alignment, the People's Republic of China occupied a special position within the third world.

THE NATIONS OF THE PACIFIC

There are several other countries in East Asia and the Pacific—Taiwan, the Philippines, and the two Koreas—that are part of the third world.

Taiwan

The "Republic of China" was founded when Generalissimo Chiang Kai-shek retreated to Taiwan in 1949. After his death in 1975, his son, Chiang Ching-kuo, succeeded him as head of state and of the leading Kuomintang or Nationalist Party. The keynotes of Taiwan's domestic policy have been economic growth and political stability. The effects of the oil crisis and growing dissatisfaction with one-party rule caused occasional unrest, but never a serious crisis. The main concern has been over Taiwan's international role. As the United States established close relations with Communist China, a Chinese invasion of Taiwan became a possibility. Washington at the time warned that such an act would be "of grave concern to the United States," but Peking asserted that Taiwan's relations with the "motherland" was entirely a Chinese internal affair.

The Philippines

Taiwan's neighbor, the Republic of the Philippines, is in a far less fortunate position as far as economic development and political stability are concerned.

More than half of its 50 million people live in dire poverty and its economy depends heavily on foreign loans. Since gaining its independence in 1946, the Philippines has been plagued by constant civil, ethnic, and religious unrest, causing thousands of deaths. The country is kept from utter chaos by the "constitutional authoritarianism" of President Ferdinand Marcos, who assumed power in 1965 and imposed martial law in 1972. His undemocratic and repressive regime has been accused of economic corruption and political fraud. There are a number of opposition parties and a large guerrilla force, the New People's Army. The main support of Marcos has come from the United States, which maintains some 17,000 troops on its 22 military bases in the Philippines and has more than $3 billion invested there. With so much at stake, the United States seems ready to overlook the gross violations of human and civil rights of which the Marcos regime has been accused.

South Korea

In its close ties to the United States, the Republic of Korea is not unlike the Philippines or, for that matter, Taiwan. Under a mutual defense treaty of 1953, America still had 38,000 troops stationed in Korea in 1982. Economically, due to large-scale American aid, Korea has made considerable strides since the Korean War thirty years ago. Its main problems have been with the unequal distribution of wealth. The early years of the new republic were dominated by its first President, Syngman Rhee, who was elected in 1948 and resigned in 1960, in the face of growing disorders. The following year General Park Chung Hee staged a coup. His rule, while economically beneficial, became increasingly authoritarian. Under a new constitution in 1972, Park assumed the presidency for life and stepped up repression of the growing opposition, especially among intellectuals and students. In 1979, Park was assassinated by the director of his own Central Intelligence Agency. After another coup, his place was taken by General Chun Doo Hwan, who had himself elected president for a seven-year term under a new constitution. An invitation to the United States in 1981 showed that Chun enjoyed the support of the Reagan administration, despite reports of continued unrest and violations of human rights.

North Korea

While all the nations discussed in this section thus far have clearly tended toward the United States, the other part of Korea, while dependent on its Communist neighbors for economic and military support, has tried to steer a more nonaligned course. The Democratic People's Republic of Korea for close to forty years has been ruled by its Communist party under the "Great Leader Comrade Kim Il Sung." Like Mao Zedong, Kim has been the center of a personality cult bordering on deification, and to ensure continuity and stability, his eldest son, Kim Jong Il, has been groomed for succession. North Korea's economy, highly centralized and strictly planned, has made much progress on its own, and its hardworking people enjoy a satisfactory standard of living. There are no official relations with the United States, and relations with the Soviet Union have been closer than with China. The North Koreans, however, have refused to take sides in the Sino-Soviet dispute. Occasional proposals from one or the other of the two Koreas for reunification have failed to find a satisfactory solution.

Japan

The most important among the nations of the western Pacific, Japan, is clearly not a member of the third world. As one of the leading economic powers, it rather belongs to the industrialized second world. Because of its geographic location, however, and its importance in Far Eastern affairs, it seems justified to include Japan in our discussion here.

Japan regained its full sovereignty in the peace treaty signed in 1951. At that time the divine monarchy of Emperor Hirohito had already been transformed into a democratic government. The most influential figure in early postwar reconstruction was General Douglas MacArthur, America's military governor. With one brief interruption, Japan has been ruled by the moderate Liberal Democratic party. Because of its rapid industrialization, the country has suffered from the usual problems of massive urbanization, housing shortages, air and water pollution, and such. There have been occasional disturbances, especially among students and the parties of the left. But the majority of Japanese—well-trained, highly-disciplined, and hard-working—have been willing instruments in their country's miraculous economic growth.

In its foreign policy, Japan has been a close ally of the United States. Under a Treaty of Mutual Cooperation and Security, concluded in 1960 and extended in 1970, the United States guaranteed Japan's defense in return for continued bases there. Under the constitution of 1946, Japan forswore any military force of its own, but it later developed a 240,000-man self-defense force. The United States, however, would like to see a still greater contribution to common defense. The main problems between the two countries have been economic: the increasingly unfavorable balance of American trade vis-à-vis Japan. Efforts to improve the situation through voluntary restraints on the part of Japan have been only partly successful.

Relations with the Soviet Union have been correct rather than cordial. Diplomatic ties were resumed in 1956, but continued Soviet occupation of the Kuril Islands, added to traditional rivalries, has prevented closer relations. In dealing with its other Asian neighbors, Japan has followed a policy of trade and aid, in an effort to eradicate the memories of Japanese aggression in the Second World War. Relations with China were resumed in 1972 and a treaty of friendship was signed in 1978. In its ceaseless search for markets and access to raw materials, the major concerns of Japan have been with economic rather than military security.

SOUTHEAST ASIA

The region east of India and south of China saw more political changes after the Second World War than any other part of Asia. Prior to 1945 only Thailand (Siam) was fully independent. In the

years that followed, Burma, Indonesia, Vietnam, Laos, Cambodia, Malaysia, and Singapore gained their sovereignty. Southeast Asia was a wealthy region, producing most of the world's natural rubber, and more than half its tin and rice. Like all third world areas, Southeast Asia was predominantly agricultural; but, except for Indonesia, it did not suffer from overpopulation. Despite its rich natural resources, the living standard of the region was very low. What Southeast Asia needed was a better-balanced regional economy with more varied commodities and increased industrialization.

Vietnam, Laos, and Cambodia (Kampuchea)

With the exception of Thailand, every country of Southeast Asia experienced Communist revolts of varying severity. In the countries that formerly made up French Indochina—Vietnam, Laos, and Cambodia—Communist takeovers were finally successful after drawn-out and bloody civil wars.

The most important of these countries, Vietnam, owed its liberation from French colonial rule to the veteran Communist leader Ho Chi Minh and his independence movement, the Viet Minh. The final defeat of French forces came in 1954 with the battle of Dien Bien Phu. The same year a conference in Geneva divided Vietnam at the seventeenth parallel, calling for reunification after elections in 1956.

These elections were never held. In 1955 a noncommunist nationalist, Ngo Dinh Diem, established a Republic of (South) Vietnam. He had strong American support, but his repressive regime was opposed by the Communist Viet Cong, supplied from the North. As time went on, American personnel increased from a few hundred to half a million men. In 1963 a military coup, supported by the United States, killed Diem in the vain hope of setting-up a more popular regime. Beginning in 1965, major bombing attacks were launched against North Vietnam. But American involvement prolonged rather than resolved the Vietnam conflict. In the light of mounting criticism at home and abroad, President Nixon in 1969 began a policy of gradual

Refused permission to settle in Malaysia, these "boat people" are set adrift on the South China Sea (1979).

withdrawal. A peace settlement was finally reached in 1973 and two years later Vietnam had become reunited under Communist rule.

Ho Chi Minh had died in 1969 and his position taken over by a system of collective leadership in which Pham Van Dong, premier in Hanoi since 1955, and Le Duan, first secretary of the Vietnam Communist party, were prominent. Since 1975 the Socialist Republic of Vietnam had found its going more and more difficult. Ambitious plans to improve its economy required massive foreign aid, but such aid was curtailed because of Vietnam's intervention against Laos and Cambodia, and the expulsion from Vietnam of large numbers of refugees, the "boat people," mostly Chinese. In retaliation, China in 1978 terminated its aid and in 1979 briefly invaded Vietnam.

The other two states of Indochina, Laos and Cambodia, were significant chiefly as pawns in a power struggle between Vietnam and the Soviet Union on the one hand and Thailand and Communist China on the other. Both countries had traditionally been buffers between Vietnam and Thailand. After gaining control over all of Vietnam in 1975, the government of Pham Van Dong ousted the fanatic Communist regime of the

Khmer Rouge under Pol Pot in Cambodia, using Laos as a staging area. The Khmer Rouge, moving into Thailand, helped rekindle the old conflict between that country and Vietnam. To China and to a lesser extent the United States, the Vietnamization of Indochina appeared as a further step in the expansion of Soviet power in Asia.

The Association of Southeast Asian Nations (ASEAN)

To counteract the spread of communism in Southeast Asia, the non-Communist nations of the area took various countermeasures. Some of them joined the Southeast Asia Treaty Organization (SEATO), of which the United States was a member. It was established in 1954 for mutual defense against aggression and subversion, but did not prove very effective and was dissolved again in 1977. The Association of Southeast Asian Nations (ASEAN), a nonmilitary alliance of Indonesia, Malaysia, Thailand, Singapore, and the Philippines, formed in 1967, was more useful. Its members cooperated on international, political and economic issues, and in 1979 ASEAN protested Vietnam's invasion of Cambodia.

In looking at the individual nations of

Southeast Asia, we find a wide variety of political and economic problems that defy generalizations. The largest country is Indonesia, with some 13,000 islands and more than 150 million people. The Republic of Indonesia proclaimed its independence in 1945, after more than three centuries of Dutch rule. The leading figure during its first two decades was President Achmed Sukarno, whose "guided democracy" was but a thinly veiled and not always benevolent dictatorship. Economic difficulties at home and intermittent clashes with the new federation of Malaysia abroad finally led to Sukarno's ouster by the army in 1966 and his replacement as president by General Suharto, army chief of staff. While Sukarno had been moving closer to Communist China, Suharto followed a policy of nonalignment and closer relations with the non-Communist members of ASEAN. His "new order" program of austerity and economic development depended heavily on western aid, mostly from the United States. Suharto's several reelections provided political stability, but Indonesia's economic situation, despite its vast natural resources, especially oil, remained precarious.

Among the remaining nations of Southeast Asia, the Kingdom of Thailand holds a unique position. Never having been subject to colonial rule, it is a constitutional monarchy with a king who is revered but has little power. In the last forty years, the country has seen a succession of more or less corrupt military regimes. Constitutional changes in 1979 reconfirmed the power of the prime minister, usually a general, but increased his dependence on elected civilian representatives. Thailand's economy remains largely agricultural. Industrialization has brought a high living standard to urban Thailand, but the majority of its 48 million people are still farmers. Thailand's overriding concern in recent years has been with foreign affairs. Until 1975, economic and military relations with the United States had been close; however, this changed with the collapse of South Vietnam. Thailand now established diplomatic relations with China and American forces were asked to withdraw. In the late 1970s, incursions of large numbers of refugees from Laos, Cambodia, and Viet-

nam and clashes with Vietnamese forces along the Thailand-Cambodian frontier once again strengthened Thailand's ties with the United States. Vastly outnumbered by seasoned Vietnamese forces, Thailand depends on American and Chinese aid to hold its own.

THE MIDDLE EAST IN THE "THIRD WORLD"

Our discussion of events in the Far East since the Second World War has shown the term "third world" to be quite vague at best. It describes nations that vary so widely in economic development and political orientation that it is difficult to find common terms to describe them. To call them "less developed countries," as some authors euphemistically do, covers too wide a range, as does the term "nonaligned." The latter, as we have seen, applies to very few Asian countries. These ambiguities we must keep in mind as we turn to the nations of the Middle East and their position in the third world.

Arab Nationalism

One of the most turbulent scenes of rebellion against western influence after the Second World War was the mostly Arab Middle East, the area bridging Asia and Africa, from Egypt in the west to Iran in the east. Before 1945, the only independent Arab states were Egypt, Saudi Arabia, Yemen, and Iraq. Since then all the rest have won their freedom. Most of the Middle East was extremely backward and desperately poor. However, it was also of great strategic importance; it contained half the world's oil resources; and it was the religious center of hundreds of millions of Arab and non-Arab Moslems. Outwardly, the Arab world was united by its opposition to foreign domination and its resentment of Israel. But below the surface there were many divisive forces. To present a united front to the outside world, the Arab nations organized the Arab League in 1945. But behind this front, Arab differences persisted.

To meet the threat posed by Communist support of Arab nationalism, Britain, Turkey, Iran, Iraq, and Pakistan signed the Baghdad Pact in 1955. When Iraq dropped out of the alliance in 1958,

President Suharto of Indonesia and President Reagan at the White House (1982).

a new Central Treaty Organization (CENTO) was formed. It included the United States, which, under the "Eisenhower Doctrine" of 1957, had already promised armed assistance against Communist aggression to any nation in the Middle East that requested it.

The Arab Republic of Egypt

The most vociferous proponent of Arab nationalism was President Gamal Abdel Nasser of Egypt, who had taken over in 1954, a year after the Egyptian

monarchy was abolished. Following a neutralist course, Nasser's Egypt accepted large-scale aid from the West and East alike. When the western powers in 1956 withdrew their support for the Aswan Dam, a huge power project on the Nile, Nasser retaliated by nationalizing the Suez Canal. The ensuing invasion of Egypt by England, France, and Israel might have resulted in a major war, had not the United Nations insisted on the withdrawal of foreign troops. Meanwhile Egypt was left in control of the Canal, and the Aswan Dam was completed in

1970 with financial aid from the Soviet Union. By that time Nasser was receiving large-scale Soviet military support as well, and thousands of Russian "advisers and experts" were reported to be in Egypt.

Nasser died in 1970 and was succeeded by Muhammad Anwar Sadat. The new president proved to be far more moderate and conciliatory toward the western powers. In 1972 he ordered the expulsion of virtually all Russians from Egypt, and as time went on he secured far-reaching economic aid from the United States and some oil-rich Arab states. Sadat's most courageous and statesmanlike act was his visit to Jerusalem in 1977 and the subsequent Camp David negotiations, leading to the Egyptian-Israeli peace treaty of 1979. Before it could be fully implemented, however, Sadat, having been forced into a more authoritarian position by economic and social problems, was assassinated late in 1981. His successor, Hosni Mubarak, continued to be faced with economic difficulties and opposition from Muslim fundamentalists at home, and troubles with Israel abroad.

Arabs Against Israel

The main danger to peace in the Middle East was the intermittent war between the Arabs and Israel. The war started in 1948–49, when Israel's neighbors invaded the newly independent country, only to be beaten and evicted. From that time an uneasy armistice prevailed. The Arabs refused to recognize Israel, and hundreds of thousands of Arab refugees, made homeless by the partition of Palestine, helped keep the conflict alive. Full-scale fighting was briefly resumed during the Suez crisis in 1956, when Israeli forces made a quick dash for the Suez Canal. Again in 1967, in a furious six-day war, Israel took the Sinai Peninsula and some other territory. Egypt's and Syria's attempts to regain these lands led to another bloody conflict, the Yom Kippur War of 1973, in which Israel won another resounding victory.

The Israelis vowed to retain their conquests until a final and stable peace could be agreed on; they believed that they were fighting for the very survival of their nation. Yet the occupation and possible annexation of Arab lands only exacerbated the Arab-Israeli conflict. Beginning in 1972, a rash of bombings, airplane highjackings, and assassinations by Palestine Arab terrorists and retaliations by Israeli commandos intensified the crisis. The demand of the Palestine Liberation Organization (PLO) under Yasir Arafat was for return of the Arab lands occupied by Israel and the creation of a separate Palestinian state.

The stalemate that had existed since 1973 came to an end in 1977, when President Sadat approached Israel with a series of peace proposals. His counterpart in Jerusalem was Prime Minister Menachem Begin, whose coalition of conservative parties, the Likud, had recently defeated the Labor Party under Shimon Peres. Hopes for a final settlement, however, proved premature. Israel lived up to some provisions of the peace treaty of 1979, such as the evacuation of the Sinai Peninsula. But when it came to evacuating the West Bank taken from Jordan and the Golan Heights taken from Syria, the Begin government hesitated. The main obstacle proved to be the PLO. Israel refused to recognize that organization and discuss Palestinian autonomy, unless in return the PLO ceased its activ-

President Nasser greets fellow Egyptians after having nationalized the Suez Canal (1956).

Sadat, Carter, and Begin after signing the Egyptian-Israeli Peace Treaty (March 26, 1979).

ISRAEL IN 1983

ities and recognized Israel's right to exist. In 1981, Israel started bombing PLO headquarters in Beirut and in 1982 invaded Lebanon. Begin's belligerency, meanwhile, including a pre-emptive air strike against an Iraqi nuclear reactor in 1981, led to Israel's condemnation by the UN Security Council and to sharp criticism from its most loyal and steadfast friend, the United States.

The Republic of Iraq

The most serious danger to Israel in the past has come from Egypt and Syria. The rest of the Arab states were too small to pose much of a threat, with one exception. Iraq at all times has been strongly anti-Israel, and according to most observers it has the most promising future of all Arab states. The government of Iraq, repressive politically, has been enlightened economically by using its large oil revenues for industrial development, of which the nuclear reactor destroyed by Israel was an example. Since the overthrow of the monarchy in 1958, Iraq has been ruled by a number of military strong-men of whom the latest, Sadam Hussein, took over in 1979. It was Hussein who, in 1980, launched an attack upon neighboring Iran. He hoped that it

---

Anwar el-Sadat Addresses the Israeli Knesset
November 20, 1977

I have chosen to set aside all precedents and traditions known by warring countries. In spite of the fact that occupation of Arab territories is still there, the declaration of my readiness to proceed to Israel came as a great surprise that stirred many feelings and confounded many minds. Some of them even doubted its intent. . . .

I have chosen to come to you with an open heart and an open mind. I have chosen to give this great impetus to all international efforts exerted for peace. I have chosen to present to you in your own home, the realities, devoid of any scheme or whim. Not to maneuver, or win a round, but for us to win together, the most dangerous of rounds embattled in modern history, the battle of permanent peace based on justice.

It is not my battle alone. Nor is it the battle of the leadership in Israel alone. It is the battle of all and every citizen in all our territories, whose right it is to live in peace. It is the commitment of conscience and responsibility in the hearts of millions.

When I put forward this initiative, many asked what is it that I conceived as possible to achieve during this visit and what my expectations were. And as I answer the questions, I announce before you that I have not thought of carrying out this initiative from the precepts of what could be achieved during this visit. I have come here to deliver a message. I have delivered the message and may God be my witness.

I repeat with Zacharia: Love, right and justice. From the holy Koran I quote the following verses: "We believe in God and in what has been revealed to us and what was revealed to Abraham, Ishmael, Isaac, Jacob and the 13 Jewish tribes. And in the books given to Moses and Jesus and the prophets from their Lord, who made no distinction between them." So we agree, Salam Aleikum—peace be upon you.

From Anwar el-Sadat, *In Search of Identity: An Autobiography* (New York: Harper & Row, 1977/78), p. 343.

would settle a long-standing border dispute and other differences. But the war did not bring the easy victory Iraq had expected, and it added further to the tensions of the Middle East.

The Islamic Republic of Iran

The turmoils in the Middle East, of course, were of deep concern to the two superpowers. The break between Egypt and the Soviet Union, and America's key role in the efforts to resolve the Arab-Israeli conflict, sharply curtailed Soviet influence in the region. Throughout that conflict, the Russians closely sided with the Arabs and the PLO, and they continued to supply arms to Syria and Iraq, to whom they were linked by security treaties. In 1978, furthermore, the Soviet Union gained influence on the periphery by supporting the newly-emerged pro-Soviet regimes in Afghanistan, Ethiopia, and the People's Democratic Republic of Yemen. At the same time the United States was strengthening its ties not only with Egypt but with the two other leading states of the Middle East, Saudi Arabia and Iran. The sudden turn of Iran against the United States in 1979, therefore, could not help but seriously affect the balance between the superpowers, especially when followed by the Soviet invasion of Afghanistan.

Iran (called Persia until 1935) was a constitutional monarchy, ruled since 1941 by Shah Mohammad Reza Pahlavi. He was known as the "reform shah" because of his radical attempts to modernize his country. The rapid pace of these changes and the authoritarian manner in which they were introduced caused mounting opposition among vested interests and religious leaders. Iran maintained close relations with the United States, which provided massive economic and military aid. When financial difficulties forced curtailment of reforms, opposition spread to the urban masses. Attempts to meet protests by ruthless repression alternating with token concessions proved useless. In early 1979, the Shah and his family left Iran for a "vacation." He never returned.

The leading figure in the ensuing revolution was a religious leader, the Ayatollah Ruhollah Khomeini, who had been exiled by the Shah. He was widely revered by the masses and, while holding no official position, had the decisive voice in all matters. The new government immediately cut all military relations with the United States and nationalized large segments of the economy. Khomeini's special concern was with the re-revival of Islamic traditions. Belonging to the fundamentalist Shi'ite branch of Islam (see p. 304), in opposition to the more numerous Sunnites, Khomeini injected a strongly religious note into Iranian politics. Stressing the Shi'ite-Sunni split, which existed in other Islamic nations as well, emphasized a further source of tension in the Middle East.

The most startling act under the Khomeini regime was the seizure by revolutionary militants of more than fifty hostages at the American Embassy in Teheran in November 1979, in hopes of forcing the surrender of the Shah. The hostages were not released until January 1981, after worldwide protests, ineffective boycotts, and an abortive rescue effort. Meanwhile, in 1980 Iran had for the first time elected a president. Abol Hassan Bani Sadr was a moderate and for that reason was caught between the religious extremists of the right and their radical opponents on the left. He was dismissed in 1981 after serving only seventeen months. Since then Iran has been in a virtual state of civil war. Only the war with Iraq brought some diversion. Relations with the United States remained interrupted; moreover, Moslem opposition to "godless communism" also worked against closer relations with the Soviet Union. Iran was thus one of the world's truly nonaligned powers.

The Republic of Turkey

One other third-world power in the Middle East deserves a brief mention. Like Iran, Turkey is a non-Arab state. Nominally a democracy, the army has frequently intervened in times of crisis and there have been several prominent military premiers and presidents, notably General Ismet Inönü, close friend of Kemal Atatürk, the founder of modern Turkey. The latest military coup was by General Kenan Evren, who became president in 1980. Economically Turkey has

The Ayatollah Khomeini in Tehran, February 1979.

depended heavily on economic aid from the United States and from the European Economic Community, of which Turkey hopes to become a member. In its foreign policy, Turkey has tried to get along with both superpowers. However, despite occasional strains with the United States, the Turks have always leaned closely to the West, as shown by their membership in NATO. Turkey's main foreign disputes have been with Greece over their respective claims on the island of Cyprus. These differences have lessened the military effectiveness of the two NATO partners in the Mediterranean.

THE AWAKENING OF AFRICA

As we turn from the third world of Asia to that of Africa, the situation becomes infinitely complex. The dark continent was the last to be swept by the tide of nationalism. From only four sovereign states in 1950, the number by 1983 had grown to fifty-one. The former colonial powers had virtually eradicated tropical diseases, but the resultant population growth had not been matched by a similar increase in food supplies. Most of Africa, therefore, remained underfed. Added to poverty was extreme diversity, with no tradition of political unity and with some seven hundred different native dialects. The one sentiment common to all Africans was anticolonialism. Just as it did everywhere else, nationalism in Africa demanded immediate independence, even though people might not be ready for it. This rush into freedom caused severe growing pains for most of the new nations.

The Islamic States of North Africa

The countries along the southern coast of the Mediterranean Sea form another logical subgroup within the third world. They have much in common. As part of the Roman Empire, their region had early contacts with western Europe; their people were mostly Islamic; and during the colonial era the majority were under French rule. One major difference in the area exists between those countries with large oil resources—Algeria and

Libya—and the rest. Belonging to the Arab world, all these states shared in the conflict with Israel. Most of them were nonaligned, but some tended more toward one or the other of the superpowers.

American relations have been closest with Morocco, Tunisia, and the Sudan. Morocco, under King Hassan II, has received considerable military aid from the United States and has favored the Egyptian-Israeli peace treaty. Its main problem has been with the adjacent and as yet unassigned Western Sahara, which is claimed by both Morocco and Mauritania. Tunisia, since 1957 under President Habib Bourguiba, has been pro-western, except on the issue of Israel. The Sudan under President Gaafar Nimeiri is one of Egypt's few Arab friends. Several attempts against his regime, instigated by Libya with Soviet involvement, led to tension between the Sudan and those two countries.

The most troublesome country in the region has been Libya. Once among the poorest nations of North Africa, it is now, thanks to the discovery of oil in the Libyan Desert, the richest. Its president, Colonel Muammar Qaddafi, has been an unpredictable troublemaker. After concluding a major arms deal with the Soviet Union in 1975, he began supporting international terrorists and intervened in Egypt in 1977 and in neighboring Chad in 1980. Nevertheless, while the United States considers Libya to be in the Soviet camp, America still buys 40 percent of that country's oil, and Libya continues to employ some two thousand American technicians. Political relations were virtually broken in 1981, but mutually advantageous economic contacts continued.

Next to Egypt and Libya, the most prominent country in North Africa is Algeria. In an effort to reduce traditional ties to France, Algerians, under President Chadhi Bendjedid, in 1979 began moving closer to the United States. In 1980, Algeria was instrumental in negotiating the release of American hostages from Iran. The United States in return continued as the largest purchaser of Algerian oil. On some issues, such as Israel, the two countries differed, with Algeria remaining the strongest supporter of the PLO. Like most African states, Algeria tries to steer a middle course, reaping advantages from both East and West.

Africa South of the Sahara

Most victories of African nationalism occurred in the central part of the continent, south of the Sahara Desert, in areas inhabited by poverty-stricken, primitive, and largely illiterate native tribes. All African states were founded as democracies, but lack of political experience and ethnic disunity soon gave rise to one-party systems and strong-man rule. American involvement in Central Africa was less active than elsewhere. Under a policy of "noninterventionism," the United States preferred to have the African states solve their own problems. The Soviet Union and its ally Cuba, on the other hand, were less hesitant and in states like Angola, Ethiopia, and Somalia gained considerable influence.

It is impossible here to discuss more than a few of the new Central African states. One of the largest and most troubled was the Republic of Zaire. It was ruled since 1965 by President Mobuto Sese Seko and his Popular Movement of the Revolution (MPR). Zaire is rich in natural resources, especially copper, but has been beset by regional strife, especially in Katanga province. As Mobuto's regime became increasingly corrupt and repressive, the economy, due to haphazard socialization, or "Zairization," became more and more dependent on foreign aid. Zaire has been kept alive by the former colonial powers, Belgium and France, and by the United States. To let its economy collapse would lead to utter chaos.

In contrast to Zaire, the Federal Republic of Nigeria was one of the most successful of the new African states. Its major problem was to cope with its ethnic and linguistic diversity. Between 1967 and 1970, civil war between Hausa-Fulanis and Ibos led to the short-lived secession of the Ibo Republic of Biafra. Nigeria initially was under military rule; not until 1979 was President Shehu Shagari, a civilian, elected under a new democratic constitution. With its 80 million people, Nigeria was the world's fourth largest democracy. Much of the country's economic success was due to the production and export of oil. The resulting wealth made possible far-reaching reforms, such as the introduction of free universal primary education. Unequal distribution of prosperity, however, caused economic and social tensions. Relations with the United States were close and mutually beneficial, with America buying the major share of Nigeria's oil.

As the two examples above show, it is impossible to generalize about the states of black Africa. The Republic of Kenya is a further illustration. Its evolution from a British colony plagued by Mau Mau terrorism in the 1950s into a free republic in the 1960s owed much to its first president and "Father of the Nation," Jomo Kenyatta. Upon his death in 1978, he was succeeded by Daniel Arap Moi. Both of them were leaders of the only political party, the Kenya African National Union (KANU). While Kenya is thus a one-party state, compared to other such states it has enjoyed relative tolerance and the rule of law. In contrast to neighboring Tanzania, its economy remains free and attractive to outside investors. As in Zaire, there has been corruption at the top, and, as in Nigeria, the gap between rich and poor remained wide. It was economic rather than political discontent that caused a rare outbreak of violence in 1982. Kenya's foreign and economic orientation was clearly toward the West.

The early history of third-world countries was often associated with some leading figure—Joseph Mobuto of Zaire, Jomo Kenyatta of Kenya, Kwame Nkrumah of Ghana, Julius Nyerere of Tanzania. One of the most notorious of these strong men was Idi Amin of Uganda. The first decade of that new nation had been dominated by the incompetent Milton Obote and his Uganda People's Congress (UPC). In 1971, Obote was ousted by a charismatic army sergeant, Idi Amin. There followed an eight-year nightmare of lawlessness and terror, costing thousands of lives. Amin was ousted by Tanzanian troops in 1979 and constitutional government under Milton Obote was restored in 1980. In the meantime, Uganda's potentially healthy economy had been wrecked almost beyond repair, an example of the

Mobuto Sese Seko, president of Zaire, and Valéry Giscard d'Estaing in Paris (1979).

Jomo Kenyatta (1893–1978), first president of Kenya (1964–78).

dangers of too rapid transition from colonialism to freedom.

Southern Africa:
Whites Against Blacks

There was one region in Africa where
the black quest for political power continued to be resisted. In the Republic of
South Africa, as in Rhodesia and in the
Portuguese colonies of Angola and Mo-
zambique, small white minorities controlled political and economic affairs.
Increasingly, however, this white power
came under attack from black nationalism.

In South Africa, where the white
minority constituted only 18 percent of
the total population, the government in
1948 introduced a policy of strict racial
segregation, or *apartheid*. It provided for
complete separation of the races, restricted franchise for nonwhites, forced
resettlement of Africans, and established
separate schools with lower standards for
black children. In 1966 Prime Minister
Henrik V. Verwoerd, a leading advocate
of *apartheid*, was assassinated; but his
successors, Balthazar J. Vorster and, since
1978, Pieter W. Botha, continued the

A Ghanian man whose shirt
is printed with the portrait
of Kwame Nkrumah, the
first president of Ghana.

policy of segregation. South Africa's racist policies, meanwhile, led to increasingly violent confrontations at home and
the censure of most of the civilized world
abroad. In the face of such protests, the
South African government somewhat
alleviated the worst abuses of urban
apartheid. But these measures will merely
postpone the inevitable showdown between blacks and whites.

South Africa has followed similar
delaying tactics with respect to neighboring Namibia, formerly South-West
Africa. A German colony before the First
World War and a League of Nations
mandate thereafter, Namibia has been
ruled by South Africa for over half a
century. Agitation by the South-West
African People's Organization (SWAPO)
for Namibia's independence found support among the governments of Western
Europe, Canada, and the United States
but has been resisted by South Africa.
The emergence of an independent state
in the area could only have repercussions
among blacks in South Africa.

As far as Rhodesia was concerned, its
ruling white minority constituted only 3
percent of the population. Outside pressures to gain political equality for the
black majority ran into stubborn resistance from the white regime of Ian Smith.
It took a bitter seven-year civil war before the new nation of Zimbabwe came
into existence in 1980. Its first prime
minister was Robert Mugabe, head of the
Zimbabwe African National Union
(ZANU). A Marxist, Mugabe nevertheless maintained a free market economy;
and, though a former guerilla leader, he
pursued a policy of conciliation with the
white minority. Whites continued to play
an essential part in the economy, producing nearly half of the country's
exports. Mugabe's moderation attracted
substantial economic aid, especially from
Western Europe. His reliance on persuasion rather than force made him one of
Africa's most respected leaders.

By the time Zimbabwe was founded,
the oldest two colonies in Africa, Mo-
zambique and Angola, had already won
their independence from Portugal. They
each became a people's republic in 1975,
Marxist in their domestic affairs and
aligned with the Soviet Union and Cuba

The United States and South Africa

Sadly, US foreign policy and American businesses have not been a
force for change in South Africa. We have attempted to gently modify
the Nationalists' repugnant racial programs while failing to address
the main issue. The white Nationalist government is a part of the
problem in South Africa, not part of the solution. Apartheid is enforced by repression on a massive scale, condoned or directed by the
Nationalists. Given the intransigence of the current South African
government, further US investment in South Africa only serves to
prop up the white minority. The Congress and the administration
must be willing to face this dilemma if we are seriously interested in
avoiding a violent racial confrontation in South Africa. Step-by-step
economic and political pressure on South Africa would represent a
reasonable counterpoint to the current do-nothing attitude which
prevails among top US political and economic policymakers. The
United States is in no position to prescribe the solution to South
Africa's racial problems. But, we are under no obligation to expand
and strengthen ties with South Africa under the present circumstances.

From Congressman Thomas Downey, "Justice under Apartheid," *Commonweal*,
(1978) Vol. 105, pp. 721–22.

abroad. This left the escalating conflict between whites and blacks in South Africa as the major problem on the African continent.

LATIN AMERICA IN THE THIRD WORLD

The last major area in the third world that we must briefly consider is Latin America. Again it differs from the other regions. Except for some islands in the Caribbean, the nations of Latin America gained their independence more than a century ago. They include a number of industrial states that do not fit the pre-industrial model of most third world countries; and their economies range from the dire poverty of Haiti to the easy affluence of Venezuela. We have already touched on some of the problem areas and their relations with the United States and shall add to what we have said earlier (see p. 807).

Cuba

The most worrisome country in the western hemisphere for the United States continued to be Castro's Cuba. For a while after the confrontation of 1962, there were some signs of improvement in American-Cuban relations and in time de facto contacts were reestablished. But in the 1970s and early 1980s, as Cuba intervened first in Africa (Angola and Ethiopia) and then in Central America (Nicaragua and El Salvador), the rapprochement came to a halt. In 1980 when Castro permitted Cubans to join relatives already in the United States, the resulting exodus testified to widespread opposition, aggravating relations between the two countries. Cuba's economy continued to fall short of its goals and depend heavily on Soviet aid. By necessity as well as inclination, therefore, Cuba continued to be firmly within the Russian orbit.

Mexico

The major power in Central America, Mexico, while leaning toward the United States, considers itself nonaligned. In the 1970s and early 1980s, its foreign policy

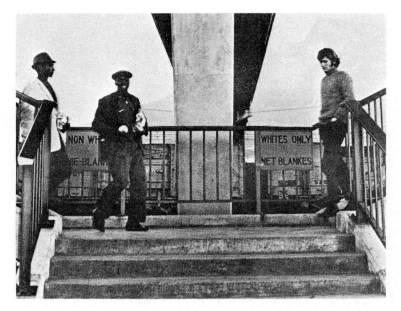

Whites versus nonwhites in South Africa.

became quite independent, maintaining friendly relations with Cuba, and favoring radical movements in Nicaragua and El Salvador. Mexico's government has been described as a six-year presidential dictatorship, under which a president is elected for a nonrenewable six-year term, usually from the leading Institutional Revolutionary Party (PRI). Mexico underwent a sudden boom with the discovery of fabulous oil deposits in the 1970s. Its overall economic health, however, leaves much to be desired. While a few Mexicans became extremely wealthy, the masses remained dismally poor. Declining agriculture and a rapidly increasing population make food a major concern. There has been growing unrest, some of it relieved by Mexican migration to the United States. The two countries are linked by close economic ties; but memories of past "American imperialism" continue to cast their shadows.

Argentina, Brazil, Chile

One of Latin America's main characteristics has been its long tradition of military dictatorships. We shall deal here only with the three largest countries; however, their experiences could be duplicated by virtually all the rest.

Argentina has a long tradition of strong-man rule. Its best-known dictator,

CENTRAL AND SOUTH AMERICA IN 1983

GULF OF MEXICO

MEXICO

CUBA

DOMINICAN REPUBLIC

BELIZE

JAMAICA

HAITI

PUERTO RICO (UNITED STATES)

GUATEMALA

HONDURAS

EL SALVADOR

CARIBBEAN SEA

NICARAGUA

COSTA RICA

PANAMA

VENEZUELA

GUYANA

SURINAME

FRENCH GUIANA

COLOMBIA

GALAPAGOS
ISLANDS
(ECUADOR)

ECUADOR

PERU

BRAZIL

BOLIVIA

PARAGUAY

CHILE

ARGENTINA

URUGUAY

PACIFIC OCEAN

ATLANTIC OCEAN

FALKLAND ISLANDS
(GREAT BRITAIN)

MILES
0   800

Juan Perón, ruled for ten years after World War II, and again briefly in the 1970s. In 1976, a military junta seized power. The regime of General Jorge Videla (1976–80) was accused of numerous murders and human rights violations; but under his successors, repression became somewhat less. Argentina was plagued by huge deficits and record inflation, leading to social unrest and terrorism. The Falkland crisis of 1982 created a brief diversion, but defeat at the hands of the British further aggravated the situation.

In Brazil, the army took over in 1964, installing a series of military leaders, most important among them Ernesto Geisel (1974–79) and his successor, João Baptista Fugueiredo. Beginning in 1977, there were some slight signs of democratization, or "decompression." After much economic progress in the early 1970s,

Brazil's development again slowed down and discontent mounted. In the early 1980s, violent crimes, land seizures and looting were frequent. Like Argentina, Brazil was strongly anticommunist, yet nonaligned. Relations of both countries with the United States were correct, rather than cordial.

While Argentina and Brazil had frequently experienced dictatorships in their past, Chile had been rare among Latin American nations for having almost always had elected governments. The last such, under Salvador Allende, came to power in 1970. An avowed Marxist, Allende embarked on a program of socialization and resumed relations with Cuba and Communist China. In 1973, he was overthrown and killed in a military coup. The United States, as was later shown, had supported the opposition to Allende. The new president, General Augusto Pinochet, soon emerged as a full-fledged dictator. In its economic measures, his regime was surprisingly liberal, hoping to solve Chile's difficulties through free market policies. Pinochet's brutal violations of human rights led to estrangement under President Carter, but his strong anticommunism was welcomed by the Reagan administration.

"THE NORTH" AND "THE SOUTH"

The third world, as our discussion has shown, includes a wide variety of countries—some of them rich, most of them poor; some of them old, most of them new; some of them on the threshold of the second world, and others still so desperately poor that we might speak of a fourth world. Some twenty-eight of the poorest nations have a quarter of the world's population and a per capita income of less than $200 per year (see table, p. 823).

The history of the third world is closely related to decolonization. As more and more non-white peoples gained their independence, common concerns naturally drew them together. There were a number of Asian-African conferences in the 1950s, the first at Bandung, Indonesia, in 1955. They were still concerned with ideological and racial issues. It was only in the 1960s, when deliberations shifted to economic problems, that these meetings became more purposeful. As time went on, they brought together not only Asians and Africans, but people from other parts of the world, especially from Latin America. The next step was a further widening of the debate, not only within the third world but between the poorer nonindustrial nations of the South and the rich industrial nations of the North.

In time there have developed a large number of international organizations devoted wholly or in part to economic improvement. There are the large regional bodies: the Organization of American States (OAS); the Organization of African Unity (OAU); the Association of South East Asian Nations (ASEAN); and the League of Arab States. Then there are the smaller economic groupings devoted to economic planning and marketing in specific areas, more than twenty all told. And finally, there are hundreds of mostly private agencies—from the African Groundnut Council to the Zinc Development Association—all of them trying to make an economically more successful world. If planning could do it, we would be living in paradise.

But we are not. When it comes to sharing, nations, like individuals, are selfish. Why do the OPEC nations, once poor themselves, not share their newfound wealth with their poorer brethren? Why does the United States give aid only where it profits most? Why do former colonial countries like France and Great Britain prefer to help their one-time dependencies? How long will it be before both East and West realize that poverty is a global disease calling for universal cures?

From time to time, doctors and patients meet to see what can be done, as they did at Cancun, Mexico, in 1981. On that occasion, the South's richest nation, Saudi Arabia, with a per capita income of $7,300 faced the North's poorest nation, Great Britain, with a per capita income of $6,300. But both of them were confronted with the *world's* poorest nation, Bangladesh, with a per capita income of $90. How will it end?

Juan Perón (1895–1974) president of Argentina 1946–55 and 1973–74.

Starving Biafran children, rationed to two cups of milk a week.

Suggestions for Further Reading

Note: Asterisk denotes a book available in paperback edition.

General G. Kurian, ed., *Encyclopedia of the Third World*, 2 vols. (1978), is a good reference work. M. Harrington, *The Vast Majority* (1977), surveys the subject. The end of colonialism is surveyed in R. Emerson, *From Empire to Nation: The Rise to Self-Assertion of Asian and African Peoples** (1960). See also, S. C. Easton, *The Twilight of European Colonialism: A Political Analysis* (1960). R. Strausz-Hupé and W. H. Hazard, *The Idea of Colonialism* (1958), corrects some misconceptions about colonial rule. G. Myrdal, *The Challenge of World Poverty* (1970), deals with the third world's greatest problem. See also A. Hoogvelt, *The Sociology of Developing Societies* (1977). On the superpowers and the third world, see B. P. Kiernan, *The United States, Communism, and the Emerging World* (1972), which is critical of American policy; and W. R. Duncan, ed., *Soviet Policy in the Third World* (1981).

South Asia R. J. Kozicki, *International Relations of South Asia* (1981), is an annotated bibliography. A good general survey is W. Wolpert, *Roots of Confrontation in South Asia* (1982). On individual nations, R. Hardgrave, Jr., *India: Government and Politics in a Developing Nation**, 3rd ed. (1980), is an excellent source of information. See also, S. Wolpert, *A New History of India*, 2nd ed. (1982). A. Lall, *The Emergence of Modern India* (1981), is by a former Indian ambassador to the United Nations. V. S. Naipaul, *India: A Wounded Civilization* (1977), is a compassionate book. On Pakistan, see L. Ziring, *Pakistan: The Enigma of Political Development* (1981), which deals with internal problems; see also, L. Blinkenberg, *India-Pakistan: The History of Unresolved Conflicts* (1972). W. N. Brown, *The United States and India, Pakistan, Bangladesh*, 3rd ed. (1972), is a standard work. On Afghanistan, see L. Dupree, *Afghanistan* (1973). The background of the current crisis is treated in J. C. Griffiths, *Afghanistan: Key to a Continent* (1981), and N. P. Newell and R. S. Newell, *The Struggle for Afghanistan** (1981).

Communist China The literature on Communist China is vast. W. S. Morton, *China: Its History and Culture* (1981), is a readable introduction. See also, O. E. Clubb, *Twentieth Century China*, 2nd ed. (1972). J. C. F. Wang, *Contemporary Chinese Politics: An Introduction** (1980), is an excellent source of information. F. W. Houn, *A Short History of Chinese Communism** (1973), is a survey. E. F. Rice, *Mao's Way** (1975), and F. Wakeman, Jr., *History and Will: Philosophic Perspectives of Mao Tse-tung's Thought** (1975), deal with the key figure. V. Shue, *Peasant China in Transition, 1949–1956* (1980), covers the period of communization. J. S. Prybyla, *The Chinese Economy: Problems and Policies**, 2nd ed. (1981), covers the post-Mao years. See also, C. Howe, *China's Economy: A Basic Guide** (1979). J. F. Copper, *China's Global Role** (1980), assesses China's rank in the hierarchy of world powers. M. Oksenberg and R. B. Oxnam, eds., *Dragon and Eagle: United States-China Relations Past and Future* (1978), is a collection of essays by China specialists. See also, M. Schaller, *The United States and China in the Twentieth Century* (1979).

The Nations of the Pacific D. Lach and E. Wehrle, *International Politics in East Asia Since World War II** (1975), and R. N. Clough, *East Asia and U.S. Security** (1975), are good general works. J. C. Thomson, P. W. Stanley, and J. C. Perry, *Sentimental Imperialists: The American Experience in East Asia* (1981), analyzes the complexity of East Asian relations. See also, J. A. Cohen, *Taiwan and American Foreign Policy** (1971). On Korea, see R. A. Scalapino and Chung-sik Lee, *Communism in Korea* (1974), and Koon Woo Nahm, *The North Korean Communist Leadership, 1945–1965* (1974). E. O. Reischauer, *Japan: The Story of a Nation* (1974), is an excellent general work. A. W. Burks, *Japan: Profile of a Postindustrial Power** (1981), is a useful introduction. Tadashi Fukutake, *Japanese Society Today**, 2nd ed. (1982), is a critical Japanese assessment. K. Kawai, *Japan's American Interlude* (1960), deals with the early postwar years. J. C. Perry, *Beneath the Eagle's Wings: Americans in Occupied Japan* (1980), is a fine interpretive study.

Southeast Asia Some of the works cited in the previous section also deal with this subject. Good general surveys are L. E. Williams, *Southeast Asia: A History* (1976); D. Steinberg et al., *In Search of Southeast Asia* (1971); and R. N. Kearney, *Politics and Modernization in South and Southeast Asia** (1974). J. Wong, *ASEAN Economics in Perspective* (1979), is a comparative study of Southeast Asian nations. J. M. Van

Der Kroef, *Communism in South-East Asia* (1980), deals with one of the region's major problems. C. A. Buss, *Southeast Asia and the World Today* (1980), places the area in a wider perspective. The following deal with individual nations: W. T. Neill, *Twentieth Century Indonesia** (1973); A. M. Sievers, *The Mystical World of Indonesia: Culture and Economic Development in Conflict* (1974); and H. Crouch, *The Army and Politics in Indonesia* (1978). The literature on Indochina and Vietnam is large. J. A. Davidson, *Indo-China—Signposts in the Storm** (1979) presents a survey. B. Fall, *The Two Vietnams*, 2d ed. (1966) is a classic. On the Vietnam War see F. Fitzgerald, *Fire in the Lake** (1973); J. A. Buttinger, *Vietnam: The Unforgettable Tragedy* (1976); and T. Hodgkin, *Vietnam: The Revolutionary Path* (1980). On Malaysia, see G. P. Means, *Malaysian Politics* (1976); and S. S. Bedlington, *Malaysia and Singapore: The Building of New States** (1978). The Philippines, sometimes considered part of Southeast Asia, are treated in B. F. Day, *The Philippines: Shattered Showcase of Democracy in Asia* (1974); and D. A. Rosenberg, ed., *Marcos and Martial Law in the Philippines* (1979). On Thailand, see D. Davies, *Thailand: The Rice Bowl of Asia* (1974); W. Bradley et al., *Thailand, Domino by Default?** (1977); and W. Donner, *The Five Faces of Thailand* (1978).

The Middle East P. Mansfield, *The Middle East: A Political and Economic Survey* (1980); and J. M. Landau, ed., *Man, State and Society in the Contemporary Middle East* (1972), are good general works. W. R. Polk, *The United States and the Arab World*, 3rd ed. (1975), is a standard work. See also, P. Mangold, *Superpower Intervention in the Middle East* (1978). On Egypt, see P. F. Vatikiotis, *Nasser and His Generation* (1978); and R. W. Baker, *Egypt's Uncertain Revolution under Nasser and Sadat* (1978). On Iraq, see M. Khadduri, *Socialist Iraq: A Study in Iraqi Politics Since 1968* (1978); and H. Batatu, *The Old Social Classes and the Revolutionary Movements of Iraq* (1979). The Iranian problem is discussed in G. Lenczowski, ed., *Iran under the Pahlavis* (1978); and R. K. Ramazani, *Iran's Foreign Policy, 1941–1973* (1975). B. Rubin, *Paved with Good Intentions: The American Experience and Iran* (1980), is insightful and objective. W. F. Weiker, *The Modernization of Turkey: From Ataturk to the Present Day* (1981), is a comprehensive assessment of Turkey's last fifty years. There are many books on Israel. H. M. Sachar, *A History of Israel* (1976), is a good survey. On foreign policy, see S. J. Roberts, *Survival or Hegemony? The Foundations of Israeli Foreign Policy* (1973). N. Safran, *Israel: The Embattled Ally* (1979), deals with relations between the United States and Israel. S. Mishal, *West Bank/East Bank: The Palestinians in Jordan, 1949–1967* (1978), treats a major problem in Arab-Israel relations.

Africa Most books on Africa deal with individual nations. Some more general works include R. Gibson, *African Liberation Movements: Contemporary Struggles Against White Minority Rule* (1972); H. F. Jackson, *From the Congo to Soweto: U.S. Foreign Policy Toward Africa Since 1960* (1982); J. Dunn, ed., *West African States, Failures and Promise: A Study in Comparative Politics** (1978), and J. D. Hargreaves, *The End of Colonial Rule in West Africa* (1979), emphasize British policy in West Africa. A. Horne, *Savage War of Peace* (1978), discusses Algeria's struggle for independence. One of the major new nations of East Africa is treated in B. U. Mwansasu and C. Pratt, eds., *Towards Socialism in Tanzania* (1979); and J. Iliffe, *A Modern History of Tanganyika* (1979). Much has been written about recent events in the southern part of the continent. R. W. Hull, *Southern Africa: Civilizations in Turmoil** (1981), deals with the racial and ethnic conflicts of the area. D. Martin and P. Johnson, *The Struggle for Zimbabwe* (1981), is comprehensive and informative. On the Republic of South Africa, see G. M. Carter, *Which Way is South Africa Going?* (1980); and N. Phillips, *The Tragedy of Apartheid* (1960). On America's attitude toward South Africa, see A. O. Hero and J. Barratt, eds., *The American People and South Africa* (1981).

Latin America The works on Latin America cited in Chapter 34 ("The Americas") are also relevant here. Other good general books are R. W. Duncan, *Latin American Politics* (1976); S. B. Tanzer, *Economic Nationalism in Latin America* (1976); B. Loveman and T. M. Davies, *The Politics of Antipolitics: The Military in Latin America* (1978); H. Handelman and T. G. Sanders, eds., *Military Government and the Movement Toward Democracy in South America* (1981); and O. C. Stoetzer, *The Organization of American States: An Introduction* (1976). On U.S. relations with the area, see C. Blasier, *The Hovering Giant: U.S. Responses to Revolutionary Change in Latin America** (1978); and J. B. Martin, *United States Policy in the Caribbean* (1978). The following deal with individual nations: G. W. Grayson, *The Politics of Mexican Oil* (1981); J. A. Hellman, *Mexico in Crisis** (1978); F. Ward, *Inside Cuba Today* (1978); D. L. Herman, *Christian Democracy in Venezuela* (1980); D. S. Palmer, *Peru: The Authoritarian Tradition* (1981); D. P. Werlich, *Peru: A Short History* (1978); E. S. Milenki, *Argentina's Foreign Policies* (1978); L. Sobel, *Argentina and Peron, 1970–1975* (1975); L. Randall, *An Economic History of Argentina in the 20th Century* (1977); S. A. Hewlett, *The Cruel Dilemmas of Development: Twentieth Century Brazil* (1980); W. H. Koebel, *Modern Chile* (1976); J. P. Canto, *Economic and Social Progress of the Republic of Chile* (1977).

Epilogue

Looking back over the events of the last forty years, it appears that the Second World War ushered in a wholly new era in world history. It has been variously called an Age of Anxiety, Age of Anarchy, or Age of Uncertainty, reflecting a sense of bewilderment in the face of ceaseless change. Rarely have so many crucial developments reached crisis proportions so rapidly; and never has a generation been confronted with so many changes and challenges.

THE PROBLEMS WE FACE

Most of these challenges, even seemingly sudden ones, have their roots in the past. It is difficult to say which is the most pressing current problem. The one that has existed longest is the relentless growth of population.

The "Population Explosion"

We have already dwelt on the problem earlier (see pp. 581, 797). Already before the Second World War, improvements in medicine and public health in the more highly developed countries had substantially lowered the death rate and prolonged the average life span. Since then, these advances have spread to the rest of the world. The results have been a dramatic increase in population. While it took a whole century before 1930 to double the world's population from 1 to 2 billion, present estimates are that the number of people at the end of this century will exceed 6 billion (see the "World Population" chart in the color map supplement). Demographers now predict that there will be a leveling-off of population growth in the next century, resulting in a stable world population of some 11 billion.

The most sensible way to cope with the unprecedented problems posed by this "population explosion," would be to curb and control the increase. Modern methods of birth control make large-scale population planning possible. In general, the more affluent industrialized societies have been more successful in slowing their population growth than the poorer nonindustrialized regions. Aside from contraception, population control can be effected by abortion, which has by now been legalized in nearly two-thirds of the world. But age-old prejudices and religious scruples still work against the general acceptance of either method of control.

The Decay of the Environment

The gravest danger from uncontrolled population growth is that in time enough food may not be available to keep these masses alive. There have already been severe famines in some parts of the world, notably in India and Africa. Some of these calamities have been due to climate, chiefly to lack of rainfall, leading to the spreading of deserts. Present estimates are that over the next twenty-five years, one-third of the earth's arable land may be lost as a result of natural causes or human mismanagement. As more and more people come to live in industrial and urban areas, many of life's basic amenities—clean air, pure water, peace and quiet—are rapidly becoming things of the past.

The awareness of pollution as a threat to our environment is of quite recent origin. While governments are trying to save society from suffocating in smog or being buried in refuse, the voracious appetites of growing populations for the luxuries and conveniences of modern technology make any remedial efforts holding actions at best. While some of the world's underdeveloped regions are existing on the brink of starvation, the more advanced countries are facing a different crisis, resulting from their consumer-oriented economies and their thoughtless waste of the world's dwindling supply of energy.

The energy crisis and the need to discover new energy sources is one of the foremost problems of our time. With petroleum the major source of energy, the meteoric rise of oil prices a decade ago ushered in a seemingly permanent worldwide economic crisis. Since then there has been increased use of such alternate sources as coal and natural gas, and a shift to new sources—solar and nuclear energy. But use of the latter is hampered by wide-spread popular fear of the possible dangers from nuclear reactors.

Poverty

It has become customary to divide the countries of the world into rich nations and poor nations. In 1975, more than 50 percent of the world's population had an annual income of less than five hundred dollars, while 10 percent earned more than five thousand dollars per year. To bridge this gap is one of the greatest challenges facing the world today (see p. 823).

The war on poverty, at first confined to the world's underdeveloped regions, in time was also being waged closer to home. While the American government was feeding people in faraway lands, millions of its own citizens went hungry; and while the United States was helping to improve housing conditions abroad, millions of Americans live in slums and ghettos. It was primarily among minorities—black and hispanic—that these economic and social injustices prevailed. In response to the growing militancy of the black community, war was finally declared on poverty. Some progress was made during the 1960s and 1970s, but much still remains to be done.

The struggle for racial justice had its counterparts in other industrialized countries, notably Great Britain. The most glaring examples of political, social, and economic inequalities are still found in South Africa, where a white minority vainly tries to stem the tide toward equal rights for all.

Women's Rights

Ethnic groups were not the only ones fighting against economic and social injustices. Other protests came from women, gays, the elderly, and the young. Women's liberation gained momentum in the early 1970s. In the economic sphere, jobs traditionally reserved for men began to be opened to women, although still rarely at equal pay. To provide a constitutional basis for women's rights, Congress in 1972 passed an Equal Rights Amendment (ERA). But when several state legislatures refused to ratify it, the amendment failed to become law. The federal government, meanwhile, introduced a program of "affirmative action" to enforce equal opportunity regardless of sex or race. Still progress toward full equality for women as well as blacks remains an unfulfilled promise and an uphill struggle.

Human Rights

By the mid-1970s, the fight for political and economic equality had turned into a worldwide concern for human rights. At a conference in Helsinki, Finland, in 1975, thirty-five Communist and non-communist nations affirmed such basic rights as free speech and freedom of movement. This Helsinki accord encouraged dissidents in several countries, notably the Soviet Union and Poland, to criticize the shortcomings of their regimes. In 1977, President Carter made human rights one of the main issues of America's foreign policy. Yet five years later, only about 36 percent of the world's population lived in total freedom, while 43 percent was not free, and the rest only partly so.

THE INDIVIDUAL IN THE NUCLEAR AGE

The major problems of our time—population explosion, decay of the environment, poverty, and curtailment of human rights—if met imaginatively and courageously, could easily help make the better world that people had dreamed of for so long. However, one further problem exceeds in magnitude all the others and, unlike the others, seems to defy solution.

Fear of Nuclear War

By the early 1980s, fear of a nuclear war had become an overriding concern of a growing number of people. Ever since the Second World War, political leaders have tried to banish this fear by finding ways of abolishing or controlling nuclear weapons. They are still trying (see p. 815). Meanwhile the stockpiling of nuclear weapons has become such as to make a more limited nuclear conflict unlikely. Given the balance of terror between the two superpowers, such a war would inevitably escalate into a nuclear holocaust. The result of such a holocaust would most likely be not only the end of our species but the end of life on earth.

The realization of this ever-present danger dawned on us only gradually, after the system of deterrence had been perfected to a point of no return. The fear of nuclear war has given birth to a worldwide peace movement. But most people still seem to be unaware of the danger of a nuclear holocaust and the likelihood that it will cause the death of the earth.

The Biological Revolution

While physics has touched off a nuclear revolution that threatens human survival, biology is making discoveries that may deeply affect and alter human existence. Some of these discoveries—artificial insemination, the transplant of human and artificial organs, and the use of drugs to control moods—are already put to use. Other research—test-tube babies, the postponement of death, genetic engineering, even the creation of life from inert matter—is still in the experimental stage. In their sum total, the discoveries that biology holds in store amount to a veritable Biological Revolution.

Discoveries and practices that so completely change the traditional pattern of human existence raise staggering ethical questions. They have led some biologists to question whether man is ready thus to tamper with his heredity. Meanwhile the experiments in the laboratories continue.

The Mind Perplexed

An avalanche of unprecedented changes crowded into the span of a single generation has left most people bewildered. In their search for understanding, they have turned to a variety of old and new doctrines, none of which seems to provide the inner security they are looking for. The temper of our time is a mixture of anticipation and apprehension, optimism and pessimism, confidence and anxiety.

The philosophy of existentialism well illustrates this blend of hope and despair. Its antecedents go back to the nineteenth century, but its vogue dates from the Second World War. The existentialists, men like Jean-Paul Sartre in France or Karl Jaspers in Germany, maintain that the individual, rather than the abstract concept of humanity, constitutes true reality. They affirm the loneliness of man in a strange and hostile world. Such loneliness, far from leading to desperation, is seen as a challenge, a call to action, since "man's destiny is within himself."

While some people are searching for a new philosophy to fit a new age, others find existing doctrines sufficient to their needs. To the true communist believer, Marxist doctrine still provides ready-made answers to most problems. There was a time when communism had a large following in the West, especially among intellectuals. But most of these people have long since become disillusioned, and new converts to communism in the free world are few. Instead, a modified form of humane socialism has gained ground among the so-called New Left. Its adherents are equally opposed to American capitalism and the bureaucratized communism of the Soviet Union.

Communism's one-time rival, fascism, also has lost most of the following it once had. One of its ingredients, nationalism, is still a potent force, especially in the new nations of Asia and Africa. Where it is used by unscrupulous leaders for selfish ends, nationalism rivals communism as a danger to world peace.

Some of the ground lost by communism and fascism has been reclaimed by religion. There are many reasons for this revived interest in religion, foremost among them the widely felt need for some central belief, some principle of authority, in a time of great intellectual uncertainty and emotional stress. The return to religion has taken many different forms and has involved not only a revival of interest in the traditional faiths of the West, but a new interest on the part of many westerners in the religions of the East. A noteworthy trend among western religions in recent years has been ecumenicalism, that is, the effort to overcome age-old differences and to work toward religious unity.

The Revolt of Youth

These are some of the ways in which people were trying to cope with their feelings of uncertainty and anxiety. There were others. One large segment of society—the younger generation—was particularly shaken by the vicissitudes of a world they had no part in making. During the 1950s, young people everywhere were reproached by their elders for the passivity with which they faced the turmoil of the times. There were some "beatniks" and "angry young men," but they were exceptions in an otherwise "quiet generation."

All this changed during the 1960s, as students began to rebel against society. Not only in the United States but the world over, the older generation was faced with a new cause for concern in an already deeply troubled world. Most of the unrest was centered in the world's large universities, where huge enrollments, combined with antiquated regulations, tended to dehumanize education. From the universities the revolt spread to the schools and into the streets. Although the aims of the youthful rebels differed from place to place, the young people were united in their opposition to what they thought their elders stood for—meaningless discipline, social injustice, and senseless wars. Some of the young expressed their protest by withdrawal rather than action, by ignoring traditional manners and mores and becoming "hippies." Others believed that only by attacking the existing "establishment" would they find a way to realize the better world of which they dreamed.

The revolt of youth ended as suddenly as it had begun. In the early 1970s, the academic climate became peaceful again. Some of the young continued protesting, but more peacefully, against war, pollution, nuclear reactors, and other social ills and injustices. In retrospect, the confrontation between generations had brought about some notable changes, not only within the universities but without. Youth's openness to new ideas, its freedom from prejudice, and its advocacy of a less inhibited life style had jolted the older generation out of many of its traditional and outworn habits and attitudes.

An Age of Violence or an Age of Compassion?

Unrest among students was only one manifestation of discontent with the existing order. During the late 1970s another more violent form of protest erupted, as terrorists launched a campaign of bombings, arson, and murder against the forces in political and economic control. Like the student revolt, terrorism struck almost everywhere, except in the communist world. Seen in conjunction with other forms of violence—airplane highjackings, killing of hostages, and a steadily rising crime wave—the world seemed to have entered upon an age of violence, uncontrolled any longer by the forces of law and order. It may be that the constant blood-letting of a half century of virtually uninterrupted warfare had inured mankind to the terror of death. More people have been killed by their fellow men in this century than during any other time in history.

Balanced against this seeming disregard for human life must be the growing awareness of the interdependence of the human family and the growing sense of responsibility among the more priviliged for the less fortunate members of that family. The present generation, of course, is only a mere incident in the long-range story of human development. But in retrospect this age may some day appear as one of the most creative phases of history. As an age in which the threat of a nuclear holocaust forced man to learn from his past mistakes; an age in which peaceful competition between rival ideologies brought forth economic and cultural progress; and an age in which fruitful debate and cooperation among peoples created a society in which such progress was shared by all.

Suggestions for Further Reading

Note: Asterisk denotes a book available in paperback edition.

The Problems We Face

The literature on the contemporary world is vast and growing daily. The following is only a small selection from the thousands of books dealing with the issues discussed in the Epilogue. Good introductions to the "population explosion" are W. D. Borrie, *The Growth and Control of World Population* (1970); and T. McKeown, *The Modern Rise of Population* (1976). On the continuing debate surrounding Malthus' predictions of inevitable poverty, see W. W. Cochrane, *The World Food Problem: A Guardedly Optimistic View** (1969). The question of birth control is discussed in G. J. Hardin, ed., *Population, Evolution and Birth Control*, 2nd ed. (1969), and A. F. Zimmerman, *Catholic Viewpoint on Overpopulation* (1961). The effect of population growth on the environment is treated in W. F. Longgood, *The Darkening Land* (1972); H. W. Helfrich, ed., *Agenda for Survival: The Environmental Crises** (1970); and K. Montague and P. Montague, *No World Without End: The New Threats to Our Biosphere* (1976).

The depressing subject of world poverty is dealt with in M. Harrington, *The Vast Majority: A Journey to the World's Poor* (1977); and possible remedies are discussed in O. Schachter, *Sharing the World's Resources* (1976). See also G. Chaliand, *Revolution in the Third World* (1977). America's poor are the subject of S. Lens, *Poverty: Yesterday and Today* (1973), a historical approach, and M. N. Danielson, *The Politics of Exclusion** (1976), treated topically. On the women's liberation movement, W. H. Chafe, *The American Woman: Her Changing Social, Economic, and Political Roles, 1920–1970** (1974), and G. G. Yates, *What Women Want: The Ideologies of the Movement* (1975), are historical treatments. See also B. A. Babcock et al., *Sex Discrimination and the Law: Causes and Remedies* (1975).

The Individual in the Nuclear Age

On the debate over the dangers of nuclear energy, see R. E. Webb, *The Accident Hazard of Nuclear Power Plants** (1976); R. S. Lewis, *The Nuclear-Power Rebellion: Citizens vs. the Atomic Industrial Establishment* (1972); and R. J. Lifton and R. Falk, *The Political and Psychological Case Against Nuclearism** (1983). J. Schell, *The Fate of the Earth** (1982), deals with the catastrophic results of a nuclear holocaust. Attempts at nuclear disarmament are discussed by A. Myrdal, *The Game of Disarmament: How the United States and Russia Run the Armaments Race* (1977); and its urgency is stressed in W. Epstein, *The Last Chance: Nuclear Proliferation and Arms Control* (1976). The best introduction to the biological revolution is P. B. Medawar and J. S. Medawar, *The Life Science: Current Ideas in Biology* (1977). Other, more alarmist, works are J. Goodfield, *Playing God: Genetic Engineering and the Manipulation of Life* (1977); M. Rogers, *Biohazard* (1977); and N. Wade, *The Ultimate Experiment: Man-made Evolution* (1977).

A good introduction to existentialism is W. A. Kaufmann, ed., *Existentialism, from Dostoevsky to Sartre*, rev. ed. (1975). See also G. Brée, *Camus and Sartre: Crisis and Commitment* (1972); and R. Aron, *Marxism and the Existentialists* (1969). On the recent revival of religious interest, see C. Y. Glock and R. N. Bellah, eds., *The New Religious Consciousness** (1976); D. F. Wells and J. D. Woodbridge, *The Evangelicals: What They Believe, Who They Are, Where They Are Changing* (1976); and M. E. Marty, *A Nation of Believers* (1976). The revolt of youth is treated in M. Crozier, *The Stalled Society** (1973); L. S. Feuer, *The Conflict of Generations* (1969); and B. R. Wilson, *The Youth Culture and the Universities* (1970). The best general work on terrorism is W. Laqueur, *Terrorism* (1977). See also F. J. Hacker, *Crusaders, Criminals, Crazies: Terror and Terrorism in Our Time* (1977); and J. Schreiber, *The Ultimate Weapon: Terrorists and World Order* (1978).

Source of Illustrations

397: *t* © 1966 by Macmillan. From Basil Davidson's *A History of Africa; l* Philadelphia Museum of Art: Given by Mrs. G. Brinton Roberts

399: *1t* Alinari/Editorial Photocolor Archives; *rt* Giraudon; *b* The Bettmann Archive

401: From A. Chavero's *Antiquedades Mexicanas,* 1892

402: Museo di Capodimonte, Naples

404: Phot. Bibl. nat. Paris

405: Bradley Smith

406: Musées des Beaux-Arts, Kassel

407: Nederlands Scheepvaart Museum, Amsterdam

408: The Royal Library, Stockholm

409: Reproduced by Courtesy of the Trustees of the British Museum

411: Musée Cantonal des Beaux-Arts, Lausanne

412: *t* Giraudon; *b* Musée Condé, Chantilly

413: Alinari/Editorial Photocolor Archives

Chapter 19

416: Rijksmuseum, Amsterdam

418: The Metropolitan Museum of Art, Rogers Fund, 1942

419: Reproduced by Courtesy of the Trustees, The National Gallery, London

421: Giraudon

423: Historical Pictures Service, Inc., Chicago

424: National Portrait Gallery, London

425: National Portrait Gallery, London

426: By Courtesy of the Rijksmuseum, Amsterdam

427: The Bettmann Archive

428: Historical Pictures Service, Inc., Chicago

429: Rare Books and Manuscripts Div., The New York Public Library, Astor, Lenox and Tilden Foundations

430: Historical Pictures Service, Inc., Chicago

431: Culver Pictures

435: From *Adventures in the Wilderness* by Wissler et al., vol. 1 in the *Yale Pageant of America* series, by permission of the United States Publishers Assn., Inc.

439: Crown Copyright. Victoria and Albert Museum, London

440: Rare Books and Manuscripts Division, The New York Public Library, Astor, Lenox and Tilden Foundations

441: Reproduced by Courtesy of the Trustees of the British Museum

443: Moll's *Map of America,* 1709–20

444: From Horizon's *History of Russia.* © 1970 by American Heritage

Chapter 20

447: Musée du Louvre, Paris

448: Phot. Bibl. nat. Paris

449: Bibliothèque Nationale, Paris

450: Phot. Bibl. nat. Paris

451: Phot. Bibl. nat. Paris

452: Archives Photographiques, Paris

453: Historical Pictures Service, Inc., Chicago

455: By permission of The British Library

457: Culver Pictures

458: The Bettmann Archive

459: Reproduced by Courtesy of the Trustees of the British Museum

460: Picture Collection, The Branch Libraries, The New York Public Library

461: BBC Hulton Picture Library

462: Kunthistorisches Museum, Vienna

463: *t* The Bettmann Archive; *b* Musée du Louvre, Paris

464: Giraudon

465: Photo Hachette

467: Novosti Press Agency, London

468: By Courtesy of the Rijksmuseum, Amsterdam

469: *t* Russian Folk Illustration 1881; *b* Novosti Press Agency, London

Chapter 21

472: New York Public Library

475: Phot. Bibl. nat. Paris

476: *t* National Portrait Gallery, London; *b* David Eugene Smith Collection, Rare Book and Manuscript Library, Columbia University

477: BBC Hulton Picture Library

479: The Bettmann Archive

480: Photo Researchers, Inc.

481: The Metropolitan Museum of Art, Harris Brisbane Dick Fund, 1953

483: The Bettmann Archive

485: John R. Freeman, London

487: © 1959 by Dover Publications, Inc. From Diderot's *Encyclopaedia*

490: © 1959 by Philosophical Library. From Rune's *Pictorial History of Philosophy*

491: Giraudon

493: Original in the Mozart Museum, Salzburg

Chapter 22

496: Giraudon

499: Historical Pictures Service, Inc., Chicago

500: New York Public Library, Rare Book Division

501: *t* Reproduced by Courtesy of the Trustees of the British Museum; *b* Lord Townshend Collection/ American Heritage Publishing Co.

502: Historical Pictures Service, Inc., Chicago

503: From Diderot's *Encyclopaedia*

504: Giraudon

505: Bildarchiv Foto Marburg

506: Picture Collection, The Branch Libraries, The New York Public Library

507: Historical Pictures Service, Inc., Chicago

509: Crown Copyright. Victoria and Albert Museum, London

510: Library of Congress

512: By Courtesy of Staatliche Münzsammlung, Munich

518: Courtesy of the Pennsylvania Academy of Fine Arts

519: Library of Congress

Chapter 23

523: Giraudon

524: BBC Hulton Picture Library

526: Phot. Bibl. nat. Paris

527: *t* Musée du Louvre, Paris; *b* Phot. Bibl. nat. Paris

528: Bibliothèque Nationale, Paris

529: Reproduced by Courtesy of the Trustees of the British Museum
530: Bibliothèque Nationale, Paris
531: Bibliothèque Nationale, Paris
532: John R. Freeman, London
533: The Bettmann Archive
534: Phot. Bibl. nat. Paris
536: From *Description de l'Egypte,* 1809–1826
537: Giraudon
538: Giraudon
540: Anne S. K. Brown Military Collection, Brown University Library
542: Photo Copyright Musée de l'Armée, Paris

Chapter 24
544: Ets J. E. Bulloz
546: Teresa Fitzherbert Print Room; Royal Library, Windsor Castle
547: *t* John R. Freeman, London; *b* Archives Photographiques, Paris
549: The Mansell Collection
550: Giraudon
551: National-Galerie, Berlin (destroyed 1945)
553: Bildarchiv Foto Marburg
554: Culver Pictures
555: The Metropolitan Museum of Art. Bequest of Seth Low, 1929
556: *t* Photo Hachette; *b* The Bettmann Archive
557: *t* Musée du Louvre, Paris; *b* Historical Pictures Service, Inc., Chicago
558: The Pierpont Morgan Library, New York
560: *t* The Mansell Collection; *b* Historical Pictures Service, Inc., Chicago
562: *t* The Bettmann Archive; *b* John R. Freeman, London
563: Österreichische Nationalbibliothek, Vienna
567: By permission of the British Library

Chapter 25
570: Deutsches Museum, Munich
573: *t* Picture Collection, The Branch Libraries, The New York Public Library; *b* British Crown Copyright, Science Museum, London
574: The Mansell Collection
575: The Mansell Collection
576: The Mansell Collection
577: The Mansell Collection
578: BBC Hulton Picture Library
579: *t* The Bettmann Archive; *b* BBC Hulton Picture Library
580: Reproduced by Courtesy of the Trustees of the British Museum
581: Brown Brothers
582: Tate Gallery, London
583: Picture Collection, The Branch Libraries, The New York Public Library
585: Picture Collection, The Branch Libraries, The New York Public Library
587: Historical Pictures Service, Inc., Chicago
590: The Dickens House, London
591: *t* Gernsheim Collection, Humanities Research Center, The University of Texas at Austin; *b* Sovfoto

Chapter 26
594: BBC Hulton Picture Library
596: *t Punch Magazine*/Picture Collection, The Branch Libraries, The New York Public Library; *b* Culver Pictures
597: Mayer & Pierson, Gernsheim Collection, Austin, Texas
599: Culver Pictures
601: Ferrier and Solier, Courtesy of the International Museum of Photography, Rochester, New York
602: The Bettmann Archive
603: *t* Brown Brothers; *b* Österreichische Nationalbibliothek, Vienna
604: The Bettmann Archive
605: Gernsheim Collection, Humanities Research Center, The University of Texas at Austin
607: HBJ Collection
611: Gernsheim Collection, Humanities Research Center, The University of Texas at Austin
612: HBJ Collection
614: *t* The Granger Collection, New York; *b* Phot. Bibl. nat. Paris

617: *t* Katherine Young/Archiv für Kunst und Geschichte; *b* BBC Hulton Picture Library

Chapter 27
620: National Museum of Tanzania, Dar-es-Salaam
622: *t* Western Union Corporation; *b* Reproduced with permission of AT & T Co.
623: *t* Library of Congress
624: *tl* New York Historical Society; *tr* Andrew Jackson; Thomas Sully; National Gallery of Art, Washington, D.C., Andrew Mellon Collection, 1942; *b* In the Collection of the Corcoran Gallery of Art
626: From Benson J. Lossing's *Pictorial History of the Civil War in the United States of America.* Reprinted with Permission of the Lost Cause Press
627: *t* United States Army Photo; *b* Library of Congress
628: Library of Congress
629: The Dentzel Collection
630: Union Pacific Railroad Company
631: Library of Congress
633: Culver Pictures
636: From R. A. Foster's *Pictures for Little Englanders,* 1876, By permission of the British Library
637: Ullstein-Bilderdienst
639: John R. Freeman, London
640: Brown Brothers
641: *t* Library of Congress; *b* The Bettmann Archive
642: The Bettmann Archive
643: Board of Global Ministries, United Methodist Church

Chapter 28
646: The Metropolitan Museum of Art, gift of Frederic H. Hatch, 1926.
648: *t* Brown Brothers; *b* London Transport Executive
649: Charts on p. 220 of *Western Civilization,* Vol. II, 2nd Ed., edited by William L. Langer et al. Copyright © 1969, 1975 by Harper & Row Publishers, Inc. Reprinted by permission.

650: Brown Brothers
651: Ets J. E. Bulloz
652: *t* Reproduced by Courtesy of the Trustees of the British Museum; *b* BBC Hulton Picture Library
653: Gernsheim Collection, Humanities Research Center, The University of Texas at Austin
655: The Granger Collection, New York
656: Phot. Bibl. nat. Paris
657: H. Roger-Viollet
658: BBC Hulton Picture Library
659: The Bettmann Archive
660: Gernsheim Collection, Humanities Research Center, The University of Texas at Austin
661: *t* Katherine Young/Archiv Für Kunst und Geschichte; *b* Brown Brothers
663: Sovfoto
664: Sovfoto
665: Historical Pictures Service, Inc., Chicago
666: Courtesy of American Museum of Natural History
667: The Bettmann Archive
670: Gernsheim Collection, Humanities Research Center, The University of Texas at Austin
671: The Granger Collection, New York

Chapter 29
675: The Press Association Limited
679: *t* Picture Collection, The Branch Libraries, The New York Public Library
680: *t* BBC Hulton Picture Library; *m* Philadelphia Museum of Art, Louis E. Stern Collection; *b* The Tate Gallery, London
685: United Press International, Inc.
686: Historical Pictures Service, Inc., Chicago
688: Picture Collection, The Branch Libraries, The New York Public Library
690: The Bettmann Archive
692: The Press Association, London
693: *t* United Press International, Inc.; *b* BBC Hulton Picture Library

Chapter 30
698: Imperial War Museum, London
700: *t* Imperial War Museum, London; *b* Historical Pictures Service, Inc., Chicago
702: Culver Pictures
703: Imperial War Museum, London
704: National Archives, Washington, D.C.
706: *t* "L'Illustration," Sygma; *b* John R. Freeman, London
707: Sovfoto
709: Imperial War Museum, London
710: U.S. Signal Corps/National Archives, Washington, D.C.
712: BBC Hulton Picture Library
713: Culver Pictures
714: "L'Illustration," Sygma
716: The Bettmann Archive
717: Gernsheim Collection, Humanities Research Center, The University of Texas at Austin
718: Wide World Photos
720: *t* The Chase Manhattan Museum of Money of the World; *b* United Press International, Inc.
721: BBC Hulton Picture Library

Chapter 31
724: Dr. Erich Salomon/Magnum Photos, Inc.
726: Library of Congress
728: Culver Pictures
729: Brown Brothers
730: Brown Brothers
731: The Granger Collection, New York
732: Wide World Photos
733: Dr. Erich Salomon
734: Wide World Photos
735: Culver Pictures
736: Times Newspapers, Ltd.
737: *t* Earl Leaf, Rapho-Guillumette/PRI; *b* Wide World Photos
739: *t* Courtesy of Ford Motor Company; *m* © 1973 by National Housewares Manufacturers Assoc. From *The Housewares Story; b* The Marconi Company
740: Clark University Archives

741: Courtesy of Dr. Margaret Mead/American Museum of Natural History
742: *t* BBC Hulton Picture Library; *b* Brown Brothers
743: S.P.A.D.E.M., Paris/V.A.G.A., New York, 1983

Chapter 32
746: Wide World Photos
748: *t* The Lenin State Library of The U.S.S.R., Moscow; *b* © by The New York Times Company. Reprinted by Permission.
749: Sovfoto
750: *t* John R. Freeman, London; *b* Sovfoto
753: Brown Brothers
757: Library of Congress
758: United Press International, Inc.
759: Gernsheim Collection, Humanities Research Center, The University of Texas at Austin
761: Bildarchiv Preussischer Kulturbesitz, Berlin
762: Frederic Lewis
763: Gernsheim Collection, Humanities Research Center, The University of Texas at Austin
764: *both* Brown Brothers
765: Gernsheim Collection, Humanities Research Center, The University of Texas at Austin
768: *t* CBS News; *b* Associated Press Photo, London/Wide World Press
769: United Press International, Inc.

Chapter 33
772: Wide World Photos
774: Wide World Photos
775: Times Newspapers, Ltd.
776: *t* Wide World Photos; *b* American Heritage Publishing Co.
777: Sovfoto
779: National Archives, Washington, D.C.
781: Keystone
782: United States Coast Guard Photo

786: *t* United Nations; *b* Imperial War Museum, London
787: © 1961 *Punch* (Rothco)
789: Fenno Jacobs/Black Star
791: Wide World Photos

Chapter 34
796: White House Photograph, National Archives
798: Pictorial Parade
799: Wide World Photos
800: Pictorial Parade
801: Keystone
802: Regis Bossu/Sygma
804: *t* Wide World Photos; *b* United Press International, Inc.

805: *t* United Press International, Inc.; *b* © 1963 Ebony Magazine
806: Wide World Photos
808: *t* United Nations; *b* Pictorial Parade
809: Wide World Photos, Inc.
810: Erich Lessing/Magnum Photos, Inc.
812: United Press International, Inc.
814: Camera Press/Photo Trends

Chapter 35
821: Alain Nogues/Sygma
822: *t* United Press International, Inc.; *b* Wide World Photos
825: *t* United Press International, Inc.; *b* Eastfoto

826: *t* Wide World Photos; *b* Fox Butterfield/New York Times Pictures
830: J. Pavlovsky/Sygma
831: Whitehead/Sygma
833: *t* Wide World Photos; *b* United Press International, Inc.
835: United Press International, Inc.
837: *t* Melloul/Sygma; *b* Pascale Villiers Le Moy/Sygma
838: Marilyn Silverstone/Magnum Photos, Inc.
839: Andrew Bailey, Camera Press/Photo Trends
841: *t* Diego Goldberg/Sygma; *b* Popperfoto, London

A

Abbasid Caliphate, 176, 218, 301–05, 309
Abdul-Hamid II, 690
Abelard, 222–24, 225; *Sic et Non*, 222, 223
abortion, 844
Abraham, 18–19, 170
Abu-Bekr, 171, 173
Abu'l Abbas, 176
Abul Fazl: quoted, 326
Abyssinia, 681, 715
Acadia, 442, 454
Acaemeneid Empire (Persia), 126
Acre, 229, 307, 308–09
Acropolis, 43
Action Française, 657
Actium, battle of, 77
Act of Settlement (1701), 459, 461, 501
Act of Union (1707), 461
Adams, Henry, 648
Addison, Joseph, 492
Aden, 397
Adenauer, Konrad, 788, 800–01
Adler, Victor, 660
Admiral Graf Spee (battleship), 773
Adrianople, 316; battle of, 113; Treaty of (1829), 556, 595
Adua, battle of, 661, 681
advertising, 649
Aegean Sea: ancient trade and settlements, 12, 13, 14, 16, 26, 28–31
Aehrenthal, Aloys von, 690
Aeschylus, 43; *Oresteia* trilogy, 44
Aëtius, 116
"affirmative action" program, 845
Afghanistan, 175, 324, 683, 684, 815, 825, 835
Afghan Lodi Dynasty (India), 325
Africa, 506, 589; central, 680–81; east, 687; European imperialism in, 633, 636, 643, 679–83; explorations in, 393, 396–97; famine in, 844; nationalism in, 836; Roman expeditions in, 93; slaves from, 400–01, 409, 439, 440, 500; and Third World, 791–92, 841; west, 511, 600, 681. *See also* North Africa; South Africa
African Groundnut Council, 841
Agadir, 691
Agincourt, battle of, 284
Agnew, Spiro, 806
agriculture, 435; in ancient Middle East, xxxvi, xxxviii, 4–6, 9, 10; and capitalism, 364–65, 629, 631; improved technology for, lvii, 581, 649; land reclaimed for, lviii, 209; open-field system, 572; revolution in, 499, 501, 571–73; three-field system, 206, 572. *See also* individual countries
Agrippa, 77, 80
Agrippina, 85
Ahmose, 15, 16
Ainu, 339–40
Aix-la-Chapelle, 548–49; Treaty of, 508
Ajanta, 130
Akbar, 326–28
Akhnaton, 16
Alais, Peace of (1629), 420
Alamanni, 153
Alaska, 555, 628
Ala-ud-Din, Delhi sultan, 325

Albania, 690, 692–93, 702, 759, 769, 775, 789, 810
Alberti, Leon Battista: *On the Family,* 353
Albigensian heresy, 245, 253, 255
Albuquerque, Alfonso de, 397
Alcuin, 183
Alexander III, Pope, 242
Alexander VI, Pope, 363, 372, 399
Alexander I, Tsar of Russia, 539–40, 541, 546, 548–49, 556, 558
Alexander II, Tsar of Russia, 596, 616–17, 662, 705
Alexander III, Tsar of Russia, 662
Alexander the Great, xxxix, xliii, xliv, 24, 50–51, 54, 57, 63, 126
Alexandra, Empress of Russia, 664, 703
Alexandria, xliii, xliv, 50, 52, 54, 76, 88, 92, 96, 112, 159, 176, 229, 394
Alexius Comnenus, Byzantine Emperor, 305–06, 307
Alfonso X, King of Castile, 241; *Siete Partidas,* 241
Alfred the Great, 190–91, 200
Algeciras, Act of (1906), 689, 691
Algeria, 317, 600, 679, 781, 799, 836–37
Ali, 173, 174, 176
Allende (Gossens), Salvador, 807, 841
Allen of Hurwood, Lord, 761
Alliance for Progress, 807
Allied Control Council, 785
Allied Military Control Commission, 712, 715, 718
Allied Powers: First World War, 699–705, 707–20, 748; post–Second World War, 784–91; Second World War, 773, 774–77, 779–83
alphabets, xxxvii, xxxviii, 17–18, 31, 168. *See also* writing
Alsace, 188, 432
Alsace-Lorraine, 187, 610, 658, 688, 700, 708
Alva, Ferdinand Alvarez de Toledo, Duke of, 406, 410
Ambrose, St., 114, 119
America, 363, 365, 408, 450, 453; Catholic Church in, 400–03; discovery of, 393, 398–99; metals from, 400, 403–04, 417
American Federation of Labor, 630, 730
American Indians, xxxiv, 399, 400–02, 403, 439, 443, 624, 632
American Revolution, 408, 517–20, 588, 623; ideals of, 462, 520, 529
Amiens Cathedral, 232
Amin Dada, Idi, 837
Amos, 18, 21
Amsterdam, 365, 405, 407, 435
Anabaptists, 384–85, 390, 405
Anagni: attack at, 264, 271
Analects of Confucius, The, 136
anarchism, 591, 617, 662
anatomy, 359, 474, 476
Anaxagoras, 45
Andalusia, 404
Anderson, Thornton: quoted, 315
Andropov, Yuri, 809–10
Angkor Wat, 131–32
Angles, 145. *See also* Anglo-Saxons
Anglicanism, 385–88, 424–28
Anglo-German Agreement (1935), 761
Anglo-German Heligoland Treaty (1890), 687

Anglo-Russian Entente (1907), 684, 689, 695
Anglo-Saxon Chronicle, 200, 211, 212
Anglo-Saxons, 155; Britain under, liii, lv, 116, 143, 145, 151–53, 199–202, 210–12; literature, 200. *See also* Germanic kingdoms; Germanic tribes
Angola, 837, 838–39
Anjou, 235, 238, 239
Anjou, François Hercule, Duke of, 406
Ankara, 316
An Lu-shan, 331, 332
Anna Comnena: quoted, 307
Anne, Queen of England, 422, 459–60, 461, 501
Anti-Comintern Pact (1936), 760
Anti-Corn Law League, 566
Antigonus, King of Macedon, 51
Antioch, 52, 112, 159, 176, 305–06, 309
anti-semitism, 655, 758–59
Antoninus Pius, Roman Emperor, 87
Antony, Mark, 75–77
Antwerp, 365, 398, 405, 406, 407, 454
apartheid, 814, 838, 845
Apollonius, 52
Apuleius: *Golden Ass,* 95
Aquinas, St. Thomas, lxii, 250, 263–65, 294, 303, 353; quoted, 263
Aquitaine, 156, 181, 235, 238, 239, 255, 267, 269, 270, 281
Arab Empire: Abbasid dynasty, 176, 218, 301–05, 309; aristocracy, 174, 176; conquests of, liv, 51, 118, 164, 167, 173, 175–76, 299; culture, 167, 168, 174–75, 176; decline, 303–05, 309; government and administration, 174–75, 299, 303–04; military, 303, 304; North Africa under, 162, 175; Ommiad dynasty, 173–76, 304; philosophers, 302–03; scholars, lx–lxii, lxiv, 174–75, 247, 263, 299, 302–03, 317–18; science, lx, lxx, 53, 167, 168, 198, 224, 245–46, 294, 302, 473; Spain under, 155, 175, 204, 259, 366–67; trade and commerce, 175, 176, 179, 301, 330, 394, 395–97. *See also* Moslems
Arabia, 7, 81, 167–68, 170, 173, 317; religion, 168–73
Arabic numerals, 129, 302
Arab League, 831
Arabs: conflict with Jews, 735, 791, 814, 831, 833–34; invasion of India, 323; nationalism, 831–32; terrorists, 833
Arafat, Yasir, 833
Aragon, lxvii, 240, 289, 366–68, 402
Arakcheiev, Alexis, 556
Aramaeans, 17
Arberry, A. J.: quoted, 170
Arcadius, Roman Emperor, 115
archeology: in China, 132; in Crete, 12–13; in Egypt, 15; in Greece, 28; and Hebrew scriptures, 18, 19; in India, 3; in Pompeii, 3, 492; in Rome, 58, 92; Stone Age, 4
architecture: baroque, 451, 481; Buddhist, 127, 331; church, 120, 162, 219, 220–22, 231–33, 263, 291; classical, 492; Egyptian, 11, 15, 32, 42; functional, 631, 743; Georgian, 492; Gothic, lx, 220–22, 231–33, 263, 291–92, 494; Greek, 32, 42, 67, 94; Hindu, 326; medieval, lx, 219,

architecture (*continued*)
220–22, 231–33, 263, 552; of Mesopotamia, 6, 7, 11; Moslem, 175, 303; Roman, 67, 94, 118, 162, 355; Romanesque, lx, 222; Turkish, 317. *See also* individual countries

Argentina, 632, 798, 839–40

Arianism, 108, 114, 117–18, 119, 144, 145, 149, 154, 155

aristocracy, 208, 235, 499; vs. monarchy, 497, 512, 517. *See also* nobility; individual countries

Aristophanes, 46, 52; *Clouds, The*, 44; *Lysistrata*, 44

Aristotle, xlii, xliv, lx, 46, 49, 53, 145, 146, 167, 223, 245–47, 263–64, 294, 300, 302, 353, 474, 477–78; *Politics*, 292

Arius, 108, 114

Arkwright, Richard, 573

Armenia, 167, 173, 687

Arminians, 434

Arminius (Herman), 81

Armstrong, Neil A., 816

Arnold, Matthew, 671

art: baroque, 480–81; Buddhist, 127, 130; Christian, l, 120; "golden ages" of, 414; manuscript illumination, 292, 300; and Romanticism, 553; and science, 669–71; Stone Age, 4. *See also* painting; individual countries

Arthurian legend, 234

Artois, Charles Philippe, Count of, 528, 556–57. *See also* Charles X, King of France

Ashoka (Mauryan emperor), 127

Asia, 633; East, 122; imperialism in, 683–84; nationalism in, 643, 824; and Third World, 792. *See also* Southeast Asia; individual countries

Asia Minor, xxxvii, xli, xliii, 14, 16, 30, 713; Byzantine reconquest of, 299, 305–06, 308; conquered by Persia, 23, 39–40, 50; Greek city–states in, 26, 31, 38, 40, 41, 48, 49, 51, 71; religions of, 54, 57, 90–91, 124; under Rome, xliv, lii, liv, 64, 71, 72, 87, 117, 159, 162, 166; under Turks, 217–18, 305–06, 307, 310, 316

Association of Southeast Asian Nations (ASEAN), 830–31, 841

Assyrian Empire, 16, 18, 22, 30

astrolabe, 395

astronomy: in ancient Middle East, xxxix, 8, 45; Arabs, 168, 198, 246, 302; Greek, 53, 130, 246; Indian, 129–30; medieval, 198, 246; Roman, 95–96; in Scientific Revolution, 473–77

Asturias, 155, 156, 240

Aswan Dam, 832–33

Atatürk, Kemal, 835

Athens, ancient, 30, 34–36, 38, 40–42, 52, 54, 64, 71; arts, 42–43; drama, 36, 43–44, 46; festivals of Dionysis in, 36, 43, 53; government, xli, 33, 34–35, 38, 41–42, 47, 48–49; historians and philosophers, 44–49; imperialism of, 47; navy, 34, 38–39, 40, 47, 48; Peloponnesian War, xlii, 46–47; Persian Wars, 24, 26, 36, 38–40, 44–45. *See also* Greece, ancient

Atlantic Charter, 784

atomic weapons, 742, 783–84, 791–92, 797, 846. *See also* nuclear power

Atoms for Peace Program, 816

Attila, King of the Huns, 116

Attlee, Clement, 786, 798

Attu, 783

Augsburg, Peace of (1555), 381–82, 393, 429–30

Augustenburg, Duke of, 607

Augustine of Canterbury, St., 152–53, 153n

Augustine of Hippo, St., 145, 449; *City of God, The*, 115, 119; *Confessions*, 119

Augustus (Octavian), Roman Emperor, xlvi–xlvii, 75–77, 79–84, 89

Augustus II (the Strong), King of Poland, 463

Aurangzeb (Mughal emperor), 327–28

Aurelian, Roman Emperor, 100, 103

Auschwitz, 779

Austerlitz, battle of, 538

Australia, 613, 633, 634, 647, 649

Austria: *Anschluss*, 755, 759, 764, 765–67; foreign affairs, 497, 499, 505, 513–14, 557, 559, 596, 598, 612, 617, 676–78, 687, 688–93, 716, 762; and French Revolutionary Wars, 531–32, 533; government and politics, 604, 607, 659, 709, 759; in Habsburg Empire, lxvii, 290–91, 295, 367, 370, 402, 430, 431, 432, 453–54, 463–64, 470, 505, 516, 540, 547–50, 554, 557–58, 562–66, 598, 601–03; industrialization, 574–76, 660; and Italian unification wars, 601–03, 606–07; labor, 652, 661; mercantilism, 438; and Napoleonic Wars, 536, 538–39, 542; nationalism in, 559, 563, 568, 604; post-First World War, 712, 713, 714, 720, 727, 731; post-Second World War, 787, 812; and Prussia, 598, 603, 604–09, 610; Seven Years' War, 509–11; socialism in, 660–61; social reform, 659, 660, 661; War of the Austrian Succession, 507–09

Austria-Hungary, 604, 659–61, 674, 677, 689, 693; First World War, 693–95, 699–704, 706, 708–09; nationalities in, 647, 659–61, 674, 708. *See also* Austria; Hungary

Austrian Netherlands, 454, 505, 516. *See also* Belgium authoritarianism, 747, 759, 807

Avanti, 753

Avars, 165, 183

Averroës, 302–03

Avignon: papacy in, lxv, lxix, 271–72, 277–78, 359–60

Axis Powers, 763, 769, 773–76, 779–83

Ayub Khan, Mohammed, 822

Azores, lxx, 396

Azov, 468

Aztec Empire, 400, 439

B

Babeuf, "Gracchus," 535

Babur, 326

Babylonian Captivity, 22, 272n; and Avignon papacy, lxv, lxix, 272, 277, 278, 344

Babylonian civilization, 6–8, 22; architecture, 6–7; legal code, 8; mathematics

and astronomy, 8, 45; religion, 6, 8. *See also* Mesopotamia

Bach, Johann Sebastian, 493

Bacon, Francis, 475–76, 478

Bacon, Roger, 264

Badoglio, Pietro, 781

Bagehot, Walter, 648; *Physics and Politics*, 634, 667

Baghdad, 175, 176, 301–02, 309; Pact (1955), 831–32

Bahamas, 398

Bahmini dynasty (India), 325

Bakunin, Mikhail, 591, 617, 651

balance of power: European, 347, 417, 454–55, 470, 497–99, 519, 541–42, 545, 547, 595, 598, 612, 618, 674–78, 686–89; international, 793, 796, 812

Balboa, Vasco de, 399

Baldwin, Count of Flanders, 308

Baldwin, Stanley, 733

Baldwin of Lorraine, 305

Balfour Declaration, 735

Balkan League, 692

Balkans, 162, 165, 244, 316, 781, 785; Byzantine influence in, liv, 301, 308; early history, 51, 61, 98, 113–14, 115, 117, 159, 166; European imperialism in, 674, 676–78, 689–91; First World War, 700, 702; nationalism in, 676, 678; under Ottoman Empire, 539, 595, 676; Second World War, 775–76; Wars, 692–93

Baltic states, 229, 466, 469, 662, 704, 727, 748, 774; post-Second World War, 785, 787

Balzac, Honoré de, 590, 670

Bancroft, George, 621

Bandung Conference (1955), 841

Bangladesh, 824–25, 841

Bani-Sadr, Abolhassan, 835

banking: European, 348, 365, 398; government control of, 630; medieval, 230, 253, 275

Bank of England, 437, 460, 798

Bannockburn, Battle of, 267, 281

Baptists, 385, 388, 456

Barani: quoted, 325

Barbados, 440

barbarians: and Roman Empire, xlix, l, 109–19; ruled North China, 140–41

baroque style, 480–81

Barras, Paul, 536

Bartók, Béla, 743

Basel, 382; Council of, 376

Basham, A. L.: quoted, 126, 127

Basil II, Byzantine Emperor, 304

Bastille: fall of, 526–27

Batavia, 407

Battle of the Bulge, 782

Bavaria, 431, 433, 463, 508, 565, 709, 714; Duke of, 196, 197; in Middle Ages, 154, 156, 181, 187

Bayle, Pierre, 353; *Historical and Critical Dictionary*, 483

Baylen, Battle of, 541

Bay of Pigs, 813

Bay of Salamis, 38

Beauvais Cathedral, 232

Bebel, August, 659

Beccaria, Cesare di, 489

Becker, Carl L.: quoted, 487

M

MacArthur, Douglas, 783, 804, 828
Maccabees, 54
MacDonald, Ramsay, 732
MacDowell, Edward, 631
Macedon, Kingdom of, xlii–xliii, xliv, 48, 49–51, 64, 65, 76. *See also* Alexander the Great
Macedonia, 692–93
Macedonian dynasty (Byzantine), 299–304
Machiavelli, Niccolò, 354, 366, 370, 420, 474, 507, 755; *Discourses on Livy*, 354; *Prince, The*, 354–55
machines. *See* technology
Madagascar, 681
Madeira, 295, 396
Madras, 130, 440, 508
Madrid, 541
Maecenas, 82
Magdeburg, 377, 431, 432
Magellan, Ferdinand, 399
Magenta: battle at, 603
Magna Carta, 238, 257, 258
Magyars, lvi, lvii, lviii, 190, 191, 196, 563, 604, 659–60
Mahabharata, 128, 197
Mahan, Alfred T.: *Influence of Sea Power upon History, The*, 691
Mahāvīra, 125
Mahmud of Ghazni, 324
Maimonides, 303
Maine, U.S.S., 685
Maintenon, François d'Aubigne, Marquise de, 450
Mainz, Archbishop of, 378
Makin, 783
Malacca, 329, 397, 407
Malay Peninsula, 329, 783
Malaysia, 812–13
Malcolm, G. A.: quoted, 684
Mallarmé, Stéphane, 671
Malthus, Thomas Robert: *Essay on the Principle of Population*, 580–82, 665–66, 825
Mamelukes, 308–10, 311
Mamluk Dynasty (India), 324
man: and anti-intellectualism, 743–44; and behavioral sciences, 739–41; empiricism, 484; individualism, 349, 356, 482, 550; natural goodness of, 586, 589; natural laws, 483, 488–91; natural rights, 461, 484, 579; in prehistory, 3–6; and progress, 489, 665, 666; rationalism, 483–84, 488–89, 550; relativism, 482–83; Renaissance, 349, 352–57 *passim*; and theory of evolution, 666–67, 669
Manchester, 550, 585
Manchu dynasty (China), 338, 636–40
Manchukuo. *See* Manchuria
Manchuria, 334, 642, 684, 738, 760, 763, 787
Mandel, William M., 831
Manicheanism, 105, 119, 331
Mann, Thomas: *Magic Mountain*, 742
mansabdars, 326–27
manuscript illumination, 292, 300, 327
Manzikert, battle of, 218, 305
Mao Zedong, 738, 793, 811, 821, 825–26, 828
Marathon, battle of, 24, 38

Marcos, Ferdinand, 828
Marcus Aurelius, Roman Emperor, xlviii, 87, 96, 98, 99, 100
Maria Louise (wife of Napoleon I), 541
Maria Theresa, Austrian Empress, 505, 507–08, 511, 513, 516, 606; quoted, 514
Maria Theresa, Queen of France, 422, 433, 450
Marie Antoinette, Queen of France, 529, 531
Marius, 70–71
Marlborough, John Churchill, 1st Duke of, 454, 481
Marne, battle of the, 700
Mars, 816
Marseillaise, 532
Marshall Plan, 789–90, 799, 803
Marsilius of Padua: *Defensor pacis*, 279
Martial, 95
Martin V, Pope, 360
Martinique, 440
Martov, Julius, 663
Marwick, A.: quoted, 704
Marx, Karl, 567, 586–90, 591, 650–51, 652, 667, 705, 740, 752, 755; *Communist Manifesto*, 567, 587–89; *Das Kapital*, 587
Marxism, 579, 586–90, 650–51, 747, 750, 808, 811, 192
Mary, Duchess of Burgundy, 366, 367, 405
Mary I, Queen of England, 387, 408, 424
Mary II, Queen of England, 458–60
Mary Stuart, Queen of Scots, 408–09, 410, 411, 424
Masaccio, 355–56
Masaryk, Jan, 790
Masaryk, Thomas, 660, 727
Massachusetts, 437, 442, 519
Massachusetts Bay Company, 442
Massilia, 31
Masurian Lakes: battle at, 701
materialism philosophy, 665, 740, 744
material progress, 489, 571, 632, 647, 668, 671, 730, 739
mathematics: advances in, 477; Arabic, 198, 302; Babylonian, 8, 45; Chinese, 338; Greek, xli, lii, lx, 53, 145, 245; Indian, 129, 130, 302; medieval, 198, 245, 291, 294; Renaissance, 359; and science, 473–79; and theory of relativity, 742; western, and Aristotelian logic, 49
Matsu, 813
Matteotti, Giacomo, 754
Mattingly, Garrett: quoted, 410
Maurice, Frederick Denison, 591
Mauritania, 836
Maurras, Charles, 657
Mauryan dynasty (India), 126–27
Maximian, Roman Emperor, 103
Maximilian, Duke of Bavaria, 429–30
Maximilian I, Holy Roman Emperor, 366, 367
Maximilian, Mexican Emperor, 628
mayors of the palace, 156, 179
Mazarin, Jules, 421–22, 428, 448, 452
Mazzini, Giuseppe, 562–63, 603
McCarthy, Joseph, 804
McKinley, William, 685; quoted, 684
Mead, Margaret, 741
Mecca, 168–70, 172, 173–74

Medes, 23
Medici, Catherine de', 411–12
Medici, Cosimo de', 348
Medici, Lorenzo de' (the Magnificent), 348, 363
Medici, Marie de', 419
Medici, Piero de', 348
Medici family, 346, 348, 353, 354
medicine, 476, 478, 644; Arabic, 224, 245, 302; Greek, 53, 95, 245; improvements in, 739, 825; medieval, 224, 245; Renaissance, 359
Medina (Medinet-en-Nabi), 170
Mediterranean, 317; in ancient world, xxxix, 7, 9, 15, 16–17, 18, 26, 29, 30, 32, 51–52, 61, 71, 89, 98, 99; in medieval times, 179, 189
Mediterranean Agreements (1887), 678
Megara, 47
Mehemet Ali, Viceroy of Egypt, 555
Memel, 769
Memling, Hans, 293
Menander, 52
Mencius, 136, 336
Mensheviks, 663, 705
mercantilism, 434, 435–39, 440, 442–43, 448, 490–91, 500, 571, 581, 623, 633
Merovingian dynasty (Franks), 153–56, 182, 186, 192
Merriman, R. B.: quoted, 402
Mersen, Treaty of (870), 188
Mesopotamia, 3, 4, 18, 50, 709; under Arabs, 173, 174, 176, 217; Chaldean Empire, 22–23; early civilization, xxxvi–xxxviii, 6–9, 10, 11; foreign invaders in, xliii, 7–9, 11–12, 21–22, 309; influence of, 13, 14, 16, 19; under Persia, 23, 40, 44–45; under Rome, 87; trade, 14, 15, 17, 52; under Turks, 304, 317. *See also* Babylonian civilization
Messenia, 37
metallurgy, lxx, 295, 363–64
metals: from Americas, 400, 403–04, 417; explorations for, 395–96; and trade regulation, 438
Methodists, 456, 490, 493
Metternich, Klemens von, 545–48, 550, 557–58, 563, 567, 568, 595, 675, 693
Meung, Jean de, 266
Mexico, 632, 750, 839; French in, 601, 609, 628, 633; Mexican War, 625, 628, 633; Spanish conquests in, 400–01, 403; Zimmermann Telegram, 705
Mexico City, 628
Michelangelo, 356
microscope, 480
Middle Ages, European: agriculture, lviii, lxiv, 151, 193, 204–07, 209, 214, 219, 275; Anglo-Saxon England, 152–53, 199–202, 210–11; Arab Empire, 167–76; banking, 230, 253, 275; and Byzantine Empire, lx, lxiii–lxiv, 218, 301, 305–06, 307–08; Carolingian Empire, 156, 179–91, 192; culture, lx, lxiv, 219, 220–22, 231–35, 263, 265, 266, 290–93, 552; division of labor in, 207–08, 275; Eastern Roman Empire, 145, 155, 159–67; economic and political disorders in late, 275–91, 344; economy, lxiv, lxvi, 204–09, 253–54, 263, 275, 300, 312, 437; education and

Russia (*continued*)

World War, 694–95, 699–707; foreign affairs, 444, 466, 497, 505, 513–14, 542, 547, 548, 554, 557, 559, 588, 612, 628, 662, 676–78, 687–93; government and politics, 434, 444, 469, 512, 615–17, 664, 705; imperialism of, 638, 639, 674, 676, 683–84, 688; industry and business, 469, 574, 575, 576, 649, 662–63, 705; intelligentsia of, 615, 617; labor, 652, 663, 705; land distribution, 513, 616, 664; literature, 670; military of, 468–69, 699; *mir* of, 616, 617, 664; under Mongols, lxiii–lxiv, 309, 310–11, 312–16; Napoleonic Wars, 537, 538–39, 540, 541–42; nobility, lxiv, 315, 370, 469, 497, 505, 512–13, 615, 616; Orthodox Church in, lxiv, 301, 310, 313, 469, 513, 596, 615; peasants and serfs, 311, 313–14, 316, 469, 498, 499, 505, 513, 615, 616, 617, 663–64, 705; and Prussia, 505, 596, 606, 607, 610, 676; Revolution of 1905, 663–64, 705; Russo-Finnish War, 773–74, 776; Russo-Japanese War, 642–43, 663, 684, 686, 688, 786; Russo-Turkish wars, 468, 513, 514, 556, 676; Seven Years' War, 509–11; Slavophils of, 615–16; socialism in, 617, 663; social reform, 647, 663, 664; society, 313, 556, 663; uprisings in, 434, 513, 615; viking settlements in, 189–90, 310; westernization of, 312–13, 467–70, 615–16. *See also* Russian Revolution; Soviet Union

Russia Company, 437
Russian Revolution, 589; of February, 705–06; of October, 706–07
Russo-Finnish War, 773–74, 777
Russo-Japanese War, 642–43, 663, 684, 686, 688, 786
Russo-Turkish wars, 468, 513, 514, 556, 676
Ruthenians, 563
Rutherford, Ernest, 741
Rykov, Alexei, 749–50, 752
Ryswick, Treaty of (1697), 453, 464

S

Saar, 658, 711, 760–61
Sadat, Anwar el-Muhammad, 833; quoted, 834
Sadowa: battle at, 608, 609
Sagres, 396
St. Bartholomew's Day Massacre, 412
St. Denis, 220–22, 223
St. Germain: Treaty of, 712–13
St. Helena, 542
St. Petersburg, 469, 705
St. Pierre, 511
St. Sophia Church, 162, 164
Sainte-Chapelle, 232
Saint-Simon, Count Henri de, 585–86
Sakhalin, 642, 787
Sakharov, Andrei, 809
Sakyamuni. *See* Buddha
Saladin, 306–07, 308
Salamanca University, 247
Salerno, 224
Salisbury, Robert Gascoyne-Cecil, 3rd Marquess of, 652–53, 687
Salvian: quoted, 114
Samarkand, 175, 324

Samoan Islands, 631, 685, 686
San Francisco: Conference (1945), 786; treaty signing in, 793
Sanskrit, 124, 326
San Stefano, Treaty of (1878), 676
Santa Anna, Antonio López de, 632
Sarajevo, 661, 693–94
Saratoga, battle of, 519–20
Sardinia, 65, 454. *See also* Piedmont-Sardinia
Sartre, Jean-Paul, 846
Sassanids, 98
Satsuma Rebellion, 641
Sattar, Abdus, 824
Saudi Arabia, 831, 835, 841
Saul, King of the Hebrews, 19
Saul of Tarsus. *See* Paul, St.
Savonarola, Girolamo, 375, 376
Savoy, 187, 454, 533, 602–03
Saxons, 183, 191, 195–96. *See also* Anglo-Saxons
Saxony, 181, 187, 216, 430, 432, 463; Duke of, 196; King of, 539
Sayyia dynasty (India), 325
Scandinavia, lv, lxiii, lxvii, 155, 179, 188, 245; invasions and settlements by Northmen (vikings) of, lvi, lvii, lviii. 188–91, 209, 211, 310, 393, 394. *See also* Denmark; Norway; Sweden
Scarlatti, Alessandro, 481
Scharnhorst, Gerhard von, 541
Schlesinger, Arthur, Jr.: quoted, 813
Schleswig-Holstein, 607–08
Schlieffen Plan, 695, 700
Schmidt, Helmut, 800
scholarship: classical, 145–46, 179, 183–84, 198–99, 224, 245–46, 263–65, 302, 344, 350–51, 352–53, 376; critical, 353; historical, 482–83, 552, 741; Renaissance, 345, 348–53; scholastic method, 224, 225; scientific, 353, 473–80, 489. *See also* Middle Ages; individual countries
Schönberg, Arnold, 743
Schonbrunn Palace, 481
Schönerer, Georg von, 660
Schuman Plan, 803
Schurz, Carl: quoted, 565
Schuschnigg, Kurt von, 765
Schwarzenberg, Prince Felix, 564, 604
science: applied, 665; and art, 669–71; Biological Revolution, 846; cult of, 664–65; and Darwinism, 665–69; and Enlightenment, 571; experimentation in, 476–79; and improvement of life, 738–39; and religion, 477, 479–80, 482, 668–69; Renaissance, 359, 474; revolution in, 473–80, 483; and witchcraft, 414. *See also* Middle Ages; individual countries
Scipio Africanus, 64, 69
Scotland, 87, 143, 461; and England, lxvi, 267, 281, 408–09, 425–26, 427, 460–61; Enlightenment in, 485; religion in, 152, 278, 383–84, 409, 424, 460–61
sculpture: baroque, 481; Christian, 120; Egyptian, 11, 32; Greek, 32, 42–43, 52, 67; Indian, 130; medieval, 266, 293; Renaissance, 344, 355–56; Roman, 67, 94, 118, 355; secular, 266
Sebastopol: siege of, 596–97
Second International, 651

Second Reform Bill (1867), 614, 617
Second World War, 783; air raids, 774, 775, 781, 784; in Asia and Pacific, 777–78, 779, 782–84, 787; in Europe and Africa, 699, 732, 738, 769, 773–77, 779–82; at sea, 773, 776, 781, 782–84; treaties of, 787–88, 793
Sedan: battle at, 610
Selective Service Act (1941), 779
Seleucid Empire, 51, 52, 54, 64
Seleucus, 51
Seljuk Turks, 304, 316. *See also* Turks
Semites, 7, 9, 12, 16
Seneca, 85, 95
Septimius Severus, Roman Emperor, 98, 99
Serbia, 660, 676, 678, 690, 692–93; First World War, 693–95, 700, 702, 708, 709
Serbs, 301, 316, 555, 563
serfdom, 18, 110, 111, 462, 465, 466; decline and abolition of, 283, 516, 568, 616, 617, 705; under feudalism, 193, 195, 208, 211–12. *See also* individual countries
Servetus, Michael, 385
Seven Years' War, 506, 509–11, 518, 524
Seville, 403
Sèvres, Treaty of (1920), 713
sex: in literature, 743
Seyss-Inquart, Artur, 765
Sforza family, 346, 349
Shafer, Boyd C.: quoted, 553
Shaftesbury, Anthony Ashley Cooper, 1st Earl of, 457, 461
Shakespeare, William, 414, 428; *Julius Caesar*, 75
Shang dynasty (China), 132
Shankara (Indian philosopher), 322
Shantung Peninsula, 639, 699, 710–11, 737, 738
Shaw, George Bernard, 650
Sherman Antitrust Act (1890), 630, 631
Shi-ites, 304, 835
Shimonoseki, Treaty of (1895), 639
Shinto, 340, 641–42
shipping, lxx, 285, 295, 339, 435, 574, 575, 613, 622
Shiva, 128, 322
Shotoku, Prince, 340
Siam, 323, 684. *See also* Thailand
Sibelius, Jan, 743
Siberia, 444, 664, 683–84, 705
Sicily, xliv, lviii, 18, 31, 32, 33, 47, 48, 63, 65, 68, 190, 210, 302, 454, 505; under Holy Roman Empire, lxv, 242, 243, 258, 260–62; revolution of 1848, 562; Second World War, 781
Siddharta Gnatama. *See* Buddha
Sieyès, Emmanuel Joseph, Abbé, 536; *What Is the Third Estate?*, 525
Sigismund, Holy Roman Emperor, 360
Sikhism, 326
Silesia, 291, 507–09, 511, 516, 574
Simons, Menno: quoted, 384
Sinai Peninsula, 833
Singapore, 829
Sinn Fein movement, 736
Sino-Japanese War, 639, 642, 688, 779
Sinyavsky, Andrei, 809
Sistine Chapel, 356